Management

Skills and Application　　　　　　　　　Eleventh Edition

Leslie W. Rue

Professor Emeritus of Management
Robinson College of Business
Georgia State University

Lloyd L. Byars

Professor of Management
College of Management
Georgia Institute of Technology

 McGraw-Hill Irwin

Boston　Burr Ridge, IL　Dubuque, IA　Madison, WI　New York　San Francisco　St. Louis
Bangkok　Bogotá　Caracas　Kuala Lumpur　Lisbon　London　Madrid　Mexico City
Milan　Montreal　New Delhi　Santiago　Seoul　Singapore　Sydney　Taipei　Toronto

MANAGEMENT: SKILLS AND APPLICATION

Published by McGraw-Hill/Irwin, a business unit of The McGraw-Hill Companies, Inc., 1221 Avenue of the Americas, New York, NY, 10020. Copyright © 2005, 2003, 2000, 1997, 1995, 1992, 1989, 1986, 1983, 1980, 1977 by The McGraw-Hill Companies, Inc. All rights reserved. No part of this publication may be reproduced or distributed in any form or by any means, or stored in a database or retrieval system, without the prior written consent of The McGraw-Hill Companies, Inc., including, but not limited to, in any network or other electronic storage or transmission, or broadcast for distance learning.

Some ancillaries, including electronic and print components, may not be available to customers outside the United States.

This book is printed on acid-free paper.

1 2 3 4 5 6 7 8 9 0 QPD/QPD 0 9 8 7 6 5 4

ISBN   0-07-293593-6

Vice president and editor-in-chief: *Robin J. Zwettler*
Editorial director: *John E. Biernat*
Senior sponsoring editor: *Andy Winston*
Senior developmental editor: *Christine Scheid*
Marketing manager: *Lisa Nicks*
Producer, Media technology: *Mark Molsky*
Project manager: *Kristin Puscas*
Production supervisor: *Gina Hangos*
Designer: *Mary E. Kazak*
Supplement producer: *Betty Hadala*
Senior digital content specialist: *Brian Nacik*
Cover design: *Jenny El-Shamy*
Cover illustration: *© Getty Images*
Typeface: *10/12 Palatino*
Compositor: *ElectraGraphics, Inc.*
Printer: *Quebecor World Dubuque Inc.*

Library of Congress Cataloging-in-Publication Data

Rue, Leslie W.

    Management : skills and application / Leslie W. Rue, Lloyd L. Byars.— 11th ed.
      p. cm.
    Includes bibliographical references and index.
    ISBN 0-07-293593-6 (alk. paper)
    1. Management. I. Byars, Lloyd L. II. Title.
  HD31.R797 2005
  658—dc22

                      2004046600

www.mhhe.com

To Penny and Linda, our wonderful wives of 36 and 34 years respectively.

Preface

We are extremely pleased that this book has gone into eleven editions. We believe that the book's endurance is due largely to the feedback and assistance we have received from instructors and students who have used the book. Relying on the suggestions of these groups as well as our own thoughts, we have attempted to improve the book with each new addition. This edition is no exception. The section below summarizes the major changes in this edition:

New to This Edition

- Information Systems for Managers has been eliminated as a separate chapter. This and other related material have been placed in appropriate spots throughout the book.
- The remaining chapters of the Contemporary issues section (International Business and Legal, Ethical, and Social Responsibilities of Management) have been moved to section two of the book. This helps broaden the student's foundation before introducing the more traditional management functions.
- Approximately two-thirds of the "Management Illustrations" used throughout the text are new to this edition, making them very up-to-date.
- Many of the referenced research studies and data have been supplemented with additional and more recent studies.
- Approximately 70 percent of the chapter previews are new to this edition.

Structure of the Chapters

Most of the text's pedagogy has been retained from the last edition. Look for these features in each chapter:

- Learning Objectives—chapter-opening guidelines for students to use as they read. This list of key objectives provides the reader a roadmap for venturing into the text.
- Chapter Previews—real-life, up-to-date vignettes that illustrate one or more of the major points covered in the respective chapters. Preview analysis questions are presented at the end of each vignette to help the student relate the chapter material to the preview.
- Management Illustrations—brief, chapter-related corporate examples found in boxes throughout the chapters. These illustrations present more than 60 examples of concepts contained in the text, and most contain urls on the companies detailed in them.
- Corporate/Organization References—more than 200 references to actual corporations and organizations. We are extremely proud of these references that best serve to bridge the gap between theory and practice. Look for them in the text itself, chapter previews, and management illustrations.
- Margin Glossary—key terms defined where mentioned in the text. This feature is especially helpful to students reviewing chapter material for study and/or testing.

- Review Questions—these questions, at the end of each chapter, tie directly back to the learning objectives. By tying the chapter concepts together from beginning to end, students can evaluate their understanding of key constructs and ideas.

- Skill-Building Questions—end-of-chapter questions designed to promote critical thinking. These questions ask students to get to a deeper level of understanding by applying, comparing, contrasting, evaluating, and illustrating ideas presented in the chapter.

- Skill-Building Exercises—end-of-chapter tools for students and instructors. These exercises can be assigned on the spot in class or as homework.

- Case Incidents—end-of-chapter short cases for students. These incidents present lifelike situations requiring management decisions related to the material covered in the respective chapters. As with the skill-building exercises, these can be assigned in class or as homework.

The Teaching Package

A variety of support materials help the instructor in teaching this dynamic field of management. These key items available with the eleventh edition of the text are described below:

- Lecture Resource Manual and Test Bank

    The Lecture Resource Manual and Test Bank, thoroughly updated by Thomas Lloyd of Westmoreland County Community College, is the instructor's tool box for enhancing student learning. The instructor's manual contains brief chapter overviews; lecture outlines that include topical headings; definitional highlights; coordination points for key terms, review questions, and learning objectives; suggested answers to in-text questions; and transparency masters. The popular "Barriers to Student Understanding" feature addresses areas that are most often stumbling blocks for students. In this section, a series of suggestions guide the instructor in preparing for difficulties, covering easily misunderstood concepts, and aiding the student learning experience through directed discussion. The Test Bank section, completely revised and updated by Thomas Kaplan of Mary Baldwin College, includes true-false, multiple choice, and essay questions tied to the chapter learning objectives and classified according to the level of difficulty.

- PowerPoint presentation software contains tables and graphs from the text as well as extra material.

- Instructor's Resource CD-ROM (007-293594-4)—Contains all of the supplements listed above, including downloads of figures from the text for your use in PowerPoint presentation slides you create.

- Manager's Hot Seat Videos (007-29359-52) or DVD—Available in both VHS and DVD format, watch real managers handle difficult situations in the workplace. These improvised videos show how issues like diversity, discrimination, telecommuting, and teams really shape the way business is done. Teaching notes provide background information and extensive teaching ideas for the VHS tapes. The DVD is completely interactive and self-contained, and can be utilized in or out of the classroom. Ask your sales representative how to get the DVD for yourself and/or students.

- Online Learning Center *www.mhhe.com/rue11e*—With a wealth of material for both student and professor, our Online Learning Center gives plenty of material to supplement course or classroom, or find more study aids. Make use of our instructor resources, Internet exercises, interactive skills modules, career information, and flash cards to help enhance and review.

Acknowledgments

We think the McGraw-Hill/Irwin sales staff is the best in the industry and we thank them for their continued efforts on our behalf. Our thanks, also, to the members of the McGraw-Hill/Irwin in-house staff who have provided their support throughout this revision.

We have relied on the assistance of so many people throughout this book's history. As we come now to the eleventh edition we wish to thank all of those who have been involved with this project and to make special mention of those involved in the most recent reviewing and marketing research processes:

Kathryn Aten
University of Oregon

Laura Barnes
Averett College–Virginia Beach

Candace Barnett
Mercer University

Sue Biedermann
Texas State University–San Marcos

William Deskin
Davenport University

Joe Downing
Southern Methodist University

Norb Elbert
Eastern Kentucky University

Shirley Fedorovich
Embry-Riddle Aeronautical University

Alan Heffner
Mary Washington College

Mary Beth Klinger
College of Southern Maryland

Karla Leavelle
George Mason University

Joanne Leoni
Johnson & Wales University–North Miami Campus

Ricardo Rivera
Embry-Riddle Aeronautical University

Randy Rose
Averett University–Vienna

John Urbanski
Francis Marion University

Douglas Woundy
Averett University

Marilyn Young
University of Texas–Tyler

We are indebted to our families, friends, colleagues, and students for the numerous comments, ideas, and support that they have provided. A special thanks goes to our assistant, Charmelle Todd, for her work on this revision.

In our continuing efforts to improve this text, we earnestly solicit your feedback. You are the reason for this book's endurance!

Leslie W. Rue

Lloyd L. Byars

About the Authors

Leslie W. Rue

is professor emeritus of management and former holder of the Carl R. Zwerner chair of Family Owned Enterprises in the Robinson College of Business at Georgia State University. He received his Bachelor of Industrial Engineering (with honor) and his Master of Industrial Engineering from Georgia Institute of Technology. He received his Ph.D. in Management from Georgia State University.

Prior to joining Georgia State University, Dr. Rue was on the faculty of the School of Business, Indiana University at Bloomington, Indiana. He has worked as a data processing project officer for the U.S. Army Management Systems Support Agency, in the Pentagon, and as an industrial engineer for Delta Airlines. In addition, Dr. Rue has worked as a consultant and trainer to numerous private and public organizations in the areas of planning, organizing, and strategy.

Dr. Rue is the author of over 50 published articles, cases, and papers that have appeared in academic and practitioner journals. In addition to this book, he has coauthored numerous other textbooks in the field of management. Several of these books have gone into multiple editions.

Dr. Rue has just celebrated his 36th wedding anniversary. He has two daughters, a son, and three grandsons. His hobbies include the restoration of antique furniture and antique wooden speedboats.

Lloyd L. Byars

received his Ph.D. from Georgia State University. He also received a Bachelor of Electrical Engineering and a Master of Science in Industrial Management from Georgia Tech. He has taught at Georgia State University, Clark Atlanta University, and is currently professor of management, College of Management at the Georgia Institute of Technology.

Dr. Byars has published articles in leading professional journals and is also the author of four textbooks that are used in colleges and universities. He has served on the editorial review board of the *Journal of Systems Management* and the *Journal of Management Case Studies.*

Dr. Byars has worked as a trainer and consultant to many organizations, including Duke Power Company, Georgia Kraft Company, Kraft, Inc., South Carolina Electric and Gas Company, the University of Florida–Medical School, the Department of the Army, and the U.S. Social Security Administration. Dr. Byars also serves as a labor arbitrator, certified by both the Federal Mediation and Conciliation Service and the American Arbitration Association. He has arbitrated cases in the United States, Europe, Central America, and the Caribbean.

Dr. Byars has been married to Linda S. Byars for 34 years. They have two daughters, a son, and one grandson.

Brief Contents

Contents

Part 1

Foundations

Gettyimages/Duncan Smith

1

Introduction to Management

Learning Objectives

After studying this chapter, you will be able to:

1. Define management.
2. Describe the levels of management.
3. Discuss the functions of management.
4. Explain the roles of a manager.
5. Describe the skills required to perform the work of management.
6. Explain how principles of management are developed.
7. Discuss the increasing role of women and minorities in management.
8. Define the glass ceiling facing women and minorities.
9. Explain diversity.
10. Define entrepreneur.
11. Define small business.
12. Outline three requirements for encouraging entrepreneurship in medium-sized and large businesses.
13. Describe user-friendly computers.

Chapter Preview

Carly Fiorina was born in 1954 in Austin, Texas. She received the nickname Carly in high school. Her mother was an abstract artist and her father was a law professor who taught at Stanford and other universities. As a child, she lived in London, Ghana, Palo Alto, and other places. She graduated from Stanford with a degree in medieval history. She then attended law school for one semester at UCLA and dropped out. As a young adult, Carly was briefly married, taught English in Europe, and worked as a receptionist for a commercial brokerage firm. It was there, while writing deals for brokers, that she became interested in business. After obtaining an MBA in marketing from the University of Maryland, she went to work as a sales representative for AT&T. She reached a level of management at AT&T where she managed the spin-off of Lucent Technologies from AT&T.

In 1999, Carly Fiorina was hired by Hewlett-Packard (HP) as CEO to turn around a company that was desperately in need of change. HP had failed to capitalize on the personal computer and Internet revolutions. Under Fiorina's leadership, HP conducted the largest technology merger ever: the $19 billion deal with Compaq.

Source: Shari Caudron, "Don't Mess with Carly," *Workforce,* July 2003, pp. 28–35.

Analyzing Management Skills

Go to the Internet and find articles relating to the management style of Carly Fiorina. What is the style of management used by Ms. Fiorina?

Applying Management Skills

In the jobs you have held either prior to entering college or during your college career, what skills did effective managers have?

Businesses today operate in a world of constant change. Technology and society are changing more rapidly than ever before. Concern for the environment has forced companies to think about how their actions affect the quality of the air, land, and water. Competition is fiercer than ever, because companies from all over the world now try to sell their products and services to the same customers. Workplaces have become increasingly diverse, as minorities, women, and new immigrants participate in growing numbers. All these changes have created new challenges for managers—the people who operate businesses.

What Is Management?

management
A form of work that involves coordinating an organization's resources—land, labor, and capital—toward accomplishing organizational objectives.

Management is the process of deciding how best to use a business's resources to produce goods or provide services. A business's resources include its employees, equipment, and money.

To see why managers are important, think about the roles they play in the automobile industry. Some managers on the assembly line schedule work shifts and supervise the men and women who manufacture and assemble the vehicles. Other managers in the engineering department develop new product features and make sure that safety standards are met. Managers also plan for the future, thinking about the vehicles the company will be producing in the next decade. Without management, automobile manufacturers could not conduct business efficiently.

All organizations, from one-person businesses to giant corporations, need managers. Small businesses may be managed by one or just a few managers. Large and medium-sized companies may have many levels of management.

Levels of Management

All but the very smallest organizations need more than one manager to coordinate their resources. Large companies generally have many managers at three different levels.

Senior Management

top or senior management
Establishes the objectives of the business, formulates the actions necessary to achieve them, and allocates the resources of the business to achieve the objectives.

The highest level is known as **senior management**. Senior management has several important functions. First, it establishes the goals, or objectives, of the business.[1] Second, it decides what actions are necessary to meet those goals. Finally, it decides how to use the company's resources. This level of management usually includes the chairperson of the company's board of directors, the chief executive officer (CEO), the chief operating officer (COO), and the company's senior vice presidents. Senior managers are not involved in the company's day-to-day problems. Instead, they concentrate on setting the direction the company will follow.

Middle Management

middle management
Responsible for implementing and achieving organizational objectives; also responsible for developing departmental objectives and actions.

Middle management is responsible for meeting the goals that senior management sets. Middle managers include department heads and district sales managers. This level of management sets goals for specific areas of the business and decides what the employees in each area must do to meet those goals. For example, senior management might set a goal of increasing company sales by 15 percent in the next year. To meet that objective, middle management might develop a new advertising campaign for one of the company's products.

Supervisory Management

supervisory management
Manages operative employees; generally considered the first or lowest level of management.

The lowest level of management is **supervisory management**. Supervisory managers make sure that the day-to-day operations of the business run smoothly. They are in charge of the people who physically produce the company's products or provide its services. Forepersons, crew leaders, and store managers are all examples of supervisory managers.

Large companies usually have all three kinds of managers. At JCPenney, for example, supervisory managers run stores and departments within stores. These managers are responsible for making sure that the daily operations of the store run well. Middle managers oversee districts. These managers are responsible for making sure that all store managers within their district are performing well. Middle managers also may suggest ideas for increasing sales, improving service, or reducing costs within their districts. Senior managers include JCPenney's CEO and senior vice presidents. These managers make decisions about the company's policies, products, and organizational strategy. A decision to increase salaries throughout the company would be made by senior management, for example.

FIGURE 1.1
The Management Pyramid

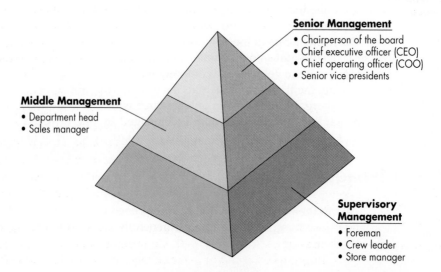

Senior Management
- Chairperson of the board
- Chief executive officer (CEO)
- Chief operating officer (COO)
- Senior vice presidents

Middle Management
- Department head
- Sales manager

Supervisory Management
- Foreman
- Crew leader
- Store manager

FIGURE 1.2
Levels of Business Management
Large companies usually have at least three levels of management. Each level is responsible for a different set of functions.

> **1. Senior Management**
> Senior management is responsible for setting goals for the business, deciding what actions are necessary to meet them, and determining how best to use resources. This level of management usually includes the chairperson of the board of directors, the CEO, the COO, and the company's senior vice presidents.
>
> **2. Middle Management**
> Middle management is responsible for achieving the goals set by senior management. Middle management includes company department heads and district sales managers.
>
> **3. Supervisory Management**
> Supervisory management is responsible for the people who physically produce the company's products or provide its services. Forepersons, crew leaders, and store managers are all examples of supervisors.

The three levels of management form a *hierarchy,* or a group ranked in order of importance. As can be seen in Figure 1.1, the management hierarchy is shaped like a pyramid, with very few senior managers at the top and many supervisory managers at the bottom. Figure 1.2 further describes the different levels of management.

The Management Process

There are several ways to examine how management works. One way is to divide the tasks managers perform into categories. A second way is to look at the roles different types of managers play in a company. A **role** is a set of behaviors associated with a particular job. A third way is to look at the skills managers need to do their jobs. Each of these ways of thinking about management will help you understand the management process.

role
Set of behaviors associated with a particular job.

Management Tasks

Managers in all organizations—from small businesses to large companies—engage in some basic activities. These activities can be divided into five categories:

planning
Deciding what objectives to pursue during a future period and what to do to achieve those objectives.

1. **Planning.** A manager decides on company goals and the actions the company must take to meet them. A CEO who sets a goal of increasing sales by 10 percent in the next year by developing a new software program is engaged in planning.

organizing
Grouping activities, assigning activities, and providing the authority necessary to carry out the activities.

2. **Organizing.** A manager groups related activities together and assigns employees to perform them. A manager who sets up a team of employees to restock an aisle in a supermarket is organizing.

3. **Staffing.** A manager decides how many and what kind of people a business needs to meet its goals and then recruits, selects, and trains the right people. A restaurant manager's staffing duties include interviewing and training waiters.

staffing
Determining human resource needs and recruiting, selecting, training, and developing human resources.

4. **Leading.** A manager provides the guidance employees need to perform their tasks. This helps ensure that company goals are met. A manager leads by keeping the lines of communication open. Holding regular staff meetings where employees can ask questions about their projects and responsibilities is a good example of leading.

5. **Controlling.** A manager measures how the business performs to ensure that financial goals are being met. Controlling requires a manager to analyze accounting records and to make changes if financial standards are not being met.

FIGURE 1.3
Relative Amount of Emphasis Placed on Each Function of Management

leading
Directing and channeling human behavior toward the accomplishment of objectives.

controlling
Measuring performance against objectives, determining the causes of deviations, and taking corrective action where necessary.

conceptual skills
Involve understanding the relationship of the parts of a business to one another and to the business as a whole. Decision making, planning, and organizing are specific managerial activities that require conceptual skills.

human relations skills
Involve understanding people and being able to work well with them.

Many management activities overlap. Organizing, for example, is difficult without a plan. Keeping good employees on the job is difficult if a workplace is poorly organized and lacks leadership.

Figure 1.3 shows how different levels of management focus on different activities. Senior managers divide their time about equally among the five activities. Middle managers spend most of their time leading and controlling. Supervisory managers spend little time planning and a lot of time controlling.

Management Roles

Managers have authority, or power, within organizations and use it in many ways. To best use their authority, managers take on different roles. Most management roles fall into one of three categories: interpersonal roles, information-related roles, and decision-making roles.[2]

Interpersonal roles include a manager's relationships with people. A manager plays an interpersonal role by providing leadership within the company or interacting with others outside the organization.

Information-related roles require a manager to provide knowledge, news, or advice to employees. A manager fills this role by holding meetings or finding other ways of letting employees know about important business activities. *Decision-making roles* are those a manager plays when making changes in policies, resolving conflicts, or deciding how best to use resources. Figure 1.4 gives examples and definitions of the three types of roles.

Management Skills

A third way of looking at the management process is by examining the kinds of skills required to perform a particular job.[3] Three types of skills have been identified.

1. **Conceptual skills** are those that help managers understand how different parts of a business relate to one another and to the business as a whole. Decision making, planning, and organizing are managerial activities that require conceptual skills.

2. **Human relations skills** are those that managers need to understand and work well with people. Interviewing job applicants, forming partnerships with other businesses, and resolving conflicts all require good human relations skills.

FIGURE 1.4
Definitions of Management Roles

Source: Adapted from Henry Mintzberg, *The Nature of Managerial Work* (New York: Harper & Row, 1972), pp. 54–99.

	Information-Related	
Interpersonal Roles	**Roles**	**Decision-Making Roles**
Figurehead: Manager serves as official representative of the organization or unit.	*Monitor:* Manager receives and collects information.	*Entrepreneur:* Manager initiates change.
Relationship builder: Manager interacts with peers and with people outside the organization to gain information.	*Communicator:* Manager distributes information within the organization.	*Disturbance handler:* Manager decides how conflicts between subordinates should be resolved and steps in when a subordinate suddenly leaves or an important customer is lost.
Leader: Manager guides and motivates staff and acts as a positive influence in the workplace.	*Spokesperson:* Manager distributes information outside the organization.	*Resource director:* Manager decides how the organization will use its resources.
		Negotiator: Manager decides to negotiate major contracts with other organizations or individuals.

technical skills
Involve being able to perform the mechanics of a particular job.

3. **Technical skills** are the specific abilities that people use to perform their jobs. Operating a word processing program, designing a brochure, and training people to use a new budgeting system are all technical skills.

Not all management skills are easy to place in a single category. Most fall into more than one. In order to develop a company advertisement, for example, a manager must have conceptual, human relations, and technical skills. Managers would need conceptual skills to develop the advertisement's message. They would need human relations skills to assemble and motivate the team of people who create the advertisement. Training the team by teaching them a computer graphics program would require technical skills.

All levels of management require some combination of these skills. Different skills are more important at different levels of management, as Figure 1.5 shows.

FIGURE 1.5
Mix of Skills Used at Different Levels of Management

Conceptual skills are most important at the senior management level. Technical skills are most important at lower levels of management, particularly at the supervisory level. Human relations skills are important at all levels of management.

Principles of Management

Managers often use certain rules when deciding how to run their businesses. These rules are known as principles of management.

principle
A basic truth or law.

A **principle** is a basic truth or law. The principle, or law, of gravity explains why objects fall to the ground when they are dropped. The principle of inertia explains why objects at rest remain at rest. Scientists prove that principles are true by performing controlled experiments. These experiments test a *hypothesis,* or an idea about the way something works. Once the experiment has been repeated many times with the same results, the hypothesis is accepted as a law, or principle.

Developing principles of management is more complicated than developing scientific principles. Carrying out a controlled experiment in the business world is difficult to do, because researchers cannot control all of the factors the way they can in a laboratory. To test the effect of a particular business practice, researchers would need to study companies that were exactly alike in every way except the business practice being studied. In the real world, however, companies differ in many ways. It is unlikely that researchers would find identical companies to study.

Because controlled management experiments are so difficult to carry out, most management principles are developed through observation and deduction. *Deduction* is the process of drawing a general conclusion from specific examples. For instance, a researcher may observe that employees in 15 companies work more efficiently when their supervisors treat them well. In this case, the researcher may deduce that a pleasant work environment contributes to productivity. This conclusion might then become a management principle.

Management principles are more likely to change than physical principles. They also are likely to be interpreted differently by different people. For this reason management principles are best viewed as guides to action rather than rigid laws. A manager follows management principles most of the time. If, however, a principle clearly does not apply to a specific situation, an experienced manager will not use it. An important part of being a manager is recognizing when a principle should be followed and when it should not. Being able to change and adapt, particularly during times of uncertainty, is an important management skill.

Until recently, many managers followed the management principle that all employees need to arrive at work at the same time. They also believed that people who worked in offices needed to dress a certain way. In the past several years, managers at many companies adopted a new way of thinking about work schedules. Many companies now allow their employees to work flexible schedules, or flextime. Some even allow their employees to work at home. Attitudes about dress codes also have changed, with many businesses allowing their employees to dress casually.

Diversity and Management

For many years, the managers of most large and medium-sized U.S. businesses were almost exclusively white males. As recently as the 1950s and 1960s, women in the workforce filled primarily service and support roles, acting as secretaries, teachers, salesclerks, and waitresses, for instance. Many minority workers, especially those lacking education, were confined to menial jobs such as custodial work and manual labor. In the last three decades of the twentieth century, however, more and more women and minorities have joined the workforce. They also have attained positions as high-level managers in companies of all sizes. Furthermore, they presently serve in senior-level management jobs in the federal, state, and local governments.

glass ceiling
Refers to a level within the managerial hierarchy beyond which very few women and minorities advance.

Despite these changes, most senior managers in the country are still white men. The problems women and minorities have had winning promotions to senior management positions gave rise to the term **glass ceiling.** This is the invisible barrier that prevents women and minorities from moving up in the world of business.

As in many other fields, such as sports and space exploration, the glass ceiling is steadily becoming a window of opportunity. Top managers, especially CEOs, are highly visible and often inseparable from their companies. Therefore, having a woman—such as Hewlett-Packard's Carly Fiorina—in the top spot can be an advantage. It also can be the spark that is needed to trigger more promotions of women to senior managerial positions. As businesses and government agencies downsize, or lay off workers to cut costs, many of those opting for attractive retirement benefits are senior white males. Their departure opens the door for women and minorities eager to move into the highest ranks of management.

As the glass ceiling falls, the challenges presented by a multicultural workplace increase. Employees and managers alike must be sensitive to these challenges. One example of the need for increased sensitivity involves religious holidays, which are celebrated at different times throughout the year by Muslims, Christians, Jews, and other religious groups. Managers need to be aware of the needs of their staff when it comes to these holidays, and workers need to be responsible about arranging to take these days off. Management Illustration 1.1 describes diversity at UPS.

What Is Diversity?

diversity
Including people of different genders, races, religions, nationalities, ethnic groups, age groups, and physical abilities.

Diversity in the workforce means including people of different genders, races, religions, nationalities, ethnic groups, age groups, and physical abilities. The increasing diversity of the workplace represents a major social change in the United States.

The trend toward greater diversity is expected to continue over the next 50 years, as the proportion of nonwhites and immigrants in the U.S. population grows. In fact, diversity is increasing so quickly in the United States that the percentage of non-Hispanic whites is projected to fall from 68 percent in 2010 to just 52.8 percent by 2050 (see Figure 1.6).

FIGURE 1.6
Projected U.S. Population, by Demographic Group, 2000–2050 (percent of population)

Source: U.S. Census Bureau, www.census.gov/ populations/nations/nsrh/ nprh9600.txt.

Demographic Group	2010	2020	2030	2040	2050
Non-Hispanic white	68.0	64.3	60.6	56.6	52.8
Non-Hispanic black	12.6	12.9	13.1	13.3	13.6
Hispanic	13.8	16.3	18.9	21.7	24.5
Non-Hispanic American Indian, Eskimo, and Aleut	0.7	0.8	0.8	0.8	0.9
Non-Hispanic Asian and Pacific Islander	4.8	5.7	6.6	7.5	8.2
Total	100.0	100.0	100.0	100.0	100.0

"At UPS, it's not where you're from or what you look like, it's how much you care and how good you are at your job," says Hugo Parades, UPS District Manager, who is responsible for almost 4,000 employees and thousands of customers. Evidence of UPS's commitment to diversity is widespread in the firm. Approximately one-third of UPS's 325,000 employees are minorities, and 21 percent are women. Diversity is prevalent on all levels, too—27 percent of the firm's officials and managers are minorities and women. Senior Vice President Calvin Darden, who is head of U.S. operations and is rumored as being in line to become CEO, is African American.

Not only is the company committed to diversity within the firm, it also has a Supplier Diversity Program that encourages small, minority, and women-owned businesses—resulting in more than $100 million in purchases from these suppliers. The firm's customers are international and also reflect the firm's commitment to diversity.

Diversity within the organization has paid off for UPS: consistently ranked as one of *Fortune*'s "50 Best Companies for Minorities," UPS is also ranked 55th on *Fortune*'s list of America's top 500 companies. Its steady $30 billion in annual revenue and solid stock price reflect how diversity within a large company creates winning results.

Source: "Best Companies for Minorities," *Fortune,* July 8, 2002; www.pressroom.ups.com.

This change in the work environment has important implications for managers. In the twenty-first century, managers will have to handle greater cultural diversity to be effective.

Reasons for Creating a Diverse Workforce

Companies are seeking diverse workforces because

- Employee population is increasingly diverse.
- Customer population is increasingly diverse.
- Retaining top talent means recruiting individuals from all backgrounds.
- Increasing diversity minimizes the risk of litigation.

By creating a culture that is open to different behavioral styles and that incorporates a wide range of views, diversity can improve corporate decision making. Greater diversity allows a company to respond to diverse groups of customers (see Figure 1.7).

To bring together all of the people who work for them, managers must avoid stereotyping. They must create a work environment in which prejudice is not tol-

FIGURE 1.7
The Changing American Workplace
Advances in civil rights and demographic changes in the United States have made the workplace much more diverse than it was 30 years ago. Today, managers must understand how to work with people from diverse backgrounds.

1. **The Workplace in the 1960s**
   Until the 1970s, white males dominated most businesses in the United States. For the most part, managers managed people who came from backgrounds that were similar to their own.

2. **The Workplace in the Year 2002**
   By the year 2002, most workplaces included women and minorities. Increasing diversity has helped companies understand the needs of their increasingly diverse customer bases.

3. **The Workplace in the Mid-Twenty-First Century**
   By the middle of the twenty-first century, minorities will make up almost half of the population. In response to these changes, the workplace is expected to become even more diverse than it is today.

erated and diversity is welcomed and respected. Employees need to feel that they are valued and respected for who they are. Managers should always be sensitive to the backgrounds of their employees and should foster a diverse and understanding corporate culture.

Entrepreneurship and Management

professional manager
An individual who performs the basic management functions for the ongoing organization.

entrepreneur
An individual who conceives the idea of what product or service to produce, starts the organization, and builds it to the point where additional people are needed.

Senior, middle, and supervisory managers are all **professional managers.** Professional managers are paid to perform management functions within a company. Like other employees, they receive salaries for the work they do. Professional managers work for businesses, but they do not own them.

Entrepreneurs are people who launch and run their own businesses. When they start out, they must perform many of the basic management functions that professional managers perform. As their companies grow, they sometimes hire professional managers.

Many large companies, including Estée Lauder, Kellogg, and General Electric, were started by entrepreneurs. Gary Comer, for example, started a small mail-order company in 1963. Today his company, Lands' End, is a multimillion dollar company whose clothing is sold all over the world. The company has thousands of employees and many professional managers.

Being an entrepreneur is much riskier than being a professional manager. Without the right skills and a lot of hard work, entrepreneurs can go out of business and lose all the money invested in their company. Starting and owning a company can be more rewarding than working for a company, however. Successful entrepreneurs can create prosperous businesses that provide high incomes and a feeling of personal accomplishment.

Entrepreneurs and professional managers often have different personal characteristics. Entrepreneurs tend to be more independent than managers, and they may have less formal education. Some entrepreneurs jump from job to job before starting their own businesses.

Entrepreneurs start with an idea for creating or modifying a product or service that they believe in. Entrepreneurs like the idea of making decisions and being their own bosses. They often find tremendous satisfaction in their work, and their financial rewards can be great. Being an entrepreneur means working long hours and making decisions about every aspect of a business. It also means taking risks. Unlike professional managers, entrepreneurs invest money in their businesses and risk losing all of it if their business does not succeed. Without entrepreneurs, there would be no new businesses and fewer exciting developments, or innovations, in business and industry. Management Illustration 1.2 describes a new business.

Entrepreneurs own their businesses, but they can choose among several different types of ownership. Some entrepreneurs are *sole proprietors,* or people who run their businesses single-handedly. Certain types of work are particularly well suited to this form of ownership—medicine, dentistry, and accounting, for example. Many store owners are also sole proprietors. Other entrepreneurs may form partnerships, especially when a large sum of money is involved. One or more partners may supply the money while another runs the business. Two or more people may also run a business together. Still other small businesses may choose to *incorporate,* or become a corporation, to avoid being held personally liable for financial losses. Some entrepreneurs choose to own franchises.

Gary Burrell and Min Kao had dinner together at the Olathe, Kansas, Red Lobster. Both of them were frustrated that their employer, a division of AlliedSignal, did not seem to be interested in a product that they found to be interesting. The product was global positioning system (GPS) receivers. GPS is a navigation system that can help lost people figure out where they are.

To further their dream, Burrell and Kao founded their business and named it Garmin Ltd.; they located the business in Olathe, Kansas. Sales of GPS receivers will reach $4.7 billion in 2003 in North America and are forecast to more than double by 2008. Garmin's revenue is up 23 percent annually since 1996 and was $465 million in 1993. Profits are at $142 million. Together, Burrell and Kao control 45 percent of Garmin's outstanding shares (they never received any venture capital funds). Based on the company's market value, Kao is worth $970 million and Burrell, $810 million.

Source: Arik Hesseldahl, "Taking the World by Hand," *Forbes*, October 27, 2003, p. 90.

Importance of Small Businesses

small business
A company that is independently owned and operated and is not dominant in its field; generally has fewer than 100 employees.

A **small business** is a company that is independently owned and operated. Some small businesses, such as neighborhood flower shops, restaurants, or dry-cleaning stores, serve local areas. Other small businesses, such as mail-order and Internet companies, serve customers all over the world. Owners of small businesses often perform all management tasks.

The Small Business Administration (SBA), the government agency that lends money to small businesses, considers a business small if it has fewer than 100 employees. According to this definition, more than 98 percent of the businesses in the United States are small businesses. These small businesses play an important role in the U.S. economy. They employ millions of American workers and sell billions of dollars of products and services.

Small businesses tend to produce more innovations than larger businesses. Many of the most important high-technology companies in the country, including Intel, Apple, and Microsoft, began as small businesses. Microsoft is one of the largest companies in the world, and its founder, Bill Gates, is one of the world's richest people. Some of today's small companies may eventually become corporate giants.

Entrepreneurship in Large and Medium-Sized Businesses

Many large and medium-sized organizations have begun to encourage their managers to become more innovative and to take more risks. At Dell Computer, for example, CEO and founder Michael Dell encourages his employees to take risks by allowing them to work independently, make mistakes, and learn from the process. He sets hard-to-meet targets and encourages his employees to stretch themselves to meet them. His approach has helped Dell become one of the most successful companies in the country.

Businesses that want to encourage managers to think more like entrepreneurs must find ways to support and encourage people who develop new products and services. Like Michael Dell, they must be willing to accept failure and to encourage people even after a new idea fails. Entrepreneurship within a large or medium-sized company is sometimes called *intrapreneurship*. Intrapreneurs take risks, but not with their own investments.

The Challenge of the New Information Age

Successful implementation of the basic planning, organizing, and controlling functions of management requires that managers have adequate information. This means managers must first identify and then acquire the necessary information. Identifying and acquiring adequate information historically have been two of the biggest challenges of managers. The advent of the computer age has greatly altered not only the availability of information but also the manner in which it is identified and acquired.

user-friendly computer
Computer that requires very little technical knowledge to use.

The phenomenal improvements in computer hardware have been accompanied by improvements in software and user compatibility. Modern computers are much more **user friendly** than those of the past. Managers today do not need to know sophisticated programming languages and computer jargon to use computers. The use of computers in the management process is discussed throughout this book.

Organization of This Book

This book is divided into six sections:

- Part I: Foundations
- Part II: Contemporary Issues
- Part III: Planning Skills
- Part IV: Organizing and Staffing Skills
- Part V: Directing Skills
- Part VI: Controlling Skills

Part I provides an overview of the management process. Chapter 1 defines management and describes the functions and skills of management. Chapter 2 presents a historical view of management. Chapter 3 describes the importance of communication skills in management. Chapter 4 focuses on the decision-making skills required in management.

Part II analyzes contemporary issues in management. Chapter 5 describes the internationalization of business. Chapter 6 focuses on ethics and social responsibility.

Part III focuses on planning skills in management. Chapter 7 describes the planning process, including its objectives, strategy issues, and the principles of strategic management. Chapter 8 focuses on applying planning skills to the operations processes of the organization.

Part IV analyzes the organizing and staffing skills of management. Chapters 9 and 10 describe organization principles and the development of organizational structures. Chapter 11 discusses the role of formal and informal work groups in businesses. Chapter 12 describes the staffing process. Chapter 13 describes the process of training and developing employees and managers.

Part V analyzes the directing skills of management. Chapters 14 and 15 examine motivation in business and the importance of leadership in improving organizational performance. Chapter 16 describes approaches to managing conflict and stress. Chapter 17 focuses on managing change and culture.

Part VI explores the controlling skills of management. Chapter 18 describes the controlling function of management. Chapter 19 discusses appraising and rewarding performance as a method of control and direction. Chapter 20 describes the application of managerial control in the operations processes.

Summary

1. *Define management.* Management is a form of work that involves coordinating an organization's resources—land, labor, and capital—to accomplish organizational objectives.

2. *Describe the levels of management.* Three levels of management exist. Top management establishes the goals of the organization and the actions necessary to achieve them. Middle management develops departmental goals and actions necessary to achieve organizational objectives. Supervisors manage operative employees.

3. *Discuss the functions of management.* The functions of management are
   - Planning: deciding what objectives to pursue during a future period and what to do to achieve those objectives.
   - Organizing: grouping activities, assigning activities, and providing the authority necessary to carry out the activities.
   - Staffing: determining human resource needs and recruiting, selecting, training, and developing human resources.
   - Leading: directing and channeling human behavior toward the accomplishment of objectives.
   - Controlling: measuring performance against objectives, determining causes of deviations, and taking corrective action where necessary.

4. *Explain the roles of a manager.* The roles of a manager fall into three major categories: interpersonal, informational, and decisional. Formal authority and status together generate certain interpersonal roles. The interpersonal roles, in turn, determine the informational roles of the manager. Finally, access to information, authority, and status place the manager at a central point in the organizational decision-making process.

5. *Describe the skills required to perform the work of management.* The three skills required in management are
   - Conceptual skills: involve understanding the relationship of the parts of a business to one another and to the business as a whole. Decision making, planning, and organizing are separate managerial activities that require conceptual skills.
   - Human relations skills: involve understanding people and being able to work well with them.
   - Technical skills: involve being able to perform the mechanics of a particular job.

6. *Explain how principles of management are developed.* Typically, principles are developed through a controlled experiment process. However, management principles are developed through observation and deduction.

7. *Discuss the increasing role of women and minorities in management.* The number of women in the civilian labor force has grown faster than the growth rate of the total number of people employed. Women and minorities have also had a higher percentage growth rate than the overall growth rate of employment in managerial and professional jobs.

8. *Define the glass ceiling facing women and minorities.* The glass ceiling refers to a level within the managerial hierarchy beyond which very few women and minorities advance.

9. *Explain diversity.* Diversity means including people of different genders, races, religions, nationalities, ethnic groups, age groups, and physical abilities.

10. *Define entrepreneur.* An entrepreneur conceives the idea of what product or service to produce, starts the organization, and builds it to the point where additional people are needed.

11. *Define small business.* A small business is a company that is independently owned and operated and is not dominant in its field. As a rule, small businesses have fewer than 100 employees.

12. *Outline three requirements for encouraging entrepreneurship in medium-sized and large businesses.* Organizations must develop a system that supports and encourages people to

champion their new ideas or products; they must tolerate failures; and they must have effective communication systems.

13. *Describe user-friendly computers.* User-friendly computers require very little technical knowledge to use.

Review Questions

1. What is management?
2. Describe the levels of management.
3. Name and describe the basic management functions.
4. Define the basic skills required in management.
5. How are principles of management developed?
6. Define entreneurship.
7. Distinguish between a professional manager and an entrepreneur.
8. What is a small business?
9. What are three essential characteristics for developing an entrepreneurial spirit in larger corporations?
10. Explain how the composition of the managerial workforce is changing in terms of gender and race.
11. Define glass ceiling and give examples of how it affects women and minorities.
12. Define diversity.
13. Define user-friendly.

Skill-Building Questions

1. Management has often been described as a universal process, meaning the basics of management are transferable and applicable in almost any environment. Do you believe a good manager in a bank could be equally effective in a college or university? Explain your reasoning.
2. How does one decide who is and who is not a manager in a given organization? For example, is the operator of a one-person business, such as a corner grocery store, a manager? Explain.
3. Do you think management can be learned through books and study or only through experience?
4. Discuss the following statement: All entrepreneurs are managers, but not all managers are entrepreneurs.
5. Explain how you would deal with the difficulties and challenges of the glass ceiling.

Skill-Building Exercise 1.1

Success of a Business

Have each student go to the library and bring back to class an actual example of an entrepreneurial business and a small business. Possible sources of information include *Venture, Inc., Business Week,* or *The Wall Street Journal.*

Each student should then prepare a five-minute report on the following:

a. History of the organization.
b. Main product of the organization.
c. Reasons for success.
d. Role of management.

Skill-Building Exercise 1.2

Online Research

In this chapter, you have learned about the field of management. For more information, go to *Business Week* online at www.businessweek.com. Locate an article on a business that interests you. Write a summary of the article and present your findings to the class.

Skill-Building Exercise 1.3

Required Attributes of a Manager

The following ads were taken from the want ads section of a newspaper. All company names and locations have been disguised.

1. Choose the job that is most attractive to you.
2. Your instructor will form you into groups with other students that selected the same job as you. Your group should then develop a list of required and desirable skills for the job.
3. Each group should be prepared to present and defend their list before the class.

CORPORATE MANAGER

CONSOLIDATIONS AND BUDGETS

Challenging career opportunity with moderate-size international machinery manufacturer with primary manufacturing locations overseas. Report to V.P.-Finance. Responsible for monthly consolidations, analysis, and financial reports. Prepare annual consolidated budgets and periodically monitor performance.

5 years' relevant experience in similar environment, familiarity with foreign exchange transactions preferred. Must be intelligent, self-disciplined, high-energy professional. We offer competitive compensation and benefits package. For prompt, totally confidential consideration please forward full resume including earnings history to: Vice President, Employee Relations.

A&B MODERN MACHINERY CO., INC.

An Equal Opportunity Employer M/F/HC

MANAGER SYSTEMS DEVELOPMENT

American Health Care Plans, which operates a number of HMOs across the country is seeking an experienced professional who can take a leadership role in the development of state-of-the-art claims processing systems. This position will report to the VP of MIS, and will involve extensive interaction with claims operational personnel as well as the programmer analysts who are implementing the new systems.

The ideal candidate will have a management, accounting, or computer science degree with a strong emphasis on information systems. The candidate's background should include at least five years in systems development and operational management in an insurance environment. Health insurance, experience and advanced degree are pluses.

We are looking for a very special person, who will bring intelligence, leadership, and creativity to the position. The selected candidate must also be able to take on expanding responsibilities as the company grows. We offer a competitive compensation package and a full range of benefits.

Qualified persons respond by sending resume and salary requirements to our Personnel Director.

American Health Care Plans

An Equal Opportunity Employer

Human Resource Manager

Jackson & Brown's Professional Products Division, the world leader in the development, manufacture, and sale of contact lenses, currently seeks a Human Resource Manager. Responsibilities will include managing personnel policies, practices, and procedures in the area of employee relations, training, organizational development, recruitment, and compensation.

The successful candidate will have a bachelor's degree, preferably in a business related field and 5 years' experience as a generalist in Human Resources. 1-2 years must be in a supervisory capacity. This highly visible position will report directly to the Vice President of Human Resources, Professional Products Division.

For immediate reply, send your resume to: Ms. Jane L. Doe, Professional Products Division.

Jackson & Brown

An Equal Opportunity Employer

VICE PRESIDENT OF MARKETING

... Office Automation Systems

Established Midwest manufacturer has an outstanding career opportunity available for an experienced, marketing professional.

You will be responsible for developing marketing plans and overseeing subsequent activities. Specific duties include:

- Market Analysis
- Product/Pricing Strategy
- Field Sales Support
- Advertising & Promotion
- Revenue Reporting and Projection

This is a prestigious opportunity to work in an industry-leading corporation, international in scope, to assure that our present and future products meet customers requirements and increase our market share. Career growth potential is exceptional. Benefits and salary are executive level. To apply, rush an outline of your qualification to the address below. All responses will be kept in inviolable secrecy. We are proud to be an equal opportunity employer.

Skill-Building Exercise 1.4

Are You an Entrepreneur?

In recent years, entrepreneurs, or folks who do things their own way, have become a highly analyzed species, but often the data uncovered have been so voluminous as to confuse rather than clarify.

Among the most confused, perhaps, are thousands of would-be entrepreneurs whose friends tell them they aren't equipped with the qualities for success.

Recognizing this, Northwestern Mutual Life Insurance Co., which considers its own agents to be entrepreneurial, wondered what it is that makes a good entrepreneur. And so it commissioned a test.

Professor John Braun, a psychologist at the University of Bridgeport, is the author of this somewhat revealing—if not entirely scientific—quiz that aims to clarify your understanding.

- Significantly high numbers of entrepreneurs are children of first-generation Americans. If your parents were immigrants, add one to your score. If not, subtract one.
- As a rule, successful entrepreneurs weren't top achievers in school. If you were a top student, deduct four. If not, add four points.
- Entrepreneurs weren't especially enthusiastic about group activities in school. If you enjoyed such activities, subtract one. If not, add it.
- As youngsters, entrepreneurs often preferred to be alone. Did you prefer aloneness? If so, add one. Otherwise, subtract it.
- Those who started childhood enterprises, such as lemonade stands, or who ran for elected office at school can add two because enterprise is easily traced to an early age. Those who weren't enterprising must subtract two.
- Stubbornness as a child seems to translate into determination to do things one's own way. If you were stubborn enough to learn the hard way, add one. Otherwise, subtract it.
- Caution may involve unwillingness to take risks. Were you a cautious child? If so, drop four points. Otherwise, add them.
- If you were more daring than your playmates, add four.
- If the opinions of others matter a lot to you, subtract one. Add one otherwise.
- Weariness with daily routine is sometimes a motivating factor in starting a business. If this would be a factor in your desire to go out on your own, add two points. Otherwise, deduct them.
- If you enjoy work, are you willing to work overnight? Yes, add two. No, deduct six.
- Add four more if you would be willing to work as long as it takes with little or no sleep to finish a job. No deductions if you wouldn't.
- Entrepreneurs generally enjoy their activity so much they move from one project to another without stopping. When you complete a project successfully, do you immediately begin another? Yes, plus two. No, minus two.
- Would you be willing to spend your savings to start a business? If so, add two, and deduct that many if you aren't.
- Add two more if you'd be willing to borrow from others to supplement your own funds. If not, you lose two points.
- If you failed, would you immediately work to start again? Yes gives you four, no takes that many away.
- Subtract another point if failure would make you look for a good-paying job.
- Do you believe entrepreneurs are risky? Yes, minus two. No, plus two.
- Add a point if you write out long-term and short-term goals. Otherwise, subtract one.
- You win two points if you think you have more knowledge and experience with cash flow than most people. You lose them if you don't.
- If you're easily bored, add two. Deduct two points if you aren't.
- If you're an optimist, add two. If you're a pessimist, erase two.

Scoring

If you score 35 or more, you have everything going for you. Between 15 and 35 suggests you have background, skills, and talent to succeed. Zero to 15 indicates you ought to be successful with application and skill development.

Zero to minus 15 doesn't rule you out, but it indicates you would have to work extra hard to overcome a lack of built-in advantages and skills. And if you score worse than minus 15, your talents probably lie elsewhere.

Source: Northwestern Mutual Life Insurance Company. Used with permission.

Case Incident 1.1

The Expansion of Blue Streak

Arthur Benton started the Blue Streak Delivery Company five years ago. Blue Streak initially provided commercial delivery services for all packages within the city of Unionville (population 1 million).

Art started with himself, one clerk, and one driver. Within three years, Blue Streak had grown to the point of requiring 4 clerks and 16 drivers. It was then that Art decided to expand and provide statewide service. He figured this would initially require the addition of two new offices, one located at Logantown (population 500,000) in the southern part of the state and one at Thomas City (population 250,000) in the northern part of the state. Each office was staffed with a manager, two clerks, and four drivers. Because both Logantown and Thomas City were within 150 miles of Unionville, Art was able to visit each office at least once a week and personally coordinate the operations in addition to providing general management assistance. The statewide delivery system met with immediate success and reported a healthy profit for the first year.

The next year, Art decided to expand and include two neighboring states. Art set up two offices in each of the two neighboring states. However, operations never seemed to go smoothly in the neighboring states. Schedules were constantly being fouled up, deliveries were lost, and customer complaints multiplied. After nine months, Art changed office managers in all four out-of-state offices. Things still did not improve. Convinced that he was the only one capable of straightening out the out-of-state offices, Art began visiting them once every two weeks. This schedule required Art to spend at least half of his time on the road traveling between offices.

After four months of this activity, Art began to be tired of the constant travel; operations in the two neighboring states still had not improved. In fact, on each trip Art found himself spending all his time putting out fires that should have been handled by the office managers.

Art decided to have a one-day meeting that all of his office managers would attend to discuss problems and come up with some answers. At the meeting, several issues were raised. First, all of the managers thought Art's visits were too frequent. Second, most of the managers did not seem to know exactly what Art expected them to do. Finally, each of the managers believed they should have the authority to make changes in their office procedures without checking with Art before making the change.

Questions

1. What suggestions would you offer to Art to improve his operation?
2. What management skills must Art master if he is to resolve his problems and continue to grow?

Case Incident 1.2

Wadsworth Company

Last year, Donna Carroll was appointed supervisor of the small parts subassembly department of Wadsworth Company. The department employed 28 people. Donna had wanted the promotion and thought her 15 years of experience in various jobs at the company qualified her for the job.

Donna decided to have two group leaders report to her. She appointed Evelyn Castalos and Bill Degger to these new positions. She made it clear, however, that they retained their present operative jobs and were expected to contribute to the direct productive efforts. Evelyn is ambitious and a highly productive employee. Bill is a steady, reliable employee.

Work assignment decisions were to be made by Evelyn. She took on this responsibility with great enthusiasm and drew up work-scheduling plans covering a period of one month. She believed productivity could be increased by 8 percent due primarily to work assignment improvements. She went regularly from workplace to workplace, checking the finished volume of work at each station. Bill assumed, at the suggestion and support of Donna, the task of training new employees or retraining present employees on new work coming into the department.

Donna spent most of her time preparing and reading reports. She made certain to be friendly with most of the other supervisors. She talked with them frequently and helped them fill out forms and reports required by their jobs. She also frequently circulated among the employees of her department, exchanging friendly remarks. However, when an employee asked a question concerning work, Donna referred the person to either Evelyn or Bill.

Some of the employees complained among themselves that the work assignments were unfair. They contended that favorites of Evelyn got all the easy jobs and, although the present volume of work had increased, no extra help was being hired. Several times the employees talked with Donna about this, but Donna referred them to Evelyn each time. Likewise, many of the employees complained about Bill's performance. They based their opinions on the apparent lack of knowledge and skill the new employees had after receiving training from Bill.

Questions

1. Do you think the duties Evelyn and Bill are handling should have been delegated by Donna?
2. What difficulties do you see for Evelyn and Bill in being both group leaders and operative employees?
3. Do you consider Evelyn and Bill to be managers? Why or why not?

References and Additional Readings

1. Throughout this book, the terms *objectives* and *goals* will be used interchangeably.
2. Henry Mintzberg, "The Manager's Job: Folklore and Fact," *Harvard Business Review,* July–August 1975, pp. 49–61.
3. See Robert L. Katz, "The Skills of an Effective Administrator," *Harvard Business Review,* September–October 1987, pp. 90–102.

2

The Management Movement

Learning Objectives

After studying this chapter, you will able to:

1. Explain why management did not emerge as a recognized discipline until the twentieth century.
2. Describe the three facets of the U.S. Industrial Revolution.
3. Discuss the role the captains of industry played in the development of modern organizations.
4. Define scientific management, and outline the role Frederick W. Taylor and his contemporaries played in its development.
5. Summarize Henri Fayol's contributions to modern management.
6. Discuss the human relations thrust in management, with emphasis on the role of the Hawthorne experiments.
7. Define the management process period, the management theory jungle, the systems approach, and the contingency approach.
8. Compare the major differences in the American, Japanese, and Theory Z organizations.
9. Summarize the eight characteristics of excellent companies identified by Peters and Waterman.
10. Explain why the international aspects of management are currently being emphasized.
11. Discuss some predictions as to how managers might manage in the twenty-first century.

Chapter Preview

One of the greatest management challenges of the twentieth century was the Manhattan Project, that vast endeavor to produce the atomic bomb. Whatever one thinks of the final result of the project, the accomplishment of harnessing and focusing a huge number of talented, temperamental, single-minded scientists and engineers represents a marvel of leadership. Other great historical tasks such as building the great pyramids of Egypt and South America, the digging of the Panama Canal, and placing a person on the Moon were no less complicated. All great tasks have been completed because of great leaders and pioneers of management thought.

One great example of successful leadership and application of management thought was the Manhattan Project's General Leslie Groves. He was known for his willingness to let ideas succeed or fail on their merit rather than on his own managerial instincts. He recognized that there was rarely a single best way to accomplish a task. In other words, in an almost Darwinian situation, if the manager will let ideas compete fairly the fittest idea will usually survive.

The great contributors to management thought described in this chapter all had unique ideas, went against the established thoughts of their day, learned from their peers, were never willing to accept defeat, and persevered when criticized. Their gift to contemporary business managers is the set of tools with which to mold and create the ideas and success of the future. Our responsibility is to use the tools wisely.

Source: Bill Walsh, "Managing the Monster," *Forbes,* October 9, 1995, p. 17.

Analyzing Management Skills

What are the benefits of understanding how management theory and practice has changed over the past 100 years? How might you use this information as a manager?

Applying Management Skills

Recall or imagine a workplace task that you found inefficient or tedious. Imagine that your manager asks you for suggestions to improve the procedure for completing the task. What would be your general approach for improving the procedure?

A knowledge of the history of any discipline is necessary to understanding where the discipline is and where it is going. Management is no exception. For example, how often have you read a news story covering a particular incident and formed an opinion only to change it when you understood the events leading up to the incident? Many of today's managerial problems began during the early management movement. Understanding the historical evolution of these problems helps the modern manager cope with them. It also helps today's managers develop a feel for why the managerial approaches that worked in earlier times do not necessarily work today. The challenge to present and future managers is not to memorize historical names and dates; it is to develop a feel for why and how things happened and to apply this knowledge to the practice of management.

Some forms of management have existed since the beginning of time. Ever since one human tried to direct another, management thought has been developing. While there are numerous isolated examples of very early management practices and theories (see Figure 2.1 and Management Illustration 2.1), the development of management thought as we know it is a relatively modern concept. The age of industrialization in the nineteenth century and the subsequent emergence of large corporate organizations called for new approaches to management. The

FIGURE 2.1
Very Early
References to
Management

Source: Daniel Wren, *The Evolution of Management Thought*, 3rd ed. (New York: John Wiley & Sons, 1987), pp. 13–18.

1792–1750 B.C.	King Hammurabi of Babylon issued a unique code of 282 laws that governed business dealings and a host of other societal matters.	551–479 B.C.	Confucius of China advocated that governmental offices should go to men based on merit and proven ability.
1750 B.C.	Viziers were created in Egypt. Viziers acted as a type of professional manager for the king.	469–399 B.C.	Socrates of Greece observed that managerial skills were transferable.
1300 B.C.	Moses of the Bible was counseled by Jethro, his father-in-law, as to how to organize his people.	384–322 B.C.	Aristotle of Greece exhibited numerous insights into management, touching on the topics of specialization, departmentalization, centralization, and leadership.

environment that led up to and surrounded the emergence of management thought is the subject of this chapter.

U.S. Industrial Revolution

As the name suggests, the U.S. Industrial Revolution encompassed the period when the United States began to shift from an almost totally agrarian society to an industrialized society. The year 1860 is generally thought of as the start of the Industrial Revolution in this country.

Daniel Wren has described the Industrial Revolution in America as having three facets: power, transportation, and communication.[1] Many new inventions, such as the steam engine, allowed industries to expand and locate in areas that at one time were devoid of factories and other signs of progress. Industry was no longer dependent on water and horses for its power.

Transportation moved through periods of industrial and commercial traffic on canals, railroads, and eventually efficient road systems. However, progress always brings its own set of unique problems. Communication lines were extended, decisions had to be made within a rapidly changing framework, scheduling difficulties arose, and new markets developed. All of these changes required new management skills.

Communication by way of the telegraph, telephone, and radio changed the way U.S. organizations functioned. Speed and efficiency dramatically increased. The trend away from an agrarian society forced many behavioral changes on the workers of the land. Schedules, work tasks, workloads, compensation, and safety were hotly debated issues well into the twentieth century.

Captains of Industry

Once industrialization began, it continued at a rapid pace. By the end of the nineteenth century, the economy had shifted from a mainly agrarian one to an economy heavily involved with manufactured goods and industrial markets.[2]

Niccolo Machiavelli (1469–1527) was born in Florence, Italy, into an old Tuscan family. In his late twenties, Machiavelli became a leading figure in the Republic of Florence where he served as first secretary of the council of the republic for 14 years. Following a shift in power in the republic, Machiavelli was dismissed from his office, arrested, tortured, and imprisoned. Orders from Pope Leo X resulted in Machiavelli finally being released from prison. Machiavelli spent the last 14 years of his life in retirement in Florence. During these retirement years, Machiavelli wrote several books on history and politics. He is best known for his book *The Prince*, written in 1513 (but not published until 1532).

Machiavelli's basic assumption was that all people are bad and ever ready to display a vicious nature, whenever they may find an opportunity to do so. Therefore, Machiavelli reasoned that rulers and leaders were justified in using any management style that suited their purpose. In other words, he believed that the ends always justified the means. He believed that rulers should not be concerned with being virtuous but rather should use whatever means, no matter how wicked, to achieve the desired results of making people obey. It is in this light that *Machiavellian* has come to mean an unscrupulous, crafty, and cunning management style.

Sources: Daniel A. Wren, *The Evolution of Management Thought,* 2nd ed. (New York: John Wiley & Sons, 1979), p. 35; and *The World Book Encyclopedia* (Chicago: World Book—Childcraft International Inc., 1979), p. 10.

During the last quarter of the nineteenth century, American business was dominated and shaped by captains of industry. These captains of industry included John D. Rockefeller (oil), James B. Duke (tobacco), Andrew Carnegie (steel), and Cornelius Vanderbilt (steamships and railroads). In contrast to the laissez-faire attitudes of previous generations, these individuals often pursued profit and self-interest above all else. Although their methods have been questioned, they did obtain results. Under these individuals, giant companies were formed through mergers in both the consumer and producer goods industries. They created new forms of organizations and introduced new methods of marketing. For the first time, nationwide distributing and marketing organizations were formed. The birth of the corporate giant also altered the business decision-making environment.

For the empire building and methods of the captains of industry, previous management approaches no longer applied. Government began to regulate business. In 1890, the Sherman Antitrust Act, which sought to check corporate practices "in restraint of trade," was passed.

By 1890, previous management methods were no longer applicable to U.S. industry. No longer could managers make on-the-spot decisions and maintain records in their heads. Corporations had become large scale, with national markets. Communication and transportation had expanded and spurred great industrial growth. Technological innovations contributed to industrial growth: The invention of the internal combustion engine and the use of electricity as a power source greatly speeded industrial development at the close of the nineteenth century.

However, despite what seemed to be an ideal climate for prosperity and productivity, wages were low.[3] Production methods were crude, and worker training was almost nonexistent. There were no methods or standards for measuring work. Work had not been studied to determine the most desirable way to complete a task. The psychological and physical aspects of a job such as boredom, monotony, and fatigue were not studied or even considered in the design of most jobs.

At this point in the development of management, the engineering profession made significant contributions. Engineers designed, built, installed, and made operative the production systems. It was only natural, then, for them to study the methods used in operating these systems.

Scientific Management and Frederick W. Taylor

The development of specialized tasks and of departments within organizations had come with the rapid industrial growth and the creation of big business. One person no longer performed every task but specialized in performing only a few tasks. This created a need to coordinate, integrate, and systematize the work flow. The time spent on each item could be significant if a company was producing several thousand items. Increased production plus the new need for integrating and systematizing the work flow led engineers to begin studying work flows and job content.

The spark generally credited with igniting the interest of engineers in general business problems was a paper presented in 1886 by Henry Towne, president of the Yale and Towne Manufacturing Company, to the American Society of Mechanical Engineers. Towne stressed that engineers should be concerned with the financial and profit orientations of the business as well as their traditional technical responsibilities.[4] A young mechanical engineer named Frederick Winslow Taylor was seated in the audience. Towne's talk sparked an idea in Taylor's mind for studying problems at Midvale Steel Company. During his years at Midvale Steel Company, Taylor worked with and observed production workers at all levels. It did not take him long to figure out that many workers put forth less than 100 percent effort. Taylor referred to this tendency to restrict output as **soldiering.** Because soldiering conflicted with Taylor's Quaker-Puritan background (Management Illustration 2.2 discusses Taylor's background), it was hard for him to understand and accept. He decided to find out why workers soldiered.

Taylor quickly saw that workers had little or no reason to produce more; most wage systems of that time were based on attendance and position. Piece-rate systems had been tried before but generally failed because of poor use and weak standards. Taylor believed a piece-rate system would work if the workers believed the standard had been fairly set and management would stick to that standard. Taylor wanted to use scientific and empirical methods rather than tradition and custom for setting work standards. Taylor's efforts became the true beginning of scientific management.

Taylor first formally presented his views to the Society of Mechanical Engineers in 1895.[5] His views were expanded in book form in 1903 and again in 1911.[6] **Scientific management,** as developed by Taylor, was based on four main principles:

1. The development of a scientific method of designing jobs to replace the old rule-of-thumb methods. This involved gathering, classifying, and tabulating data to arrive at the "one best way" to perform a task or a series of tasks.
2. The scientific selection and progressive teaching and development of employees. Taylor saw the value of matching the job to the worker. He also emphasized the need to study worker strengths and weaknesses and to provide training to improve employee performance.
3. The bringing together of scientifically selected employees and scientifically developed methods for designing jobs. Taylor believed that new and scientific methods of job design should not merely be put before an employee; they should also be fully explained by management. He believed employees would

soldiering
Describes the actions of employees who intentionally restrict output.

scientific management
Philosophy of Frederick W. Taylor that sought to increase productivity and make the work easier by scientifically studying work methods and establishing standards.

Frederick Winslow Taylor was born in Germantown, Pennsylvania, in 1856 of Quaker-Puritan stock. From his boyhood, Taylor had sought to improve everything he saw. Other kids viewed him as weird, since he seemed more interested in laying out the ball field correctly than in playing the game.

His parents wanted him to be a lawyer like his father and hence enrolled him at Phillips Exeter Academy to prepare for Harvard. Though Taylor passed the Harvard exams with honors, his poor health and eyesight forced him to take up an apprenticeship as a pattern maker and machinist with the Enterprise Hydraulic works at Philadelphia in 1874. At the end of his apprenticeship period, Taylor joined Midvale Steel as a common laborer and rose to machinist, to gang boss of the machinists, to foreman of the shop, to master mechanic in charge of repairs and maintenance throughout the plant, and to chief engineer in the short span of six years.

After a three-year stint as general manager at Manufacturing Investment Company, Taylor set up practice as a consulting engineer for management. It was as a consultant to Bethlehem Steel Company that Taylor made his greatest contribution to management with his time and motion studies. Employees willing to follow Taylor's "one best way" of doing a job found that their productivity soared and that they could double or even triple their old pay. As the pace of work accelerated, some employees rebelled, and complaints against Taylor by organized labor even landed him in front of a Senate investigatory panel in 1912.

Recently, some scholars have challenged the methodology and accuracy of Taylor's studies. The assertion is that Taylor drew erroneous conclusions by simplifying his experiments and data collection. Even if these recent accusations are true, Taylor's imprint on management cannot be denied. As stated by populist critic Jeremy Rifkin, "His work principles have been transported to every sector of the globe and have been responsible for converting much of the world's population to the modern time frame."

The world of management was indeed poorer when Taylor died of pneumonia a day after his fifty-ninth birthday. The epitaph on his grave in Philadelphia reads "Frederick W. Taylor, Father of Scientific Management" and rightly so.

Sources: Daniel A. Wren, *The Evolution of Management Thought* (New York: Ronald Press, 1972); Alan Farnham, "The Man Who Changed Work Forever," *Fortune*, July 21, 1997, p. 114; John Greco, "Frederick Winslow Taylor (1856–1915): The Science of Business," *Journal of Business Strategy*, September–October 1999, p. 28; and Charles D. Wrege and Richard M. Hodgetts, "Frederick W. Taylor's 1899 Pig Iron Observations: Examining Fact, Fiction and Lessons for the New Millennium," *Academy of Management Journal*, December 2000, pp. 1283–91. For more information about Bethlehem Steel Company, please visit its website at www.bethsteel.com. You can read more about Frederick Winslow Taylor by visiting the Taylor Archive website at www.lib.stevens-tech.edu.

show little resistance to changes in methods if they understood the reasons for the changes and saw a chance for greater earnings for themselves.

4. A division of work resulting in an interdependence between management and workers. Taylor believed if they were truly dependent on each other, cooperation would naturally follow.[7]

For both management and employees, scientific management brought a new attitude toward their respective duties and toward each other.[8] It was a new philosophy about the use of human effort. It emphasized maximum output with minimum effort through the elimination of waste and inefficiency at the operative level of the organization.[9] A methodological approach was used to study job tasks. This approach included research and experimentation methods (scientific methods). Standards were set in the areas of personnel, working conditions, equipment, output, and procedures. The managers planned the work; the employees performed it. The result was closer cooperation between managers and employees.

The scientific study of work also emphasized specialization and division of labor. Thus, the need for an organizational framework became more and more apparent. The concepts of line and staff emerged. In an effort to motivate employees,

In 1899, a man named Henry Noll loaded 48 tons of pig iron in one day as part of a scientific management experiment conducted by Frederick W. Taylor for Bethlehem Steel. From that experiment, Taylor developed a high-incentive work program with a set sequence of work and rest motions. The program—described in Taylor's *Principles of Scientific Management*—was designed to more than triple the amount a worker could load in a day. The Taylor method was adopted by companies all over the country.

When the results of the experiment were published, Henry Noll—under the pseudonym "Schmidt"—was described only as an ambitious and healthy 27-year-old man. In a social commentary published 12 years later, Upton Sin-clair described Taylor's method as inhumane and accused him of unfairly inducing "Schmidt" to perform 362 percent more work for 61 percent more pay.

In response to the criticism, Taylor and others made several unsuccessful attempts to find Henry Noll, and rumors began to surface that he had died of overexertion. In 1914, he was finally found and pronounced healthy by a physician. Henry Noll—"Schmidt"—died of a natural death in 1925.

Source: Ann Kovalenko, *The Sunday Call-Chronicle,* Allentown, PA, December 6, 1964.

wage incentives were developed in most scientific management programs. Once standards were set, managers began to monitor actual performance and compare it with the standards. Thus began the managerial function of control.

Scientific management is a philosophy about the relationship between people and work, not a technique or an efficiency device. Taylor's ideas and scientific management were based on a concern not only for the proper design of the job but also for the worker. This aspect has often been misunderstood. Taylor and scientific management were (and still are) attacked as being inhumane and aimed only at increasing output. In this regard, scientific management and Taylor were the targets of a congressional investigation in 1912.[10] The key to Taylor's thinking was that he saw scientific management as benefiting management and employees equally: Management could achieve more work in a given amount of time; the employee could produce more—and hence earn more—with little or no additional effort. In summary, Taylor and other scientific management pioneers believed employees could be motivated by economic rewards, provided those rewards were related to individual performance. Management Illustration 2.3 provides an interesting story related to Frederick Taylor.

Other Scientific Management Pioneers

Several disciples and colleagues of Taylor helped to promote scientific management. Carl Barth was often called the most orthodox of Taylor's followers. He worked with Taylor at Bethlehem Steel and followed him as a consultant when Taylor left Bethlehem. Barth did not alter or add to scientific management to any significant degree; rather, he worked to popularize Taylor's ideas.

Morris Cooke worked directly with Taylor on several occasions. Cooke's major contribution was the application of scientific management to educational and municipal organizations. Cooke worked hard to bring management and labor together through scientific management. His thesis was that labor was as responsible for production as management was. Cooke believed increased production would improve the position of both.[11] Thus, Cooke broadened the scope of scientific management and helped gain the support of organized labor.

FIGURE 2.2
Lillian M. Gilbreth:
First Lady of
Management

Source: From Daniel A.
Wren, *Evolution of
Management Thought*, 4th
Edition. Copyright © 1994
John Wiley & Sons, Inc. This
material is used by
permission of John Wiley &
Sons, Inc.

- First female member of the Society of Industrial Engineers (1921).
- First female member of the American Society of Mechanical Engineers.
- First female selected to attend the National Academy of Engineering.
- First woman to receive the degree of Honorary Master of Engineering (University of Michigan).
- First female professor of management at an engineering school (Purdue University, 1935).
- First female professor of management at Newark College of Engineering.
- First and only female recipient of the Gilbreth Medal (1931).
- First female awarded the Gantt Gold Medal.
- First and only recipient of the CIOS Gold Medal.
- Received over 20 honorary degrees and served five U.S. presidents as an adviser.

Henry Lawrence Gantt worked with Taylor at both Midvale Steel and Bethlehem Steel. Gantt is best known for his work in production control and his invention of the Gantt chart, which is still in use today. The Gantt chart graphically depicts both expected and completed production. (Gantt charts are discussed in Chapter 8.) Gantt was also one of the first management pioneers to state publicly the social responsibility of management and business. He believed the community would attempt to take over business if the business system neglected its social responsibilities.[12]

Frank and Lillian Gilbreth were important to the early management movement both as a husband-and-wife team and as individuals. The Gilbreths, inspired by Taylor and scientific research, were among the first to use motion picture films to study hand and body movements to eliminate wasted motion. Frank Gilbreth's major area of interest was the study of motions and work methods. Lillian Gilbreth's primary field was psychology. Following Frank's untimely death in 1924 (he was in his mid-50s), Lillian continued their work for almost 50 years until her death in 1972. During this time, Lillian's work emphasized concern for the worker, and she showed how scientific management should foster rather than stifle employees. Because of her many achievements (see Figure 2.2), Lillian Gilbreth became known as the First Lady of Management. By combining motion study and psychology, the Gilbreths contributed greatly to research in the areas of fatigue, monotony, micromotion study, and morale.

Fayol's Theory of Management

Henri Fayol, a Frenchman, was the first to issue a complete statement on a theory of general management. Though popular in Europe in the early 1900s, the theory did not really gain acceptance in America until the late 1940s. Today, Fayol's greatest contribution is considered to be his theory of management principles and elements. Fayol identified the following 14 principles of management:

1. *Division of work:* concept of specialization of work.
2. *Authority:* formal (positional) authority versus personal authority.
3. *Discipline:* based on obedience and respect.
4. *Unity of command:* each employee should receive orders from only one superior.
5. *Unity of direction:* one boss and one plan for a group of activities having the same objective.

6. *Subordination of individual interests to the general interest:* a plea to abolish the tendency to place individual interest ahead of the group interest.
7. *Remuneration:* the mode of payment of wages was dependent on many factors.
8. *Centralization:* the degree of centralization desired depended on the situation and the formal communication channels.
9. *Scalar chain* (line of authority): shows the routing of the line of authority and formal communication channels.
10. *Order:* ensured a place for everything.
11. *Equity:* resulted from kindness and justice.
12. *Stability of tenured personnel:* called for orderly personnel planning.
13. *Initiative:* called for individual zeal and energy in all efforts.
14. *Esprit de corps:* stressed the building of harmony and unity within the organization.

Fayol developed his list of principles from the practices he had used most often in his own work. He used them as general guidelines for effective management but stressed flexibility in their application to allow for different and changing circumstances.

Fayol's real contribution, however, was not the 14 principles themselves (many of which were the products of the early factory system) but his formal recognition and synthesis of these principles. In presenting his principles of management, Fayol was probably the first to outline what today are called the *functions of management.* In essence, he identified planning, organizing, commanding, coordinating, and controlling as elements of management. He most heavily emphasized planning and organizing because he viewed these elements as essential to the other functions.

The works of Taylor and Fayol are essentially complementary. Both believed proper management of personnel and other resources is the key to organizational success. Both used a scientific approach to management. The major difference is in their orientation. Taylor stressed the management of operative work, whereas Fayol emphasized the management of organization.

Period of Solidification

period of solidification
A period in the 1920s and 1930s in which management became recognized as a discipline.

The 1920s and most of the 1930s were a **period of solidification** and popularization of management as a discipline. The acceptance of management as a respectable discipline was gained through several avenues. Universities and colleges began to teach management; by 1925, most schools of engineering were offering classes in management.[13] Professional societies began to take an interest in management. Much of the management pioneers' work was presented through the American Society of Mechanical Engineers. After the turn of the century, many other professional societies began to promote management. By the mid-1930s, management was truly a recognized discipline. Figure 2.3 summarizes the major events leading to this recognition.

The Human Relations Thrust

The Great Depression of 1929–32 saw unemployment in excess of 25 percent. Afterward, unions sought and gained major advantages for the working class. In this period, known as the Golden Age of Unionism, legislatures and courts actively

FIGURE 2.3
Significant Events Contributing to the Solidification of Management

- First conference on Scientific Management, October 1911.
- First doctoral dissertation on subject of scientific management by H. R. Drury at Columbia University, 1915.
- Founding of professional management societies: Society to Promote the Science of Management, 1912; Society of Industrial Engineers, 1917; American Management Association, 1923; Society for Advancement of Management, 1936.
- First meeting of management teachers, December 1924.

supported organized labor and the worker. The general climate tended to emphasize understanding employees and their needs (as opposed to focusing on the methods used to conduct work). Figure 2.4 summarizes several of the most important pro-union laws passed during the 1920s and 1930s. A major research project, known as the Hawthorne studies, is generally recognized as igniting the interest of business in the human element of the workplace.[14]

The Hawthorne Studies

Hawthorne studies
Series of experiments conducted in 1924 at the Hawthorne plant of Western Electric in Cicero, Illinois; production increased in relationship to psychological and social conditions rather than to the environment.

The **Hawthorne studies** began in 1924 when the National Research Council of the National Academy of Sciences began a project to define the relationship between physical working conditions and worker productivity. The Hawthorne plant of Western Electric in Cicero, Illinois, was the study site. First, the researchers lowered the level of lighting, expecting productivity to decrease. To their astonishment, productivity increased. Over the next several months, the researchers repeated the experiment by testing many different levels of lighting and other variables. Regardless of the level of light, output was found to increase.

Baffled by the results, in early 1927 the researchers called in a team of psychologists from Harvard University led by Elton Mayo. Over the next five years, hundreds of experiments were run involving thousands of employees. In these experiments, the researchers altered such variables as wage payments, rest periods, and length of workday. The results were similar to those obtained in the illumination experiments: Production increased, but with no obvious relationship to the environment. After much analysis, the researchers concluded that other factors besides the physical environment affected worker productivity. They found that employees reacted to the psychological and social conditions at work, such as informal group pressures, individual recognition, and participation in decision making.

FIGURE 2.4
Significant Pro-Union Legislation during the 1920s and 1930s

Railway Labor Act of 1926	Gave railway workers the right to form unions and engage in collective bargaining; established a corresponding obligation for employers to recognize and collectively bargain with the union.
Norris–La Guardia Act of 1932	Severely restricted the use of injunctions to limit union activity.
National Labor Relations Act of 1935 (Wagner Act)	Resulted in full, enforceable rights of employees to join unions and to engage in collective bargaining with their employer, who was legally obligated to do so.
Fair Labor Standards Act of 1938	Established minimum wages and required that time-and-a-half be paid for hours worked over 40 in one week.

The Hawthorne studies were comprised of four major categories of experiments. The illumination experiments took place before the Harvard researchers were involved. In these experiments, the level of illumination was altered in one test group, and the resulting outputs were then compared to the outputs of another group not subjected to changes in illumination. Only when the intensity of illumination was reduced to moonlight level was there any appreciable decline in productivity. The relay assembly test room experiments were concerned with evaluating the effects of improved material conditions, methods of work, relief from fatigue, reduced monotony, and wage incentives on group output. All of these factors were found to have little effect on output. The interview program involved interviewing over 20,000 workers to gain information about their attitudes and sentiments. Out of these interviews came the first insights as to the influence of the work group on the outputs of the group's individual members. The bank wiring observation room experiments were designed to further investigate the influence of the group on individual group members. This experiment tested the effect of a group piecework incentive pay plan on the output of the work group in a bank wiring room. The researchers concluded from this experiment that output is actually a form of social behavior, and that, if a worker is to be accepted, he or she must act in accordance with the standards of the group.

Source: Alan C. Filley and Robert J. House, *Managerial Process and Organizational Behavior* (Glenview, IL: Scott, Foresman and Co., 1969), pp. 19–21. For more information on studies conducted by the National Academy of Sciences, go to its website at www.nas.edu.

The researchers also discovered that the attention shown to the employees by the experimenters positively biased their productivity. This phenomenon has since become known as the *Hawthorne effect*. Yet another finding was the significance of effective supervision to both productivity and employee morale. While the methods used and the conclusions reached by the Hawthorne researchers have been questioned, they did generate great interest in the human problems in the workplace and focused attention on the human factor.[15] Management Illustration 2.4 describes the specific phases of the Hawthorne studies.

Early Champions of Human Relations

Mary Parker Follett was not a businesswoman in the sense that she managed her own business. However, through her writings and lectures, she had a great impact on many business and government leaders. While concerned with many aspects of the management process, her basic theory was that the fundamental problem of any organization is to build and maintain dynamic yet harmonious human relations within the organization.[16] In 1938, Chester Barnard, president of New Jersey Bell Telephone for many years, published a book that combined a thorough knowledge of organizational theory and sociology.[17] Barnard viewed the organization as a social structure and stressed the psychosocial aspects of organizations. Effectively integrating traditional management and the behavioral sciences, Barnard's work had a great impact on managers and teachers of management.

The Professional Manager

The career manager, or professional manager, did not exist until the 1930s. Until this time, managers were placed into one of three categories: owner-managers, captains of industry, or financial managers. The owner-managers dominated until after the Civil War. The captains of industry controlled organizations from the 1880s through the turn of the century. The financial managers operated in much the same ways the captains of industry did, except that they often did not own the enterprises they controlled and operated. The financial managers dominated from around 1905 until the early 1930s, when the Great Depression severely weakened public confidence in business organizations.

In the late 1930s, the professional manager emerged. The *professional manager* is a career person who does not necessarily have a controlling interest in the enterprise for which he or she works. Professional managers realize their responsibility to three groups: employees, stockholders, and the public. With expanded technology and more complex organizations, the professional manager became more and more prevalent.

Changing Styles of Management

As organizations grew in size and complexity, managers began stressing the importance of employees and their needs. As managers studied the employees and developed theories about employees' behavior, new styles and methods of managing emerged.

One innovative style of managing was developed by James F. Lincoln of Lincoln Electric Company in 1913. Lincoln realized that effective cooperation requires rewards. Thus, he designed a plan that coupled an incentive system with a request for cooperation. Lincoln emphasized the basic need of all individuals to express themselves. Specifically, the plan contained the following components:

1. An advisory board of employees.
2. A piece-rate method of compensation wherever possible.
3. A suggestion system.
4. Employee ownership of stock.
5. Year-end bonuses.
6. Life insurance for all employees.
7. Two weeks of paid vacation.
8. An annuity pension plan.
9. A promotion policy.

The development of Lincoln Electric Company can be attributed to its innovative management. It certainly has been successful. For several decades, Lincoln workers have consistently been among the highest paid in their industry in the world, averaging almost double the total pay of employees in competing companies. Lincoln's selling price has consistently been lower than that of any comparable product, and the company has consistently paid a dividend since 1918.

Another innovative manager, Henry Dennison (1877–1952), believed the strengths of an organization come from its members and the sources of power are the incentives, habits, and traditions that influence people in an organization.[18] Dennison believed an organization has the greatest strength if all of its members are strongly motivated; their actions do not lose effectiveness through friction, conflicts, or imbalance; and their actions move in a single direction, reinforcing one another. He believed management's primary purpose is to provide conditions under which employees work most readily and effectively. Instead of designing an organizational structure first, Dennison advocated finding "like-minded" people, grouping them, and then developing the total organizational structure. In summary, Dennison believed management's attention must focus on causes and effects in the field of human behavior. Dennison successfully practiced his management approach in the 1920s and 1930s at Dennison Manufacturing Company, which was also one of the early companies to implement the Taylor system of scientific management.

Charles McCormick and William Given, Jr., were top managers who worked independently and who both applied a human relations philosophy to their organizations. Both McCormick's and Given's styles of management were based on employee involvement in the decision-making process.

McCormick multiple-management plan
Developed by Charles McCormick, a plan that uses participation as a training and motivational tool by selecting promising young employees from various company departments to form a junior board of directors.

McCormick, a manufacturer of spices and extracts, developed and made famous the **McCormick multiple-management plan.**[19] This plan used participation as a training and motivating tool by selecting 17 promising young people from various departments within the company to form a junior board of directors. The junior board met with the senior board once a month and submitted its suggestions. Besides the immediate benefit of providing suggestions, the junior board provided early identification of management talent, opened communication lines, and relieved senior board members of much of the detailed planning and research. The huge success of the junior board led to the creation of sales and factory boards that operated in much the same way. McCormick's model of developing junior executive boards was used in numerous companies by 1938 and in nearly 400 companies by the late 1940s.[20]

bottom-up management
Philosophy popularized by William B. Given that encouraged widespread delegation of authority to solicit the participation of all employees from the bottom to the top of the organization.

Shoe and Foundry Company encouraged widespread delegation of authority to gain the involvement of "all those down from the **bottom up.**"[21] Given's approach promoted considerable managerial freedom in decision making, the free interchange of ideas, and the recognition that managerial growth involves some failure. Given believed the judgment, initiative, and creativeness of all employees in an organization provide a better end result than the autocratic administration of any single individual.

Scanlon plan
Incentive plan developed in 1938 by Joseph Scanlon to give workers a bonus for tangible savings in labor costs.

In 1938, Joseph Scanlon developed a productivity plan that gave employees a bonus for tangible savings in labor costs. The **Scanlon plan** was unique in at least three respects. First, joint management and union committees were formed to discuss and propose labor-saving techniques. Second, group rewards, rather than individual rewards, were made for suggestions. Third, employees shared in reduced costs rather than increased profits.[22] Scanlon believed participation was desirable not only to create a feeling of belonging but also to show clearly the role of employees and unions in suggesting improvements.

Management Process Period

process approach to management
Focuses on the management functions of planning, controlling, organizing, staffing, and leading.

The participative forms of management developed in the 1930s gave rise to the **process approach to management** in the late 1940s.[23] This approach attempted to identify and define a process for attaining desired objectives. The process approach led management to become concerned primarily with identifying and refining the functions or components of the management process. For this reason, the process approach is sometimes referred to as the *functional approach.*

As we have said, Henri Fayol was the first management scholar to present explicitly a functional analysis of the management process. Fayol identified planning, organizing, commanding, coordination, and control as functions of management. However, Fayol's work was not readily available in English until 1949, so his ideas were virtually unknown in this country until then.

Oliver Sheldon, an Englishman, also gave an early breakdown of the management process.[24] In 1923, Sheldon defined management as the determination of business policy, the coordination of the execution of policy, the organization of the business, and the control of the executive.

In 1935, Ralph C. Davis was the first American to publish a functional breakdown of the management process.[25] He subdivided it into three functions: planning, organizing, and controlling.

All of these management scholars made early reference to a functional approach to management. But the concept was not widely accepted until Constance Starrs's translation made Fayol's work widely available in 1949. Thus, Fayol was truly responsible for founding the process approach to management.

Other Approaches

The late 1950s saw a new era in the study of management. Uneasy with the process approach to management, production managers and industrial engineering scholars began testing mathematical and modeling approaches to quantify management. As a result, mathematical and decision theory schools of thought developed for the study of management. The decision theory school was based largely on economic theory and the theory of consumer choice. The mathematical school viewed management as a system of mathematical relationships.

At about the same time the mathematical school was flourishing, behavioral scientists were studying management in terms of small-group relations; they depended heavily on psychology and social psychology. Drawing on the work of Chester Barnard and sociological theory, another school saw management as a system of cultural interrelationships. An empirical school of thought was developed by those scholars using the case approach. Their basic premise was that effective management can be learned by studying the successes and failures of other managers.

management theory jungle
Term developed by Harold Koontz referring to the division of thought that resulted from the multiple approaches to studying the management process.

Harold Koontz was the first management scholar to discuss this fragmentation movement in detail.[26] Koontz accurately referred to this division of thought as the **management theory jungle.** Many conferences and discussions followed Koontz's analysis in an attempt to untangle the theory jungle and unite the various schools of thought. While some progress was made, a unified theory of management has yet to be realized.

The Systems Approach

The fragmentation period of the late 1950s and early 1960s was followed by an era of attempted integration. Many management theorists sought to use a systems approach to integrate the various management schools. A system is "an assemblage or combination of things or parts forming a complex or unitary whole."[27]

systems approach to management
A way of thinking about the job of managing that provides a framework for visualizing internal and external environmental factors as an integrated whole.

The **systems approach to management** was viewed as "a way of thinking about the job of managing . . . [which] provides a framework for visualizing internal and external environmental factors as an integrated whole."[28] Under this approach, the organization is seen as an open system that is influenced by its internal and external environmental factors. The organization then, in turn, influences these same internal and external environmental factors; hence, a dynamic interplay is created. In essence, the manager is asked to view the human, physical, and informational facets of the manager's job as linked in an integrated whole.

One popular thrust was to use a systems approach to integrate the other schools of management into the traditional functional approach. The idea was to integrate the human relations and mathematical approaches into the appropriate functional areas. Thus, while studying planning, a systems approach might include mathematical forecasting techniques.

The Contingency Approach

contingency approach to management
Theorizes that different situations and conditions require different management approaches.

The 1970s were characterized by the so-called contingency approach. In the **contingency approach to management,** different situations and conditions require different management approaches. Proponents believe there is no one best way to manage; the best way depends on the specific circumstances. Recognizing the rarity of a manager who thinks one way to manage works best in all situations, one might ask, "What is new about this approach?" What is new is that contingency theorists have often gone much further than simply saying, "It all depends." Many contingency theories outline in detail the style or approach that works best under certain circumstances. Contingency theories, many of which are discussed in this book, have been developed in areas such as decision making, organizational design, leadership, planning, and group behavior.

The Japanese Management Movement and Theory Z

Theory Z
A theory developed by William Ouchi that attempts to integrate American and Japanese management practices by combining the American emphasis on individual responsibility with the Japanese emphasis on collective decision making, slow evaluation and promotion, and holistic concern for employees.

The tremendous economic success many Japanese companies enjoyed following World War II drew worldwide attention to their management practices. As management scholars studied Japanese management, they identified certain characteristics that differed somewhat from traditional American approaches. In general terms, Japanese managers encouraged more employee participation in decision making, they showed a deeper concern for the personal well-being of employees, and they placed great emphasis on the quality of their products and services. Top management acted more as a facilitator of decision making than as an issuer of edicts. The flow of information and initiatives from the bottom to the top of the organization was emphasized. Japanese organizations also tended to be characterized by lifetime employment and nonspecialized career paths for employees.

Realizing there are many valuable lessons to be learned from the Japanese, William Ouchi developed a theory, called **Theory Z,** that attempts to integrate American and Japanese management practices.[29] Theory Z combines the American emphasis on individual responsibility with the Japanese emphasis on collective decision making, slow evaluation and promotion, and holistic concern for employees. Other factors recommended by Ouchi, such as length of employment and career path characteristics, represent compromises between traditional American and Japanese practices. Figure 2.5 summarizes the profile of traditional American and Japanese organizations as well as Ouchi's Theory Z organization.

Search for Excellence

In 1982, Thomas J. Peters and Robert H. Waterman, Jr., released a book, *In Search of Excellence,* that has since become the best-selling management-related book ever published.[30] Working as management consultants at a time when Japanese

FIGURE 2.5
Comparison of Japanese, American, and Theory Z Organizations

Source: Adapted from William Ouchi, *Theory Z* (Reading, MA: Addison-Wesley Publishing, Inc., 1984), pp. 58, 71–88.

Japanese-Type Organization
1. Lifetime employment
2. Collective decision making
3. Collective responsibility
4. Slow evaluation and promotion
5. Implicit control mechanisms
6. Nonspecialized career path
7. Holistic concern for employee as a person

American-Type Organization
1. Short-term employment
2. Individual decision making
3. Individual responsibility
4. Rapid evaluation and promotion
5. Explicit control mechanisms
6. Specialized career path
7. Segmented concern for employee as an employee

Theory Z–Type Organization
1. Long-term employment
2. Consensual, participative decision making
3. Individual responsibility
4. Slow evaluation and promotion
5. Implicit, informal control with explicit, formalized measures
6. Moderately specialized career paths
7. Holistic concern, including family

In Search of Excellence
Book by Thomas J. Peters and Robert H. Waterman, Jr., that identifies 36 companies with an excellent 20-year performance record. The authors identified eight characteristics of excellence after interviewing managers in each company.

management styles were receiving worldwide attention (in the late 1970s), Peters and Waterman asked, "Can't we learn something from America's most successful companies?" Using a combination of subjective criteria and six measures of financial success covering a 20-year period (1961 through 1980), the authors identified a final subsample of 36 American companies. According to the authors' criteria, these companies had demonstrated excellent performance over the 20-year time frame studied. Most of the 36 companies in the final subsample were well-known companies such as IBM, McDonald's, Delta Air Lines, and Eastman Kodak. After interviewing each company in the subsample and analyzing their findings, Peters and Waterman identified eight "attributes of excellence," summarized in Figure 2.6.

While Peters and Waterman's work has been criticized as being overly subjective and not based on sound research methods, it has caused many managers to rethink their ways of doing things.[31] Specifically, Peters and Waterman reemphasized the value of on-the-job experimentation and creative thinking, the need to place the customer first, and the need to treat employees as human beings. Management Illustration 2.5 discusses what has happened to some of Peters and Waterman's "excellent companies."

The Emphasis on Quality

Beginning in the late 1970s, gathering steam throughout the 1980s, and reaching its height in the early 1990s was an emphasis on overall quality of the product or service. The quality of American products and services had reached a low by the early 1970s. This phenomenon, coupled with the quality successes of the Japanese,

FIGURE 2.6
Peters and Waterman's Eight Characteristics of Excellent Companies

Source: Thomas J. Peters and Robert H. Waterman, Jr., *In Search of Excellence* (New York: Harper & Row, 1982), pp. 13–16.

Characteristics of Excellence	Description of Characteristics
1. A bias for action	A tendency to get on with things; a willingness to experiment.
2. Close to the customer	The provision of unparalleled quality/service; a willingness to listen to the customer.
3. Autonomy and entrepreneurship	Encouragement of practical risk taking and innovation; tolerance of a reasonable number of mistakes as a part of the innovative process.
4. Productivity through people	Rank-and-file employees are viewed as the root source of quality and productivity gains; employees are treated with respect and dignity; enthusiasm and trust are encouraged.
5. Hands on; value driven	The company philosophy and values are clearly communicated; managers take a hands-on approach.
6. Stick to the knitting	Companies diversify only into businesses that are closely related; emphasis is on internal growth as opposed to mergers.
7. Simple form; lean staff	Companies have simple structure with clear lines of authority; headquarters staff is kept small.
8. Simultaneous loose-tight properties	Autonomy is pushed down to the lowest levels, but at the same time certain core values are not negotiable.

forced managers to look to the quality issue as one way of improving the position of American products and services.

The major change that resulted from this increased attention to quality was a shift from finding and correcting mistakes or rejects to *preventing* them. This led to the development of total quality management (TQM), which is a management philosophy that emphasizes "managing the entire organization so that it excels in all dimensions of products and services that are important to the customer."[32] TQM is discussed at length in Chapter 20.

The International and Global Movement

In the past 25 years, many U.S. companies have turned to the international arena for new markets and opportunities. For example, in the year 2000, 28 of the 100 largest U.S. multinationals realized more than 50 percent of their revenues from international markets, and only 13 of these companies realized less than 25 percent from international markets.[33] Recent studies show that U.S. companies are investing heavily in European countries and that these same countries are also investing in the United States.[34] The recent weakening of the U.S. dollar has made almost all foreign investment in the United States even more attractive.[35]

Even companies that do not trade directly in the international and global markets are often greatly affected by foreign competition, alliances, and investment. As a result, U.S. managers are being forced to think in terms of international and global rather than local or national markets. Business emphasis will likely con-

As soon as two years after *In Search of Excellence* was published, at least 14 of the "excellent" companies highlighted by Peters and Waterman had lost some of their luster. Of the 14 companies that stumbled, 12 were inept at adapting to fundamental changes in their markets. Some maintain that overadherence to Peters and Waterman's eight characteristics, which do not emphasize reacting to broad economic and business trends, may have contributed to their problems. Others, including Peters and Waterman, argue that these companies ran into trouble because they strayed from the principles that had been key to their earlier successes. By the early 1990s, some of the stars of Peters and Waterman's original list (such as IBM) were also having difficulties. Some critics have also questioned the criteria originally used by Peters and Waterman (continuous innovation, large size, and sustained financial performance over the 20-year period from 1961 to 1980) for selecting their "excellent" companies. Critics have also questioned whether the so-called excellent firms provided exceptional returns to stockholders in either the short run or the long run.

At least two lessons can be drawn from the experiences of these companies: (1) the excellent companies of today will not necessarily be the excellent companies of tomorrow and (2) good management requires much more than following any one set of rules.

Sources: "Who's Excellent Now?" *Business Week*, November 5, 1984, pp. 76–78; and Richard Kolodny, Martin Laurence, and Arabinda Ghosh, "In Search of Excellence . . . from Whom?" *Journal of Portfolio Management*, Spring 1989, pp. 56–60.

tinue to shift to the international scene throughout the intermediate future. International management is discussed in greater detail in Chapter 5.

Management in the Twenty-First Century

As summarized in this chapter, there is little doubt that significant changes occurred in the twentieth century in all facets of American organizations and the manner in which they are managed. From a management perspective, what changes are likely to occur as we move into the twenty-first century?

The authors of the book *Beyond Workplace 2000* have made some interesting projections as to what organizations and management might look like in the twenty-first century.

- Most American companies will find that they no longer can gain a competitive advantage from further improvements in quality, service, cost, or speed, since the gap between rivals on these traditional measures of performance will all but close.

- Every American business and every employee who works for an American business will be forced to become agile, flexible, and highly adaptive, since the product or service they will provide and the business processes they will employ will be in a constant state of change.

- Every American company will be forced to develop a much better understanding of what it does truly well and will invest its limited resources in developing and sustaining superiority in that unique knowledge, skill, or capability.

- Organizational structures will become extremely fluid. No longer will there be departments, units, divisions, or functional groups in most American businesses. There will only be multidisciplinary and multiskilled teams, and every team will be temporary.

- There will be a meltdown of the barrier between leader and follower, manager and worker. Bosses, in the traditional sense, will all but disappear. While there will be a few permanent leaders external to work and project teams, these people will act more as coordinators of team activities than as traditional leaders.[36]

Time will tell if these predictions do, in fact, come true. One thing for certain is that the rate of change will continue to accelerate and both organizations and managers will be required to adapt to these changes.

Conclusion

This chapter has summarized the major events that affected management discipline from the nineteenth century to the present. But the discipline did not develop and mature at the same rate in all parts of the country. Similarly, it did not develop from a series of discrete happenings; rather, it grew from a series of major and minor events. Figure 2.7 presents a chronological summary of the major and related events in the management movement.

FIGURE 2.7
Major Components and Related Events of the Management Movement

Major Management Movements	Related Events
U.S. Industrial Revolution (before 1875)	Steam power (1790–1810) Railroad boom (1830–1850) Telegraph (1844)

Captains of industry (1875–1900)	Formation of corporate giants:
	    John D. Rockefeller (oil)
	    James B. Duke (tobacco)
	    Andrew Carnegie (steel)
	    Cornelius Vanderbilt (shipping and railroads)

Scientific management era (1895–1920)	Henry Towne, "The Engineer as Economist," 1886
	Frederick W. Taylor's work (1895–1915):
	    Carl Barth
	    Morris Cooke
	    Henry Lawrence Gantt
	    Frank and Lillian Gilbreth
	Henry Fayol, *Administration Industrielle et Generale,* 1916

Period of solidification (1920 to early 1930s)	Founding of professional management societies (1920s)
Human relations movement (1931 to late 1940s)	Hawthorne studies, led by Elton Mayo (1924–1932) Mary Parker Follett (1920–1933) Chester Barnard, *Functions of the Executive,* 1938
Management process period (early 1950s to early 1960s)	Starr's translation of Fayol's work (1949) Ralph Davis, *Top Management Planning,* 1951 George Terry, *Principles of Management,* 1953 Koontz and O'Donnell, *Principles of Management,* 1955
Management theory jungle (early to late 1960s)	Process approach Quantitative approaches Behavioral approaches *(concluded top of pg 39)*

FIGURE 2.7
Concluded

Major Management Movements	Related Events
Systems approach (late 1960s to early 1970s)	Integrating the various approaches to the study of management
Contingency approach (1970s)	Theorizes that different situations and conditions require different management approaches
Theory Z (1980s)	Combines certain characteristics of traditional Japanese and American management styles
Search for excellence (1980s)	Attempt to learn management lessons from a group of U.S. companies that experienced certain success over the 1961–80 time span
Emphasis on quality, TQM (1980s–1990s)	Emphasis on overall quality of the product or service
International movement (1980s–1990s)	Increased awareness of international and global markets and of managerial approaches
Management into twenty-first century	Extremely fluid organizations; multidisciplinary and multiskilled teams

Summary

1. *Explain why management did not emerge as a recognized discipline until the twentieth century.* Just as traffic lights were not needed before cars, management, as it now exists, was not needed before organizations became complex. Before the late nineteenth and twentieth centuries, most organizations were relatively simple. Industrialization and mass production brought large and complex organizations.

2. *Describe the three facets of the U.S. Industrial Revolution.* The three major facets of the U.S. Industrial Revolution are (1) power, (2) transportation, and (3) communication.

3. *Discuss the role the captains of industry played in the development of modern organizations.* The captains of industry, who included John D. Rockefeller, James B. Duke, Andrew Carnegie, and Cornelius Vanderbilt, built great companies. They introduced nationwide distribution and marketing methods. Because of the size and dominance of these companies, the relationship between business and government changed forever. Government passed legislation to check corporate practices in restraint of trade.

4. *Define scientific management, and outline the role Frederick W. Taylor and his contemporaries played in its development.* Scientific management is a philosophy about the use of human effort. It seeks to maximize output with minimum effort through the elimination of waste and inefficiency at the operative level. Frederick W. Taylor was the major figure responsible for popularizing scientific management through his writings and consulting. Several contemporaries of Taylor helped spread Taylor's philosophy through their own efforts. The most prominent included Carl Barth, Morris Cooke, Henry Gantt, and Frank and Lillian Gilbreth.

5. *Summarize Henri Fayol's contributions to modern management.* Henri Fayol made many contributions, but the most significant was his development of management principles and elements. The 14 principles Fayol developed are still applicable today, and his five management elements are very similar to today's functions of management.

6. *Discuss the human relations thrust in management, with emphasis on the role of the Hawthorne experiments.* Following the Great Depression, more emphasis began to be placed on understanding workers and their needs. The Hawthorne studies, which began in 1924 and lasted until 1932, focused attention on human relations and specifically on the psychological and sociological aspects of work. Mary Parker Follett also helped to popularize the human relations movement.

7. *Define the management process period, the management theory jungle, the systems approach, and the contingency approach.* The management process period took place between the late 1940s and the late 1950s. During this period, management thought focused primarily on identifying and refining the functions or components of the management process. The management theory jungle, first clearly identified by Harold Koontz, referred to the many different approaches being taken to the study of management in the late 1950s and early 1960s. The systems approach attempted to integrate the various approaches to management. The systems approach is a way of thinking about the job of managing that provides a framework for visualizing internal and external environmental factors as an integrated whole. The contingency approach to management theorizes that different situations and conditions require different management approaches and that no one approach works best in all situations.

8. *Compare the major differences in the American, Japanese, and Theory Z organizations.* In general terms, American organizations place emphasis on individual responsibility, whereas Japanese organizations place more emphasis on collective decision making, slow evaluation and promotion, and holistic concern for employees. Theory Z attempts to combine the American emphasis on individual responsibility with the Japanese emphasis on collective decision making and responsibility. Figure 2.5 summarizes the major points of each type of organization.

9. *Summarize the eight characteristics of excellent companies identified by Peters and Waterman.* In their book *In Search of Excellence,* Peters and Waterman identified eight characteristics of excellent companies (see Figure 2.6). In general, these eight characteristics emphasize the value of on-the-job experimentation and creative thinking, the need to place the customer first, and the need to treat employees as human beings.

10. *Explain why the international aspects of management are currently being emphasized.* Many of today's U.S. companies have turned to the international arena for new markets and profits. Even those companies that do not trade internationally are often greatly affected by imports or exports from other countries. Thus, almost all companies today are affected to some degree by the international aspects of management.

11. *Discuss some predictions as to how managers might manage in the twenty-first century.* Organization structures may become extremely fluid with no structured departments, units, divisions, or functional groups. The barriers between leader and follower, manager and worker will disappear. Managers will act as coordinators of team activities.

Review Questions

1. What were the three facets of the Industrial Revolution in America? Discuss the impact of each of these facets on the development of today's industry.

2. What effect did the captains of industry have on the relationships between government and industry?

3. What is scientific management? Discuss the four main principles of scientific management.

4. Discuss the major contribution to scientific management of Morris Cooke, Henry Lawrence Gantt, and Frank and Lillian Gilbreth.

5. What was Henri Fayol's major contribution to the management movement?

6. Discuss the impact of the Hawthorne studies on management thought.

7. Describe in detail the following approaches to the management process: Lincoln Electric Company, the McCormick multiple-management plan, bottom-up management, and the Scanlon plan.

8. What is the process approach to management? Discuss some of the major contributors to this approach.

9. Discuss the factors that led to the management theory jungle.

10. What is the systems approach to the management process?

11. Describe the period beginning in the late 1970s where significant emphasis was placed on the quality of products and services.

12. Describe the contingency approach to management.

13. What is Theory Z?

14. Identify the eight characteristics of successful companies reported by the authors of *In Search of Excellence*.

15. How are companies that do not trade internationally affected by international markets?

16. Discuss several predictions concerning how organizations might be structured and managed in the twenty-first century.

Skill-Building Questions

1. From the viewpoint of a practicing manager, what do you see as the major lessons to be learned from the evolution of management thought?

2. Why do you think many people have misinterpreted Frederick W. Taylor's scientific management principles as being inhumane?

3. Offer some general guidelines for applying scientific management principles in a manner that would be positively received by employees.

4. What challenges do you think will be presented by the continued internationalization of companies?

Skill-Building Exercise 2.1

What Have We Learned?

Following are excerpts from a speech made by Frederick W. Taylor in 1911:*

> If any of you will get close to the average workman in this country—close enough to him so that he will talk to you as an intimate friend—he will tell you that in his particular trade if, we will say, each man were to turn out twice as much work as he is now doing, there could be but one result to follow: namely, that one-half the men in his trade would be thrown out of work.
>
> This doctrine is preached by almost every labor leader in the country and is taught by every workman to his children as they are growing up; and I repeat, as I said in the beginning, that it is our fault more than theirs that this fallacy prevails.
>
> While the labor leaders and the workmen themselves in season and out of season are pointing out the necessity of restriction of output, not one step are we taking to counteract that fallacy; therefore, I say, the fault is ours and not theirs.

1. Do you think Taylor's position is equally applicable today? Be prepared to justify your answer.

The chairman of the American Productivity Center in Houston, C. Jackson Grayson, has warned that if management and labor cannot make their relationship less adversarial, "then we won't get the full, long-term kick in productivity that we desperately need."†

2. Looking at Taylor's and Grayson's remarks, which were made approximately 73 years apart, one has to wonder what we have learned. Many similar comparisons could be made. Why do you think managers don't seem to learn as much as they could from the past?

*Scientific Management: Address and Discussions at the Conference on Scientific Management at the Amos Truck School of Administration and Finance (Norwood, MA: Plimpton Press, 1912), pp. 23–24.

†"The Revival of Productivity," Business Week, February 13, 1984, p. 100.

Skill-Building Exercise 2.2

Finding the One Best Way

Suppose you have been assigned the simple task of stuffing 1,000 two-page flyers (8½" × 11") into a normal size envelope (4" × 9½"). The envelopes come in boxes of 250, and the flyer pages are in stacks of 1,000 each. The flyers must first be stapled together, folded, and then placed into the envelopes.

a. Get a stapler, a few envelopes, and several 8½″ × 11″ sheets of paper, and determine how you might accomplish this task. Identify where each component will be positioned and exactly how you will perform the task.

b. After you have tried your first method, see if you can determine any ways in which it might be improved.

c. Compare your method with others in your class.

Questions

1. Were you able to improve your first method in step *b*?
2. Did you pick up further improvements from others in your class (step *c*)?

Case Incident 2.1

Granddad's Company

J.R.V. Company, which manufactures industrial tools, was founded in 1905 by James R. Vail, Sr. Currently, James R. Vail, Jr., is the president of the company; his son Richard is executive vice president. James Jr. has run the company for the past 30 years in a fashion very similar to that of his father.

When the company was founded, James Sr. had been a big supporter of scientific management. He had organized the work very scientifically with the use of time and motion studies to determine the most efficient method of performing each job. As a result, most jobs at J.R.V. were highly specialized and utilized a high degree of division of labor. In addition, there was always a heavy emphasis on putting people in jobs that were best suited for them and then providing adequate training. Most employees are paid on a piece-rate incentive system, with the standards set by time and motion studies. James Jr. has largely continued to emphasize scientific management since he took over. All employees now receive two weeks' paid vacation and company insurance. Also, employees are generally paid an average wage for their industry. The present J.R.V. building was constructed in 1920, but it has had several minor improvements, such as the addition of fluorescent lighting and an employees' lunchroom.

James Jr. is planning to retire in a few years. Recently, he and Richard, his planned successor, have disagreed over the management of the company. Richard's main argument is that times have changed and time and motion studies, specialization, high division of labor, and other company practices are obsolete. James Jr. counters that J.R.V. has been successful under its present management philosophy for many years, and change would be "foolish."

Questions
1. Do you agree with Richard? Why or why not?
2. Are the principles of scientific management applicable in today's organization? Explain your answer.

Case Incident 2.2

Return to Scientific Management

Recently, a professor at State University was lecturing in a management development seminar on the topic of motivation. Each of the participants candidly discussed problems that existed in their respective organizations. Problem areas mentioned included absenteeism, turnover, and poor workmanship. The participants managed a variety of workers such as automobile assembly workers, clerical workers, computer operators, sanitation workers, and even some middle-level managers.

During the discussion, one of the participants made the following statement: "What we need to stop all of these problems is a little scientific management."

Questions
1. What do you think the person means?
2. Do you agree? Discuss.

3. Take one of the jobs in the above case and show how you could apply scientific management.

References and Additional Readings

1. Daniel Wren, *The Evolution of Management Thought,* 2nd ed. (New York: Ronald Press, 1979), p. 90.
2. Alfred D. Chandler, Jr., "The Beginnings of 'Big Business' in American Industry," *Business History Review,* Spring 1959, p. 3.
3. Harry Kelsey and David Wilderson, "The Evolution of Management Thought" (unpublished paper, Indiana University, Bloomington, IN, 1974), p. 7.
4. Henry R. Towne, "The Engineer as Economist," *Transactions, ASME* 7 (1886), pp. 428–32.
5. Frederick W. Taylor, "A Piece-Rate System," *Transactions, ASME* 16 (1895), pp. 856–83.
6. Frederick W. Taylor, *Shop Management* (New York: Harper & Row, 1903); and Frederick W. Taylor, *The Principles of Scientific Management* (New York: Harper & Row, 1911).
7. *Scientific Management: Address and Discussions at the Conference on Scientific Management at the Amos Truck School of Administration and Finance* (Norwood, MA: Plimpton Press, 1912), pp. 32–35.
8. John F. Mee, *Management Thought in a Dynamic Economy* (New York: New York University Press, 1963), p. 411.
9. John F. Mee, "Seminar in Business Organization and Operation" (unpublished paper, Indiana University, Bloomington, IN), p. 5.
10. Wren, *The Evolution of Management Thought,* pp. 136–40.
11. Ibid., p. 188.
12. Henry L. Gantt, *Organizing for Work* (New York: Harcourt Brace Jovanovich, 1919), p. 15.
13. John F. Mee, "Management Teaching in Historical Perspective," *Southern Journal of Business,* May 1972, p. 21.
14. For a detailed description of the Hawthorne studies, see Fritz G. Roethlisberger and William J. Dickson, *Management and the Worker* (Cambridge, MA: Harvard University Press, 1939).
15. For example, see Alex Carey, "The Hawthorne Studies: A Radical Criticism," *American Sociological Review,* June 1967, pp. 403–16.
16. Henry C. Metcalf and L. Urwick, eds., *Dynamic Administration: The Collected Papers of Mary Parker Follett* (New York: Harper & Row, 1940), p. 21.
17. Chester I. Barnard, *The Functions of the Executive* (Cambridge, MA: Harvard University Press, 1938).
18. Henry S. Dennison, *Organization Engineering* (New York: McGraw-Hill, 1931).
19. Charles P. McCormick, *Multiple Management* (New York: Harper & Row, 1949).
20. Ibid., p. viii; and Charles P. McCormick, *The Power of People* (New York: Harper & Row, 1949).
21. William B. Given, Jr., *Bottom Up Management* (New York: Harper & Row, 1949).
22. Joseph Scanlon, "Enterprise for Everyone," *Fortune,* January 1950, pp. 41, 55–59; and Wren, *The Evolution of Management Thought,* p. 330.
23. Mee, *Management Thought,* p. 53.
24. Oliver Sheldon, *The Philosophy of Management* (London: Sir Isaac Pitman & Sons, 1923).
25. Ralph C. Davis, *The Principles of Business Organizations and Operations* (Columbus, OH: H. L. Hedrick, 1935), pp. 12–13.
26. Harold Koontz, "The Management Theory Jungle," *Academy of Management Journal,* December 1961, pp. 174–88.
27. *Webster's Collegiate Dictionary* (New York: Random House, 1991), p. 1356.

28. Richard A. Johnson, Fremont E. Kast, and James E. Rosenzweig, *The Theory of Management Systems* (New York: McGraw-Hill, 1963), p. 3.

29. William C. Ouchi, *Theory Z* (Reading, MA: Addison-Wesley, 1981).

30. Thomas J. Peters and Robert H. Waterman, Jr., *In Search of Excellence* (New York: Harper & Row, 1982).

31. For a criticism of *In Search of Excellence*, see Daniel T. Carroll, "A Disappointing Search for Excellence," *Harvard Business Review*, November–December 1983, pp. 78–88.

32. Richard B. Chase and Nicholas J. Aquilano, *Production and Operations Management: A Life Cycle Approach*, 6th ed. (Homewood, IL: Richard D. Irwin, 1992), pp. 186–87.

33. Brian Zajac, "Global Giants," *Forbes*, July 24, 2000, pp. 335–38.

34. Anita Raghavan, "American Companies Look to Europe for Acquisitions," *The Wall Street Journal*, June 30, 2003, p. C1; and Stephen Baker, "Why Europe Keeps Gobbling Up U.S. Companies," *Business Week*, June 18, 2001, p. 56.

35. Rich Miller, Peter Coy, Christine Tierney, and David Fairlamb, "Good News! The Dollar Is Down, Why It's Falling, and Why That Should Benefit the U.S. Economy," *Business Week*, May 26, 2003, p. 36.

36. Joseph H. Boyett and Jimmie T. Boyett, *Beyond Workplace 2000* (New York: Penguin Books, 1995), pp. xiii–xiv.

Chapter

3

Developing Communication Skills

Learning Objectives

After studying this chapter, you will able to:

1. Define communication.
2. Describe the interpersonal communication process.
3. Describe problems that could arise from conflicting or inappropriate assumptions made in interpersonal communication.
4. Define semantics, and explain its role in interpersonal communication.
5. Define perception.
6. Explain how emotions may affect communication.
7. Explain the concept of feedback in communication.
8. Explain active listening.
9. Describe the grapevine.
10. Define and briefly discuss the e-mail process.
11. Define the Internet and intranets.
12. Discuss two factors that complicate communications in international business activities.

Chapter Preview

During 1990 to 1993, the most severe downturn in Silicon Valley history made it necessary for Agilent Technologies to lay off more than 14,000 people. Yet during May of 1992, *Fortune* magazine ranked Agilent number 31 on its "100 Best Places to Work" list—an improvement from number 46. In addition, Agilent's CEO, Ned Barnholt, won the IABC's award for exemplary CEO communications.

At Agilent, key messages for its employees are delivered at "coffee talks" with senior managers and business leaders, over e-mail and the company's intranet, through a twice-weekly electronic news service, and through printed newsletters. The company uses a variety of methods to track employee responses to messages such as surveys and a web-based "Pulse" program that solicits employee comments and questions, anonymously or with names attached.

Source: Ron Fuchs and Steve Beitler, "Communicating through a Downturn at Agilent," *Strategic Communication Management,* August 2003, pp. 23–24.

Analyzing Management Skills

Most people have heard the statement: Actions speak louder than words. What does this statement mean? Do you agree or disagree with the statement?

Applying Management Skills

Go on the Internet and find an example of communications within an organization. Be prepared to describe what you find.

communication
The act of exchanging information

Communication is the act of exchanging information. It can be used to inform, command, instruct, assess, influence, and persuade other people. Communication skills are important in all aspects of life, including business.

Managers use communication every day. In fact, they spend as much as three-quarters of their time communicating (see Figure 3.1). Good managers develop effective communication skills. They use these skills to absorb information, motivate employees, and deal effectively with customers and co-workers. Good communication can significantly affect a manager's success.

Communication as a Management Skill

Communicating effectively is an important management skill for several reasons:

- *Managers must give direction to the people who work for them.* Managers who fail to give clear guidance often find that employees perform their jobs poorly because they do not understand what is expected of them.
- *Managers must be able to motivate people.* Good managers use their ability to communicate to get other people excited about their jobs.

FIGURE 3.1
Communicating in the Business World

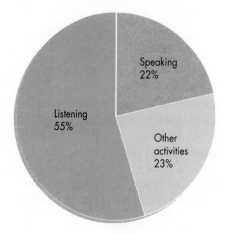

Listening 55%

Speaking 22%

Other activities 23%

- *Managers must be able to convince customers that they should do business with them.* Effective communication is the key to convincing a customer to purchase a product or service. Without good communication skills, managers will find it difficult to attract customers, even if their companies' products or services meet the customer's needs.
- *Managers must be able to absorb the ideas of others.* Business managers interact with many people, including co-workers, customers, and suppliers. To be effective, they must be able to understand and accept other people's viewpoints.
- *Managers must be able to persuade other people.* Managers often have ideas that others oppose. To persuade other people to accept their ideas, managers must be able to communicate effectively.

Interpersonal Communication

Effective communication between individuals, especially between a manager and subordinates, is critical to achieving organizational objectives and, as a result, to managing people effectively. Estimates vary, but it is generally agreed that since managers spend much of their time with their subordinates, effective communication is critical to the wise and effective use of their time.

interpersonal communication
An interactive process between individuals that involves sending and receiving verbal and nonverbal messages.

Interpersonal communication is an interactive process between individuals that involves sending and receiving verbal and nonverbal messages. The basic purpose of interpersonal communication is to transmit information so that the sender of the message is understood and understands the receiver. Figure 3.2 diagrams this dynamic and interactive process. An event or a condition generates information. The desire to share the information, or inform another person about it, creates the need to communicate. The sender then creates a message and communicates it both verbally and nonverbally. The receiver, in turn, perceives and interprets the message and (hopefully) creates a reply message as a response to it. This reply message may generate a response by the sender of the initial message, and the process continues in this fashion.

Often, however, many factors interfere and cause this process to fail. Some causes of interpersonal communication failure are conflicting or inappropriate assumptions, different interpretations of the meanings of words (semantics), differences in perception, emotions either preceding or during communication, poor listening habits, inadequate communication skills, insufficient feedback, and differences in the interpretations of nonverbal communications.

FIGURE 3.2
Interpersonal Communication Process

| Sender | Initial message communicated both verbally and nonverbally. | Receiver |

Event or condition generates information. This creates a message.

Perceives the message, derives meaning, and reacts to the message. The reaction creates a reply message to the sender.

| Sender | Reply message communicated both verbally and nonverbally (sometimes referred to as feedback). | |

Perceives message, derives meaning, and reacts to the message.

Conflicting or Inappropriate Assumptions

Have you ever thought you were being understood when you were really not? This is a common mistake made by couples, teachers, superiors, and parents. If one assumes that communication is flowing as intended, one tends to move on with the dialogue without allowing feedback to indicate whether clarity of expression and communication has been achieved. Good managers and salespeople always seek verbal or nonverbal feedback, before continuing the communication process. Remember that interpretation of meaning can always be a problem when assumptions are involved. Messages such as "Stop," "Do this right now," and "Please don't" never seem to have the same meanings to children that the adult sender intended. Sound communication usually flows from ensuring that the sender and the receiver see and understand assumptions in the same way.

Semantics

semantics
The science or study of the meanings of words and symbols.

Semantics is the science or study of the meanings of words and symbols. Words themselves have no real meaning. They have meaning only in terms of people's reactions to them. A word may mean very different things to different people, depending on how it is used. In addition, a word may be interpreted differently based on the facial expressions, hand gestures, and voice inflections used.

The problems involved in semantics are of two general types. Some words and phrases invite multiple interpretations. For example, Figure 3.3 shows different interpretations of the word *fix*. Another problem is that groups of people in specific situations often develop their own technical language, which outsiders may or may not understand. For example, physicians, government workers, and military employees are often guilty of using acronyms and abbreviations that only they understand.

Words are the most common form of interpersonal communication. Because of the real possibility of misinterpretation, words must be carefully chosen and clearly defined for effective communication.

Perception

perception
The mental and sensory processes an individual uses in interpreting information received.

Perception deals with the mental and sensory processes an individual uses in interpreting information she or he receives. Since each individual's perception is unique, people often perceive the same situation in different ways.

FIGURE 3.3
Interpretations of the Word *Fix*

An Englishman visits America and is completely awed by the many ways we use the word *fix*. For example,

1. His host asks him how he'd like his drink fixed. He meant *mixed*.

2. As he prepares to leave, he discovers he has a flat tire and calls a repairperson, who says he'll fix it immediately. He means *repair*.

3. On the way home, he is given a ticket for speeding. He calls his host, who says, "Don't worry, I'll fix it." He means *nullify*.

4. At the office the next day, he comments on the cost of living in America, and one of his colleagues says, "It's hard to make ends meet on a fixed income." She means *steady* or *unchanging*.

5. He has an argument with a co-worker. The latter says, "I'll fix you." He means *seek revenge*.

6. A cohort remarks that she is in a fix. She means *condition* or *situation*.

FIGURE 3.4
Illustrations of Perceptual Distortion

Source: Adapted from Jonathan L. Freedman, *Introductory Psychology*, 2nd ed. (Reading, MA: Addison-Wesley, 1982), p. 58.

(a)

(b)

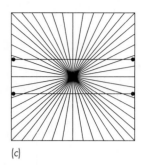

(c)

Perception begins when the sense organs receive a stimulus. The stimulus is the information received, whether it is conveyed in writing, verbally, nonverbally, or in another way. The sense organs respond to, shape, and organize the information received. When this information reaches the brain, it is further organized and interpreted, resulting in perception. Different people perceive the same information differently because no two people have the same personal experiences, memories, likes, and dislikes. In addition, the phenomenon of selective perception often distorts the intended message: People tend to listen to only part of the message, blocking out the rest for any number of reasons.

Figure 3.4 illustrates perceptual distortion. Look at the figure and answer the following questions:

1. Is the vertical line longer than the horizontal line in Figure 3.4(*a*)?
2. Is line *x* or *y* longer in Figure 3.4(*b*)?
3. Are the two horizontal lines in Figure 3.4(*c*) bowed or parallel?

Using a ruler, you can see that the vertical and horizontal lines in 3.4(*a*) are equal and that the *x* and *y* lines in 3.4(*b*) are also equal. The horizontal lines in 3.4(*c*) are also parallel. These examples illustrate the difference between the real world and the perceived world. If differences in perception exist in viewing physical objects, more subtle forms of communication such as facial expressions and hand gestures leave much room for perceptional differences.

Emotions Either Preceding or During Communication

Just as perception affects our cognitive processes during communication, emotions affect our disposition to send and receive the communication. Anger, joy, fear, sorrow, disgust, or panic (to mention only a few emotions) can all affect the way we send or receive messages. Emotional disposition is like the stage on which the communication piece plays its part: The stage can be perfectly prepared or in total disarray. The setting for the communication piece is obviously important. Communications during periods of high emotion usually have difficulty succeeding. Therefore, managers with good communication skills strive to manage the emotional as well as the physical communication environment.

Learning to Communicate

Managers communicate in writing and verbally. Before they can master either form of communication, they must be able to identify the audience, develop good listening skills, and understand the importance of feedback and nonverbal communication.

Understanding the Audience

Managers communicate with many different kinds of people. Hotel managers, for example, communicate with hotel guests, food and beverage managers, housekeepers, maintenance people, architects, travel agents, furniture salespeople, and many other types of people. They also may deal with senior management from the hotel's corporate office. Each of these groups of people represents a different audience.

To communicate effectively, managers need to determine their audience. Specifically, they need to be able to answer the following questions:

1. What does the audience already know?
2. What does it want to know?
3. What is its capacity for absorbing information?
4. What does it hope to gain by listening? Is it hoping to be motivated? Informed? Convinced?
5. Is the audience friendly or hostile?

Hotel managers communicate with the hotel's housekeeping staff about complaints by guests. In doing so, they must inform the staff of the problem and motivate them to work harder to prevent complaints in the future. They would not need to provide background material on the nature of the housekeeper's role. The audience already understands what that role includes.

If a lawsuit is filed against a hotel, managers of the hotel must inform senior management about the situation. In communicating with the hotel's senior management, they would describe what was being done to deal with the situation. They would also provide detailed background information that would allow the corporate officers to fully understand the situation.

Developing Good Listening Skills

One of the most important skills a manager can develop is the ability to listen (see Figure 3.5). Good listening skills enable managers to absorb the information they need, recognize problems, and understand other people's viewpoints.

active listening
Absorbing what another person is saying and responding to the person's concerns.

Managers need to learn to listen actively. **Active listening** involves absorbing what another person is saying and responding to the person's concerns (see Figure 3.6). Learning to listen actively is the key to becoming a good communicator.

Most people do not listen actively. Tests indicate that immediately after listening to a 10-minute oral presentation, the average listener has heard, comprehended, accurately evaluated, and retained about half of what was said. Within 48 hours, the effectiveness level drops to just 25 percent. By the end of a week, listeners recall only about 10 percent or less of what they heard.

Managers need to work at being active listeners. Many people daydream or think about an unrelated topic when someone else is talking. Some people become angry by a speaker's remarks and fail to fully absorb what the person is saying. Others become impatient and interrupt, preferring to talk rather than listen.

FIGURE 3.5
Are You a Good Listener?

- Are you open to what other people say to you, or do you make up your mind about things before you hear other people's views?
- Do you become bored when other people speak?
- Do you interrupt people when they are speaking?
- Do you daydream at meetings?
- Are you hesitant to ask clarifying questions?

FIGURE 3.6
Using Active
Listening

1. **Listening**
   Knowing how to listen is an important part of dealing with customers. Using active listening skills helps managers understand why customers are dissatisfied.

2. **Responding**
   The way managers respond to complaints can be just as important as the way they solve the customer's problem. Businesspeople should always be courteous and friendly when dealing with customers. They should demonstrate interest in determining what went wrong and figuring out what they can do to solve the problem.

3. **Making Sure the Customers Are Satisfied**
   Managers need to determine whether they have satisfied the customers' needs. To do so, they must interpret the feedback they receive from the customers..

Learning to listen actively involves the following steps:

1. *Identify the speaker's purpose.* What is the speaker trying to achieve? Why is the speaker speaking?
2. *Identify the speaker's main ideas.* Which of the points are the key points? Which points need to be addressed by the listener?
3. *Note the speaker's tone as well as his or her body language.* Is the speaker angry? Nervous? Confident?
4. *Respond to the speaker with appropriate comments, questions, and body language.* Use facial expressions and body language to express the emotions you want to express. Establish eye contact, sit up straight, and lean toward the speaker to show interest. Ask a question or make a comment from time to time to show that you are listening attentively.

Selecting Feedback

Effective communication is a two-way process. Information must flow back and forth between sender and receiver. The flow from the receiver to the sender is called **feedback.** It informs the sender whether the receiver has received the correct message; it also lets the receiver know if he or she has received the correct message. For example, asking a person if she or he understands a message often puts the person on the defensive and can result in limited feedback. Instead of asking if a person understands a message, it is much better to request that the receiver explain what he or she has heard.

In an experiment designed to show the importance of feedback in the communication process, one person was asked to verbally describe to a group of people the layout of the rectangles shown in Figure 3.7. The group members were

feedback
The flow of information from the receiver to the sender.

FIGURE 3.7
Rectangles in
Communication
Experiment

Source: From Harold J. Leavitt, *Managerial Psychology.* Copyright © 1972 The University of Chicago Press. Reprinted with permission.

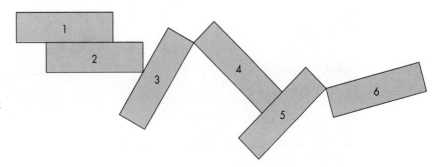

required to draw the layout based on the verbal description. The group received only a verbal description of the layout. The experiment was conducted in two ways. First, the group was not allowed to ask questions while the layout was being described, and the person describing the layout was hidden from view so the group could not see the person's facial expressions or other nonverbal communications. Thus, no feedback was present. In the second trial, the group was allowed to ask questions as the layout was being described, and the speaker was openly facing the group. Thus, feedback was present. The results showed the layout was described more quickly to the group when no feedback was allowed. However, feedback greatly improved the accuracy and the group's degree of confidence in the accuracy of their drawings.

Understanding the Importance of Nonverbal Communication

paralanguage
A form of nonverbal communication that includes the pitch, tempo, loudness, and hesitations in the verbal communication.

People have a great capacity to convey meaning through nonverbal means of expression. One form of nonverbal communication, called **paralanguage,** includes the pitch, tempo, loudness, and hesitations in the verbal communication. People also use a variety of gestures in nonverbal communication. In America, for example, one can raise an eyebrow to indicate disapproval, interest, concern, or attention. In Japan, however, that raised eyebrow would be considered an obscene gesture.

People also communicate nonverbally by how close they stand to each other. Body posture and eye contact also communicate messages. For example, lack of eye contact can communicate indifference or shyness.

In summary, nonverbal communication is an important supplement to verbal communication and sometimes can even change the meaning of verbal communication. Nonverbal communication is an effective way to communicate emotions. When combined with verbal communication, it gives managers powerful tools for transmitting information to employees.

Written Communication

Managers communicate in writing every day. They send e-mails, write letters, and draft reports. To communicate effectively, managers must be able to write clearly, concisely, and persuasively.

Before actually writing a business document, managers need to think about what they want to achieve. They must identify the purpose of the document, the audience, and the main point they want to convey. Using a form like that shown in Figure 3.8 can help them work through this stage of the writing process.

FIGURE 3.8
Identifying the Purpose, Audience, and Main Point of a Document

Purpose
- Why am I writing this document?
- What action do I want the reader to take after reading it?

Audience
- Who will read this document?
- How much does the reader already know about the topic?
- How will the reader use the document?
- Are there any special sensitivities of which I should be aware?

Main Message
- What is the main message I want to convey in this document?
- How will I support that message?

FIGURE 3.9 **Suggestions for Improving Written Communication Skills**

	Examples	
Tips	**Weak Writing**	**Strong Writing**
Use language that is easy to understand. Avoid using jargon or bureaucratic language.	Interfacing with foreign counterparts is likely to continue in the future at an accelerated pace.	We plan to work closely with foreign partners.
Use short, simple sentences.	After three years of declining sales, corporate management decided to adopt a quality-improvement program, which was instituted in all production units last month, with plans for expansion throughout the company by early April.	Sales fell for three consecutive years. In response, corporate management put a quality-improvement program in place in all production units. By April, it hopes to expand the program throughout the company.
Use restrained, moderate language that is not overly emotional.	Sales were terrible this year!	Sales were weaker than management had expected.
Avoid the passive voice in favor of the active voice.	The decision was made to create two new brochures.	The marketing department decided to create two new brochures.
Use gender-neutral language. Avoid sexist language.	Every man in this company does his best to increase company profits.	Everyone in our company does his or her best to increase company profits.

Principles of Good Writing

Many business managers have difficulty writing well. To improve their writing, managers can apply several basic principles:

1. *Write as simply and clearly as possible.* Avoid writing in a way that is difficult to understand.
2. *Be sure that the content and tone of the document are appropriate for the audience.* Do not waste readers' time communicating information they already know. However, do not assume they are as familiar with the topic as you are. Always use a polite tone, especially when writing to customers.
3. *Proofread the document.* If you are using a computer, use the spell-check function. If you are not using a computer, use a dictionary to check the spelling of words you do not know. Always read the document for incorrect grammar or usage.

Figure 3.9 offers suggestions for improving written communication skills.

Oral Communication

Not all business communication is done in writing. In fact, most business communication is done orally.

Some oral communication is formal and takes place at meetings or interviews. Most oral communication is informal. It takes place in offices and hallways, next to the water fountain, in the cafeteria, and over the telephone.

The Importance of Oral Communication

Communicating well verbally is important for managers. Successful managers use their oral communication skills to give clear instructions, motivate their staffs, and persuade other people.

FIGURE 3.10   Techniques for Speaking Effectively

Technique	Example
Enumeration (listing key points)	Our department is looking for people with excellent technical ability, outstanding communication skills, and the desire to contribute to a team.
Generalization followed by examples	We continue to demonstrate our commitment to staff education. Last year we sent almost half of our employees to seminars and training sessions. This year, we expect to include up to 75 percent of all employees in staff education.
Cause and effect	We increased our sales force by 25 percent in the Northeast region in 2001. As a result, sales rose by more than $2 million.
Comparison and contrast	Our newest portable computer is as light as our competitors' and has as much computing power. It is $400 less expensive than our competitors' product, however.

Being able to communicate effectively also is important because it can set the tone within a department or company. In some departments, managers say "good morning" to as many co-workers as they can. They invite their employees to discuss problems with them. In other departments, managers isolate themselves from lower-level employees and make no effort to communicate. These small differences can have a big effect on employee morale.

Developing Oral Communication Skills

All businesspeople need to be able to speak effectively (see Figure 3.10). Whether they are talking to a colleague or presenting a keynote address before thousands of people, they need to follow the same rules of thumb:

1. *Make emotional contact with listeners by addressing them by name where possible.* When talking face-to-face, establish eye contact.
2. *Avoid speaking in a monotone.* Use your voice to emphasize important words within a sentence.
3. *Be enthusiastic and project a positive outlook.* Focus on what is going right, rather than what is going wrong.
4. *Avoid interrupting others.* Even if you know what the other person is going to say, avoid cutting other people off or finishing their sentences for them.
5. *Always be courteous.* Avoid getting angry when other people are talking, even if you disagree with what they are saying.
6. *Avoid empty sounds or words, such as "uh," "um," "like," and "you know."* Sprinkling your speech with empty fillers will make you sound unprofessional.

Choosing the Best Method of Communication

Managers need to master both written and verbal communication skills. They also need to understand when to use each kind of skill. In general, verbal communication is most appropriate for sensitive communications, such as reprimanding or dismissing an employee. Written communication is most appropriate for communicating routine information, such as changes in company policies or staff. Choosing the best method of communication will help you relay information in an appropriate and professional manner.

Communicating within the Organization

In order to be an effective manager, the importance of the grapevine and e-mail must be understood.

The Grapevine

grapevine
Informal channels of communication within an organization

Many informal paths of communication also exist in organizations. These informal channels are generally referred to as the **grapevine.** During the Civil War, intelligence telegraph lines hung loosely from tree to tree and looked like grapevines. Messages sent over these lines were often garbled; thus, any rumor was said to be from the grapevine. Grapevines develop within organizations when employees share common hobbies, home towns, lunch breaks, family ties, and social relationships. The grapevine always exists within the formal organizational structure. However, it does not follow the organizational hierarchy; it may go from secretary to vice president or from engineer to clerk. The grapevine is not limited to nonmanagement personnel; it also operates among managers and professional personnel.

The grapevine generally has a poor reputation because it is regarded as the primary source of distorted messages and rumors. However, management must recognize that the grapevine is often accurate. Management must also recognize that information in the grapevine travels more rapidly than information in the formal channels of communication. Finally, management must recognize the resilience of the grapevine. No matter how much effort is spent improving the formal channels of communication, grapevines will always exist.

Because the grapevine is inevitable, management should use it to complement formal channels of communication. In utilizing the grapevine, honesty is always the best policy. Rumors and distorted messages will persist, but honest disclaimers by management will stop the spread of inaccurate information.[1] Management Illustration 3.1 describes how a large South African company uses the grapevine.

E-mail

Especially valuable to communication in today's organizations is the use of electronic mail systems, or e-mail, provided by networked and online systems. The e-mail system provides for high-speed exchange of written messages through the use of computerized text processing and computer-oriented communication networks. The primary advantages of this system are that it saves time, eliminates wasted effort (such as unanswered or repeat phone calls), provides written records (if necessary) of communications without the formality of memos, and enables communication among individuals who might not communicate otherwise.

The Internet

Internet
A global collection of independently operating, but interconnected, computers.

The **Internet** is a global collection of independently operating, but interconnected, computers.[2] Frequently referred to as the *information superhighway*, the Internet is actually a network of computer networks. Think of the Internet as analogous to the interstate highway system; just as the interstate system connects to different cities via many different routes, the Internet connects computers around the world via a number of different electronic pathways.

The real value of the Internet to managers is the information that it makes available. Through the Internet, managers can access massive amounts of information by accessing computers around the world that are linked together through the Internet. E-mail uses the Internet.

After a company survey revealed that many employees felt they couldn't discuss some topics without retribution and believed that management were not always transparent in their dealings with staff, The Liberty Group in South Africa (a large financial company listed on the Johannesburg Stock Exchange) introduced an official employee grapevine on the company intranet. "We realized that staff needed to query company rumors and concerns anonymously," says internal communications manager Shani Webster.

To enable this, a special form has been provided on the intranet allowing employees to send anonymous queries.

Every rumor or query received—usually between 2 and 10 a day—is passed on to the relevant executive for a response, which is then published on the intranet.

Sensitive issues dealt with so far include employee reactions to a hefty bonus received by the company's CEO, which were published together with his response, providing the reasons and history behind the bonus.

Source: Mandy Thatcher, "The Grapevine: Communication Tool or Thorn in Your Side?" *Strategic Communication Management,* August 2003, p. 32.

Intranets

intranet
A private, corporate, computer network that uses Internet products and technologies to provide multimedia applications within organizations.

An **intranet** is a private, corporate, computer network that uses Internet products and technologies to provide multimedia applications within organizations.[3] An intranet connects people to people and people to information and knowledge within the organization; it serves as an "information hub" for the entire organization. Most organizations set up intranets primarily for employees, but they can extend to business partners and even customers with appropriate security clearance. Research has found that the biggest applications for intranets today are internal communications, followed by knowledge sharing and management information systems.[4]

Communication in International Business Activities

Communication in international business activities becomes more complicated in both the verbal and nonverbal communication processes. In verbal communication, the obvious problem of dealing with different languages exists. More than 3,000 languages are spoken, and about 100 of these are official languages of nations. English is the leading international language, and its leadership continues to grow. However, as anyone who has studied a modern language knows, verbally communicating with a person in another language complicates the communication process.

The nonverbal communication process is even more complicated. Cultural differences play a significant role in nonverbal communication. For example, in the United States, people tend to place themselves about three feet apart when standing and talking. However, in the Middle East, individuals are likely to stand only a foot or so apart while conversing. This closeness obviously could intimidate an American manager.

There are no simple answers to the problems in communicating in international business activities. However, there are two things the manager should do: (1) learn the culture of the people with whom he or she communicates and (2) write and speak clearly and simply. Most people will have learned English in school and will not understand jargon or slang. As expansion into international business contin-

The use of your hands is one method used to communicate to another person. The use of the handshake is familiar to most people. This ancient practice of indicating that one is unarmed is fairly universal. However, there are plenty of entrenched local alternatives such as the Japanese bow or the Indian namaste. Nonetheless, frequent hand gripping can be essential in some countries. In France, it is de rigueur at the start and end of the day, at least between men. In contrast, hand contact between men and women is unacceptable within the Islamic world. While conversing, a general flailing of hands and arms may go unnoticed in Italy, but in Japan it may be considering threatening. Also, in some countries it is highly offensive to point with the finger. Furthermore, in many parts of the world—such as the Middle East—eating or accepting food with the left hand is considered unclean.

Source: "Business—Culture Differences—Mind the Banana Skins," *Accountancy,* October 1, 2001, p. 37.

ues, these simple rules will become increasingly important. Management Illustration 3.2 describes several methods of communicating in the international setting.

Summary

1. *Define communication.* Communication is the act of transmitting information.

2. *Describe the interpersonal communication process.* Interpersonal communication occurs between individuals. It is an interactive process that involves a person's effort to attain meaning and respond to it. It involves sending and receiving verbal and nonverbal messages.

3. *Describe problems that could arise from conflicting or inappropriate assumptions made in interpersonal communication.* Misunderstandings can occur when a speaker thinks he or she was being clear or was understood. Questions that go unanswered, points that are misunderstood, and meanings that are misinterpreted are examples of potential problems.

4. *Define semantics, and explain its role in interpersonal communication.* Semantics is the science or study of the meanings of words and symbols. Because of the possibility of misinterpretation, words must be carefully chosen and clearly defined to enable effective communication.

5. *Define perception.* Perception deals with the mental and sensory processes an individual uses in interpreting information received.

6. *Explain how emotions may affect communication.* Emotions affect one's disposition to send and receive communication. Anger, joy, fear, sorrow, disgust, or panic can all affect the way one sends and receives messages. Communications during periods of high emotion are often subject to distortion.

7. *Explain the concept of feedback in communication.* Feedback is the flow of information from the receiver to the sender. For communication to be effective, information must flow back and forth between sender and receiver.

8. *Explain active listening.* Active listening involves absorbing what another person is saying and responding to the person's concerns.

9. *Describe the grapevine.* The grapevine consists of the informal channels of communication that develop within the organization as a result of common hobbies, home towns, lunch breaks, family ties, and social relationships among employees.

10. *Define and briefly discuss the e-mail process.* The electronic mail, or e-mail, system provides for high-speed exchange of written messages through the use of computerized text processing and computer-oriented communication networks.

11. *Define the Internet and intranets.* The Internet is a global collection of independently operating, but interconnected, computers. An intranet is a private, corporate, computer network that uses Internet products and technologies to provide multimelia applications within organizations.

12. *Discuss two factors that complicate communications in international business activities.* Communicating in a foreign language complicates the communication process. Cultural differences exhibited through nonverbal communications are also complicating factors.

Review Questions

1. What is communication?
2. Define interpersonal communication.
3. Give an illustration of a conflicting assumption.
4. What is semantics?
5. What is perception, and what role does it play in communication?
6. How should one deal with emotions in communication?
7. What is feedback, and how does it affect the communication process?
8. What is active listening?
9. Explain the importance of nonverbal communication in interpersonal communication.
10. Describe the following organizational communication systems:
    a. E-mail communication system
    b. Grapevine
11. Define the Internet and intranets.
12. Describe two factors that complicate communications in international business.

Skill-Building Questions

1. Describe some ways the grapevine can be used effectively in organizations.
2. Explain why many managers frequently raise the following question: "Why didn't you do what I told you to do?"
3. Discuss the following statement: Meanings are in people, not words.
4. "Watch what we do, not what we say." Is this a good practice in organizations? Explain.
5. Poor communication of the organization's objectives is often given as the reason for low organizational performance. Do you think this is usually a valid explanation? Why or why not?

Skill-Building Exercise 3.1

Perception Test

Take a maximum of 10 minutes to complete the following test.

1. In 1963, if you went to bed at 8 o'clock P.M. and set the alarm to get up at 9 o'clock the next morning, how many hours of sleep would you get?
2. If you have only one match and enter a room in which there is a kerosene lamp, an oil stove, and a wood-burning stove, which would you light first?
3. Some months have 30 days; some have 31. How many have 28 days?
4. If a doctor gave you three pills and told you to take one every half-hour, how long would they last?
5. A man builds a house with four sides, and it is rectangular in shape. Each side has a southern exposure. A big bear comes wandering by. What color is the bear?
6. I have in my hand two U.S. coins that total 55 cents in value. One is not a nickel. Please bear that in mind. What are the two coins?
7. Divide 30 by ½ and add 10. What is the answer?

8. Take two apples from three apples, and what do you have?

9. An archaeologist found some gold coins dated 34 B.C. How old are they?

10. How many animals of each species did Moses take aboard the ark with him?

**Skill-
Building
Exercise 3.2**

We Americans supposedly speak the English language. However, anyone who has ever visited England knows that the English often use different words and phrases than we do. Can you identify what the English words or phrases in the left column below would be if spoken by an American?

_____ chemist	*a.* elevator
_____ phone engaged	*b.* mailbox
_____ ring-up	*c.* orchestra seat
_____ round up	*d.* line
_____ wines and spirits	*e.* can
_____ chipped potatoes	*f.* subway
_____ give way	*g.* hood
_____ to let	*h.* newsstand
_____ ta!	*i.* taxes
_____ it's mommy's go	*j.* suspenders
_____ half five	*k.* aisle
_____ mind your step	*l.* apartment
_____ a bit dear	*m.* janitor
_____ way out	*n.* hardware dealer
_____ bonnet	*o.* truck
_____ stall	*p.* exit
_____ flat	*q.* drugstore
_____ kiosk	*r.* busy
_____ ironmonger	*s.* too expensive
_____ pillar box	*t.* watch your step
_____ porter	*u.* call
_____ tin	*v.* go halfway around circle and straight up
_____ lift	*w.* liquor store
_____ queue	*x.* french fries
_____ lorry	*y.* yield
_____ rates	*z.* for rent
_____ braces	*aa.* bid adieu
_____ gangway	*bb.* it's mommy's turn
_____ underground	*cc.* five-thirty

**Skill-
Building
Exercise 3.3**

What's Your Communication Style?

Carefully read each statement and its four endings. Grade these by assigning a 4 to the ending that most describes you, a 3 to the next ending most like you, a 2 to the next ending most like you, and a 1 to the ending least like you. Once you have assigned a number, you may not use that number again in the set of four endings. For example, you may not assign a grade of 4 to both 1*a* and 1*b*.

1. I am most likely to impress my co-workers as

   a. Down to earth, practical, and to the point.   *a* _____

   b. Emotional, sensitive to my own and others' feelings.   *b* _____ *c.* Cool, logical, patient.   *c* _____

    d. Intellectual and somewhat aloof.   *d* _____

2. When I am assigned a project, I am most concerned that the project will be

    a. Practical, with definite results that will justify my time and energy on it. *a* _____

    b. Stimulating, involving lively interaction with others. *b* _____

    c. Systematically or logically developed. *c* _____

    d. Breaking ground and advancing knowledge. *d* _____

3. In reacting to individuals whom I meet socially, I am likely to consider whether

    a. They are assertive and decisive. *a* _____

    b. They are caring. *b* _____

    c. They seem thorough and exact. *c* _____

    d. They seem highly intelligent. *d* _____

4. When confronted by others with a different opinion, I find it most useful to

    a. Pinpoint the key differences, and develop compromises so that speedy decisions can be made. *a* _____

    b. Put myself in the others' shoes, and try to understand their point of view. *b* _____

    c. Keep calm and present my material clearly, simply, and logically. *c* _____

    d. Create new proposals. *d* _____

5. Under pressure, I suspect I may come through to others as being

    a. Too concerned with wanting immediate action, and pushing for immediate decisions. *a* _____

    b. Too emotional and occasionally carried away by my feelings. *b* _____

    c. Highly unemotional, impersonal, too analytical and critical. *c* _____

    d. Snobbish, condescending, intellectually superior. *d* _____

6. When lecturing to a group, I would like to leave the impression of being

    a. A practical and resourceful person who can show the audience how to, for example, streamline a procedure. *a* _____

    b. A lively and persuasive individual who is in touch with the audience's emotions and moods. *b* _____

    c. A systematic thinker who can analyze the group's problems. *c* _____

    d. A highly innovative individual. *d* _____

Now transcribe the numbers that you wrote beside each ending to the appropriate spaces below. Total the columns for questions 1–3 and for questions 4–6. The initials at the bottom of the columns—S, F, T, and I—stand for the different communication styles: senser, feeler, thinker, and intuitor. The column with the highest total for questions 1–3 is your communication style under relaxed conditions, and the column with the highest total for questions 4–6 is your style under stress conditions. Once you have defined your particular style, check the table at the end of the exercise for the positive and negative traits associated with it. Note that you may have the positive traits without the negative ones or vice versa.

	a	*b*	*c*	*d*			*a*	*b*	*c*	*d*
1.	__	__	__	__		4.	__	__	__	__
2.	__	__	__	__		5.	__	__	__	__
3.	__	__	__	__		6.	__	__	__	__
Total	S	F	T	I		**Total**	S	F	T	I

Source: Phyllis Kuhn, "Sharpening Your Communication Skills," *Medical Laboratory Observer*, March 1987. Used with permission from Medical Laboratory Observer. Copyright © 1987 by Nelson Publishing, Inc. www.mlo-online.com

Some Traits Linked to Each Communication Style

Positive	Negative
Intuitor	
Creative	Fantasy-bound
Idealistic	Impractical
Intellectual	Too theoretical
Feeler	
Caring	Wishy-washy
Conscientious	Guilt-ridden
Persuasive	Manipulative
Thinker	
Exact, precise	Nitpicker
Deliberate	Rigid
Weighs all alternatives	Indecisive
Senser	
Decisive	Impulsive
Assertive	Aggressive
Enjoys producing quick results	Lacks trust in others' ability
Technically skillful	Self-involved, status seeking

Skill-Building Exercise 3.4

Sexist/Nonsexist Language

As part of communicating that an organization is truly committed to supporting a highly qualified and diverse workforce, managers should take every opportunity to demonstrate the use of nonsexist language.

1. Try to identify a nonsexist word to use in place of each of the following words that may carry a sexist connotation:

Man-hours	Salesman
Watchman	Spokesman
Girl Friday	Foreman
Repairman	Draftsman
Layout man	Policeman
Man-made	Freshman

2. List additional words or terms that you think might carry a sexist connotation.

Case Incident 3.1

Who Calls the Shots?

The financial reports for the last quarter of operations for Brighton Cabinet Company were just received by the company's president, John Branner. After looking over the reports, John decided the purchasing department was paying too much for the company's raw materials, which include plywood, paneling, and flakeboard. He immediately called Joe Scott, vice president of manufacturing, and informed him of the decision. Exhibit 1 gives a partial organizational chart for Brighton Cabinet Company.

Joe called Bill Sloane, the supervisor of purchasing, and said, "Mr. Branner is upset over the cost figures for raw materials last quarter. You were well above budget. He wants them brought down this quarter!"

As Bill hung up the phone, he asked himself who figured out the budget for his department and if they realized plywood had gone up from $6.05 to $6.75 a sheet. Bill had been instructed to cut costs, and he was determined to do so. Two days later, Bill found a supplier who would sell Brighton plywood for $5.95 a sheet. He ordered a two-week supply.

On delivery, Bill's suspicions were confirmed. The plywood was of a poorer quality, but it would work. Bill decided to continue to buy the less expensive plywood.

EXHIBIT 1
Partial Organization
Chart for Brighton
Cabinet Company

A month later, Bill was approached by Ted Brown, supervisor of the assembly department, who asked, "Bill, what's with this plywood? All of a sudden, we've been having a lot of it split on us while trying to nail and staple the pieces together." Bill replied, "Well, Ted, Mr. Branner sent orders down for me to cut costs. I don't know how else to do it other than purchasing the lower-grade plywood. It was the only way out." Things were left as they were, and the quarter ended.

The financial reports for the quarter showed a drop in sales and profits. According to forecasts and trends of previous years, the profits and sales should have been higher. John Branner immediately called Mary Strickland, vice president of marketing, to his office and demanded an explanation. Mary explained,

It seems that we have lost a couple of major builders as customers. They seem to think that our competitors have something better to offer. I have investigated the situation and have found that our cabinets are splitting more on installation because we are using a lower-grade plywood now. I talked to Joe Scott. He told me you had ordered him to cut costs, and the purchase of the lower grade was one of the few ways that costs could be reduced.

John immediately ordered Joe to begin purchasing plywood of the necessary quality. Joe then informed Bill. Later that day, Bill asked Joe what should be done with the three-week supply of the lower-grade plywood. "That's your problem," Joe snapped. Apparently, he had gotten a good chewing out from Branner.

After making several calls, Bill decided the only good offer for the plywood was made by the company that sold it to Brighton. But it would pay only 60 percent of what it cost Brighton. Bill agreed to the price, wanting to get rid of it to make room for the new supplies that would be coming in.

Three days later, Bill was called into Joe's office. Joe asked, "Bill, who gave you permission to sell that plywood at that price?" "No one," Bill replied. "It was my decision. It was the best deal I could find, and I needed to get it out to make room for the new supplies coming in."

"Well, Bill, with decisions like that, this company won't last very long," Joe commented. "You should have used up the other plywood a little at a time by mixing it with the higher-grade plywood. Don't let this happen again!"

Questions

1. How did this problem begin, and how could it have been avoided?
2. Describe the communication failures that occurred in this case.
3. Is Bill really responsible? Who else, if anyone, is responsible?
4. Comment on Joe Scott's talk with Bill at the end of the case.

References and Additional Readings

1. For additional information, see Mandy Thatcher, "The Grapevine: Communication Tool or Thorn in Your Side?" *Strategic Communication Management*, August 2003, pp. 30–34.

2. Byron J. Finch, *The Management Guide to Internet Resources* (New York: McGraw-Hill), 1997, p. 2. Much of this section is drawn from this source.

3. Paul Barker, "The Evolving Corporate Intranet," *Telecommunications*, December 1997, pp. 67–70.

4. Ibid.

Chapter

4

Decision-Making Skills

Learning Objectives

After studying this chapter, you will be able to:

1. Explain the difference between decision making and problem solving.
2. Distinguish between programmed and nonprogrammed decisions.
3. Explain the intuitive approach to decision making.
4. Discuss two rational approaches to decision making.
5. List the different conditions under which managers make decisions.
6. Explain the role values play in making decisions.
7. Summarize the positive and negative aspects of group decision making.
8. Define creativity and innovation, and outline the basic stages in the creative process.
9. Identify several specific tools and techniques that can be used to foster creative decisions.
10. List the six stages in creative decision making.
11. Explain the role of a management information system (MIS).

Chapter Preview

Managers who run dynamic organizations always seem to make great decisions at precisely the proper time. Most great managers seem to have the following decision-making characteristics in common: They accept change, listen to customers, decentralize authority, hire carefully, teach continuously, and control costs. They don't do just one of these things right; they do all of them right.

Steve Spurrier was the winningest coach in the University of Florida history at 122–27–1 in 12 seasons. He was also one of the highest-paid coaches in college football, making more than 2 million dollars a year. He was coaching at his alma mater and seemed to have everything going his way. Yet surprisingly, Spurrier resigned as the University of Florida coach on January 4, 2002. At his January 7 farewell news conference in Gainesville, Florida, Spurrier spoke of a longtime desire to see if his methods could work in the National Football League. "I'm intrigued to see if my style of offense, my style of coaching, can be successful at the NFL level," he said. "I need to find that out before I completely hang it up. Before I call my last play." A week later, Spurrier was hired as the new head coach for the

Washington Redskins of the NFL. Spurrier's contract was for approximately $25 million for five years. After two poor seasons (with a combined record of 12 wins and 20 losses) in Washington, Spurrier resigned as coach in December 2003.

Source: Chris Harry, "Redskins Go to Fun 'N Gun; Pro Football: After Schottenheimer Is Fired, Spurrier Agrees to Five-Year, $25 Million Contract to Become Washington's Fourth Coach in 13 Months," *Los Angeles Times,* January 14, 2002, p. D7.

Analyzing Management Skills

What factors do you think affected Steve Spurrier's decision to leave college football and move on to the National Football League? Do you think that some of these same factors affect the decisions of managers?

Applying Management Skills

Imagine you are in charge of purchasing a new computer system for your workplace or college. What type of research would you do? What factors would you consider before making your decision?

Some authors use the term d*ecision maker* to mean *manager.* However, although managers are decision makers, not all decision makers are managers. For example, a person who sorts fruit or vegetables is required to make decisions, but not as a manager. However, all managers, regardless of their positions in the organization, must make decisions in the pursuit of organizational goals. In fact, decision making pervades all of the basic management functions: planning, organizing, staffing, leading, and controlling. Although each of these functions requires different types of decisions, all of them require decisions. Thus, to be a good planner, organizer, staffer, leader, and controller, a manager must first be a good decision maker.

decision process
Process that involves three stages: intelligence, design, and choice. Intelligence is searching the environment for conditions requiring a decision. Design is inventing, developing, and analyzing possible courses of action. Choice is the actual selection of a course of action.

Herbert Simon, a Nobel prize winner, has described the manager's **decision process** in three stages: (1) intelligence, (2) design, and (3) choice.[1] The intelligence stage involves searching the environment for conditions requiring a decision. The design stage entails inventing, developing, and analyzing possible courses of action. Choice, the final stage, refers to the actual selection of a course of action.

The decision process stages show the difference between management and nonmanagement decisions. Nonmanagement decisions are concentrated in the last (choice) stage. The fruit/vegetable sorter has to make a choice regarding only the size or quality of the goods. Management decisions place greater emphasis on the intelligence and design stages. If the decision-making process is viewed as only the choice stage, managers spend very little time making decisions. If, however, the decision-making process is viewed as not only the actual choice but also the intelligence and design work needed to make the choice, managers spend most of their time making decisions.

decision making
In its narrowest sense, the process of choosing from among various alternatives.

Decision Making versus Problem Solving

The terms *decision making* and *problem solving* are often confused and therefore need to be clarified. As indicated earlier, **decision making**, in its narrowest sense, is the process of choosing from among various alternatives. A *problem* is any deviation

problem solving
Process of determining the appropriate responses or actions necessary to alleviate a problem.

from some standard or desired level of performance. **Problem solving,** then, is the process of determining the appropriate responses or actions necessary to alleviate a problem. Problem solving necessarily involves decision making, since all problems can be attacked in numerous ways and the problem solver must decide which way is best. On the other hand, not all decisions involve problems (such as the person sorting fruit and vegetables). However, from a practical perspective, almost all managerial decisions do involve solving or at least avoiding problems.

Programmed versus Nonprogrammed Decisions

programmed decisions
Decisions that are reached by following an established or systematic procedure.

nonprogrammed decisions
Decisions that have little or no precedent; they are relatively unstructured and generally require a creative approach by the decision maker.

Decisions are often classified as programmed or nonprogrammed. **Programmed decisions** are reached by an established or systematic procedure. Normally, the decision maker knows the situation in a programmable decision. Routine, repetitive decisions usually fall into this category. Managerial decisions covered by organizational policies, procedures, and rules are programmed in that established guidelines must be followed in arriving at the decision.

Nonprogrammed decisions have little or no precedent. They are relatively unstructured and generally require a more creative approach by the decision maker; the decision maker must develop the procedure to be used. Generally, nonprogrammed decisions are more difficult to make than programmed decisions. Deciding on a new product, a new piece of equipment, and next year's goals are all nonprogrammed decisions.

Decision Making with Computers

With the continuing increase in technology, computers are being used more and more to help managers make decisions. The development of artificial intelligence and related software has reached the point where computers can not only provide managers with data to help make decisions, but the computers themselves can actually execute certain managerial decisions.

The Intuitive Approach to Decision Making

intuitive approach
Approach used when managers make decisions based largely on hunches and intuition.

When managers make decisions solely on hunches and intuition (the **intuitive approach**), they are practicing management as though it were wholly an art based only on feelings. While intuition and other forms of judgment do play a role in many decision situations, problems can occur when managers ignore available facts and rely only on feelings. When this happens, managers sometimes become so emotionally attached to certain positions that almost nothing will change their minds. They develop the "don't bother me with the facts—my mind is made up" attitude. George Odiorne isolated the following emotional attachments that can hurt decision makers:

1. Fastening on unsubstantiated facts and sticking with them.
2. Being attracted to scandalous issues and heightening their significance.
3. Pressing every fact into a moral pattern.
4. Overlooking everything except what is immediately useful.
5. Having an affinity for romantic stories and finding such information more significant than any other kind, including hard evidence.[2]

Such emotional attachments can be very real and can lead to poor decisions. They most often affect managers or decision makers who are "living in the past" and either will not or cannot modernize their thinking. An example is the manager who insists on making decisions just as the founder of the company did 40 years ago.

Odiorne offers two suggestions for managers and decision makers engulfed by emotional attachments.[3] First, become aware of biases and allow for them. Undiscovered biases do the most damage. Second, seek independent opinions. It is always advisable to ask the opinion of some person who has no vested interest in the decision. Intuition does play a role in decision making. The key is to not ignore facts when they are available. "Good companies not only can learn. They've also learned to forget," says Professor C. K. Prahalad of the University of Michigan in his co-authored book *Competing for the Future*.[4]

Rational Approaches to Decision Making

Approaches to decision making that attempt to evaluate factual information through the use of some type of deductive reasoning are referred to as *rational approaches.* The following sections discuss two types of rational approaches.

The Optimizing Approach

The physical sciences have provided a rational approach to decision making that can be adapted to management problems. The **optimizing approach** (sometimes called the *rational* or *scientific approach*) to decision making includes the following steps:

1. Recognize the need for a decision.
2. Establish, rank, and weigh the decision criteria.
3. Gather available information and data.
4. Identify possible alternatives.
5. Evaluate each alternative with respect to all criteria.
6. Select the best alternative.

Once the need to make the decision is known, criteria must be set for expected results of the decision. These criteria should then be ranked and weighed according to their relative importance.

Next, factual data relating to the decision should be collected. After that, all alternatives that meet the criteria are identified. Each is then evaluated with respect to all criteria. The final decision is based on the alternative that best meets the criteria.

Limitations of the Optimizing Approach

The optimizing approach to decision making is an improvement over the intuitive approach, but it is not without its problems and limitations. The optimizing approach is based on the concept of "economic man." This concept postulates that people behave rationally and their behavior is based on the following assumptions:

1. People have clearly defined criteria, and the relative weights they assign to these criteria are stable.
2. People have knowledge of all relevant alternatives.

optimizing approach
Includes the following steps: recognize the need for a decision; establish, rank, and weigh criteria; gather available information and data; identify possible alternatives; evaluate each alternative with respect to all criteria; and select the best alternative.

3. People have the ability to evaluate each alternative with respect to all the criteria and arrive at an overall rating for each alternative.

4. People have the self-discipline to choose the alternative that rates the highest (they will not manipulate the system).

Consider the following difficulties with the above approach. First, these assumptions are often unrealistic; decision makers do not always have clearly defined criteria for making decisions. Second, many decisions are based on limited knowledge of the possible alternatives; even when information is available, it is usually less than perfect. Third, there is always a temptation to manipulate or ignore the gathered information and choose a favored (but not necessarily the best) alternative.

Due to the limitations of the optimizing approach, most decisions still involve some judgment. Thus, in making decisions, the manager generally uses a combination of intuitive and rational approaches.

The Satisficing Approach

Believing the assumptions of the optimizing approach to be generally unrealistic, Herbert Simon, in attempting to understand how managerial decisions are actually made, formulated his **principle of bounded rationality.** This principle states, "The capacity of the human mind for formulating and solving complex problems is very small compared with the size of the problems whose solution *is* required for objectively rational behavior—or even for a reasonable approximation to such objective rationality."[5] Basically, the principle of bounded rationality states that human rationality has definite limits. Based on this principle, Simon proposed a decision model of the "administrative man," which makes the following assumptions:

1. A person's knowledge of alternatives and criteria is limited.
2. People act on the basis of a simplified, ill-structured, mental abstraction of the real world; this abstraction is influenced by personal perceptions, biases, and so forth.
3. People do not attempt to optimize but will take the first alternative that satisfies their current level of aspiration. This is called *satisficing*.
4. An individual's level of aspiration concerning a decision fluctuates upward and downward, depending on the values of the most recently identified alternatives.

The first assumption is a synopsis of the principle of bounded rationality. The second assumption follows naturally from the first. If limits to human rationality do exist, an individual must make decisions based on limited and incomplete knowledge. The third assumption also naturally follows from the first assumption: If the decision maker's knowledge of alternatives is incomplete, the individual cannot optimize but can only satisfice. **Optimizing** means selecting the best possible alternative; **satisficing** means selecting the first alternative that meets the decision maker's minimum standard of satisfaction. Assumption four is based on the belief that the criteria for a satisfactory alternative are determined by the person's current level of aspiration. **Level of aspiration** refers to the level of performance a person expects to attain, and it is impacted by the person's prior successes and failures.

Figure 4.1 represents the satisficing approach to decision making. If the decision maker is satisfied that an acceptable alternative has been found, she or he se-

principle of bounded rationality
Assumes people have the time and cognitive ability to process only a limited amount of information on which to base decisions.

optimizing
Selecting the best possible alternative.

satisficing
Selecting the first alternative that meets the decision maker's minimum standard of satisfaction.

level of aspiration
Level of performance that a person expects to attain; determined by the person's prior successes and failures.

FIGURE 4.1
Model of the
Satisficing
Approach

Source: Adapted from James
G. March and Herbert A.
Simon, *Organizations* (New
York: John Wiley & Sons,
1958), p. 49.

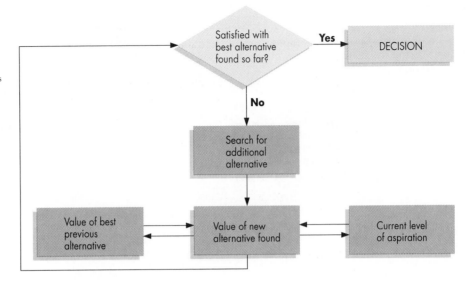

lects that alternative. Otherwise the decision maker searches for an additional alternative. In Figure 4.1, the double arrows indicate a two-way relationship: The value of the new alternative is influenced by the value of the best previous alternative; the value of the best previous alternative is in turn influenced by the value of the new alternative. As the arrows indicate, a similar two-way relationship exists between the value of the new alternative and the current level of aspiration. The net result of this evaluation determines whether or not the decision maker is satisfied with the alternative. Thus, the "administrative man" selects the first alternative that meets the minimum satisfaction criteria and makes no real attempt to optimize.

The Decision Maker's Environment

A manager's freedom to make decisions depends largely on the manager's position within the organization and on its structure. In general, higher-level managers have more flexibility and discretion. The patterns of authority outlined by the formal organization structure also influence the flexibility of the decision maker.

Another important factor in decision-making style is the purpose and tradition of the organization. For example, a military organization requires a different style of decision making than a volunteer organization does.

The organization's formal and informal group structures also affect decision-making styles. These groups may range from labor unions to advisory councils.

The final subset of the environment includes all of the decision maker's superiors and subordinates. The personalities, backgrounds, and expectations of these people influence the decision maker.

Figure 4.2 shows the major environmental factors within an organization that affect decision makers in an organization. In addition to these major organizational factors, there are always other factors in the general environment that can import a decision. Some of these factors might include industry norms, the labor market, the political climate, and competition. Successful managers must develop

FIGURE 4.2
Environmental
Factors Influencing
Decision Making in
an Organization

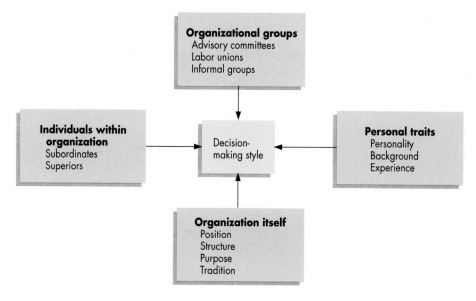

an appreciation for the different environmental forces that both influence them
and are influenced by their decisions.

Conditions for Making Decisions

Decisions are not always made with the same amount of available information.
The best decision often depends on what happens later. Consider the simple decision of whether to take an umbrella when going outside. The more desirable alternative is determined by whether or not it rains, but this is not under the control
of the decision maker. Figure 4.3 gives combinations of alternatives and states of
nature and their respective outcomes for the individual trying to decide whether
or not to take an umbrella when going outside.

Certainty

**situation of
certainty**
Situation that occurs
when a decision
maker knows exactly
what will happen and
can often calculate the
precise outcome for
each alternative.

Knowing exactly what will happen places the decision maker in a **situation of
certainty**. In such a situation, the decision maker can calculate the precise outcome for each alternative. If it is raining, the person knows the outcome of each
alternative and therefore can choose the best alternative (take an umbrella).
Rarely, however, are decisions made in today's organizations under a condition of
certainty. A manager deciding between a delivery by air (taking a set time to arrive at a set cost) or one by truck (also taking a set time to arrive at a set cost)
would be an example of a decision made under a condition of certainty.

FIGURE 4.3
Umbrella Decision
Alternatives and
Outcomes

	State of Nature	
Alternative	**No Rain**	**Rain**
Take umbrella	Dry, but inconvenient	Dry
Do not take umbrella	Dry, happy	Wet

Risk

Unfortunately, the outcome associated with each alternative is not always known in advance. The decision maker can often obtain—at some cost—information regarding the different possible outcomes. The desirability of getting the information is figured by weighing the costs of obtaining the information against the information's value. A decision maker is in a **situation of risk** if certain reliable but incomplete information is available. In a situation of risk, some ideas of the relative probabilities associated with each outcome are known. If the weather forecaster has said there is a 40 percent chance of rain, the decision maker is operating in a situation of risk.

The precise probabilities of the various outcomes usually are not known. However, reasonably accurate probabilities based on historical data and past experiences often can be calculated. When no such data exist, it is difficult to estimate probabilities. In such cases, one approach is to survey individual opinions.

Under conditions of risk, the decision maker can use expected value analysis to help arrive at a decision. With this technique, the expected payoff of each known alternative is mathematically calculated based on its probability of occurrence. One potential shortcoming of expected value analysis is that it represents the average outcome if the event is repeated many times. That is of little help if the act occurs only once. For example, airplane passengers are not interested in average fatality rates; rather, they are interested in what happens on their particular flight.

Uncertainty

When the decision maker has very little or no reliable information on which to evaluate the different possible outcomes, he or she is operating in a situation of uncertainty. Under a **situation of uncertainty,** the decision maker has no knowledge concerning the probabilities associated with different possible outcomes. For example, a person who is going to New York and has not heard a weather forecast for New York will have no knowledge of the likelihood of rain and hence will not know whether or not to carry an umbrella.

If the decision maker has little or no knowledge about which state of nature will occur, one of several basic approaches may be taken. The first is to choose the alternative whose best possible outcome is the best of all possible outcomes for all alternatives. This is an optimistic, or gambling, approach and is sometimes called the **maximax approach.** A decision maker using this approach would not take the umbrella because the best possible outcome (being dry without being inconvenienced) could be achieved only with this alternative.

A second approach for dealing with uncertainty is to compare the worst possible outcomes for each alternative and select the one that is least bad. This is a pessimistic approach and is sometimes called the **maximin approach.** In the umbrella example, the decision maker would compare the worst possible outcome of taking an umbrella to that of not taking an umbrella. The decision maker would then decide to take an umbrella because it is better to be dry than wet.

A third approach is to choose the alternative with the least variation among its possible outcomes. This is a **risk-averting approach** and results in more effective planning. If the decision maker chooses not to take an umbrella, the outcomes can vary from being dry to being wet. Thus, the risk-averting decision maker would take an umbrella to ensure staying dry.

---

situation of risk
Situation that occurs when a decision maker is aware of the relative probabilities of occurrence associated with each alternative.

situation of uncertainty
Situation that occurs when a decision maker has very little or no reliable information on which to evaluate the different possible outcomes.

maximax approach
Selecting the alternative whose best possible outcome is the best of all possible outcomes for all alternatives; sometimes called the *optimistic* or *gambling approach* to decision making.

maximin approach
Comparing the worst possible outcomes for each alternative and selecting the one that is least undesirable; sometimes called the *pessimistic approach* to decision making.

risk-averting approach
Choosing the alternative with the least variation among its possible outcomes.

Many companies and boards of directors are now taking a more proactive stance for managing all types of risks faced by the organizations' decision makers. For example the J. A. Jones Company of Charlotte, NC, has been developing a risk management system since October 2001. Jones, a $3 billion global diversified services company, is creating an ongoing management, measurement, and monitoring system to be used across all levels of the company for managing risks. One of the first steps in the process was to find the best methods for monitoring risk/reward relationships and to create a simple process for integrating these methods into the day-to-day practices of decision makers. Eric J. Gerner, vice president of corporate risk strategies, has sum-marized this approach as follows: "This doesn't change who's responsible for managing the risks, and it's not a re-placement for good judgment. Our aim was to provide a good decision-making process for good judgment. We want people identifying, planning, and communicating key risks as early as possible. The framework creates that ability."

The company views this process as an ongoing en-deavor and believes that as of mid-2003 it was "about halfway through our journey."

Source: Bruce W. Fraser, "Managing Risk Proactively," *Strategic Finance,* April 2003, pp. 36–40.

Figure 4.4 summarizes the different approaches to making a decision under conditions of uncertainty. Management Illustration 4.1 discusses how one com-pany is developing a companywide system to help managers deal with risks of all types.

Timing the Decision

To properly time a decision, the need for a decision must be recognized. That is not always easy. The manager may simply not be aware of what is going on, or the problem requiring a decision may be camouflaged. Some managers always seem to make decisions on the spot; others tend to take forever to decide even a simple matter. The manager who makes quick decisions runs the risk of making bad de-cisions. Failure to gather and evaluate available data, consider people's feelings, and anticipate the impact of the decision can result in a quick but poor decision.

FIGURE 4.4
Possible Approaches to Making Decisions under Uncertainty

Approach	How It Works	Related to the Umbrella Example
Optimistic or gambling approach (maximax)	Choose the alternative whose best possible outcome is the best of all possible outcomes for all alternatives.	Do not take umbrella
Pessimistic approach (maximin)	Compare the worst possible outcomes of each of the alternatives, and select the alternative whose worst possible outcome is least undesirable.	Take umbrella
Risk-averting approach	Choose the alternative that has the least variation among its possible alternatives.	Take umbrella

North American Enterprises, Inc., was founded in Tucson, Arizona, in 1989 by Joseph Lovallo. At the time, Joseph Lovallo had to persuade Italian pasta maker Mario Rummo to allow him to import pasta to America. Today, North American Enterprises has a headquarters in Tucson, five warehouses around the country, and a 3,500-square-foot fulfillment center in Tempe that produces gift baskets. The company supplies pasta to at least 700 U.S. restaurants and six of nine Costco regions across the country. Three of Joseph Lovallo's children, Grant, Lisa, and Lesley, now work in the business in different but complementary roles.

The Lovallos believe that being relatively small and a family company gives them certain advantages over others, especially in the ability to make quick and timely decisions.

Lisa Lovallo, chief operating officer, says, "If you're going to be small, you'd better be fast." Lisa points out that at North American Enterprises, customers don't have to wade through layers of management to get a decision. "You're talking to somebody who can actually make a decision here. We don't have to waste a lot of time with me going back to corporate, and then talking to the marketing guy. The marketing guy is my brother. If we need to change that on that packaging, to meet that requirement, we can do it—and as a matter of fact, we can do it tomorrow."

Source: Tiffany Kjos, "Tucson, Arizona, Pasta Importer Expands into Gourmet Markets with Own Brand," *Knight Ridder Tribune Business News,* October 28, 2002, p. 1.

Just as risky is the other extreme: the manager who listens to problems, promises to act, but never does. Nearly as bad is the manager who responds only after an inordinate delay. Other familiar types are the manager who never seems to have enough information to make a decision, the manager who frets and worries over even the simplest decisions, and the manager who refers everything to superiors.

Knowing when to make a decision is complicated because different decisions have different time frames. For instance, a manager generally has more time to decide committee appointments than he or she has to decide what to do when three employees call in sick. No magic formula exists to tell managers when a decision should be made or how long it should take to make it. The important thing is to see the importance of properly timing decisions. Management Illustration 4.2 discusses how one company believes that it has a distinct advantage over many of its competitors by being able to make quick and timely decisions.

The Role of Values in Decision Making

value
A conception, explicit or implicit, that defines what an individual or a group regards as desirable. People are not born with values; rather, they acquire and develop them early in life.

A **value** is a conception, explicit or implicit, defining what an individual or a group regards as desirable.[6] Values play an important role in the decision-making process. People are not born with values; rather, they acquire and develop them early in life. Parents, teachers, relatives, and others influence an individual's values. As a result, every manager and every employee brings a certain set of values to the workplace.

A person's values have an impact on the selection of performance measures, alternatives, and choice criteria in the decision process. Differences in values often account for the use of different performance measures. For example, a manager concerned primarily with economic values would probably measure performance differently than a manager concerned mainly with social values. The former might look only at profit; the latter might think only of customer complaints.

Differences in values may also generate different alternatives. A viable alternative to one person may be unacceptable to another because of differences in

FIGURE 4.5
George England's
Major Categories of
Values

Source: George England,
"Personal Value Systems of
Managers and
Administrators," *Academy of
Management Proceedings,*
August 1973, pp. 81–94.

Pragmatic mode	Suggests that an individual has an evaluative framework that is guided primarily by success–failure considerations.
Ethical/moral mode	Implies an evaluative framework consisting of ethical considerations influencing behavior toward actions and decisions that are judged to be right and away from those judged to be wrong.
Affect, or feeling, mode	Suggests an evaluative framework that is guided by hedonism: one behaves in ways that increase pleasure and decrease pain.

values. Because the final choice criteria depend on the performance measures used, they are also affected by values. For example, consider the question of laying off employees. Managers with dominant economic values would probably lay them off much quicker than would managers with high social values.

George England, who has conducted very extensive research on the role of values in the decision-making process, has identified three major categories of values (see Figure 4.5).[7] He reported the following:

1. Large individual differences in personal values exist within every group studied. In the different countries studied, some managers have a pragmatic orientation, some have an ethical/moral orientation, and some have an affect, or feeling, orientation. Some managers have a very small set of values; others have a large set and seem to be influenced by many strongly held values.

2. Personal value systems of managers are relatively stable. Edward Lusk and Bruce Oliver repeated one of George England's earlier studies and reported that values of managers had changed very little during the six years covered by their study.[8]

3. Personal value systems of managers are related to or influence the way managers make decisions. For example, those who have profit maximization as an important goal are less willing to spend money on cafeteria and restroom improvements than those who do not have profit maximization as an important value.

4. Personal value systems of managers are related to their career success as managers. Successful American managers favor pragmatic, dynamic, achievement-oriented values; less successful managers prefer more static and passive values.

5. Differences exist in the personal values of managers working in different organizational contexts. For example, the personal values of U.S. managers were found to differ from those of labor leaders.

6. Overall, the value systems of managers in the countries studied were similar; yet some distinct differences were observed. The data suggest that cultural and social factors, as opposed to level of technological and industrial development, are more important in explaining value differences and similarities.[9]

The work of England and others clearly establishes the important role values play in managers' decision-making processes. England's and other, more recent studies show that values may differ from culture to culture and that these differences may have a profound effect on resulting decisions.[10] To make sound decisions, today's managers must not only be aware of their own values but also must know those of others inside and outside the organization.

Participation in Decision Making

Most managers have opportunities to involve their subordinates and others in the decision-making process. One pertinent question is: Do groups make better decisions than individuals? Another is: When should subordinates be involved in making managerial decisions?

Group or Team Decision Making

Everyone knows the old axiom that two heads are better than one. Empirical evidence generally supports this view, with a few minor qualifications. Group performance is frequently better than that of the average group member.[11] Similarly, groups can often be successfully used to develop innovative and creative solutions to problems. Groups also take longer to solve problems than does the average person.[12] Thus, group decisions are generally better when avoiding mistakes is more important than speed.

Group performance is generally superior to that of the average group member for two reasons. First, the sum total of the group's knowledge is greater. Second, the group has a much wider range of alternatives in the decision process.

One facet of group or team decision making compares the risk people will take alone with the risk they will take in a group. Laboratory experiments have shown that unanimous group decisions are consistently riskier than the average of the individual decisions.[13] This is somewhat surprising, since group pressures often inhibit the members. Possibly people feel less responsible for the outcome of a group decision than when they act alone. More recent research has found that groups make decisions best described as more polar than do individuals acting alone.[14] "More polar" means that groups tend to make decisions that are more extreme than those they would make as individuals. Figure 4.6 summarizes the positive and negative aspects of group decision making.

Barriers to Effective Decision Making

Although it is desirable to study how to make decisions, managers must also work to remove barriers that limit the effectiveness of those decisions. Daniel Wheeler and Irving Janis identified four basic barriers to effective decision making. Barrier one is *complacency:* The decision maker either does not see danger

FIGURE 4.6
Positive and Negative Aspects of Group (Team) Decision Making

Positive Aspects	Negative Aspects
1. The sum total of the group's knowledge is greater.	1. One individual may dominate or control the group.
2. The group possesses a much wider range of alternatives in the decision process.	2. Social pressures to conform can inhibit group members.
3. Participation in the decision-making process increases the acceptance of the decision by group members.	3. Competition can develop to such an extent that winning becomes more important than the issue itself.
4. Group members better understand the decision and the alternatives considered.	4. Groups have a tendency to accept the first potentially positive solution while giving little attention to other possible solutions.

signs or opportunity or ignores data from the environment that would affect decision making. Barrier two is called *defensive avoidance:* The decision maker denies the importance of danger, the opportunity, or the responsibility for taking action. *Panic* is the third barrier: Frantic attempts to solve a problem rarely produce the best results. The final barrier is *deciding to decide:* Accepting the responsibility and challenge of decision making is critical to overall effectiveness.[15] All of these barriers must be dealt with to create an environment that stimulates effective and creative decision making.

Making Creative Decisions

If the optimizing approach to decision making is based on unrealistic assumptions and the intuitive and satisficing approaches often result in less than optimal decisions, what can managers do to improve their decision-making process? One option that has produced positive results in numerous organizations is to encourage creative decisions and innovation at all levels. This section discusses some techniques to foster creative decisions within an organization.

The Creative Process

creativity
Coming up with an idea that is new, original, useful, or satisfying to its creator or to someone else.

innovation
Process of applying a new and creative idea to a product, service, or method of operation.

Creativity and innovation may seem similar but are actually quite different processes. **Creativity** is the thinking process involved in producing an idea or a concept that is new, original, useful, or satisfying to its creator or to someone else. **Innovation** refers to doing new things. Creativity involves coming up with a new idea, whereas innovation involves implementing the new idea. In the 1995 hit movie *Apollo 13,* the phrase "Houston, we have a problem" was not a simplistic one. A sound creative process and dynamic engineering applications brought home three weary space travelers. Corporate management usually does not have to deal with life-threatening decisions such as those facing the staff and engineers of mission control. However, the development of a climate that fosters creative thinking is often very similar. The following five-step creative process is generally thought to help establish an environment for creative decision making:

1. *Preparation.* The manager investigates thoroughly to make sure that all parts of the problem are fully understood and that all facts and ideas relevant to the problem have been identified.
2. *Concentration.* The manager commits to solving the problem in a timely manner.
3. *Incubation of ideas and information.* The manager recognizes that the accepted way of solving a problem is not always the best way. (Allow the creative spark to catch fire.)
4. *Illumination.* The manager connects a problem with an acceptable solution. (This step is often called the *Eureka connection.*)
5. *Verification.* The manager tests the solution and accepts the result.[16]

Although these steps often overlap, they provide a sound beginning point for the development of creative solutions that are critical to the success of the modern organization.

Establishing a Creative Environment

Probably the single most important factor that influences creativity and innovation by organizational members is the climate, or environment, in which they work. Certainly a manager's boss can have an impact on the type of climate established, but ultimately it is the individual manager who sets the tone for his or her area of responsibility. If a manager is genuinely interested in creative ideas, most employees are aware of it. The opposite is also true: Most employees realize when a manager is not interested in creativity.

People-based management skills and positive leadership can encourage a climate of creativity. To avoid hampering creativity, the manager must

- Instill trust—eliminate the fear of failure of an idea.
- Develop effective internal and external communication. Upward and lateral communication encourage innovation.
- Seek a mix of talent within the organization. A blend of different personality types and interactions encourages creative problem solving.
- Reward useful ideas and solutions.
- Allow for some flexibility in the existing organizational structure so that new ideas and creative solutions will not be eliminated by tradition.

Tools to Foster Creativity

In addition to establishing the proper environment, managers can use several techniques to encourage creativity. The following sections describe some of these techniques.

Brainstorming

brainstorming
Presenting a problem to a group and allowing group members to produce a large quantity of ideas for its solution; no criticisms are allowed initially.

Alex F. Osborn developed brainstorming as an aid to producing creative ideas for an advertising agency. Basically, **brainstorming** involves presenting a problem to a group of people and allowing them to present ideas for solution to the problem. Brainstorming is intended to produce a large quantity of ideas or alternatives and generally follows a definite procedure.

In the first phase, members of the group are asked to present ideas off the tops of their heads. Group members are told that quantity rather than quality of ideas is the goal. Questions submitted by the group leader usually include How can we use this differently?, How can we change?, How can we substitute this?, or How can we combine this? Four basic rules for the first phase are as follows:

1. No criticism of ideas is allowed.
2. No praise of ideas is allowed.
3. No questions or discussion of ideas is allowed.
4. Combinations of and improvements on ideas that have been previously presented are encouraged.

During the second phase, the merits of each idea are reviewed. This review often leads to additional alternatives. Furthermore, alternatives with little merit are eliminated in this phase. In the third phase, one of the alternatives is selected, frequently through group consensus. Management Illustration 4.3 describes how one company has successfully used online brainstorming.

Gordon Technique

Gordon technique
Differs from brainstorming in that no one but the group leader knows the exact nature of the real problem under consideration. A key word is used to describe a problem area.

William J. J. Gordon developed a technique for the consulting firm of Arthur D. Little, Inc., to spur creative problem solving. The technique was initially devised to get creative ideas on technical problems. The **Gordon technique** differs from brainstorming in that no one but the group leader knows the exact nature of the

Brainstorming is one area where online technology is delivering more than expected. Through the use of online brainstorming, companies are able to significantly and economically boost creativity.

Diane Watkins is a senior marketing specialist for State Farm Insurance in suburban Philadelphia. Watkins, who specializes in automobile and homeowners insurance, helps agents make the most of their sales territories.

In the spring of 2001, Watkins put her 10 best tips in writing and posted them to a discussion board on State Farm's nationwide in-house website. Within a few days of posting her list, a dozen agents had added tips of their own to the in-house website. One agent from Flushing, New York, for example, explained how to get referrals in the Asian community. Others discussed ways to entice auto-only customers into buying other types of insurance offered by State Farm. By early June of that same year, more than 40 agents from across the country had joined in the discussion, and hundreds more had read the postings. Interestingly, State Farm had offered no rewards or incentives to encourage agent participation.

Source: George Anders, "Inside Job," *Fast Company,* September 2001, pp. 176–84.

real problem under consideration. A key word is used to describe a problem area; the group then explores that area, using the key word as a starting point. For instance, the word *conservation* may be used to start a discussion on energy conservation. The key word would direct discussion and suggestions on conservation to other areas in addition to the one under question. Proponents of the Gordon technique argue that it generates better-quality ideas because the discussion is not limited to one particular area as is the case with brainstorming.

Nominal Group Technique

nominal group technique (NGT)
Highly structured technique for solving group tasks; minimizes personal interactions to encourage activity and reduce pressures toward conformity.

The **nominal group technique (NGT)** is a highly structured technique designed to keep personal interactions at a minimum. It involves the following steps:

1. *Listing.* Each group member, working alone, develops a list of probable solutions to a group task.
2. *Recording.* Each member offers an item from his or her listing in a round-robin manner to the group leader, who records the ideas on a master list in full view of the group. Some organizations today even have specially designed rooms with computers that project responses onto a large screen for all participants to see. The round-robin process continues until the leader has recorded all items on each person's list.
3. *Voting.* Each member records on an individual ballot his or her preference with respect to the priority or importance of the items appearing on the master list.

No verbal interaction is allowed during the first three steps. The results of the voting are tabulated, and scores are posted on the master list. Then the process continues as follows:

4. *Discussion.* Each item is discussed for clarification and valuation.
5. *Final voting.* Each member votes a second time with respect to the priority of the ideas generated.[17]

The NGT has been found to generate more unique ideas than brainstorming does. However, both the NGT and brainstorming suffer from the problem that occurs when the participants are so close to the problem under study that they are blind to what appear to be obvious solutions.

Brainwriting

brainwriting
Technique in which a group is presented with a problem situation and members anonymously write down ideas, then exchange papers with others, who build on ideas and pass them on until all members have participated.

In the **brainwriting** approach, group members are presented with a problem situation and then asked to jot their ideas on paper without any discussion. The papers are not signed. The papers are then exchanged with others, who build on the ideas and pass the papers on again until all members have had an opportunity to participate.

Synectics

synectics
Creative problem-solving technique that uses metaphorical thinking to "make the familiar strange and the strange familiar."

Synectics is a relatively new technique used in creative problem solving. Synectics uses metaphorical thinking to "make the familiar strange and the strange familiar." Analogies are the best method for doing this. There appear to be several basic forms from which to springboard ideas:

- *Personal analogies.* Place yourself in the role of the object.
- *Direct analogies.* Make direct comparisons.
- *Symbolic analogies.* Look at the problem in terms of symbols.
- *Fantasy analogies.* Imagine the most perfect solution.

As an illustration of the fantasy analogy method, or "goal wishing," the participants fantasize about how a particular problem could be solved if there were no physical constraints. After developing a list of wishful solutions, the participants are encouraged to come up with the most absurd solutions they can imagine. Often at least one or two of these solutions can be refined into practical solutions.

A word of caution is in order regarding all of these techniques. Much controversy exists regarding their effectiveness as aids to creativity. Two researchers addressed this issue: "The evidence on balance does not seem encouraging enough to propose that managers who are seeking an extremely creative idea to help them on a problem situation should resort to a brainstorming session."[18] On the other hand, these same researchers concluded that brainstorming may generate a wider variety of solutions to a problem.

In conclusion, none of the previously described techniques is a complete answer for improving creativity within organizations. Each should be viewed as a tool that can help in some situations when the proper environment has been established. Management Illustration 4.4 describes how one company has used unorthodox environments to boost creative efficiency and productivity.

A Model for Creative Decision Making

This section presents a practical model that can lead to better and more creative decisions.[19] While this model incorporates parts of the rational approach, its emphasis is on encouraging the generation of new ideas. Figure 4.7 outlines the stages of this model.

Stage 1: Recognition

When a problem or a decision situation exists, it is useful to first describe the circumstances in writing. An effective approach is to simply write out the facts in narrative form. This stage should include a description of the present situation, as well as when and where pertinent events occurred or will occur.

Stage 2: Fact Finding

After the decision situation has been described in written form, the next step is to systematically gather additional information concerning the current state of affairs. Questions asked in this stage usually begin with *who, what, where, when, how*

Some big-name companies have found that holding meetings in nontraditional environments such as on horseback, on playgrounds, and even in locker rooms can significantly encourage creativity. One example is Budweiser in Canada.

Mike Robitaille is the Toronto-based brand manager for Budweiser in Canada. Faced with generating new marketing ideas for his company's NFL partnership, Robitaille and Tom Monahan, a creativity consultant, formed teams made up of Budweiser employees and NFL staffers. After a brief skills clinic, the teams were then engaged in a two-hour football scrimmage. Afterward, a brainstorming session was held in the Toronto Blue Jays' locker room.

Another meeting sponsored by Robitaille took place at a Toronto boxing club. The group first spent 90 minutes jumping rope and punching bags and then brainstormed at ringside for the rest of the day. (It is interesting to note that many of Robitaille's participants are women.)

In yet another situation Robitaille had his marketing team don cowboy duds, go for a two-hour morning horseback ride, cook lunch over an open fire, and then brainstorm amid the serene mountain vistas.

In each of the above examples, Robitaille wanted to put his teams into situations where they could better think like and relate to their clients—Bud consumers.

Source: Sara J. Welch, "Here, There and Everywhere," *Successful Meetings,* August 2001, pp. 76–79.

---

many, how much, or similar words. The intent of the fact-finding stage is to organize available information about the decision situation.

Stage 3: Problem Finding

The fact-finding stage is concerned primarily with the present and the past; the problem-finding stage is oriented toward the future. In a sense, this stage might be viewed as problem redefining or problem analysis. The overriding purpose of this stage is to rewrite or restate the problem in a manner that will encourage more creative solutions. In light of stages 1 and 2, the decision maker should attempt to restate the problem in several different ways, with the ultimate goal of encouraging a broader range of solutions. For example, the decision situation "Shall I use my savings to start a new business?" could be restated, "In what ways might I finance my new business?" The first statement elicits a much narrower range of possible solutions than does the second. Similarly, "Shall I fire this employee?" could be restated, "Should I transfer, punish, retrain, or fire this employee, or should I give him/her another chance?"

After listing several restatements of the problem, the decision maker should select the one that most closely represents the real problem and has the greatest

FIGURE 4.7
Model for Creative Decision Making

Source: Bruce Meyers, unpublished paper, Western Illinois University, 1987.

Stage		Activity
1	Recognition	To investigate and eventually
2	Fact finding	define a problem or decision
3	Problem finding	situation.
4	Idea finding	To generate possible alternatives or solutions (ideas).
5	Solution finding	To identify criteria and evaluate ideas generated in stage 4.
6	Acceptance finding	To work out a plan for implementing a chosen idea.

number of potential solutions. At this point, the decision situation should be defined in a manner that suggests multiple solutions.

Stage 4: Idea Finding

This stage aims to generate a number of different alternatives for the decision situation. In this stage, a form of brainstorming is used, following two simple rules: (1) no judgment or evaluation is allowed and (2) all ideas presented must be considered. The purpose of these rules is to encourage the generation of alternatives, regardless of how impractical they seem at first. A good approach is for the decision maker to list as many ideas as possible that relate to the problem. The decision maker should then go back and consider what might be substituted, combined, adopted, modified, eliminated, or rearranged to transform any of the previously generated ideas into additional ideas.

Stage 5: Solution Finding

The purpose of this stage is to identify the decision criteria and evaluate the potential ideas generated in stage 4. The first step is for the decision maker to develop a list of potential decision criteria by listing all possibilities. Once a list of potential criteria has been developed, the decision maker should pare down the list by selecting the most appropriate criteria. Naturally, the decision maker should aim for a manageable number of criteria (normally fewer than seven). The next step is to evaluate each idea generated in stage 4 against the selected criteria. Usually many ideas from stage 4 can be eliminated by simple inspection. The remaining ideas should then be evaluated against each criterion using some type of rating scale. After each idea has been evaluated against all criteria, the best solution usually becomes obvious.

Stage 6: Acceptance Finding

This final stage attempts to identify what needs to be done to successfully implement the chosen idea or solution. This stage not only addresses the *who, when, where,* and *how* questions but should also attempt to anticipate potential objections to the decision.

While the above model is certainly not perfect, it does encourage managers to go beyond bounded rationality and to make better decisions than they would by following the satisficing approach.

Management Information Systems

management information system (MIS)
Integrated approach for providing interpreted and relevant data that can help managers make decisions.

Management information systems (MISs), also called *management reporting systems,* support the day-to-day operational and tactical decision-making needs of managers. MISs are designed to produce information needed for the successful management of a process, department, or business.[20] An MIS provides information that managers have specified in advance as adequately meeting their information needs.[21] Usually the information made available by an MIS is in the form of periodic reports, special reports, and outputs of mathematical simulations.[22]

In the broader sense, management information systems have existed for many years, even before computers. However, in most people's mind, the term *MIS* implies the use of computers to process data that managers will use to make operational decisions. The information an MIS provides describes the organization or

FIGURE 4.8
Characteristics of an MIS

Source: From *Information Technology in Business*, 2nd edition, by J. A. Senn. Copyright © 1998 by Pearson Education, Inc. Reprinted by permission of Pearson Education, Inc., Upper Saddle River, NJ.

- Uses data captured and stored as a result of transaction processing.
- Reports data and information rather than details of transaction processing.
- Assists managers in monitoring situations, evaluating conditions, and determining what actions need to be taken.
- Supports recurring decisions.
- Provides information in prespecified report formats, either in print or on-screen.

one of its major parts in terms of what has happened in the past, what is happening now, and what is likely to happen in the future.[23]

It is important to note that an MIS is not the same as data processing. **Data processing** is the capture, processing, and storage of data, whereas an MIS uses those data to produce information for management in making decisions to solve problems. In other words, data processing provides the database of the MIS.

data processing
Capture, processing, and storage of data.

Transaction-processing systems substitute computer processing for manual recordkeeping procedures. Examples include payroll, billing, and inventory record systems. By definition, transaction processing requires routine and highly structured decisions. It is actually a subset of data processing. Therefore, an organization can have a very effective transaction-processing system and not have an MIS. Figure 4.8 summarizes the characteristics of management information systems.

transaction-processing system
Substitutes computer processing for manual recordkeeping procedures.

Many MISs have been developed for use by specific organizational subunits. Examples of MISs intended to support managers in particular functional areas include operational information systems, marketing information systems, financial information systems, and human resource information systems. Several specific MISs used by organizational subunits are discussed in later chapters.

Summary

1. *Explain the difference between decision making and problem solving.* In its narrowest sense, decision making is the process of choosing from among various alternatives. Problem solving is the process of determining the appropriate responses or actions necessary to alleviate a deviation from some standard or desired level of performance. From a practical perspective, almost all managerial decisions involve solving or avoiding problems, and therefore, it is not necessary to distinguish between managerial decision making and managerial problem solving.

2. *Distinguish between programmed and nonprogrammed decisions.* Programmed decisions are reached by following an established or systematic procedure. Nonprogrammed decisions have little or no precedent and generally require a more creative approach by the decision maker.

3. *Explain the intuitive approach to decision making.* In the intuitive approach, managers make decisions based on hunches and intuition. Emotions and feelings play a major role in this approach.

4. *Discuss two rational approaches to decision making.* One rational approach, optimizing, involves the following six steps: (1) recognize the need for a decision; (2) establish, rank, and weigh the criteria; (3) gather available information and data; (4) identify possible alternatives; (5) evaluate each alternative with respect to all criteria; and (6) select the best alternative. A second rational approach, satisficing, is based on the principle of bounded rationality. In the satisficing approach, the decision maker selects the first alternative that meets his or her minimum standard of satisfaction.

5. *List the different conditions under which managers make decisions.* Managers normally make decisions under the conditions of certainty, risk, or uncertainty.

6. *Explain the role values play in making decisions.* A manager's values affect the selection of performance measures, alternatives, and choice criteria in the decision process.

7. *Summarize the positive and negative aspects of group decision making.* Positive aspects include the following: (1) The sum total of the group's knowledge is greater; (2) the group possesses a much wider range of alternatives in the decision process; (3) participation in the decision-making process increases the acceptance of the decision by group members; and (4) group members better understand the decision and the alternatives considered. Negative aspects include the following: (1) One individual may dominate or control the group; (2) social pressures to conform can inhibit group members; (3) competition can develop to such an extent that winning becomes more important than the issue itself; and (4) groups have a tendency to accept the first potentially positive solution while giving little attention to other possible solutions.

8. *Define creativity and innovation, and outline the basic stages in the creative process.* Creativity is the thinking process involved in producing an idea or a concept that is new, original, useful, or satisfying to its creator or to someone else. Innovation is doing new things. The creative process generally has five stages: (1) preparation, (2) concentration, (3) incubation, (4) illumination, and (5) verification.

9. *Identify several specific tools and techniques that can be used to foster creative decisions.* Tools to foster creative decisions include brainstorming, the Gordon technique, the nominal group technique, brainwriting, and synectics.

10. *List the six stages in creative decision making.* The model for creative decision making encompasses the following six steps: (1) recognition, (2) fact finding, (3) problem finding, (4) idea finding, (5) solution finding, and (6) acceptance finding.

11. *Explain the role of a management information system (MIS).* An MIS supports the day-to-day operational and tactical decision-making needs of managers. An MIS provides information that managers have specified in advance as adequately meeting their information needs. Usually the information made available by an MIS is in the form of periodic reports, special reports, and outputs of mathematical simulations.

Review Questions

1. What are the three stages in the decision-making process?
2. What is the difference between decision making and problem solving?
3. Discuss the intuitive approach to decision making.
4. Discuss the optimizing approach to decision making.
5. What criticisms can be made concerning the optimizing approach to decision making?
6. Discuss the satisficing approach to decision making, and explain the difference between satisficing and optimizing.
7. Distinguish among the decision situations of certainty, risk, and uncertainty.
8. What are values? What relationship exists between values and managerial success?
9. Outline some positive and negative aspects of group decision making.
10. What are the four barriers to effective decision making?
11. Describe the five-step process for creating an environment that fosters creative decision making.
12. Describe the following aids to creativity:
    a. Brainstorming
    b. Gordon technique
    c. Nominal group technique
    d. Brainwriting
    e. Synectics
13. Describe the six-stage model of creative decision making.
14. How does a transaction-processing system differ from an MIS?

Skill-Building Questions

1. Identify a significant decision recently made by a major company (you might look in *Business Week* or *The Wall Street Journal*). In the decision you identify, did the manager or managers satisfice or optimize?

2. What factors do you think affect the amount of risk a manager is willing to take when making a decision?

3. Comment on the following statement: "Groups always make better decisions than individuals acting alone."

4. How many creative uses can you think of for a brick? Now ask a five- to seven-year-old child the same question. How do you account for the differences? Why do you think children might be more creative than adults?

5. Think of a new form of a product or service to solve something that bugs you, for example, trash can lids that won't stay shut. (Many primary-grade creativity classes do this as a learning exercise in creativity.)

6. When you go into a fast-food store and the salesperson keys your order into the cash register, how might this information be used as part of an MIS?

Skill-Building Exercise 4.1

Lost at Sea

You are adrift on a private yacht in the South Pacific. Due to a fire of unknown origin, much of the yacht and its contents have been destroyed. The yacht is now slowly sinking. Your location is unclear because critical navigational equipment was destroyed and you and the crew were distracted in trying to bring the fire under control. Your best estimate is that you are approximately 1,000 miles south-southwest of the nearest land.

Following is a list of 15 items that are intact and undamaged after the fire. In addition to these articles, you have a serviceable rubber life raft with oars large enough to carry yourself, the crew, and all the items listed. The total contents of all survivors' pockets are a package of cigarettes, several books of matches, and five one-dollar bills.

Your task is to rank the following 15 items in terms of their importance to your survival. Place the number 1 by the most important item, the number 2 by the second most important, and so on through number 15, the least important.

_6_ Sextant
_4_ Shaving mirror
_7_ Five-gallon can of water
_10_ Mosquito netting
_3_ One case of U.S. Army C rations
_7_ Maps of the Pacific Ocean
_13_ Seat cushion (flotation device approved by the Coast Guard)
_11_ Two-gallon can of oil-gas mixture
_14_ Small transistor radio
_12_ Shark repellent
_2_ 20 square feet of opaque plastic
_9_ One quart of 160-proof Puerto Rican rum
_8_ 15 feet of nylon rope
_13_ Two boxes of chocolate bars
_5_ Fishing kit

After everyone has completed the above rankings, your instructor will divide the class into teams or groups. Your group is to then rank the same items, using a group consensus method. This means the ranking for each of the 15 survival items must be agreed on by each group member before it becomes part of the group decision. Consensus is difficult to reach. Therefore, not every ranking will meet with everyone's complete approval. As a group, try to make each ranking one with which all group members can at least partly agree. Here are some guides to use in reaching consensus:

1. Avoid arguing for your own individual judgments. Approach the task on the basis of logic.
2. Avoid changing your mind for the sole purpose of reaching agreement and avoiding conflict. Support only solutions with which you agree at least somewhat.
3. Avoid conflict-reducing techniques such as majority vote, averaging, or trading.
4. View differences of opinion as a help rather than a hindrance in decision making.

Source: Adapted from John E. Jones and J. William Pfeiffer, eds., *The 1975 Annual Handbook for Group Facilitators* (La Jolla, CA: University Associates, Inc., 1975).

Skill-Building Exercise 4.2

Creativity Exercise

Most of us believe we are more creative than we really are. Take a maximum of four minutes each on solving the following three problems.

a. Draw four straight lines connecting the dots in the following diagram without lifting your pencil (or pen) off the paper. You are permitted to cross a line, but you cannot retrace any part of a line.

```
 •      •      •


 •      •      •


 •      •      •
```

b. What do the following words have in common (other than they are all in the English language)?

CALMNESS   FIRST
CANOPY   SIGHING
DEFT   STUN

c. Place 10 circles of the same size in five rows with four circles in each row.

After you have attempted each of the above problems, be prepared to discuss the following questions:

1. Why do you think these "simple" problems were difficult for you?
2. Do you think grade school children tend to do better or worse than adults on problems such as these? Why?

Case Incident 4.1

Getting Out of the Army

Jay Abbott is confident that his future will be secure and financially rewarding if he decides to remain in the Army. He entered more than 10 years ago as a commissioned officer after completing his college education on an ROTC scholarship. At age 32, Jay has progressed to the rank of captain and is currently being considered for promotion to major. He has no reason to believe he will not be promoted. He has been successful in all of his appointments, is well liked by everyone—his peers, superiors, and subordinates—and has an unblemished record.

However, at the 10-year mark, Jay had second thoughts about staying in the Army and has been thinking about leaving ever since. He has felt more and more resentful that the Army has affected a large part of his personal life. Although he had always preferred to wear his hair shorter than most young men do, he resented the fact that even if he wanted to let it grow out or grow sideburns, he couldn't do it. It was the principle of the whole idea: the intrusion of the Army into his personal life. That this intrusion extended to his wife and children bothered him even more.

Jay's wife, Ellen, was finishing her master's thesis. This took up a large portion of her free time; yet her lack of involvement in the officer's clubs was frowned on. There was just no such thing as a private family life in Jay's position. He didn't even have much time to spend with the family. His job required long hours of work, including weekend duty, which left little time for his wife and two daughters, ages seven and nine. Another problem was that Ellen, who held a degree in design engineering, was unable to pursue any kind of real career, something that was important to both of them.

These thoughts raced through Jay's mind over and over again as he tried to decide what would be best for him and his family. The Army had a lot of positive aspects, he kept reminding himself: He was already earning $40,000 a year, and with his nearly certain promotion, this would rise to $46,000. Also, he was being recommended for the Army's command and general staff college. There was little chance he would not be approved; completing the program would make his future even brighter. If he stayed, he would be able to retire in just 10 more years (at age 42) with a permanent retirement income of half his final salary plus free medical and dental coverage. By then, he figured, he would probably be a lieutenant colonel with a base pay of about $61,000; at worst, he would retire a major. At 42, he would have plenty of time to devote to a second career if he so desired.

On the other hand, regardless of how attractive the benefits seemed, salaries in the armed services had not kept pace with the rising rate of inflation: Congress had held the lid on raises at less than 3 percent, and no changes in this position were evident for the next few years. In fact, Jay had read several newspaper articles indicating that Congress was considering reducing benefits for the armed services, the 20-year retirement specifically.

After doing some checking, Jay learned that the training and experience received in the Army were valuable to civilian employers. Commissioned in the signal corps, he had vast experience in the area of telecommunications. He had recently completed a tour as an instructor in a service school. He had also been in many positions of leadership during his term in the Army. At 32, he probably had more firsthand managerial experience than most civilian managers. He knew that large organizations were currently hiring young ex-military officers at salaries $10,000 to $15,000 higher than those of recent college graduates.

Questions

1. What should Jay do?
2. What factors should Jay consider in his decision?
3. What role would values play in Jay's decision?

Case Incident 4.2

Going Abroad

You supervise 12 engineers. Their formal training and work experience are very similar, so you can use them interchangeably on projects. Yesterday, your manager informed you that an overseas affiliate has requested four engineers to go abroad on extended loan for six to eight months. For a number of reasons, he argued and you agreed, this request should be met from your group.

All your engineers are capable of handling this assignment; from the standpoint of present and future projects, there is no special reason any one engineer should be retained over any other. Somewhat complicating the situation is the fact that the overseas assignment is in a generally undesirable location.

Questions

1. How would you select who should go abroad on extended loan?
2. What are some major factors that would influence your decision process?

Source: Victor H. Vroom, "A New Look at Managerial Decision Making," *Organizational Dynamics,* Spring 1973.

References and Additional Readings

1. Herbert A. Simon, *The New Science of Management Decision* (New York: Harper & Row, 1960), p. 2.

2. George S. Odiorne, *Management and the Activity Trap* (New York: Harper & Row, 1974), pp. 128–29; and George S. Odiorne, *The Change Resisters* (Englewood Cliffs, NJ: Prentice Hall, 1981), pp. 15–25.

3. Odiorne, *Management and the Activity Trap*, pp. 142–44.

4. "Go-Go Goliaths," *Business Week*, February 13, 1995, p. 66.

5. Herbert A. Simon, *Model of Man* (New York: John Wiley & Sons, 1957), p. 198.

6. William D. Guth and Renato Tagiuri, "Personal Values and Corporate Strategy," *Harvard Business Review*, September–October 1965, pp. 124–25.

7. George England, "Personal Value Systems of Managers and Administrators," *Academy of Management Proceedings*, August 1973, pp. 81–94.

8. Edward J. Lusk and Bruce L. Oliver, "American Managers' Personal Value Systems Revisited," *Academy of Management Journal*, September 1974, pp. 549–54.

9. England, "Personal Value Systems," pp. 82–87.

10. For example, see H. S. Badr, E. R. Gray, and B. L. Kedia, "Personal Values and Managerial Decision Making: Evidence from Two Cultures," *Management International Review*, Fall 1982, pp. 65–73; and H. J. Davis and S. A. Rasool, "Values Research and Managerial Behavior: Implications for Devising Culturally Consistent Managerial Styles," *Management International Review*, July 1988, pp. 11–19.

11. Irving Lorge, David Fox, Joel Davitz, and Marlin Brenner, "A Survey of Studies Contrasting the Quality of Group Performance and Individual Performance, 1930–1957," *Psychological Bulletin*, November 1958, pp. 337–72; Frederick C. Miner, Jr., "Group versus Individual Decision Making: An Investigation of Performance Measures, Decision Strategies, and Process Losses/Gains," *Organizational Behavior and Human Performance*, February 1984, pp. 112–24; and K. L. Bettenhausen, "Five Years of Group Research: What We Have Learned and What Needs to Be Addressed," *Journal of Management*, June 1991, pp. 345–81.

12. M. E. Shaw, "A Comparison of Individuals and Small Groups in the National Solution of Complex Problems," *American Journal of Psychology*, July 1932, pp. 491–504; Lorge et al., "A Survey of Studies"; and W. E. Watson, K. Kumar, and L. K. Michaelson, "Cultural Diversity's Impact on Interaction Process and Performance: Comparing Homogeneous and Diverse Task Groups," *Academy of Management Journal*, June 1993, pp. 590–602.

13. M. Wallach, N. Kogan, and D. J. Bem, "Group Influence on Individual Risk Taking," *Journal of Abnormal and Social Psychology*, August 1962, pp. 75–86; and N. Kogan and M. Wallach, "Risk Taking as a Function of the Situation, the Person, and the Group," in *New Directions of Psychology*, vol. 3, ed. G. Mardler (New York: Holt, Rinehart & Winston, 1967).

14. D. G. Meyers, "Polarizing Effects of Social Interaction," in *Group Decision Making*, ed. H. BranStatter, J. Davis, and G. Stock-Kreichgauer (New York: Academic Press, 1982).

15. Daniel D. Wheeler and Irving L. Janis, *A Practical Guide for Making Decisions* (New York: Macmillan, 1980), pp. 17–36.

16. Graham Walles, *The Art of Thought* (New York: Harcourt Brace Jovanovich, 1976), p. 80.

17. Gene E. Burton, Dev S. Pathok, and David B. Burton, "The Gordon Effect in Nominal Grouping," *University of Michigan Business Review*, July 1978, p. 8; and Nells Zuech, "Identifying and Ranking Opportunities for Machine Vision in a Facility," *Industrial Engineering*, October 1992, pp. 42–44.

18. T. Richards and B. L. Freedom, "Procedures for Managers in Idea-Deficient Situations: An Examination of Brainstorming Approaches," *Journal of Management Studies*, February 1978, pp. 43–55.

19. The basis for this model and much of this discussion were contributed by Bruce Meyers, associate professor of management at Western Illinois University.

20. James A. Senn, *Information Technology in Business*, 2nd ed. (Englewood Cliffs, NJ: Prentice Hall, 1998), p. 615.

21. James A. O'Brien, *Management Information Systems*, 3rd ed. (Burr Ridge, IL: Richard D. Irwin, 1996), p. 370.

22. Raymond McLeod, Jr., *Management Information Systems*, 4th ed. (New York: Macmillan, 1990), p. 30.

23. Ibid.

Part 2

Contemporary Issues

5. International Business
6. Legal, Ethical, and Social Responsibilities of Management

Gettyimages/PhotoLink

Chapter

5

International Business

Learning Objectives

After studying this chapter, you will be able to:

1. Explain why countries trade with each other.
2. Explain why companies export and import.
3. Explain how and why countries restrict international trade.
4. Describe a global economy.
5. Explain e-commerce.
6. Describe a free trade area.
7. Describe the strategies organizations use to compete in the global economy.
8. Describe various ways used by companies to sell their products or services in the international market.

Chapter Preview

Coke, GE, McDonald's, and Boeing attribute their success in international business to decisions made years ago to localize their global businesses. All employ hundreds of thousands of people overseas and attempt to bend their products and selling strategies to fit local tastes. In Belgium, Coke ran a promotion featuring Coke cans designed by Belgian fashion stylists. In Saudi Arabia, Abdul Mejid Abdullah, a top singer, is Coke's celebrity endorser. In France, McDonald's sells fresh fruit and Danone water in addition to fries and Coca-Cola. The seating and ambiance of its restaurants there have proved so conducive to sales that a French architect is now designing new stores for the United States. To better penetrate the European market, Boeing three years ago stopped flying salespeople in from Seattle and hired a group of powerful country presidents with political ties to local governments. Boeing CEO Phil Condit decided "we had to become a truly global company and not a large American company that was successful globally," says Boeing spokesperson Charles Miller.

American businesses also own many local brands and companies. Ford, for instance, owns Volvo and Jaguar; PepisCo owns Walkers snack foods in Britain; Procter & Gamble owns Ariel washing detergent in Europe. "European and American *business* is so intertwined that it's not easy to separate who is who," says Alex Cohen, an American lawyer with Latham & Watkins in London who advises European clients. "How many people realize which consumer brands are actually owned by Europeans and which are owned by American companies?"

Source: Janet Guyan, "Brand America," *Fortune,* October 27, 2003, p. 179.

Analyzing Management Skills

What risks are involved in operating in a global industry?

Applying Management Skills

Choose one of your favorite American products. To which foreign country would you choose to sell the product? Explain why and how you would sell the product in that country.

Over the past 50 years, companies from all over the world have begun operating globally. Nike operates factories in Vietnam and Indonesia. The Gap owns stores in Canada, France, Germany, Great Britain, and Japan. Perrier and Evian sell bottled water in dozens of countries outside of France. Nokia, a Finnish company, dominates the cellular phone market. Consumers everywhere own products made in other countries.

international trade
The exchange of goods and services by different countries.

International trade consists of the exchange of goods and services by different countries. It includes the purchase of American blue jeans in China and the purchase of Belgian chocolate in the United States.

Most of the world today depends on international trade to maintain its standard of living. American manufacturers sell automobiles, heavy machinery, clothing, and electronic goods abroad. Argentine cattle ranchers ship beef to consumers in dozens of foreign countries. Saudi Arabian oil producers supply much of the world with oil. In return, they purchase food, cars, and electronic goods from other countries.

Countries trade for several different reasons. One country may not be able to produce a good it wants. France, for example, cannot produce oil because it has no oil fields. If it wants to consume oil, it must trade with oil-producing countries. Countries also may trade because they have an advantage over other countries in producing particular goods or services.

Absolute Advantage

absolute advantage
The ability to produce more of a good than another producer.

Different countries are endowed with different resources. Honduras, for example, has fertile land, a warm and sunny climate, and inexpensive labor. Compared with Honduras, Great Britain has less fertile soil, a colder and rainier climate, and more expensive labor. Given the same combination of inputs (land, labor, and capital), Honduras would produce much more coffee than Great Britain. It has an absolute advantage in the production of coffee. An **absolute advantage** is the ability to produce more of a good than another producer with the same quantity of inputs.

Comparative Advantage

law of comparative advantage
Producers should produce the goods they are most efficient at producing and purchase from others the goods they are less efficient at producing.

Countries need not have an absolute advantage in the production of a good to trade. Some countries may be less efficient at producing *all* goods than other countries. Even countries that are not very efficient producers are more efficient at producing some goods than others, however. The **law of comparative advantage** states that producers should produce the goods they are most efficient at producing and purchase from others the goods they are less efficient at producing. According to the law of comparative advantage, individuals, companies, and countries should specialize in what they do best.

Exporting and Importing

exports
Goods and services that are sold abroad.

imports
Goods and services purchased abroad.

International trade takes place when companies sell the goods they produce in a foreign country or purchase goods produced abroad. Goods and services that are sold abroad are called **exports**. Goods and services that are purchased abroad are called **imports**.

The United States is the largest exporter in the world, exporting about $700 billion worth of goods and services a year. It also is the world's largest importer, purchasing about $900 billion worth of foreign goods and services annually.

Exports

Exports represent an important source of revenue for many companies. Northwest Airlines, for example, earns about a third of its revenues outside the United States. IBM earns almost 40 percent of its revenues abroad.

Why Do Companies Export?

About 95 percent of the world's consumers live outside the United States. Companies that sell their products exclusively within the United States miss out on the opportunity to reach most of the world's consumers. To increase their sales, companies like Procter & Gamble spend millions of dollars trying to identify what customers in foreign countries want.

Companies also seek out export markets in order to diversify their sources of revenue. *Diversification* is engaging in a variety of operations. Businesses like to diversify their sales so that sluggish sales in one market can be offset by stronger sales elsewhere.

How Do Companies Identify Export Markets?

To determine if there is sufficient demand for their products or services overseas, companies analyze demographic figures, economic data, country reports, consumer tastes, and competition in the markets they are considering. Business managers contact the International Trade Administration of the U.S. Department of Commerce, foreign consulates and embassies, and foreign and international trade organizations. They also visit the countries they are considering and conduct surveys in order to assess consumer demand.

Businesses also need to find out what restrictions they may face as exporters. All countries require exporters to complete certain kinds of documents. Some countries also insist that foreign companies meet specific requirements on packaging, labeling, and product safety. Some also limit the ability of exporters to take money they earn from their exports out of the country.

Imports

American companies import billions of dollars worth of goods and services every year. They import consumer goods, such as television sets and automobiles, and industrial goods, such as machines and parts. They import raw materials, such as petroleum, and food products, such as fruits and vegetables. They import these goods in order to use them to produce other goods or to sell them to customers.

Imports of Materials

Many companies import some or all of the materials they use in order to reduce their production costs. Manufacturers of appliances, for example, import steel from Japan because it is less expensive than steel manufactured in the United States.

Some companies use imported inputs because domestically made inputs are not available or their quality is not as good as that of imported goods. Jewelry designers import diamonds and emeralds, which are not produced in the United States. Fashion designers use imported cashmere wool, which is softer than domestic wool.

Imports of Consumer Goods

Companies also import products that they can resell in their own countries. Automobile dealers import cars and trucks from Europe and Asia. Wholesalers and retailers import clothing from Thailand, electronic goods from Japan, and cheese from France.

Companies import these goods because consumers want to purchase them. Some of these goods, such as garments from Asia, are less expensive than domestically manufactured products. Others, such as Saabs and Volvos, are popular despite costing more than domestically produced goods.

The Trade Balance

balance of trade
Difference between the value of the goods a country exports and the value of the goods it imports.

The **balance of trade** is the difference between the value of the goods a country exports and the value of the goods it imports. A country that exports more than it imports runs a *trade surplus*. A country that imports more than it exports runs a *trade deficit*.

For many years the United States has run a trade deficit. This means that the value of the goods and services it buys from other countries exceeds the value of the goods and services it sells to other countries. Other countries, such as Japan, have run huge trade surpluses. In these countries, the value of exports exceeds the value of imports.

Foreign Exchange

Companies that purchase goods or services from foreign countries must pay for them with foreign currency. If a U.S. company purchases goods from Japan, for example, it must pay for them in yen. If it purchases goods from Switzerland, it must pay for them in Swiss francs.

Companies purchase foreign currency from banks, which convert each currency into dollars. The value of one currency in terms of another is the foreign exchange rate.

Exchange rates can be quoted in dollars per unit of foreign currency or units of foreign currency per dollar. The exchange rate for the Swiss franc, for example, might be 1.5 to the dollar. This means that one dollar is worth 1.5 Swiss francs and one Swiss franc is worth 1/1.5 dollar, or $0.67.

China is coming under growing international pressure, led by the United States, to revalue its currency, the yuan. The criticism has so far focused on the size of the bilateral trade surplus that China is running with the United States, which for 2002 stood at US$100 billion. Across the United States, China is being blamed for job losses in the manufacturing sector, which in the last three years have amounted to 3 million jobs.

China is likely to continue resisting pressure from the United States to revalue or float its exchange rate. It appears that some reform of the current exchange rate system is possible. The Chinese government now appears to accept that the rapid inflow of funds into the country is causing problems for the domestic economy. Reform, therefore, is likely to focus on reducing pressure on the inflow of funds. The government has already relaxed restrictions on the amount of money that Chinese tourists can take abroad, it is allowing companies to keep a bigger share of their foreign-exchange earnings, and it has also announced plans which will allow some Chinese firms to buy foreign bonds and stocks. To reduce pressure from the United States and other foreign governments, the Chinese may also consider fixing the yuan to a basket of foreign currencies, including the euro. This would reduce pressure on the European currency, which is so far taking the brunt of the falling U.S. dollar. It may also lead to a realignment of other Asian currencies. Due to the growing importance of China's economy within the region, Asian countries are unlikely to allow their currencies to revalue without the yuan doing so first.

Source: "China Under Pressure to Revalue," *Asia Monitor: China and North East Asia Monitor,* November 2003, p. 1.

Most exchange rates fluctuate from day to day. Managers involved in international trade must follow these fluctuations closely, because they can have a dramatic effect on profits. Consider, for example, an American electronics store that wants to purchase 10 million yen worth of Japanese stereos, camcorders, and cameras. If the exchange rate of the yen is 115 to the dollar, the U.S. company must pay $86,956 to purchase 10 million yen worth of Japanese equipment (10 million yen/115 yen per dollar). If the value of the yen rises so that a dollar is worth only 100 yen, the company would have to spend $100,000 to purchase the same value of Japanese goods (10 million yen/100 yen per dollar). Management Illustration 5.1 explains some foreign exchange problems.

Protectionism

International trade can benefit all trading partners. It also may hurt some domestic producers, however. A U.S. manufacturer of watches may find it difficult to compete with a Taiwanese producer, who pays his workers a fraction of what workers in the United States earn. Competition from the Taiwanese producer may force the U.S. company out of business.

To help domestic manufacturers compete against foreign companies, governments sometimes impose protectionist measures, such as tariffs, quotas, and other types of restrictions. All of these measures reduce the volume of international trade.

Tariffs

tariffs
Government-imposed taxes charged on goods imported into a country.

A **tariff** is a tax on imports. The purpose of a tariff is to raise the price of foreign goods in order to allow domestic manufacturers to compete. The United States imposes tariffs on many goods, including most textiles and apparel. This means that a Korean company that sells men's shirts in the United States must pay an import tax on every one of its shirts that enters the country. The purpose of this tax is to

Some U.S. officials argue that the 40-year-old embargo against Cuba clearly no longer works and have called to have it lifted; others have demanded that it should be tightened, by banning financial remittances from émigrés in the United States, for example. In Cuba itself, some residents have suggested that their president believes he can swap a few of the jailed dissidents for the five Cuban spies currently serving long sentences in the United States. Another interpretation making the rounds in Havana is that the crackdown was meant to feed Cuba's never-ending war rhetoric, which the regime hopes will distract the population from the dire economic situation. Cuba's financial woes have been caused mostly by mismanagement (and were recently aggravated by two hurricanes), but the problems are real. The all-important sugar industry is near collapse, with this year's raw sugar production expected to be 80 percent lower than in 1989 (when the Soviet Union ended its subsidies). Last year, almost half of Cuba's 156 sugar mills were shut down, leaving some 100,000 workers jobless. Tourism, the other main source of hard currency, has slumped as a result of the September 11, 2001, attacks.

Cuba's disastrous economic situation has grown so dire, in fact, that merely acquiring enough food to eat has become a full-time preoccupation. The creeping dollarization of consumer goods has made survival on a salary paid in local currency mathematically impossible; American dollars were made legal in 1993 and today are simply indispensable. As for the regime's traditional counterargument—that health and education are still free and excellent—it no longer carries much weight. Hospitals are decrepit, basic medicines are unavailable (except in foreigners-only pharmacies), schools indoctrinate instead of teaching, and, as Cubans say, "One is not always either sick or learning." In Havana, using public transportation is a time-consuming ordeal, public phones work sporadically, and water and power fail on a daily basis. Outside the capital, the situation is even worse. Of course tourists, whisked around the country in air-conditioned buses on mojito-salsa-cigar holidays, remain immune from (and oblivious to) the privations.

Source: Theresa Bond, "The Crackdown in Cuba," *Foreign Affairs,* September–October 2003, pp. 118–31.

---

quota
Establishes the maximum quantity of a product that can be imported or exported during a given period.

embargo
Involves stopping the flow of exports to or imports from a foreign country.

global economy
Economy in which companies compete actively with businesses from around the world.

make it more difficult for foreign manufacturers of textiles and apparel to compete with American companies in the United States.

Quotas

Quotas are restrictions on the quantity of a good that can enter a country. The United States imposes quotas on many kinds of goods. For example, it allows just 1.6 million tons of raw sugar to enter the country from abroad. This quota raised the price of raw sugar, making goods that use sugar, such as candy and cold cereal, more expensive. It hurt American companies and individuals that consume sugar, but it helped American companies and individuals that produce sugar.

Embargoes

An **embargo** is a total ban on the import of a good from a particular country. Embargoes usually are imposed for political rather than economic reasons. Since 1961, for example, the United States has imposed an embargo on Cuba, whose regime it opposes. This embargo bans the importation of goods from Cuba and the export of U.S. goods to Cuba. Management Illustration 5.2 describes the Cuban embargo in more depth.

The Rise of the Global Economy

Many factors have led to the rise of the **global economy,** an economy in which companies compete actively with businesses from all over the world. These factors include improvements in communications technology, the rise in democracy in the world, and the elimination of trade restrictions.[1]

Improvements in Telecommunications Technology

Improvements in telecommunications technology have had an enormous impact on international trade. Exchanges of information that once took weeks now take seconds, as a result of the development of fax machines and e-mail.

Development of the Internet also has led to *e-commerce,* or sales made over the World Wide Web. E-commerce has enabled even small companies to reach consumers in foreign countries by marketing their products on websites.

Political Changes

The political changes that have taken place since the late 1980s have dramatically increased opportunities for businesses. As a result of the end of the cold war with Russia and the thawing of relations with China, American companies have earned billions of dollars selling products and services in markets from which they were once excluded. Holiday Inn, for example, now runs a hotel in Warsaw. Colgate-Palmolive has a facility in Huangpu, China. Both of these companies, and thousands of others, have benefited from the spread of capitalism.

Free Trade Areas

free trade area
A region within which trade restrictions are reduced or eliminated.

To promote international trade and limit protectionism, countries create free trade areas. A **free trade area** is a region within which trade restrictions are reduced or eliminated.

The largest free trade area in the world is in North America. Under the terms of the North American Free Trade Agreement (NAFTA) of 1994, businesses in the United States, Mexico, and Canada can sell their products anywhere in North America without facing major trade restrictions.

Consumers in all three countries have benefited from lower prices on North American imports. The price of a blouse imported from Canada or a pair of shoes imported from Mexico, for example, is lower than it used to be, because the price no longer includes a tariff.

Many producers have also benefited from NAFTA by increasing their exports within North America. American grain farmers, for example, have increased their sales to Mexico as a result of NAFTA. U.S. automobile sales to Mexico also have risen.

NAFTA has forced some American workers to lose their jobs, however. Sara Lee laid off more than a thousand American workers after it moved some of its operations to Mexico. Many other companies have also reduced their workforces in this country to take advantage of lower labor costs south of the border.

Doing Business Globally

Thousands of U.S. businesses, large and small, participate in the global marketplace. Some companies, such as Benetton, build factories in foreign countries or set up retail outlets overseas. Others, such as Harley-Davidson, export their products throughout the world and import materials from other countries.

Forms of International Operations

Companies can sell their products or services in foreign countries in various ways. Small companies often work through local companies, which are familiar with local markets. Large companies often establish sales, manufacturing, and distribution facilities in foreign countries.

Working through a Foreign Intermediary

Companies that are not willing or able to invest millions of dollars in operations abroad often export their products through foreign intermediaries. A *foreign intermediary* is a wholesaler or agent who markets products for companies that want to do business abroad. In return for a commission, the agent markets the foreign company's product.

Working through a foreign intermediary saves a company the expense of setting up facilities in a foreign country. It also ensures that the company is represented by someone familiar with local conditions. Foreign intermediaries usually work for many foreign companies at a time, however. Thus, they are not likely to devote as much time to a single company's products as the company's own sales force would.

Signing a Licensing Agreement with a Foreign Company

Another way companies can reach foreign consumers is by licensing a foreign company to sell their products or services abroad. A *licensing agreement* is an agreement that permits one company to sell another company's products abroad in return for a percentage of the company's revenues.

TGI Friday's, a Dallas-based restaurant company, has used licensing agreements to expand its operations overseas. Signing such agreements enabled it to open branches in Singapore, Indonesia, Malaysia, Thailand, Australia, and New Zealand. Without such agreements, it might not have been able to penetrate those markets.

Forming a Strategic Alliance

Some companies can expand into foreign markets by forming *strategic alliances* with foreign companies. A strategic alliance involves pooling resources and skills in order to achieve common goals. Companies usually form strategic alliances to gain access to new markets, share research, broaden their product lines, learn new skills, and expand cross-cultural knowledge of management groups.

One of the largest strategic alliances in recent years was the 1998 merger between two of the world's largest automakers, Daimler-Benz, which produces Mercedes-Benz vehicles, and Chrysler. The American automaker benefited from the merger by gaining access to the European market—something it had been unable to do on its own. The German partner benefited by improving access to U.S. consumers, thus increasing sales.

multinational corporation (MNC) Business that maintains a presence in two or more countries, has a considerable portion of its assets invested in and derives a substantial portion of its sales and profits from international activities, considers opportunities throughout the world, and has a worldwide perspective and orientation.

Becoming a Multinational Corporation

Companies willing to make a significant financial commitment often establish manufacturing and distribution facilities in foreign countries. A business with such facilities is known as a **multinational corporation (MNC)** (see Figure 5.1).

Businesses become multinational corporations for several reasons. Some do so in order to sell their products or services in other countries. McDonald's, for example, maintains restaurants in 116 foreign countries. Sales to customers in these countries represent half of the company's total revenue.

Companies also expand abroad in order to take advantage of inexpensive labor costs. For example, Tarrant Apparel, a U.S. manufacturer of blue jeans, weaves most of its fabric in Mexico. It also has most of its jeans sewn in Mexico, where labor is cheaper than in the United States.[2]

FIGURE 5.1
**Multinational
Corporations**
There are many
ways for companies
to do business
globally.
Multinational
corporations often
purchase their
materials abroad or
manufacture or
assemble their
products abroad.
They also sell their
products in foreign
countries.

1. **Imported Materials**
   Multinational corporations may import materials used to manufacture their products. General Motors (GM), the largest automobile producer in the United States, works with more than 30,000 suppliers worldwide. Many of these suppliers are overseas.

2. **International Production**
   Multinational companies may produce their products in other countries. GM has manufacturing, assembly, or component operations in 50 countries. It operates abroad in order to improve service or reduce costs.

3. **International Sales**
   Multinational companies sell their products in other countries. GM cars and trucks are sold in Africa, Asia and the Pacific, Europe, the Middle East, and North America. Foreign sales represent a significant share of the company's total sales.

Challenges of Working in an International Environment

Working for a multinational corporation presents many challenges. Managers must learn to deal with customers, producers, suppliers, and employees from different countries. They must become familiar with local laws and learn to respect local customs. They must try to understand what customers and employees want in countries that may be very different from the United States.

Understanding Foreign Cultures

Business managers from different countries see the world differently. Japanese managers, for example, tend to be more sensitive to job layoffs than American managers. Asian and African managers often have different views about the role of women in the workplace than American managers do.

Managers who work in foreign countries need to be aware of different cultural attitudes. They also need to understand business customs in different countries (see Figure 5.2). Not knowing how to act in a foreign country can cause managers embarrassment, and it can cause them to miss out on business opportunities. Showing up for a business meeting without a tie might be acceptable in Israel, for example, but it would be completely out of place in Switzerland. Demonstrating

FIGURE 5.2
**Examples of
Foreign Business
Practices.**

Country	Business Practice
China	Food is extremely important. All business transactions require at least one and usually two evening banquets. The first banquet is given by the host, the second by the guest.
Indonesia	Even foreigners are expected to arrive late to social occasions. It is generally appropriate to arrive about 30 minutes after the scheduled time.
Singapore	Businesspeople exchange business cards in a formal manner, receiving the card with both hands and studying it for a few moments before putting it away.
Saudi Arabia	Businesspeople greet foreigners by clasping their hand, but they do not shake hands.
Switzerland	Business is conducted very formally. Humor and informality are inappropriate.

great respect to a superior would be appreciated in Indonesia, but it would send the wrong signal in the Netherlands, where equality among individuals is valued.

Coalitions of Cooperating Countries and Trading Blocs

International businesses must also deal with coalitions of cooperating countries that are established to improve the economic conditions of the member countries. One coalition is the European Union. Organized in 1957, the European Union's membership includes Great Britain, Italy, France, Germany, Denmark, Ireland, Greece, Belgium, Luxembourg, the Netherlands, Spain, and Portugal. Its purpose is to reduce tariffs on goods sold among member countries. Also, it is an attempt to eliminate the fiscal, technical, and border barriers between member countries that over several decades have increased the costs of goods and services in Europe and reduced the international competitiveness of European companies. Europe was to be a single market with exciting potential for multinational corporations. Many problems still exist in implementing the changes necessary for Europe to become one market. It also remains to be seen whether the democratic movement in Eastern Europe, the reunification of Germany, and the demise of the Soviet Union will lead some of those countries and republics to join the European Union or form a new trading bloc of some other configuration.

Another coalition is the Organization of Petroleum Exporting Countries (OPEC), which includes many of the oil-producing countries of the world. Its purpose is to control oil prices and production levels among member countries. Today, OPEC's effectiveness is limited because several member countries sell and produce at levels considerably different from official OPEC standards.

Today, three large trading blocks exist: Europe; the North American Alliance of the United States, Canada, and Mexico (NAFTA); and Pacific Asia (Pacific Rim countries), with Japan being the dominant country in that region. Other members of the Pacific Rim trading bloc are China, Korea, Taiwan, Indonesia, Malaysia, the Philippines, Thailand, Hong Kong, and Singapore. These three large trading blocs will provide many opportunities and pose many threats for multinational organizations.

Political Changes

One of the most dramatic illustrations of how political changes influence the international business environment was the breakup of the Soviet Union and the fall of communist governments in Eastern Europe in the early 1990s. The end of the Soviet Union and the creation of the Commonwealth of Independent States (CIS) is likely to lead to many opportunities for Western businesses. In addition, the political and economic upheavals in Bulgaria, Hungary, Poland, Romania, and the countries formerly known as Czechoslovakia and Yugoslavia have caused significant changes in how these countries conduct their own international business activities and how they relate to businesses from foreign countries.

Human Rights and Ethics

Should multinational firms close their plants in countries where human rights abuses are common and accepted ethical boundaries are violated? This is a valid issue, but U.S. managers must remember that business ethics have not yet been globalized; the norms of ethical behavior continue to vary widely even in Western capitalist countries. Thus, questions such as Should Coca-Cola establish minimum labor standards for all of its bottlers around the world to prevent abuses of workers in certain countries? seem highly appropriate in the United States. However, such questions present dilemmas for multinational firms that are accompanied by ethical predicaments and hard choices. In each situation, the multinational firm must strike a balance among the values and ideals of all of its various publics. No clear and easy choices exist.

Summary

1. *Explain why countries trade with each other.* Countries trade for several different reasons. One country may not be able to produce a good it wants. Another reason is that one of the countries may have an absolute advantage over another country. Another reason is that countries produce according to the law of comparative advantage.

2. *Explain why companies export and import.* One reason for exporting is to increase sales. Companies also export to diversify their sources of revenue. Companies import goods in order to use them to produce other goods or to sell them to customers. Companies also import products that they can resell in their own countries.

3. *Explain how and why countries restrict international trade.* To help domestic manufacturers compete against foreign companies, governments sometimes impose protectionist measures, such as tariffs, quotas, and other types of restrictions.

4. *Describe a global economy.* A global economy is one in which companies compete actively with businesses from all over the world.

5. *Explain e-commerce.* E-commerce refers to sales made over the World Wide Web.

6. *Describe a free trade area.* A free trade area is a region within which trade restrictions are reduced or eliminated.

7. *Describe the strategies organizations use to compete in the global economy.* Companies can sell their products or services in foreign countries in various ways. Small companies often work through local companies, which are familiar with local markets. Large companies often establish sales, manufacturing, and distribution facilities in foreign countries.

8. *Describe various ways used by companies to sell their products or services in the international market.* Companies sell their products by working through a foreign intermediary, signing a licensing agreement with a foreign company, forming a strategic alliance, or becoming a multinational corporation.

Review Questions

1. Define international trade.
2. What is absolute advantage? Law of comparative advantage?
3. Define export. Import.
4. What is the balance of trade?
5. What does foreign exchange mean?
6. What is a tariff? A quota? An embargo?
7. What is a global economy?
8. Describe a free trade area.
9. What ways can companies use to sell their products or services in foreign countries?

Skill-Building Questions

1. Do you think the old saying "When in Rome, do as the Romans do" applies to international business activities? Explain your answer.
2. What problems might you face if you were asked to serve as a manager in a foreign country?
3. What are some typical U.S. management practices that would be difficult to apply in foreign countries?

4. The fastest-growing market for U.S. cigarette manufacturers is in international markets. What ethical problems do you see in exporting cigarettes to foreign markets?

5. What do you think could be some potential pitfalls of entering into a strategic alliance?

6. Do you think NAFTA is a good idea? Develop five pro arguments and five con arguments for the establishment of NAFTA. What do you think will be the next country to join the NAFTA agreement? Justify your answer.

Skill-Building Exercise 5.1

Blunders

Multinational corporations have occasionally experienced unexpected troubles due to culture, language, and custom differences. The following examples demonstrate problems encountered by some companies with regard to product and company names:

- When Chevrolet introduced its Nova in Puerto Rico, sales were less than brisk. When spoken, the word *nova* sounded like "no va," which in Spanish means "it doesn't go."
- Ford introduced a low-cost truck, the Fiera, into some less developed countries and also experienced slow sales. *Fiera* means "ugly old woman" in Spanish.
- A private Egyptian airline, Misair, proved to be rather unpopular with French people. When pronounced in French, the name means "misery."
- The phonetic pronunciation of Esso in Japanese means "stalled car." Obviously this name did not go over well in Japan.

Questions

1. Assume you have been considering opening a McDonald's franchise in either Central America or Spain. Develop a list of internationally related factors you would need to investigate in evaluating the feasibility of this idea.

2. Prioritize the list you developed in question 1.

Source: These examples are taken from David A. Ricks, *Big Business Blunders: Mistakes in Multinational Marketing* (Homewood, IL: Richard D. Irwin, 1983), pp. 37–47.

Skill-Building Exercise 5.2

Market Penetration

Your company is a manufacturer of consumer soaps and detergents. You have been working for the company for seven years and have recently been promoted to a new position of manager of international business activities. Presently, your company does little business in Europe.

The president of your company has recognized the vast potential of the European community and asked you to develop some recommendations for expanding into Europe—both Eastern and Western Europe. He has voiced the opinion that a plant should be built somewhere in Europe. However, he has also stated this is not essential and you are free to recommend any approach you would like to take to do business in Europe.

Your professor will break the class into teams to prepare this exercise. Prepare a 10-minute presentation on your recommendations.

Case Incident 5.1

Profiles

In the July–August 1989 issue of the *International Executive*, many statements were made as to how the Japanese viewed Americans and how they viewed themselves. Some of these included:

- Americans are too liberal, and they take too many risks. They don't always do their homework.
- We look at long-term earnings, five years ahead. Americans tend to look only at the next financial quarter or so. Japanese stockholders don't have as much involvement, power, or clout as American stockholders do.

- Americans are always identifying themselves or each other by race or religion or something. In Japan, we're just all the same.
- We are a very proud people. We do believe we are unique and different. Americans should never assume that we want to be like them.

Questions

1. Do any of these statements surprise you? If yes, why?
2. What implications would the last statement have for American business?
3. Do you have any views about the Japanese? Write down one of your views for discussion in class.

Source: Editorial of the *International Executive,* July–August 1989, pp. 39–41.

Case Incident 5.2

Imposed Quotas

A labor union official of the Textile Workers of America was alleged to have made the following statement:

> Foreign imports of textiles have cost American jobs and tax revenues. In order to slow down the disruptive impacts on American society, quotas should be placed on imports into the United States for those goods and product lines that are displacing significant percentages of U.S. production and employment.

Questions

1. Do you agree with the union official? Explain.
2. Do you believe import quotas should be established for certain industries? Which ones?
3. Does the United States benefit or lose from international business activity?

References and Additional Readings

1. See, for example, V. Kumar and Anish Nagpal, "Segmenting Global Markets: Look before You Leap," *Marketing Research* 13, no. 1 (2001), pp. 8–19.
2. For more information on multinational companies, see Marc S. Mentzer, "Two Heads Are Better Than One If Your Company Spans the Globe," *Academy of Management Executive,* May 1999, pp. 89–90.

Chapter

Legal, Ethical, and Social Responsibilities of Management

Learning Objectives

After studying this chapter, you will be able to:

1. Identify the six areas of law that affect business organizations.
2. Identify the types of taxes that affect business profits.
3. Explain the differences between copyrights, patents, and trademarks.
4. Define intellectual property.
5. Define ethics.
6. Explain a code of ethics.
7. Identify four categories of laws relating to ethics in business.
8. Explain social responsibility.

Chapter Preview

In 2001 and 2002, alleged fraud and other misdeeds at firms such as Adelphia, Enron, HealthSouth, Tyco International, and WorldCom led to demands for reform in corporate ethics. Congress reacted quickly and passed the Sarbanes-Oxley Act in July 2002. This act was designed not only to increase the financial accountability of public companies but also covers a broad range of corporate behavior. For example, Sections 302 and 906 of the Sarbanes-Oxley Act require chief executive officers (CEO) and chief financial officers (CFO) to personally certify in each annual and quarterly report filed with the Securities and Exchange Commission (SEC) that they have reviewed the report and that, based on their knowledge, it doesn't contain any material misstatements or omissions. In addition, they must certify that the financial statements and other financial information included in the report fairly represent the company's financial condition and results of operations. False certification of financial information carries penalties for CEOs and CFOs: $1 million in fines and/or up to 10 years' imprisonment if the violation was "knowing," and $5 million in fines and/or up to 20 years' imprisonment if the violation was "willful." The law went into effect for reports filed after August 29, 2002.

Source: Alan Levinsohn, "Legal Liability for Your Financial Reporting," *Strategic Finance*, September 2003, pp. 1–2.

Analyzing Management Skills

Look up the Sarbanes-Oxley Act on the Internet and be prepared to describe other behaviors that could lead to fines and/or imprisonment for corporate managers.

Applying Management Skills

What actions could your school or workplace take to make it more socially responsible?

Congress and state and local legislatures pass many laws that regulate businesses. The federal, state, and local governments enforce these laws. If businesses do not comply with these laws, they may be subject to legal sanctions, such as fines, penalties, loss of license, or even jail. Many companies hire a government affairs manager, who makes sure that the company knows the laws that regulate its activities. The government affairs manager also makes sure that the company keeps up with new laws and does not become liable for their actions.

regulations
Rules that government agencies issue to implement laws.

Regulations are rules that government agencies issue to implement laws. Businesses spend a lot of time and money making sure they comply with laws and regulations and do not face unwanted liability.

There are six important areas of law that affect business operations:

1. *Corporate law.* Corporate law regulates how businesses can set themselves up to operate as companies.
2. *Tax law.* Tax law regulates how much money businesses must pay the government to help provide services for the public.
3. *Intellectual property law.* Intellectual property law regulates how businesses can protect inventions and new products.
4. *Consumer law.* Consumer law protects individuals against business activities that might be harmful to them.
5. *Commercial law.* Commercial law regulates how businesses enter into contracts with other businesses and with consumers.
6. *Licensing and zoning law.* Licensing laws regulate who can go into certain businesses. Zoning laws regulate where they can establish operations.

Corporate Law

Not all businesses are alike. Some companies are enormous, with more than 100,000 employees and offices in many states and even in other countries. Some are small, with only a couple of partners working together in a single office. Still others are run by just one person. There are laws regulating three kinds of business entities or ownership: sole proprietorships, partnerships, and corporations.

Sole Proprietorships

sole proprietorship
A business owned by a single individual, or proprietor.

The simplest kind of business is a **sole proprietorship**. A sole proprietorship is a business owned by a single individual, or proprietor. Small businesses often are sole proprietorships, and entrepreneurs often are sole proprietors. Sole proprietors set up businesses after checking with state and local officials about licenses, zoning regulations, and other requirements. Sole proprietors have many advantages. First, they control the entire business and keep all the profits. Second, sole proprietors can make decisions quickly. Additionally, sole proprietors usually pay fewer taxes than other kinds of businesses.

There are several disadvantages of sole proprietorship, however. Sole proprietors have full responsibility for the business. If the business runs into financial trouble, for instance, the owner has full liability for all debts. A sole proprietor may have to use personal savings or even sell a house or car to pay debts from a business. In addition, sole proprietorships can fail entirely if, for example, the owner becomes ill or disabled. Despite these disadvantages, sole proprietorships are popular in the United States.

Partnerships

partnership
An association of two or more persons who jointly own a for-profit business.

A **partnership** is an association of two or more persons who jointly own a for-profit business. The Uniform Partnership Act, which governs general partnerships, requires them to meet two requirements. First, a partnership must be owned by two or more persons. Under the law, a "person" can be a corporation or another organization as well as an individual. Second, partners must share the profits from their business.

A partnership allows partners to combine their talents and their financial resources. Partners share responsibility for making decisions, and a partnership pays less in taxes than a corporation. With two people rather than one, a partnership may have an easier time getting a loan than a sole proprietorship.

The biggest disadvantage of a partnership is that the partners, like sole proprietors, have unlimited liability for business debts. Even if only one partner is responsible for a business's debts, all the partners are responsible for paying them. A second disadvantage is that partners may disagree on how the business should be run or how profits should be shared. Such disagreements can hurt the business.

Corporations

corporation
A business formed under state or federal statutes that is authorized to act as a legal person.

A **corporation** is a business formed under state or federal statutes that is authorized to act as a legal person. A corporation exists apart from its owners and can be taxed and sued like an individual. Corporate owners have limited liability. This means they cannot lose their personal resources if the corporation fails. Only the corporation loses.

Corporations have many advantages. Like partnerships, they offer stockholders limited liability and a share of the profits. Stockholders have no management responsibilities. Corporations can raise money by selling stock. They generally have an easier time getting credit than any other type of business.

Corporations have two major disadvantages, however. First, they must comply with many more federal and state laws than either sole proprietorships or partnerships. Corporations must register with a state government agency to begin a business, while a sole proprietor can begin a business at any time. Second, corporations pay more taxes than any other type of business. They pay special taxes to the state and federal governments as well as a tax on profits.

Tax Law

The type of ownership managers choose for their businesses often depends on the types of taxes involved. Taxes are monies paid by corporations and individuals and are used to fund government programs and services, such as highways and schools.

Income Tax

income tax
A tax levied against a business's profits.

Businesses pay several different types of taxes, but the most important tax is called an income tax. An **income tax** is a tax levied against a business's profits. For example, if a business earns $100,000 in profits this year, and the income tax rate is 30 percent, the business will pay the government $30,000 in taxes.

Property Tax

property tax
Tax levied against the property, buildings, and land owned by a business.

Businesses also must pay property taxes. **Property taxes** are taxes levied against the property, buildings, and land owned by a business. Property taxes are based on an assessed valuation of the building or land. An *assessed valuation* is the amount that a piece of property is worth, according to a tax assessor. For example, the assessed valuation of land and buildings in the heart of Manhattan in New York City is extremely high because there is very little space to construct new buildings. The business owners of property and land in New York City would pay more in taxes than business owners in many other parts of the country.

Taxes may hurt businesses by taking away part of their profits. To make up for these losses, businesses often pass on costs by charging consumers more money for products.

Withholding Federal Taxes

Businesses also collect taxes from workers. The government requires businesses to withhold income taxes from employees' earnings and send them to the federal government. Without the help of business, it would be very difficult for the federal government to collect taxes from working people.

Managers make important decisions because of taxes. For example, a manager may decide to relocate the business's operations because of more favorable taxes in another state. In the late 1990s, for example, the Caterpillar Corporation, a major equipment manufacturer, moved its operations from Illinois to Texas because the taxes were more favorable in the state of Texas. When managers develop strategic plans for making profits, they always need to take the effect of taxes into account.

Intellectual Property Laws

Taxes can cut into a company's profits, but there are also laws that protect business profit. For example, businesses are protected by intellectual property laws. Intellectual property laws protect the inventions and new ideas of businesses.

Our society could not survive without new inventions. Inventions lead to advances in fields such as medicine that improve our quality of life. In the business world, inventions lead to new products. The three kinds of intellectual property protections are patents, trademarks, and copyrights.

Patents

Inventors and companies come up with thousands of inventions every year. Just think about it—television, CDs, cellular phones, bar codes at grocery stores—our world is full of new technological devices made possible by creative inventors.

Some inventors work on their own, while others work for companies. A company can protect its inventions by applying for a patent. A **patent** is the document the federal government issues to inventors and companies that gives them the exclusive right to make, use, and sell their inventions for 17 years. When the 17 years are up, other companies can begin selling that invention. The inventor of each type of new product must apply for another patent.

patent
The document the federal government issues to inventors and companies that gives them the exclusive right to their inventions for 17 years.

Trademarks

A **trademark** is a word, name, symbol, or slogan a business uses to identify its own goods and set them apart from others. Companies apply to the federal government's patents and trademark office when they want to establish a new trademark. Once a company owns its trademark, no other company can use it. Registered trademarks are good for 10 years, and companies can renew them every additional 10 years.

Trademarks are powerful selling tools. Nike puts its trademark on every item of athletic wear it makes, from shoes to underwear. In many countries of the world, wearing Nike goods is a status symbol.

trademark
A word, name, symbol, or slogan a business uses to identify its own goods.

Copyrights

John Grisham's novels are widely read in the United States and abroad. When Grisham writes the novel, he copyrights the manuscript so that no one else can publish his work without his permission. A **copyright** is the protection provided to a creative work. It can be used to protect literary works, musical compositions, plays, dances, paintings, movies, maps, and computer programs. The owner of the copyright, usually the person who creates the work, is the only one with the legal right to reproduce the work, sell it, or allow others to use it. Under copyright law, photocopying pages of a book can be illegal without the author's or publisher's permission.

copyright
The protection provided to a creative work.

Consumer Law

Some laws, such as intellectual property laws, protect businesses. Other laws are designed to protect consumers. *Consumers* are individuals who buy goods and services for their own use. You and the members of your family are consumers every time you buy food, clothing, drugs, or any other item from a business. To protect consumers from unfair business practices, the federal and state governments have established consumer protection laws.

Consumers should understand consumer laws so they know their rights when dealing with businesses. For example, many consumers who buy used cars from dealerships may not know that the law requires dealers to tell buyers certain things about that car, including how many miles it has been driven. Knowing what a car dealer must tell you about buying a car protects both you and the dealer.

The Federal Trade Commission

If you think that someone in business has treated you unfairly, you can write a letter of complaint to the Federal Trade Commission (FTC).

The FTC, an agency of the federal government, will take action against a company if it receives enough consumer complaints to establish a "pattern of wrongdoing." For example, if a large number of people complain that a catalog company is making false promises about its merchandise, the FTC will investigate the complaint.

The FTC has many rules governing all kinds of sales. For instance, the Used Car Rule requires dealers to tell customers important information about a used car. The Telemarketing Sales Rule helps protect consumers from being bombarded with unwanted telemarketing calls by placing limitations on companies that sell or promote by telephone. Some of the FTC rules have been very successful. For example, many consumers would be surprised to find an article of clothing without a care label that tells you how to wash and dry the clothing.

Other Rules That Protect Consumers

There are other laws and agencies that protect consumers as well. For example, the Food and Drug Administration (FDA) protects consumers against problems with mislabeled and impure foods, drugs, cosmetics, and medical devices. The FDA approves all new drugs before they are sold. The Fair Packaging and Labeling Act requires manufacturers of foods, drugs, cosmetics, and medical devices to clearly label products with the name of the manufacturer, the contents, and the amount the package contains. Labels on packaged foods must provide complete nutritional information as well.

Commercial Law

In addition to complying with laws regulating their dealings with consumers, businesses must comply with commercial laws that regulate their contracts and dealings with other businesses. The basic commercial law document is called the Uniform Commercial Code.

Contracts

contract
An agreement between two parties to carry out a transaction.

Businesses must follow laws governing how they can enter into contracts. A contract is an agreement between two parties to carry out a transaction, such as the sale of goods from a seller to buyer. Contracts create an obligation between the parties, or those agreeing to the contract, that can be enforced in a court of law. For example, when McDonald's agrees to purchase orange juice from Minute Maid to sell in its restaurants, the two companies enter into a contract that is legally enforceable.

Most people enter into different kinds of contracts during their lives. When they buy cars, expensive pieces of furniture, computers, and houses, they generally sign a contract. The contract describes the item being sold, sets out the terms of payment, and states whether the item can be returned.

Businesses enter into contracts daily. Like individuals, they buy things, such as office supplies and computer equipment. They also may lease items, such as furniture or even temporary employees. In each instance, they become a party to a contract.

Contracts must follow very specific rules if they are to stand up in a court of law. Anyone signing a contract—an individual, a representative of a group, the manager of a company—must know exactly what is in the contract and make sure the contract is properly prepared.

Contracts are often difficult to break. If you sign a contract and do not live up to your end of the bargain, the other party can take you to court. You have the same option if the other party does not complete the contract. It's always best to review contracts carefully beforehand. Knowing what you are signing is the best way to avoid problems with a contract later on.

Because most businesses deal in amounts of goods worth more than $500, most business sales contracts are written contracts. To satisfy the Uniform Commercial Code, written contracts must contain certain information. They must state that the parties involved have agreed to the sale and must give the quantity of the goods involved. The exact quantity is important because courts will enforce a contract only for the amount of the goods listed in the contract.

Business Sales Contracts

Business sales contracts are often short, simple documents that meet the requirements of the Uniform Commercial Code. When businesses write a contract for a very large quantity of goods, however, the contract often is many pages long. Suppose the National Aeronautic and Space Administration (NASA), a branch of the federal government, orders parts to build a new shuttle from Boeing Corporation. A space shuttle is a complicated machine that must be extremely safe. The contract must describe the parts using exact measurements that may be tiny fractions of an inch. It must list everything used to make the parts. Because the parts may have more than one component, the contract must provide details for each component. It must break down the costs so that NASA can see what it is paying for each item, no matter how small.

Licensing and Zoning Law

Government passes rules on commercial law to make sure that businesses follow rigid standards when they make deals with other businesses. In addition, state and local governments pass licensing and zoning laws that regulate who can operate a business and where owners can set up shop.

State and local governments use licensing as a way to limit and control people who plan to enter certain types of businesses. For example, if you wanted to start a restaurant, you would need to apply for a license from the local department of food and beverage control. The government may deny your application if it thinks there already are more than enough restaurants in the area.

Government officials can take away a license from a business that is not complying with laws and regulations. For example, the department of sanitation inspects local restaurants to make sure that they are complying with health codes, such as storing foods properly and keeping bathrooms sanitary. If the restaurant is not complying with the rules, the department of sanitation will issue a warning or possibly suspend the restaurant's license to operate. A government agency also has the power to completely revoke a restaurant's license, which means that the restaurant would have to close and go out of business altogether.

Local governments also may regulate businesses through building codes, which regulate physical features or structures of buildings. Building codes may regulate the maximum height, minimum square feet of space, and the types of materials that can be used in constructing an office. Finally, local governments regulate where a building can be built through zoning ordinances and regulations. For example, businesses can operate in commercially zoned areas but not residential areas. Finally, it is important to note that other legislation that affects businesses and management is discussed throughout this book.

The Importance of Ethics

ethics
A set of moral principles or values that govern behavior.

Individuals make personal decisions about what they believe is right or wrong. These decisions are based on their ethics. **Ethics** are a set of moral principles or values that govern behavior. All individuals develop their own set of ethical rules, which help them decide how to behave in different situations.

Like individuals, businesses develop ethics to help them determine how to behave. These ethics reflect a company's beliefs about what actions are appropriate and fair among people.

The role of ethics in management decisions is difficult. Management issues often are emotionally charged, and many types of ethical problems may arise in business situations. What should managers do if they are aware of unethical practices in their businesses? Should they blow the whistle and risk their jobs? Should they quit and allow unethical practices to continue? Should they ignore the practices? These are only a few of the difficult ethical decisions managers face.[1]

Codes of Ethics

code of ethics
A document that outlines the principles of conduct to be used in making decisions within an organization.

To help managers know how to respond ethically to different business situations, many companies have developed codes of ethics. A **code of ethics** is a document that outlines the principles of conduct to be used in making decisions within an organization. Most corporations in the United States have codes of ethics.

Content of Ethical Codes

Codes of ethics are formal documents that are shared with all employees. Some of the areas they cover include the following:

- Honesty.
- Adherence to the law.
- Product safety and quality.
- Health and safety in the workplace.
- Conflicts of interest.
- Employment practices.
- Selling and marketing practices.
- Financial reporting.
- Pricing, billing, and contracting.
- Trading in securities/using confidential information.
- Acquiring and using information about competitors.
- Security.
- Payments to obtain business.
- Political activities.
- Protection of the environment.

Honesty

- Offer full disclosure and withdraw from discussions and decisions when our business judgment appears to be in conflict with a personal interest.
- Respect the rights and property of others, including their intellectual property.
- Compete fairly without collaboration with competitors to divide markets, set prices, restrict production, allocate customers, or otherwise restrain competition.
- Assure that no payments or favors are offered to influence others to do something wrong.
- Keep records that are accurate and include all payments and receipts.
- Exercise good judgment in the exchange of business courtesies, meals, and entertainment by avoiding activities that could create even the appearance that our decisions could be compromised.
- Refuse to speculate in company stock through frequent buying and selling or through other forms of speculative trading.

Respect for People

- Exercise the basic virtues of respect, dignity, kindness, courtesy, and manners in all work relationships.
- Recognize and avoid behaviors that others may find offensive, including the manner in which we speak and relate to one another and the materials we bring into the workplace, both printed and electronically.
- Respect the right and obligation of every employee to resolve concerns relating to ethics questions in the course of our duties without retribution and retaliation.
- Give all employees the same opportunity to have their questions, issues, and situations fairly considered while understanding that being treated fairly does not always mean that we will all be treated the same.
- Trust one another to use sound judgment in our use of company business and information systems.
- Understand that even though Texas Instruments has the obligation to monitor its business information systems activity, we will respect privacy by prohibiting random searches of individual employees' communications.
- Recognize that conduct socially and professionally acceptable in one culture and country may be viewed differently in another.

Merely establishing a code of ethics does not prevent unethical behavior. To be effective, codes of ethics must be enforced. In fact, ethical codes that are not enforced probably do more harm than good. For this reason, it is important that companies discipline employees who violate their codes of ethics.

Texas Instruments has developed a detailed code of ethics. As Management Illustration 6.1 shows, the company's code of ethics stresses honesty and respect for people.

Behaving Ethically

Businesspeople regularly make ethical decisions. These decisions have important consequences for both individuals and their companies. Behaving unethically can hurt, or even end, a businessperson's career. It can cause a company to lose millions of dollars or even go out of business altogether. Behaving ethically helps employees gain the trust of the people with whom they work. It can also help businesses gain the trust of customers, suppliers, and others.

Behaving Honestly

In many situations, the ethical course of action is clear-cut. Ethical employees never steal from their employers. They never lie about the hours they work. They never falsify documents. Employees who engage in any of these actions threaten their careers. They also risk causing severe damage to their employers.

Employee Theft

Employers trust their employees not to steal from them. Employees who behave ethically do not violate that trust.

Dishonest employees steal from their employers in a variety of ways. Some embezzle money or steal supplies or inventory from their employers. Some accept bribes from people who want to do business with their company. Others submit false expense accounts.

Lying about Hours Worked

Employees who behave ethically are honest about the hours they work. Employees who work at home, for example, accurately report how long they work. They do not take advantage of the fact that their managers cannot check to see if they are actually at their desks.

Ethical employees also show up at work unless they are ill or need to be away from their jobs for a legitimate reason. They do not pretend to be sick in order to stay home when they should be at work.

Falsifying Records

One of the worst ethical lapses an employee can commit is falsifying records. This can cause very grave damage to a company's reputation. It can even cause people to become ill or die. A manager at a pharmaceutical company, for example, who falsifies records documenting the side effects of the drugs the company produces can cause people who take the drug to die. A production supervisor who falsifies documents to indicate that computer parts were checked can cause his company to sell defective products. Years of excellent corporate performance can be wiped out by these kinds of unethical actions.

Dealing with Ethical Dilemmas

Ethical dilemmas are situations in which the ethical course of action is not clear. Such situations arise regularly in the business world. Consider the following examples:

1. Your boss informs you confidentially that one of your friends is going to be fired. Your friend is about to buy a house. Should you warn your friend that he is about to be fired, even though you promised your boss that you would not?

2. Your colleague has been violating your company's code of ethics by accepting expensive gifts from a salesperson who does business with your company. Should you notify your supervisor?

FIGURE 6.1
Solving Ethical Dilemmas

Source: L. Nash, "Ethics without the Sermon," *Harvard Business Review* 59 (1981), p. 78.

1. Have you defined the problem accurately?

2. How would you define the problem if you stood on the other side of the fence?

3. Whom could your decision or action injure? Can you discuss the problem with the affected parties before you make your decision?

4. Are you confident that your position will be as valid over a long period of time as it seems now?

5. Could you disclose without qualm your decision or action to your boss, your CEO, the board of directors, your family, and society as a whole?

FIGURE 6.2
Ethical Problems in the Business World
Having a code of ethics and a personal sense of what is right and wrong can help business managers choose the right course of action.

1. **Normal Interactions between Business Acquaintances**
   Many interactions between people doing business together are considered a normal part of doing business. Managers often take clients out to lunch or invite them to play golf, for example. These kinds of interactions help businesspeople get to know each other.

2. **Questionable Interactions between Business Acquaintances**
   Some interactions between business acquaintances are questionable. A manager who sends a client an expensive gift, for example, could be seen as trying to bribe the client into doing business with his or her company. Businesses often provide their employees with guidelines on the types of gifts they consider acceptable.

3. **Illegal Interactions between Business Acquaintances**
   Paying bribes to attract business is unethical and illegal. Managers who engage in this kind of activity could face legal action and go to jail.

3. One of your employees has not been performing her job properly. You know that she has been having serious personal problems, and you have tried to be understanding. However, your entire staff is suffering because of poor performance by this key team member. What should you do?

One way of approaching ethical dilemmas like these is to answer the series of questions shown in Figure 6.1. Talking to people you trust can also help you develop solutions to ethical problems. Figure 6.2 explains some of the ethical problems in business.

Laws Relating to Ethics in Business

Over the years, various laws have been enacted that directly relate to the issue of ethics in business. These laws apply to competitive behavior, consumer protection, and environmental protection.

Competitive Behavior

Since the late nineteenth century the federal government has regulated companies to make sure that they do not engage in anticompetitive behavior. All companies operating in the United States must abide by these laws. Enforcement of these laws is handled by the Antitrust Division of the Justice Department and by the Federal Trade Commission.

The Sherman Act

As you learned in Chapter 2, the Sherman Antitrust Act of 1890 makes it illegal for companies to monopolize trade. Under the law, mergers can be prohibited if the new company that results from the merger will control too large a share of the market. The purpose of the law is to ensure that companies remain able to compete fairly.

The Clayton Act

The Clayton Act of 1914 makes it illegal to charge different prices to different wholesale customers. This means that a manufacturer of steel, for example, cannot charge one price to General Motors and another price to Chrysler.

The Clayton Act also bans the practice of requiring a customer to purchase a second good. Manufacturers of computer hardware, for example, cannot require customers to purchase software as well.

The Wheeler-Lea Act

The Wheeler-Lea Act of 1938 bans unfair or deceptive acts or practices, including false advertising. Under the act, businesses must inform consumers of possible negative consequences of using their products. Labeling of cigarette packages is an example of the kind of disclosure required by the Wheeler-Lea Act.

Consumer Protection

Several laws protect consumers in the United States against unethical and unsafe business practices. These laws cover food and drugs, other manufactured products, and loans.

Food and Drugs

The Federal Food, Drug, and Cosmetic Act of 1938 bans the sale of impure, improperly labeled, falsely guaranteed, and unhealthful foods, drugs, and cosmetics. The law is enforced by the Food and Drug Administration (FDA), which has the power to force manufacturers to stop selling products it considers unsafe.

Consumer Products

The Consumer Product Safety Commission (CPSC) was established in 1972. It establishes minimum product safety standards on consumer products. If a product is found to be defective, the Consumer Product Safety Commission has the authority to force the manufacturer to recall the product. For example, in 1999 the CPSC recalled a quarter of a million Nike water bottles. The bottles were recalled because the cap was not attached properly, possibly causing users to choke.

Loans

A series of laws protects U.S. consumers against unfair lending practices. Under the Truth in Lending Act of 1968, creditors are required to let consumers know how much they are paying in finance charges and interest. The Equal Credit Opportunity Act of 1975 prohibits creditors from making credit decisions on the basis of discriminatory practices.

Environmental Protection

Since the late 1960s, environmental protection has been an important social and economic issue in the United States. This concern has been reflected in the many laws designed to protect the environment.

The National Environmental Policy Act of 1969

The key piece of legislation in environmental protection is the National Environmental Policy Act of 1969. This law created the Environmental Protection Agency (EPA), whose mission is to protect human health and safeguard the air, water, and land.

Since 1969, many environmental laws affecting businesses have been passed. These laws include the Clean Air Act, the Toxic Substances Control Act, and the Clean Water Act. All of these laws are enforced by the EPA.

The Clean Air Act of 1970

The Clean Air Act of 1970 is the comprehensive federal law that regulates air emissions. The original act set maximum air pollution standards for each of the 50 states. In 1990, the act was amended to deal with problems of acid rain, ground-level ozone, stratospheric ozone depletion, and toxic substances in the air.

The Toxic Substances Control Act of 1976

The Toxic Substances Control Act of 1976 was enacted to give the EPA the ability to track the 75,000 industrial chemicals currently produced in or imported into the United States. The EPA screens these chemicals and can require reporting or testing of those that may pose an environmental or human health hazard.

The Clean Water Act of 1977

The Clean Water Act of 1977 gives the EPA the authority to set standards on the type and quantity of pollutants that industries can put into bodies of water. The law makes it illegal to discharge any pollutant into navigable waters unless a permit is obtained.

Ethical Standards and Culture

Standards of business ethics differ around the world. This means that business practices that are acceptable in one country may be considered unethical in others.

Business managers working in foreign countries must be aware of these different ethical standards. They must set guidelines for their companies on how to operate both within their own culture and in other cultures.

Corporate Gift Giving

Gift-giving customs differ around the world. In some cultures, gifts are expected; failure to present them is considered an insult. In Japan, for example, lavish gift giving is an important part of doing business. Gifts are usually exchanged at the first meeting.

In the United States, government officials are not allowed to accept expensive gifts from businesses. Regardless of local practices, American managers operating abroad must abide by the standards set in the United States.

Intellectual Property

intellectual property
Ownership of ideas; gives creators of the intellectual property the exclusive right to market and sell their work.

Intellectual property refers to ownership of ideas, such as inventions, books, movies, and computer programs. In many countries, including the United States, creators of intellectual property have the exclusive right to market and sell their work. These rights are guaranteed through patent, trademark, and copyright laws. These types of protection ensure that only the creators of intellectual property profit from their work.

Intellectual property protection is very important to business. Without such laws, a computer company could market a best-selling game created by another computer company. A pharmaceutical company could manufacture and sell drugs developed by another drug company.

Although the United States has tough laws governing intellectual property, enforcing those laws is a problem, particularly in the software industry. In 1999, the Justice Department, the FBI, and the Customs Service began cracking down on piracy and counterfeiting of computer software and other products in the United States.

Rules concerning intellectual property rights differ in some countries. In China and India, for example, the government does not enforce such rights. As a result, some Chinese companies copy and sell foreign computer programs. Some publishers in India reprint foreign textbooks, selling them as if they had published them themselves. In the United States, someone who engages in this practice is guilty of plagiarism and can be sued in a court of law. Intellectual property must be respected in the American workplace.

Social Responsibility

social responsibility
The obligation that individuals or businesses have to help solve social problems.

Social responsibility refers to the obligation that individuals or businesses have to help solve social problems. Most companies in the United States feel some sense of social responsibility.[2]

Businesses' concept of their role in society has changed dramatically over the past century. Views toward social responsibility evolved through three distinct schools of thought: profit maximization, trusteeship management, and social involvement.

Profit Maximization

In the nineteenth and early twentieth centuries, business owners in the United States believed that their role was simply to maximize the profits their companies earned. Dealing with social problems was not considered a legitimate business activity.

Trusteeship Management

Thinking about the role of business changed in the 1920s and 1930s, when a philosophy known as *trusteeship management* became popular. This philosophy recognized that owners of businesses had obligations to do more than just earn profits. They also had obligations to their employees, their customers, and their creditors. Most businesspeople continued to hold this view until the 1960s.

Social Involvement

During the 1960s, many people began to believe that corporations should use their influence and financial resources to address social problems. They believed corporations should help solve problems such as poverty, crime, environmental destruction, and illiteracy.

stakeholders
The people—employees, customers, suppliers, and the community—who are affected by the actions of a business.

According to this view, businesses should be responsible corporate citizens, not just maximizers of profit. Businesses have obligations to all of the people affected by their actions, known as stakeholders. **Stakeholders** include a company's employees, customers, suppliers, and the community.

Since the 1960s, corporations have increasingly demonstrated their commitment to social change. One example of this commitment is the increased diversity in the workplace. Over the past 35 years, most corporations have made efforts to diversify their workforces by hiring and promoting more women and minorities. Many businesses also have established workshops to help their employees understand people from different backgrounds.

Measuring Social Responsibility

Corporations demonstrate their sense of social responsibility in various ways. Performance in each of these areas is measured as part of a social audit.

Philanthropy and Volunteerism

One way a company demonstrates its sense of social responsibility is by contributing time and money to charitable, cultural, and civic organizations. Corporate philanthropy, or efforts to improve human welfare, can take many forms. Computer giant Compaq (now merged with Hewlett-Packard), for example, provides technology, product, and cash contributions to organizations throughout the United States. It also has planted seedlings in Australia, supported an institute for people with disabilities in India, and refurbished a school in Brazil. All of these activities reflect the company's sense of social responsibility.

Some companies grant employees paid time off to participate in charitable activities. Many high-tech companies, for example, allow their employees to volunteer for the U.S. Tech Corps, which sends employees from technology companies to work in public schools. Other corporations allow employees time off to donate blood, participate in food and clothing drives, or raise money for such causes as the United Way.

Many corporations also donate money by matching charitable donations made by their employees. In this way companies both encourage employee giving and make their own contributions to philanthropic causes.

Environmental Awareness

Another way companies demonstrate their sense of social responsibility is by limiting the damage their operations cause to the environment. They do so by creating production processes that are as environmentally friendly as possible.

Businesses also can affect the environment by establishing policies that reduce pollution. Encouraging employees to carpool, for example, reduces toxic emissions and conserves gasoline. Using biodegradable products also helps protect the environment.

Sensitivity to Diversity and Quality of Work Life

One of the most important ways a company can demonstrate its sense of social responsibility is through its workforce. Socially responsible businesses maintain ethnically diverse workforces that reflect the societies in which they operate. McDonald's, for example, has created a diverse work environment. At least 70 percent of McDonald's restaurant management and 25 percent of the company executives are minorities and women.

Companies also can demonstrate their social responsibility by adopting policies that contribute to the quality of life of their workers. Flexible work hours, for example, allow workers to better meet their families' needs. On-site day care centers make life easier for employees with young children.

Actions Necessary to Implement Social Responsibility

The biggest obstacle to organizations assuming more social responsibility is pressure by financial analysts and stockholders who push for steady increases in earnings per share on a quarterly basis. Concern about immediate profits makes it difficult to invest in areas that cannot be accurately measured and still have returns that are long run in nature. Furthermore, pressure for short-term earnings affects corporate social behavior; most companies are geared toward short-term profit goals. Budgets, objectives, and performance evaluations are often based on short-run considerations. Management may state a willingness to lose some short-term profit to achieve social objectives. However, managers who sacrifice profit and seek to justify these actions on the basis of corporate social goals may find stockholders unsympathetic.

Organizations should also carefully examine their cherished values, short-run profits, and others, to ensure that these concepts are in tune with the values held

The old mind-set that corporate philanthropy equals writing checks is just that—old. Hands-on philanthropy is the newest trend in the world of corporate giving, not to mention in employee motivation.

Suzanne Apple, vice president of community affairs for Atlanta-based Home Depot, believes many employees are looking for a sense of purpose, and that's what makes them stay at Home Depot. "A lot of employees, especially the younger ones, say they came because of the company's commitment," she says. Branded Team Depot, the company's volunteer efforts are focused in two areas, which are closely linked to its home improvement business: affordable housing and disaster preparation and relief. Working toward affordable housing "comes from the fact that we have unique resources," Apple says. Home Depot strives to be one of the first organizations to get involved in local relief efforts after a natural disaster.

Team Depot's partners include Habitat for Humanity, a nonprofit that builds affordable houses in partnership with the people who need them, and the Red Cross. "Employees get really excited about activities like Habitat for Humanity. They see the value and significance of what they're doing," says Jonathan Roseman, the company's director of community relations.

LensCrafters, the optometry company headquartered in Cincinnati, also has an established employee volunteer program, which evolved into a business strategy that strengthens employee loyalty and company pride. Its Give the Gift of Sight (GOS) program started in 1988 with used glasses drives in its stores. The glasses were distributed to needy people in the community. The idea for used glasses drives came from the Lions Clubs, which have collected them for 30 years, and are now a LensCrafters partner. "When you're looking for a cause or a philanthropic activity you don't have to reinvent the wheel. People are doing things similar to what you do as a company," says GOS director Susan Knobler.

Source: Elana Harris, "Corporate Giving Goes Both Ways," *Sales and Marketing Management*, December 2000, p. 104.

---

by society. This should be a constant process, because the values society holds are ever-changing.

Organizations should reevaluate their long-range planning and decision-making processes to ensure that they fully understand the potential social consequences. Plant location decisions are no longer merely economic matters. Environmental impact and job opportunities for disadvantaged groups are examples of other factors to consider.

Organizations should seek to aid both governmental agencies and voluntary agencies in their social efforts. This should include technical and managerial help as well as monetary support. Technological knowledge, organizational skills, and managerial competence can all be applied to solving social problems.

Organizations should look at ways to help solve social problems through their own businesses. Many social problems stem from the economic deprivation of a fairly large segment of our society. Attacking this problem could be the greatest social effort of organizations.

Another major area in which businesses are active is corporate philanthropy. Corporate philanthropy involves donations of money, property, or work by organizations to socially useful purposes. Many companies have directed their philanthropic efforts toward education, the arts, and the United Way. Contributions can be made directly by the company, or a company foundation can be created to handle the philanthropic program. Management Illustration 6.2 describes philanthropic programs at Home Depot and LensCrafters.

social audit
A method used by management to evaluate the success or lack of success of programs designed to improve the social performance of the organization.

Conducting a Social Audit

One method of measuring the success of a firm is to conduct a social audit. A **social audit** allows management to evaluate the success or lack of success of programs designed to improve the social performance of the organization. Rather than looking exclusively at economic and financial measures, the social audit can be a beginning point for encouraging environmental and social strategies that really work.

One suggested method for accomplishing the social audit and reacting to the information includes the following steps:

1. Examine social expectations, sensitivity, and past responses.
2. Examine and then set social objectives and meaningful priorities.
3. Plan and implement strategies and objectives in each program area.
4. Set budgets for resources necessary for social action and make a commitment to acquire them.
5. Monitor accomplishments or progress in each program area.

To ensure that stockholders, stakeholders, and the general public know about the commitment and accomplishments of social programs, most large corporations publish their successes in their annual reports. These firms make social responsibility an integral part of their mission statements. True commitment goes beyond the self-serving and selective nature of public relations. Most experts agree that socially responsible firms will eventually be rewarded by their markets and stakeholders.

Summary

1. *Identify the six areas of law that affect business organizations.* The six areas of law that affect business organizations are corporate law, tax law, intellectual property law, consumer law, commercial law, and licensing and zoning law.

2. *Identify the types of taxes that affect business profits.* These are income taxes, property taxes, and withholding federal taxes.

3. *Explain the differences between copyrights, patents, and trademarks.* A patent is the document the federal government issues to inventors and companies that gives them the exclusive right to make, use, and sell their inventions for 17 years. A trademark is a word, name, symbol, or slogan a business uses to identify its own goods and set them apart from others. Companies apply to the federal government's patents and trademark office when they want to establish a new trademark. Once a company owns its trademark, no other company can use it. Registered trademarks are good for 10 years, and companies can renew them every additional 10 years. A copyright is the protection provided to a creative work.

4. *Define intellectual property.* Intellectual property laws protect the inventions and new ideas of businesses. The three kinds of intellectual property protections are patents, trademarks, and copyrights.

5. *Define ethics.* Ethics are a set of moral principles or values that govern behavior.

6. *Explain a code of ethics.* A code of ethics is a written document that outlines the principles of conduct to be used in making decisions within an organization.

7. *Identify four categories of laws relating to ethics in business.* These laws apply to competitive behavior, consumer protection, and environmental protection.

8. *Explain social responsibility.* Social responsibility refers to the role of business in solving current social issues over and above legal requirements.

Review Questions

1. What are the six areas of law that affect business organizations?
2. Explain the laws regulating the three kinds of business entities or ownership.
3. Describe the three kinds of intellectual property protections.

4. What is the Uniform Commercial Code?
5. Define ethics.
6. What is a code of ethics?
7. What is intellectual property?
8. Identify the laws that deal with ethical issues in business.
9. Explain social responsibility.

Skill-Building Questions

1. Why does the government regulate businesses?
2. What are three ways in which corporations can demonstrate a sense of social responsibility?
3. Why are ethical codes more common today than they were 50 years ago?
4. James F. Lincoln stated: "'Do unto others as you would have them do unto you' is a proper labor–management policy." Do you agree or disagree? Why?

Skill-Building Exercise 6.1

Where Do You Stand?

Read each of the following situations and decide how you would respond. Be prepared to justify your position in a class discussion.

Situation 1: Family versus Ethics

Jim, a 56-year-old middle manager with children in college, discovers that the owners of his company are cheating the government out of several thousand dollars a year in taxes. Jim is the only employee in a position to know this. Should Jim report the owners to the Internal Revenue Service at the risk of endangering his own livelihood, or should he disregard the discovery to protect his family's livelihood?

Situation 2: The Roundabout Raise

When Joe asks for a raise, his boss praises his work but says the company's rigid budget won't allow any further merit raises for the time being. Instead, the boss suggests the company "won't look too closely at your expense accounts for a while." Should Joe take this as authorization to pad his expense account because he is simply getting the money he deserves through a different route, or should he not take this roundabout "raise"?

Situation 3: The Faked Degree

Bill has done a sound job for over a year; he got the job by claiming to have a college degree. Bill's boss learns Bill actually never graduated. Should his boss dismiss him for a false résumé? Should he overlook the false claim, since Bill is otherwise conscientious and honorable and dismissal might ruin Bill's career?

Situation 4: Sneaking Phone Calls

Helen discovers that a co-worker makes about $100 a month in personal long-distance telephone calls from an office telephone. Should Helen report the employee or disregard the calls, since many people make personal calls at the office?

Situation 5: Cover-Up Temptation

José discovers that the chemical plant he manages is creating slightly more water pollution in a nearby lake than is legally permitted. Revealing the problem will bring negative publicity to the plant, hurt the lakeside town's resort business, and scare the community. Solving the problem will cost the company well over $100,000. It is unlikely that outsiders will discover the problem. The violation poses no danger whatever to people; at most, it will endanger a small number of fish. Should José reveal the problem despite the cost to his company, or should he consider the problem as a mere technicality and disregard it?

Situation 6: Actual Salary

Dorothy finds out that the best-qualified candidate for a job really earned only $18,000 a year in his last job, not the $28,000 he claimed. Should Dorothy hire the candidate anyway, or should she choose someone considerably less qualified?

Source: *The Wall Street Journal,* Eastern Edition, by Roger Rickles. Copyright © 1983 by Dow Jones & Co., Inc. Reproduced with permission of Dow Jones & Co., Inc., via Copyright Clearance Center.

Skill-Building Exercise 6.2

Truthfulness in Advertising

Advertising claims may be totally inaccurate ("sticker price is a low $11,998" may omit all transportation costs, state taxes, dealer charges, and factory options, which together add 25 percent to 30 percent to the price of a car). Other claims are greatly exaggerated ("12-hour relief from sore throat pain"), verbally misleading ("you'll have to eat 12 bowls of Shredded Wheat to get the vitamins and nutrition in 1 bowl of Total"), or visually misleading (healthy, active people shown in pleasant social situations to advertise liquor, beer, or cigarettes).

Questions

From magazines, newspapers, or television, select an advertisement you believe to be untruthful.

1. Why do you think the claims are untruthful?
2. Into what group (inaccurate, exaggerated, or misleading) do you think they fall?

Source: La Rue Tone Hosmer, *The Ethics of Management* (Homewood, IL: Richard D. Irwin, 1987), p. 86.

Case Incident 6.1

Lightbulb Sellers

You receive the following telephone call: "Hello, Mr. Smith. This is Sam. I am a handicapped person." Sam wants to sell you a high-priced lightbulb, guaranteed to last up to five years. He may also want to sell you vitamins and household cleaning solutions. The lightbulbs sold in this manner cost about twice as much as they do at a local hardware store.

However, few of the lightbulb sales organizations are charities. They are for-profit companies whose business is selling lightbulbs by phone. United Handicapped Workers, Lifeline Industries Inc., Handicapped Workers of America, United Handicapped Workers of Charlotte (North Carolina), and American Handicapped Workers are among the larger for-profit companies selling lightbulbs by phone.

The people who make the phone calls are normally paid an hourly wage, a commission, or some combination of the two. The fact that you are dealing with a for-profit business is not always clear, even though the caller may say, "We're not asking for charity or a handout."

Questions

1. Do you believe the practices of these organizations are ethical? Explain.
2. What are the pros and cons of these practices?

Source: "Lightbulb Sellers' Employers Often Not Charity," *Atlanta Journal and Constitution,* May 28, 1990, p. B3.

Case Incident 6.2

Bonuses at Drexel Burnham Lambert

Drexel Burnham Lambert, former Wall Street junk bond powerhouse, filed for Chapter 11 protection from its creditors February 13, 1990. The firm's management announced its assets would be sold and it would cease doing business. The bankruptcy claim threw into jeopardy the claims of hundreds of creditors.

On February 24, 1990, it was announced that Drexel Burnham had paid out $260 million in cash and stock bonuses in the two months before it filed for bankruptcy protection. Of the total bonuses, $150 million was paid in December 1989 and $110 million was paid in January 1990. People inside the firm have said some executives were paid more than $10 million in bonuses.

Questions

1. Do creditors of Drexel Burnham have any options under present laws against the firm's actions?

2. What reasons could be offered for paying these bonuses?

Source: Kurt Eichenwald, "Drexel Asserts Bonuses Come to $260 Million," *New York Times,* February 24, 1990, p. 37L.

References and Additional Readings

1. See Dennis W. Organ, "Business Ethics 101?" *Business Horizons*, January–February 2003, pp. 1–2.

2. For additional information, see Ronald Paul Hill, Debra Stephens, and Iain Smith, "Corporate Social Responsibility: An Examination of Individual Firm Behavior," *Business and Society Review,* September 2003, pp. 339–64.

3

Planning Skills

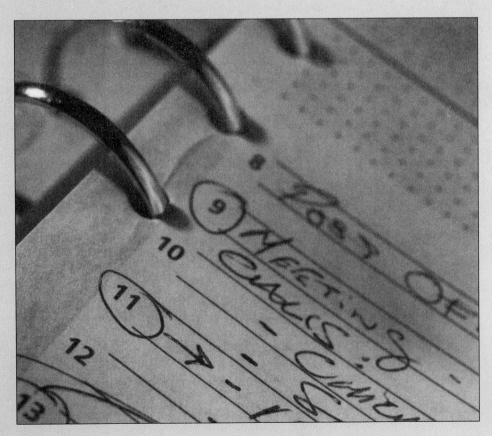

7

The Basics of Planning and Strategic Management

Learning Objectives

After studying this chapter, you will be able to:

1. Define planning and distinguish between formal and functional plans.
2. Contrast strategic planning with operational planning.
3. Define strategy and explain the various levels of strategies.
4. Define strategic management and explain the strategic management process.
5. Explain the differences between missions, objectives, policies, procedures, and rules.
6. Discuss the components of a SWOT analysis.
7. Define a strategic business unit (SBU).
8. Discuss what organizational factors need to be evaluated in implementing a strategic plan.

Chapter Preview

In the early 1980s, Howard Schultz predicted that consumers would support a new type of "coffee bar," serving specialty coffee and espresso products. Under his leadership, Starbucks grew from a homey little coffee shop in Seattle into a multimillion dollar corporation. In its early years, the company focused on domestic growth, infrastructure, and product development. In 1992, the company first went public, raising $29 million for expansion. A secondary offering in late 1994 netted around $180 million. Since going public, Starbucks has raised almost $500 million.

Speaking in 2000, Schultz said, "Five years ago our strategic intent was to build the leading brand of specialty coffee in North America. Five years later we have fulfilled that promise. And our strategic objectives now are much different, and that is to maintain our leadership position in North America and to build an enduring global band around the world."

Today, Starbucks has locations in Europe, Japan, Puerto Rico, Mexico, South America, and China. By mid-2003, Starbucks had 470 stores in Japan. As of the same time, Starbucks had 69 stores in China.

Sources: Karyn Stauss, "Howard Schultz: Starbucks' CEO Serves a Blend of Community, Employee Commitment," *Nation's Restaurant News,* January 2000, pp. 162–63; Jason Singer and Martin Fackler, "In Japan, Adding Beer, Wine to Latte List," *The Wall Street Journal,* July 14, 2003, p. B1; and Geoffrey A. Fowler, "Converting the Masses: Starbucks in China," *Far Eastern Economic Review,* July 17, 2003, p. 34.

Analyzing Management Skills

Why do you think it is important for a company like Starbucks to regularly refine and update its strategic objectives? What other functions might annual strategic planning sessions serve?

Applying Management Skills

What trends do you think will influence businesses in the next 10 years? If you opened a business today, what things would you do to plan for its future success?

The Planning Process

planning
Process of deciding what objectives to pursue during a future time period and what to do to achieve those objectives.

Planning is the process of deciding what objectives to pursue during a future time period and what to do to achieve those objectives. It is the primary management function and is inherent in everything a manager does. This chapter discusses the basics of the planning function and how this function relates to strategic management.

Why Plan?

It is futile for a manager to attempt to perform the other management functions without having a plan. Managers who attempt to organize without a plan find themselves reorganizing on a regular basis. The manager who attempts to staff without a plan will be constantly hiring and firing employees. Motivation is almost impossible in an organization undergoing continuous reorganization and high employee turnover.

Planning enables a manager or an organization to actively affect rather than passively accept the future. By setting objectives and charting a course of action, the organization commits itself to "making it happen." This allows the organization to affect the future. Without a planned course of action, the organization is much more likely to sit back, let things happen, and then react to those happenings in a crisis mode.

Planning provides a means for actively involving personnel from all areas of the organization in the management of the organization. Involvement produces a multitude of benefits. First, input from throughout the organization improves the quality of the plans; good suggestions can come from any level in the organization. Involvement in the planning process also enhances the overall understanding of the organization's direction. Knowing the big picture can minimize friction among departments, sections, and individuals. For example, through planning,

A recent study investigating the import of planning on U.S. small business failures found that very little formal planning goes on in U.S. small business. However, non-failed firms were found to engage in more planning than similar failed firms did prior to failure. A "failure" was defined in this study as a bankruptcy with losses to creditors. Firms with less than 500 employees were considered "small."

Recently failed firms were randomly selected and matched with non-failed firms on the basis of age, size, industry, and location. One hundred fifty-two matched-pair cases were used in the study. Five specific questions were asked of each respondent.

The five questions all asked whether the firm engaged in specific planning related activities. The questions were arranged in an order which presumed an increasing intensity and sophistication in planning. The general assumption was that a firm must produce some type of written planning document to be considered sufficiently formal and substantive.

Source: Stephen C. Perry, "The Relationship between Written Business Plans and the Failure of Small Businesses in the U.S.," *Journal of Small Business Management,* July 2001, pp. 201–08.

the sales department can understand and appreciate the objectives of the production department and their relationship to organizational objectives. Involvement in the planning process fosters a greater personal commitment to the plan; the plan becomes "our" plan rather than "their" plan. Positive attitudes created by involvement also improve overall organizational morale and loyalty.

Planning can also have positive effects on managerial performance. Studies have demonstrated that employees who stress planning earn high performance ratings from supervisors.[1] They have also shown that planning has a positive impact on the quality of work produced.[2] While some have proven inconclusive, several studies have reported a positive relationship between planning and certain measures of organizational success, such as profits and goals.[3] One explanation that would fit all the findings to date is that good planning, as opposed to the mere presence or absence of a plan, is related to organizational success. Management Illustration 7.1 discusses a recent study related to planning in small businesses.

A final reason for planning is the mental exercise required to develop a plan. Many people believe the experience and knowledge gained throughout the development of a plan force managers to think in a future- and contingency-oriented manner; this can result in great advantages over managers who are static in their thinking.

Formal Planning

formal plan
Written, documented plan developed through an identifiable process.

All managers plan. The difference lies in the methods they employ and the extent to which they plan. Most planning is carried out on an informal or casual basis. This occurs when planners do not record their thoughts but carry them around in their heads. A **formal plan** is a written, documented plan developed through an identifiable process. The appropriate degree of sophistication depends on the needs of the individual managers and the organization itself. The environment, size, and type of business are factors that typically affect the planning needs of an organization.

Functional Plans

functional plans
Originate from the functional areas of an organization such as production, marketing, finance, and personnel.

Plans are often classified by function or use. The most frequently encountered types of **functional plans** are sales and marketing plans, production plans, financial plans, and personnel plans. Sales and marketing plans are for developing new products or services and selling both present and future products or services. Production plans deal with producing the desired products or services on a timely schedule. Financial plans deal primarily with meeting the financial commitments and capital expenditures of the organization. Personnel plans relate to the human resource needs of the organization. Many functional plans are interrelated and interdependent. For example, a financial plan would obviously be dependent on production, sales, and personnel plans.

The Planning Horizon: Short Range, Intermediate, and Long Range

short-range plans
Generally cover up to one year.

long-range plans
Typically span at least three to five years; some extend as far as 20 years into the future.

The length of the planning horizon is relative and varies somewhat from industry to industry, depending on the specific environment and activity. What may be long range when operating in a rapidly changing environment, such as the electronics industry, may be short range when operating in a relatively static environment, such as the brick manufacturing industry. In practice, however, **short-range plans** generally cover up to one year, whereas **long-range plans** span at least three to five years, with some extending as far as 20 years into the future. While long-range planning is possible at any level in the organization, it is carried out primarily at the top levels.

Intermediate plans cover the time span between short-range and long-range plans. From a pragmatic standpoint, intermediate plans generally cover from one to three or one to five years, depending on the horizon covered by the long-range plan. Usually intermediate plans are derived from long-range plans and short-range plans are derived from intermediate plans. For example, if the long-range plan calls for a 40 percent growth in sales by the end of five years, the intermediate plan should outline the necessary steps to be taken over the time span covering one to five years. Short-range plans would outline what actions are necessary within the next year.

Operational versus Strategic Plans

strategic planning
Analogous to top-level long-range planning; covers a relatively long period; affects many parts of the organization.

operations or tactical planning
Short-range planning; done primarily by middle- to lower-level managers, it concentrates on the formulation of functional plans.

Strategic planning is analogous to top-level, long-range planning. It is the planning process applied at the highest levels of the organization, covering a relatively long period and affecting many parts of the organization. **Operations** or **tactical planning** is short-range planning and concentrates on the formulation of functional plans. Production schedules and day-to-day plans are examples of operational plans.

However, the distinctions between strategic and operations planning are relative, not absolute. The major difference is the level at which the planning is done. Strategic planning is done primarily by top-level managers; operational planning is done by managers at all levels in the organization and especially by middle- and lower-level managers.

Contingency Plans

contingency plans
Address the what-ifs of the manager's job; gets the manager in the habit of being prepared and knowing what to do if something does go wrong.

Regardless of how thorough plans are, there will always be things that go wrong. What goes wrong is often beyond the control of the manager. For example, the economy takes an unexpected dip, a machine breaks down, or the arrival of a new piece of equipment is delayed. When such things happen, managers must be prepared with a backup, a contingency, plan. **Contingency plans** address the what-ifs of the manager's job. Contingency planning gets the manager in the habit of being prepared and knowing what to do if something does go wrong. Naturally, contingency plans cannot be prepared for all possibilities. What managers should do is identify the most critical assumptions of the current plan and then develop contingencies for problems that have a reasonable chance of occurring. A good approach is to examine the current plan from the point of view of what could go wrong. Contingency planning is most needed in rapidly changing environments.

Before studying the planning process further, it is necessary to develop a clear understanding of strategy and its various forms. These forms are discussed in the next section.

Strategy

strategy
Outlines the basic steps management plans to take to reach an objective or a set of objectives; outlines how management intends to achieve its objectives.

The word *strategy* originated with the Greeks about 400 B.C.; it pertained to the art and science of directing military forces.[4] A **strategy** outlines the basic steps that management plans to take to reach an objective or a set of objectives. In other words, a strategy outlines how management intends to achieve its objectives.

Levels of Strategy

Strategies exist at three primary levels in an organization and are classified according to the scope of what they are intended to accomplish. The three levels are corporate, business, and functional strategies.

Corporate Strategies

corporate (grand) strategies
Address which businesses an organization will be in and how resources will be allocated among those businesses.

Strategies that address which businesses the organization will be in and how resources will be allocated among those businesses are referred to as **corporate strategies.** Corporate strategies are sometimes called **grand strategies.** They are established at the highest levels in the organization, and they involve a long-range time horizon. Corporate strategies are concerned with the overall direction of the organization, specifically tied to mission statements, and generally formulated by top corporate management. Four basic corporate strategy types are recognized: growth, stability, defensive, and combination.

growth strategy
Used when the organization tries to expand, as measured by sales, product line, number of employees, or similar measures.

Growth strategies are used when the organization tries to expand in terms of sales, product line, number of employees, or similar measures. Under this concept, an organization can grow through concentration of current businesses, vertical integration, and diversification. Kellogg and McDonald's use concentration strategies—focusing on extending the sales of their current products or services—very successfully. A. G. Bass (maker of the famous "preppie" shoe, Bass Weejuns) believes vertical integration, in which a company moves into areas it previously served either as a supplier to or as a customer for its current products or services, to be a superior growth strategy. The final growth strategy is exemplified by Coca-Cola's purchase of Minute Maid Orange Juice in the early 1980s and its more recent purchase of Dasani spring waters. Diversification can take several forms, but concentric (in related fields) is the most common.

stability strategy
Used when the organization is satisfied with its present course (status quo strategy).

Stability strategies are used when the organization is satisfied with its present course. Management will make efforts to eliminate minor weaknesses, but generally its actions will remain the status quo. Stability strategies are most likely to be successful in unchanging or very slowly changing environments. Growth is possible under a stability strategy, but it will be slow, methodical, and nonaggressive. Most organizations elect a stability strategy by default rather than by any conscious decision or plan.

defensive (retrenchment) strategy
Used when a company wants or needs to reduce its operations.

Defensive or **retrenchment strategies** are used when a company wants or needs to reduce its operations. Most often they are used to reverse a negative trend or to overcome a crisis or problem. The three most popular types are *turn-*

FIGURE 7.1
Major Types and Subtypes of Corporate Strategies

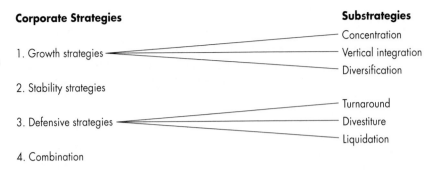

around (designed to reverse a negative trend and get the organization back to profitability), *divestiture* (the company sells or divests itself of a business or part of a business), and *liquidation* (the entire company is sold or dissolved).

combination strategy
Used when an organization simultaneously employs different strategies for different parts of the company.

Combination strategies are used when an organization simultaneously employs different strategies for different parts of the company. Most multibusiness companies use some type of combination strategy, especially those serving several different markets. Coca-Cola, for example, pursued a combination strategy in 1989 when it divested its Columbia Pictures division while expanding its soft-drink and orange juice businesses.

Figure 7.1 summarizes the major types and subtypes of corporate strategies.

Business Strategies

business strategies
Focus on how to compete in a given business.

Business strategies, the second primary level of strategy formulation, focus on how to compete in a given business. Narrower in scope than a corporate strategy, a business strategy generally applies to a single business unit. Though usually situational in nature, most of these strategies can be classified as overall cost leadership, differentiation, or focus.[5]

Overall cost leadership is a strategy designed to produce and deliver the product or service for a lower cost than the competition. Cost leadership is usually attained through a combination of experience and efficiency. More specifically, cost leadership requires close attention to production methods, overhead, marginal customers, and overall cost minimization in such areas as sales and research and development (R&D). Achieving an overall low-cost position usually requires that the company develop some unique advantage or advantages over its competitors. Examples include a high market share, favorable access to raw materials, use of state-of-the-art equipment, or special design features that make the product easy to manufacture. Wal-Mart and Home Depot have adopted this strategy with great success.

Differentiation aims to make the product or service unique in its category, thus permitting the organization to charge higher-than-average prices. Differentiation can take many forms, such as design or brand image, quality, technology, customer service, or dealer network. The basic purpose of a differentiation strategy is to gain the brand loyalty of customers and a resulting lower sensitivity to price. Following a differentiation strategy does not imply that the business should have little concern for costs but, rather, that the major competitive advantage sought is through differentiation.

Depending on what is required to achieve differentiation, a company may or may not find it necessary to incur relatively high costs. For example, if high-quality materials or extensive research is necessary, the resulting product or service may be priced relatively high. When this is the case, the idea is that the uniqueness of

FIGURE 7.2
Levels of Strategies

Corporate Strategy

Addresses which businesses an organization will be in and how resources will be allocated among those businesses; describes the way the organization will pursue its objectives.

Business Strategy

Focuses on how to compete in a given business.

Functional Strategy

Concerned with the activities of the different functional areas of the organization, short-range step-by-step methods to be used (tactics).

functional strategies
Concerned with the activities of the different functional areas of the business.

strategic management
Formulation, proper implementation, and continuous evaluation of strategic plans; determines the long-run directions and performance of an organization. The essence of strategic management is developing strategic plans and keeping them current.

the product or service will create a willingness on the part of the customers to pay the premium price. While such a strategy can be very profitable, it may or may not preclude gaining a high share of the market. For example, Rolex demands a very high price for its watches and makes a profit, but it has a very small market share.[6] Ralph Lauren Polo sportswear and Mercedes-Benz are other examples of products that used a differentiation strategy. Differentiation can be achieved through a superior product (Microsoft), a quality image (Mercedes-Benz), or a brand image (Polo sportswear).

Focus is a third type of business strategy. Companies that use this method focus on, or direct their attention to, a narrow market segment. The segment may be a special buyer group, a geographical market, or one part of the product line. With a focus strategy, the firm serves a well-defined but narrow market better than competitors that serve a broader or less defined market. A "tall men's" clothing store is an example of a company following a focus strategy. Colgate-Palmolive, for example, has determined that to reach Hispanics successfully, it must capitalize on shared traits of this growing segment. Its 70 percent market share of toothpaste sold to Hispanics is largely attributed to understanding that three-quarters of Hispanics who watch TV or listen to radio do so with Spanish-language stations. Colgate-Palmolive has heavy sponsorship of favorite programs on these stations.[7]

Functional Strategies

The third primary level of strategy is functional strategies. **Functional strategies** are narrower in scope than business strategies and deal with the activities of the different functional areas of the business—production, finance, marketing, human resources, and the like. Functional strategies support the business strategies and are primarily concerned with how-to issues. Usually functional strategies are in effect for a relatively short period, often one year or less. Figure 7.2 summarizes the different levels of strategies.

The Strategic Management Process

Strategic Management

The rapid rate of change in today's business world is making it increasingly necessary that managers keep their plans current. **Strategic management** is the application of the basic planning process at the highest levels of the organization. Through the strategic management process, top management determines the long-run direction and performance of the organization by ensuring careful formulation, proper implementation, and continuous evaluation of plans and strategies. The essence of strategic management is developing strategic plans and keeping them current as changes occur internally and in the environment. It is possible to prepare a formal plan with a well-defined strategy and not practice strategic management. In such a situation, the plan could become outmoded as changes occur in the environment. Practicing strategic management does not ensure that an organization will meet all change successfully, but it does increase the odds.

Although guided by top management, successful strategic management involves many different levels in the organization. For example, top management may ask middle- and lower-level managers for input when formulating top-level plans. Once top-level plans have been finalized, different organizational units may be asked to formulate plans for their respective areas. A proper strategic management process helps ensure that plans throughout the different levels of the organization are coordinated and mutually supportive.

Organizations that consciously engage in strategic management generally follow some type of formalized process for making decisions and taking actions that affect their future direction. In the absence of a formal process, strategic decisions are made in a piecemeal fashion. An informal approach to strategy, however, does not necessarily mean the organization doesn't know what it is doing. It simply means the organization does not engage in any type of formalized process for initiating and managing strategy.

The strategic management process includes setting the organization's mission; defining what business or businesses the organization will be in; setting objectives; developing, implementing, and evaluating strategies; and adjusting these components as necessary. While the basic process is similar in most organizations, differences exist in the formality of the process, levels of managerial involvement, and degree of institutionalization of the process.

formulation phase
First phase in strategic management, in which the initial strategic plan is developed.

Although different organizations may use somewhat different approaches to the strategic management process, most successful approaches share several common components and a similar sequence. The strategic management process is composed of three major phases: (1) formulating the strategic plan, (2) implementing the strategic plan, and (3) evaluating the strategic plan. The **formulation phase** is concerned with developing the initial strategic plan. The **implementation phase** involves implementing the strategic plan that has been formulated. The **evaluation phase** stresses the importance of continuously evaluating and updating the strategic plan after it has been implemented. Each of these three phases is critical to the success of the strategic management process. A breakdown in any one area can easily cause the entire process to fail.

implementation phase
Second phase in strategic management, in which the strategic plan is put into effect.

Formulating Strategy

The formulation stage of the strategic management process involves developing the corporate- and business-level strategies to be pursued. The strategies ultimately chosen are shaped by the organization's internal strengths and weaknesses and the threats and opportunities the environment presents.

evaluation phase
Third phase in strategic management, in which the implemented strategic plan is monitored, evaluated, and updated.

The first part of the formulation phase is to obtain a clear understanding of the current position and status of the organization. This includes identifying the mission, identifying the past and present strategies, diagnosing the organization's past and present performance, and setting objectives for the company's operation.

Identifying Mission

mission
Defines the basic purpose(s) of an organization: why the organization exists.

An organization's mission is actually the broadest and highest level of objectives. The **mission** defines the basic purpose or purposes of the organization (for this

FIGURE 7.3
Objectives of the Company Mission

Source: Adapted from William R. King and David I. Cleland, *Strategic Planning and Policy* (New York: Van Nostrand Reinhold, 1978), p. 124.

1. To ensure unanimity of purpose within the organization.
2. To provide a basis for motivating the use of the organization's resources.
3. To develop a basis, or standard, for allocating organizational resources.
4. To establish a general tone or organizational climate; for example, to suggest a businesslike operation.
5. To serve as a focal point for those who can identify with the organization's purpose and direction and to deter those who cannot do so from participating further in its activities.
6. To facilitate the translation of objectives and goals into a work structure involving the assignment of tasks to responsible elements within the organization.
7. To specify organizational purposes and the translation of these purposes into goals in such a way that cost, time, and performance parameters can be assessed and controlled.

reason, the terms *mission* and *purpose* are often used interchangeably). Basically, an organization's mission outlines why the organization exists. A mission statement usually includes a description of the organization's basic products or services and a definition of its markets or sources of revenue. Figure 7.3 outlines the objectives of a typical mission statement. Figure 7.4 presents actual mission statements from three well-known companies.

Defining *mission* is crucial. It is also more difficult than one might imagine. Peter Drucker emphasizes that an organization's purpose should be examined and defined not only at its inception or during difficult times but also during successful periods.[8] If the railroad companies of the early 1900s or the wagon makers of the 1800s had made their organizational purpose to develop a firm position in the transportation business, they might hold the same economic positions today that they enjoyed in earlier times.

Drucker argues that an organization's purpose is determined not by the organization itself but by its customers.[9] Customer satisfaction with the organization's

FIGURE 7.4
Examples of Mission Statements

Company	Mission Statement
FedEx	FedEx Corporation will produce superior financial returns for its shareowners by providing high value-added logistics, transportation, and related information services through focused operating companies. Customer requirements will be met in the highest quality manner appropriate to each market segment served. FedEx Corporation will strive to develop mutually rewarding relationships with its employees, partners, and suppliers. Safety will be the first consideration in all operations. Corporate activities will be conducted to the highest ethical and professional standards.
Harley-Davidson	We fulfill dreams through the experience of motorcycling, by providing to motorcyclists and to the general public an expanding line of motorcycles and branded products and services in selected market segments.
Pfizer	We will become the world's most valued company to patients, customers, colleagues, investors, business partners, and the communities where we work and live.

product or service defines the purpose more clearly than does the organization's name, statutes, or articles of incorporation. Drucker outlines three questions that need to be answered to define an organization's present business. First, management must identify the customers: where they are, how they buy, and how they can be reached. Second, management must know what the customer buys. For instance, does the Rolls-Royce owner buy transportation or prestige? Finally, what is the customer looking for in the product? For example, does the homeowner buy an appliance from Sears, Roebuck & Company because of price, quality, or service?

Management must also identify what the future business will be and what it should be. Drucker presents four areas to investigate. The first is market potential: What does the long-term trend look like? Second, what changes in market structure might occur due to economic developments, changes in styles or fashions, or competition? For example, how have oil prices affected the automobile market structure? Third, what possible changes will alter customers' buying habits? What new ideas or products might create new customer demand or change old demands? Consider the impact of the cell phone on the demand for pay telephones. Finally, what customer needs are not being adequately served by available products and services? The introduction of overnight package delivery by FedEx is a well-known example of identifying and filling a current customer need. Figure 7.5 presents several excerpts of actual mission statements as they relate to certain components.

Identifying Past and Present Strategies

Before deciding if a strategic change is necessary or desirable, the past and present strategies used by the organization need to be clearly identified. General questions to be addressed include the following: Has past strategy been consciously developed? If not, can past history be analyzed to identify what implicit strategy has evolved? If so, has the strategy been recorded in written form? In either case, a strategy or a series of strategies, as reflected by the organization's past actions and intentions, can usually be identified.

Diagnosing Past and Present Performance

To evaluate how past strategies have worked and determine whether strategic changes are needed, the organization's performance record must be examined. How is the organization currently performing? How has the organization performed over the last several years? Is the performance trend moving up or down? Management must address all of these questions before attempting to formulate any type of future strategy. Evaluating an organization's performance usually involves some type of in-depth financial analysis and diagnosis. Management Illustration 7.2 describes how the business strategy of Sam's Clubs unintentionally changed with declining results.

Once management has an accurate picture of the current status of the organization, the next step in formulating strategy is to decide what the long-, intermediate-, and short-range objectives should be in light of the current mission. However, these objectives cannot be accurately established without examining the internal and external environments. Thus, establishing the long- and intermediate-range objectives and analyzing the internal and external environments are concurrent processes that influence each other.

objectives
Statements outlining what the organization is trying to achieve; give an organization and its members direction.

Setting Objectives

If you don't know where you are going, how will you know when you get there? **Objectives** are statements outlining what the organization is trying to achieve;

FIGURE 7.5   **Identifying Mission Statement Components: A Compilation of Excerpts from Actual Corporate Mission Statements**

1. Customer-market	We believe our first responsibility is to the doctors, nurses, and patients, to mothers and all others who use our products and services. (Johnson & Johnson)
	To anticipate and meet market needs of farmers, ranchers, and rural communities within North America. (CENEX)
2. Product-service	AMAX's principal products are molybdenum, coal, iron ore, copper, lead, zinc, petroleum and natural gas, potash, phosphates, nickel, tungsten, silver, gold, and magnesium. (AMAX)
3. Geographic domain	We are dedicated to the total success of Corning Glass Works as a worldwide competitor. (Corning Glass)
4. Technology	Control Data is in the business of applying microelectronics and computer technology in two general areas: computer-related hardware and computing-enhancing services, which include computation, information, education, and finance. (Control Data)
	The common technology in these areas relates to discrete particle coatings. (NASHUA)
5. Concern for survival	In this respect, the company will conduct its operation prudently, and will provide the profits and growth which will assure Hoover's ultimate success. (Hoover Universal)
6. Philosophy	We are committed to improve health care throughout the world. (Baxter Healthcare)
	We believe human development to be the worthiest of the goals of civilization and independence to be the superior condition for nurturing growth in the capabilities of people. (Sun Company)
7. Self-concept	Hoover Universal is a diversified, multi-industry corporation with strong manufacturing capabilities, entrepreneurial policies, and individual business unit autonomy. (Hoover Universal)
8. Concern for public image	We are responsible to the communities in which we live and work and to the world community as well. (Johnson & Johnson)
	Also, we must be responsive to the broader concerns of the public, including especially the general desire for improvement in the quality of life, equal opportunity for all, and the constructive use of natural resources. (Sun Company)

Source: From John A. Pearce II and F. R. David, "Corporate Mission Statements: The Bottom Line," *Academy of Management Executive,* May 1987. Reprinted with permission.

long-range objectives
Go beyond the current fiscal year; must support and not conflict with the organizational mission.

short-range objectives
Generally tied to a specific time period of a year or less and are derived from an in-depth evaluation of long-range objectives.

they give the organization and its members direction and purpose. Few managers question the importance of objectives; they question only what the objectives should be.

Long-range objectives generally go beyond the organization's current fiscal year. Long-range objectives must support and not conflict with the organizational mission. However, they may be quite different from the organizational mission, yet still support it. For instance, the organizational mission of a fast-food restaurant might be to provide rapid, hot-food service to a certain area of the city. One long-range objective might be to increase sales to a specific level within the next four years. Obviously, this objective is quite different from the organizational mission, but it still supports the mission.

Short-range objectives should be derived from an in-depth evaluation of long-range objectives. Such an evaluation should result in a listing of priorities of the long-range objectives. Then short-range objectives can be set to help achieve the long-range objectives.

Objectives should be clear, concise, and quantified when possible. Affected personnel should clearly understand what is expected. Normally, multiple objectives

The original business strategy of Sam's Club was to cater specifically to the needs of small business members as opposed to the needs of individual consumers. In recent years, Sam's has drifted from its original strategy by eliminating core small business items from its product mix, increasing expenses by making the clubs more aesthetically pleasing, and focusing too much on individual members, known as Sam's Advantage Members.

Weak sales and profit performance in 2002 resulted in a management change. The new management team, comprised of Wal-Mart Stores vice chairman Tom Coughlin,

Sam's Club CEO Kevin Turner, and executive vice president of merchandising Doug McMillon, is going back to putting emphasis on small business customers. For example, clubs are offering gold key hours from 7 A.M. to 10 A.M. when only business members can shop. Sam's is also making sure that its product mix offers staple items that small businesses purchase most frequently.

Source: Mike Troy, "Sam's Rewrites Business Plan," *DSN Retailing Today,* June 9, 2003, p. 73.

should be used to reflect the desired performance of a given organizational unit or person. From a top-level perspective, objectives should span all major areas of the organization. A problem with one overriding objective is that it is often achieved at the expense of other desirable objectives. For example, if production is the only objective, quality may suffer in attempts to realize maximum production. While objectives in different areas may serve as checks on one another, they should be reasonably consistent among themselves.

Objectives should be dynamic; that is, they should be reevaluated as the environment and opportunities change. Objectives for organizations usually fall into one of four general categories: (1) profit oriented, (2) service to customers, (3) employee needs and well-being, and (4) social responsibility. Even nonprofit organizations must be concerned with profit in the sense that they generally must operate within a budget. Another scheme for classifying organizational objectives is (1) primary, (2) secondary, (3) individual, and (4) societal. Primary objectives relate directly to profit. Secondary objectives apply to specific units of the organization (e.g., departmental objectives). Individual objectives directly concern the organization's employees. Finally, societal objectives relate to the local, national, and global communities. The following section outlines areas for establishing objectives in most organizations:[10]

1. *Profitability.* Measures the degree to which the firm is attaining an acceptable level of profits; usually expressed in terms of profits before or after taxes, return on investment, earnings per share, or profit-to-sales ratios.

2. *Markets.* Reflects the firm's position in its marketplace, expressed in terms of share of the market, dollar or unit volume in sales, or niche in the industry.

3. *Productivity.* Measures the efficiency of internal operations expressed as a ratio of inputs to outputs, such as number of items or services produced per unit of time.

4. *Product.* Describes the introduction or elimination of products or services; expressed in terms of when a product or service will be introduced or dropped.

5. *Financial resources.* Reflects goals relating to the funding needs of the firm; expressed in terms of capital structure, new issues of common stock, cash flow, working capital, dividend payments, and collection periods.

6. *Physical facilities.* Describes the physical facilities of the firm; expressed in terms of square feet of office or plant space, fixed costs, units of production, or similar measurements.

7. *Research and innovation.* Reflects the research, development, or innovation aspirations of the firm; usually expressed in terms of dollars to be expended.

8. *Organization structure.* Describes objectives relating to changes in the organizational structure and related activities; expressed in terms of a desired future structure or network of relationships.

9. *Human resources.* Describes the human resource assets of the organization; expressed in terms of absenteeism, tardiness, number of grievances, and training.

10. *Social responsibility.* Refers to the commitments of the firm regarding society and the environment; expressed in terms of types of activities, number of days of service, or financial contributions.

Policies

policies
Broad, general guides to action that constrain or direct the attainment of objectives.

To help in the objective-setting process, the manager can rely to some extent on policies and procedures developed by the organization. **Policies** are broad, general guides to action that constrain or direct objective attainment. Policies do not tell organizational members exactly what to do, but they do establish the boundaries within which they must operate. For example, a policy of "answering all written customer complaints in writing within 10 days" does not tell a manager exactly how to respond, but it does say it must be done in writing within 10 days. Policies create an understanding among members of a group that makes the actions of each member more predictable to other members.

procedure
Series of related steps or tasks expressed in chronological order for a specific purpose.

rules
Require specific and definite actions to be taken or not to be taken in a given situation.

Procedures and rules differ from policies only in degree. In fact, they may be thought of as low-level policies. A **procedure** is a series of related steps or tasks expressed in chronological order for a specific purpose. Procedures define in step-by-step fashion the methods through which policies are achieved. Procedures emphasize details. **Rules** require specific and definite actions to be taken or not to be taken in a given situation. Rules leave little doubt about what is to be done. They permit no flexibility or deviation. Unlike procedures, rules do not have to specify sequence. For example, "No smoking in the conference room" is a rule. In reality, procedures and rules are subsets of policies. The primary purpose is guidance. The differences lie in the range of applicability and the degree of flexibility. A no-smoking rule is much less flexible than a procedure for handling customer complaints. However, a rule can have a clear relationship to an objective. For example, a no-smoking rule may help the organization reach a stated objective of "a cleaner and safer corporate environment."

SWOT Analysis

SWOT is an acronym for an organization's strengths, weaknesses, opportunities, and threats. A SWOT analysis is a technique for evaluating an organization's internal strengths and weaknesses and its external opportunities and threats. A major advantage of using a SWOT analysis is that it provides a general overview of an organization's strategic situation.[11] The underlying assumption of a SWOT analysis is that managers can better formulate a successful strategy after they have carefully reviewed the organization's strengths and weaknesses in light of the threats and opportunities the environment presents.

An organization's strengths and weaknesses are usually identified by conducting an internal analysis of the organization. The basic idea of conducting an internal analysis is to perform an objective assessment of the organization's current strengths and weaknesses. What things does the organization do well? What things does the organization do poorly? From a resource perspective, what are the organization's strengths and weaknesses?

The threats and opportunities presented by the environment are usually identified by methodically assessing the organization's external environment. An organization's **external environment** consists of everything outside the organization, but the focus of this assessment is on the external factors that have an impact on its business. Such factors are classified by their proximity to the organization: They are either in its broad environment or in its competitive environment. Broad environmental factors are somewhat removed from the organization but can still influence it. General economic conditions and social, political, and technological trends represent major factors in the broad environment. Factors in the competitive environment are close to the organization and come in regular contact with it. Stockholders, suppliers, competitors, labor unions, customers, and potential new entrants represent members of the competitive environment.

Managers use many different qualitative and quantitative methods for forecasting broad environmental trends. Qualitative techniques are based primarily on opinions and judgments, whereas quantitative techniques are based primarily on the analysis of data and the use of statistical techniques. Both methods can be helpful depending on the circumstances and the information available.

The five forces model of competition is a tool developed by Michael Porter to help managers analyze their competitive environment. This model suggests that the competitive environment can be assessed by analyzing the import of and interactions among five major forces in the competitive or industry environment: (1) suppliers, (2) buyers, (3) competitive rivalry among firms currently in the industry, (4) product or service substitutes, and (5) potential entrants into the industry.[12] By using this tool to access the competitive environment, managers can then better select the most appropriate business level strategy to pursue. Figure 7.6 summarizes the five forces model of competition.

An assessment of the external environment emphasizes the fact that organizations do not operate in a vacuum and are very much affected by their surroundings. Figure 7.7 lists several factors that managers should consider when assessing an organization's strengths and weaknesses and the threats and opportunities posed by the environment. The most important result of a SWOT analysis is the ability to draw conclusions about the attractiveness of the organization's situation and the need for strategic action.[13] Management Illustration 7.3 discusses how one

external environment
Consists of everything outside the organization.

FIGURE 7.6
Five Forces Model of Competition

Source: M. E. Porter, *Competitive Strategy* (New York: Free Press, 1980).

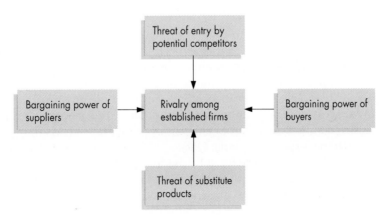

FIGURE 7.7   SWOT Analysis—What to Look for in Sizing Up a Company's Strengths, Weaknesses, Opportunities, and Threats

Potential Internal Strengths

- Core competencies in key areas
- Adequate financial resources
- Well-thought-of by buyers
- An acknowledged market leader
- Well-conceived functional area strategies
- Access to economies of scale
- Insulated (at least somewhat) from strong competitive pressures
- Proprietary technology
- Cost advantages
- Better advertising campaigns
- Product innovation skills
- Proven management
- Ahead on experience curve
- Better manufacturing capability
- Superior technological skills
- Other?

Potential External Opportunities

- Ability to serve additional customer groups or expand into new markets or segments
- Ways to expand product line to meet broader range of customer needs
- Ability to transfer skills or technological know-how to new products or businesses
- Integrating forward or backward
- Falling trade barriers in attractive foreign markets
- Complacency among rival firms
- Ability to grow rapidly because of strong increases in market demand
- Emerging new technologies

Potential Internal Weaknesses

- No clear strategic direction
- Obsolete facilities
- Subpar profitability because . . .
- Lack of managerial depth and talent
- Missing some key skills or competencies
- Poor track record in implementing strategy
- Plagued with internal operating problems
- Falling behind in R&D
- Too narrow a product line
- Weak market image
- Weak distribution network
- Below-average marketing skills
- Unable to finance needed changes in strategy
- Higher overall unit costs relative to key competitors
- Other?

Potential External Threats

- Entry of lower-cost foreign competitors
- Rising sales of substitute products
- Slower market growth
- Adverse shifts in foreign exchange rates and trade policies of foreign governments
- Costly regulatory requirements
- Vulnerability to recession and business cycle
- Growing bargaining power of customers or suppliers
- Changing buyer needs and tastes
- Adverse demographic changes
- Other?

Source: From Arthur A. Thompson, Jr., and A. J. Strickland III, *Strategic Management: Concepts and Cases*, 8th ed. Copyright © 1995 The McGraw-Hill Companies, Inc. Reprinted with permission.

company changed its strategy as a result of perceived changes in its external environment.

Comparing Strategic Alternatives

The goal in this stage of the formulation process is to identify the feasible strategic alternatives (in light of everything that has been done up to this point) and then select the best alternative. Given the mission and long-range objectives, what are the feasible strategic alternatives? The results of the SWOT analysis also limit the feasible strategic alternatives. For example, the results of an internal financial analysis could severely restrict an organization's options for expansion. Similarly, the results of an external analysis of population trends might also limit an organization's expansion plans. Once a set of feasible alternatives has been defined, the final strategic choice must be made.

The evaluation and final choice of an appropriate strategic alternative involves the integration of the mission, objectives, internal analysis, and external analysis. In this phase, management attempts to select the corporate strategy that offers the

Enesco Group Inc., located in Itasca, Illinois, is a maker of collectible figurines and other giftware. In 1996, Enesco's biggest selling product, a figurine known as Precious Moments, produced about $206 million in sales and accounted for 40 percent of total sales. By 2002, Precious Moments sales had dropped to about $96 million and represented 38 percent of a far smaller total amount.

Daniel DalleMolle was brought in from Newell Rubbermaid Inc. as president and CEO in March 2001, when Enesco was well into its revenue slide. Believing that the collectibles markets had weakened significantly and would continue to weaken, DalleMolle decided to change Enesco from a collectibles company into a giftware company. Part of the strategy for accomplishing this shift was to move into mass markets, such as Wal-Mart. It was decided to make a much cheaper Precious Moments in the form of a trinket to sell for as little as $2.99 (the original Precious Moments figures sold for between $24.99 and $300.00 each). The idea is to promote the brand, hoping that Wal-Mart customers might later find a gift shop where the collectible figurines remain exclusively. DalleMolle is also looking to acquire giftware makers that will take the company into higher-end retailers.

Source: Jeff Bailey, "Small Business Enterprise: What to Do When Your Hot Item Starts to Cool; Figurine Maker Seeks Out New Ideas for Marketing, Expands Line, Cuts Cost," *The Wall Street Journal,* September 16, 2003, p. B10.

---

organization its best chance to achieve its mission and objectives through actions that are compatible with its capacity for risk and its value structure. Once the corporate strategy has been identified, additional substrategies must be selected to support it.

In the case of diversified, multibusiness organizations, comparing strategic alternatives involves assessing the attractiveness of each business as well as the overall business mix. A **strategic business unit (SBU)** is a distinct business that has its own set of competitors and can be managed reasonably independently of other businesses within the organization.[14] The elements of an SBU vary from organization to organization but can be a division, a subsidiary, or a single product line. In a small organization, the entire company may be a SBU.

strategic business unit (SBU)
Distinct business that has its own set of competitors and can be managed reasonably independently of other businesses within the organization.

Implementing Strategy

After the corporate strategy has been carefully formulated, it must be translated into organizational actions. Given that the corporate strategy and business-level strategies have been clearly identified, what actions must be taken to implement them? Strategy implementation involves everything that must be done to put the strategy in motion successfully. Necessary actions include determining and implementing the most appropriate organizational structure, developing short-range objectives, and establishing functional strategies.

Organizational Factors

Not only does an organization have a strategic history; it also has existing structures, policies, and systems. Although each of these factors can change as a result of a new strategy, each must be assessed and dealt with as part of the implementation process.

Even though an organization's structure can always be altered, the associated costs may be high. For example, a reorganization may result in substantial hiring and training costs for newly structured jobs. Thus, from a practical standpoint, an organization's current structure places certain restrictions on strategy implementation.

The strategy must fit with current organizational policies, or the conflicting policies must be modified. Often past policies heavily influence the extent to

FIGURE 7.8
The Strategic Management Process

which future policies can be altered. For example, A. T. Cross Company, manufacturer of world-renowned writing instruments, has a policy of unconditionally guaranteeing its products for life. Because customers have come to expect this policy, Cross would find it difficult to discontinue it.

Similarly, organizational systems that are currently in place can affect how the strategy might best be implemented. These systems can be either formal or informal. Examples include information systems, compensation systems, communication systems, and control systems.

Functional Strategies

As introduced earlier in this chapter, functional strategies are the means by which business strategies are operationalized. Functional strategies outline the specific short-range actions to be taken by the different functional units of the organization (production, marketing, finance, human resource, etc.) to implement the business strategies. The development of functional strategies generally requires the active participation of many levels of management. In fact, input by lower levels of management at the development stage is essential to the successful implementation of functional strategies.

Evaluating and Controlling the Strategic Plan

After the strategic plan has been put into motion, the next challenge is to monitor continuously the organization's progress toward its long-range objectives and mission. Is the corporate strategy working, or should revisions be made? Where are problems likely to occur? The emphasis is on making the organization's managers aware of the problems that are likely to occur and of the actions to be taken if they do arise. As discussed earlier in this chapter, continuously evaluating and responding to internal and environmental changes is what strategic management is all about.

Figure 7.8 summarizes the strategic management process and its major components.

Summary

1. *Define planning and distinguish between formal and functional plans.* Planning is the process of deciding which objectives to pursue during a future time period and what to do to achieve those objectives. Formal planning occurs when a written, documented plan is developed through an identifiable process. Functional plans originate from the

functional areas of an organization, such as production, marketing, finance, and personnel.

2. *Contrast strategic planning with operational planning.* Strategic planning covers a relatively long period, affects many parts of the organization, and includes the formulation of objectives and the selection of the means for attaining those objectives. Operational or tactical planning is short range and concentrates on the formulation of functional strategies.

3. *Define strategy and explain the various levels of strategies.* A strategy outlines the basic steps management must take to reach an objective or a set of objectives. Corporate strategies (growth, stability, defensive, or combination) address what businesses an organization will be in and how resources will be allocated among those businesses. Business strategies (overall cost leadership, differentiation, and focus) concentrate on how to compete in a given business or industry. Functional strategies (production, marketing, finance, and personnel) deal with the activities of the different functional areas of the business.

4. *Define strategic management and explain the strategic management process.* Strategic management is the process of determining the long-run direction and performance of an organization by ensuring careful formulation, proper implementation, and continuous evaluation of plans and strategies. The major phases of the strategic management process are (1) formulating the strategic plan, (2) implementing the strategic plan, and (3) continuously evaluating and updating the strategic plan.

5. *Explain the differences between missions, objectives, policies, procedures, and rules.* The organization's mission defines the basic purpose or purposes of the organization and usually includes a description of the organization's basic products or services and a definition of its markets or sources of revenue. Objectives are statements outlining what the organization is trying to achieve; they give the organization and its members direction and purpose. Objectives can be long, intermediate, or short range in nature. Policies are broad, general guides to action that constrain or direct the attainment of objectives. Policies do not tell the organization what to do, but they do establish the boundaries within which it must operate. Procedures are a series of related steps or tasks expressed in chronological order for a specific purpose. Procedures emphasize details. Finally, rules require specific and definite actions to be taken or not to be taken in a given situation. Unlike procedures, rules do not have to specify sequence; they permit no flexibility or deviation.

6. *Discuss the components of a SWOT analysis.* SWOT is an acronym for an organization's strengths, weaknesses, opportunities, and threats. A SWOT analysis is a technique for evaluating an organization's internal strengths and weaknesses and its external opportunities and threats. A major advantage of using a SWOT analysis is that it provides a general overview of the organization's strategic situation.

7. *Define a strategic business unit (SBU).* An SBU is a distinct business that has its own set of competitors and can be managed reasonably independently of other businesses within the organization.

8. *Discuss what organizational factors need to be evaluated in implementing a strategic plan.* Not only does an organization have a strategic history; it also has existing structures, policies, and systems. Although each of these factors can change as a result of a new strategy, each must be assessed and dealt with as part of the implementation process.

Review Questions

1. Define planning. What questions does planning answer?
2. Why is it necessary to plan? Distinguish between formal and functional planning. How is most planning conducted?
3. What is the difference between strategic planning and operational planning? Between long-range and short-range planning?

4. What is a contingency plan?

5. Define strategy.

6. What are the major forms of strategy?

7. What are the four types of corporate strategy? What are the three forms of business strategy?

8. What are the steps in the strategic management process?

9. Define mission, objective, policy, procedure, and rule.

10. What does SWOT stand for?

11. Define a strategic business unit (SBU).

Skill-Building Questions

1. Why should one plan? What are the benefits of planning?

2. If you were serving as a strategic management consultant, how might you respond to the following question: How can I plan for next year when I don't even know what I'm going to do tomorrow?

3. As discussed on pages 130 and 131, strategic management is an activity that must emanate from top management. Given this, why should you, as a first-line or middle manager, be concerned with strategic management?

4. Comment on the following statement: Most organizations succeed or fail based on their ability to react to environmental changes.

Skill-Building Exercise 7.1

Developing a Personal Career Plan

One of the common threads many successful people share is that they developed a sense of direction relatively early in life. At the same time, it is common for people to enter and even graduate from college with little idea of what they want to do. Similarly, many people reach middle age only to ask, "How did I end up here?"

Questions

1. Apply the concepts discussed in this chapter and develop, in outline form, a 10-year plan for your own career.

2. Your outline need only be a few pages long. Begin with a statement of mission and work down through each step in the strategic management model. Be sure and include a SWOT analysis. Make your plan as realistic as possible.

3. Identify the major assumptions and environmental trends on which you based your plan.

4. What parts of your plan do you think will be the hardest to achieve?

The following article gives great guidance for developing your own career plan: Patricia Buhler, "Managing in the 90s," *Supervision*, May 1997, pp. 24–26.

Skill-Building Exercise 7.2

Ten Most Admired Companies

Every year, *Fortune* magazine publishes the results of a survey that attempts to identify the most admired among the largest companies in the United States. For 2004, the survey included 10,000 executives, directors, and analysts and 592 companies. The companies identified as the 10 most admired (in descending order) were

1. Wal-Mart
2. Berkshire Hathaway
3. Southwest Airlines
4. General Electric
5. Dell Computer

6. Microsoft
7. Johnson & Johnson
8. Starbucks
9. FedEx
10. IBM

The companies that scored the lowest on the most admired list for 2004 (in descending order) were

583.	Royal Ahold	588.	Fleming
584.	Tyco International	589.	Allete
585.	Trump Hotels and Casino Resorts	590.5.	Kmart*
586.	US Airways Group	590.5.	Tenet*
587.	Federal-Mogul	592.	UAL

* These companies tied.

Looking at the above lists, identify one or more trends or forces in the external environment that likely have affected the performance or ranking of these companies. Be prepared to share your ideas with the class.

Source: Ann Harrington, "America's Most Admired Companies," *Fortune,* March 8, 2004, pp. 80–82, 116.

Skill-Building Exercise 7.3

Making Assumptions

Translate the demographic data below into a set of assumptions for (*a*) a small community hospital, (*b*) an urban school system, and (*c*) Ford Motor Company.

How does this demographic data rank in importance with other environmental trends that might affect each of these organizations?

Percentage Increase in Population by Age Groups, 1980–1990

Ages	1980–1985	1985–1990	1980–1990
Under 15	3.4	70	10.6
15–17	–11.6	–10.3	–20.1
18–24	–5.4	–9.7	–13.6
25–34	10.2	3.0	13.5
35–44	22.2	16.6	42.4
45–54	–0.9	12.4	11.5
55–65	2.4	–4.1	–1.9
Over 65	9.6	9.1	19.6

Skill-Building Exercise 7.4

Environmental Forces

Summarized below are the descriptions of two environmental forces that could have an influence on the automobile industry. Describe the threats and opportunities that might face General Motors as a result of these environmental forces.

Social

Studies of social and economic trends in the 1990s present the auto industry with an enormous population of buyers who are predisposed to purchase and will have the financial means to buy new cars on a regular basis. Three demographic groups that will be particularly significant to the industry are baby boomers, women, and the elderly.

Maturing baby boomers will have far more disposable income available for automobile purchases, and a sizable upscale segment will favor luxury cars and sport-utility vehicles. Baby boomers and the elderly also will increase demand for recreational vehicles (RVs) while reducing the need for station wagons and minivans as their families mature. A large and growing blue-collar segment of the boomers, however, favors American cars and domestic minivans.

Women will increasingly become more involved in new-car purchases and are expected to exercise as much power in the automotive market as men. Automotive marketing successes of the 90s will be generated by advertising that prominently features women.

The final dominant group, which represents a "graying of America," is buyers 55 and older. They constitute 25 percent of new-car buyers, and this statistic will increase. Older buyers will look for features that make driving safer and easier, including electronic systems to warn drivers who are getting drowsy, nonglare instrument panels, and simplified electronic controls.

Technological

The cars of tomorrow will be loaded with convenience features and intelligent systems: smart computers that run the engine and transmission more efficiently, electronic suspension systems, radar obstacle detection to help drivers avoid accidents, and navigation systems that will help drivers avoid traffic jams while video screens indicate alternate routes. Self-tinting glass and infrared technology that enhances night vision also will be available. Antilock brakes, air bags, and traction control will become standard.

The use of space-age plastics will increase because they are lightweight, less expensive than steel, and noncorrosive. New techniques for making models and prototypes quickly and inexpensively using sophisticated computers are the wave of the future, and 10,000 electric cars are slated for use in southern California in the next five years.

The extensive use of robotic technology in production will increase, and automobile manufacturers will develop cars for the future that will run on alternative fuels.

Skill-Building Exercise 7.5

Word Associations

This exercise is designed to demonstrate how the establishment of a realistic and specific goal can help you improve your performance. You will be given four words and your task is to identify a fifth word that has a common association with each of the four words in a given set. For example, what word has a common association with each of the following?

sleeping   contest   spot   shop

The answer is *beauty*.

Now that you understand the game, time yourself and see how many of the following sets you can do in *two* minutes.

1. cross	baby	blood	ribbon	_____
2. touch	palate	soap	sell	_____
3. tree	cup	cake	forbidden	_____
4. dust	movie	gaze	sapphire	_____
5. alley	date	snow	spot	_____
6. rest	post	linen	fellow	_____
7. opera	no	box	stone	_____
8. storage	shoulder	comfort	cream	_____
9. business	suit	wrench	shine	_____
10. bug	rest	fellow	cover	_____

Your instructor will give you the correct answers. Based on the number you got right, set the following goal for the next exercise:

If you got 1 or 2 correct, your new goal is 4.

If you got 3 or 4 correct, your new goal is 7.

If you got 5 or more correct, your new goal is 9.

Do you consider this new goal challenging? Impossible? Now, striving to make your new goal, see how many of the following sets you can do in *two* minutes.

1. days	biscuit	collar	ear	_____
2. play	breast	pox	wire	_____
3. guy	crack	up	man	_____
4. ball	trouser	fruit	house	_____
5. dress	good	star	prayer	_____
6. stone	jacket	fever	pages	_____
7. bathtub	wedding	telephone	key	_____
8. horse	brake	left	box	_____
9. right	pike	your	stile	_____
10. bulldog	cuff	toast	windows	_____

Your instructor will give you the correct answers. How did you do relative to your score on the first set? Do you think that having a specific goal affected your score on the second exercise?

Source: This exercise is adapted from Henry Tosi and Jerald W. Young, *Management Experiences and Demonstrations* (Homewood, IL: Richard D. Irwin, 1982), pp. 35–38, 166, 183.

Case Incident 7.1

First in the Market

Juan Peron is a process engineer employed by Vantage Engineering, Inc., and assigned to the research laboratory in the Advanced Products Division (APD). Vantage is a well-established manufacturer of military hardware. APD's general purpose is to conduct research to improve the company's military hardware products. However, the laboratory director was recently given permission to develop spin-off products for possible sale on the open market.

Juan spent his first year in APD assisting on various project assignments. At the end of that year, he was put in charge of a special project to research a chemically processed wood for specialty applications. During the initial stages of the project, Juan spent most of his time in the laboratory becoming familiar with the basic aspects of the treatment process. However, he soon tired of the long, tedious experimental work and became more and more eager to move quickly into the promotion and marketing of the product. This desire was soon realized. An article in a recent national trade publication had generated keen interest in a similar wood product, and as a result, Vantage immediately allocated several thousand dollars to the development and marketing of the chemically processed wood. Simultaneously, a minor reorganization occurred, placing Juan and his project under the direction of Greg Waites, a close friend of Juan's. Thus, Juan had an opportunity to get out of the lab and become involved in the more desirable promotion and marketing aspects.

Juan and Greg soon began traveling nationally, discussing the new product with potential customers. Traveling enabled Juan to spend less and less time in the lab, and as a result many of the experiments required to determine the performance characteristics of the new product were left unfinished. As the number of companies demonstrating an interest in purchasing small quantities for trial applications grew, Juan suggested to Greg that a small pilot plant be constructed. In response to Greg's concerns regarding the performance characteristics of the wood, Juan assured him the preliminary tests indicated the wood could be successfully produced. Juan contended that Vantage had to get a head start on the newly created market before everyone else got into the game, that they should build the pilot plant immediately to fill the sudden influx of orders and then worry about completing the performance tests. Greg, seeing the advantages of getting into the market first, finally agreed, and construction of the pilot plant began shortly thereafter.

During construction, Juan and Greg continued traveling to promote the wood. When the pilot plant was near completion, Juan went to Vantage's personnel department and requested that three laborers be hired to operate the plant. Juan intended to personally direct the technical operations and thus saw no need to establish elaborate job descriptions for the positions.

A week later, Juan had his three employees. Due to a workload reduction in the Electronics Division of Vantage, the employees filling these positions had taken the laborer jobs to avoid being laid off. One had been a purchasing agent, and the others had been electronics technicians. At the beginning of the workday, Juan would drop by the plant and give directions to the crew for the entire day before departing to make sales calls. No formal leader had been appointed, and the three laborers, knowing little about the chemical process involved, were instructed to "use common sense and ingenuity."

A month after the plant operations had gotten under way, a major producer of archery bows requested an order for 70,000 bow handles to be delivered in time to be sold for the upcoming hunting season. It was too good to be true! Juan knew that if they accepted the order, the first year of operations would be guaranteed to be in the black. On receiving the product specifications, Juan persuaded Greg to sign the contract, arguing that they would be throwing all their hard work down the drain if they didn't. Subsequently, a crash program was established at the plant to get the order out on time.

One month after the final shipment of handles had been made, Juan hired a junior engineer, Libby Adams, to conduct the performance experiments that had been disbanded while the plant was getting the rush order out. Libby examined some of the experimental handles and discovered hairline cracks at various stress points that had not appeared during the initial examination. She immediately went to Juan's office to inform him of the problem and found Juan and Greg sitting there with a telegram from the archery company. It stated that several retail merchants had returned bows with hairline cracks in the handles and that the archery company would seek a settlement for its entire investment in the handles.

Vantage paid the settlement and subsequently canceled the wood project.

Questions

1. What caused the wood project to fail?
2. Would a more effective strategy on the part of Juan and Greg have helped ensure the success of the project?
3. At what stage of the strategic management process did the breakdown occur?
4. What general observations can be made to prevent such a situation from occurring again?

Source: From Patricia Buhler, "Managing in the 90s," *Supervision,* May 1997. Reprinted by permission of © National Research Bureau, 320 Valley Street, Burlington, Iowa 52601.

Case Incident 7.2

Hudson Shoe Company

John Hudson, president of Hudson Shoe Company, and his wife spent the month of February on a long vacation in Santo Oro in Central America. After two weeks, Mr. Hudson became restless and started thinking about an idea he had considered for several years but had been too busy to pursue—entering the foreign market.

Mr. Hudson's company, located in a midwestern city, was started some 50 years earlier by his father, now deceased. It has remained a family enterprise, with his brother David in charge of production, his brother Sam the comptroller, and his brother-in-law Bill Owens taking care of product development. Bill and David share responsibility for quality control; Bill often works with Sam on administrative matters and advertising campaigns. Many competent subordinates are also employed. The company has one of the finest reputations in the shoe industry. The product integrity is to be envied and is a source of great pride to the company.

During John's stay in Santo Oro, he decided to visit some importers of shoes. He spoke to several and was most impressed with Señor Lopez of Bueno Compania. After checking Señor Lopez's bank and personal references, his impression was confirmed. Señor Lopez said he would place a small initial order if the samples proved satisfactory. John immediately phoned his office and requested the company rush samples of its best-sellers to Señor Lopez. These arrived a few days before John left for home. Shortly after arriving home, John was pleased to receive an order for 1,000 pairs of shoes from Señor Lopez.

John stayed in touch with Lopez by telephone; within two months after the initial order, Hudson Shoe received an order for 5,000 additional pairs of shoes per month. Business continued at this level for about two years until Señor Lopez visited the plant. He was impressed and increased his monthly order from 5,000 to 10,000 pairs of shoes.

This precipitated a crisis at Hudson Shoe Company, and the family held a meeting. They had to decide whether to increase their capacity with a sizable capital investment or drop some of their customers. They did not like the idea of eliminating loyal customers but did not want to make a major investment. David suggested they run a second shift, which solved the problem nicely.

A year later, Lopez again visited and left orders for 15,000 pairs per month. He also informed them that more effort and expense was now required on his part for a wide distribution of the shoes. In addition to his regular 5 percent commission, he asked John for an additional commission of $2 per pair of shoes. When John hesitated, Lopez assured him that Hudson could raise its selling price by $2 and nothing would be lost. John felt uneasy but went along because the business was easy, steady, and most profitable. A few of Hudson's smaller customers had to be dropped.

By the end of the next year, Lopez was placing orders for 20,000 pairs per month. He asked that Hudson bid on supplying boots for the entire police force of the capital city of Santo Oro. Hudson received the contract and within a year, was supplying the army and navy of Santo Oro and three other Central American countries with their needs.

Again, several old Hudson customers could not get their orders filled. Other Hudson customers were starting to complain of late deliveries. Also, Hudson seemed to be less willing to accept returns at the end of the season or to offer markdown allowances or advertising money. None of this was necessary with its export business. However, Hudson Shoe did decide to cling to its largest domestic customer—the largest mail-order chain in the United States.

In June of the following year, Lopez made a trip to Hudson Shoe. He informed John that in addition to his $2 per pair, it would be necessary to give the minister of revenue $2 per pair if he was to continue granting import licenses. Moreover, the defense ministers, who approved the army and navy orders in each country where they did business, also wanted $2 per pair. Again, selling prices could be increased accordingly. Lopez informed John that shoe manufacturers in the United States and two other countries were most eager to have this business at any terms. John asked for 10 days to discuss this with his partners. Lopez agreed and returned home to await their decision. The morning of the meeting of the board of directors of the Hudson Shoe Company, a wire was received from the domestic chain stating it would not be buying from Hudson next season. John Hudson called the meeting to order.

Questions

1. What were the objectives of Hudson Shoe?
2. What policies existed?
3. How would you evaluate John Hudson's plans?
4. What would you do if you were John Hudson?

References and Additional Readings

1. J. J. Hemphill, "Personal Variables and Administrative Styles," in *Behavioral Science and Educational Administration* (Chicago: National Society for the Study of Education, 1964), chap. 8.
2. A. L. Comrey, W. High, and R. C. Wilson, "Factors Influencing Organization Effectiveness: A Survey of Aircraft Workers," *Personnel Psychology* 8 (1955), pp. 79–99.
3. For a discussion of these studies, see John A. Pearce II, Elizabeth B. Freeman, and Richard D. Robinson, Jr., "The Tenuous Link between Formal Strategic Planning and Financial Performance," *Academy of Management Review,* October 1987, pp. 658–73; and

Mike Schraeder, "A Simplified Approach to Strategic Planning," *Business Process Management Journal* 8, no. 1 (2002), pp. 11–21.

4. George A. Steiner, *Top Management Planning* (New York: Macmillan, 1969), p. 237.

5. Michael E. Porter, *Competitive Strategy: Techniques for Analyzing Industries and Competitors* (New York: Free Press, 1980).

6. Porter, *Competitive Strategy*, pp. 37–38.

7. Patricia Braus, "What Does 'Hispanic' Mean?" *American Demographics*, June 1993, pp. 46–49, 58.

8. Peter F. Drucker, *The Practice of Management* (New York: Harper & Row, 1954), p. 51.

9. Ibid., pp. 50–57.

10. Anthony Raia, *Managing by Objectives* (Glenview, IL: Scott, Foresman, 1974), p. 38.

11. Arthur A. Thompson, Jr., and A. J. Strickland III, *Strategic Management: Concepts and Cases*, 7th ed. (Burr Ridge, IL: Richard D. Irwin, 1993), p. 87.

12. Porter, *Competitive Strategy*.

13. Thompson and Strickland, *Strategic Management*, p. 90.

14. George A. Steiner, John B. Miner, and Edmond R. Gray, *Management Policy and Strategy*, 2nd ed. (New York: Macmillan, 1982), p. 189.

Chapter

Operations Management and Planning

Learning Objectives

After studying this chapter, you will be able to:

1. Define operations management.
2. Describe an operating system, and identify the two basic types of operating systems.
3. Differentiate among product/service design, process selection, and site selection decisions.
4. Explain what a materials-handling system is.
5. Describe and give an example of the three basic classifications of facilities layouts.
6. Explain the sociotechnical approach to job design.
7. Describe several computer-related technologies that are currently playing major roles in production/operations management.
8. Outline the three major steps in developing an aggregate operations plan.
9. Summarize the differences between resource allocation and activity scheduling.
10. Distinguish between Gantt charts, the critical path method (CPM), and the program evaluation and review technique (PERT).

Chapter Preview

Igus Inc., which is located in Germany, makes more than 28,000 different products that are used in everything from assembly lines to the movable stage for Broadway's *Beauty and the Beast.* Because of the unpredictability of its customers' needs, Igus has to be able to react quickly and is in a state of almost constant innovation. What's different about Igus is the plant's design that enables it to operate exceptionally flexibly. Employees buzz around the plant's enormous space—about the size of three football fields—on shiny scooters. Very little equipment is bolted down, so machines and modular furniture can be rearranged in a moment's notice. Easily accessible, exposed overhead electrical wiring and few obstructive support columns allow Igus to expand, shrink, or relocate departments with minimal disruption. Glass walls separate the factory floor from the office area, which eliminates any real or perceived barriers between departments. The plant has only one cafeteria, one set of restrooms, and one entrance. Additionally, the parking lot has no designated spaces for managers. According to Frank Blase, Igus' president, "We're trying to be a different kind of company, and our building helps us tremendously in doing that. It creates a holistic system for how to behave."

Sources: Chuck Salter, "This Is One Fast Factory," *Fast Company,* August 2001, pp. 32–33; and Michelle Porter, "Fast and Fluid Factory," *Plants, Sites and Parks,* October–November 2001, p. 8.

Analyzing Management Skills

To what extent do you think the layout and physical facilities of the workplace are important?

Applying Management Skills

Suppose you were designing a small store for selling office supplies to college students. What are some of the major factors you would want to consider in your design?

operations management
Application of the basic concepts and principles of management to those segments of the organization that produce its goods or services.

operations planning
Designing the systems of the organization that produce goods or services; planning the day-to-day operations within those systems.

Operations management, which evolved from the field of production or manufacturing management, deals with the application of the basic concepts and principles of management to those segments of the organization that produce the organization's goods or services. Traditionally, the term *production* brings to mind such things as smokestacks, machine shops, and the manufacture of real goods. Operations management is the management of the production function in any organization—private or public, profit or nonprofit, manufacturing or service.

Operations planning is concerned with designing the systems of the organization that produce the goods or services and with the planning of the day-to-day operations within those systems. The design of the systems that produce the goods or services is a long-range and strategic planning issue, whereas the planning of the day-to-day operations is a short-range and tactical planning issue. This chapter introduces some basic concepts related to operations management, discusses the basic design-related aspects of operations, and covers the day-to-day planning of operations.

The Importance of Operations Management

The operations function is only one part of the total organization; however, it is a very important part. The production of goods or services often involves the bulk of an organization's financial assets, personnel, and expenses. The operations process also usually takes up an appreciable amount of time. Thus, because of the resources and time consumed by operations, the management of this function plays a critical role in achieving the organization's goals.

Effective operations managers directly influence employee output by (1) building group cohesiveness and individual commitment and (2) making sound technical and administrative decisions. Both tasks have become more complex and important in recent years. Society wants not only improved productivity but also an enriched work environment. Demands for expanded education, child care, enriched benefits, flextime options, and more attention to workplace safety have all caused gaps between employees and management. The human problems confronting operations management have therefore become more important and more challenging.

Most operations managers no longer manage in a stable environment with standard products. Changing technology and a strong emphasis on low costs have altered the technical and administrative problems they confront. The modern operations manager must deal not only with low costs but also with product diversity, a demand for high quality, short lead times, and a rapidly changing technology. As a result, an operations manager's problems are now greater and require much more managerial talent than ever before.

Operating Systems and Activities

operating systems
Consist of the processes and activities necessary to turn inputs into goods or services.

Operating systems consist of the processes and activities necessary to turn inputs into goods or services. Operating systems exist in all organizations; they are made up of people, materials, facilities, and information. The end result of an operating system is to add value by improving, enhancing, or rearranging the inputs. Many operating systems take a collection of parts and form them into a more valuable whole. For example, an automobile is a group of separate parts formed into a more valuable whole.

In some situations, the operating system breaks something down from a larger quantity to smaller quantities with more value. A metal shop cuts smaller parts from larger sheets of metal; a butcher produces steaks, hamburger, and other cuts from a side of beef. Both break down a larger quantity into smaller quantities with more value.

A third type of operating system produces services by turning inputs into more useful outputs. Here more emphasis is usually placed on labor and less on materials. For example, an electronics repair shop uses some materials, but the primary value results from the repairer's labor.

Figure 8.1 presents a simplified model of an operating system. The operating system is broader and more inclusive than just the conversion or transformation process. It includes not only the design and operation of the process but also many of the activities needed to get the various inputs (such as product design and scheduling) into the transformation process. Inputs can take on numerous forms (such as managers, workers, equipment, facilities, materials, or information). Many of the activities necessary to get the outputs out of the transformation process (such as inventory control and materials distribution) are also included. Management Illustration 8.1 discusses the most famous operating system in the automotive industry.

continuous flow system
Operating system used by companies that produce large amounts of similar products/services flowing through similar stages of the operating system.

Basic Types of Operating Systems

There are two basic types of operating systems. One is based on continuous flows and the other on intermittent flows. Organizations with a **continuous flow system** generally have a standardized product or service. This product or service is

The most famous operating system in the automotive industry is the Toyota Production System (TPS). Initially established in the late 1940s, the Toyota operating system is based on the concept of "lean manufacturing." Lean manufacturing is an approach to manufacturing that attempts to minimize everything, from work in process, to part counts, to labor hours. This approach not only reduces cost, it also increases pressure to get things done more quickly as well as correctly.

One of the fundamental elements that makes TPS successful is the commitment to the customer-first philosophy. However, Toyota views the customer as not only the entity that purchases the final product at the end of the process but each succeeding process or workstation or department in the production process. Under the TPS there are no artificial barriers that wall off one area from another or one department from another. Rather, the entire organization shares problems and must work together to ensure that a solution is found.

Sources: Gary Vasilash, "Three Ways to Succeed," *Automotive Design and Production,* March 2003, p. 8; Gary Convis, "Learning to Think Lean: Role of Management in a Lean Manufacturing Environment," *Automotive Manufacturing and Production,* July 2001, pp. 64–65; and Gary S. Vasilash, "Going Places and Getting Things Done: Think Operating Systems," *Automotive Manufacturing and Production,* April 1998, pp. 62–65.

often advertised and is immediately available to the customer. The post office, paper mills, petroleum refineries, assembly plants, and fast-food outlets with standardized products (such as McDonald's) are examples. The continuous type of operation has relatively large volumes of identical or similar products or services flowing through similar stages of the operating system.

intermittent flow system
Operating system used when customized products and services are produced.

The second type of operating system, the **intermittent flow** (or *job shop)* **system,** produces customized products and services. Because of its customized nature, organizations using an intermittent operating system usually do not keep an inventory of finished products or offer standardized services. Intermittent flow systems include special-order fabrication shops, hospitals, advertising agencies, and dental offices. Technological advances in the last several years have lowered the per-unit costs associated with many intermittent flow systems.

The continuous flow system usually results in lower unit costs than the intermittent flow system because of economies of scale, specialized labor, and high

FIGURE 8.1
Simplified Model of an Operating System

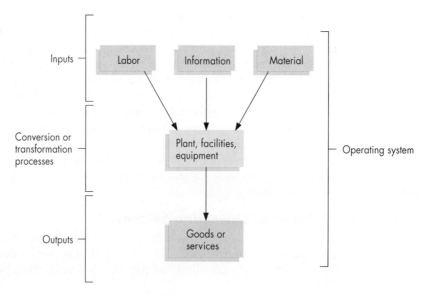

equipment use. However, continuous flow systems usually require special-purpose equipment that is less flexible and usually more expensive than general-purpose equipment. An example is the customized equipment and machinery used in an automobile assembly plant. Inputs can take on numerous forms (such as managers, workers, equipment, facilities, materials, or information).

To understand the difference between the two types of operating systems, consider the difference between McDonald's and Taco Bell. McDonald's uses a continuous flow operating system. It makes a certain number of products, based on sales history, and hopes people will buy them. Taco Bell uses an intermittent flow operating system. It does not produce anything until a customer places an order.

Product/Service Design

An organization's product or service determines the design of its operating systems. The design of a new product/service or the redesign of an existing product/service may lead to extensive systems redesign, equipment changes, new personnel, and other modifications. Consider the redesign necessary just to change from one year's automobile models to the next year's models. The design can be functionally sound, yet not economical to produce. Of course, specific functional design objectives must be achieved; however, several alternative designs are often available. When such choices exist, production costs should certainly be one criterion used in the decision.

Historically, design engineers have encountered conflict with operations managers. Design engineers are technically oriented and sometimes lack concern for production methods and costs. On the other hand, operations managers may care more about the production costs and requirements than about the functional requirements of the product. A good example of these differences occurred at Boeing Aircraft in the mid-1990s. During this period, Boeing won a $1.2 billion order from SAS; a chief component of the deal was Boeing's promise to slash the cost of its planes by one-third. However, cutting prices without knowing where the matching savings would come from was not only a gamble but an operations manager's nightmare. When asked to comment, CEO Frank Shrontz said, "We have been technically excellent but [production] process-poor, and we have to change. Now common goals and close communication between design and operations is not only a necessity at Boeing but a mandate."[1] Close communication that fosters an appreciation by both engineers and managers for the common objective of producing a functional product or service at minimum cost is certainly in the best interest of Boeing.

Process Selection

process selection
Specifies in detail the processes and sequences required to transform inputs into products or services.

Process selection includes a wide range of decisions about the specific process to be used, the basic sequences of the process, and the equipment to be employed. As suggested earlier, the product/service design decisions and the process selection decisions should be closely coordinated.

The processes and equipment used can play a large role in whether the product or service is competitive. The importance of the process selection decision has become magnified in some industries with the advent of robotics. This is clearly evident in the steel and automotive industries; the Japanese steel and automotive industries have much more modern production processes than their American counterparts. At the most basic level, the types of processes that are normally considered in managerial planning can be categorized as follows: (1) conversion processes (e.g., changing iron ore into steel sheets), (2) fabrication processes (e.g., changing raw materials into some specific form, such as in making sheet metal into a car bumper), (3) assembly processes (e.g., assembling a fender to a car), and (4) testing processes (not usually functional processes but incorporated to ensure quality control).[2] Understanding which process is needed or is in operation is thought to be a key to efficiently organizing production.

Once the overall type of operations process has been selected, specific decisions are needed regarding such factors as whether to use general- or special-purpose equipment, whether to make or buy the components, and how much to automate. In equipment decisions, several factors beyond normal cost should be considered:

1. Availability of operators.
2. Training required for operators.
3. Maintenance record and potential.
4. Availability of parts and services.
5. Supplier assistance in installation and debugging.
6. Compatibility with existing equipment.
7. Flexibility of equipment in handling product variation.
8. Safety of equipment.
9. Expected delivery date.
10. Warranty coverage.

In process selection, the overriding objective is to specify in detail the most economical processes and sequences required to transform the inputs into the desired product or service.

Facilities Layout

facilities layout
Process of planning the optimal physical arrangement of facilities, including personnel, operating equipment, storage space, office space, materials-handling equipment, and room for customer or product movement.

After the product/service design has been established, the facilities layout should be planned. **Facilities layout** is essentially the process of planning the optimal physical arrangement of facilities, which includes personnel, operating equipment, storage space, office space, materials-handling equipment, and room for customer service and movement. Facilities layout integrates all of the previous planning of the design process into one physical system. Facilities layout decisions are needed for a number of reasons, including

1. Construction of a new or an additional facility.
2. Obsolescence of current facilities.
3. Changes in demand.
4. Development of a new or redesigned product or process.
5. Personnel considerations: frequent accidents, poor working environment, or prohibitive supervisory costs.

Demand forecasts for the product or service must be considered in establishing the productive capacity of the organization. The costs of running short on space and equipment must be balanced against the costs of having idle space and equipment. A good approach is to match space needs with estimates of future demand but purchase equipment only as it is needed. This allows quick capacity expansion and avoids the costs of idle equipment.

Materials Handling

The materials used and how they are moved around in manufacturing a product or producing a service can have a significant influence on the facility layout. The size, shape, weight, density, and even the flexibility of the materials used can affect the layout. Some materials require special handling and storage with regard to factors such as temperature, humidity, light, dust, and vibration. A materials-handling system is the entire network that receives materials, stores materials, moves materials between processing points and between buildings, and positions the final product or service for delivery to the ultimate customer.

The design and layout of the facilities must be closely coordinated with the design of the materials-handling system. Materials-handling specialists James Apple and Leon McGinnis believe the chief difficulty in this area that needs to be overcome through innovative management is the failure to realize that this function should be a "factory integrator," the thread that ties the system together. In fact, process planning and the production scheduling and control systems should incorporate materials-handling system needs and limitations (such as wide aisles in the plant to accommodate forklifts) as part of their design and not ignore the complexity of the function. This new view of the materials-handling function would include attention to the (1) handling unit and container design, (2) micromovement (within a production workplace), (3) macromovement (between operations), (4) staging and storage of materials, and (5) control system for directing and tracking activity.[3]

In light of this view, consider two divergent trends currently taking place in the U.S. manufacturing environment. At one extreme is a movement toward simplicity with less mechanization (surprisingly, this trend is also occurring in Japan, which already has the advantage of flexibility). At the other extreme is the tendency to develop highly complex and automated systems. Today's manager must be ready to learn about and adapt to both trends. While the design of any materials-handling system depends on the specifics of the situation, the principles outlined in Figure 8.2 generally apply.

Basic Layout Classifications

Most layouts are one of three types: product layout, process layout, or fixed-position layout. Which type of layout is used usually depends on the type of product or service produced.

FIGURE 8.2
Materials-Handling Principles

Source: From *Production & Operations Management*, 5th edition—HSIE 5th edition, by Norman Gaither. Copyright © 1992. Reprinted with permission of South-Western College Publishing, a division of Thomson Learning.

1. Materials should move through the facility in direct flow patterns, minimizing zigzagging or backtracking.
2. Related production processes should be arranged to provide for direct material flows.
3. Mechanical materials-handling devices should be designed and located, and material storage locations should be selected so that human effort expended through bending, reaching, lifting, and walking is minimized.
4. Heavy or bulky materials should be moved the shortest distance through locating the processes that use them near receiving and shipping areas.
5. The number of times each material is moved should be minimized.
6. Systems flexibility should allow for unexpected situations such as materials-handling equipment breakdowns, changes in production system technology, and future expansion of production capacities.
7. Mobile equipment should carry full loads at all times; empty and partial loads should be avoided.

product layout
Facilities layout that arranges equipment or services according to the progressive steps by which the product is made or the customer is served.

Product layouts usually occur in continuous flow operating systems. In a **product layout,** equipment or services are arranged according to the progressive steps by which the product is made or the customer is serviced. A product layout is generally used when a standardized product is made in large quantities. The assembly line is the ultimate product layout. Automobile assembly plants, cafeterias, and standardized testing centers are normally product layout oriented. In a product layout, all the equipment or services necessary to produce a product or completely serve a customer are located in one area.

A product layout is efficient because it simplifies production planning. It also allows workers to specialize in a small number of simple tasks. This kind of layout can cause problems. First, workers who perform a limited number of repetitive tasks often grow bored. Second, an assembly line can move only as fast as the slowest link in the chain.

process layout
Facilities layout that groups together equipment or services of a similar functional type.

Process layouts are generally used in intermittent flow operating systems. In a **process layout,** equipment or services of a similar functional type are arranged or grouped together. All X-ray machines are grouped together; all reproduction equipment is grouped together; all drilling machines are grouped together; and so forth. Custom fabrication shops, hospitals, and restaurants are usually arranged in this fashion. With a process layout, a product/customer moves from area to area in the desired sequence of functional operations. When the product or service is not standardized or when the volume of similar products or customers in service at any one time is low, a process layout is preferred because of its flexibility.

The main advantage of the process layout is that employees perform a wider variety of tasks than do people working on assembly lines. As a result, they are less likely to become bored at their jobs and more likely to perform well. A disadvantage of the process layout is that it requires high-skilled workers.

fixed-position layout
A type of facilities layout where the product is too large to move and remains in one place.

The third type of layout is the **fixed-position layout.** In this, the product is too large to move and remains in one place. Manufacturing of very large products, such as ships or airplanes, and construction of most houses and buildings use a fixed-position layout. A disadvantage of the fixed-position layout is that it is not always as efficient as a product layout or process layout.

Site Selection

Management should carefully consider site location. It is easy to become overly engrossed in the operating details and techniques and ignore the importance of site location. Location is an ongoing question; it does not arise only when a facility is outgrown or obsolete. Location decisions relate to offices, warehouses, service centers, and branches, as well as the parent facility. Each site selection decision involves the total production/distribution system of the organization. Therefore, not only the location of new facilities should be examined; the location of present facilities should also be regularly reviewed for the most effective production/distribution system.

Several options exist for expanding capacity when the present facility is overcrowded:

1. Subcontract work.
2. Add another shift.
3. Work overtime.
4. Move operation to a larger facility.

FIGURE 8.3
Factors to Be
Considered in Site
Location

1. Revenue
   a. Location of customers and accessibility
   b. Location of competitors
2. Operating costs
   a. Price of materials
   b. Transportation costs: materials, products, people
   c. Wage rates
   d. Taxes: income, property, sales
   e. Utility rates
   f. Rental rates
   g. Communication costs
3. Investment
   a. Cost of land
   b. Cost of construction
4. Other limiting factors
   a. Availability of labor with appropriate skills
   b. Availability of materials, utilities, supplies
   c. Union activity
   d. Community attitudes and culture
   e. Political situation
   f. Pollution restrictions
   g. Climate
   h. General living conditions

5. Expand the current facility.
6. Keep the current facility and add another facility elsewhere.

A decision to expand on site, move the entire operation to a larger facility, or add another facility elsewhere means management faces a location decision. A survey of Fortune 500 firms showed that 45 percent of expansions were on site, 43 percent were in new plants at new locations, and only 12 percent were relocations. The popularity of on-site expansions was thought to be due to the advantages of keeping management together, reducing construction time and costs, and avoiding splitting up operations. However, there are arguments for building new plants or relocating. According to Lee Krajewski and Larry Ritzman, reasons for taking these actions might be poor materials handling, employee "job bumping," increasingly complex production control, and a simple lack of space.[4]

Two primary concerns still tend to dominate the location decision, however. The first is financial in nature. Figure 8.3 indicates the principal considerations affecting the financial decision. The second, and no less important, concern is the quality-of-life factor. Most firms are finding out, as Saturn Corporation did when it located in Spring Hill, Tennessee, that attractiveness of location (beauty, terrain, climate, etc.), business climate and community interest, proximity to sources of quality education, availability of well-established employee training facilities and resources, and a climate conducive to innovative entrepreneurship are factors that cannot be ignored in a location decision.[5] The final choice of the site should be a compromise on all the above factors. Management Illustration 8.2 describes some of the criteria used by Owens-Illinois in selecting the location of its newest glass container plant.

Job Design

job design
Designates the specific work activities of an individual or a group of individuals.

Job design specifies the work activities of an individual or a group of individuals. Job design answers the question of how the job is to be performed, who is to perform it, and where it is to be performed.

The job design process generally proceeds in three phases:

1. The specification of individual tasks.
2. The specification of the method of performing each task.
3. The combination of individual tasks into specific jobs to be assigned to individuals.[6]

Owens-Illinois, Inc., first announced plans to build a new 500,000-square-foot glass container plant in February 2003. Right after the announcement, company officials began working with local economic development boards, state and local government officials, environmental agencies, and civic leaders in northeast Colorado and southeast Wyoming to select a precise location.

The company evaluated potential sites based on operational and logistical criteria, including proximity to its customer base and accessibility to natural gas, power, highways, railroads, and labor pool. The location selected for the plant was near Windsor, Colorado.

Construction is slated to begin as soon as designs are finalized and permit applications have been approved. Owens-Illinois hopes to start production at the new plant in January 2005.

Source: "Owens-Illinois Selects Colorado for New Glass Container Plant," *Toledo Business Journal,* October 1, 2003, p. 27.

Phases 1 and 3 determine the content of the job; phase 2 identifies the specific methods to be used to perform the job.

Job Content

job content
Aggregate of all the work tasks the jobholder may be asked to perform.

Job content is the sum of all the work tasks the jobholder may be asked to perform. Starting with the scientific management movement, job design focused on the most efficient way to do a job. This usually meant minimizing short-run costs by minimizing unit operation time. Thus, the number of tasks a jobholder was assigned was small. The obvious problem with this approach is that the job can become overly routine and repetitive, which leads to motivational problems in the form of boredom, absenteeism, turnover, and perhaps low performance. One fact greatly complicates the job design process: Different people react differently to similar jobs. In other words, what is boring and routine to one person is not necessarily boring and routine to another. Figure 8.4 illustrates the most commonly recognized advantages and disadvantages of job specialization.

Job Methods

job method
Manner in which the human body is used, the arrangement of the workplace, and the design of the tools and equipment used.

The next step in the job design process is to determine the precise methods to be used to perform the job. The optimal **job method** is a function of the manner in which the human body is used, the arrangement of the workplace, and the design of the tools and equipment used.[7] The main purpose of job method design is to find the one best way to do a job. Normally, job methods are determined after the basic process and physical layout have been established.

Motion study is used in designing jobs. It involves determining the necessary motions and movements to perform a job or task and then designing the most efficient method for putting these motions and movements together.

ergonomics
Study of the interface between people and machines.

Ergonomics is the study of the interface between people and machines. A primary concern of ergonomics is that the equipment and the workplace be designed to make jobs as physically easy as possible.

Job methods designers have traditionally concentrated on manual tasks. However, the basic concept of finding the one best way applies to all types of jobs.

Job Characteristics

Job design can also be described in terms of five key characteristics:

FIGURE 8.4
Advantages and Disadvantages of Specialization of Labor

Source: Richard B. Chase, F. Robert Jacobs, and Nicholas J. Aquilano, *Operations Management for Competitive Advantage*, 10th ed., 2003, p. 127; copyright © by The McGraw-Hill Companies. Reproduced with permission of The McGraw-Hill Companies.

Advantages of Specialization	
To Management	**To Labor**
1. Rapid training of the workforce. 2. Ease in recruiting new workers. 3. High output due to simple and repetitive work. 4. Low wages due to ease of substitutability of labor. 5. Close control over work flow and workloads.	1. Little or no education required to obtain work. 2. Ease in learning job.
Disadvantages of Specialization	
To Management	**To Labor**
1. Difficulty in controlling quality since no one person has responsibility for entire product. 2. Worker dissatisfaction leading to hidden costs arising from turnover, absenteeism, tardiness, grievances, and intentional disruption of production process. 3. Reduced likelihood of improving the process because of workers' limited perspective. 4. Limited flexibility to change the production process to produce new or improved products.	1. Boredom stemming from repetitive nature of work. 2. Little gratification from work itself because of small contribution to each item. 3. Little or no control over the workplace, leading to frustration and fatigue (in assembly-line situations). 4. Little opportunity to progress to a better job since significant learning is rarely possible on fractionated work.

- Skill variety
- Task identity
- Task significance
- Autonomy
- Feedback

Skill variety refers to the number of different skills an employee needs to perform a job. Security officers who only check people's bags as they enter a building have little skill variety in their jobs. People whose jobs demand little skill variety often become bored at work.

Task identity refers to the degree to which a job allows an employee to complete an entire task rather than just part of the task. Mechanics who work at small garages have a high degree of task identity because they are responsible for every aspect of the job of repairing cars. In contrast, mechanics on assembly lines that do nothing but check transmissions have a lower degree of task identity.

Task significance refers to the level of impact a job has on the whole organization. Employees who feel that their work affects the organization generally have high job satisfaction. Employees who feel that their jobs do not affect others rarely share this feeling.

Autonomy refers to the independence employees have to make decisions about how to perform their jobs. Checkout clerks in supermarkets have almost no job autonomy. In contrast, supermarket store managers are able to decide how they spend their time. They evaluate the tasks they need to accomplish during the day and perform them in the order they choose. Most people prefer to have some autonomy in their jobs.

Feedback involves the extent to which managers let employees know how they are performing. Feedback is discussed in depth in Chapter 19. In general, employees like to receive feedback about their job performance.

Jobs that rank high in these five characteristics tend to be more desirable than those that don't.

The Physical Work Environment

The physical work environment—temperature, humidity, ventilation, noise, light, color, and so on—can affect employee performance and safety. Studies clearly show that adverse physical conditions do have a negative impact on performance, but the degree of influence varies from person to person.

The importance of safety in the design process was reinforced by the **Occupational Safety and Health Act (OSHA) of 1970.** Designed to reduce job injuries, the act gives very specific federal safety guidelines for almost all U.S. organizations.

In general, the work area should allow for normal lighting, temperature, ventilation, and humidity. Baffles, acoustical wall materials, and sound absorbers should be used to reduce unpleasant noises. Exposure to less than ideal conditions should be limited to short periods. All of these measures will minimize potential physical or psychological damage to employees.[8]

Sociotechnical Approach

The sociotechnical concept was introduced in the 1950s by Eric Trist and his colleagues at the Tavistock Institute of Human Relations in London.[9] The **sociotechnical approach** rests on two premises. First, in any organization that requires people to perform certain tasks, a joint system is operating; this joint system combines the social and technological systems. Second, the environment of every sociotechnical system is influenced by a culture, its values, and a set of generally accepted practices.[10] The concept stresses that the technical system, the related social system, and the general environment should all be considered when designing jobs.

The sociotechnical approach is very situational; few jobs have identical technical requirements, social surroundings, and environments. This approach requires that the job designer carefully consider the role of the worker within the system, the task boundaries, and the autonomy of the work group. Using the sociotechnical approach, Louis Davis has developed the following guidelines for job design:

1. The need for the content of a job to be reasonably demanding for the employee in terms other than sheer endurance and yet provide some variety (but not necessarily novelty).
2. The need to be able to learn on the job and go on learning.
3. The need for some minimum area of decision making that the individual can call his or her own.
4. The need for some minimum degree of social support and recognition at the workplace.
5. The need to be able to relate what the individual does and what he or she produces to the person's social life.
6. The need to feel that the job leads to some sort of desirable future.[11]

Occupational Safety and Health Act (OSHA) of 1970
Federal legislation designed to reduce job injuries; established specific federal safety guidelines for almost all U.S. organizations.

sociotechnical approach
Approach to job design that considers both the technical system and the accompanying social system.

computer-aided design (CAD)
Generates various views of different components and assemblies.

Begun as a small business in 1961, Petersen, Inc., is now one of the foremost fabrication and machinery companies in the United States. Petersen's current facilities encompass over 300,000 square feet and include some of the latest fabrication and machinery equipment available.

Petersen recently used Solid Edge CAD software to design a new 200-ton trash compactor. Tom Burkland, vice president of engineering, estimates the company saved roughly $200,000 by designing the compactor with the Solid Edge CAD software. Certain features of the CAD software enabled Petersen's engineers to simulate the running of the compactor and identify potential interferences in parts. Using this data, the engineers were able to decrease the outside dimensions of the machine by 40 percent.

Burkland estimates that the new CAD system has enabled Petersen's engineers to be about 50 percent more productive while simultaneously saving the company from a 60 percent hiring increase. These and other associated cost savings have allowed Petersen to invest more money in training and thus "get everyone farther up the learning wire."

Source: Michelle Lang, "No Time to Waste," *Design News,* September 22, 2003, p. 50.

Computer Technology and the Design Process

computer-aided engineering (CAE)
Uses a product's characteristics to analyze its performance under different parameters.

In recent years, computers have come to play a major role in production/operations technology. The term *factories of the future* has become popular and generally refers to the use of computers in various parts of the operating system. **Computer-aided design (CAD)** may be defined as carrying out all structural or mechanical design processes of a product or component at a specially equipped computer terminal.[12] CAD can be used to generate various views of different components and assemblies. With CAD, designs can be developed, analyzed, and changed much faster than by using conventional drawing methods. Management Illustration 8.3 discusses how one company realized substantial cost savings by using a new CAD system.

computer-aided manufacturing (CAM)
Uses stored data regarding various products to provide instructions for automated production equipment.

Engineering analysis, when performed at a computer terminal with a CAD system, is called **computer-aided engineering (CAE).** CAE uses a product's characteristics from a CAD database and analyzes its performance under different parameters.[13] For example, several designs could be subjected to different tests and comparisons made by computer instead of actually making and testing different prototypes.

Computer-aided manufacturing (CAM) basically refers to control of the manufacturing process by computers.[14] CAM uses stored data regarding various products to provide instructions for automated production equipment. When CAD provides the design formation used by CAM, the result is called *computer-aided design and manufacturing (CAD/CAM).*

computer-integrated manufacturing (CIM)
Uses computer technology to incorporate all of the organization's production-related functions into an integrated computer system to assist, augment, or automate most functions.

Finally, **computer-integrated manufacturing (CIM)** uses computer technology to incorporate all of the organization's production-related functions into an integrated computer system to assist, augment, or automate most operations.[15] With CIM, the output of one activity or operation serves as the input to the next activity, and this system pervades the entire organization. In essence, CIM involves the integration of product design, engineering, process planning, and manufacturing through the use of computer systems. The overall goal of using CIM is to link various parts of an organization to achieve rapid response to customer orders

OzPharm is part of a multinational Australian pharmaceutical group that has been established for many years. OzPharm employs hundreds of people and manufactures medicines in several forms such as injections, tablets, and aerosols.

In the late 1980s, OzPharm was faced with increasing capital expenditures and overheads that were severely affecting profitability. This, in conjunction with tightening government regulations, led OzPharm to concentrate their attentions on the quality of their manufacturing process. To achieve excellence in product quality in manufacturing, OzPharm has gradually implemented computer-integrated manufacturing throughout its plants.

For example, OzPharm's computer system controls the movement of products throughout the warehouse. A con-veyer belt delivers materials to an automatic crave, which then stores the materials in a warehouse. When an operator needs a particular batch of product to be made, the entry order is input into the computer, which then *enacts* the crave to find and retrieve the materials in storage.

Since implementing CIM, OzPharm has realized savings of over $500,000 per year by reducing product waste, dispensing time has been reduced by almost 30 percent, and lead time from production to packaging has been reduced significantly.

Source: Amrik S. Sohal, "Computer Integrated Manufacturing in the Australian Pharmaceutical Industry," *Integrated Manufacturing Systems* 11, no. 7 (2000), pp. 444+.

or product changes, to allow fast production, and to reduce indirect labor costs.[16] Management Illustration 8.4 describes how the use of CIM has benefitted one company in Australia.

There is little doubt that operations design and planning are moving more and more toward the use of computer technology. For example, sales of mechanical CAD/CAM/CAE software have increased significantly over the past several years. Many believe that in the near future, CIM will become a reality for most manufacturers.

Day-to-Day Operations Planning

production planning
Concerned primarily with aggregate operations planning, resource allocation, and activity scheduling.

Designing an effective operating system does not ensure that the system will operate efficiently. The day-to-day operations must also be planned and then carried out. This process is called **production planning** and includes aggregate operations planning, resource allocation, and scheduling. Its overriding purpose is to maintain a smooth, constant flow of work from start to finish so that the product or service will be completed in the desired time at the lowest possible cost.

Aggregate Operations Planning

aggregate operations planning
Concerned with overall operations and balancing major sections of the operating system; matches the organization's resources with demands for its goods and services.

Aggregate operations planning (also known as *aggregate production planning*) deals with overall operations and with balancing the major parts of the operating system. The objective of the aggregate operations plan is to minimize the cost of resources required to meet demand over the period covered.[17] This is achieved by matching the organization's resources with the demands for its goods or services. Specifically, the plan should find the production rates that satisfy demand requirements while minimizing the costs of workforce and inventory fluctuations. Aggregate operations plans generally look 6 to 18 months into the future.

The first step in developing an aggregate operations plan is to obtain a demand forecast for the organization's goods or services. The second step involves evaluating the impact of the demand forecasts on the organization's resources—plant

FIGURE 8.5
Sample Gantt Chart

Source: Adapted from
Elwood S. Buffa, *Modern
Production Management*, 4th
ed. (New York: John Wiley &
Sons, Inc., 1973), p. 576.

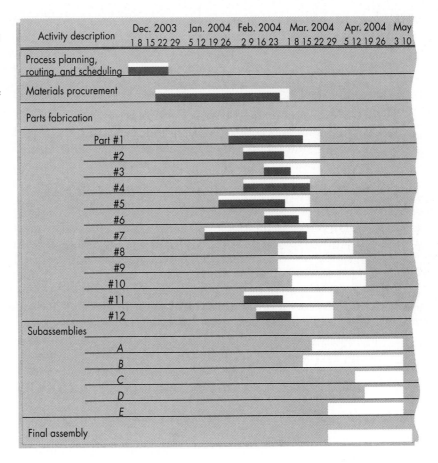

capacity, workforce, raw materials, and the like. The final step is to develop the best plan for using the organization's current and expected resources to meet the forecast demand. The aggregate operations plan determines production rates, workforce needs, and inventory levels for the entire operating system over a specified period.

One of the oldest and simplest methods of graphically showing both expected and completed production is the Gantt chart. Developed by Henry L. Gantt in the early 1900s, the main feature of the **Gantt chart** is that it shows work planned and work accomplished in relation to time. Figure 8.5 presents a typical Gantt chart.

From a planning perspective, Gantt charts require operations managers to clearly think through the sequence of events necessary to complete the tasks being charted. From a control perspective, Gantt charts emphasize the element of time by readily pointing out any actual or potential slippages. One criticism of the Gantt chart is that it can require considerable time to incorporate scheduling changes such as rush orders. To accommodate such scheduling changes rapidly, mechanical boards using movable pegs or cards have been developed.

Gantt chart
Planning and controlling device that graphically depicts work planned and work accomplished in their relation to each other and to time.

resource allocation
Efficient allocation of people, materials, and equipment to meet the demand requirements of the operating system.

Resource Allocation

Resource allocation is the efficient allocation of people, materials, and equipment to meet the demand requirements of the operating system. It is the natural outgrowth of the aggregate production plan. The materials needed must be determined and ordered; the work must be distributed to the different departments and workstations; personnel must be allocated; and time allotments must be set for each stage of the process.

Due to resource scarcities, resource allocation has become critical in recent times. Increased competition, both domestic and foreign, has also heightened its importance. Proper resource allocation can mean great cost savings, which can give the needed competitive edge.

Numerous mathematical and computer-assisted tools and techniques can assist in resource allocation. Linear programming, the critical path method (CPM), and the program evaluation and review technique (PERT) are some of the most often used approaches. The last two are discussed in the following section.

Critical Path Method (CPM) and Program Evaluation and Review Technique (PERT)

critical path method (CPM)
Planning and control technique that graphically depicts the relationships among the various activities of a project; used when time durations of project activities are accurately known and have little variance.

program evaluation and review technique (PERT)
Planning and control technique that graphically depicts the relationships among the various activities of a project; used when the durations of the project activities are not accurately known.

Network analysis focuses on finding the most time-consuming path through a network of tasks and identifying the relationships among the different tasks. The Gantt chart concept formed the foundation for network analysis.[18] The most popular network analysis approaches are the **critical path method (CPM)** and the **program evaluation and review technique (PERT).** These two techniques were developed almost simultaneously in the late 1950s. CPM grew out of a joint study by Du Pont and Remington Rand Univac to determine how to best reduce the time required to perform routine plant overhaul, maintenance, and construction work.[19] PERT was developed by the Navy in conjunction with representatives of Lockheed Aircraft Corporation and the consulting firm of Booz, Allen, & Hamilton to coordinate the development and production of the Polaris weapons system.

CPM and PERT both result in a network representation of a project. The network is composed of sequential activities and events. An activity is the work necessary to complete a particular event, and it usually consumes time. Events denote a point in time, and their occurrence signifies the completion of all activities leading to the event. All activities originate and terminate at events. Activities are usually represented by arrows in a network, while events are represented by a circle.

The path through the network that has the longest duration (based on a summation of estimated individual activity times) is referred to as the *critical path*. If any activity on the critical path lengthens, the entire project duration lengthens.

Figure 8.6 shows a project represented by both a Gantt chart and a project network. The project network has two distinct advantages over the Gantt chart:

FIGURE 8.6   **Project Represented by Gantt Chart and a Project Network**

A. Gantt chart

B. Project network

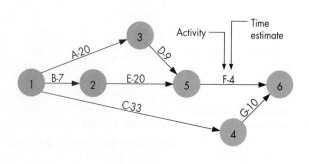

(1) the interdependencies of the activities are noted explicitly, and (2) the activities are shown in greater detail. In addition, from a practical standpoint, Gantt charts become very difficult to visualize and work with for projects involving more than 25 activities.

The major difference between CPM and PERT concerns the activity time estimates. CPM is used for projects whose activity durations are accurately known and whose variance in performance time is negligible. PERT is used when the activity durations are more uncertain and variable. CPM is based on a single estimate for an activity duration, whereas PERT is based on three time estimates for each activity: an optimistic (minimum) time, a most likely (modal) time, and a pessimistic (maximum) time.

Project network analysis can provide information beyond simple project planning and control. By knowing the critical activities, the project manager can best allocate limited resources and can make more accurate time–cost trade-offs.

Routing

routing
Finds the best path and sequence of operations for attaining a desired level of output with a given mix of equipment and personnel.

Routing finds the best path and sequence of operations for attaining a desired level of output with a given mix of equipment and personnel. Routing looks for the best use of existing equipment and personnel through careful assignment of these resources. An organization may or may not have to analyze its routing system frequently; it depends on the variety of products or services it offers.

Flowcharts and diagrams are used to locate and end inefficiencies in a process by analyzing the process in a step-by-step fashion. Most charting procedures divide the actions in a given process into five types: operation, transportation, inspection, delay, and storage. Figure 8.7 defines each of these types of actions.

assembly chart
Depicts the sequence and manner in which the various components of a product or service are assembled.

flow process chart
Outlines what happens to a product or service as it progresses through the facility.

Two types of charts frequently used are the assembly chart and the flow process chart. An **assembly chart** depicts the sequence and manner in which the various parts of a product or service are assembled. A **flow process chart** outlines what happens to the product as it moves through the operating facility. Flow process

FIGURE 8.7
Flowcharting Activities

Source: From H. B. Maynard, *Industrial Engineering Handbook*, 1963. Copyright © 1963 by The McGraw-Hill Companies. Reproduced with permission of The McGraw-Hill Companies.

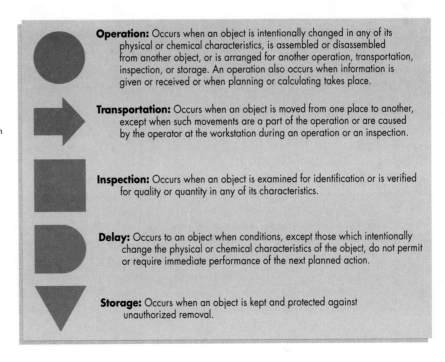

Operation: Occurs when an object is intentionally changed in any of its physical or chemical characteristics, is assembled or disassembled from another object, or is arranged for another operation, transportation, inspection, or storage. An operation also occurs when information is given or received or when planning or calculating takes place.

Transportation: Occurs when an object is moved from one place to another, except when such movements are a part of the operation or are caused by the operator at the workstation during an operation or an inspection.

Inspection: Occurs when an object is examined for identification or is verified for quality or quantity in any of its characteristics.

Delay: Occurs to an object when conditions, except those which intentionally change the physical or chemical characteristics of the object, do not permit or require immediate performance of the next planned action.

Storage: Occurs when an object is kept and protected against unauthorized removal.

FIGURE 8.8
Flow Process Chart: Present Method for Completing Authorization-to-Investigate Form

Source: From *Production and Operations Management*, 6th edition—HSIE 6th edition, by Norman Gaither. Copyright © 1994. Reprinted with permission of South-Western College Publishing, a division of Thomson Learning.

charts can also map the flow of customers through a service facility. Figure 8.8 shows a flow process chart for the processing of a form for an insurance company.

Activity Scheduling

activity scheduling
Develops the precise timetable to be followed in producing a product or service.

Activity scheduling develops the precise timetable to be followed in producing the product or service. It also includes dispatching work orders and expediting critical and late orders. Scheduling does not involve deciding how long a job will take (which is part of job design); rather, it determines when the work is to be done. Scheduling is the link between system design and operations planning and control. Once the initial schedule has been set, the system is ready for operation. Of course, scheduling is an ongoing activity in an operating system.

A scheduling system design must be based on knowledge of the operating system for which it is being designed. Scheduling for intermittent systems is very complex because of the larger number of individual orders or customers that must flow through the system. Many types of scheduling tools, such as the Gantt chart, the critical path method, and the program evaluation and review technique, have been developed to help overcome scheduling problems.

Scheduling for high-volume continuous flow systems is often a process of matching the available resources to the production needs as outlined by the aggregate plan. Computer simulation is used to assist in the scheduling of continuous flow systems by estimating the impact of different scheduling decisions on the system.

Summary

1. *Define operations management.* Operations management is the application of the basic concepts and principles of management to those segments of the organization that produce its goods or services.

2. *Describe an operating system, and identify the two basic types of operating systems.* An operating system consists of the processes and activities necessary to transform various inputs into goods or services. The two basic types of operating systems are those based on continuous flows and those based on intermittent flows. Continuous flow systems generally have a standardized product or service. Intermittent flow systems usually produce customized products and services.

3. *Differentiate among product/service design, process selection, and site selection decisions.* Product/service design decisions deal with how the product or service will be designed. The design must be such that it can be economically produced. Process selection includes a wide range of decisions concerning the specific process to be used, the basic sequences of the process, and the equipment to be used. Site selection decisions are concerned with where to locate a new or an additional facility.

4. *Explain what a materials-handling system is.* A materials-handling system is the entire network that receives materials, stores materials, moves materials between processing points and between buildings, and positions the final product or service for delivery to the ultimate customer.

5. *Describe and give an example of the three basic classifications of facilities layouts.* The three basic types of layouts are process layouts, product layouts, and fixed-position layouts. With a process layout, equipment or services of a similar functional type are arranged or grouped together. Custom fabrication shops and hospitals are examples of organizations that use process layouts. With a product layout, the equipment or services are arranged according to the progressive steps by which the product is made or the customer is serviced. Automobile assembly plants and cafeterias are examples of organizations that use product layouts. With a process layout, equipment or services of a similar functional type are arranged or grouped together. Custom fabrication shops and hospitals are examples of organizations that use process layouts. With a fixed-position layout the product is too large to move and remains in place. Manufacturing of very large products such as ships or airplanes use the fixed-position layout.

6. *Explain the sociotechnical approach to job design.* The sociotechnical approach to job design considers not only the technical system and the task to be done but also the accompanying social system.

7. *Describe several computer-related technologies that are currently playing major roles in production/operations management.* Computer-aided design is carrying out all structural or mechanical design processes of a product or component at a specially equipped computer terminal. CAD is used in product design to generate various views of different components and assemblies. CAE is when engineering analysis is performed at a computer terminal with a CAD system. CAE uses a product's characteristics to analyze its performance under different parameters. Computer-aided manufacturing (CAM) uses stored data regarding various products to provide instructions for automated production equipment. When CAD provides the design information used by CAM, the result is called computer-aided design and manufacturing (CAD/CAM).

Computer-integrated manufacturing (CIM) uses computer technology to incorporate all of the organization's production-related functions into an integrated computer system to assist, augment, or automate most operations.

8. *Outline the three major steps in developing an aggregate operations plan.* The first step in developing an aggregate operations plan is to obtain a demand forecast for the organization's goods or services. The second step involves evaluating the impact of the demand forecasts on the organization's resources. The third step is to develop the best plan for using the organization's current and expected resources to meet the forecast demand.

9. *Summarize the differences between resource allocation and activity scheduling.* Resource allocation is concerned with the efficient allocation of people, materials, and equipment to meet the demand requirements of the operating system. This includes distributing the workload and determining how much time should be allotted for each stage in the production process. Activity scheduling develops the precise timetable to be followed when producing the product or service. Activity scheduling does not involve determining how long a job will take; rather, it determines when the work is to be done.

10. *Distinguish between Gantt charts, the critical path method (CPM), and the program evaluation and review technique (PERT).* Gantt charts graphically depict work planned and work accomplished in relation to time. CPM and PERT both result in a network representation of a project or a group of activities. CPM and PERT have two distinct advantages over Gantt charts: (1) The interdependencies of the activities are noted explicitly, and (2) the activities are shown in greater detail. The major difference between CPM and PERT centers on activity time estimates. CPM is used for projects whose activity durations are accurately known. PERT is used when the activity durations are more uncertain and variable.

Review Questions

1. What is operations management?
2. Describe an operating system.
3. Describe the two basic types of operating systems.
4. What is the overriding objective of the process selection decision?
5. At the most basic level of process selection, what are the four primary types?
6. Discuss several factors that should be considered in site location.
7. What is a process-oriented layout? A product-oriented layout? A fixed-position layout?
8. What is a materials-handling system?
9. Identify the three phases of the job design process.
10. Define ergonomics.
11. What is the sociotechnical approach to job design? Using the sociotechnical approach, give some guidelines for job design.
12. Define CAD, CAE, CAM, and CIM.
13. What is production planning?
14. Define aggregate operations planning.
15. What is the difference between resource allocation and activity scheduling?

Skill-Building Questions

1. Explain how you might take a production line approach (transferring the concepts and methodologies of operations management) to a service organization such as a branch bank.
2. Does process selection in service industries such as restaurants and hotels differ from process selection in manufacturing? If so, how?
3. Why should all of the phases in designing an operating system be integrated?

4. Discuss the following statement: Most production planning is a waste of time because it all depends on demand forecasts, which are usually inaccurate.

5. What can the computer do to help with modern assembly-line planning? How might simulations be used?

Skill-Building Exercise 8.1

Analyzing the Layout

Visit a local fast-food restaurant (McDonald's, Burger King, Hardee's, Wendy's, etc.) and sketch the basic layout of the facility on a single sheet of 8½-by-11-inch paper. Observe the flow of customers and employees through the store. Identify what specific aspects of the layout you think are particularly good. Try to identify one or more aspects of the layout that you think could be improved. Why do you think this improvement has not been made previously? Write down your findings and be prepared to discuss them in class.

Skill-Building Exercise 8.2

Disseminating Confidential Information

Every month, you are responsible for collating and stapling 500 copies of a four-page document. The documents must then be placed in manila envelopes, sealed, and have the word *CONFIDENTIAL* written on each. The four pages are printed on one side only and are numbered sequentially.

1. Assume you have a manual stapler and a felt marker at your disposal. Draw a sketch of how you would arrange your workplace for doing this task and describe the procedure you would use.

2. Assume you have the authority (within reason) to make changes in the equipment, materials, and processes used, as long as the basic task of organizing the information and labeling it as confidential is accomplished. What suggestions would you make?

Case Incident 8.1

The Lines at Sam's

Sam Baker owns and manages a cafeteria on Main Street in Dawsonville. During his two years of operation, Sam has identified several problems he has been unable to solve. One is the line that always seems to develop at the checkout register during the rush hour. Another is customers' constant complaints that the size of the helpings and the size of the pie slices vary tremendously from customer to customer. A third problem is the frequency with which the cafeteria runs out of "choice" dishes. The final problem is that every Sunday at noon, when a large crowd arrives after church, Sam invariably runs short of seating space.

Sam had worked at other food establishments for the previous 15 years, and most of them experienced similar problems. In fact, these and other, related problems have come to be expected and are therefore accepted practice for the industry. After all, Sam's former boss used to say, "You can't please everybody all the time." Sam is wondering if he should take the industry's position and just accept these problems as an inherent part of the business.

Questions

1. Do you have any suggestions for Sam? If so, what are they?

2. What other service-oriented industries can you think of that seem to take the same view toward their problems that Sam's industry does?

Case Incident 8.2

A New Building for Tot-Two

The Tot-Two Company manufactures clothes for children up to age five. Tot-Two has been growing rapidly for the past several years and is planning to build a new plant in a recently developed industrial park on the north side of town. Shirley Shaver, the plant's operations manager, has been assigned the task of drawing up a new physical layout subject to the constraints that the new building cannot exceed 7,000 square feet, including office space, and that it must be a perfect rectangle to minimize construction costs. Shirley developed the following list of departments with their respective approximate space requirements:

Shipping (400 square feet)—area for shipping all finished goods.

Receiving (400 square feet)—area for receiving all materials and supplies.

Materials supply room (300 square feet)—storage area for all incoming materials.

Spreading and cutting area (1,600 square feet)—area containing three 40-foot tables for spreading and then cutting the cloth. Many layers of cloth are spread on top of each other and cut at the same time with large portable cutters.

Pattern-making area (200 square feet)—area in which patterns are made.

Assembly area (1,200 square feet)—area for sewing the various clothing parts.

Packing area (400 square feet)—area for packing the finished goods into boxes for shipping.

Finished goods storage (500 square feet)—area for storing finished goods before shipping.

Design area (200 square feet)—area occupied by designers.

Office space (800 square feet)—space for secretaries and company officers.

Wash facilities (300 square feet)—area containing men's and women's bathrooms.

Lunch/break area (400 square feet)—area with vending machines and lunch tables.

Shirley then drew up an initial layout as illustrated below.

Designers (200 sq. ft.)	Office (800 sq. ft.)		Assembly (1,200 sq. ft.)
Lunch/break (400 sq. ft.)			
Wash facilities (300 sq. ft.)	Packing (400 sq. ft.)		
	Finished goods storage (500 sq. ft.)		Spreading and cutting (1,600 sq. ft.)
Shipping (400 sq. ft.)			
Pattern making (200 sq. ft.)	Material supply (300 sq. ft.)	Receiving (400 sq. ft.)	

Questions

1. What are the strong points of Shirley's layout? What are the weak points?
2. Redesign the layout, based on your answers to question 1.

References and Additional Readings

1. Howard Banks, "Moment of Truth," *Forbes*, May 22, 1995, pp. 51–62.
2. Richard B. Chase and Nicholas J. Aquilano, *Production and Operations Management*, 7th ed. (Burr Ridge, IL: Richard D. Irwin, 1995), pp. 60–61.
3. James M. Apple and Leon F. McGinnis, "Innovation in Facilities and Materials Handling Systems: An Introduction," *Industrial Engineering*, March 1987, pp. 33–38.
4. Lee J. Krajewski and Larry P. Ritzman, *Operations Management*, 3rd ed. (Reading, MA: Addison-Wesley, 1993), p. 348.
5. James L. Lewardowski and William P. MacKinnon, "What We Learned at Saturn," *Personnel Journal*, December 1992, pp. 30–32.
6. Louis E. Davis, "Job Design and Productivity: A New Approach," *Personnel*, March 1957, p. 420.

7. Richard A. Johnson, William T. Newell, and Roger C. Vergin, *Production and Operations Management: A Systems Concept* (Boston: Houghton Mifflin, 1974), p. 204.

8. Ibid., p. 206.

9. Peter B. Vaill, "Industrial Engineering and Socio-Technical Systems," *Journal of Industrial Engineering*, September 1967, p. 535.

10. Louis E. Davis and James C. Taylor, *Design of Jobs*, 2nd ed. (Santa Monica, CA: Goodyear Publishing, 1979), pp. 98–99.

11. Louis E. Davis, *Job Satisfaction—a Socio-Technical View*, report no. 515-1-69 (Los Angeles: University of California, 1969), p. 14.

12. Mark M. Davis, Nicholas J. Aquilano, and Richard B. Chase, *Fundamentals of Operations Management*, 4th ed. (New York: McGraw-Hill/Irwin, 2003), p. 125.

13. Roberta S. Russell and Bernard W. Taylor III, *Operations Management*, 4th ed. (Upper Saddle River, NJ: Prentice Hall, 2003), p. 101.

14. Ibid.

15. Mikell P. Groover, *Automation, Production Systems and Computer Integrated Manufacturing* (Englewood Cliffs, NJ: Prentice Hall, 1980), pp. 721–22; and James B. Dilworth, *Production and Operations Management*, 5th ed. (New York: McGraw-Hill, 1993), pp. 609–13.

16. William J. Stevenson, *Operations Management*, 7th ed. (New York: McGraw-Hill/Irwin, 2002), p. 228.

17. Richard B. Chase, F. Robert Jacobs, and Nicholas J. Aquilano, *Operations Management for Competitive Advantage* (New York: McGraw-Hill/Irwin, 2004), p. 5.

18. Evidence indicates there were other forerunners to CPM and PERT. See Edward R. Marsh, "The Harmonogram of Karol Adamiecki," *Academy of Management Journal*, June 1975, pp. 358–64.

19. Joseph J. Moder and Cecil R. Phillips, *Project Management with CPM and PERT* (New York: Van Nostrand Reinhold, 1970), p. 6.

Organizing and Staffing Skills

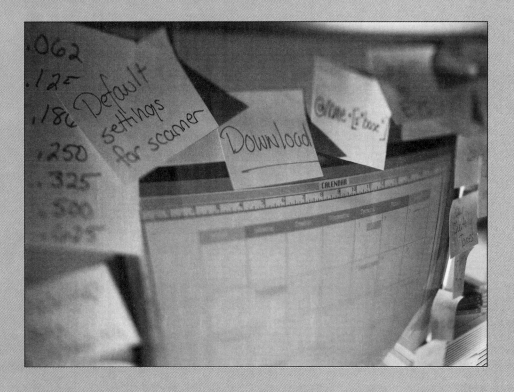

Chapter

9

Organizing Work

Learning Objectives

After studying this chapter, you will be able to:

1. Define organization, and differentiate between a formal and an informal organization.
2. Explain the importance of the organizing function.
3. List the advantages and the major disadvantage of horizontal division of labor.
4. Distinguish between power, authority, and responsibility.
5. Explain the concept of centralization versus decentralization.
6. Define empowerment.
7. List four principles of organization that are related to authority.
8. Identify several reasons managers are reluctant to delegate.
9. Recount the major factors that affect a manager's span of management.
10. Name and define three workplace changes, in addition to decentralization and empowerment, that have affected the organizing function in today's organizations.

Chapter Preview

Brenda Craig works for Standard Motor Products, Inc., which makes and distributes aftermarket automotive products to customers such as Carquest, NAPA, and Advance Automotive. Today, Brenda is going through order sheets figuring out what her co-workers are going to do that day. What's different is that Brenda is not the boss; rather, she's just doing her month-long rotation as the scheduler for her work team. Everyone in her 12-member team will rotate through the scheduling assignment as well as all the other tasks assigned to the group; in addition, they may help other work teams or vice versa. The team system used at Brenda's company thrives in what could be a divisive environment: Over half of the warehouse and plant workers are union members.

It is rare for managers to overrule decisions made by work teams. Furthermore, the evolution to self-directed teams has resulted in team members having access to financial and other data that were once only available to management. The acting union chairman, Mike Cecena, summed up the situation: "The team knows the schedule, knows the goals, the dollar amounts. We don't just show up and have somebody say, 'Here's what you're doing today.' We have a lot more information about the business."

Source: Diane Stafford, "Team-Based Decision Making Works at Edwardsville, Kansas, Auto Product Plant," *Knight Ridder Tribune Business News,* June 11, 2002, p. 1.

Analyzing Management Skills

How might involving employees in making decisions help an organization run more smoothly?

Applying Management Skills

Suppose you are in charge of building a homecoming display for your school with 10 volunteers. How would you organize them?

organization
Group of people working together in some concerted or coordinated effort to attain objectives.

Most work today is accomplished through organizations. An **organization** is a group of people working together in some type of concerted or coordinated effort to attain objectives. As such, an organization provides a vehicle for implementing strategy and accomplishing objectives that could not be achieved by individuals working separately. The process of **organizing** is the grouping of activities necessary to attain common objectives and the assignment of each grouping to a manager who has the authority required to supervise the people performing the activities.[1] Thus, organizing is basically a process of division of labor accompanied by appropriate delegation of authority. Proper organizing results in more effective use of resources.

organizing
Grouping of activities necessary to attain common objectives and the assignment of each grouping to a manager who has the authority necessary to supervise the people performing the activities.

The framework that defines the boundaries of the formal organization and within which the organization operates is the organization structure. A second and equally important element of an organization is the informal organization. The **informal organization** refers to the aggregate of the personal contacts and interactions and the associated groupings of people working within the formal organization.[2] The informal organization has a structure, but it is not formally and consciously designed.

Reasons for Organizing

informal organization
Aggregate of the personal contacts and interactions and the associated groupings of people working within the formal organization.

One of the primary reasons for organizing is to establish lines of authority. Clear lines of authority create order within a group. Absence of authority almost always leads to chaotic situations where everyone is telling everyone else what to do.

Second, organizing improves the efficiency and quality of work through synergism. *Synergism* occurs when individuals or groups work together to produce a whole greater than the sum of the parts. For example, synergism results when three people working together produce more than three people working separately. Synergism can result from division of labor or from increased coordination, both of which are products of good organization.

A final reason for organizing is to improve communication. A good organization structure clearly defines channels of communication among the members of the organization. Such a system also ensures more efficient communications.

One man draws out the wire, another straightens it, and a third cuts it, a fourth points it, a fifth grinds it at the top for receiving the head; to make the head requires two or three distinct operations; to put it on is a peculiar business, to whiten the pins is another; it is even a trade by itself to put them into the paper, and the important business of making a pin is, in this manner, divided into 18 distinct operations, which, in some manufactories, are all performed by distinct hands; though in others the same man will sometimes perform two or three of them. I have seen a small manufactory of this kind where 10 men only were employed and where some of them consequently performed two or three distinct operations. But though they were very poor and therefore but indifferently accommodated with the necessary machinery, they could, when they exerted themselves, make among them about 12 pounds of pins a day.

Source: Adam Smith, *An Inquiry into the Nature and Causes of the Wealth of Nations,* vol. 1 (London: A. Strahan and T. Cadell, 1776), pp. 7–8.

Historically, the desire to organize led to the development of an organization. The use of an organization allows people to jointly (1) increase specialization and division of labor, (2) use large-scale technology, (3) manage the external environment, (4) economize on transaction costs, and (5) exert power and control.[3] When designed and coordinated effectively, these characteristics help the organization to serve its customers with a high degree of service and productivity.

Division of Labor

Organizing is basically a process of division of labor. The merits of dividing labor have been known for centuries. Taking the simple task of manufacturing a pin, Adam Smith in 1776 demonstrated how much more efficiently the task could be performed through division of labor.[4] As explained in Management Illustration 9.1, Smith argued that it was more efficient to divide the different tasks or operations required to make an object than it was to have each employee make the entire object individually.

Labor can be divided either vertically or horizontally. Vertical division of labor is based on the establishment of lines of authority and defines the levels that make up the vertical organization structure. In addition to establishing authority, vertical division of labor facilitates the flow of communication within the organization. To illustrate how vertical division of labor can vary from company to company, consider the automobile industry in the early 1980s. At that time, Toyota had 5 levels between the chairperson and the first-line supervisor, whereas Ford had over 15.[5] For a more thorough description of the advantages of the "flat" organization, see Chapter 10.

Horizontal division of labor is based on specialization of work. The basic assumption underlying horizontal division of labor is that by making each worker's task specialized, more work can be produced with the same effort through increased efficiency and quality. Specifically, horizontal division of labor can result in the following advantages:

1. Fewer skills are required per person.
2. The skills required for selection or training purposes are easier to supply.
3. Practice in the same job develops proficiency.
4. Primarily utilizing each worker's best skills promotes efficient use of skills.

5. Concurrent operations are made possible.

6. More conformity in the final product results when each piece is always produced by the same person.

The major problem with horizontal division of labor is that it can result in job boredom and even degradation of the employee. An extreme example of horizontal division of labor is the automobile assembly line. Most people working on an automobile assembly line do a small number of very simple tasks over and over again. It usually doesn't take long for these employees to become bored. Once employees become bored, their productivity often declines, absenteeism and tardiness increase, and the quality of work goes down. Solutions to the problems created by horizontal division of labor include a reexamination of job scope, implementing job rotation, and balancing job simplification with job depth.

job scope
Refers to the number of different types of operations performed on the job.

Job scope refers to the number of different types of operations performed. In performing a job with narrow scope, the employee performs few operations and repeats the cycle frequently. The negative effects of jobs lacking in scope vary with the person performing the job, but they can include more errors and lower quality. Often job rotation, wherein workers shift in the planned sequence of activities, eliminates boredom and monotony and encourages multiple skills and cross-training.

job depth
Refers to the freedom of employees to plan and organize their own work, work at their own pace, and move around and communicate as desired.

Job depth refers to the freedom of employees to plan and organize their own work, work at their own pace, and move around and communicate as desired. A lack of job depth can result in job dissatisfaction and work avoidance, which in turn can lead to absenteeism, tardiness, and even sabotage.

Division of labor is not more efficient or even desirable in all situations. At least two basic requirements must exist for the successful use of division of labor. The first requirement is a relatively large volume of work. Enough volume must be produced to allow for specialization and keep each employee busy. The second requirement is stability in the volume of work, employee attendance, quality of raw materials, product design, and production technology.

Power, Authority, and Responsibility

power
Ability to influence, command, or apply force.

Power is the ability to influence, command, or apply force. Power is usually derived from the control of resources. **Authority** is power derived from the rights that come with a position and represents the legitimate exercise of power. Thus, authority is one source of power for a manager. Lines of authority link the various organizational components. Unclear lines of authority can create major confusion and conflict within an organization.

authority
Legitimate exercise of power; the right to issue directives and expend resources; related to power but narrower in scope.

Responsibility is accountability for the attainment of objectives, the use of resources, and the adherence to organizational policy. Once responsibility is accepted, performing assigned work becomes an obligation. The term *responsibility* as used here should not be confused with the term *responsibilities* as in the context of defining job duties.

responsibility
Accountability for the attainment of objectives, the use of resources, and the adherence to organizational policy.

Sources of Authority

As just mentioned, authority can be viewed as a function of position, flowing from top to bottom through the formal organization. According to this view, people hold authority because they occupy a certain position; once removed from the position, they lose their authority. Taking this theory one step further, one can say the American people, through the Constitution and laws, represent the ultimate source of authority in this country. The Constitution and laws guarantee the right of free enterprise. The owners of a free enterprise organization have the right to elect a board of directors and top management. Top management selects middle-level managers. This process continues down to the lowest person in the organization. This traditional view of authority is also called the *formal theory of authority.*

A second theory of authority was first outlined in 1926 by Mary Parker Follett and popularized in 1938 by Chester Barnard.[6] Called the *acceptance theory of authority,* this theory maintains that a manager's source of authority lies with his or her subordinates because they have the power to either accept or reject the manager's command. Presumably, if a subordinate does not view a manager's authority as legitimate, it does not exist. Both Follett and Barnard viewed disobeying a communication from a manager as a denial of authority by the subordinate. In summary, the acceptance theory of authority recognizes that subordinates play an active role in determining lines of authority and are not merely passive recipients in the process. This idea is somewhat similar to the contention that without followers you can have no leaders. Both elements must be present and mutually recognized for true structure to exist. Companies with a high degree of employee involvement, responsibility, and accountability appear to recognize acceptance theory as being beneficial for mutual support and encouragement between labor and management.

Centralization versus Decentralization

centralization
Little authority is delegated to lower levels of management.

decentralization
A great deal of authority is delegated to lower levels of management.

There are limitations to the authority of any position. These limitations may be external, in the form of laws, politics, or social attitudes, or they may be internal, as delineated by the organization's objectives or by the job description. The tapered concept of authority states that the breadth and scope of authority become more limited as one descends the scalar chain (see Figure 9.1).

The top levels of management establish the shapes of the funnels in Figures 9.1 and 9.2. The more authority top management chooses to delegate, the less conical the funnel becomes. The less conical the funnel, the more decentralized the organization. **Centralization** and **decentralization** refer to the degree of authority delegated by upper management. This is usually reflected by the numbers and kinds of decisions made by the lower levels of management. As they increase, the degree of decentralization also increases. Thus, an organization is never totally centralized or totally decentralized; rather, it falls along a continuum ranging from

FIGURE 9.1
Tapered Concept of Authority

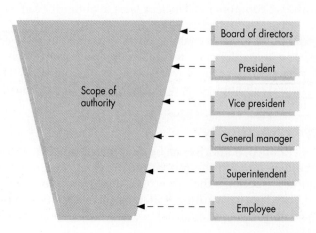

Scope of authority

Board of directors

President

Vice president

General manager

Superintendent

Employee

John W. Brown is currently and has been president and CEO of Stryker Corporation for the past 25 years. Stryker is a $2.6 billion Kalamazoo, Michigan, global manufacturer of surgical devices, orthopedic implants, and hospital beds and stretchers. When Brown became president and CEO 25 years ago, he set a staggering target of 20 percent annual growth in net earnings—a goal that has amazingly been met in all but five quarters since that time.

One of Brown's keys to success is that he oversees a decentralized organization with each of Stryker's 14 divisions focusing on a specific market. Brown leaves the day-to-day running of the business to his division heads, who operate the way they see fit. "It is tremendous autonomy, but responsibility with a capital R," says Brown. Decentralization works at Stryker because Brown has made Stryker a very numbers-oriented company. The people who thrive at Stryker are those who are entrepreneurial but also willing to be measured and rewarded based on financial goals.

Source: Michael A. Verespej, "Recession? What Recession?" *Chief Executive,* June 2002, pp. 44–47.

highly centralized to highly decentralized. In Figure 9.2, the organization represented by the diagram on the left is much more centralized than that represented by the right-hand diagram.

The trend in today's organizations is toward more decentralization. Decentralization has the advantage of allowing for more flexibility and quicker action. It also relieves executives from time-consuming detail work. It often results in higher morale by allowing lower levels of management to be actively involved in the decision-making process. The major disadvantage of decentralization is the potential loss of control. Duplication of effort can also accompany decentralization. Management Illustration 9.2 describes how one company realized outstanding results through decentralization.

Empowerment

empowerment
Form of decentralization in which subordinates have authority to make decisions.

Empowerment is a form of decentralization that involves giving subordinates substantial authority to make decisions. Under empowerment, managers express confidence in the ability of employees to perform at high levels. Employees are also encouraged to accept personal responsibility for their work. In situations where true empowerment takes place, employees gain confidence in their ability

FIGURE 9.2
Centralized versus Decentralized Authority

Scope of authority

Board of directors

President

Vice president

General manager

Superintendent

Employee

Scope of authority

Centralized   Decentralized

to perform their jobs and influence the organization's performance. Under true empowerment, employees can bend the rules to do whatever they have to do to take care of the customer.[7] One result of empowerment is that employees demonstrate more initiative and perseverance in pursuing organizational goals.

Organizations can take several actions to implement empowerment:[8]

- Whenever possible, restructure organizational units to be smaller, less complex, and less dependent on other units for decision making and action.
- Reduce to a minimum the number of hard rules for the organization.
- Emphasize a change throughout the organization that focuses on empowerment and personal accountability for delivering results.
- Provide the education and training necessary to enable people to respond to opportunities for improvement.

Accompanying the trend toward more decentralization in today's organizations is a trend toward increased empowerment of today's workforce. While some people believe that empowerment is praised loudly in public but seldom implemented, companies have experienced very positive results from having empowered their employees.

Self-Managed Work Teams

One method for empowering employees is through the use of *self-managed work teams*. Self-managed work teams (also called *self-directed* or *self-regulated work teams*) are work units without a frontline manager and empowered to control their own work.[9] The philosophy behind any type of work team is that teams can contribute to improved performance by identifying and solving work-related problems. The basic idea is to motivate employees by having them participate in decisions that affect them and their work. Self-managed work teams are teams of employees who accomplish tasks within their area of responsibility without direct supervision. Each team makes its own job assignments, plans its own work, performs equipment maintenance, keeps records, obtains supplies, and makes selection decisions of new members into the work unit.

There is no doubt that the use of self-managed work teams has grown dramatically over the last several years and will continue to grow in the future. Self-directed work teams are discussed further in Chapter 11, which is devoted to understanding all forms of work teams.

Principles Based on Authority

Because authority is a key element in managing organizations, several key concepts are relevant. Delegation, unity of command, the scalar principle, and the span of management historically have been the most important of these concepts.

Delegation: The Parity Principle

According to Herbert Engel, "As an abstract idea, delegation must be as old as the human race itself."[10] The apportioning of specific duties to members of a group by a leader seems almost as natural as it is necessary. Delegation normally occurs when one needs something done that one either cannot or chooses not to do oneself. The decision may be based on situations, skills, time, established order, or the expansion and growth of responsibilities as dictated by the group or the organization. Managers can delegate responsibility to subordinates in the sense of making subordinates responsible to them. However, this delegation to subordinates makes managers no less responsible to their superiors. Delegation of responsibility does not mean abdication of responsibility by the delegating manager. Responsibility is not like an object that can be passed from individual to individual.

parity principle
States that authority and responsibility must coincide.

The **parity principle** states that authority and responsibility must coincide. Management must delegate sufficient authority to enable subordinates to do their jobs. At the same time, subordinates can be expected to accept responsibility only for those areas within their authority.

Subordinates must accept both authority and responsibility before the delegation process has been completed. Management sometimes expects employees to seek and assume responsibility they have not been asked to assume and then bid for the necessary authority. Such a system leads to guessing games that do nothing but create frustration and waste energy.

A manager's resistance to delegating authority is natural. There are several reasons for this reluctance:

1. Fear that subordinates will fail in doing the task.
2. The belief that it is easier to do the task oneself rather than delegate it.
3. Fear that subordinates will look "too good."
4. Humans' attraction to power.
5. Comfort in doing the tasks of the previous job held.

Despite all the reasons for not delegating, there are some very strong reasons for a manager to delegate. Several phenomena occur when a manager successfully delegates. First, the manager's time is freed to pursue other tasks, and the subordinates gain feelings of belonging and being needed. These feelings often lead to a genuine commitment on the part of the subordinates. Second, delegation is one of the best methods for developing subordinates and satisfying customers. Pushing authority down the organization also allows employees to deal more effectively with customers. In its mid-1990s reengineering effort, Hallmark Cards, Inc., found that when you drive something from the top, you have to articulate clearly and communicate why it is being done.[11] By converting delegation to a shared vision, the organization has a much better chance of accomplishing its goals and objectives without resorting to adverse persuasion. Similarly, Taco Bell went from a $500 million regional company in 1982 to a $3 billion national company today because it recognized that the way to ultimately reach and satisfy customers was to empower its lower-level employees to make changes in operational strategies and tactics.[12] Successful delegation involves delegating matters that stimulate subordinates.

How to Delegate

To successfully delegate, a manager must decide which tasks can be delegated. Figure 9.3 indicates the steps the manager can follow to analyze and improve the delegation process. In addition, clearly defining objectives and standards, involving subordinates in the delegation process, initiating training that defines and encourages delegation, and supporting control efforts tend to improve the overall delegation process.

FIGURE 9.3
Steps in the Delegation Process

1. Analyze how you spend your time.
2. Decide which tasks can be assigned.
3. Decide who can handle each task.
4. Delegate the authority.
5. Create an obligation (responsibility).
6. Control the delegation.

Probably the most nebulous part of the delegation process centers around the question of how much authority to delegate. As mentioned previously, management must delegate sufficient authority to allow the subordinate to perform the job. Precisely what can and cannot be delegated depends on the commitments of the manager and the number and quality of subordinates. A rule of thumb is to delegate authority and responsibility to the lowest organization level that has the competence to accept them.

Failure to master delegation is probably the single most frequently encountered reason managers fail. To be a good manager, a person must learn to delegate.

exception principle
States that managers should concentrate on matters that deviate significantly from normal and let subordinates handle routine matters; also called *management by exception.*

The **exception principle** (also known as *management by exception*) states that managers should concentrate their efforts on matters that deviate significantly from normal and let subordinates handle routine matters. The exception principle is closely related to the parity principle. The idea behind the exception principle is that managers should concentrate on those matters that require their abilities and not become bogged down with duties their subordinates should be doing. The exception principle can be hard to comply with when incompetent or insecure subordinates refer everything to their superiors because they are afraid to make a decision. On the other hand, superiors should refrain from making everyday decisions that they have delegated to subordinates. This problem is often referred to as *micromanaging.*

Unity of Command

unity of command principle
States that an employee should have one, and only one, immediate manager.

The **unity of command principle** states that an employee should have one, and only one, immediate manager. The difficulty of serving more than one superior has been recognized for thousands of years. Recall the biblical quote, "No man can serve two masters." In its simplest form, this problem arises when two managers tell the same employee to do different jobs at the same time. The employee is thus placed in a no-win situation. Regardless of which manager the employee obeys, the other will be dissatisfied. The key to avoiding problems with unity of command is to make sure employees clearly understand the lines of authority that directly affect them. Too often managers assume employees understand the lines of authority when in fact they do not. All employees should have a basic understanding of the organizational chart for their company and where they fit on it. An organizational chart frequently clarifies lines of authority and the chain of command.

More times than not, problems relating to the unity of command principle stem from the actions of managers rather than the actions of employees. This happens most often when managers make requests of employees who do not work directly for them.

Scalar Principle

scalar principle
States that authority in the organization flows through the chain of managers one link at a time, ranging from the highest to the lowest ranks; also called *chain of command.*

The **scalar principle** states that authority in the organization flows through the chain of managers one link at a time, ranging from the highest to the lowest ranks. Commonly referred to as the *chain of command,* the scalar principle is based on the need for communication and the principle of unity of command.

The problem with circumventing the scalar principle is that the link bypassed in the process may have very pertinent information. For example, suppose Jerry goes directly above his immediate boss, Ellen, to Charlie for permission to take his lunch break 30 minutes earlier. Charlie, believing the request is reasonable, approves it, only to find out later that the other two people in Jerry's department had also rescheduled their lunch breaks. Thus, the department would be totally vacant from 12:30 to 1 o'clock. Ellen, the bypassed manager, would have known about the other rescheduled lunch breaks.

A common misconception is that every action must painstakingly progress through every link in the chain, whether its course is upward or downward. This point was refuted many years ago by Lyndall Urwick, an internationally known management consultant:

> Provided there is proper confidence and loyalty between superiors and subordinates, and both parties take the trouble to keep the other informed in matters in which they should have a concern, the "scalar process" does not imply that there should be no shortcuts. It is concerned with authority, and provided the authority is recognized and no attempt is made to evade or to supersede it, there is ample room for avoiding in matters of action the childish practices of going upstairs one step at a time or running up one ladder and down another when there is nothing to prevent a direct approach on level ground.[13]

As Henri Fayol stated years before Urwick, "It is an error to depart needlessly from authority, but it is an even greater one to keep to it when detriment to the business ensues."[14] Both Urwick and Fayol are simply saying that in certain instances, one can and should shortcut the scalar chain as long as one does not do so in a secretive or deceitful manner.

Span of Management

span of management
Number of subordinates a manager can effectively manage; also called *span of control.*

The **span of management** (also called the *span of control*) refers to the number of subordinates a manager can effectively manage. Although the British World War I general Sir Ian Hamilton is usually credited for developing the concept of a limited span of control, related examples abound throughout history. Hamilton argued that a narrow span of management (with no more than six subordinates reporting to a manager) would enable the manager to get the job accomplished in the course of a normal working day.[15]

In 1933, V. A. Graicunas published a classic paper that analyzed subordinate–superior relationships in terms of a mathematical formula.[16] This formula was based on the theory that the complexities of managing increase geometrically as the number of subordinates increases arithmetically.

Based on his personal experience and the works of Hamilton and Graicunas, Lyndall Urwick first stated the concept of span of management as a management principle in 1938: "No superior can supervise directly the work of more than five, or at the most, six subordinates whose work interlocks."[17]

Since the publication of Graicunas's and Urwick's works, the upper limit of five or six subordinates has been continuously criticized as being too restrictive. Many practitioners and scholars contend there are situations in which more than five or six subordinates can be effectively supervised. Their beliefs have been substantiated by considerable empirical evidence showing that the limit of five or six subordinates has been successfully exceeded in many situations.[18] Urwick has suggested these exceptions can be explained by the fact that senior workers often function as unofficial managers or leaders.[19]

In view of recent evidence, the span of management concept has been revised to state that the number of people who should report directly to any one person should be based on the complexity, variety, and proximity of the jobs, the quality of the people filling the jobs, and the ability of the manager.

While much effort is given to ensuring that a manager's span of management is not too great, the opposite situation is often overlooked. All too frequently in organizations, situations develop in which only one employee reports to a particular manager. While this situation might very well be justified under certain circumstances, it often results in an inefficient and top-heavy organization. The pros

FIGURE 9.4
Factors Affecting
the Span of
Management

Factor	Description	Relationship to Span of Control
Complexity	Job scope Job depth	Shortens span of control
Variety	Number of different types of jobs being managed	Shortens span of control
Proximity	Physical dispersion of jobs being managed	Lengthens span of control
Quality of subordinates	General quality of the employees being managed	Lengthens span of control
Quality of manager	Ability to perform managerial duties	Lengthens span of control

and cons of flat organizations (wide spans of management, few levels) versus tall organizations (narrow spans of management, many levels) are discussed at length in the next chapter. Figure 9.4 summarizes the factors affecting the manager's span of management.

Workplace Changes in Organizations

The trends toward increased decentralization and empowerment of employees were discussed earlier in this chapter. Other trends relating to organizations of the workplace include flextime, telecommuting, and job sharing.

Flextime, or flexible working hours, allows employees to choose, within certain limits, when they start and end their workday. Usually the organization defines a core period (such as 10 A.M. to 3 P.M.) when all employees will be at work. It is then left to each employee to decide when to start and end the workday as long as the hours encompass the core period. Some flextime programs allow employees to vary the hours worked each day as long as they meet some specific total, which is usually 40 hours. The percentage of wage and salary employees with flexible schedules has increased from 15 percent in 1991 to 29 percent in 2001, according to figures from the Bureau of Labor Statistics.[20] Close to six of every ten major firms offer flextime, according to a recent Hewitt Associates employer survey.[21]

Flextime has the advantage of allowing different employees to accommodate different lifestyles and schedules. Other potential advantages include avoiding rush hours and having less absenteeism and tardiness. From the employer's viewpoint, flextime can have the advantage of providing an edge in recruiting new employees and also in retaining hard-to-find qualified employees. Also, organizations with flextime schedules have reported an average increase of 1 to 5 percent in productivity.[22] On the downside, flextime can create communication and coordination problems for supervisors and managers.

Telecommuting is the practice of working at home, while traveling and being able to interact with the office or working at a satellite office. Today's information technology (PCs, the Internet, cellular phones, etc.) has made telecommuting a reality for many companies. According to the International Telework Association & Council (ITAC), teleworkers now number 28 million employees nationwide.[23] Although the majority of Fortune 1000 firms offer telecommuting, more than half report that only between 1 and 5 percent of employees actually participate in such programs.[24] Advantages of telecommuting include lower turnover, less travel

Every Wednesday, Barbara Cafero and Robin Como commute on the train to New York together. Since 1993, Cafero and Como have shared the same major account contract manager's job at Xerox. Cafero negotiates pricing and contracts for Xerox's major accounts on Monday and Tuesday, Como takes over on Thursday and Friday. On Wednesday, both are in the office.

Wanting to balance work with a broader home life, Cafero and Como prepared a detailed proposal for how their job sharing would work. When they presented this proposal to their managers, both women found them supportive and even excited. After 10 years the job sharing is still working, with tangible advantages to both the employees and the company. "It's spending more time with my three children," Cafero says, "to be there at the school play or to be there in the house when they get home." The advantages to Xerox include retaining two tenured, high-performing employees.

Source: Amanda Beeler, "It Takes Two," *Sales and Marketing Management,* August 2003, p. 38.

---

time, avoiding rush hour, avoid distractions at the office, being able to work flexible hours, and lower real estate costs for employers. Potential disadvantages of telecommuting are insurance concerns relating to the health and safety of employees working at home. Another drawback is that some state and local laws restrict just what work can be done at home.

Job sharing is a relatively new concept whereby two or more part-time employees perform a job that would normally be held by one full-time employee. Job sharing can be in the form of equally shared responsibilities or split duties, or a combination of both. Approximately 28 percent of major firms in the United States offer some type of job sharing, according to the recent Hewitt Associates employer survey.[25] Job sharing is especially attractive to people who want to work but not full-time. A critical factor relating to job sharing is how benefits are handled. Often benefits are prorated between the part-time employees. Some organizations allow job-sharing employees to purchase full health insurance by paying the difference between their prorated benefit and the premium for a full-time employee. Management Illustration 9.3 discusses an example of job sharing at Xerox.

Summary

1. *Define organization, and differentiate between a formal and an informal organization.* An organization is a group of people working together in some type of concerted or coordinated effort to attain objectives. As such, an organization provides a vehicle for accomplishing objectives that could not be achieved by individuals working separately. The framework that defines the boundaries of the formal organization and within which the organization operates is the organization structure. The informal organization refers to the aggregate of the personal contacts and interactions and the associated groupings of people working within the formal organization. The informal organization has a structure, but it is not formally and consciously designed.

2. *Explain the importance of the organizing function.* The organizing function determines how organizational resources will be employed to achieve goals. It also establishes lines of authority, improves the efficiency and quality of work through synergism, and improves communication by defining channels of communication in the organization.

3. *List the advantages and the major disadvantage of horizontal division of labor.* Horizontal division of labor can result in the following advantages: (1) fewer skills are required per person; (2) it is easier to supply the skills required for selection or training purposes;

(3) practice in the same job develops proficiency; (4) primarily utilizing each worker's best skills promotes efficient use of skills; (5) concurrent operations are made possible; and (6) there is more conformity in the final product if each piece is always produced by the same person. The major disadvantage of horizontal division of labor is that it can result in job boredom and even degradation of the worker.

4. *Distinguish between power, authority, and responsibility.* Power is the ability to influence, command, or apply force. Power is derived from the control of resources. Authority is power derived from the rights that come with a position; it is the legitimate exercise of power. Responsibility is accountability for the attainment of objectives, the use of resources, and the adherence to organizational policy. Once responsibility is accepted, performing assigned work becomes an obligation.

5. *Explain the concept of centralization versus decentralization.* Centralization and decentralization refer to the degree of authority delegated by upper management. This is usually reflected by the numbers and kinds of decisions made by the lower levels of management. As they increase, the degree of decentralization also increases. Thus, an organization is never totally centralized or totally decentralized: rather, it falls along a continuum ranging from highly centralized to highly decentralized.

6. *Define empowerment.* Empowerment is a form of decentralization that involves giving subordinates substantial authority to make decisions.

7. *List four principles of organization that are related to authority.* Four principles of organization related to authority are (1) the parity principle, (2) the unity of command principle, (3) the scalar principle, and (4) span of management.

8. *Identify several reasons managers are reluctant to delegate.* A manager's resistance to delegating authority is natural. Several reasons managers are reluctant to delegate include the following: (1) fear of subordinates failing; (2) it is easier for the manager to do the task than to teach a subordinate how to do it; (3) fear that subordinates will look "too good"; (4) humans' attraction to power; and (5) comfort in doing those tasks that should be delegated.

9. *Recount the major factors that affect a manager's span of management.* The major factors that affect a manager's span of management are (1) the complexity of the job being managed, (2) the variety among the jobs being managed, (3) the physical proximity of the jobs to one another, (4) the general quality of the subordinates being managed, and (5) the ability of the manager to perform the different managerial duties.

10. *Name and define three workplace changes, in addition to decentralization and empowerment, that have affected the organizing function in today's organizations.* The use of flextime, telecommuting, and job sharing has affected today's organizations. Flextime allows employees to choose, within certain limits, when they start and end their workday. Telecommuting is the process of working away from a traditional office—usually at home. Job sharing is where two or more part-time employees perform a job that would normally be held by one full-time employee.

Review Questions

1. What is an organization? Define the management function of organizing. Define organization structure. What is an informal organization?
2. Discuss the reasons for organizing.
3. What is the difference between horizontal and vertical division of labor? What is the difference between job scope and job depth?
4. Define power, authority, and responsibility.
5. Discuss two approaches to viewing the sources of authority.
6. What is the difference between a highly centralized and a highly decentralized organization?
7. Explain the concept of empowerment. What are self-managed work teams?

8. What is the parity principle? How does the parity principle relate to the exception principle?

9. Describe three components of the delegation process.

10. Why are many managers reluctant to delegate authority?

11. What is the unity of command principle?

12. What is the scalar principle?

13. What is the span of management?

14. Define the following: flextime, telecommuting, and job sharing.

Skill-Building Questions

1. Do you think division of labor has been overemphasized in today's highly mechanized and efficient society?

2. Comment on the following statement, which is attributed to Robert Heinlein: "A human being should be able to change a diaper, plan an invasion, butcher a hog, conn a ship, design a building, write a sonnet, balance accounts, build a wall, set a bone, comfort the dying, take orders, give orders, cooperate, act alone, solve equations, analyze new problems, pitch manure, program a computer, cook a tasty meal, fight efficiently, and die gallantly. Specialization is for insects."

3. Identify and discuss a job that has a relatively wide job scope and narrow job depth. Identify a job that has a relatively narrow job scope and a wide job depth.

4. As a manager, would you prefer a relatively large (more than seven subordinates) or small (seven or fewer subordinates) span of management? Why? What are the implications of your choice?

5. Many people believe that the concept of empowerment receives a lot more talk than action. Why do you think this could be true?

6. Do you think you would like to telecommute? Why or why not?

Skill-Building Exercise 9.1

Promotion Possible: A Role Play

Your instructor will ask some class members to role play either the president or the current assistant sales manager in the following scenario.

The assistant sales manager of ABC Company has been in that job for six months. Due to poor sales over the past 18 months, the sales manager (his or her boss) has just been fired. The president of ABC then offers this job to the assistant sales manager subject to the following stipulations:

• You cannot increase the advertising budget.

• You must continue to let Metro-Media, Inc., handle the advertising.

• You cannot make any personnel changes.

• You will accept full responsibility for the sales for this fiscal year (which started two months ago).

The role play will simulate a meeting between the president and the assistant sales manager to discuss the offer. You can make any reasonable assumptions you think are necessary to play the role assigned to you.

Skill-Building Exercise 9.2

Minor Errors

Recently you have noticed that one of the staff members on the same level as your boss has been giving you a hard time concerning reports you submit to her. Having reviewed recent reports, you have discovered a few minor errors you should have caught; but in your opinion, they are not significant enough to warrant the kind of criticism you've been receiving. Your boss and this particular manager have a history of bad relations, which may be one reason for her attitude and actions.

As you think about how to best handle the situation, you consider these alternatives:

a. Talk to the manager in private and ask her why she is being so critical.

b. Do nothing. It is probably a temporary situation; to bring undue attention to it will only make matters worse.

c. Since your boss may get involved, discuss it with her and ask advice on what to do.

d. Work harder to upgrade the reports; make sure there will be nothing to criticize in the future.

e. Discuss it with your boss, but minimize or downplay the situation by letting her know that you believe constructive criticism of this type is usually healthy.

Other alternatives may be open to you, but assume these are the only ones you have considered.

1. *Without discussion* with anyone, decide which of these approaches you would take now. Be prepared to defend your choice.
2. What principle of organization most closely relates to this situation?
3. To what extent do you think this is an organizing problem as opposed to a personality problem?

Case Incident 9.1

A Good Manager?

Francis S. Russell is assistant general manager and sales manager for Webb Enterprises. At the moment, this self-styled perfectionist is sitting up in bed, checking his TTD sheet for tomorrow. The TTD (Things to Do) itemizes his daily activities, placing them on an exact time schedule. Never one to browbeat subordinates, Russell has his own special way of reminding people that time is money. Ever since the days when he was the best salesperson the company ever had, he had worked harder than the rest. It had paid off, too, because in only two years (when old Charlie retired), he was the heir apparent to the general managership. As this thought crossed Russell's mind, his immediate pride was replaced with a nagging problem. Where was he going to find the time to do all the things his position required? He certainly couldn't afford to just maintain the status quo. Then his mind forced him to plan tomorrow's activities and the problem was pushed into the background for future consideration.

(We see below a portion of Russell's well-planned day.)

TTD—October 16

7:15 Breakfast with Johnson (Purchasing). Get information on his cataloging system. Maybe combine with sales department and avoid duplication.

8:30 Meeting with Henry (assistant sales manager). Tell him exactly how the sales meeting for out-of-state representatives should be conducted. Caution—he's shaky on questions.

9:15 Discuss progress on new office procedures manual with Charlie (general manager). (He's irritated because I've dragged my heels on this. Let him know I've got Newman working on the problem.)

9:45 Assign Pat Newman the job of collecting data and sample copies regarding office manuals in other companies in our industry. Set up a system for him to use in analysis.

10:45 Call on Acliff Printing. A potentially big customer. (As Russell jotted down some information on this client, he reflected that it was a shame no one else on his staff could really handle the big ones the way he could. This thought was pleasing and bothersome at the same time.)

12:00 Lunch with J. Acliff (reservations at Black Angus).

3:00 Meet with Frank Lentz (advertising assistant) and check his progress on the new sales campaign. (Russell thought about Lentz's usual wild ideas and hoped that he had followed the general theme and rough sketches he had prepared.)

    7:30   Chamber of Commerce meeting. (Look up Pierce Hansen—he may be able to help on the Acliff account.)

Questions

1. Do you think Francis is a highly motivated employee trying to do a good job? Explain your answer.
2. What problems do you see concerning Francis' effectiveness as a manager?
3. Assuming you were Charlie, the general manager, what solutions would you recommend?

Case Incident 9.2

The Vacation Request

Tom Blair has a week's vacation coming and really wants to take it the third week in May, which is the height of the bass fishing season. The only problem is that two of the other five members of his department have already requested and received approval from their boss, Luther Jones, to take off that same week. Afraid that Luther would not approve his request, Tom decided to forward his request directly to Harry Jensen, who is Luther's boss and who is rather friendly to Tom (Tom has taken Harry fishing on several occasions). Not realizing that Luther has not seen the request, Harry approves it. Several weeks pass before Luther finds out, by accident, that Tom has been approved to go on vacation the third week of May.

The thing that really bugs Luther is that this is only one of many instances in which his subordinates have gone directly to Harry and gotten permission to do something. Just last week, in fact, he overheard a conversation in the washroom to the effect that, "If you want anything approved, don't waste time with Luther, go directly to Harry."

Questions

1. What should Harry have done?
2. Who is at fault, Harry or Tom?
3. What if Luther confronts Harry with the problem and he simply brushes it off by saying he is really only helping?

References and Additional Readings

1. Harold Koontz and Cyril O'Donnell, *Management: A Systems and Contingency Analysis of Managerial Functions*, 6th ed. (New York: McGraw-Hill, 1976), p. 274.
2. Chester L. Barnard, *Functions of the Executive* (Cambridge, MA: Harvard University Press, 1938), pp. 114–15.
3. Gareth R. Jones, *Organizational Theory* (Reading, MA: Addison-Wesley, 1995), p. 9.
4. Adam Smith, *The Wealth of Nations* (New York: Modern Library, 1917); originally published in 1776.
5. Thomas J. Peters and Robert H. Waterman, Jr., *In Search of Excellence* (New York: Harper & Row, 1982), p. 313.
6. Mary Parker Follett, *Freedom and Co-Ordination* (London: Management Publication Trust, 1949), pp. 1–15 (the lecture reproduced in *Freedom and Co-Ordination* was first delivered in 1926); and Barnard, *Functions,* p. 163.
7. John Tschol, "Empowerment: The Key to Customer Service," *American Salesman,* November 1997, pp. 12–15.
8. Robert B. Shaw, "The Capacity to Act: Creating a Context for Empowerment," in *Organizational Architecture: Designs for Changing Organizations,* ed. David A. Nadler, Marc S. Gerstein, and Robert B. Shaw (San Francisco: Jossey-Bass, 1992), p. 169.
9. Renee Beckhams, "Self-Directed Work Teams: The Wave of the Future?" *Hospital Material Management Quarterly,* August 1998, pp. 48–60.

10. Herbert M. Engel, *How to Delegate* (Houston: Gulf, 1983), p. 6.

11. Michael Hammer and James Champy, *Reengineering the Corporation* (New York: Harper Business, 1993), pp. 168, 180–81.

12. Ibid., pp. 180–81.

13. L. F. Urwick, *The Elements of Administration* (New York: Harper & Row, 1943), p. 46.

14. Henri Fayol, *General and Industrial Management* (London: Sir Isaac Pitman & Sons, 1949), p. 36; first published in 1916.

15. Sir Ian Hamilton, *The Soul and Body of an Army* (London: Edward Arnold, 1921), p. 229.

16. V. A. Graicunas, "Relationship in Organization," *Bulletin of the International Management Institute* (Geneva: International Labour Office, 1933); reprinted in *Papers on the Science of Administration,* ed. L. Gulick and L. F. Urwick (New York: Institute of Public Administration, 1937), pp. 181–87.

17. L. F. Urwick, "Scientific Principles and Organizations," *Institute of Management Series No. 19* (New York: American Management Association, 1938), p. 8.

18. For a brief discussion of such situations, see Leslie W. Rue, "Supervisory Control in Modern Management," *Atlanta Economic Review,* January–February 1975, pp. 43–44.

19. L. F. Urwick, "V. A. Graicunas and the Span of Control," *Academy of Management Journal,* June 1974, p. 352.

20. Sarah Hale, "The Orlando Sentinel, Fla., Small Business Toolbox Column," *Knight Ridder Tribune Business News,* July 15, 2002, p. 1.

21. "Hewitt Study Shows Work/Life Benefits Hold Steady Despite Recession," press release, May 13, 2002, © 2003, Hewitt Associates.

22. Brian Gill, "Flextime Benefits Employees and Employers," *American Printer,* February 1998, p. 70.

23. Donald D. Davis and Karen A. Polonko, "Telework America 2001 Summary," © 2002–2003, International Telework Association & Council.

24. Susan J. Wells, "Making Telecommuting Work," *HR Magazine,* October 2001, pp. 34–35.

25. "Hewitt Study Shows Work/Life Benefits Hold Steady Despite Recession."

Chapter 10

Organizing Structure

Learning Objectives

After studying this chapter, you will be able to:

1. Discuss the different stages an organization goes through as it grows and matures.
2. Explain what an organization chart is.
3. List several factors that can affect which structure is the most appropriate for a given organization.
4. Describe the general relationship between an organization's strategy and its structure.
5. Define outsourcing, and summarize its potential benefits as well as its potential drawbacks.
6. Describe a contingency approach to organizing.
7. Identify the different types of departmentation.
8. Briefly describe each of the following types of organizational structure: line structure, line and staff structure, matrix structure, horizontal structure, and virtual organization.
9. Describe several trends that have taken place regarding the popularity of different types of organization structures.
10. Describe how committees can be made more effective.
11. Explain the difference between an inside and an outside board of directors.

Chapter Preview

In business, decentralization and organizational flattening typically involve eliminating several layers of management, often leaving managers overwhelmed with as many as a dozen direct subordinates. The U.S. Marines, on the other hand, have pushed decision-making authority down the line while retaining a simple hierarchical structure. The Marines' "rule of three" states that each Marine has three, and only three, things to worry about. In terms of organizational structure, the "rule of three" means each corporal has a three-person fire team; each sergeant has a squad of three fire teams; each lieutenant and a staff sergeant have a platoon of three squads; and so on, up to generals.

From a functional viewpoint, the rule of three dictates that each Marine should limit his or her attention to three tasks or goals. When strategizing, each Marine should boil an infinite world of possibilities down to three alternative courses of action; anything more might lead to confusion. The rule of three results in an organizational hierarchy that might seem extremely narrow and tall since there are typically six full layers of management in between an infantry private and the colonel commanding his or her regiment. However, when the action starts, the layers collapse on an as-needed basis. Marines at all levels begin making decisions in responses to fast-changing situations—without so much as consulting the chain of command. Even privates are expected to take whatever initiative is necessary to complete a mission. Major General John Admire, commander of an infantry division at Camp Pendleton, sums up the Marines' view, "If your decision-making loop is more streamlined than your enemy's, then you set the pace and course of the battle."

The Marines believe that the key to making their organizational structure work is recruiting effective decision makers for lower levels. The lowest ranks are consistently told that their performance not only contributes to the bottom line but rather it is the bottom line. The higher the level of a Marine officer, the quicker he or she is to give credit to the lower ranks. Few organizations make hiring and training of managers as high a priority as the Marines.

Sources: David H. Freedman, "Grunts Rule," *Across the Board,* March–April 2001, p. 13; and David H. Freedman, "Corps Values," *Inc.,* April 1998, pp. 54–56.

Analyzing Management Skills

Would you describe the Marines' organizational structure as flat or tall? Why? Do you think the Marines' structure has captured the best points of both flat and tall organizations? Explain your answer.

Applying Management Skills

Have you ever been in or observed a work situation where you felt customer service was being hindered by the organization's structure? What would you do differently if you could change the structure?

organization structure
Framework that defines the boundaries of the formal organization and within which the organization operates.

Organization structure is the framework that defines the boundaries of the formal organization and within which the organization operates. The structure of an organization reflects how groups compete for resources, where responsibilities for profits and other performance measures lie, how information is transmitted, and how decisions are made. Many people believe a good manager or a competent employee should be able to perform well regardless of the organization structure and environment. They believe that if managers or employees are good enough, they can overcome any obstacles the organization structure presents. Others believe that given the right organization structure, anyone should be able to perform in an acceptable fashion. The truth lies somewhere in between. An appropriate organization structure certainly helps foster good performance.

FIGURE 10.1
Organization
Growth and Change

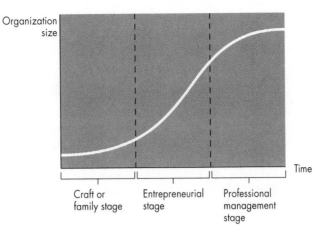

Organization
size

Time

Craft or
family stage

Entrepreneurial
stage

Professional
management
stage

Organization Growth Stages

Figure 10.1 shows in general terms the stages an organization goes through as it grows and matures. The craft or family stage is characterized by the absence of formal policies, objectives, and structure. The operations of the organization at this stage generally center on one individual and one functional area. During the entrepreneurial stage, the organization grows first at an increasing and then a decreasing rate. An atmosphere of optimism pervades the entire organization as sales and profits rise rapidly. By the third stage of growth, the entrepreneur has been replaced by or evolved into a professional manager who performs the processes of planning, organizing, staffing, motivating, and controlling.[1] Profits are realized more from internal efficiency and less from external exploitation of the market. At this stage, the organization becomes characterized by written policies, procedures, and plans.

As the organization moves through the craft stage and into the entrepreneurial stage, an organization structure must be developed. This is a critical stage for the organization. If an appropriate structure is not established and utilized, the entrepreneur may lose control and the entire organization may collapse. An organization structure must be developed that allows the organization to adapt to change in its environment.

Organization Charts

An organization chart uses a series of boxes connected with one or more lines to graphically represent the organization's structure. Each box represents a position within the organization, and each line indicates the nature of the relationships among the different positions. The organization chart not only identifies specific relationships but also provides an overall picture of how the entire organization fits together. As organizations become larger and more complex, it becomes increasingly difficult to represent all of the relationships accurately.

Factors Affecting Organization Structure

Several factors can affect which structure is the most appropriate for a given organization. A structure that is appropriate for a high-tech company that employs 50,000 people in eight countries will probably not be appropriate for a small retail business with just a dozen employees. Strategy, size, environment, and technology are some of the important factors found to be mostly closely related to organization structure.

Strategy

A major part of an organization's strategy for attaining its objectives deals with how the organization is structured. An appropriate structure will not guarantee success, but it will enhance the organization's chances for success. Business leaders, athletic coaches, and military leaders all stress that to succeed one must not only have a good strategy but also be prepared to win (mentally and structurally). In addition to clarifying and defining strategy through the delegation of authority and responsibility, the organization structure can either facilitate or inhibit strategy implementation.

In a groundbreaking study of organizational strategy, Alfred D. Chandler described a pattern in the evolution of organizational structures.[2] The pattern was based on studies of Du Pont, General Motors, Sears, and Standard Oil Company, with corroborating evidence from many other firms. The pattern Chandler described was that of changing strategy, followed by administrative problems, leading to decline in performance, revised structure, and a subsequent return to economic health. In summary, Chandler concluded that structure follows strategy; in other words, changes in strategy ultimately led to changes in the organization's structure. Chandler's work related particularly to growth and to the structural adjustments made to maintain efficient performance during market expansion, product line diversification, and vertical integration.

Although subsequent research has supported the idea of a relationship between strategy and structure, it is clear that strategy is not the only variable that has a bearing on structure.[3] The process of matching structure to strategy is complex and should be undertaken with a thorough understanding of the historical development of the current structure and of other variables, including size, environment, and technology.

mechanistic systems
Organizational systems characterized by a rigid delineation of functional duties, precise job descriptions, fixed authority and responsibility, and a well-developed organizational hierarchy through which information filters up and instructions flow down.

organic systems
Organizational systems characterized by less formal job descriptions, greater emphasis on adaptability, more participation, and less fixed authority.

Size

There are many ways to measure the size of an organization, but sales volume and number of employees are the most frequently used factors. While no hard-and-fast rules exist, certain characteristics generally relate to an organization's size. Small organizations tend to be less specialized (horizontal division of labor), less standardized, and more centralized. Larger organizations tend to be more specialized, more standardized, and more decentralized. Thus, as an organization grows in size, certain structural changes naturally occur.

Environment

A landmark study relating organization to environment was conducted by Tom Burns and G. M. Stalker in the United Kingdom.[4] By examining some 20 industrial firms in both a changing industry and a more stable, established industry, Burns and Stalker focused on how a firm's pattern of organization was related to certain characteristics of the external environment. The researchers identified two distinct organizational systems. **Mechanistic systems** are characterized by a rigid delineation of functional duties, precise job descriptions, fixed authority and responsibility, and a well-developed organizational hierarchy through which information filters up and instructions flow down. **Organic systems** are characterized by less formal job descriptions, greater emphasis on adaptability, more participa-

FIGURE 10.2
Structural Differences between Mechanistic and Organic Systems

Source: Adapted from Tom Burns and G. W. Stalker, *The Management of Innovation* (London: Tavistock, 1961), pp. 119–22.

Characteristics of Mechanistic and Organic Organizations	
Mechanistic	**Organic**
Work is divided into narrow, specialized tasks.	Work is defined in terms of general tasks.
Tasks are performed as specified unless changed by managers in the hierarchy.	Tasks are continually adjusted as needed through interaction with others involved in the task.
Structure of control, authority, and communication is hierarchical.	Structure of control, authority, and communication is a network.
Decisions are made by the specified hierarchical level.	Decisions are made by individuals with relevant knowledge and technical expertise.
Communication is mainly vertical, between superior and subordinate.	Communication is vertical and horizontal, among superiors, subordinates, and peers.
Communication content is larzgely instructions and decisions issued by superiors.	Communication content is largely information and advice.
Emphasis is on loyalty to the organization and obedience to superiors.	Emphasis is on commitment to organizational goals and possession of needed expertise.

tion, and less fixed authority. Burns and Stalker found that successful firms in stable and established industries tended to be mechanistic in structure, whereas successful firms in dynamic industries tended to be organic in structure. See Figure 10.2 for a more complete evaluation of the structural differences between mechanistic and organic systems.

Paul Lawrence and Jay Lorsch conducted a later study dealing with organization structure and its environment.[5] Their original study included 10 firms in three distinct industrial environments. Reaching conclusions similar to those of Burns and Stalker, Lawrence and Lorsch found that to be successful, firms operating in a dynamic environment needed a relatively flexible structure, firms operating in a stable environment needed a more rigid structure, and firms operating in an intermediate environment needed a structure somewhere between the two extremes.

Numerous other studies have been conducted in the past several years investigating the relationship between organization structure and environment. In general, most have concluded that the best structure for a given organization is contingent on the organization's environment to some degree.[6] However, managerial style and corporate culture may also have an impact as interpretative agents of the environment. Microsoft's Bill Gates, Nike's Phil Knight, and Pixar's Steve Jobs have all moved their companies in the direction of the organic model so they could swiftly move into new and as yet untapped markets and product lines.

Organization and Technology

Numerous studies have also been conducted investigating potential relationships between technology and organization structure. One of the most important of these studies was conducted by Joan Woodward in the late 1950s.[7] Her study was based on an analysis of 100 manufacturing firms in the southeast Essex area of England. Woodward's general approach was to classify firms along a scale of "technical complexity" with particular emphasis on three modes of production: (1) unit or small-batch production (e.g., custom-made machines), (2) large-batch or mass production (e.g., an automotive assembly plant), and (3) continuous flow or process production (e.g., a chemical plant). The unit or small-batch production mode represents the lower end of the technical complexity scale, while the continuous flow mode represents the upper end.

After classifying each firm into one of the preceding categories, Woodward investigated a number of organizational variables. Some of her findings follow:

1. The number of levels in an organization increased as technical complexity increased.
2. The ratio of managers and supervisors to total personnel increased as technical complexity increased.
3. Using Burns and Stalker's definition of organic and mechanistic systems, organic management systems tended to predominate in firms at both ends of the scale of technical complexity, while mechanistic systems predominated in firms falling in the middle ranges.
4. No significant relationship existed between technical complexity and organizational size.

A few years later, Edward Harvey undertook a similar study.[8] Rather than using Woodward's technical complexity scale, Harvey grouped firms along a continuum from technical diffuseness to technical specificity. Technically diffused firms have a wider range of products, produce products that vary from year to year, and produce more made-to-order products. Harvey's findings were similar to Woodward's in that he found significant relationships between technology and several organizational characteristics.

The general conclusion reached in the Woodward and Harvey studies was that a relationship clearly exists between organizational technology and a number of aspects of organization structure. Many additional studies have investigated the relationship between technology and structure. While they have reported some conflicting results, most studies have found a relationship between technology and structure.[9]

Changes Affecting Organization Structure

In recent years, dramatic improvements in communication technology have introduced new ways of conducting business. These new practices have affected the structure of many organizations. Outsourcing has resulted from improved communication technology and is having an effect on the structure of many organizations. **Outsourcing** is the practice of subcontracting certain work functions to an outside entity. Whether outsourcing is a response to downsizing or a natural extension of downsizing, it is a practice that will significantly affect the workplace and organizational charts. Work functions that are frequently being outsourced include accounting and finance functions, human resources, information technology, and even contract manufacturing. According to the Outsourcing Institute, outsourcing expenditures of all types have gone from virtually no activity in 1980 to $150 billion in 1998 and a projected $320 billion in 2004.[10]

Outsourcing has numerous potential benefits, including the following:[11]

outsourcing
Practice of subcontracting information systems work to an independent outside source.

- Allowing the organization to emphasize its core competencies by not spending time on routine areas that can be outsourced.

When United Airlines closed its maintenance hubs in Indianapolis and Oakland in the summer of 2003, thousands of mechanics' jobs were outsourced. United has since begun outsourcing more functions such as cargo handling, airplane cleaning, and fuel purchasing. Collectively, bankrupt United hopes to save about $900 million a year through outsourcing and other cost-cutting moves. Amos Kazzaz, vice president of financial planning and analysis at United's parent company, UAL Corporation, explained the outsourcing moves: "There are always those who are specialists. We looked to outside parties who can do it better."

Specifically, United expects to save only about $5 million on $2.8 billion in annual fuel expenses by turning over fuel purchasing and hedging operations to Morgan Stanley Capital Group. However, the big benefit is that Morgan Stanley will carry the inventory and free up about $250 million in working capital. The company expects to save more than $20 million by outsourcing plane cleaning services. The question is whether the projected savings will become reality and if these savings are enough to ensure United's survival.

Source: Paul Merrion, "Outsourcing Files UAL into Uncharted Skies," *Crain's Chicago Business*, October 13, 2003, p. 3.

- Reducing operating costs by utilizing others who can do the job more efficiently.
- Accessing top talent and state-of-the-art technology without having to own it.
- Fewer personnel headaches.
- Improving resource allocation by allowing growth to take place more quickly.

Of course, there are potential drawbacks to outsourcing.[12] One overriding concern is that a large number of jobs are being lost to other countries through outsourcing. For example, it has been estimated that almost 600,000 high-skilled U.S. jobs will leave by 2005 and that more than 3 million will leave by 2015.[13] Other specific drawbacks include

contingency (situational) approach to organization structure
States that the most appropriate structure depends on the technology used, the rate of environmental change, and other dynamic forces.

- Loss of control and being at the mercy of the vendor.
- Loss of in-house skills.
- Threat to the morale of the workforce if too many areas are dominated by outside vendors.
- No guarantee that it will save money or provide higher service standards.

As with most management approaches, outsourcing is not a cure-all. Care must be taken that a long-term strategy evolves out of the use of outsourcing, not just a short-term fix to reduce costs. In the right situations, outsourcing can work well; but it almost always requires good management, good contracts, and realistic expectations. Management Illustration 10.1 discusses United Airlines' attempt to cut costs through outsourcing.

A Contingency Approach

The previous discussions emphasize the fact that several factors affect an organization's structure. The knowledge that there is no one best way to organize (i.e., the design is conditional) has led to a **contingency (situational) approach** to organizing. Figure 10.3 shows the previously discussed variables and others that can help determine the most appropriate organization structure. The contingency approach should be viewed as a process of assessing these relevant variables and

FIGURE 10.3
Variables Affecting Appropriate Organization Structure

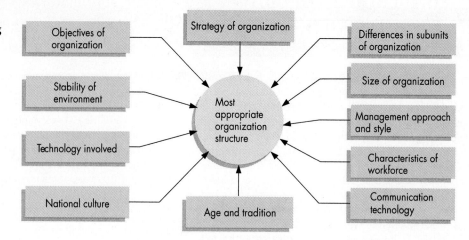

then choosing the most appropriate structure for the situation. Because most of the relevant variables are dynamic, management should periodically analyze and appraise the organization's structure in light of any relevant changes.

Departmentation

departmentation
Grouping jobs into related work units.

While thousands of different organization structures exist, almost all are built on the concept of departmentation. **Departmentation** involves grouping jobs into related work units. The work units may be related on the basis of work functions, product, geography, customer, technique, or time.

Work Functions

functional departmentation
Defining organizational units in terms of the nature of the work.

Functional departmentation occurs when organization units are defined by the nature of the work. Although different terms may be used, most organizations have four basic functions: production, marketing, finance, and human resources. Production refers to the actual creation of something of value, either goods, services, or both. Marketing involves product or service planning, pricing the product or service with respect to demand, evaluating how to best distribute the good or service, and communicating information to the market through sales and advertising. Any organization, whether manufacturing or service, must provide the financial structure necessary for carrying out its activities. The human resource function is responsible for securing and developing the organization's people.

Each of these basic functions may be broken down as necessary. For instance, the production department may be split into maintenance, quality control, engineering, manufacturing, and so on. The marketing department may be grouped into advertising, sales, and market research. Figure 10.4 charts a typical functional departmentation.

The primary advantage of functional departmentation is that it allows for specialization within functions. It also provides for efficient use of equipment and resources, potential economies of scale, and ease of coordination within the function itself. However, functional departmentation can have some negative effects. For example, suboptimization of goals occurs when members of a functional group develop more loyalty to the functional group's goals than to the organization's goals. For example, the marketing department might be overzealous in selling products even when production cannot meet any additional demand. If the

FIGURE 10.4
Functional
Departmentation

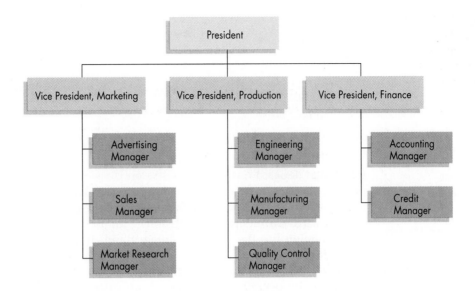

group's goals and the organization's goals are not mutually supportive, such activity can lead to problems. Conflict may also develop among different departments striving for different goals. In addition, employees who are locked into their functions have a restricted view of the organization. Finally, the rather narrow functional scope of managers may be a disadvantage when a multidisciplinary approach would be more advantageous.

Product

**product
departmentation**
Grouping all
activities necessary to
produce and market a
product or service
under one manager.

Under **product departmentation,** all the activities needed to produce and market a product or service are usually under a single manager. This system allows employees to identify with a particular product and thus develop esprit de corps. It also facilitates managing each product as a distinct profit center. Product departmentation provides opportunities for training for executive personnel by letting them experience a broad range of functional activities. Problems can arise if departments become overly competitive to the detriment of the overall organization. A second potential problem is duplication of facilities and equipment. Product departmentation adapts best to large, multiproduct organizations. Figure 10.5 illustrates how a company might be structured using product departmentation.

Geographic

**geographic
departmentation**
Defining
organizational units
by territories.

Geographic departmentation is most likely to occur in organizations that maintain physically dispersed and autonomous operations or offices. Departmentation by geography permits the use of local employees or salespeople. This can create customer goodwill and an awareness of local feelings and desires. It can also lead to a high level of service. Of course, having too many locations can be costly.

FIGURE 10.5
Product
Departmentation

FIGURE 10.6
Customer
Departmentation

Customer

customer departmentation
Defining organizational units in terms of customers served.

Customer departmentation is based on division by customers served. A common example is an organization that has one department to handle retail customers and one department to handle wholesale or industrial customers. Figure 10.6 shows departmentation by customer for Johnson & Johnson. This type of departmentation has the same advantages and disadvantages as product departmentation. For example, if the professional group and the pharmaceutical group in Figure 10.6 became too competitive with each other for corporate resources, the organization's overall performance could suffer.

Other Types

Several other types of departmentation are possible. Departmentation by simple numbers is practiced when the most important ingredient for success is the number of employees. Organizing for a local United Way drive would be an example. Departmentation by process or equipment is another possibility. A final type of departmentation is by time or shift. Organizations that work around the clock may use this type of departmentation.

Hybrid Departmentation

hybrid departmentation
Occurs when an organization simultaneously uses more than one type of departmentation.

Typically, as an organization grows in size, it adds levels of departmentation. A small organization may have no departmentation at first. As it grows, it may departmentalize first on one basis, then another, and then another. For example, a large sales organization may use product departmentation to create self-contained divisions; then each division might be further divided by geography and then by type of customer. **Hybrid departmentation** occurs when an organization simultaneously uses more than one type of departmentation. As Figure 10.7 illustrates, many different department mixes are possible for a given organization. Which one is best depends on the specific situation.

Types of Organization Structures

There are several basic types of structures that organizations may use. Traditionally, these have been the line structure, the line and staff structure, or the matrix structure. Recently, new types of structures and organizations have evolved and are evolving to take advantage of the new communication and logistical technology available. These new structures include the horizontal structure and the virtual organization. Each of these types of structures is discussed in the following sections.

line structure
Organization structure with direct vertical lines between the different levels of the organization.

Line Structure

In a *line organization*, authority originates at the top and moves downward in a line. All managers perform *line functions*, or functions that contribute directly to company profits. Examples of line functions include production managers, sales representatives, and marketing managers.

FIGURE 10.7   **Possible Departmentation Mixes for a Sales Organization**

The most important aspect of the **line structure** is that the work of all organizational units is directly involved in producing and marketing the organization's goods or services. This is the simplest organization structure and is characterized by vertical links between the different levels of the organization. All members of the organization receive instructions through the scalar chain. One advantage is a clear authority structure that promotes rapid decision making and prevents "passing the buck." A disadvantage is that it may force managers to perform too broad a range of duties. It may also cause the organization to become too dependent on one or two key employees who are capable of performing many duties. Because of its simplicity, line structure exists most frequently in small organizations. Figure 10.8 represents a simplified line structure.

line and staff structure
Organization structure that results when staff specialists are added to a line organization.

staff functions
Functions that are advisory and supportive in nature; designed to contribute to the efficiency and maintenance of the organization.

Line and Staff Structure

The addition of staff specialists to a line-structured organization creates a **line and staff structure.** As a line organization grows, staff assistance often becomes necessary. **Staff functions** are advisory and supportive in nature; they contribute to the efficiency and maintenance of the organization. **Line functions** are directly

FIGURE 10.8
A Simplified Line Structure

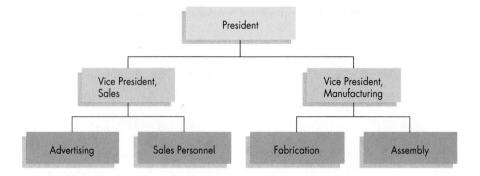

line functions
Functions and activities directly involved in producing and marketing the organization's goods or services.

involved in producing and marketing the organization's goods or services. They generally relate directly to the attainment of major organizational objectives, while staff functions contribute indirectly. Staff people are generally specialists in one field, and their authority is normally limited to making recommendations to line people. Typical staff functions include research and development, personnel management, employee training, and various "assistant to" positions. Figure 10.9 shows a simplified line and staff organization structure.

Line and Staff Conflict

The line and staff organization allows much more specialization and flexibility than does the simple line organization; however, it sometimes creates conflict. Some staff specialists resent the fact that they may be only advisers to line personnel and have no real authority over the line. At the same time, line managers, knowing they have final responsibility for the product, are often reluctant to listen to staff advice. Many staff specialists think they should not be in a position of having to sell their ideas to the line. They believe the line managers should openly listen to their ideas. If the staff specialist is persistent, the line manager often resents even more that the staff "always tries to interfere and run my department." The staff specialist who does not persist often becomes discouraged because "no one ever listens."

Matrix Structure

The matrix (sometimes called *project*) form of organization is a way of forming project teams within the traditional line-staff organization. A project is "a combination of human and nonhuman resources pulled together in a temporary organization to achieve a specified purpose."[14] The marketing of a new product and the construction of a new building are examples of projects. Because projects have a

FIGURE 10.9
A Simplified Line and Staff Structure

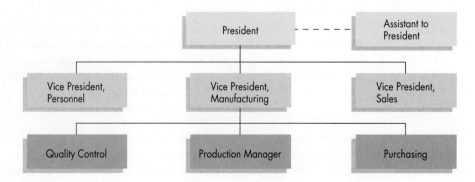

temporary life, a method of managing and organizing them was sought so that the existing organization structure would not be totally disrupted and would maintain some efficiency.

matrix structure
Hybrid organization structure in which individuals from different functional areas are assigned to work on a specific project or task.

Under the **matrix structure,** those working on a project are officially assigned to the project and to their original or base departments. A manager is given the authority and responsibility to meet the project objectives in terms of cost, quality, quantity, and time of completion. The project manager is then assigned the necessary personnel from the functional departments of the parent organization. Thus, a horizontal-line organization develops for the project within the parent vertical-line structure. Under such a system, the functional personnel are assigned to and evaluated by the project manager while they work on the project. When the project or their individual work on it is done, the functional personnel return to their departments or begin a new project, perhaps with a new project team. Figure 10.10 shows a matrix structure.

A major advantage of matrix structure is that the mix of people and resources can readily be changed as project needs change. Other advantages include the emphasis placed on the project by use of a project team and the relative ease with which project members can move back into the functional organization once the project has ended. In addition, employees are challenged constantly, and interdepartmental cooperation develops along with expanded managerial talent due to the multitude of roles the project manager must undertake.

FIGURE 10.10   **Illustrative Matrix Structure**

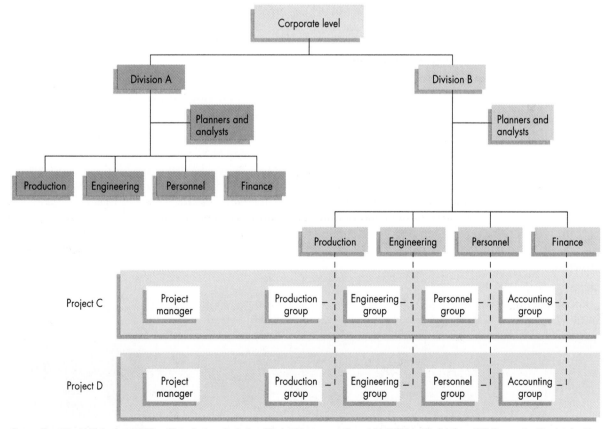

Source: From David Cleland and William King, *Systems Analysis and Project Management.* Copyright © 1983 by The McGraw-Hill Companies. Reprinted with permission.

One serious problem with the matrix structure is that it can violate the principle of unity of command. A role conflict can develop if the authority of the project manager is not clearly delineated from that of the functional managers. In such a case, the people assigned to the project may receive conflicting assignments from the project manager and their functional managers. A second problem occurs when the personnel assigned to a project are still evaluated by their functional manager, who usually has little opportunity to observe their work on the project. Third, matrix structures are often costly to implement, are only marginally accepted because they defy tradition, and put undue stress on communication networks.

Horizontal Structure

horizontal structure
Consists of two groups. One group is composed of senior management who are responsible for strategic decisions and policies. The second group is composed of empowered employees working together in different process teams.

A relatively new type of structure is the **horizontal structure** (also called *team structure*). The pure form of a horizontal structure consists of two core groups. One group is composed of senior management who are responsible for strategic decisions and policies. The second group is composed of empowered employees working together in different process teams. Figure 10.11 illustrates a basic horizontal structure. Characteristics of a horizontal organization include the following:

1. The organization is built around three to five core processes, such as developing new products, with specific performance goals assigned. Each process has an owner or champion.
2. The hierarchy is flattened to reduce supervision.
3. Teams manage everything, including themselves. They're held accountable for performance goals.
4. Customers, not stock appreciation or profitability, drive performance.
5. Team performance, not just the individual, is rewarded. Staffers are encouraged to develop multiple skills and are rewarded for it.
6. Customer contact is maximized with employees.
7. Emphasis is on informing and training all employees. "Don't just spoon-feed information on a 'need to know' basis."[15]

Rather than focusing on financial or functional goals, the horizontal organization emphasizes customer satisfaction. Information is processed at the local level by process teams. Local problems can often be resolved quickly by the process team, thus permitting the organization to operate with flexibility and responsiveness.[16]

FIGURE 10.11
Horizontal Structure

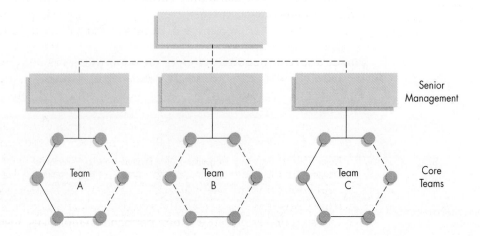

Elizabeth Arden International is a global cosmetics and perfumery company owned by Unilever. In the early 1990s, the company was plagued with duplication of processes within individual countries, inefficient third-party distributors, and excessively high inventory holding costs. Marketing was also out of control due to little coordination among national subsidiaries.

Recognizing its problems, the company put in place a horizontal structure with eight teams of 10–15 people (300 in total) led by a project director and reporting to a steering committee. The company spent the better part of two years implementing the new structure.

The transition was particularly difficult for the company's general managers whose role was significantly altered. No longer overseeing a wide array of functions, the general managers now concentrated on market intelligence, new product and service opportunities, and customer sales and service. Of the original 15 general managers, only 2 remain.

While the transition was painful, it has been profitable. Overall, the company has realized a 30 percent reduction in administrative costs, a 60 percent reduction in personnel, and a 50 percent cut in required working capital.

Source: Marcie Krempel, "Arden's Makeover," *Business Europe*, June 2, 1999, p. 4.

Additional advantages of the horizontal organization include increased efficiency, improved work culture and morale, and more satisfied customers. Kraft Foods, Ford Motor Company, General Electric, British Airways, AT&T, Motorola, Saab, Tesco, and American Express Financial Advisors have all made efforts to implement a horizontal structure in at least a part of their organizations. Management Illustration 10.2 describes why and how an international European company transitioned to a horizontal structure.

The Virtual Organization

virtual organization
Temporary network of independent companies—suppliers, customers, and even rivals—linked by information technology to share skills, costs, and access to one another's markets.

A **virtual organization** is one in which business partners and teams work together across geographical or organizational boundaries by means of information technology.[17] In a virtual organization, co-workers often do not see each other on a regular basis. Three common types of virtual organizations have been identified.[18] One type exists when a group of skilled individuals form a company by communicating via computer, phone, fax, and videoconference. A second type occurs when a group of companies, each of which specializes in a certain function such as manufacturing or marketing, partner together. A third type occurs when one large company outsources many of its operations by using modern technology to transmit information to its partner companies so that it can focus on its specialty.

Virtual organizations create a network of collaborators that come together to pursue a specific opportunity. Once the opportunity has been realized, the collaborators usually disband and form new alliances to pursue new opportunities. Thus, virtual organizations are fluid, flexible, and constantly changing. Figure 10.12 illustrates a basic type of virtual organization.

Technology plays a central role in allowing virtual organizations to form. Integrated computer and communication technology are the means by which the different collaborators are put together. To illustrate one example of how a virtual organization might work, suppose you head a large company.[19] It's Christmas season, and your company needs an additional 100 customer service representatives. Once the Christmas rush is over, these additional service representatives won't be needed, so it makes no sense to hire permanent employees. Instead, you hire 100

FIGURE 10.12
Virtual
Organization

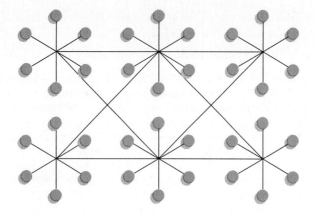

flat structure
Organization with
few levels and
relatively large spans
of management at
each level.

people who work at home and have their own computers. The physical locations of these *virtual employees* doesn't matter; they can be in Cleveland, Hong Kong, or Singapore. The virtual employees dial into the company's database and become an extension of the company. Whenever a customer calls in, all information about that customer appears on the computer screen of the virtual employee handling the call; hence, the widely scattered employees can operate as if they are all at the same location. Once the Christmas rush is over, the collaboration is dissolved.

As outlined in Figure 10.13, virtual organizations have many potential benefits and challenges. Many people believe that some form of virtual organization is the wave of the future. Management Illustration 10.3 describes how Boeing has proposed to utilize a virtual organization structure.

Trends in Organization Structure

tall structure
Organization with
many levels and
relatively small spans
of management.

Several trends in organization structures have emerged over the last several decades. Beginning in the 1950s and 1960s, much attention was focused on the virtues of flat versus tall organization structures. A **flat structure** has relatively few levels and relatively large spans of management at each level; a **tall structure** has many levels and relatively small spans of management (see Figure 10.14). A classic study in this area was conducted by James Worthy.[20] Worthy studied the morale of over 100,000 employees at Sears and Roebuck during a 12-year period.

FIGURE 10.13
**Benefits and
Challenges of
Transitioning to a
Virtual
Organization**

Sources: Maggie Biggs,
"Tomorrow's Workforce,"
Infoworld, September 18,
2000, p. 59; and Sonny Ariss,
Nick Nykodym, and Aimee
A. Cole-Laramore, "Trust
and Technology in the
Virtual Organization,"
*S.A.M. Advanced Management
Journal,* Autumn 2002, pp.
22–25.

Benefits	Challenges
Increases productivity.	Leaders must move from a control model to a trust method.
Decreases the cost of doing business.	
Provides the ability to hire the best talent regardless of location.	New forms of communication and collaboration will be required.
Allows you to quickly solve problems by forming dynamic teams.	Management must enable a learning culture and be willing to change.
Allows you to more easily leverage both static and dynamic staff.	Staff reeducation may be required.
Improves the work environment.	It can be difficult to monitor employee behavior.
Provides better balance for professional and personal lives.	
Provides competitive advantage.	

Boeing has proposed building a virtual organization to train screeners at airports and to train airline flight crews on how to counter terrorist threats. These businesses would be new territory for Boeing. However, the company does have experience in training pilots, designing training software and systems, and securing government approval for courses. Boeing services are particularly attractive to foreign governments that see Boeing's familiarity with the Federal Aviation Administration (FAA) as a big plus. Boeing envisions a potential large international market as international airports are likely to need to meet some type of standard in order for flights to leave there and come into the United States.

Boeing's international training proposals, as well as its domestic proposals, are based on partnership arrangements with other entities; hence, the formation of a type of virtual organization. Basically, Boeing will contribute aerospace expertise and its partners will handle related topics, such as law enforcement.

Source: David Bowmaster, "Boeing Poised for New Business of Airport Security," *Knight Ridder Tribune Business News,* February 22, 2002, p. 1.

His study noted that organizations with fewer levels and wider spans of management offered the potential for greater job satisfaction. A wide span of management also forced managers to delegate authority and develop more direct links of communication—another plus. On the other hand, Rocco Carzo and John Yanouzas found that groups operating in a tall structure had significantly better performance than those operating in a flat structure.[21] Other studies have also shown conflicting results. Therefore, one cannot conclude that all flat structures are better than all tall structures, or vice versa.[22]

In general, Japanese organizations historically have had fewer middle managers and flatter structures than American organizations. However, the downsizing many American organizations have experienced in the last several years has resulted in flatter structures with wider spans of control.

Beginning in the early 1980s with the publication of the best-selling book *In Search of Excellence* by Thomas Peters and Robert Waterman, emphasis shifted to the concept of a simple form and a lean staff. Historically, as organizations grow and meet with success, they tend to evolve into increasingly complex structures. How this occurs varies; frequently, a major cause is an increase in staff positions, especially at high levels. Many managers seem to feel a need for more staff and a

FIGURE 10.14
Flat versus Tall Structures

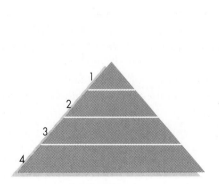

Span of management 8:1
Four levels
Flat structure

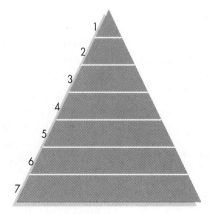

Span of management 5:1
Seven levels
Tall structure

more complex structure as the organization grows. They seem inclined to equate staff size with success.

In their study, Peters and Waterman found that many of the best-performing companies had maintained simple structures with small staffs.[23] One reason is that a simple form with a lean staff allows an organization to adjust more rapidly to a fast-changing environment. It is also conducive to innovation. A simple form and a lean staff are naturally intertwined in that one breeds the other: A simple form requires fewer staff, and a lean staff results in a simple form.

More recently, many organizations have abandoned the more traditional line and staff structures in favor of horizontal structures and virtual organizations. All indications are that these trends will continue. As more and more employees become empowered, companies will put increased emphasis on managing through teams. Similarly, as communications technology continues to improve, many companies will evolve into virtual organizations.

Committees

committee
Organization structure in which a group of people are formally appointed, organized, and superimposed on the line or line and staff structure to consider or decide certain matters.

Committees represent an important part of most traditional organization structures. A **committee** is a group of people formally appointed and organized to consider or decide certain matters. From a structural standpoint, committees are superimposed on the existing line, line and staff, or matrix structure. Committees can be permanent (standing) or temporary (ad hoc) and are usually in charge of, or supplementary to, the line and staff functions.

Teams are the counterpart to committees in nontraditional horizontal structures and virtual organizations. Because of their importance in today's organizations, the next chapter is devoted to understanding teams.

Using Committees Effectively

Managers can do many things to avoid the pitfalls and increase the efficiency of a committee. The first step is to define clearly its functions, scope, and authority. Obviously, the members must know the purpose of the committee to function effectively. If it is a temporary committee, the members should be informed of its expected duration. This will help avoid prolonging the life of the committee unnecessarily. Those responsible for establishing a committee should carefully communicate the limits of the committee's authority. This should be done very soon after the committee has been established.

In addition, careful thought should go into the selection of the committee members and chairperson. Size is always an important variable; generally, committees become more inefficient as they grow in size. A good rule of thumb is to use the smallest group necessary to get the job done. It is more important to select capable members than representative members. It is also important to pick members from the same approximate organizational level. Members from higher levels may inhibit the actions and participation of the other members. Figure 10.15 lists several methods for selecting committee members and chairpeople and outlines advantages and disadvantages for each method.

board of directors
Carefully selected committee that reviews major policy and strategy decisions proposed by top management.

Boards of Directors

A **board of directors** is really a type of committee that is responsible for reviewing the major policy and strategy decisions proposed by top management. A board of directors can be characterized as either an inside or an outside board. On an *inside board,* a majority of the members hold management positions in the organization;

FIGURE 10.15
Methods of
Selecting
Committees

Method	Advantages/Disadvantages
Appointment of chairperson and members	Promotes sense of responsibility for all. May result in most capable members. Members may not work well together.
Appointment of chairperson who chooses members	Will probably get along well. Lack of sense of responsibility by members. May not be most capable or representative.
Appointment of members who elect chairperson	Lack of sense of responsibility by chairperson. May not choose best chairperson for the job. Election of chairperson may lead to split in the committee.
Volunteers	Will get those who have greatest interest in the outcome or those who are least busy. Lack of responsibility. Potential for splits among committee members is great.

on an *outside board*, a majority of the members do not hold or have not held a position with the organization. While insiders who are members of a board ordinarily have other duties related to the strategic management process by virtue of their corporate position, the role the board plays as an entity should be basically the same for both types. Board members do not necessarily need to own stock; they should be chosen primarily for what they can and will contribute to the organization.

Although most boards of directors restrict their inputs to the policy and strategy level and do not participate in the day-to-day operations of the organization, their degree of involvement varies widely from board to board. For many years, boards were used primarily as figureheads in many organizations, contributing little to the organization. However, this trend has been changing over the last several years. Recent lawsuits against boards of directors concerning their liabilities regarding the day-to-day operation of the organization have increased the risks of serving on boards.[24] Because of this, boards are becoming more active than they have been in the past. Moreover, some people now require liability insurance coverage before they will serve on a board of directors. An even more recent development is the tendency of shareholders to demand that the chairperson of the board be an outsider who is not employed in another capacity by the organization. Every diligent board of directors should address itself on behalf of the shareholders to this key issue: What is the standard of performance of the company's management—not what the company earned last year or this year, but what it *should* have earned?[25]

Summary

1. *Discuss the different stages an organization goes through as it grows and matures.* The first stage an organization goes through is the craft or family stage, which is characterized by the absence of formal policies, objectives, and structure. Operations at this stage generally center around one individual and one functional area. The second stage is the entrepreneurial stage, in which the organization grows first at an increasing and then at a decreasing rate. By the third stage, the entrepreneur has been replaced by a professional manager and profits are realized more from internal efficiency and less from a rapidly growing market.

2. *Explain what an organization chart is.* An organization chart uses a series of boxes connected with one or more lines to graphically represent the organization's structure.

3. *List several factors that can affect which structure is the most appropriate for a given organization.* Some of the most important variables that can affect an organization's structure are strategy, size, environment, and technology.

4. *Describe the general relationship between an organization's strategy and its structure.* Early research by Chandler reported that changes in strategy ultimately lead to changes in an organization's structure. Although subsequent research has supported the idea of some relationship between strategy and structure, it is clear that strategy is not the only variable that affects structure.

5. *Define outsourcing, and summarize its potential benefits as well as its potential drawbacks.* Outsourcing is the practice of subcontracting certain work functions to an outside entity. The potential benefits of outsourcing include allowing the organization to emphasize its core competencies; reducing operating costs; fewer personal headaches; accessing top talent and state-of-the-art technology; and improving resource allocations. Potential drawbacks include loss of control; loss of in-house skills; and threats to the morale of employees.

6. *Describe a contingency approach to organizing.* The contingency approach to organization states that the most appropriate structure depends on many situational variables, including strategy, environment, size, technology, and employee characteristics. When taking a contingency approach, a manager should first analyze these variables and design a structure to fit the situation.

7. *Identify the different types of departmentation.* Departmentation refers to the grouping of activities into related work units. Departmentation may be undertaken on the basis of work function, product, geography, customer, or time worked (shift). Hybrid departmentation occurs when an organization simultaneously uses more than one type of departmentation.

8. *Briefly describe each of the following types of organization structures: line structure, line and staff structure, matrix structure, horizontal structure, and virtual organization.* A line structure is the simplest organization structure; it has direct vertical links between the different organizational levels. The addition of staff specialists to a line organization creates a line and staff structure. A matrix structure is a structure in which individuals from different functional areas are assigned to work on a specific project or task. Under a matrix structure, those working on a project are officially assigned to the project and to their original or base departments. In its pure form, a horizontal structure consists of two core groups. One group is composed of senior management who are responsible for strategic decisions and policies. The second group is composed of empowered employees working together in different process teams. A virtual organization is one in which business partners and teams work together across geographical or organizational boundaries by means of information technology.

9. *Describe several trends that have taken place regarding the popularity of different types of organization structures.* Beginning in the 1950s and 1960s, much attention was focused on the virtues of flat versus tall organizations. In the early 1980s, emphasis shifted to the concept of a simple form and a lean staff. More recently, many organizations have abandoned the more traditional line and staff structures in favor of horizontal structures and virtual organizations.

10. *Describe how committees can be made more effective.* The first step is to define clearly the committee's functions, scope, and authority. The next step is to carefully review who will serve on the committee. Size and member capability are extremely important.

11. *Explain the difference between an inside and an outside board of directors.* With an inside board, a majority of the members hold management positions in the organization; with an outside board, a majority of the members do not hold or have not held a position with the organization.

Review Questions

1. Describe the different stages an organization goes through as it grows and matures.
2. What is an organization chart?
3. What several factors can affect an organization's structure?

4. Discuss the relationship between an organization's strategy and its structure.

5. Discuss the relationship between an organization's technology and its structure.

6. What is outsourcing?

7. What is the contingency approach to organizing?

8. Describe the following:
   a. Functional departmentation
   b. Product departmentation
   c. Geographic departmentation
   d. Customer departmentation
   e. Hybrid departmentation

9. Explain the following:
   a. Line structure
   b. Line and staff structure
   c. Matrix structure
   d. Horizontal structure
   e. Virtual organization

10. What factors contribute to potential conflict between line and staff personnel in a line and staff organization?

11. What are the advantages of a flat structure? What are the advantages of a tall structure?

12. What types of organization structures have organizations moved toward in recent times?

13. How can committees be made more effective?

Skill-Building Questions

1. As a practicing manager, how could you justify the use of a matrix structure given that it potentially violates the unity of command principle?

2. Do you think the contingency approach to organizing is a useful concept that can be implemented, or is it really a cop-out?

3. Discuss this statement: When the appropriate organization structure is determined and implemented, a firm no longer has to worry about structure.

4. Recognizing that most organizations' staffs expand considerably as the organization grows, respond to the following statement: There is no way to grow and keep the corporate staff small.

5. If you were an employee and your company embarked on a large-scale outsourcing program, how do you think you would react?

6. Do you think that virtual organizations are going to become more and more prominent in the future? Why or why not?

Skill-Building Exercise 10.1

Applied Departmentation

Suppose you have just been hired as the vice president in charge of sales at COMBO Enterprises, Inc. COMBO manufactures, sells, and distributes both land and water vehicles. The land vehicles are bicycles powered by a two-horsepower, two-cycle engine. Basically, you have developed a method to adapt an off-the-shelf chain saw motor to a popular French-produced bicycle. The water vehicles use the same chain saw motor adapted to a standard canoe, which is fitted with a special propeller and rudder.

The advantage over the existing competition is that, due to the light weight of the motor being used, the bicycles and canoes can also be used manually with very little loss of efficiency compared to nonmotorized bicycles and canoes. Your market surveys have shown that a large market exists for such a product.

COMBO serves both civilian and military markets for both the land and water vehicles. Presently COMBO has a plant in a medium-size eastern city and one in a medium-size western city. The eastern plant handles all business east of the Mississippi River, while the western plant handles business west of the Mississippi.

1. Design what you think would be the best way to organize the sales (marketing) division of the company.
2. Design an alternative structure for your division.
3. Why do you prefer one structure over the other?
4. Design a matrix structure for this situation (if you did not use one in question 1 or 2). What would be the pros and cons of such a structure in this situation?

Skill-Building Exercise 10.2

The Composition of Boards

Referring to the lists of most admired companies as identified by *Fortune* magazine (see Skill-Building Exercise 7.1, pages 142–43), go to the library or get on the Internet and research the board of directors for any five companies from the top of the most admired list and five from the bottom of the list. Determine how many outside directors and how many inside directors are serving each company. This information can be found in each company's annual report or in *Standard & Poor's Register of Corporations*, which is published annually.

1. Do most of these large, publicly held companies have a majority of inside or outside directors?
2. Are there any obvious differences in the composition of the boards of those companies from the top of the most admired list as compared to those from the bottom of the list?
3. Do you think the trend in large companies is toward more inside or more outside directors?

Case Incident 10.1

Who Dropped the Ball?

In October 2003, Industrial Water Treatment Company (IWT) introduced KELATE, a new product that was 10 times more effective than other treatments in controlling scale buildup in boilers. The instantaneous demand for KELATE required that IWT double its number of service engineers within the following year.

The sudden expansion caused IWT to reorganize its operations. Previously, each district office was headed by a district manager who was assisted by a chief engineer and two engineering supervisors. In 2004, this structure changed. The district manager now had a chief engineer and a manager of operations. Four engineering supervisors (now designated as group leaders) were established. They were to channel all work assignments through the manager of operations, while all engineering-related problems were to be handled by the chief engineer. Each group leader supervised 8 to 10 field service engineers (see Exhibit 1).

Bill Marlowe, district manager for the southeast district, has just received a letter from an old and very large customer, Sel Tex, Inc. The letter revealed that when Sel Tex inspected one of its boilers last week, it found the water treatment was not working properly. When Sel Tex officials contacted Wes Smith, IWT's service engineer for the area, they were told he was scheduled to be working in the Jacksonville area the rest of the week but would get someone else down there the next day. When no one showed up, Sel Tex officials were naturally upset; after all, they were only requesting the engineering service they had been promised.

Bill Marlowe, upset over the growing number of customer complaints that seemed to be crossing his desk in recent months, called Ed Jones, chief engineer, into his office and showed him the letter he had received from Sel Tex.

Ed: Why are you showing me this? This is a work assignment foul-up.

Bill: Do you know anything about this unsatisfactory condition?

Ed: Sure, Wes called me immediately after he found out. Their concentration of KELATE must have gone up, since they're getting corrosion and oxygen on their tubes. I told Peter Adinaro, Wes's group leader, about it, and I suggested he schedule someone to visit Sel Tex.

EXHIBIT 1   Partial Organizational Chart for IWT

Bill: OK, Ed, thanks for your help. [Bill then calls Peter Adinaro into his office.] Peter, two weeks ago Ed asked you to assign someone to visit Sel Tex because of a tube corrosion problem they are having. Do you remember?

Peter: Oh, sure! As usual, Wes Smith called Ed instead of me. I left a message for Dick to assign someone there because my whole group was tied up and I couldn't spare anyone. I thought Dick would ask another group leader to assign someone to check it out.

Bill: Well, thanks for your help. Tell Dick to come on in here for a second.

Dick Welsh, manager of operations, came into Bill's office about 20 minutes later.

Bill: Dick, here's a letter from Sel Tex. Please read it and tell me what you know about the situation.

Dick: [After reading the letter] Bill, I didn't know anything about this.

Bill: I checked with Pete, Wes's group leader, and he tells me he left a message for you to assign someone since his group was all tied up. Didn't you get the message?

Dick: Have you taken a look at my desk lately? I'm flooded with messages. Heck, I'm the greatest message handler of all times. If I could schedule my people without having all the engineering headaches unloaded on me, I wouldn't have all these messages. Sure, it's possible that he left a message, but I haven't seen it. I will look for it, though. Anyway, that letter sounds to me like they've got an engineering problem, and Ed should contact them to solve it.

Bill: I'll write Sel Tex myself and try to explain the situation to them. You and I will have to get together this afternoon and talk over some of these difficulties. See you later, Dick.

Questions

1. What problems does Bill Marlowe face?
2. Are the problems related to the way IWT is organized, or are they related to the employees?
3. How could these problems be resolved?

Case Incident 10.2

A New Organization Structure

Yesterday, Tom Andrews was officially promoted to his new job as hospital administrator for Cobb General Hospital. Cobb General is a 600-bed hospital located in a suburban area of New Orleans. Tom is extremely excited about the promotion but at the same time has some serious doubts about it.

Tom has worked at Cobb General for three years and had previously served as the associate administrator of the hospital. Although associate administrator was his official job title, he was really more of an errand boy for the former administrator, Bill Collins. Because of Tom's educational background (which includes a master of hospital administration degree) and his enthusiasm for the hospital, Tom was offered the administrator's job last week after the hospital's board of directors had asked for Bill Collins's resignation.

Tom was now looking at the organization chart for the hospital, which had been pieced together over the years by Bill Collins (see Exhibit 1). In reality, each time a new unit had been added or a new function started, Bill merely had the person report directly to him. Tom is worried about his ability to handle all of the people currently reporting to him in his new position.

Questions

1. Do you agree with Tom's concern? Why?
2. How would you redraw the organizational chart?

EXHIBIT 1   Organization Structure—Cobb General Hospital

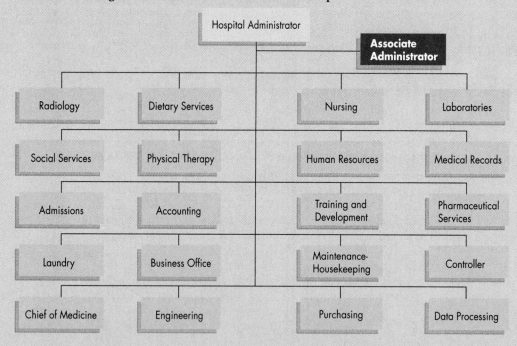

References and Additional Readings

1. Alan Filley and Robert House, *Managerial Process and Organizational Behavior* (Glenview, IL: Scott, Foresman, 1969), pp. 443–55.

2. A. D. Chandler, *Strategy and Structure* (Cambridge, MA: MIT Press, 1962).

3. Some relevant research includes J. Child, "Organization Structure, Environment, and Performance: The Role of Strategic Choice," *Sociology* 6 (1972), pp. 1–22; R. Rumelt, *Strategy, Structure, and Economic Performance* (Boston: Harvard Business School, Divi-

sion of Research, 1974); and Stephen P. Robins, *Organization Theory: Structure, Design, and Application* (Englewood Cliffs, NJ: Prentice Hall, 1990).

4. Tom Burns and G. M. Stalker, *The Management of Innovation* (London: Tavistock Institute, 1962).

5. Paul Lawrence and Jay Lorsch, "Differentiation and Integration in Complex Organizations," *Administrative Science Quarterly*, June 1967, pp. 1–47; and Paul Lawrence and Jay Lorsch, *Organization and Environment* (Homewood, IL: Richard D. Irwin, 1969). Originally published in 1967 by Division of Research, Graduate School of Business Administration, Harvard University.

6. Robins, *Organization Theory.*

7. Joan Woodward, *Industrial Organization: Theory and Practice* (London: Oxford University Press, 1965).

8. Edward Harvey, "Technology and the Structure of Organizations," *American Sociological Review*, April 1968, pp. 247–59.

9. Robins, *Organization Theory.*

10. Bruce McIndoep, "Crazy Like a Fox: Outsourcing Your Sales Force," *The Outsourcing Institute: Articles & Info;* www.outsourcing.com, accessed on November 4, 2003.

11. Laure Edwards, "When Outsourcing Is Appropriate," *Wall Street and Technology*, July 1998, pp. 96–98, and "Outsourcing: What's In, What's Out," *Employee Benefits*, October 6, 2003, p. 39.

12. Ibid.

13. Kathleen Madigan and Michael J. Mandel, "Outsourcing Jobs: Is It Bad?" *Business Week*, August 25, 2003, p. 36.

14. David Cleland and William King, *Systems Analysis and Project Management*, 3rd ed. (New York: McGraw-Hill, 1983), p. 187.

15. Cliff McGoon, "After Downsizing . . . Then What?" *Communication World*, May 1994, pp. 16–19.

16. Ronald K. Chung, "The Horizontal Organization: Breaking Down Functional Silos," *Business Credit*, May 1994, pp. 21–24.

17. Joyce Chutchian-Ferranti, "Virtual Corporation," *Computerworld*, September 1999, p. 33.

18. Ibid., p. 37.

19. This example is drawn from Samuel E. Bleecker, "The Virtual Organization," *Futurist*, March–April 1994, p. 9.

20. James Worthy, "Organization Structure and Employee Morale," *American Sociological Review* 15 (1956), pp. 169–79.

21. Rocco Carzo, Jr., and John Yanouzas, "Effects of Flat and Tall Organization Structure," *Administrative Science Quarterly* 114 (1969), pp. 178–91.

22. Dan R. Dalton, William D. Todor, Michael J. Spendolini, Gordon J. Fielding, and Lyman W. Porter, "Organization Structure and Performance: A Critical Review," *Academy of Management Review*, January 1980, pp. 49–54.

23. Thomas J. Peters and Robert W. Waterman, Jr., *In Search of Excellence* (New York: Harper & Row, 1982), pp. 306–17.

24. Richard M. Miller, "The D&O Liability Dilemma," *Chief Executive*, November–December 1988, pp. 34–39.

25. Harold Geneen, *Managing* (Garden City, NY: Doubleday, 1984), p. 259.

11

Understanding Work Teams

Learning Objectives

After studying this chapter, you will be able to:

1. Describe formal and informal work groups.
2. Define group norms.
3. Explain group cohesiveness.
4. Define group conformity.
5. Outline the conditions under which individual members tend to conform to group norms.
6. Define groupthink.
7. Understand the concept of team building.
8. Explain idiosyncrasy credit.
9. Describe a quality circle.
10. Explain self-directed work teams.
11. Define virtual work teams.

Chapter Preview

To meet and anticipate the growing level of demand, increase its market share, and remain the number one motorcycle manufacturer in the world, Harley-Davidson has undertaken several expansion projects. One such project was located in Kansas City. This facility began full production in 1998 and produced the Harley-Davidson's Sportster models. This facility was to operate on a team-based structure that was completely new for Harley-Davidson. The facility has three distinct groups—the plant leadership group (overall focus is plantwide issues and operation objectives), the process operations group (overall focus is processwide issues and strategies), and the natural work group (overall focus is daily operations and actions). All employment in the facility is team-based. Every employee throughout the organization belongs to a group or, at times, multiple groups. Under this system, manufacturing productivity has increased by 88 percent, with a 50 percent reduction in scrap and damaged components. Production costs declined between 30 and 45 percent. Prior to the installation of the system, the customers had to wait anywhere from 16 to 24 months for their motorcycle. Customer satisfaction with the Harley-Davidson Sportster has improved by 200 percent, and the waiting period has been reduced to two weeks or less.

Source: Joe Singer and Steve Duvall, "High-Performance Partnering by Self-Managed Teams in Manufacturing," *Engineering Management Journal,* December 2000, pp. 9–15.

Analyzing Management Skills

Why do you think Harley-Davidson has achieved such improvement from the use of a team-based structure? Is such a system applicable to all organizations?

Applying Management Skills

Go to the library and find other examples of organizations using a team-based organizational structure. What successes or failures did you find?

All organizations depend on groups to achieve success. In organizations, a group is two or more people who interact to meet a shared goal. Groups of students may organize fund-raising or social events. A shared sense of purpose sets a group apart from just a gathering of people. In general, organizations contain two kinds of groups: formal work groups and informal work groups.

Formal Work Groups

formal work group
Work group established and formally recognized by the organizing function of management.

Management establishes **formal work groups** to carry out specific tasks. Formal groups may exist for a short or long period of time. A task force is an example of a formal group. These groups have a single goal, such as resolving a problem or designing a new product.

A different type of formal work group is the *command,* or *functional,* group. This group consists of a manager and all the employees he or she supervises. Unlike a task group, the command group's work is ongoing and not confined to one issue or product.

Informal Work Groups

informal work group
Work group that results from personal contacts and interactions among people and is not formally recognized by the organization.

Informal work groups are formed voluntarily by members of an organization. They develop from personal contacts and interactions among people. Groups of employees who lunch together regularly and office cliques are examples of informal work groups.

A special type of informal group is the *interest group.* Its members share a purpose or concern. For example, women executives might form a group to share ideas about issues that women in management face.

Work is a social experience. Employees interact while performing job duties in offices, factories, stores, and other workplaces. Friendships emerge naturally from these contacts. Informal groups formed around mutual interests fill important social needs. In earlier centuries, groups like extended families, churches, and small towns met these needs. Today people socialize mostly with people they meet at work.

Informal work groups affect productivity, the morale of other employees, and the success of managers. They can be the result of—and can help create—a shared sense of loyalty. This is especially prevalent in high-risk occupations, such as fire fighting and police work.

Informal work groups often develop in areas where employees work close together (such as offices with cubicles) and among employees in the same field (such as accounting or graphic design). Employees may band together to share fears or complaints. In such cases, informal groups work against organization goals.

Studies have identified the power of informal work groups in organizations. The Hawthorne studies discovered that groups may set their own productivity levels and pressure workers to meet them. In one group, workers who produced more or less than the acceptable levels met with name-calling, sarcasm, ridicule, and in some cases, a blow on the arm. The Hawthorne studies concluded that informal organizations with their own social systems exist within formal organizations.[1]

In general, management does not recognize informal groups that revolve around friendships, interests, or shared working space and tasks. Yet an understanding of these groups can improve managers' work with formal groups. Employees join informal groups to meet a social need. They often gain great satisfaction from these groups. Managers seek to duplicate this satisfaction in formal work groups.

Group Norms

group norms
Informal rules a group adopts to regulate and regularize group members' behavior.

Group norms are the informal rules a group adopts to regulate the behavior of group members.[2] They may be extremely simple—a group that lunches together may maintain a rigid seating order. They may include expectations that group members will remain loyal to each other under any circumstances. Whatever the norms, group members are expected to hold to them. Members who break the rules often are shut out.

Norms don't govern every action in a group, only those important for group survival. For instance, a working group's norms would affect its productivity levels, operating procedures, and other work-related activities. Norms may not be written down or even spoken. Rather, group members use their actions to show new members how to behave.

Group Behavior

Think about the informal groups of friends and classmates you have belonged to at school or in your neighborhood. However they develop, informal work groups share similar types of behaviors. They include cohesiveness, conformity, and groupthink.

Group Cohesiveness

group cohesiveness
Degree of attraction each member has for the group, or the "stick-togetherness" of the group.

Group cohesiveness is the degree of attraction among group members, or how tightly knit a group is.[3] The more cohesive a group, the more likely members are to follow group norms. A number of factors affect the cohesiveness of informal work groups—size, success, status, outside pressures, stability of membership, communication, and physical isolation.

Size is a particularly important factor in group cohesiveness. The smaller the group, the more cohesive it is likely to be. A small group allows individual members to interact frequently. Members of large groups have fewer chances to interact; therefore, these groups tend to be less cohesive.

Think about how two close friends operate when they study together. Because they know each other well and talk easily, they have no trouble working together. Now imagine three new people in the study session. Everyone might not agree on the best way to cover material. It may be hard to work with different people. This might cause the study group to fall apart.

Success and status affect group cohesiveness. The more success a group experiences, the more cohesive it becomes. Several factors contribute to a group's status. For instance, highly skilled work groups tend to have more status than less-skilled groups. Like groups that meet their goals, high-status groups tend to be more cohesive than other informal work groups. These relationships are circular—success and status bring about cohesiveness, and cohesiveness brings about status and success.

Outside pressures, such as conflicts with management, can increase group cohesiveness. If a group sees management's requests as a demand or threat, it becomes more cohesive. In these situations, members may develop an "us against them" mentality.

A stable membership and easy lines of communication improve group cohesiveness. Long-standing members know each other well and are familiar with group norms. Employees who work in the same area socialize easily. In a production line, however, conversation is difficult and groups are less cohesive.

Finally, physical isolation from other employees may increase group cohesiveness. The isolation forces workers into close contact with each other and strengthens bonds.

Group Conformity

group conformity
Degree to which the members of the group accept and abide by the norms of the group.

Group conformity is the degree to which group members accept and follow group norms. A group generally seeks to control members' behavior for two reasons. First, independent behavior can cause disagreements that threaten a group's survival. Second, consistent behavior creates an atmosphere of trust that allows members to work together and socialize comfortably. Members are able to predict how others in the group will behave.

Individual members tend to conform to group norms under certain conditions:

- When group norms are similar to personal attitudes, beliefs, and behavior.
- When they do not agree with the group's norms but feel pressure to accept them.
- When the rewards for complying are valued or the sanctions imposed for non-compliance are devalued.

Group Pressure and Conformity

Researchers have studied the influence of group pressure on individual members. One study of group conformity took place at a textile firm in Virginia.[4] A textile employee began to produce more than the group norm of 50 units per day. After two weeks, the group started to pressure this worker to produce less, and she quickly dropped to the group's level. After three weeks, all the members of the group were moved to other jobs except for this worker. Once again, her production quickly climbed to double the group norm (see Figure 11.1).

FIGURE 11.1
Effect of Group Norms on a Member's Productivity

Source: Lester Coch and J. R. P. French, Jr., "Overcoming Resistance to Change," *Human Relations* (1948), pp. 519–20.

Groupthink

groupthink
Dysfunctional syndrome that cohesive groups experience that causes the group to lose its critical evaluative capabilities.

When group members lose their ability to think as individuals and conform at the expense of their good judgment, **groupthink** occurs.[5] Members become unwilling to say anything against the group or any member, even if an action is wrong. William Golding explored the concept of groupthink in his novel *The Lord of the Flies*. This book illustrates what can happen when individuals are removed from society and are left to create their own rules.

Keeping a group together under any circumstance is a goal in itself. Groups with this goal believe that the group is indestructible and always right. Group members justify any action, stereotype outsiders as enemies of the group, and pressure unwilling members to conform. In business, groupthink is disruptive because it affects employees' ability to make logical decisions.

The Importance of Formal Work Groups

Formal work groups play an important part in helping an organization meet its goals. Groups have more knowledge and information than individuals. They make communicating and solving problems easier. This creates a more efficient and effective company.

The importance of managing groups effectively is becoming recognized in the business world. Employees must work closely to improve production and maintain a competitive edge. Changes in the workforce are bringing men and women from different backgrounds together. Managers must work with groups to overcome cultural and gender differences. These, and other factors, make managing work groups one of management's most important tasks.

Influencing Work Groups

Studies at the Hawthorne plant, where researchers documented the existence of informal work groups, looked at the effects of various changes on workers' productivity. Researchers varied job factors, including the way workers were paid and supervised, lighting, the length of rest periods, and the number of hours worked. Productivity rose with each change.

Hawthorne effect
States that giving special attention to a group of employees (such as involving them in an experiment) changes their behavior.

This result led to the coining of the term **Hawthorne effect.** As you may remember from Chapter 2, the Hawthorne effect states that giving special attention to a group of employees changes the employees' behavior. The results of the studies show that when groups of employees are singled out for attention, they tend to work more efficiently.

Building Effective Work Groups

Members of informal work groups often develop a shared sense of values and group loyalty. Formal groups rarely share these qualities because they are assigned to rather than voluntary. Managers are responsible for developing shared values and group loyalty in formal work groups.

linking-pin concept
Because managers are members of overlapping groups, they link formal work groups to the total organization.

The linking-pin concept is one way of describing management's role in work groups. The **linking-pin concept** holds that because managers are members of overlapping groups, they link formal work groups to the total organization. Managers improve communication and ensure that organizational and group goals are met. In other words, managers themselves are the linking pins (see Figure 11.2).

team building
Process by which the formal work group develops an awareness of those conditions that keep it from functioning effectively and then requires the group to eliminate those conditions.

Building effective formal work groups often is called team building. **Team building** is the process of establishing a cohesive group that works together to achieve its goals.[6] A team will be successful only if its members feel that working conditions are fair to all. A team can fail, even in a supportive organization, if a manager does not encourage fair play.

The success of a group or team can be measured in the same way as the success of organizations. Successful organizations and groups both meet their goals by using their resources well. Managers encourage teamwork by selecting group members carefully, creating a positive work environment, building trust, and increasing group cohesiveness. Figure 11.3 describes three steps to use in building productive teams. Management Illustration 11.1 shows how Bell Atlantic formed effective teams.

Creating Groups

For a group to succeed, members must be able to perform the tasks assigned by management. Selecting the right individuals is key to the success of a group. The first step is to identify qualified people. Then management must make the group attractive to these individuals.

FIGURE 11.2   **Linking-Pin Concept**

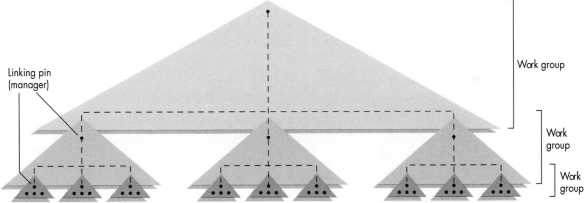

Source: Rensis Likert, *New Patterns of Management.* Copyright © 1961 The McGraw-Hill Companies, Inc. Reprinted with permission.

FIGURE 11.3
Steps for Building Productive Teams

> **1. Selecting Individuals**
> The first step in building an effective team is finding the right people. Group members need to have the right skills and the right personality fit.
>
> **2. Building Trust**
> The second step is to build trust among group members and between the group and management.
>
> **3. Encouraging Group Cohesiveness**
> The third step is to develop a cohesive group that conforms to group norms. Managers can improve group cohesiveness by keeping groups small, giving them clear goals, and rewarding them as a team.

For most employees, a formal work group is attractive because it increases pay and offers some satisfaction. If employees see that joining a formal group can provide them with the same satisfaction that an informal group can, they are more likely to participate willingly.

Environment also can be important to the success of a group. An important requirement for meeting group goals is a suitable place to work. How the office is laid out and other physical factors will affect the group's ability to work together successfully.

Building Trust

Trust is essential among group members and between groups and management. A successful group effort means sharing responsibilities and making decisions together. Group members must feel that the entire group is willing and able to work together successfully to achieve goals. Without trust, groups can't set or stick to production norms.

Managers must have faith in their employees. They also must recognize the interests of the organization, the group, and the employees. Effective managers should become personally involved, take a real interest in group members, share information, and exhibit honesty.

Influencing Group Cohesiveness and Conformity

Think about teams you have belonged to at school or summer camp. These successful teams often are highly competitive and eager to succeed. Effective work groups share these characteristics. Both types of groups also draw their primary satisfaction from a sense of accomplishment, which comes from a job well done.

Managers can affect formal group performance levels by studying the degree of group conformity. Formal groups must be cohesive and dedicated to high performance norms in order to succeed. Managers can influence group cohesiveness by

- Keeping groups small.
- Selecting group members carefully.
- Finding a good personality fit between new and old employees.
- Developing an office layout that improves communication.
- Creating clear goals.
- Inspiring group competition.
- Rewarding groups rather than individuals.
- Isolating groups from each other.

Created in 1984 when the U.S. government forced telecommunications giant AT&T to deregulate, Bell Atlantic Corporation had as its mission to provide comprehensive telephone services to business and residential customers in the mid-Atlantic region of the United States. In 2000, Bell Atlantic merged with GTE, and the company is now known as Verizon. From the company's inception, Bell Atlantic management faced numerous business challenges, including a changing regulatory environment, exploding competition for phone and communications services, and an increase in product offerings as a result of changing technologies.

Bell Atlantic operated 45 consumer call centers, staffed with about 6,000 sales consultants, that provided sales and service support to residential customers. Call centers were converted to a team structure over the course of a two-year period. The basic job function of the sales consultant remained the same in both the teamed and the nonteamed offices, but the organizational structure for the teamed offices changed. These changes included

- An office committee made up of sales consultants and an assistant manager who helped to identify, coordinate, and communicate team needs.
- Physically grouping team members together and changing furniture to remove high walls.

- Training focused on team processes, cooperative communication, and problem-solving skills.
- Weekly team meetings to discuss results, solve problems, or cross-train team members.
- A performance feedback system that related individual results, team results, and summary data about other teams' performance, creating an environment of acknowledgment and learning that many sales consultants lauded. The feedback system also helped to identify "best practice" sales consultants, who were then asked to share their skills with other team members.

The increase in the products-sold rate is the most telling measure of the revenue impact of teaming. Analysis shows that a teamed sales consultant, on average, would generate over $21,000 per year in sales revenues more than a nonteamed sales consultant. Multiplying the average gain of $21,312 times the 6,000 Bell Atlantic sales consultants, the potential revenue gain from teaming is over $127 million!

Source: Priscilla Wisner, *Strategic Finance,* February 2001, pp. 58–65.

---

idiosyncrasy credit
Phenomenon that occurs when certain members who have made or are making significant contributions to the group's goals are allowed to take some liberties within the group.

High individual performance with poor team performance is not what winning is about, either in sports or in business. Individuals must surrender their egos so that the end result is bigger than the sum of its parts. When this happens, the team works together like fingers on a hand.

Some members of groups will always be permitted to depart from group norms. This phenomenon is known as the idiosyncrasy credit. The **idiosyncrasy credit** occurs when individuals who have played a significant role in a group are allowed some freedom within the group. People in this position have often helped develop a group's norms. Because the group's norms often are the same as their own, those who could use the idiosyncrasy credit often do not.

Quality Circles

quality circle
Composed of a group of employees (usually from 5 to 15 people) who are members of a single work unit, section, or department; the basic purpose of a quality circle is to discuss quality problems and generate ideas that might help improve quality.

One type of formal work group is the quality circle. A **quality circle** is a group of employees, usually from 5 to 15 people, from a single work unit (such as a department) who share ideas on how to improve quality. The goal of a quality circle is to involve employees in decision making. Membership is almost always voluntary, and members share a common bond—they perform similar tasks.

Japan has used quality circles since the early 1960s. The idea arrived in the United States after executives from Lockheed Corporation visited Japan in the 1970s and saw the circles in action. Lockheed used quality circles to improve quality and save several million dollars.

Conducting meetings on *Star Trek* was simple enough. When Captain Kirk needed to speak with someone, he raised him or her on a handheld communicator or talked to an image on a video screen. For face-to-face encounters, Scotty easily beamed the participants aboard the *Enterprise.* Though conducting meetings in the corporate world has yet to reach that level of sophistication, virtual teamwork has come a long way over the past decade.

For example, CNA Insurance Cos. in Chicago used collaboration technology to solve a particularly pressing problem prior to a large convention. "We were going crazy," said Christy Keener, senior vice president of organization development, who had to set up a meeting to review strategies and overall direction. Before attending, 350 participants needed to review documents and discuss them. "We couldn't possibly make this happen without collaborative technology," she said.

CNA brought in consultants from Collaboration Architects LLC, of Falls Church, Virginia, to set up an externally hosted virtual team portal. The website, which is accessible by anyone in the company, has buttons for teams, e-learning, a knowledge database, and announcements, as well as an insurance industry news feed.

Prior to the meeting, CNA staff used portal functions such as project status reports, budgeting tools, document logs, responsibility matrices, project summaries, goals, and a general discussion space to review key documents, make changes, and respond to revisions others had made. Result: All participants were fully briefed in advance, and the convention was successful. With everyone up to speed already, management could launch into the more pivotal issues, confident that everyone in attendance knew exactly what he or she was talking about.

Source: Drew Robb, "Virtual Workplace," *HR Magazine,* June 2002, pp. 105–10.

Quality circles have benefits other than increasing employee participation.[7] They encourage communication and trust among members and managers. They are an inexpensive way to provide employees with training while giving them a sense of control over their work lives. Most important, however, they may solve problems that have been around for years. Quality circles create strong lines of communication. "Me" becomes "us" in a good quality circle. A more current program on quality called a *six sigma* program is discussed in Chapter 20.

Self-Directed Work Teams

self-directed work teams (SDWT)
Teams in which members are empowered to control the work they do without a formal supervisor.

Another type of formal work group is the **self-directed work team (SDWT).** SDWTs are empowered to control the work they do without a formal supervisor. Each SDWT has a leader who normally comes from the employees on the team. Most of these teams plan and schedule their work, make operational and personnel decisions, solve problems, set priorities, determine what employee does what work, and share leadership responsibilities. The positive and negative aspects of team decision making are discussed in more detail in Chapter 4.

Virtual Work Teams

Virtual work teams were largely nonexistent a decade ago. Today, globalization, technology, and fast responses to customer needs have led organizations to establish virtual work teams. Virtual work teams are responsible for making or implementing important decisions for the business, mainly using technology-supported communication, with the team members working and living in different locations. It is likely that this form of work team over time will be more widely used. Management Illustration 11.2 discusses how a virtual workplace would function.

Groups and Leaders

When an informal group selects a leader, members choose the person most capable of satisfying the group's needs. The group gives this leader authority and can take this authority away at any time. This leader needs strong communication skills, especially in setting objectives for the group, giving directions, and summarizing information.

To see how informal groups choose leaders, imagine a group of people shipwrecked on an island. The group's first goal is to find food, water, and shelter. The individual best equipped to help the group survive would naturally become the leader. Later, the group's goal might change to getting off the island. The original leader may no longer be the best person to help meet this new goal, and a new leader could emerge. The process may continue through several leaders.

Gaining Acceptance

Managers assigned to formal work groups must work to gain acceptance as leaders. They generally do not have the same authority as leaders of informal groups. The formal authority granted by top management is no guarantee that a manager will effectively guide a group.

Think about how you respond to your teachers. You respect teachers who know their subject well, communicate information effectively, treat students with respect, and make fair judgments. Managers working with formal groups can use these same behaviors to gain the trust and respect of employees.

Managers must keep track of those changes within the organization that might affect the group. At times, they may have to modify group goals to meet new organizational goals. For example, an organization faced with strong competition may need to make decisions rapidly rather than rely on groups to come up with a solution. In these cases, managers must be ready to make immediate decisions for the group.

Encouraging Participation

Building an effective team requires a nontraditional managerial approach. In a traditional organizational structure, managers direct the employees who work for them. As part of a team, however, managers encourage participation and share responsibility, acting more like a coach than a manager.

One way of encouraging team spirit is to provide the group with a vision. People who organize groups to support social causes often use this approach. For example, one person may rally a community around a project such as reclaiming a vacant lot for a park. In the business world, managers can offer team members the possibility of designing a state-of-the-art product or service.

Managers lead by example. Their attitude and performance become the standard for group norms. A manager who believes that a group must listen to and support all members might create a group of top managers who share this feeling. Employees who see managers functioning within a cohesive group are more likely to work effectively in groups themselves.

Summary

1. *Describe formal and informal work groups.* Formal work groups are established by the organizing function. Their structure and membership are established and recognized by management. Informal work groups result from personal contacts and interactions of people within the organization and are not formally recognized by the organization.

2. *Define group norms.* Group norms are the informal rules a group adopts to regulate and regularize group members' behavior.

3. *Explain group cohesiveness.* Group cohesiveness refers to the degree of attraction each member has for the group, or the stick-togetherness of the group.

4. *Define group conformity.* Group conformity is the degree to which the members of a group accept and abide by the norms of the group.

5. *Outline conditions under which individual members tend to conform to group norms.* Members tend to conform to group norms when the norms are congruent with their personal attitudes, beliefs, and behavioral predispositions; when the norms are inconsistent with their personal attitudes, beliefs, or behavioral predispositions but the group exerts strong pressures to comply; and when the rewards for complying are valued or the sanctions imposed for noncompliance are devalued.

6. *Define groupthink.* Groupthink is a dysfunctional syndrome that cohesive groups experience that causes the group to lose its critical evaluative capabilities.

7. *Understand the concept of team building.* Team building is the process of establishing a cohesive group that works together to achieve its goals.

8. *Explain idiosyncrasy credit.* Idiosyncrasy credit refers to a phenomenon that occurs when certain members of a group who have made or are making significant contributions to the group's goals are allowed to take some liberties within the group.

9. *Describe a quality circle.* A quality circle is composed of a group of employees (usually from 5 to 15 people) who are members of a single work unit, section, or department and whose basic purpose is to discuss quality problems and generate ideas to help improve quality.

10. *Explain self-directed work teams.* SDWTs are empowered to control the work they do without a formal supervisor.

11. *Define virtual work teams.* Virtual work groups are responsible for making or implementing important decisions, using technology-supported communication, with the team members working and living in different locations.

Review Questions

1. Describe a formal work group.
2. Describe an informal work group.
3. What is the Hawthorne effect?
4. What is a group norm?
5. What is group cohesiveness?
6. What is group conformity?
7. What are some suggestions for building group cohesiveness?
8. Outline the conditions under which individual members of a group tend to conform to group norms.
9. What is idiosyncrasy credit?
10. Explain the linking-pin concept.
11. What is team building?
12. What is a quality circle?
13. What is a self-directed work team?
14. Define virtual work teams.

Skill-Building Questions

1. Do you think it is possible to eliminate the need for informal work groups? Explain.
2. Discuss the following statement: The goals of informal work groups are never congruent with the goals of the formal organization.
3. Some employees are described as "marching to the beat of a different drummer." In light of the discussion in this chapter, what does this statement mean to you?

4. Cite one business example and one social example of what you perceive to be group-think mentality.

5. Why do you think quality circles can be effective?

Skill-Building Exercise 11.1

Characteristics of Effective Work Groups

You have been a member of many groups in your lifetime. Some of these groups include both formal and informal groups. Examples of such groups might include your Sunday school class, your neighborhood playmates when you were younger, your soccer or base-ball team, and your co-workers at your summer job. Whether a formal or informal work group, all of us have been members of a group at some time. Some of the groups have been quite effective, and some have been quite ineffective.

Recall the most effective and the most ineffective groups of which you have been a member. Prepare a description of the characteristics of both groups. Be prepared to make a five-minute presentation of these characteristics in class.

Skill-Building Exercise 11.2

Crash Project

You are told that you and your work group have two weeks to implement a new program. You think two weeks are insufficient and you and your employees would have to work around the clock to complete it in that time. Morale has always been high in your group; yet you know some people just don't like overtime. As you think about how best to handle the situation, you consider these alternatives:

1. Tell your group the company is being pretty unreasonable about this: "I don't see what the big rush is. But it's got to be done, so let's all pitch in and help, shall we?"

2. Tell your group that you have told Bob Smith (your boss) you have a superb group of people: "If anyone in the company could get the job done, we could."

3. Tell the group your job is on the line: "If you want me around for a while, you will have to make a heroic effort."

4. Tell your group you don't want to hear any griping: "This is the nature of the job, and anyone who thinks he or she can't devote the extra time had better start looking for another job."

5. Tell the group the job must be done and ask them to make suggestions on how it can be completed within the deadline.

Other alternatives may be open to you, but assume these are the only ones you have considered.

Without discussion with anyone, decide which of these approaches you would take and be prepared to defend your choice.

Case Incident 11.1

One of the Gang?

Recently, Ruth Brown was appointed as the supervisor of a group of word processors in which she was formerly one of the rank-and-file employees. When she was selected for the job, the department head told her the former supervisor was being transferred because she could not get sufficient work out of the group. He also said the reason Ruth was selected was that she appeared to be a natural leader, she was close to the group, and she knew the tricks they were practicing to restrict output. He told Ruth he believed she could lick the problem and he would stand behind her.

He was right about Ruth knowing the tricks. When she was one of the gang, not only did she try to hamper the supervisor, but she was the ringleader in the group's efforts to make life miserable for her. None of them had anything personal against the supervisor; all of them considered it a game to pit their wits against hers. There was a set of signals to inform the employees the supervisor was coming so that everyone would appear to be working hard. As soon as she left the immediate vicinity, everyone would take it easy. Also, the employees would act dumb to get the supervisor to go into lengthy explanations and demonstrations while they stood around. They complained constantly, and without justification, about the materials and the equipment.

At lunchtime, the employees would ridicule the company, tell the latest fast one they had pulled on the supervisor, and plan new ways to harass her. All of this seemed to be a great joke. Ruth and the rest of the employees had a lot of fun at the expense of the supervisor and the company.

Now that Ruth has joined the ranks of management, it is not so funny. She is determined to use her managerial position and knowledge to win the group over to working for the company instead of against it. She knows that if this can be done, she will have a top-notch group. The employees know their stuff, have a very good team spirit, and, if they would use their brains and efforts constructively, could turn out above-average production.

Ruth's former colleagues are rather cool to her now; but this seems natural, and she believes she can overcome it in a short time. What concerns her is that Joe James is taking over her old post as ringleader of the group, and the group is trying to play the same tricks on her that it did on the former supervisor.

Questions

1. Did the company make a good selection in Ruth? Explain.
2. What suggestions would you make to Ruth?
3. Are work groups necessarily opposed to working toward organizational goals? Explain.

Case Incident 11.2

Talkative Mike

Mike was an exceptionally friendly and talkative man—to the extent that he bothered his supervisor by frequently stopping the whole work crew to tell them a joke or a story. It didn't seem to bother Mike that it was during working hours or that somebody other than his crew might be watching. He just enjoyed telling stories and being the center of attention. The trouble was that the rest of the crew enjoyed him too.

The supervisor had just recently taken over the department, and he was determined to straighten out the crew. He thought he would have no problem motivating such a friendly person as Mike. Because the crew was on a group incentive, the supervisor believed he could get them to see how much they were losing by standing around and talking. But there was no question about it: Mike was the informal leader of the crew, and they followed him just as surely as if he were the plant manager.

Mike's crew produced extremely well. When they worked—and that was most of the time—their output could not be equaled. But the frequent nonscheduled storytelling breaks did bother the supervisor. Not only could that nonproductive time be converted to badly needed production, but they also were setting a poor example for the other crews and the rest of the department.

The supervisor called Mike in to discuss the situation. His primary emphasis was on the fact that Mike's crew could make more money by better using their idle time. Mike's contention was, "What good is money if you can't enjoy it? You sweat your whole life away to rake in money, and then all you've got to show for it is a lot of miserable years and no way of knowing how to enjoy what's left. Life's too short to spend every minute trying to make more money." The discussion ended with Mike promising the group would quiet down; if their production didn't keep up, the supervisor would let him know.

Things did improve for a while; but within a week or so, the old pattern was right back where it had been. The supervisor then arranged to talk with the other members of the crew individually. Their reactions were the same as Mike's. As before, some improvements were noted at first; then the crew gradually reverted to the old habits.

Questions

1. Do you agree with Mike and his group?
2. Does the supervisor really have a complaint in light of the fact that Mike's group produces well above average?
3. If you were the supervisor, what would you do next?

References and Additional Readings

1. Elton Mayo, *The Human Problems of an Industrial Civilization* (Cambridge, MA: Harvard University Graduate School of Business Administration, 1946).

2. Daniel C. Feldman, "The Development and Enforcement of Group Norms," *Academy of Management Review,* January 1984, p. 47.

3. For a further discussion of components of group cohesion, see Joseph P. Stokes, "Components of Group Cohesion: Intermember Attraction, Instrumental Value, and Risk Taking," *Small Group Behavior,* May 1983, pp. 163–73.

4. Lester Coch and John R. P. French, Jr., "Overcoming Resistance to Change," *Human Relations,* 1948, pp. 519–20.

5. Irving Janis, *Victims of Groupthink: A Psychological Study of Foreign Policy Decisions and Fiascos* (Boston: Houghton Mifflin, 1973), p. 9.

6. See Paul E. Brauchle and David W. Wright, "Fourteen Team-Building Tips," *Training and Development Journal,* January 1992, pp. 32–36. Also see Mahmoud Salem, Harold Lazarus, and Joseph Cullen, "Developing Self-Managing Teams: Structure and Performance," *Journal of Management Development* 11 (1992), pp. 24–32.

7. Everett E. Adam, Jr., "Quality Circle Performance," *Journal of Management,* March 1991, pp. 25–39.

Chapter 12

Staffing

Learning Objectives

After studying this chapter, you will be able to:

1. Outline the human resource planning process.
2. Define job analysis, job description, job specification, and skills inventory.
3. Define equal employment opportunity.
4. Describe the recruitment process.
5. Define affirmative action plan.
6. Discuss reverse discrimination.
7. Define tests, test validity, and test reliability.
8. Discuss the different types of employment interviews.
9. Discuss potential problems in the interviewing process.

Chapter Preview

Some businesses feel preemployment testing is essential, especially in a tight labor market where the pool of available workers is depleted of the best and brightest. Seattle aircraft-maker Boeing uses a preemployment assessment test for hourly-paid mechanics and electricians who perform assembly work and is happy with the results. "Our managers have noticed that once people come on line after taking the preemployment tests, they tend to be better performers and show up for work," said Linda Sawin, manager of assessment services in Boeing's human resources department.

The four-hour-long test measures work aptitude, including math, verbal, and spatial aspects, along with testing of comprehensive mechanical and electrical components. Boeing, which has 180,000 employees, conducts specialized preemployment testing for management positions. It also uses an oral, behavioral-based interview on college campuses for recruiting salaried engineering and business positions. "It's just a small piece of the recruitment puzzle, but it really levels the playing field," Sawin said. The test neutralizes the old nepotistic adage, "Your father worked here so you can have a job here too." "It really makes everyone equal. Some will do better than others, but that's how you identify people who will perform better on the job."

Source: Gilbert Nicholson, "Pre-Employment Screening," *Workforce,* October 2000, pp. 72–77.

Analyzing Management Skills

Do you feel that diversity should be a goal of the hiring process in organizations? What benefits do you think come from having diversity as a goal in hiring?

Applying Management Skills

What different ideas or viewpoints have you gained from a person or persons from a different cultural background?

The staffing function of management involves securing and developing people to perform the jobs created by the organizing function. The goal of staffing is to obtain the best available people for the organization and to develop the skills and abilities of those people. Obtaining the best available people generally involves forecasting personnel requirements and recruiting and selecting new employees. Developing the skills and abilities of an organization's employees involves employee development as well as the proper use of promotions, transfers, and separations. The staffing function is complicated by numerous government regulations. Furthermore, many of these regulations are subject to frequent change.

Unfortunately, many staffing activities have traditionally been conducted by human resource/personnel departments and have been considered relatively unimportant by line managers. However, securing and developing qualified personnel should be a major concern of all managers because it involves the most valuable asset of an organization: human resources.

Human Resource Planning

human resource planning (HRP)
Process of "getting the right number of qualified people into the right job at the right time." Also called *personnel planning.*

Human resource planning (HRP), also referred to as *personnel planning,* has been defined as the process of "getting the right number of qualified people into the right job at the right time."[1] Put another way, HRP is "the system of matching the supply of people—internally (existing employees) and externally (those to be hired or searched for)—with the openings the organization expects to have for a given time frame."[2]

HRP involves applying the basic planning process to the human resource needs of the organization. Once organizational plans are made and specific objectives set, the HRP process attempts to define the human resource needs to meet the organization's objectives.[3]

The first basic question addressed by the planning process is: Where are we now? Human resource planning frequently answers this question by using job analysis and skills inventories.

job analysis
Process of determining, through observation and study, the pertinent information relating to the nature of a specific job.

Job Analysis and Skills Inventory

Job analysis is the process of determining, through observation and study, the pertinent information relating to the nature of a specific job. The end products of a job analysis are a job description and a job specification. A **job description** is a written statement that identifies the tasks, duties, activities, and performance results required in a particular job. The job description should be used to develop fair and comprehensive compensation and reward systems. In addition, the accuracy of the

job description
Written statement that identifies the tasks, duties, activities, and performance results required in a particular job.

FIGURE 12.1
Relationship between Job Analysis, Human Resource Planning, Recruitment, and Selection

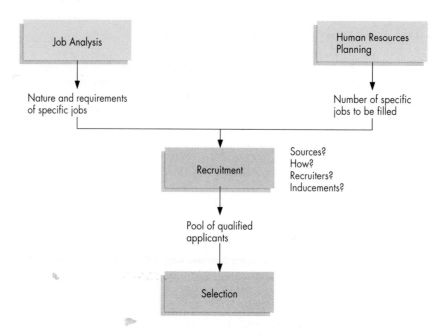

job specification
Written statement that identifies the abilities, skills, traits, or attributes necessary for successful performance in a particular job.

skills inventory
Consolidates information about the organization's current human resources.

job description can help or hinder recruiters in their efforts to attract qualified applicants for positions within the company. A **job specification** is a written statement that identifies the abilities, skills, traits, or attributes necessary for successful performance in a particular job. In general, a job specification identifies the qualifications of an individual who could perform the job. Job analyses are frequently conducted by specialists from the human resource department. However, managers should have input into the final job descriptions for the jobs they are managing. Figure 12.1 shows the relationship among job analysis, human resource planning, recruitment, and selection.

Through conducting job analysis, an organization defines its current human resource needs on the basis of existing or newly created jobs. A **skills inventory** consolidates information about the organization's current human resources. The skills inventory contains basic information about each employee of the organization, giving a comprehensive picture of the individual. Through analyzing the skills inventory, the organization can assess the current quantity and quality of its human resources.

Thomas Patten has outlined seven broad categories of information that may be included in a skills inventory:[4]

1. Personal data history: age, sex, marital status, etc.
2. Skills: education, job experience, training, etc.
3. Special qualifications: memberships in professional groups, special achievements, etc.
4. Salary and job history: present salary, past salary, dates of raises, various jobs held, etc.
5. Company data: benefit plan data, retirement information, seniority, etc.
6. Capacity of individual: scores on tests, health information, etc.
7. Special preferences of individual: location or job preferences, etc.

The primary advantage of a computerized skills inventory is that it offers a quick and accurate evaluation of the skills available within the organization. Combining the information provided by the job analysis and the skills inventory enables the organization to evaluate the present status of its human resources.[5]

Specialized versions of the skills inventory can also be devised and maintained. One example would be the management inventory, which would separately evaluate the specific skills of managers such as strategy development, experiences (e.g., international experience or language skill), and successes or failures at administration or leadership.

In addition to appraising the current status of its human resources, the organization must consider anticipated changes in the current workforce due to retirements, deaths, discharges, promotions, transfers, and resignations. Certain changes in personnel can be estimated accurately and easily, whereas other changes are more difficult to forecast.

Forecasting

human resource forecasting
Process that attempts to determine the future human resource needs of the organization in light of the organization's objectives.

The second basic question the organization addresses in the planning process is: Where do we want to go? **Human resource forecasting** attempts to answer this question with regard to the organization's human resource needs. It is a process that attempts to determine the future human resource needs of the organization in light of the organization's objectives. Some of the many variables considered in forecasting human resource needs include sales projections, skills required in potential business ventures, composition of the present workforce, technological changes, and general economic conditions. Given the critical role human resources play in attaining organizational objectives, all levels of management should be involved in the forecasting process.

Human resource forecasting is presently conducted largely on the basis of intuition; the experience and judgment of the manager are used to determine future human resource needs. This assumes all managers are aware of the future plans of the total organization. Unfortunately, this is not true in many cases.

Transition

In the final phase of human resource planning, the transition, the organization determines how it can obtain the quantity and quality of human resources it needs to meet its objectives as reflected by the human resource forecast. The human resource forecast results in a statement of what the organization's human resource needs are in light of its plans and objectives. The organization engages in several transitional activities to bring its current level of human resources in line with forecast requirements. These activities include recruiting and selecting new employees, developing current or new employees, promoting or transferring employees, laying off employees, and discharging employees. Given the current trend of downsizing in many organizations, some human resource departments now maintain a replacement chart for each employee. This confidential chart shows a diagram of each position in the management hierarchy and a list of candidates who would be qualified to replace a particular person should the need arise. Generally, the coordination of all the activities mentioned earlier is delegated to a human resource or personnel department within the organization.

Legal Considerations

Due to discriminatory personnel practices by many organizations, government regulation now plays a vital role in human resource planning. The following paragraphs describe the significant government bills and laws that have affected human resource planning.

Equal Pay Act of 1963
Prohibits wage discrimination on the basis of sex.

The **Equal Pay Act of 1963,** which became effective in June 1964, prohibits wage discrimination on the basis of sex. The law states,

> No employer . . . shall . . . discriminate . . . between employees on the basis of sex by paying wages . . . at a rate less than the rate at which he pays wages to employees of the opposite sex . . . for equal work on jobs the performance of which requires equal skill, effort, and responsibility and which are performed under similar working conditions.[6]

Title VII of the Civil Rights Act of 1964
Designed to eliminate employment discrimination related to race, color, religion, sex, or national origin in organizations that conduct interstate commerce.

Title VII of the Civil Rights Act of 1964 is designed to eliminate employment discrimination related to race, color, religion, sex, or national origin in organizations that conduct interstate commerce. The act as amended covers the following types of organizations:

1. All private employers of 15 or more employees.
2. All educational institutions, public and private.
3. State and local governments.
4. Public and private employment agencies.
5. Labor unions with 15 or more members.
6. Joint labor–management committees for apprenticeship and training.

equal employment opportunity
The right of all people to work and to advance on the bases of merit, ability, and potential.

Congress passed the Civil Rights Act to establish guidelines for ensuring equal employment opportunities for all people. **Equal employment opportunity** refers to the right of all people to work and to advance on the bases of merit, ability, and potential. One major focus of equal employment opportunity efforts has been to identify and eliminate discriminatory employment practices. Such practices are any artificial, arbitrary, and unnecessary barriers to employment when the barriers operate to discriminate on the basis of sex, race, or another impermissible classification.

Age Discrimination in Employment Act
Passed in 1968, initially designed to protect individuals ages 40 to 65 from discrimination in hiring, retention, and other conditions of employment. Amended in 1978 to include individuals up to age 70. Specifically, forbids mandatory retirement at 65 except in certain circumstances.

Great strides in promoting diversity have been made since 1964. However, to Debra D. Richards, an African American communications manager for a large insurance company, change has been very slow. "At times, I think we're making progress toward a multicultural environment, but on a day-to-day level, all I have to do is look around me and look at the people in leadership positions," she said. To many people, race and sex still color a supervisor's perception of abilities.[7]

The **Age Discrimination in Employment Act** went into effect on June 12, 1968. Initially it was designed to protect individuals 40 to 65 years of age from discrimination in hiring, retention, compensation, and other conditions of employment. In 1978, the act was amended and coverage was extended to individuals up to age 70. Specifically, the act now forbids mandatory retirement at age 65 except in certain circumstances.

Rehabilitation Act of 1973
Prohibits discrimination in hiring of persons with disabilities by federal agencies and federal contractors.

The **Rehabilitation Act of 1973** prohibits discrimination in hiring of individuals with disabilities by federal agencies and federal contractors. The **Americans with Disabilities Act (ADA) of 1990** gives individuals with disabilities sharply increased access to services and jobs. Both acts have given citizens with disabilities protection in the workplace and increased opportunities to compete for jobs.

Americans with Disabilities Act (ADA) of 1990
Gives individuals with disabilities sharply increased access to services and jobs.

The **Civil Rights Act of 1991** permits women, minorities, persons with disabilities, and persons who are religious minorities to have a jury trial and sue for punitive damages of up to $300,000 if they can prove they are victims of intentional hiring or workplace discrimination. The law covers all employers with 15 or more employees. Prior to the passage of this law, jury trials and punitive damages were not permitted except in intentional discrimination lawsuits involving

Civil Rights Act of 1991
Permits women, persons with disabilities, and persons who are religious minorities to have a jury trial and sue for punitive damages if they can prove intentional hiring and workplace discrimination. Also requires companies to provide evidence that the business practice that led to the discrimination was not discriminatory but was related to the performance of the job in question and consistent with business necessity.

Family and Medical Leave Act (FMLA)
Enables qualified employees to take prolonged unpaid leave for family- and health-related reasons without fear of losing their jobs.

racial discrimination. The law places a cap on the amount of damages a victim of nonracial, intentional discrimination can collect. The cap is based on the size of the employer.

A second aspect of this act concerned the burden of proof for companies with regard to intentional discrimination lawsuits. In a series of Supreme Court decisions beginning in 1989, the Court began to ease the burden-of-proof requirements on companies. This act, however, requires that companies provide evidence that the business practice that led to the discrimination was not discriminatory but was related to the performance of the job in question and consistent with business necessity.

The **Family and Medical Leave Act (FMLA)** was enacted in 1993 to enable qualified employees to take prolonged unpaid leave for family- and health-related reasons without fear of losing their jobs. Under the law, employees can use this leave if they are seriously ill, if an immediate family member is ill, or in the event of the birth, adoption, or placement for foster care of a child.

The results of discrimination are not always as obvious as hiring and firing practices. Communication, managerial and promotional career paths, and networking that are essential to employees' success in the workplace also can be affected by indirect discrimination. Herminia Ibarra found that minority managers had more racially heterogeneous and fewer intimate network relationships, different advancement potential because of different network configurations, fewer high-status ties, and generally fewer career benefits.[8]

Figure 12.2 summarizes the laws related to equal employment opportunity.

FIGURE 12.2 Summary of Equal Opportunity Laws

Law	Year	Intent	Coverage
Equal Pay Act	1963	Prohibits sexual-based discrimination in rates of pay for men and women working in the same or similar jobs.	Private employers engaged in commerce or in the production of goods for commerce and with two or more employees; labor organizations.
Title VII, Civil Rights Act (as amended in 1972)	1964	Prohibits discrimination based on race, sex, color, religion, or national origin.	Private employers with 15 or more employees for 20 or more weeks per year, educational institutions, state and local governments, employment agencies, labor unions, and joint labor–management committees.
Age Discrimination in Employment Act (ADEA)	1967	Prohibits discrimination against individuals who are 40 years of age and older.	Private employers with 20 or more employees for 20 or more weeks per year, labor organizations, employment agencies, state and local governments, and federal agencies with some exceptions.
Rehabilitation Act (as amended)	1973	Prohibits discrimination against persons with disabilities and requires affirmative action to provide employment opportunity for these individuals.	Federal contractors and subcontractors with contracts in excess of $2,500, organizations receiving federal financial assistance, federal agencies.

(continued on next page)

FIGURE 12.2   Summary of Equal Opportunity Laws (concluded)

Law	Year	Intent	Coverage
Vietnam-Era Veterans Readjustment Assistance Act	1974	Prohibits discrimination in hiring disabled veterans with 30 percent or more disability rating, veterans discharged or released for a service-connected disability, and veterans on active duty between August 5, 1964, and May 7, 1975. Also requires written affirmative action plans for certain employers.	Federal contractors and subcontractors with contracts in excess of $10,000. Employers with 50 or more employees and contracts in excess of $50,000 must have written affirmative action plans.
Pregnancy Discrimination Act (PDA)	1978	Requires employers to treat pregnancy just like any other medical condition with regard to fringe benefits and leave policies.	Same as Title VII, Civil Rights Act.
Immigration Reform and Control Act	1986	Prohibits hiring of illegal aliens.	Any individual or company.
Americans with Disabilities Act	1990	Increases access to services and jobs for persons with disabilities.	Private employers with 15 or more employees.
Civil Rights Act	1991	Permits women, minorities, persons with disabilities, and persons who are religious minorities to have a jury trial and to sue for punitive damages if they can prove intentional hiring and workplace discrimination. Also requires companies to provide evidence that the business practice that led to the discrimination was not discriminatory but was related to the position in question and consistent with business necessity.	Private employers with 15 or more employees.
Family and Medical Leave Act (FMLA)	1993	Enables qualified employees to take prolonged unpaid leave for family- and health-related reasons without fear of losing their jobs.	Private employers with 15 or more employees.

Promotion from Internal and External Sources

An organization that has been doing an effective job of selecting employees has one of the best sources of supply for filling job openings: its own employees. Promotion from within is very popular with growing and dynamic organizations. If internal sources prove to be inadequate, external sources are always available. Though usually more costly and time consuming to pursue, external sources such as employment agencies, consulting firms, employee referrals, and employment advertisements can be valuable resources for an organization. Figure 12.3 summarizes the advantages and disadvantages of using internal and external sources for human resource needs.

FIGURE 12.3
Advantages and
Disadvantages of
Internal and
External Sources

Source: R. L. Mathis and
J. H. Jackson, *Personnel:
Contemporary Perspectives and
Applications,* West Publishing
Company, 1994.

Advantages	Disadvantages
Internal	
• Morale of promotee • Better assessment of abilities • Lower cost for some jobs • Motivator for good performance • Causes a succession of promotions • Have to hire only at entry level	• Inbreeding • Possible morale problems of those not promoted • Political infighting for promotions • Need strong management-development program
External	
• New blood bringing new perspectives • Cheaper and faster than training professionals • No group of political supporters in organization already • May bring industry insights	• May not select someone who will fit the job or organization • May cause morale problems for internal candidates not selected • Longer adjustment or orientation time

Peter Principle
Tendency of
individuals in a
hierarchy to rise to
their levels of
incompetence.

With respect to internal promotions, one interesting proposition is the so-called Peter Principle. Proposed by Laurence J. Peter, the **Peter Principle** states that in a hierarchy such as a modern organization, individuals tend to rise to their levels of incompetence.[9] In other words, people routinely get promoted in organizations and ultimately reach a level at which they are unable to perform. Organizations that maintain tight control in the human resource area, adhere to skills inventories, and conduct careful job analyses can minimize this effect.

Recruitment

recruitment
Seeking and
attracting a supply of
people from which
qualified candidates
for job vacancies can
be selected.

Recruitment involves seeking and attracting a supply of people from which qualified candidates for job vacancies can be selected. The amount of recruitment an organization must do is determined by the difference between the forecasted human resource needs and the talent available within the organization. After the decision to recruit has been made, the sources of supply must be explored. Management Illustration 12.1 describes some actions that CVS, the large drugstore chain, has taken to increase its labor pool.

Legal Influences

The previously discussed legislation has also had a profound impact on the recruitment activities of organizations. For example, the courts have ruled reliance on word-of-mouth or walk-in methods of recruitment to be a discriminatory practice where females and minorities are not well represented at all levels within the organizations.[10]

The Equal Employment Opportunity Commission (EEOC) offers the following suggestions to help eliminate discrimination in recruitment practices:[11]

• Maintain a file of unhired female and minority applicants who are potential candidates for future openings. Contact these candidates first when an opening occurs.

• Utilize females and minorities in recruitment and in the entire human resource process.

Green Thumb, Inc., is a national nonprofit organization best known as America's leader in the field of older worker training and employment. Its mission is to strengthen families, communities, and the nation by providing older and disadvantaged individuals with opportunities to learn, work, and serve others. Founded in 1965, Green Thumb was first chartered to use the "green thumbs" of retired farmers to improve our nation's parks and highways. The four-state pilot project soon evolved into one of the most innovative and cost-effective of all workforce initiatives, the Senior Community Service Employment Program. Over its history, Green Thumb has expanded its services to bring workforce opportunities each year to more than 40,000 mature workers, dislocated workers, welfare recipients, and adults with special needs in 44 states and Puerto Rico.

In acknowledgment of those American companies that recognize the importance of mature workers to their success, Green Thumb each year identifies several "Outstanding Employers of Older Workers." These awards honor those companies that have developed exemplary models promoting senior worker image, encourage aging-friendly workplaces, actively recruit, hire and retain older workers, and offer special programs such as training and flexible work schedules.

CVS employs 100,000, of whom 15,003 are mature workers. CVS began a concerted effort to proactively recruit older workers in 1992, when less than 7 percent of their workforce was 55 and over.

Today, older workers represent a diverse array of corporate job categories, including professional and managerial positions. There are 177 pharmacists and two store managers over the age of 70. Of the two employees over 90, one is a full-time pharmacist; the other is a greeting cards merchandiser. CVS has more than 4,100 CVS/pharmacy stores in 31 states and the District of Columbia.

Steve Wing, Director of Government Programs for CVS, says, "Older workers reflect a diverse workforce which helps in serving a diverse customer base that includes many older people. Some older workers are really fantastic; they serve as role models for younger people and excel in such areas as customer service."

Source: Adapted from news release dated September 13, 2001. For more information on Green Thumb, see *www.greenthumb.org*.

- Place classified ads under "Help Wanted" or "Help Wanted, Male–Female" listings. Be sure the content of ads does not indicate any sex, race, or age preference or qualification for the job.
- Advertise in media directed toward women and minorities.
- All advertising should include the phrase "equal opportunity employer."

Research has shown that organizations that are aware of protective legislation and EEOC guidelines are more likely to promote diversity, conform to accepted hiring practices, be identity conscious in their recruitment efforts, and generally go beyond symbolic efforts to improve conditions for protected groups.[12] The diverse workplace is a reality, and growth-oriented companies use that fact as a positive rather than a negative influence on the staffing of their organizations.

Selection

The selection process involves choosing from those available the individuals most likely to succeed in the job. The process is dependent on proper human resource planning and recruitment. Only when an adequate pool of qualified candidates is available can the selection process function effectively. The ultimate objective of the selection process is to match the requirements of the job with the qualifications of the individual.

Who Makes the Decision?

The responsibility for hiring is assigned to different levels of management in different organizations. Often the human resource/personnel department does the initial screening of recruits, but the final selection decision is left to the manager of the department with the job opening. Such a system relieves the manager of the time-consuming responsibility of screening out unqualified and uninterested applicants. Less frequently, the human resource/personnel department is responsible for both the initial screening and the final decision. Many organizations leave the final choice to the immediate manager, subject to the approval of higher levels of management. In small organizations, the owner or the top manager often makes the choice.

An alternative approach is to involve peers in the selection decision. Traditionally, peer involvement has been used primarily with professionals and those in upper levels of management, but it is becoming more popular at all levels of the organization. With this approach, co-workers have an input into the final selection decision.

Legal Considerations in the Selection Process

The selection process has been of primary interest to the government, as evidenced by the number of laws and regulations in effect that prohibit discrimination in the selection of employees. One action frequently required of organizations is the development of an affirmative action plan. An **affirmative action plan** is a written document outlining specific goals and timetables for remedying past discriminatory actions. All federal contractors and subcontractors with contracts over $50,000 and 50 or more employees are required to develop and implement written affirmative action plans, which are monitored by the Office of Federal Contract Compliance Programs (OFCCP). While Title VII and the EEOC require no specific type of affirmative action plan, court rulings have often required affirmative action when discrimination has been found.

A number of basic steps are involved in the development of an effective affirmative action plan. Figure 12.4 presents the EEOC's suggestions for developing an affirmative action plan.

Organizations without affirmative action plans will find it makes good business sense to identify and revise employment practices that have discriminatory effects before the federal government requires such action. Increased legal action and the record of court-required affirmative action emphasize the advantage of writing and instituting an affirmative action plan.

However, the growing number of reverse discrimination suits may have a significant impact on affirmative action programs. **Reverse discrimination** is providing preferential treatment for one group (e.g., minority or female) over another group (e.g., white male) rather than merely providing equal opportunity. The first real test case in this area was the *Bakke* case of 1978.[13] Allen Bakke, a white male, brought suit against the medical school of the University of California at Davis. He charged he was unconstitutionally discriminated against when he was denied admission to the medical school while some minority applicants with lower qualifications were accepted. The Supreme Court ruled in Bakke's favor but at the same time upheld the constitutionality of affirmative action programs.

In another case in 1979, the Supreme Court heard a challenge, brought by a white worker, Brian F. Weber, to an affirmative action plan collectively bargained by a union and an employer.[14] This case questioned whether Title VII of the Civil Rights Act of 1964 as amended prohibited private employers from granting racial preference in employment practices. The Court, in a 5–2 opinion, held that it did not and that the voluntary quota was permissible. The *Weber* decision also hinted at the Court's criteria for a permissible affirmative action plan: (1) The plan must

---

affirmative action plan
Written document outlining specific goals and timetables for remedying past discriminatory actions.

reverse discrimination
Providing preferential treatment for one group (e.g., minority or female) over another group (e.g., white male) rather than merely providing equal opportunity.

FIGURE 12.4
EEOC's Suggestions for Developing an Affirmative Action Plan

Source: *Affirmative Action and Equal Employment,* vol. 1 (Washington, DC: U.S. Equal Employment Opportunity Commission, 1974), pp. 16–64.

1. The chief executive officer of an organization should issue a written statement describing his or her personal commitment to the plan, legal obligations, and the importance of equal employment opportunity as an organizational goal.
2. A top official of the organization should be given the authority and responsibility to direct and implement the program. In addition, all managers and supervisors within the organization should clearly understand their own responsibilities for carrying out equal employment opportunity.
3. The organization's policy and commitment to the policy should be publicized both internally and externally.
4. Present employment should be surveyed to identify areas of concentration and underutilization and to determine the extent of underutilization.
5. Goals and timetables for achieving the goals should be developed to improve utilization of minorities, males, and females in each area where underutilization has been identified.
6. The entire employment system should be reviewed to identify and eliminate barriers to equal employment. Areas for review include recruitment, selection, promotion systems, training programs, wage and salary structure, benefits and conditions of employment, layoffs, discharges, disciplinary action, and union contract provisions affecting these areas.
7. An internal audit and reporting system should be established to monitor and evaluate progress in all aspects of the program.
8. Company and community programs that are supportive of equal opportunity should be developed. Programs might include training of supervisors regarding their legal responsibilities and the organization's commitment to equal employment and job and career counseling programs.

be designed to break down old patterns of segregation; (2) it must not involve the discharge of innocent third parties; (3) it must not have any bars to the advancement of white employees; and (4) it must be a temporary measure to eliminate discrimination. However, in a 1989 case (*Martin v. Wilks*), the Supreme Court ruled that white employees could bring reverse discrimination claims against court-approved affirmative action plans.[15] In another case (*City of Richmond v. J. A. Crosan Company*), the Court ruled that government affirmative action programs that put whites at a disadvantage were illegal. Finally, in the case involving the University of Texas law school, the Court ruled that the school could not use race as a factor in admissions. As these examples indicate, managers must stay abreast of legislation and judicial rulings in this area, because constant changes and revised interpretations appear to be inevitable.

Selection Procedure

Figure 12.5 presents a suggested procedure for selecting employees. The preliminary screening and preliminary interview eliminate candidates who are obviously not qualified for the job. In the preliminary screening of applications, personnel data sheets, school records, work records, and similar sources are reviewed to determine characteristics, abilities, and the past performance of the individual. The preliminary interview is then used to screen out unsuitable or uninterested applicants who passed the preliminary screening phase.

Testing

tests
Provide a sample of behavior used to draw inferences about the future behavior or performance of an individual.

One of the most controversial areas of staffing is employment testing. **Tests** provide a sample of behavior that is used to draw inferences about the future behav-

FIGURE 12.5
Steps in the Selection Process

Steps in Selection Process	Possible Criteria for Eliminating Potential Employee
• Preliminary screening from application blank, résumé, employer records, etc.	Inadequate educational level or performance/experience record for the job and its requirements.
• Preliminary interview	Obvious disinterest and unsuitability for job and its requirements.
• Testing	Failure to meet minimum standards on job-related measures of intelligence, aptitude, personality, etc.
• Reference checks	Unfavorable reports from references regarding past performance.
• Employment interview	Inadequate demonstration of ability or other job-related characteristics.
• Physical examination	Lack of physical fitness required for job.
• Personal judgment	Intuition and judgment resulting in the selection of a new employee. Inadequate demonstration of ability or other job-related characteristics.

aptitude tests
Measure a person's capacity or potential ability to learn.

psychomotor tests
Measure a person's strength, dexterity, and coordination.

job knowledge tests
Measure the job-related knowledge possessed by a job applicant.

proficiency tests
Measure how well the applicant can do a sample of the work that is to be performed.

interest tests
Determine how a person's interests compare with the interests of successful people in a specific job.

psychological tests
Attempt to measure personality characteristics.

polygraph tests
Record physical changes in the body as the test subject answers a series of questions; popularly known as *lie detector tests.*

test validity
Extent to which a test predicts a specific criterion.

test reliability
Consistency or reproducibility of the results of a test.

ior or performance of an individual. Many tests are available to organizations for use in the selection process.[16] Tests used by organizations can be grouped into the following general categories: aptitude, psychomotor, job knowledge and proficiency, interests, psychological, and polygraphs.

Aptitude tests measure a person's capacity or potential ability to learn. **Psychomotor tests** measure a person's strength, dexterity, and coordination. **Job knowledge tests** measure the job-related knowledge possessed by a job applicant. **Proficiency tests** measure how well the applicant can do a sample of the work to be performed. **Interest tests** are designed to determine how a person's interests compare with the interests of successful people in a specific job. **Psychological tests** attempt to measure personality characteristics. **Polygraph tests,** popularly known as *lie detector tests,* record physical changes in the body as the test subject answers a series of questions. By studying recorded physiological measurements, the polygraph examiner then makes a judgment as to whether the subject's response was truthful or deceptive.

Employment testing is legally subject to the requirements of validity and reliability. **Test validity** refers to the extent to which a test predicts a specific criterion. For organizations, the criterion usually used is performance on the job. Thus, test validity generally refers to the extent to which a test predicts future job success or performance. The selection of criteria to define job success or performance is a difficult process, and its importance cannot be overstated. Obviously, test validity cannot be measured unless satisfactory criteria exist.

Test reliability refers to the consistency or reproducibility of the results of a test. Three methods are commonly used to determine the reliability of a test. The first method, called *test-retest,* involves testing a group of people and then retesting them later. The degree of similarity between the sets of scores determines the reliability of the test. The second method, called *parallel forms,* entails giving two separate but similar forms of the test. The degree to which the sets of scores coincide determines the reliability of the test. The third method, called *split halves,* divides the test into two halves to determine whether performance is similar on both halves. Again, the degree of similarity determines the reliability. All of these methods require statistical calculations to determine the degree of reliability of the test.

In the past, organizations have frequently used tests without establishing their validity or reliability. As a result of such practices, testing came under a great deal of attack. The previously discussed Civil Rights Act of 1964 includes a section specifically related to the use of tests:

> nor shall it be an unlawful employment practice for an employer to give and to act upon the results of any professionally developed ability test provided that such a test, its administration, or action upon the results is not designed, intended, or used to discriminate because of race, color, religion, sex, or national origin.[17]

Two Supreme Court decisions have had a profound impact on the use of testing by organizations. First, in the case of *Griggs v. Duke Power Company,* the Court ruled that any test that has an adverse impact on female or minority group applicants must be validated as job related, regardless of whether an employer intended to discriminate.[18] In *Albermarle Paper Company v. Moody,* the Supreme Court placed the burden on the employer to show that its tests are in compliance with EEOC guidelines for testing.[19]

Finally, in 1978, the EEOC, the Civil Service Commission, the Department of Justice, and the Department of Labor adopted a document titled "Uniform Guidelines on Employee Selection Procedures."[20] These guidelines established the federal government's position concerning discrimination in employment practices. The guidelines explain what private and public employers must do to prove their selection procedures, including testing, are nondiscriminatory.[21]

Polygraph and Drug Testing

As noted earlier, polygraph tests can be used for screening job applicants. The *polygraph,* or lie detector, is a device that records physical changes in the body as the test subject answers a series of questions. The polygraph records fluctuations in blood pressure, respiration, and perspiration on a moving roll of graph paper. On the basis of the recorded fluctuations, the polygraph operator makes a judgment as to whether the subject's response was truthful or deceptive.

The use of a polygraph test rests on a series of cause-and-effect assumptions: stress causes certain physiological changes in the body; fear and guilt cause stress; lying causes fear and guilt. The use of a polygraph test assumes that a direct relationship exists between the subject's responses to questions and the physiological responses recorded on the polygraph. However, the polygraph itself does not detect lies; it only detects physiological changes. The operator must interpret the data that the polygraph records. Thus, the real lie detector is the operator, not the device.

Serious questions exist regarding the validity of polygraph tests. Difficulties arise if a person lies without guilt (a pathological liar) or lies believing the response to be true. Furthermore, it is hard to prove that the physiological responses recorded by the polygraph occur only because a lie has been told. In addition, some critics argue that the use of the polygraph violates fundamental principles of the Constitution: the right of privacy, the privilege against self-incrimination, and the presumption of innocence. As a result of these questions and criticisms, Congress passed the Employee Polygraph Protection Act of 1988 that severely restricts the commercial use of polygraph tests. Those exempt from this restrictive law are (1) all local, state, and federal employees (however, state laws can be passed to restrict the use of polygraphs); (2) industries with national defense or security contracts; (3) businesses with nuclear power–related contracts with the Department of Energy; and (4) businesses and consultants with access to highly classified information.

Private businesses are also allowed to use polygraphs under certain conditions: when hiring private security personnel; when hiring persons with access to drugs; and during investigations of economic injury or loss by the employer.

In the past few years, there has also been a proliferation of drug-testing programs. Such programs have been instituted not only to screen job applicants but also to test current employees for drug use. It has been estimated that about 20 percent of the Fortune 500 companies have either instituted drug-testing programs or are contemplating their institution.

Numerous lawsuits have been filed to contest the legality of such programs. Generally, a drug-testing program is on stronger legal ground if it is limited to job applicants. Furthermore, current employees should not be subjected to drug testing on a random basis. A probable cause for drug testing, such as a dramatic change in behavior or a sudden increase in accident rates, should be established before testing. In addition, the results of drug testing should be protected to ensure confidentiality.

Background and Reference Checks

Background and reference checks usually fall into three categories: personal, academic, and past employment. Contacting personal and academic references is generally of limited value, because few people will list someone as a reference unless they feel that that person will give them a positive recommendation. Previous employers are in the best position to supply the most objective information. However, the amount and type of information that a previous employer is willing to divulge varies. Normally, most previous employers will provide only the following information—yes or no to the question if this applicant worked there, what the employee's dates of employment were, and what position he or she held.

If a job applicant is rejected because of information in a credit report or another type of report from an outside reporting service, the applicant must be given the name and address of the organization that developed the report. The reporting service is *not* required by law to give the person a copy of his or her file, but it *must* inform the person of the nature and substance of the information. Management Illustration 12.2 describes potential hazards in reference checking.

Employment Interview

The employment interview is used by virtually all organizations as an important step in the selection process. Its purpose is to supplement information gained in other steps in the selection process to determine the suitability of an applicant for a specific opening in the organization. It is important to remember that all questions asked during an interview must be job related. Equal employment opportunity legislation has placed limitations on the types of questions that can be asked during an interview.

Types of Interviews

Organizations use several types of interviews. The *structured interview* is conducted using a predetermined outline. Through the use of this outline, the interviewer maintains control of the interview so that all pertinent information on the applicant is covered systematically. Structured interviews provide the same type of information on all interviewees and allow systematic coverage of all questions deemed necessary by the organization. Furthermore, research studies have recommended the use of a structured interview to increase reliability and accuracy.[22]

There was no love lost when Scott Ginther left his job as supervisor of broadband network engineering at a San Diego telecommunications company two and a half years ago. He and his boss had clashing work styles, and Ginther agreed to quit his job gracefully. But as he began interviewing for other positions, the computer wizard worried that his former supervisor was bad-mouthing or sabotaging him in some way. He turned to L.A.-based BadReferences.com (also known as Documented Reference Check) to find out if his hunch was right. He was stunned by what he learned.

"This supervisor said a lot of really untruthful, negative things," Ginther said. "He implied that I was anal, and said I was a little too obsessive, that I like to play it safe and am not comfortable with taking risks or making big decisions. They asked him pointblank if he would hire me again and he said no. He even suggested that I should consider switching careers."

BadReferences, which uses trained court reporters to call employers, checks a reference and then prepares a written report, at a cost of $87.95. Turnaround time averages 38 days. Ginther bought the service and also hired an employment attorney to pursue a case against his previous employer, asking for an end to the defamation and for $45,000 in compensation. Largely because of the information contained in the BadReferences report, his attorney felt that the case was strong. Michael Rankin, chief services officer at BadReferences, said that when the firm's reports have been used as evidence, "we haven't lost a case in 20 years."

Source: Eilene Zimmerman, "A Subtle Reference Trap for Unwary Employers," *Workforce,* April 2003, p. 22.

Two variations of the structured interview are the semistructured and the situational interview. In the *semistructured interview,* the interviewer prepares the major questions in advance but has the flexibility to use techniques such as probing to help assess the applicant's strengths and weaknesses. The *situational interview* uses projective techniques to put the prospective employee in action situations that might be encountered on the job. For example, the interviewer may wish to see how the applicant might handle a customer complaint or observe certain important decision-making characteristics. With either method, however, interviewer bias must be guarded against.

Unstructured interviews are conducted using no predetermined checklist of questions. This type of interview uses open-ended questions such as "Tell me about your previous job." Interviews of this type pose numerous problems, such as a lack of systematic coverage of information, and are susceptible to the personal biases of the interviewer. This type of interview, however, does provide a more relaxed atmosphere.

Organizations have used three other types of interviewing techniques to a limited extent. The *stress interview* is designed to place the interviewee under pressure. In the stress interview, the interviewer assumes a hostile and antagonistic attitude toward the interviewee. The purpose of this type of interview is to detect whether the person is highly emotional. In the *board (or panel) interview,* two or more interviewers conduct the interview. The *group interview,* which questions several interviewees together in a group discussion, is also sometimes used. Board interviews and group interviews can involve either a structured or an unstructured format.

Problems in Conducting Interviews

Although interviews have widespread use in selection procedures, they can pose a host of problems. The first and one of the most significant problems is that interviews are subject to the same legal requirements of validity and reliability as other steps in the selection process. Furthermore, the validity and reliability of most interviews are questionable. One reason seems to be that it is easy for the interviewer to become either favorably or unfavorably impressed with the job applicant for the wrong reasons.

Several common pitfalls may be encountered in interviewing a job applicant. Interviewers, like all people, have personal biases, and these biases can play a role in the interviewing process. For example, a qualified male applicant should not be rejected merely because the interviewer dislikes long hair on males.

halo effect
Occurs when the interviewer allows a single prominent characteristic to dominate judgment of all other traits.

Closely related is the problem of the **halo effect,** which occurs when the interviewer allows a single prominent characteristic to dominate judgment of all other traits. For instance, it is often easy to overlook other characteristics when a person has a pleasant personality. However, merely having a pleasant personality does not ensure that the person will be a qualified employee.

Overgeneralizing is another common problem. An interviewee may not behave exactly the same way on the job that she or he did during the interview. The interviewer must remember that the interviewee is under pressure during the interview and that some people just naturally become nervous during an interview.

Conducting Effective Interviews

Problems associated with interviews can be partially overcome through careful planning. The following suggestions are offered to increase the effectiveness of the interviewing process.

First, careful attention must be given to the selection and training of interviewers. They should be outgoing and emotionally well-adjusted people. Interviewing skills can be learned, and the people responsible for conducting interviews should be thoroughly trained in these skills.

Second, the plan for the interview should include an outline specifying the information to be obtained and the questions to be asked. The plan should also include room arrangements. Privacy and some degree of comfort are important. If a private room is not available, the interview should be conducted in a place where other applicants are not within hearing distance.

Third, the interviewer should attempt to put the applicant at ease. The interviewer should not argue with the applicant or put the applicant on the spot. A brief conversation about a general topic of interest or offering the applicant a cup of coffee can help ease the tension. The applicant should be encouraged to talk. However, the interviewer must maintain control and remember that the primary goal of the interview is to gain information that will aid in the selection decision.

Fourth, the facts obtained in the interview should be recorded immediately. Generally, notes can and should be taken during the interview.

Finally, the effectiveness of the interviewing process should be evaluated. One way to evaluate effectiveness is to compare the performance ratings of individuals who are hired against assessments made during the interview. This cross-check can serve to evaluate the effectiveness of individual interviewers as well as that of the overall interviewing program.

Personal Judgment

The final step in the selection process is to make a personal judgment regarding which individual to select for the job. (Of course, it is assumed that at this point more than one applicant will be qualified for the job.) A value judgment using all of the data obtained in the previous steps of the selection process must be made in selecting the best individual for the job. If previous steps have been performed correctly, the chances of making a successful personal judgment improve dramatically.

The individual making the personal judgment should also recognize that in some cases, none of the applicants is satisfactory. If this occurs, the job should be redesigned, more money should be offered to attract more qualified candidates, or other actions should be taken. Caution should be taken against accepting the "best" applicant if that person is not truly qualified to do the job.

Transfers, Promotions, and Separations

The final step in the human resource planning process involves transfers, promotions, and separations. A transfer involves moving an employee to another job at approximately the same level in the organization with basically the same pay, performance requirements, and status. Planned transfers can serve as an excellent development technique. Transfers can also be helpful in balancing varying departmental workload requirements. The most common difficulty relating to transfers occurs when a "problem" employee is unloaded on an unsuspecting manager. Training, counseling, or corrective discipline of the employee may eliminate the need for such a transfer. If the employee cannot be rehabilitated, discharge is usually preferable to transfer.

A promotion moves an employee to a job involving higher pay, higher status, and thus higher performance requirements. The two basic criteria used by most organizations in promotions are merit and seniority. Union contracts often require that seniority be considered in promotions. Many organizations prefer to base promotions on merit as a way to reward and encourage performance. Obviously, this assumes the organization has a method for evaluating performance and determining merit. An organization must also consider the requirements of the job in question, not just the employee's performance in previous jobs. Success in one job does not automatically ensure success in another job. Both past performance and potential must be considered. This also lessens the probability that the Peter Principle effect will occur.

A separation involves either voluntary or involuntary termination of an employee. In voluntary separations, many organizations attempt to determine why the employee is leaving by using exit interviews. This type of interview provides insights into problem areas that need to be corrected in the organization. Involuntary separations involve terminations and layoffs. Layoffs occur when there is not enough work for all employees. Laid-off employees are called back if and when the workload increases. A termination usually occurs when an employee is not performing his or her job or has broken a company rule. Terminations should be made only as a last resort. When a company has hired an employee and invested resources in the employee, termination results in a low return on the organization's investment. Training and counseling often are tried before firing an individual. However, when rehabilitation fails, the best action is usually termination because of the negative impact a disgruntled or misfit employee can have on others in the organization.

Summary

1. *Outline the human resource planning process.* Human resource planning (HRP) is the process of "getting the right number of qualified people into the right jobs at the right time." Once organizational plans are made and specific objectives are set, human re-

source planning attempts to define the human resource needs to meet the organization's objectives.

2. *Define job analysis, job description, job specification, and skills inventory.* Job analysis is the process of determining, through observation and study, the pertinent information relating to the nature of a specific job. A job description is a written statement that identifies the tasks, duties, activities, and performance results required in a particular job. A job specification is a written statement that identifies the abilities, skills, traits, or attributes necessary for successful performance in a particular job. A skills inventory contains basic information about all employees of the organization.

3. *Define equal employment opportunity.* Equal employment opportunity refers to the right of all people to work and to advance on the bases of merit, ability, and potential.

4. *Describe the recruitment process.* Recruitment involves the activities of seeking and attracting a supply of people from which to select qualified candidates for job vacancies.

5. *Define affirmative action plan.* An affirmative action plan is a written document outlining specific goals and timetables for remedying past discriminatory actions.

6. *Discuss reverse discrimination.* Reverse discrimination is the provision of alleged preferential treatment for one group (e.g., minority or female) over another group (e.g., white male) rather than merely providing equal opportunity.

7. *Define tests, test validity, and test reliability.* Tests provide a sample of behavior used to draw inferences about the future behavior or performance of an individual. Test validity refers to the extent to which a test predicts a specific criterion. Test reliability refers to the consistency or reproducibility of the results of a test.

8. *Discuss the different types of employment interviews.* A structured interview is conducted using a predetermined outline. Unstructured interviews are conducted using no predetermined checklist of questions. In the stress interview, the interviewer assumes a hostile and antagonistic attitude to place the interviewee under stress. In the board (or panel) interview, two or more interviewers conduct the interview. In a group interview, several interviewees are questioned together in a group discussion.

9. *Discuss potential problems in the interviewing process.* The biggest problem concerns validity and reliability; the interviewer may be legally required to show that the interviewing method used was valid, reliable, and not discriminatory. Second, the interviewer may be favorably or unfavorably impressed with the prospective employee for the wrong reasons and let personal biases enter into his or her judgment of the applicant. Third, the halo effect can cause the interviewer to make judgments based on a dominant favorable characteristic and therefore fail to see the total individual. Finally, overgeneralizing can be a problem. The interviewer must remember that the interview is different from the job itself and that the interviewee is likely to be nervous during the interview.

Review Questions

1. How does staffing relate to the organizing function?
2. What is human resource planning?
3. What is a job analysis? A job description? A job specification? A skills inventory?
4. What is human resource forecasting?
5. Describe a model of the human resource planning process.
6. Describe the purposes of the following government legislation:
   a. Equal Pay Act of 1963.
   b. Civil Rights Act of 1964.
   c. Age Discrimination in Employment Act of 1968, as amended in 1972.
   d. Rehabilitation Act of 1973.
   e. Americans with Disabilities Act of 1990.

    f. Civil Rights Act of 1991.

    g. Family and Medical Leave Act.

  7. What is equal employment opportunity?

  8. Define affirmative action plan.

  9. What is recruitment? Describe some sources of recruitment.

 10. What is selection? Describe the steps in the selection process.

 11. What is test validity?

 12. What is test reliability? What methods are commonly used to determine test reliability?

 13. Describe two basic types of interviews.

 14. Discuss some common pitfalls in interviewing.

 15. What is a transfer? A promotion? A separation?

Skill-Building Questions

1. Discuss the following statement: An individual who owns a business should be able to hire anyone and shouldn't have to worry about government interference.

2. Discuss your feelings about reverse discrimination.

3. Many managers believe line managers should not have to worry about human resource needs and this function should be handled by the human resource department. What do you think?

4. One common method of handling problem employees is to transfer them to another department of the organization. What do you think about this practice?

5. What is EQ? How do you think you might rate on this characteristic? For what types of jobs would a high EQ be useful?

Skill-Building Exercise 12.1

Affirmative Action Debate

Your instructor will break the class into teams of four to five students. Each team should then prepare to debate one of the following statements:

1. The federal government should not require affirmative action programs for private enterprise organizations that are federal contractors or subcontractors.

2. Affirmative action programs have been very helpful to minorities and women. Private enterprise organizations should be required to have affirmative action programs.

After the debate, the instructor will list on the board the points made by each team and discuss the issues involved.

Skill-Building Exercise 12.2

The Layoff

Two years ago, your organization experienced a sudden increase in its volume of work. At about the same time, it was threatened with an equal employment opportunity suit that resulted in an affirmative action plan. Under this plan, additional women and minority members have been recruited and hired.

Presently, the top level of management in your organization is anticipating a decrease in volume of work. You have been asked to rank the clerical employees of your section in the event a layoff is necessary.

Below you will find biographical data for the seven clerical people in your section. Rank the seven people according to the order in which they should be laid off, that is, the person ranked first is to be laid off first, and so on.

Burt Green: White male, age 45. Married, four children; five years with the organization. Reputed to be an alcoholic; poor work record.

Nan Nushka: White female, age 26. Married, no children, husband has a steady job; six months with the organization. Hired after the affirmative action plan went into effect; average work record to date. Saving to buy a house.

Johnny Jones: Black male, age 20. Unmarried; one year with organization. High performance ratings. Reputed to be shy—a "loner"; wants to start his own business some day.

Joe Jefferson: White male, age 24. Married, no children but wife is pregnant; three years with organization. Going to college at night; erratic performance attributed to work/study conflicts.

Livonia Long: Black female, age 49. Widow, three grown children; two years with the organization. Steady worker whose performance is average.

Ward Watt: White male, age 30. Recently divorced, one child; three years with the organization. Good worker.

Rosa Sanchez: Hispanic female, age 45. Six children, husband disabled one year ago; trying to help support her family; three months with the organization. No performance appraisal data available.

1. What criteria did you use for ranking the employees?
2. What implications does your ranking have in the area of affirmative action?

Case Incident 12.1

Accept Things as They Are?

Jane Harris came to work at the S&J department store two years ago. In Jane's initial assignment in the finance department, she proved to be a good and hard worker. It soon became obvious to both Jane and her department head, Rich Jackson, that she could handle a much more responsible job than the one she presently held. Jane discussed this matter with Rich. It was obvious to him that if a better position could not be found for Jane, S&J would lose a good employee. As there were no higher openings in the finance department, Rich recommended her for a job in the accounting department. She was hired.

Jane joined the accounting department as payroll administrator and quickly mastered her position. She became knowledgeable in all aspects of the job and maintained a good rapport with her two employees. A short time later, Jane was promoted to assistant manager of the accounting department. In this job, Jane continued her outstanding performance.

Two months ago, Bob Thomas suddenly appeared as a new employee in the accounting department. Ralph Simpson, vice president of administration for S&J, explained to Jane and Steve Smith, head of the accounting department, that Bob was a trainee. After Bob had learned all areas of the department, he would be used to take some of the load off both Jane and Steve and also to undertake special projects for the department. Several days after Bob's arrival, Jane learned that Bob was the son of a politician who was a close friend of the president of S&J. Bob had worked in his father's successful election campaign until shortly before he joined S&J.

Last week, Steve asked Jane to help him prepare the accounting department's budget for next year. While working on the budget, Jane got a big surprise. She found that Bob had been hired at a salary of $2,400 per month. At the time of Bob's hiring, Jane, as assistant manager of the accounting department, was making only $2,000 per month.

After considering her situation for several days, Jane went to see Ralph Simpson, the division head, about the problem. She told Ralph she had learned of the difference in salary while assisting Steve with the budget and stated it was not right to pay a trainee more than a manager. She reminded Ralph of what he had said several times: that Jane's position should pay $26,000 to $28,000 per year considering her responsibility, but S&J just could not afford to pay her that much. Jane told Ralph that things could not remain as they were at present, and she wanted to give S&J a chance to correct the situation. Ralph told Jane he would get back to her in several days.

About a week later, Ralph gave Jane a reply. He stated that while the situation was unfair, he did not think S&J could do anything about it. He told her that sometimes one has to accept things as they are, even if they are wrong. He further stated that he hoped this would not cause S&J to lose a good employee.

Questions

1. What options does Jane have?
2. What influence, if any, would the federal government have in this case?

Case Incident 12.2

The Employment Interview

Jerry Sullivan is the underwriting manager for a large insurance company located in the Southwest. Recently, one of his best employees had given him two weeks' notice of her intention to leave. She was expecting a baby soon, and she and her husband had decided she was going to quit work and stay home with her new baby and her other two young children.

Today, Jerry was scheduled to start interviewing applicants for this job. The first applicant was Barbara Riley. She arrived at the company's office promptly at 9 A.M., the time scheduled for her interview. Unfortunately, just before she arrived, Jerry received a phone call from his boss, who had just returned from a three-week vacation. He wanted Jerry to bring him up to date on what had been going on. The telephone conversation lasted 30 minutes. During that time, Barbara Riley was seated in the company's reception room.

At 9:30, Jerry went to the reception room and invited her into his office. The following conversation occurred:

Jerry: Would you like a cup of coffee?

Barbara: No, I've already had one.

Jerry: You don't mind if I have a cup, do you?

Barbara: No, go right ahead. [*Jerry pauses, and rings his secretary Dorothy Cannon.*]

Jerry: Dorothy, would you fix me a cup of coffee?

Dorothy: I'll bring it in shortly. You have a call on line 1.

Jerry: Who is it?

Dorothy: It's Tom Powell, our IBM representative. He wants to talk to you about the delivery date on our new word processor.

Jerry: I'd better talk to him. [*Turning to Barbara.*] I'd better take this call. I'll only be a minute. [*He picks up his phone.*] Well, Tom, when are we going to get our machines?

This phone conversation goes on for almost 10 minutes. After hanging up, Jerry turns again to Barbara to resume the interview.

Jerry: I'm sorry, but I needed to know about those machines. We really do need them. We only have a short time, so why don't you just tell me about yourself.

At that point, Barbara tells Jerry about her education, which includes an undergraduate degree in psychology and an MBA, which she will be receiving shortly. She explains to Jerry that this will be her first full-time job. Just then the phone rings, and Jerry's secretary tells him that his next interviewee is waiting.

Jerry: [*Turns to Barbara.*] Thank you for coming in. I'll be in touch with you as soon as I interview two more applicants for this job. However, I need to ask you a couple of quick questions.

Barbara: OK.

Jerry: Are you married?

Barbara: I am divorced.

Jerry: Do you have children?

Barbara: Yes, two boys.

Jerry: Do they live with you?

Barbara: Yes.

Jerry: The reason I am asking is that this job requires some travel. Will this pose a problem?

Barbara: No.

Jerry: Thanks, and I'll be in touch with you.

Questions

1. Outline the inadequacies of this interview.
2. What information did Jerry learn?
3. What do you think of Jerry's last questions?

References and Additional Readings

1. C. F. Russ, Jr., "Manpower Systems: Part I," *Personnel Journal,* January 1982, p. 41.
2. Ibid.
3. For a description of how Robbins & Meyers, Inc., does human resource planning, see David R. Leigh, "Business Planning Is People Planning," *Personnel Journal,* May 1984, pp. 44–45.
4. Thomas H. Patten, *Manpower Planning and the Development of Human Resources* (New York: John Wiley & Sons, 1971), p. 243.
5. For a detailed discussion of skills inventories, see Donald C. Doele and Carlton W. Dukes, "Skills Inventories and Promotion Systems," in *Handbook of Human Resources Administration,* 2nd ed., ed. Joseph J. Famularo (New York: McGraw-Hill, 1986), pp. 18–1 through 18–21.
6. "Equal Pay for Equal Work under the Fair Labor Standards Act," *Interpractices Bulletin* (Washington, DC: U.S. Department of Labor, 1967), Title 29, pt. 800.
7. Wendy Zellner, "Pioneer: The Race Battle Never Ends," *Business Week,* October 17, 1994, p. 98.
8. Herminia Ibarra, "Race, Opportunity, and Diversity of Social Circles in Managerial Networks," *Academy of Management Journal* 38, no. 3 (1995), p. 673.
9. Laurence J. Peter and R. Hall, *The Peter Principle* (New York: Bantam Books, 1969). See also Laurence J. Peter, *Why Things Go Wrong* (New York: William Morrow and Company, 1985).
10. *Parham v. Southwestern Bell Telephone Company,* 433 F.2d 421 (8th Cir. 1970).
11. *Affirmative Action and Equal Employment,* vol. 1 (Washington, DC: U.S. Equal Employment Opportunity Commission, 1974), pp. 30–31.
12. Alison M. Konrad and Frank Linnehan, "Formalized HRM Structures: Coordinating Equal Employment Opportunity or Concealing Organizational Practices?" *Academy of Management Journal* 38, no. 3 (1995), p. 787.
13. *University of California Regents v. Bakke,* 483 U.S. 265 (1978).
14. *United Steelworkers v. Weber,* 99 S. Ct. 2721 (1979).
15. *Martin v. Wilks,* 104 L. Ed. 2d 835 (1989).
16. For a detailed description of a large number of tests, see *Tests and Reviews* (Highland Park, NJ: Gryphon Press, 1974).
17. Title VII, Section 703(h), Civil Rights Act of 1964.
18. *Griggs v. Duke Power Company,* 401 U.S. 424 (1971).
19. Thaddeus Holt, "A View from Albermarle," *Personnel Psychology,* Spring 1977, p. 71. Also see "EEOC Guidelines on Employment Testing," *Federal Register,* August 1, 1970, p. 12333.
20. "Uniform Guidelines on Employee Selection Procedures," *Federal Register,* August 25, 1978, pp. 38290–315.
21. For a more in-depth discussion of the current state of testing, see Dale Yoder and Paul D. Staudohar, "Testing and EEO: Getting Down to Cases," *Personnel Administrator,* February 1984, pp. 67–74.
22. E. D. Pursell, M. A. Champion, and S. R. Gaylord, "Structured Interviewing: Avoid Selection Problems," *Personnel Journal,* November 1980, p. 908.

13

Developing Employees and Managers

Learning Objectives

After studying this chapter, you will be able to:

1. Define human asset accounting.
2. Describe the orientation process.
3. Define training.
4. Define needs assessment.
5. Discuss vestibule training, apprenticeship training, and computer-based instruction.
6. List and define the most popular methods of management development.
7. Describe an assessment center.
8. List the steps involved in the evaluation of training and management development.

Chapter Preview

General Motors and McDonald's pioneered the corporate university concept. Now an estimated 1,600 corporate colleges exist at companies like Motorola, Walt Disney, Carpet One, Verizon, Sears Roebuck, and Microsoft. Many other corporations, even small to midsize businesses, are establishing corporate schools. Like the traditional college or university, corporate universities have buildings, classroom courses with instructors, catalogs, and even course numbers. In some cases, students receive degrees or certificates for such training. Some companies are having their programs accredited so employees can convert some in-house course work into college credits for graduate degrees. Robert Brado, senior vice president of Strategic Management Group, a consulting firm that specializes in helping companies develop training programs, stated as follows: "You think that employees are attracted to companies because of how much they pay. But typically, excellent training programs, such as corporate universities, are always in the top three reasons why people are attracted and why they stay."

Source: Amit Shah, Charles Sterrett, Jerry Chesser, and Jessica Wilmore, "Meeting the Need for Employee Development in the Twenty-First Century," *S.A.M. Advanced Management Journal,* Spring 2001, pp. 22–28.

Analyzing Management Skills

Do you feel that you would be more attracted to work for a company that has a good employee training program? Why or why not?

Applying Management Skills

Do you feel that management skills can be learned?

---

human asset accounting
Determining and recording the value of an organization's human resources in its statement of financial condition.

On an organization's balance sheet, such factors as cash, buildings, and equipment are listed as assets. One asset that is not listed is the value of the organization's human resources. However, businesses make huge investments in recruiting, hiring, training, and developing their human resources. **Human asset accounting** involves determining and recording the value of an organization's human resources in its statement of financial condition. Although human asset accounting is not an acceptable accounting practice for tax or financial reporting purposes, it does recognize that the quality of an organization's human resources is an important asset.

Human Resource Development Process

Enhancing the quality of an organization's human resources involves many activities. Newly hired employees must be introduced to the organization and to their jobs. They must be trained to perform their jobs. Employee assistance and union relations (if applicable) must be planned and managed. Also, current employees must regularly have their skills updated and must learn new skills. A business must also be concerned about developing the skills of its management team. Developing employee skills is a key managerial responsibility.

As Figure 13.1 shows, the human resource development process has many steps and functions. Most of these steps are not independent or mutually exclusive tasks. Instead, in the rapidly changing organization of the 2000s, the human resource department is a blend of all the needs that affect the company's workforce. The human resource department is at the heart of many important managerial decisions because of the increasing reliance on the department's skills in understanding, training, and providing tools with which to build and maintain a competitive workforce. Management Illustration 13.1 explains JCPenney's virtual university.

Orientation

orientation
Introduction of new employees to the organization, their work units, and their jobs.

Orientation is the introduction of new employees to the organization, their work units, and their jobs. Orientation comes from co-workers and the organization. The orientation from co-workers is usually unplanned and unofficial, and it can provide the new employee with misleading and inaccurate information. This is one reason it is important that the organization provide an orientation. An effective orientation program has an immediate and lasting impact on the new employee and can make the difference between a new employee's success or failure.

FIGURE 13.1
Human Resource
Wheel

Source: P. A. McLagan,
"Models for HRD Practice,"
*Training and Development
Journal* 41 (1989), p. 53.

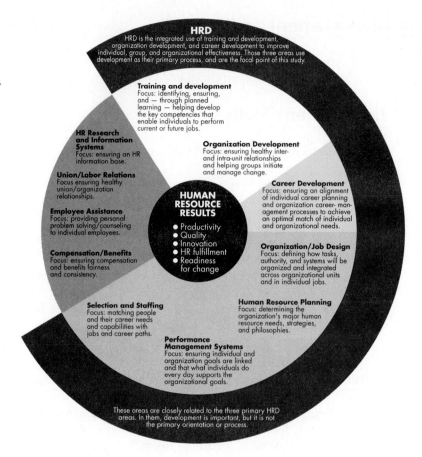

Job applicants get some orientation to the organization even before they are hired. Sometimes the orientation comes through the organization's reputation: how it treats employees and the types of products or services it provides. Also, during the selection process, applicants often learn about other general aspects of the organization and what their duties, working conditions, and pay will be. Commonly cited objectives of company orientation programs are (1) reduction of new employee stress, (2) lower start-up costs of integrating the new employee into the organization, (3) eventual reduction of turnover due to failure to understand the rules and culture of the organization, (4) reduced time required to integrate the employee into the job, and (5) helping the employee adjust to his or her work team or work environment more quickly.[1]

After the employee is hired, the organization's formal orientation program begins. For all types of organizations, orientation usually should be conducted at two distinct levels:

1. *General organizational orientation:* presents topics of relevance and interest to all employees.

2. *Departmental and job orientation:* covers topics unique to the new employee's specific department and job.

Normally, the general orientation is given by the human resource department. Departmental and job orientation are generally handled by the new employee's

In order to keep key employees and stay competitive and profitable, organizations are sometimes turning from training to highly customized learning. Competition and increasing consumer demand mean that organizations must respond quickly to change. At the same time, corporate mergers and related job cuts mean that the remaining employees have more responsibilities without the training to fulfill them. How can companies meet all these demands?

JCPenney's corporate university, The Learning Place, is run by Jane Masten from the company's headquarters in Plano, Texas. There, a production studio holds videoconferences via satellite for employees around the world. Participants use touch-pad technology to ask questions or make comments—and all the other participants can hear them,

in real time. Masten, the director of human resources development, says: "There is no bricks-and-mortar facility for our university, outside of the production studio. We've created a completely virtual university. When people need knowledge, they need it immediately. They can't wait until it can be scheduled, then hop on a plane and spend a week in a seminar." In addition to its videoconferencing capabilities, The Learning Place provides all of its training materials online, available at any time to JCPenney's 200,000 employees.

Source: Eileen M. Garger, "Goodbye Training, Hello Learning," *Workforce,* November 1999, pp. 35–42.

---

manager. Each new employee should receive a kit or packet of information to supplement the general organizational orientation program. This orientation kit is usually prepared by the human resource department and provides a wide variety of materials. It should be designed with care and provide only essential information. The orientation kit may include the following:

- Organizational chart.
- Map of the organization's facilities.
- Copy of policy and procedures handbook.
- List of holidays and fringe benefits.
- Copies of performance appraisal forms and procedures.
- Copies of other required forms (e.g., expense reimbursement form).
- Emergency and accident prevention procedures.
- Sample copy of company newsletter or magazine.
- Telephone numbers and locations of key company personnel (e.g., security).
- Copies of insurance plans.

Many organizations require employees to sign a form stating they have received and read the orientation kit. In unionized organizations, this protects the company if a grievance arises and the employee claims not to be aware of certain company policies and procedures. It is equally important that a form be signed in nonunionized businesses, particularly in light of an increase in wrongful discharge litigation. Whether signing a form actually encourages new employees to read the orientation kit is questionable, however.

Orientations do pose some difficulties. Commonly cited problems include information overload for the new employee, too much paperwork, unnecessary information, too much "selling" of the organization, lack of support of existing employees (e.g., seasoned co-workers telling new employees not to listen to the company line), lack of a long-term orientation (many orientations are done in only one day), lack of accurate follow-up, and failure to correct weaknesses in the orientation program. Reducing these difficulties is a real challenge for the human resource department.

Organizations should realize that the orientation, whether from co-workers or from the organization, will have a strong impact on the performance of new employees. Thus, it is in the company's best interest to have a well-planned, well-executed orientation program.

Training Employees

training
Acquiring skills or learning concepts to increase the performance of employees.

Training involves the employee acquiring skills or learning concepts to increase his or her performance. Generally, the new employee's manager has primary responsibility for training in how to perform the job. Sometimes this responsibility is delegated to a senior employee in the department. Regardless, the quality of this initial training can greatly influence the employee's job attitude and productivity.

Economic, social, technological, and governmental changes also influence the skills an organization needs. Changes in these areas can make current skills obsolete in a short time. Also, planned organizational changes and expansions can make it necessary for employees to update their skills or acquire new ones.

Needs Assessment

needs assessment
Systematic analysis of the specific training activities a business requires to achieve its objectives.

Training must be directed toward the accomplishment of some organizational objective, such as more efficient production methods, improved quality of products or services, or reduced operating costs. This means an organization should commit its resources only to those training activities that can best help in achieving its objectives. **Needs assessment** is a systematic analysis of the specific training activities a business requires to achieve its objectives. In general, a needs assessment can be conducted in three ways: organizational analysis, functional unit or departmental analysis, and individual employee analysis.

At the organizational level, records on absenteeism, turnover, tardiness, and accident rates provide objective evidence of problems within the organization. When problems occur, these records should be examined carefully to determine if the problems could be partially resolved through training. Employee attitude surveys can also be used to uncover training needs at both the organizational and functional unit levels. Normally, most organizations bring in an independent party to conduct and analyze the survey.

Consumer or customer surveys can also indicate problem areas that may not be obvious to the employees of the organization. Responses to a customer survey may indicate areas of training for the organization as a whole or within functional units of the organization.

A popular approach to planning the assessment process includes the following steps:

1. Define the objectives of the assessment process (what is the purpose?).
2. Identify data necessary to conduct the assessment.
3. Select a method for gathering the data (questionnaires, interviews, surveys, etc.).
4. Gather the data.
5. Analyze and verify the data.
6. Prepare a final report.

These steps may be customized to fit the individual needs of the company, but a plan always helps to produce favorable results.

Establishing Training Objectives

After training needs have been determined, objectives must be established for meeting these needs. Unfortunately, many organizational training programs have no objectives. "Training for training's sake" appears to be the maxim. This philosophy makes it virtually impossible to evaluate the strengths and weaknesses of a training program.

Effective training objectives should state what the organization, department, or individual is to be like when the training is completed. The outcomes should be in writing. Training objectives can be categorized as follows:

1. Instructional objectives:
   - What principles, facts, and concepts are to be learned in the training programs?
   - Who is to be taught?
   - When are they to be taught?
2. Organizational and departmental objectives:
   - What impact will the training have on organizational and departmental outcomes, such as absenteeism, turnover, reduced costs, and improved productivity?
3. Individual performance and growth objectives:
   - What impact will the training have on the behavioral and attitudinal outcomes of the individual trainee?
   - What impact will the training have on the personal growth of the individual trainee?

When clearly defined objectives are lacking, it is impossible to evaluate a program efficiently. However, sound training objectives can usually unlock the potential of the employee by identifying skill deficiencies and developmental opportunities, making good performance better, overcoming skill deficits, and helping the employee prepare for the future.

Methods of Training

Several methods can be used to satisfy the organization's training needs and accomplish its objectives. Some of the more commonly used methods include on-the-job training, job rotation, vestibule training, apprenticeship training, classroom training, and computer-assisted instruction.

On-the-Job Training and Job Rotation

on-the-job training (OJT)
Normally given by a senior employee or supervisor, training in which the trainee is shown how to perform the job and allowed to do it under the trainer's supervision.

On-the-job training (OJT) is normally given by a senior employee or supervisor. The trainee is shown how to perform the job and allowed to do it under the trainer's supervision.

One form of on-the-job training is *job rotation,* sometimes called *cross-training.* In job rotation, an employee learns several different jobs within a work unit or department and performs each job for a specified period. One main advantage of job rotation is that it allows flexibility in the department. For example, when one member of a work unit is absent, another can perform that job.

One advantage of OJT is that it requires no special facilities. Also, the new employee does productive work during the learning process. A major disadvantage is that the pressures of the workplace can cause training to be haphazard or neglected.

Vestibule Training

vestibule training
System in which procedures and equipment similar to those used in the actual job are set up in a special working area called a vestibule.

In **vestibule training,** procedures and equipment similar to those used in the actual job are set up in a special working area called a *vestibule.* The trainee is then taught how to perform the job by a skilled person and is able to learn the job at a comfortable pace without the pressures of production schedules.

The primary advantage of this method is that the trainer can stress theory and use of proper techniques rather than output, and the student can learn by actually doing the job. However, this method is expensive, and the employee still must adjust to the actual production environment. Vestibule training has been used to train word processor operators, bank tellers, clerks, and others in similar jobs.

Apprenticeship Training

apprenticeship training
System in which an employee is given instruction and experience, both on and off the job, in all of the practical and theoretical aspects of the work required in a skilled occupation, craft, or trade.

Apprenticeship training dates back to biblical times and is, in the simplest terms, training in those occupations requiring a wide and diverse range of skills and knowledge as well as independence of judgment. As practiced by organizations, **apprenticeship training** is a system in which an employee is given instruction and experience, both on and off the job, in all of the practical and theoretical aspects of the work required in a skilled occupation, craft, or trade. Most apprenticeship programs range from one to five years.

Classroom Training and Computer-Assisted Instruction

Classroom training is conducted off the job and is probably the most familiar method of training. Classroom training is an effective means of quickly getting information to large groups with limited or no knowledge of the subject being presented. It is useful for teaching actual material, concepts, principles, and theories. Portions of orientation programs, some aspects of apprenticeship training, and safety programs are usually presented with some form of classroom instruction. However, classroom training is used more frequently for technical, professional, and managerial employees. The most common classroom methods used for the general workforce are lecture, discussion, audiovisual methods, experiential methods, and computer-based training.

The lecture method is the simplest and least costly. A lecturer gives an oral presentation on a subject to an audience. The primary problems concern the skill of the lecturer and the ability of the audience to listen effectively. The lecture method is more effective when discussion is not only allowed but encouraged.

If expertise or lecture skills are lacking, audiovisual techniques can bring outside experts to the classroom via video or film. The method is most effective if a moderator allows periodic discussion or hands-on demonstration to complement the audiovisual presentation.

computer-based training
Training that allows the trainee to absorb knowledge from a preset computer program and advance his or her knowledge in a self-paced format.

Occasionally, experiential methods, such as case studies or role playing, are effective for the general workforce. Though most commonly associated with management training, this method usually emphasizes creative thinking, problem solution, and human behavior skills.

Computer-based training allows the employee to absorb information from a preset computer program and advance his or her knowledge in a self-paced format. This method is more effective than the old workbook method of answering questions, but it requires the use and understanding of computer equipment. Highly technical and computer-based manufacturing processes lend themselves to this method. The advantages of being able to use the full capabilities (especially the visually attractive CD-ROM feature) of the computer for learning usually outweigh the disadvantages associated with limited computer skills. One growing method of training is Internet-based training.

Making Training Meaningful

To make all types of training more meaningful, a manager should avoid several common pitfalls. Lack of reinforcement is one. An employee who is praised for doing a job well is likely to be motivated to do it well again. Praise and recognition can very effectively reinforce an employee's learning. Feedback regarding progress is critical to effective learning. Setting standards for trainees and measuring performance against the standards encourage learning.

The adage "practice makes perfect" definitely applies to the learning process. Too many managers try to explain the job quickly, then expect the person to do it perfectly the first time. Having trainees perform a job or explain how to perform it focuses their concentration and enhances learning. Repeating a job or task several times also helps. Learning is always aided by practice and repetition.

Managers sometimes also have preconceived and inaccurate ideas about what certain people or groups of people can or cannot do. A manager should realize that different people learn at different rates. Some learn rapidly; some learn more slowly. A manager should not expect everyone to catch on to the job right away. The pace of the training should be adjusted to the trainee. Also, a person who is not a fast learner will not necessarily always be a poor performer. The manager should take the attitude that all people can learn and want to learn.

Management Development

management development
Process of developing the attitudes and skills necessary to become or remain an effective manager.

Management development is concerned with developing the attitudes and skills necessary to become or remain an effective manager. To succeed, it must have the full support of the organization's top executives. Management development should be designed, conducted, and evaluated on the basis of the objectives of the organization, the needs of the managers involved, and probable changes in the organization's management team.

Needs Assessment

Numerous methods have been proposed for use in assessing management development needs. The management development needs of any organization are composed of the aggregate, or overall, needs of the organization and the development needs of each manager within the organization.

Organizational Needs

The most common method for determining organizational management development needs is an analysis of problem areas within the organization. For example, increases in the number of grievances or accidents within an area of the organization often signal the need for management development. High turnover rates, absenteeism, or tardiness may also indicate management development needs. Projections based on the organization's objectives and on changes in its management team are also used to determine overall management development needs.

Undertaking new business ventures, increased competitive threat (new competitors with new strategies), and a revised corporate vision or mission all usually call for a reevaluation of current management development. Top management must move forward through constant training, or it will begin to move backward and will lose its competitive edge that is so critical to successful business operation.

Needs of Individual Managers

The performance of the person is the primary indicator of individual development needs. Performance evaluations of each manager should be examined to determine areas that need strengthening. The existence of problem situations within a manager's work unit can also signal needs. Planned promotions or reassignments also often indicate the need for development. Outside motivators and consultants often can assist with the personal development and growth of the manager.

Establishing Management Development Objectives

After the management development needs of the organization have been determined, objectives for the overall management development program and for individual programs must be established to meet those needs. Both types of objectives should be expressed in writing and should be measurable. As mentioned earlier in this chapter, training objectives can be categorized within three broad areas: instructional, organizational and departmental, and individual performance and growth. This categorization scheme can also be used for management development objectives.

Instructional objectives might incorporate targets relating to the number of trainees to be taught, hours of training, cost per trainee, and time required for trainees to reach a standard level of knowledge. Furthermore, objectives are needed for the principles, facts, and concepts to be learned in the management development program(s). Organizational and departmental objectives are concerned with the impact the programs will have on organizational and departmental outcomes, such as absenteeism, turnover, safety, and number of grievances. Individual and personal growth objectives relate to the impact on the behavioral and attitudinal outcomes of the individual. They may also relate to the impact on the personal growth of the individuals involved in the programs.

After the overall management development objectives have been established, individual program objectives must be identified that specify the skills, concepts, or attitudes that should result. After these objectives are developed, course content and method of instruction can be specified. Figure 13.2 shows the relationship among needs assessment, objectives, identification of overall management development objectives, and identification of objectives for each individual management development program.

Methods Used in Management Development

After the company's needs have been assessed and its objectives stated, management development programs can be implemented. This section examines some of the more frequently used methods of management development. As with employee training, management development can be achieved both on and off the job. Figure 13.3 summarizes some of the more commonly used methods of management development.

FIGURE 13.2
Relationship
between Needs
Assessment and
Objectives in
Management
Development

Understudy Assignments

Generally, *understudy assignments* are used to develop an individual's capabilities to fill a specific job. An individual who will eventually be given a particular job works for the incumbent. The title of the heir to the job is usually assistant manager, administrative assistant, or assistant to a particular manager.

The advantage of understudy assignments is that the heir realizes the purpose of the training and can learn in a practical and realistic situation without being directly responsible for operating results. On the negative side, the understudy learns the bad as well as the good practices of the incumbent. In addition, understudy assignments maintained over a long period can become expensive. If an understudy assignment system is used, it generally should be supplemented with one or more of the other management development methods.

Coaching

coaching
Carried out by
experienced
managers,
emphasizes the
responsibility of all
managers for
developing
employees.

Coaching is carried out by experienced managers and emphasizes the responsibility of all managers for developing employees. Under this method of management development, experienced managers advise and guide trainees in solving managerial problems. The idea behind coaching should be to allow the trainees to develop their own approaches to management with the counsel of a more experienced person.

One advantage of coaching is that trainees get practical experience and see the results of their decisions. However, there is a danger that the coach will neglect the training responsibilities or pass on inappropriate management practices. The coach's expertise and experience are critical to the success of this method.

FIGURE 13.3
Methods Used in
Management
Development

On the Job	Off the Job
Understudy assignments	Classroom training
Coaching	Lectures
Job rotation	Case studies
Special projects and committee assignments	Role playing
	In-basket techniques
	Business games
	Assessment centers

Job Rotation

Job rotation is designed to give an individual broad experience through exposure to many different areas of the organization. With understudy assignments, coaching, and experience, the trainee generally receives training and development for one particular job. With **job rotation,** the trainee goes from one job to another within the organization, generally remaining in each job from six months to a year. This technique is used frequently by large organizations for training recent college graduates.

One advantage of job rotation is that the trainees can see how management principles can be applied in a cross section of environments. Also, the training is practical and allows the trainee to become familiar with the entire operation of the company. One serious disadvantage of this method is that the trainee is frequently given menial assignments in each job. Another disadvantage is the tendency to leave the trainee in each job longer than necessary. Both of these disadvantages can produce negative attitudes.

job rotation
Process in which the trainee goes from one job to another within the organization, generally remaining in each job from six months to a year.

Special Projects and Committee Assignments

Special projects require the trainee to learn about a particular subject. For example, a trainee may be told to develop a training program on safety. This would require learning about the organization's present safety policies and problems and the safety training procedures used by other companies. The individual must also learn to work with and relate to other employees. However, it is critical that the special assignments provide a developmental and learning experience for the trainee and not just busywork.

Committee assignments, which are similar to special projects, can be used if the organization has regularly constituted or ad hoc committees. In this approach, an individual works with the committee on its regularly assigned duties and responsibilities. Thus, the person exercises skills in working with others and learns through the activities of the committee.

Classroom Training

With classroom training, the most familiar type of training, several methods can be used. Classroom training is used not only in management development programs but also in the orientation and training activities discussed earlier in this chapter. Therefore, some of the material in this section is also applicable to those activities.

Lectures

With lecturing, instructors have control over the situation and can present the material exactly as they desire. Although the lecture is useful for presenting facts, its value in changing attitudes and teaching skills is somewhat limited.

Case Studies

The **case study,** a technique popularized by the Harvard Business School, presents real and hypothetical situations for the trainee to analyze. Ideally, the case study should force the trainee to think through problems, propose solutions, choose among the alternatives, and analyze the consequences of the decision.

One primary advantage of the case method is that it brings a note of realism to the instruction. However, case studies often are simpler than the real situations managers face. Another drawback is that when cases are discussed, the participants often lack emotional involvement; thus, attitudinal and behavioral changes

case study
Training technique that presents real and hypothetical situations for the trainee to analyze.

are less likely to occur. Also, the success of the case study method depends heavily on the skills of the instructor.

One variation of the case study is the *incident method*. The trainee is initially given only the general outline of a situation. The instructor then provides additional information as the trainee requests it. Theoretically, the incident method makes students probe the situations and seek additional information, much as they would be required to do in real life.

Role Playing

With role playing, trainees are assigned different roles and required to act out these roles in a realistic situation. The idea is for the participants to learn from playing out the assigned roles. The success of this method depends on the ability of participants to assume the roles realistically. Videotaping allows for review and evaluation of the exercise to improve its effectiveness.

In-Basket Techniques

in-basket technique
Simulates a realistic situation by requiring each trainee to answer one manager's mail and telephone calls.

The **in-basket technique** simulates a realistic situation by requiring each trainee to answer one manager's mail and telephone calls. Important duties are interspersed with routine matters. For instance, one call may come from an important customer who is angry, while a letter from a local civic club may request a donation. The trainees analyze the situations and suggest alternative actions. They are evaluated on the basis of the number and quality of decisions and on the priorities assigned to each situation. The in-basket technique has been used not only for management development but also in assessment centers, which are discussed later in this chapter.

Business Games

business game
Generally provides a setting of a company and its environment and requires a team of players to make decisions involving company operations.

Business games generally provide a setting of a company and its environment and require a team of players to make decisions involving company operations. They also normally require the use of computer facilities. In a business game, several teams act as companies within a type of industry. This method forces individuals not only to work with other group members but also to function in an atmosphere of competition within the industry.

Advantages of business games are that they simulate reality, decisions are made in a competitive environment, feedback is provided concerning decisions, and decisions are made using less than complete data. The main disadvantage is that many participants simply attempt to determine the key to winning. When this occurs, the game is not used to its fullest potential as a learning device.

Management Education

In addition to traditional on- and off-the-job training, manager development can occur within the confines of the academic or special (seminar) education environment. Expert training can occur within additional undergraduate, MBA, executive MBA, or special seminar programs. These methods rely on sources outside the corporation to control and design the educational material for managers who wish to receive additional training. At their best, these programs can provide fresh ideas, strategies, and perspectives for the manager-student. At their worst, they may lack real-world application and be a waste of time. Among the chief complaints regarding the university-based programs are that they are too lengthy, drain the energy of employees, and may encourage career moves and employment changes. The last is a particularly distressing problem considering that

Many human resource professionals study the latest human resource practices by literally going to Disney World. The Disney Institute, which is a management training business set up by Disney, conducts a four-day seminar, cosponsored by the Society for Human Resource Management, for human resource professionals. The seminar, which is called "The Walt Disney Approach to Human Resource Management," features a fast-paced, multimedia mix of substantive lectures, discussions, presentations by Disney executives, and field trips to resort facilities. Topics covered in the seminar include the following: (1) employee relations, including issues such as equal employment opportunity, Americans with Disabilities Act, and other compliance issues; procedures for investigating sexual harassment complaints; administration of collective bargaining agreements; and Internet and e-mail usage policies; (2) management training, including issues such as mentoring, personal development plans and core training programs for managers, and the use of 360-degree feedback tools; (3) compensation and benefits, including issues such as benchmarking with industry leaders, use of published and customized survey data, bonus plans, and annual performance reviews. According to George Aguel, senior vice president for Walt Disney Parks and Resorts, behind-the-scenes tours and lectures that exemplify doing business Disney style have been the most popular with participants.

Source: Rowland Stiteler, "Disney Enterprise Expands Its Programs Resort-Wide," *Meeting News,* May 6, 2002, p. 37.

many companies pay 80 percent of the tuition for advanced or additional degrees. Internet-based college courses are increasing rapidly. Management Illustration 13.2 explains what the Disney Institute does in management education.

Assessment Centers

assessment center
Utilizes a formal procedure to simulate the problems a person might face in a real managerial situation to evaluate the person's potential as a manager and determine the person's development needs.

An **assessment center** utilizes a formal procedure to evaluate an employee's potential as a manager and determine that employee's developmental needs. Assessment centers are used for making decisions about promoting, evaluating, and training managerial personnel. Basically, these centers simulate the problems a person might face in a real managerial situation. In the typical center, 10 to 15 employees of about equal organizational rank are brought together for three to five days to work on individual and group exercises typical of a managerial job. Business games, in-basket techniques, and role playing are used to simulate managerial situations. These exercises involve the participants in decision making, leadership, written and oral communication, planning, organizing, and motivating. Assessors observe the participants, rate their performance, and provide feedback to them about their performance and developmental needs.

Assessors are often selected from management ranks several levels above those of the participants. Also, psychologists from outside the organization often serve as assessors. For a program to be successful, the assessors must be thoroughly trained in the assessment process, the mechanics of the exercises to be observed, and the techniques of observing and providing feedback.

Some operational problems can arise in using assessment centers. First, the organization must recognize that they are often more costly than other methods of management assessment. Problems can also occur when employees come from different levels in the organization. When their differences become apparent, lower-level participants often defer to those at higher levels during the group exercises; thus, the assessment results are biased. Finally, certain "canned" exercises may be only remotely related to the on-the-job activity at the organization in question. Care must be taken to ensure that exercises used in the assessment center bring out the specific skills and aptitudes needed in the position for which participants are being assessed.

Evaluating Employee Training and Management Development Activities

When the results of employee training and management development are evaluated, certain benefits accrue. Less effective programs can be withdrawn to save time and effort. Weaknesses within programs can be identified and remedied. Evaluation of training and management development activities can be broken down into four areas:

1. *Reaction.* How well did the trainees like the program?
2. *Learning.* What principles, facts, and concepts were learned in the program?
3. *Behavior.* Did the job behavior of the trainees change because of the program?
4. *Results.* What were the results of the program in terms of factors such as reduced costs or reduction in turnover?

Even when great care is taken in designing evaluation procedures, it is difficult to determine the exact effects of training on learning, behavior, and results.[2] Because of this, the evaluation of training is still limited and often superficial. However, if the management development programs are carefully tied to the focus of the corporate mission, related to the organization's strategic plan, and supported with sincere commitment on the part of senior management, they provide great benefits and move the organization in the direction of positive growth. Motivating employees usually is a function of opportunities for advancement and a corporate culture that encourages change and growth. In-house training, updated knowledge of computer technology, increased ability to create and implement strategy, and empowerment are no longer extras in which only some companies are interested. They are mandates for successful competition.

Summary

1. *Define human asset accounting.* Human asset accounting involves determining and recording the value of an organization's human resources in its statement of financial condition.
2. *Describe the orientation process.* Orientation is the introduction of new employees to the organization, their work units, and their jobs.
3. *Define training.* Training is a process that involves acquiring skills or learning concepts to increase the performance of employees.
4. *Define needs assessment.* Needs assessment is a systematic analysis of the specific training activities required to achieve the organization's objectives.
5. *Discuss vestibule training, apprenticeship training, and computer-based training.* In vestibule training, procedures and equipment similar to those used in the actual job are set up in a special working area called a *vestibule,* where the trainee learns the job at a comfortable pace without the pressures of production schedules. Apprenticeship training generally lasts from two to five years and requires the trainee to work under the guidance of a skilled worker over this period. Computer-based training allows the trainee to absorb information from a preset computer program in a self-paced format.
6. *List and define the most popular methods of management development.* Understudy assignments require the person who will someday have a specific job to work for the incumbent to learn the job. With coaching, experienced managers advise and guide trainees in

solving management problems. Job rotation exposes a manager to broad experiences in many different areas of the organization. Role playing requires trainees to act out assigned roles in a realistic situation. In-basket techniques require the trainee to answer one manager's mail and telephone calls. Business games generally provide settings of the company and its environment and require a team of players to make operating decisions.

7. *Describe an assessment center.* An assessment center utilizes a formal procedure to simulate the problems a person might face in a real managerial situation to evaluate the person's potential as a manager and determine the person's development needs.

8. *List the steps involved in the evaluation of training and management development.* The four steps in the evaluation of training and management development are (1) reaction (How well did the trainees like the program?), (2) learning (What principles, facts, and concepts were learned in the program?), (3) behavior (Did the job behavior of the trainees change because of the program?), and (4) results (What were the results of the program in terms of factors such as reduced costs or reduced turnover?).

Review Questions

1. What is human asset accounting?
2. What is orientation?
3. Describe the two distinct levels at which orientation is normally conducted within organizations.
4. What is training?
5. Describe the following methods of training:
   a. On-the-job.
   b. Job rotation.
   c. Vestibule.
   d. Apprenticeship.
   e. Computer-based training.
6. What is management development?
7. Describe the following methods used in management development:
   a. Understudy assignments.
   b. Coaching.
   c. Job rotation.
   d. Special projects and committee assignments.
   e. Classroom training.
8. What is an assessment center?
9. Describe four areas in the evaluation of training and management development.

Skill-Building Questions

1. Discuss the following statement: Why should we train our employees? It is a waste of money because they soon leave and another organization gets the benefits.
2. Outline a system for evaluating a development program for supervisors.
3. Discuss the following statement: Management games are fun, but you don't really learn anything from them.
4. Why are training programs generally one of the first areas to be eliminated when an organization must cut its budget?

Skill-Building Exercise 13.1

Training Methods
Summarized below are some methods that can be used in training both operative and managerial employees. Your professor will assign one of these methods for you to explain to your class. You are to prepare a five-minute presentation describing the method, how it works, and its strengths and weaknesses.

- Role playing
- Sensitivity training
- Simulation exercises
- Wilderness training
- In-basket technique
- Incident method
- Vestibule training
- Apprenticeship training

Skill-Building Exercise 13.2

OJT

Assume you are training director for a large, local retail company. The company has seven department stores in your city. One of your biggest problems is adequately training new salesclerks. Because salesclerks represent your company to the public, the manner in which they conduct themselves is highly important. Especially critical aspects of their job include knowledge of the computerized cash register system, interaction with the customers, and knowledge of the particular products being sold.

1. Design a three-day orientation/training program for these salesclerks. Be sure to outline the specific topics (subjects) to be covered and the techniques to be used.
2. Specify what methods could be used to evaluate the success of the program.
3. Be prepared to present your program to the class.

Case Incident 13.1

Starting a New Job

Jack Smythe, branch manager for a large computer manufacturer, has just been told by his marketing manager, Bob Sprague, that Otis Brown has given two weeks' notice. When Jack had interviewed Otis, he had been convinced of the applicant's tremendous potential in sales. Otis was bright and personable, an honor graduate in electrical engineering from Massachusetts Institute of Technology who had the qualifications the company looked for in computer sales. Now he was leaving after only two months with the company. Jack called Otis into his office for an exit interview.

Jack: Come in, Otis, I really want to talk to you. I hope I can change your mind about leaving.

Otis: I don't think so.

Jack: Well, tell me why you want to go. Has some other company offered you more money?

Otis: No. In fact, I don't have another job. I'm just starting to look.

Jack: You've given us notice without having another job?

Otis: Well, I just don't think this is the place for me!

Jack: What do you mean?

Otis: Let me see if I can explain. On my first day at work, I was told that my formal classroom training in computers would not begin for a month. I was given a sales manual and told to read and study it for the rest of the day.

  The next day I was told that the technical library, where all the manuals on computers are kept, was in a mess and needed to be organized. That was to be my responsibility for the next three weeks.

  The day before I was to begin computer school, my boss told me that the course had been delayed for another month. He said not to worry, however, because he was going to have James Chess, the branch's leading salesperson, give me some on-the-job training. I was told to accompany James on his calls. I'm supposed to start the computer school in two weeks, but I've just made up my mind that this place is not for me.

Jack: Hold on a minute, Otis. That's the way it is for everyone in the first couple months of employment in our industry. Any place you go will be the same. In fact, you had it better than I did. You should have seen what I did in my first couple of months.

Questions

1. What do you think about the philosophy of this company on a new employee's first few months on the job?

2. What suggestions do you have for Jack to help his company avoid similar problems of employee turnover in the future?

Case Incident 13.2

A New Computer System

John Brown, 52, has been at State Bank for 30 years. Over the past 20 years, he has worked in the bank's investment department. During his first 15 years, the department was managed by Lisa Adams. The department consisted of Lisa, John, and two other employees. Lisa made all decisions, while the others performed manual recordkeeping functions. When Lisa retired five years ago, John held the position of assistant cashier.

Tom Smith took over the investment department after Lisa Adams retired. Tom, 56, has worked for State Bank for the past 28 years. Shortly after taking control of the department, Tom recognized that it needed to be modernized and staffed with people capable of giving better service to the bank's customers. As a result, he increased the department workforce to 10 people and installed two different computer systems. Of the 10 employees, only John and Tom are older than 33.

When Tom took over the department, John was a big help because he knew all about how the department had been run in the past. Tom considered John to be a capable worker; after about a year, he promoted John to assistant vice president.

After he had headed the department for about a year and a half, Tom purchased a computer package to handle the bond portfolio and its accounting. When the new system was implemented, John said he did not like the computer system and would have nothing to do with them.

Over the next two years, further changes came about. As the other employees in the department became more experienced, they branched into new areas of investment work. The old ways of doing things were replaced by new, more sophisticated methods. John resisted these changes; he refused to accept or learn new methods and ideas. He slipped more and more into doing only simple but time-consuming activities.

Presently, a new computer system is being acquired for the investment section, and another department is being put under Tom's control. John has written Tom a letter stating he wants no part of the new computer systems but would like to be the manager of the new department. In his letter, John said he was tired of being given routine tasks while the "young people" got all the exciting jobs. John contended that since he has been with the bank longer than anyone else, he should be given first shot at the newly created job.

Questions

1. What suggestions do you have to motivate John to train on the new computer systems?

2. What methods of training would you recommend for John?

References and Additional Readings

1. See, for example, John P. Wanous and Arnon E. Aeichers, "New Employee Orientation Programs," *Human Resource Management Review,* Winter 2000, pp. 435–52.

2. For more information, see Jack McKillip, "Case Studies in Job Analysis and Training Evaluation," *International Journal of Training and Development,* December 2001, pp. 283–90.

Part 5

Directing Skills

Gettyimages/Steve Cole

Chapter

14

Motivating Employees

Learning Objectives

After studying this chapter, you will be able to:

1. Define motivation.
2. Describe the scientific management approach to motivation.
3. Explain the equity approach to motivation.
4. Explain the hierarchy of needs.
5. Discuss the achievement-power-affiliation approach to motivation.
6. Discuss the motivation-maintenance approach to motivation.
7. Discuss the expectancy approach to motivation.
8. Explain the reinforcement approach to motivation.
9. Define job satisfaction and organizational morale.
10. Explain the importance of trust in management in motivation.

Chapter Preview

After the September 11, 2001, tragedy, the dot-com bust, and a declining economy, many companies were announcing job cuts of 20 percent or more. However, many companies such as Southwest Airlines, FedEx, AFLAC, Erie Insurance, and Nucor Corporation refused to follow a practice of laying off employees. Rather, executives at no-layoff companies argue that maintaining their workforce even in terrible times breeds fierce loyalty, higher productivity, and the innovation needed to enable them to snap back once the economy recovers. The CEO of Southwest Airlines, James F. Parker, said, "We are willing to suffer some damage, even to our stock price, to protect the jobs of our people." At steelmaker Nucor Corp., based in Charlotte, N.C., some plants are on a four-day schedule, shaving 20 percent off the average employee's $50,000 annual pay. Bonuses of senior executives, which make up 66 percent of their salaries, have been stopped.

Source: Michelle Conlin, "Where Layoffs Are a Last Resort," *Business Week,* October 8, 2001, p. 42.

Analyzing Management Skills

Do you think employees respond positively to a no-layoffs policy?

Applying Management Skills

Imagine that you own two coffee shops. Assume that the overall economy is declining. Shop 1 is losing money. Shop 2 is doing very well. What would you do to motivate employees at shop 1? Shop 2?

Statements and questions such as the following are often expressed by managers: Our employees are just not motivated. Half the problems we have are due to a lack of personal motivation. How do I motivate my employees?

The problem of motivation is not a recent development. Research conducted by William James in the late 1800s indicated the importance of motivation.[1] James found that hourly employees could keep their jobs by using approximately 20 to 30 percent of their ability. He also found that highly motivated employees will work at approximately 80 to 90 percent of their ability. Figure 14.1 illustrates the potential influence of motivation on performance. Highly motivated employees can bring about substantial increases in performance and substantial decreases in problems such as absenteeism, turnover, tardiness, strikes, and grievances. Management Illustration 14.1 describes a technique to motivate employees.

motivation
Concerned with what activates human behavior, what directs this behavior toward a particular goal, and how this behavior is sustained.

The word **motivation** comes from the Latin word *movere*, which means to move. Numerous definitions are given for the term. Usually included are such words as *aim, desire, end, impulse, intention, objective,* and *purpose.* These definitions normally include three common characteristics of motivation. First, motivation is concerned with what activates human behavior. Second, motivation is concerned with what directs this behavior toward a particular goal. Third, motivation is concerned with how this behavior is sustained.[2]

Motivation can be analyzed using the following causative sequence:

$$\text{Needs} \rightarrow \text{Drives or motives} \rightarrow \text{Achievement of goals}$$

In motivation, needs produce motives, which lead to the accomplishment of goals. Needs are caused by deficiencies, which can be either physical or psychological. For instance, a physical need exists when an individual goes without sleep for 48 hours. A psychological need exists when an individual has no friends or

FIGURE 14.1
Potential Influence of Motivation on Performance

Source: P. Hersey and K. H. Blanchard, *Management of Organizational Behavior: Utilizing Human Resources,* 4th ed., Prentice Hall, 1982.

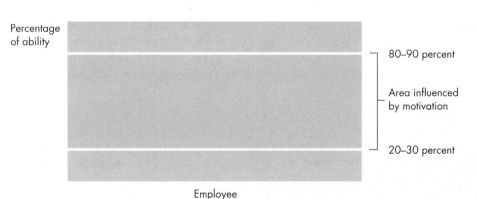

Percentage of ability

80–90 percent

Area influenced by motivation

20–30 percent

Employee

One way financial institutions can improve customer service is by encouraging employees to engage the public in a more spontaneous, lighthearted manner. The technique, known as the Fish! Philosophy, is based on an approach pioneered by Seattle's world famous Pike Place Fish Market.

The key principles of the Fish! Philosophy are

- *Play with purpose.* Work made fun gets done, especially when we choose to do serious tasks in a lighthearted, spontaneous way. "Play" is not just an activity; it's a state of mind that makes the day move quickly and sparks creative solutions.

- *Look for ways to make the customers' day.* When you make someone's day, or moment, through a small kindness or unexpected attention, you can lift someone else's spirit—as well as your own.

- *Be present to the needs of customers and co-workers.* Focus on the person or task with which you are engaged. Listen deeply. "Being there" fights burnout, for it is the half-hearted tasks we perform while juggling other thoughts that wear us out.

- *Choose your attitude.* There is an exhilarating freedom in taking responsibility for your choices. You can choose your attitude and, if you find yourself with an attitude you don't want, you can choose another.

First Essex Bank of Lawrence, Massachusetts, enjoys a solid reputation as a community bank with a loyal customer base. Its 32 branches serve the standard variety of borrowers—home owners and small businesses. The company is also the largest lender in the nation for the purchase of private aircraft, primarily single-engine airplanes. The organization has carved a reputation out of niche markets, sound strategies, and responsive service for loyal customers. First Essex adopted the Fish! Philosophy.

The bottom line still drives First Essex—and the bottom line is doing great. Sculpting a fun, engaging culture might have seemed to be a risk for First Essex, but its employees have proven that they are accountable for their work, but when the organization gave them an opportunity to have fun at the same time, it became invigorating rather than draining.

Fish! is effective at First Essex because management took a step back and invited employees to participate, rather than mandating that they had to. By allowing each department to identify the starfish, the company turned over the reigns of the program to its true leaders. When the employees shared a simple language, everyone had a common starting point from which to create the environment they wanted to work in.

Source: Michael Wilson, "No Fish Story," *Bank Marketing,* June 2002, pp. 20–24.

companions. Individual needs will be explored in much greater depth later in this chapter.

A motive is a stimulus that leads to an action that satisfies the need. In other words, motives produce actions. Lack of sleep (the need) activates the physical changes of fatigue (the motive), which produces sleep (the action or, in this example, inaction).

Achievement of the goal satisfies the need and reduces the motive. When the goal is reached, balance is restored. However, other needs arise, which are then satisfied by the same sequence of events. Understanding the motivation sequence in itself offers a manager little help in determining what motivates employees. The approaches to analyzing motivation described in this chapter help to provide a broader understanding of what motivates people. They include the following: scientific management, equity, hierarchy of needs, achievement-power-affiliation, motivation-maintenance, expectancy, and reinforcement.

Scientific Management Approach

The scientific management approach to motivation evolved from the work of Frederick W. Taylor and the scientific management movement that took place at the turn of this century. Taylor's ideas were based on his belief that existing reward systems were not designed to reward individuals for high production. He believed that when highly productive people discover they are being compensated basically the same as less productive people, then the output of highly productive people will decrease. Taylor's solution was quite simple. He designed a system whereby an employee was compensated according to individual production.

One of Taylor's problems was determining a reasonable standard of performance. Taylor solved the problem by breaking jobs down into components and measuring the time necessary to accomplish each component. In this way, Taylor was able to establish standards of performance "scientifically."

Taylor's plan was unique in that he had one rate of pay for units produced up to the standard. Once the standard was reached, a significantly higher rate was paid, not only for the units above the standard but also for all units produced during the day. Thus, under Taylor's system, employees could in many cases significantly increase their pay for production above the standard.

equity theory
Motivation theory based on the idea that people want to be treated fairly in relationship to others.

The scientific management approach to motivation is based on the assumption that money is the primary motivator. Financial rewards are directly related to performance in the belief that if the reward is great enough, employees will produce more.

Equity Approach

inequity
Exists when a person perceives his or her job inputs and outcomes to be less than the job inputs and outcomes of another person.

Equity theory is based on the idea that people want to be treated fairly in relationship to others.[3] **Inequity** exists when a person perceives his or her job inputs and outcomes to be less than the job inputs and outcomes of another person. The important point to note in this definition is that it is the person's *perception* of inputs and outcomes, not necessarily the actual inputs and outcomes. Furthermore, the other person in the comparison can be an employee in the person's work group or in another part of the organization.

inputs
What an employee perceives are his or her contributions to the organization (i.e., education, intelligence, experience, training, skills, and the effort exerted on the job).

Inputs are what an employee perceives are his or her contributions to the organization (i.e., education, intelligence, experience, training, skills, and the effort exerted on the job). Outcomes are the rewards received by the employee (i.e., pay, rewards intrinsic to the job, seniority benefits, and status).

Equity theory also postulates that the presence of inequity in a person creates tension in a person that is proportional to the magnitude of the inequity. Furthermore, the tension will motivate the person to achieve equity or reduce inequity. The strength of the motivation varies directly with the amount of inequity. A person might take several actions to reduce inequity:

need hierarchy
Based on the assumption that individuals are motivated to satisfy a number of needs and that money can directly or indirectly satisfy only some of these needs.

1. Increase inputs on the job if his or her inputs are low relative to the other person. For example, a person might work harder to increase his or her inputs on the job.
2. Reduce inputs if they are high relative to the other person's inputs and to his or her own outcomes.
3. Quit the job.
4. Request a pay increase.

Hierarchy of Needs

The **hierarchy of needs** is based on the assumption that individuals are motivated to satisfy a number of needs and that money can directly or indirectly satisfy only some of these needs. The need hierarchy is based largely on the work of

FIGURE 14.2   **Hierarchy of Needs**

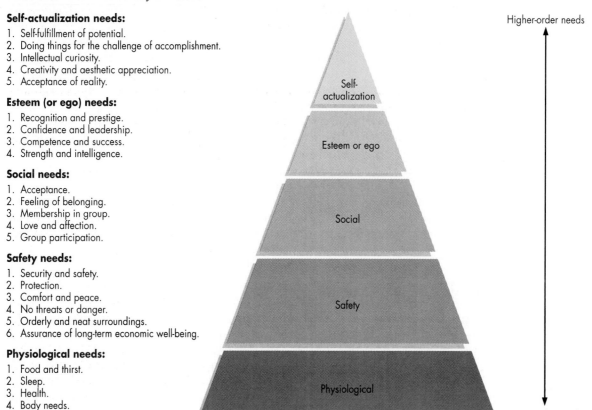

Self-actualization needs:

1. Self-fulfillment of potential.
2. Doing things for the challenge of accomplishment.
3. Intellectual curiosity.
4. Creativity and aesthetic appreciation.
5. Acceptance of reality.

Esteem (or ego) needs:

1. Recognition and prestige.
2. Confidence and leadership.
3. Competence and success.
4. Strength and intelligence.

Social needs:

1. Acceptance.
2. Feeling of belonging.
3. Membership in group.
4. Love and affection.
5. Group participation.

Safety needs:

1. Security and safety.
2. Protection.
3. Comfort and peace.
4. No threats or danger.
5. Orderly and neat surroundings.
6. Assurance of long-term economic well-being.

Physiological needs:

1. Food and thirst.
2. Sleep.
3. Health.
4. Body needs.
5. Exercise and rest.

Abraham Maslow.[4] The hierarchy of needs consists of the five levels shown in Figure 14.2.

The physiological needs are basically the needs of the human body that must be satisfied in order to sustain life. These needs include food, sleep, water, exercise, clothing, shelter, and so forth.

Safety needs are concerned with protection against danger, threat, or deprivation. Since all employees have (to some degree) a dependent relationship with the organization, safety needs can be critically important. Favoritism, discrimination, and arbitrary administration of organizational policies are all actions that arouse uncertainty and therefore affect the safety needs.

The third level of needs is composed of the social needs. Generally categorized at this level are the needs for love, affection, belonging—all are concerned with establishing one's position relative to others. This need is satisfied by the development of meaningful personal relations and by acceptance into meaningful groups of individuals. Belonging to organizations and identifying with work groups are means of satisfying these needs in organizations.

The fourth level of needs is composed of the esteem needs. The esteem needs include both self-esteem and the esteem of others. These needs influence the development of various kinds of relationships based on adequacy, independence, and the giving and receiving of indications of esteem and acceptance.

The highest-order need is concerned with the need for self-actualization or self-fulfillment—that is, the need of people to reach their full potential in applying their abilities and interests to functioning in their environment. This need is concerned with the will to operate at the optimum. The need for self-actualization or self-fulfillment is never completely satisfied; one can always reach one step higher.

The hierarchy of needs adequately describes the general order or ranking of most people's needs. However, there are several other possibilities to be considered. First, although the needs of most people are arranged in the sequence shown in Figure 14.2, differences in the sequence can occur, depending on an individual's learning experience, culture, social upbringing, and numerous other personality aspects. Second, the strength or potency of a person's needs may shift back and forth under different situations. For instance, during bad economic times, physiological and safety needs might tend to dominate an individual's behavior; in good economic times, higher-order needs might dominate an individual's behavior.

The unconscious character of the various needs should be recognized. In addition, there is a certain degree of cultural specificity of needs. In other words, the ways by which the various needs can be met tend to be controlled by cultural and societal factors. For example, the particular culture may dictate one's eating habits, social life, and numerous other facets of life.

Finally, different methods can be used by different individuals to satisfy a particular need. Two individuals may be deficient in relation to the same physiological need; however, the way in which each chooses to satisfy that need may vary considerably.

As far as motivation is concerned, the thrust of the hierarchy of needs is that the lowest-level unsatisfied need causes behavior. The hierarchy represents what Maslow thought was the order in which unsatisfied needs would activate behavior.

Many of today's organizations are applying the logic of the needs hierarchy. For instance, compensation systems are generally designed to satisfy the lower-order needs—physiological and safety. On the other hand, interesting work and opportunities for advancement are designed to appeal to higher-order needs. So the job of a manager is to determine the need level an individual employee is attempting to satisfy and then provide the means by which the employee can satisfy that need. Obviously, determining the need level of a particular person can be difficult. All people do not operate at the same level on the needs hierarchy. All people do not react similarly to the same situation.

Little research has been conducted to test the validity of the hierarchy of needs theory.[5] Its primary value is that it provides a structure for analyzing needs and, as will be seen later in this chapter, is used as a basis for other theories of motivation.

Achievement-Power-Affiliation Approach

While recognizing that people have many different needs, David C. McClelland developed the achievement-power-affiliation approach to motivation, which focuses on three needs: (1) need to achieve, (2) need for power, and (3) need for affiliation.[6] The use of the term *need* in this approach is different from the hierarchy of needs approach in that, under this approach, the three needs are assumed to be learned, whereas the needs hierarchy assumes that needs are inherent.

The need for achievement is a desire to do something better or more efficiently than it has been done before—to achieve. The need for power is basically a concern for influencing people—to be strong and influential. The need for affiliation is a need to be liked—to establish or maintain friendly relations with others.

FIGURE 14.3
Achievement-Power-Affiliation Needs

1. **The Need for Power**
   Some people are strongly motivated by the need for power. They are likely to be happiest in jobs that give them control over budgets, people, and decision making.

2. **The Need for Achievement**
   Other people are strongly motivated by the need for achievement. They are likely to be happiest working in an environment in which they can create something new.

3. **The Need for Affiliation**
   Some people are strongly motivated by the need for affiliation. These people usually enjoy working with other people. They are motivated by the prospect of having people like them.

This approach assumes that most people have developed a degree of each of these needs, but the level of intensity varies among people. For example, an individual may be high in the need for achievement, moderate in the need for power, and low in the need for affiliation. This individual's motivation to work will vary greatly from that of another person who has a high need for power and low needs for achievement and affiliation. An employee with a high need for affiliation would probably respond positively to demonstrations of warmth and support by a manager; an employee with a high need for achievement would likely respond positively to increased responsibility. Finally, under this approach to motivation, when a need's strength has been developed, it motivates behaviors or attracts employees to situations where such behaviors can be acted out. However, this does not satisfy the need; it is more likely to strengthen it further. Figure 14.3 describes this approach to motivation.

Motivation-Maintenance Approach

motivation maintenance
An approach to work motivation that associates factors of high-low motivation with either the work environment or the work itself. Also called *motivation hygiene.*

Another approach to work motivation was developed by Frederick Herzberg and is referred to by several names: the **motivation-maintenance,** two-factor, or motivation-hygiene approach.[7] Initially, the development of the approach involved extensive interviews with approximately 200 engineers and accountants from 11 industries in the Pittsburgh area. In the interviews, researchers used what is called the critical incident method. This involved asking subjects to recall work situations in which they had experienced periods of high and low motivation. They were asked to recount specific details about the situation and the effect of the experience over time.

Analysis of the interviewees' statements showed that different factors were associated with good and bad feelings. The findings fell into two major categories. Those factors that were most frequently mentioned in association with a favorably viewed incident concerned the work itself. These factors were achievement, recognition, responsibility, advancement, and the characteristics of the job. But when subjects felt negatively oriented toward a work incident, they were more likely to mention factors associated with the work environment. These included status; interpersonal relations with supervisors, peers, and subordinates; technical aspects of supervision; company policy and administration; job security; working conditions; salary; and aspects of their personal lives that were affected by the work situation.

The latter set of factors was called *hygiene* or *maintenance* factors because the researchers thought that they are preventive in nature. In other words, they do not

FIGURE 14.4
Motivation-Hygiene Factors

Hygiene Factors (Environmental)	Motivator Factors (Job Itself)
Policies and administration	Achievement
Supervision	Recognition
Working conditions	Challenging work
Interpersonal relations	Increased responsibility
Personal life	Opportunities for advancement
Money, status, security	Opportunities for personal growth

produce motivation but can prevent motivation from occurring. Thus, proper attention to maintenance factors is a necessary but not sufficient condition for motivation. The first set of factors were called *motivators*. The researchers contended that these factors, when present in addition to the maintenance factors, provide true motivation.

In summary, the motivation-hygiene approach contends that motivation comes from the individual, not from the manager. At best, proper attention to the maintenance factors keeps an individual from being highly dissatisfied but does not make that individual motivated. Both hygiene and motivator factors must be present in order for true motivation to occur. Figure 14.4 lists some examples of hygiene and motivator factors.

Job enrichment programs have been developed in an attempt to solve motivational problems by using the motivation-maintenance theory. Unlike **job enlargement,** which merely involves giving an employee more of a similar type of operation to perform, or **job rotation,** which is the practice of periodically rotating job assignments, **job enrichment** involves an upgrading of the job by adding motivator factors. Designing jobs that provide for meaningful work, achievement, recognition, responsibility, advancement, and growth is the key to job enrichment.

As can be seen from Figure 14.5, the motivation-hygiene approach is very closely related to the hierarchy of needs approach to motivation and so is subject to many of the same criticisms.

job enlargement
Giving an employee more of a similar type of operation to perform.

job rotation
Process in which the trainee goes from one job to another within the organization, generally remaining in each job from six months to a year.

job enrichment
Upgrading of the job by adding motivator factors.

FIGURE 14.5
Comparison of the Hierarchy of Needs with the Motivation-Hygiene Approach

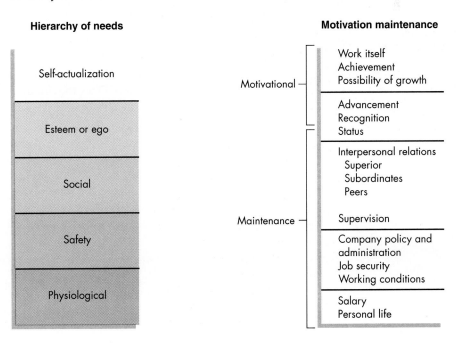

Expectancy Approach

expectancy approach
Based on the idea that employee beliefs about the relationship among effort, performance, and outcomes as a result of performance and the value employees place on the outcomes determine their level of motivation.

The **expectancy approach** to motivation was developed by Victor Vroom and is based on the idea that employee beliefs about the relationship among effort, performance, and outcomes as a result of performance and the value employees place on the outcomes determine their level of motivation.[8] Figure 14.6 outlines the expectancy approach to motivation.

The expectancy approach postulates that an employee's level of motivation depends on three basic beliefs: expectancy, instrumentality, and valence. **Expectancy** refers to the employee's belief that his or her effort will lead to the desired level of performance. **Instrumentality** refers to the employee's belief that attaining the desired level of performance will lead to certain outcomes. **Valence** refers to the employee's belief about the value of the outcomes. External factors are beyond the employee's control and often negatively influence expectancies and instrumentalities because they introduce uncertainty into the relationship. Company policies and efficiency of the equipment being used are examples of external factors.

expectancy
Employee's belief that his or her effort will lead to the desired level of performance.

The following example is intended to illustrate the expectancy approach. Assume John Stone is an insurance salesman for the ABC Life Insurance Company. John has learned over the years that he completes one sale for approximately every six calls he makes. John has a high expectancy about the relationship between his effort and performance. Since John is on a straight commission, he also sees a direct relationship between performance and rewards. Thus, his expectation that increased effort will lead to increased rewards is relatively high. Further, suppose that John's income is currently in a high tax bracket such that he gets to keep, after taxes, only 60 percent of his commissions. This being the case, he may not look on the additional money he gets to keep (the outcome) as being very attractive. The end result is that John's belief about the value of the additional money (valence) may be relatively low. Thus, even when the expectation of receiving the additional money is high, his motivation to do additional work may be relatively low.

instrumentality
Employee's belief that attaining the desired level of performance will lead to desired outcomes.

valence
Employee's belief about the value of the outcome.

Each of the separate components of the expectancy approach can be affected by the organization's practices and management. The expectancy that increased effort will lead to increased performance can be positively influenced by providing proper selection, training, and clear direction to the workforce. The expectancy that increased performance will lead to desired outcomes is almost totally under the control of the organization. Does the organization really attempt to link rewards to performance? Or are rewards based on some other variable, such

FIGURE 14.6
**Expectancy
Approach**

as seniority? The final component—the preference for the rewards being offered—is usually taken for granted by the organization. Historically, organizations have assumed that whatever rewards are provided will be valued by employees. Even if this were true, some rewards are certainly more valued than others. Certain rewards, such as a promotion that involves a transfer to another city, may be viewed negatively. Organizations should solicit feedback from their employees concerning the types of rewards that are valued. Since an organization is going to spend a certain amount of money on rewards (salary, fringe benefits, and so on), it should try to get the maximum return from its investment.

Reinforcement Approach

positive reinforcement
Providing a positive consequence as a result of desired behavior.

avoidance
Giving a person the opportunity to avoid a negative consequence by exhibiting a desired behavior. Also called *negative reinforcement.*

extinction
Providing no positive consequences or removing previously provided positive consequences as a result of undesirable behavior.

punishment
Providing a negative consequence as a result of undesired behavior.

Developed by B. F. Skinner, the general idea behind the reinforcement approach to motivation is that the consequences of a person's present behavior influence his or her future behavior.[9] For example, behavior that leads to a positive consequence is likely to be repeated, while behavior that leads to a negative consequence is unlikely to be repeated.

The consequences of an individual's behavior are called *reinforcement.* Basically, four types of reinforcement exist—positive reinforcement, avoidance, extinction, and punishment. These are summarized in Figure 14.7. **Positive reinforcement** involves providing a positive consequence as a result of desired behavior. **Avoidance,** also called *negative reinforcement,* involves giving a person the opportunity to avoid a negative consequence by exhibiting a desired behavior. Both positive reinforcement and avoidance can be used to increase the frequency of desired behavior.

Extinction involves providing no positive consequences or removing previously provided positive consequences as a result of undesirable behavior. In other words, behavior that no longer pays is less likely to be repeated. **Punishment** involves providing a negative consequence as a result of undesired behavior. Both extinction and punishment can be used to decrease the frequency of undesired behavior.

The current emphasis on the use of reinforcement theory in management practices is concerned with positive reinforcement. Examples include increased pay for increased performance, and praise and recognition when an employee does a good job. Generally, several steps are to be followed in the use of positive reinforcement. These steps include:

1. Selecting reinforcers that are strong and durable enough to establish and strengthen the desired behavior.

FIGURE 14.7
Types of Reinforcement

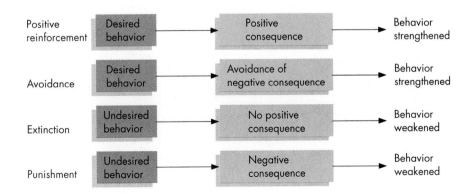

2. Designing the work environment in such a way that the reinforcing events are contingent on the desired behavior.

3. Designing the work environment so that the employee has the opportunity to demonstrate the desired behavior.[10]

The key to successful positive reinforcement is that rewards must result from performance. Several suggestions for the effective use of reinforcement have been proposed. These include the following:

1. All people should not be rewarded the same. In other words, the greater the level of performance by an employee, the greater should be the rewards.

2. Failure to respond to an employee's behavior has reinforcing consequences.

3. A person must be told what can be done to be reinforced.

4. A person must be told what he or she is doing wrong.

5. Reprimands should not be issued in front of others.

6. The consequences of a person's behavior should be equal to the behavior.[11]

In addition, positive reinforcement generally is more effective than negative reinforcement and punishment in producing and maintaining desired behavior.[12]

Integrating the Approaches to Motivation

There are many ways to look at motivation. Each approach emphasizes different contributors to motivation, or sees the same contributors from a different perspective (see Figure 14.8). No single approach provides all the answers, so it is sometimes necessary to utilize more than one approach. Management Illustration 14.2 describes how times are changing in approaches to motivation.

FIGURE 14.8
The Relationship between Different Motivation Approaches

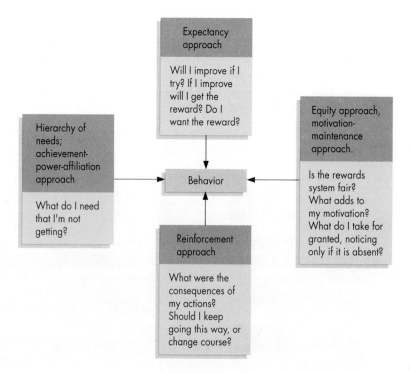

As the *New York Times* recently pointed out, in recent years American companies have increasingly required their staffs to check in their freedoms at the office door, spending "half of their waking hours in what amounts, in plain terms, to a dictatorship." But the need to keep workers happy may now force bosses to relax their iron grip. *The Wall Street Journal* reports that companies are starting to relax the anti-dating policies they introduced as insurance against sexual-harassment laws. They may be prepared to forgive mistakes that would once have resulted in dismissal, such as minor drug offenses or sexist workplace language.

Free lunch (though not to the employer) is one of many perks that more and more employers are starting to offer their staffs. Texas Instruments' concierge team will repair an employee's pickup truck. Sun Microsystems provides an in-house laundry. In-house gyms, sports clinics, and trainers are proliferating. Netscape has its own dentist; Intuit offers in-chair massage. Health care benefits are being increased to ease employee frustration with stingy managed-care organizations. Benefits are also being extended to live-in and same-sex partners.

Source: "The Real Meaning of Empowerment," *Economist*, March 25, 2000, p. 25.

Job Satisfaction

job satisfaction
An individual's general attitude about his or her job.

Job satisfaction is an individual's general attitude about his or her job. The five major components of job satisfaction are (1) attitude toward work group, (2) general working conditions, (3) attitude toward company, (4) monetary benefits, and (5) attitude toward supervision. Other major components that should be added to these five are the individual's attitudes toward the work itself and toward life in general. The individual's health, age, level of aspiration, social status, and political and social activities can all contribute to job satisfaction. Therefore, job satisfaction is an attitude that results from other specific attitudes and factors.

Job satisfaction refers to the individual's mental set about the job. This mental set may be positive or negative, depending on the individual's mental set concerning the major components of job satisfaction. Job satisfaction is not synonymous with organizational morale. **Organizational morale** refers to an individual's feeling of being accepted by, and belonging to, a group of employees through common goals, confidence in the desirability of these goals, and progress toward these goals. Morale is related to group attitudes, whereas job satisfaction is more of an individual attitude. However, the two concepts are interrelated in that job satisfaction can contribute to morale and morale can contribute to job satisfaction.

organizational morale
An individual's feeling of being accepted by, and belonging to, a group of employees through common goals, confidence in the desirability of these goals, and progress toward these goals.

The Satisfaction–Performance Controversy

For many years, managers have believed for the most part that a satisfied worker will automatically be a good worker. In other words, if management could keep all the workers "happy," good performance would automatically follow. Charles Greene has suggested that many managers subscribe to this belief because it represents "the path of least resistance."[13] Greene's thesis is that increasing employees' happiness is far more pleasant for the manager than confronting employees with their performance if a performance problem exists.

Research evidence generally rejects the more popular view that employee satisfaction leads to improved performance. The evidence does, however, provide moderate support for the view that performance causes satisfaction. The evidence also provides strong indications that (1) rewards constitute a more direct cause of satisfaction than does performance; and (2) rewards based on current performance cause subsequent performance.[14]

Research has also investigated the relationship between intrinsic and extrinsic satisfaction and performance for jobs categorized as being either stimulating or nonstimulating.[15] The studies found that the relationship did vary, depending on whether the job was stimulating or nonstimulating. These and other studies further emphasize the complexity of the satisfaction–performance relationship. One relationship that has been clearly established is that job satisfaction does have a positive impact on turnover, absenteeism, tardiness, accidents, grievances, and strikes.[16]

In addition, recruitment efforts by employees are generally more successful if the employees are satisfied. Satisfied employees are preferred simply because they make the work situation a more pleasant environment. So, even though a satisfied employee is not necessarily a high performer, there are numerous reasons for cultivating satisfied employees.

A wide range of both internal and external factors affect an individual's level of satisfaction. The top portion of Figure 14.9 summarizes the major factors that determine an individual's level of satisfaction (or dissatisfaction). The lower portion of the figure shows the organizational behaviors generally associated with satisfaction and dissatisfaction. Individual satisfaction leads to organizational commitment, while dissatisfaction results in behaviors detrimental to the organization (turnover, absenteeism, tardiness, accidents, etc.). For example, employees who like their jobs, supervisors, and other job-related factors will probably be very loyal and devoted employees. However, employees who strongly dislike their jobs or any of the job-related factors will probably be disgruntled and will often exhibit these feelings by being late, absent, or by taking more covert actions to disrupt the organization.

Satisfaction and motivation are not synonymous. Motivation is a drive to perform, whereas satisfaction reflects the individual's attitude or happiness with the situation. The factors that determine whether an individual is satisfied with the job differ from those that determine whether the individual is motivated. Satisfaction is largely determined by the comfort offered by the environment and

FIGURE 14.9
Determinants of Satisfaction and Dissatisfaction

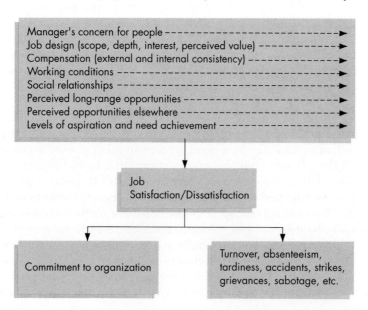

the situation. Motivation, on the other hand, is largely determined by the value of rewards and their contingency on performance. The result of motivation is increased effort, which in turn increases performance if the individual has the ability and if the effort is properly directed. The result of satisfaction is increased commitment to the organization, which may or may not result in increased performance. This increased commitment will normally result in a decrease in problems, such as absenteeism, tardiness, turnover, and strikes.

Importance of Trust in Motivation

The importance of trust in management by employees cannot be stressed enough as being absolutely essential for the success (or failure) for all motivational efforts. Without trust in management, all organizational efforts to motivate employees for improved performance is suspect. The presence of trust gives management credibility when asking for more productivity from employees.

Summary

1. *Define motivation.* Motivation is concerned with what activates human behavior, what directs this behavior toward a particular goal, and how this behavior is sustained.

2. *Describe the scientific management approach to motivation.* The scientific management approach to motivation is based on the assumption that money is the primary motivation of people: if the monetary reward is great enough, employees will work harder and produce more.

3. *Explain the equity approach to motivation.* The equity approach to motivation is based on the idea that people want to be treated fairly in relationship to others.

4. *Explain the hierarchy of needs.* The five levels of needs are physiological, safety, social, ego, and self-actualization. The physiological needs include food, sleep, water, exercise, clothing, and shelter. Safety needs are concerned with protection against danger, threat, or deprivation. Social needs are the needs for love, affection, and belonging. Ego needs include both self-esteem and the esteem of others. Self-actualization is the need of people to reach their full potential in applying their abilities and interests to functioning in their environment.

5. *Discuss the achievement-power-affiliation approach to motivation.* This approach focuses on three needs of people: achievement, power, and affiliation. The level of intensity of these needs varies among individuals, and people are motivated in situations that allow them to satisfy their most intense needs.

6. *Discuss the motivation-maintenance approach to motivation.* This approach postulates that all work-related factors can be grouped into two categories. The first category, maintenance factors, will not produce motivation but can prevent it. The second category, motivators, encourages motivation.

7. *Discuss the expectancy approach to motivation.* This approach holds that motivation is based on a combination of the individual's expectancy that increased effort will lead to increased performance, the expectancy that increased performance will lead to increased rewards, and the individual's preference for those rewards.

8. *Explain the reinforcement approach to motivation.* This approach is based on the idea that behavior that appears to lead to a positive consequence tends to be repeated, whereas behavior that appears to lead to a negative consequence tends not to be repeated.

9. *Define job satisfaction and organizational morale.* Job satisfaction is an individual's general attitude about his or her job. Organizational morale refers to an individual's feeling of being accepted by, and belonging to, a group of employees through common goals, confidence in the desirability of these goals, and progress toward these goals.

10. *Explain the importance of trust in management in motivation.* The presence of trust gives management credibility when asking for more productivity from employees.

Review Questions

1. Explain the motivation sequence.
2. Describe the following approaches to motivation:
   a. Scientific management
   b. Equity
   c. Hierarchy of needs
   d. Achievement-power-affiliation
   e. Motivation maintenance
   f. Expectancy
   g. Reinforcement
3. What is job satisfaction? What are the major components of job satisfaction?
4. What is organizational morale?
5. Discuss the satisfaction–performance controversy.
6. From a managerial standpoint, what are the real benefits of having satisfied employees?

Skill-Building Questions

1. Discuss your views on this statement: Most people can be motivated with money.
2. Do you think a very loyal employee is necessarily a good employee?
3. As a manager, would you prefer a motivated or a satisfied group of employees? Why?
4. The XYZ Company has just decided to take all of its 200 employees to Las Vegas for a three-day, expense-paid weekend to show its appreciation for their high level of performance this past year. What is your reaction to this idea?
5. Discuss the following statement: A satisfied employee is one that is not being pushed hard enough.

Skill-Building Exercise 14.1

Motivation Maintenance

This exercise is designed to illustrate the motivation-maintenance theory in terms of your personal experiences.

1. Think of a time when you were extremely motivated or "turned on" by a job (the instance could have taken place yesterday or several years ago and it could have been on a full- or part-time job) and write a brief two- or three-sentence description of the situation. After you have completed the description, list the reasons this situation had a motivational effect on you. Don't sign your name, but do pass your paper forward.
2. After completing the above, repeat the same procedure for a situation that was highly demotivating. After all the papers have been passed forward, your instructor will help you analyze them.

Skill-Building Exercise 14.2

Does Money Motivate?

You will be divided into groups of three people each. Your group will be assigned one of the two following statements:

1. Money is the primary motivator of people.
2. Money is not the primary motivator of people.

Your assignment is to prepare for a debate with another group on the validity of the statement that your group has been assigned. You will be debating a group that has the opposing viewpoint.

At the end of the debate, prepare a brief statement summarizing the key points made by your opposing group.

Case Incident 14.1

Our Engineers Are Just Not Motivated

You are a consultant to the manager of mechanical engineering for a large company (8,000 employees, $200 million annual sales) that manufactures industrial equipment. The manager has been in this position for six months, having moved from a similar position in a much smaller company.

Manager: I just can't seem to get these people to perform. They are all extremely competent, but they just don't seem to be willing to put forth the kind of effort that we expect and need if this company is going to remain successful.

Consultant: What type of work do they do?

Manager: Primarily designing minor modifications to existing equipment lines to keep up with our competition and to satisfy special customer requirements.

Consultant: How do you evaluate their performance?

Manager: Mainly on whether they meet project deadlines. It's hard to evaluate the quality of their work, since most of it is fairly routine and the designs are frequently altered later by the production engineers to facilitate production processes.

Consultant: Are they meeting their deadlines reasonably well?

Manager: No, that's the problem. What's worse is that they don't really seem too concerned about it.

Consultant: What financial rewards do you offer them?

Manager: They are all well-paid—some of the best salaries for mechanical engineers that I know of anywhere. Base pay is determined mainly on the basis of seniority, but there is also a companywide profit-sharing plan. At the end of each year, the company distributes 10 percent of its profits after taxes to the employees. The piece of the pie that you get is in proportion to your basic salary. This kind of plan was used in the company I used to work for, and it seemed to have a highly motivating effect for them. They also get good vacations, insurance plans, and all the other usual goodies. I know of no complaints about compensation.

Consultant: How about promotion possibilities?

Manager: Well, all I know is that I was brought in from the outside.

Consultant: If they are so lackadaisical, have you considered firing any of them?

Manager: Are you kidding? We need them too much, and it would be difficult and expensive to replace them. If I even threatened to fire any of them for anything short of blowing up the building, my boss would come down on me like a ton of bricks. We are so far behind on our work as it is. Besides, I'm not sure that it's really their fault entirely.

Questions

1. Why are the engineers not motivated?
2. What should management do to correct the situation?

Case Incident 14.2

The Long-Term Employee

Bill Harrison is 57 years old and has been with Ross Products for 37 years. He is on a top-paying machine-operator job and has been for the last 20 years. Bill is quite active in community affairs and takes a genuine interest in most employee activities. He is very friendly and well liked by all employees, especially the younger ones, who often come to him for advice. He is extremely helpful to these younger employees and never hesitates to help when asked. When talking with the younger employees, Bill never talks negatively about the company.

Bill's one shortcoming, as his supervisor Alice Jeffries sees it, is his tendency to spend too much time talking with other employees. This not only causes Bill's work to suffer but also, perhaps more importantly, hinders the output of others. Whenever Alice confronts Bill with the problem, Bill's performance improves for a day or two. It never takes long, however, for Bill to slip back into his old habit of storytelling and interrupting others.

Alice considered trying to have Bill transferred to another area where he would have less opportunity to interrupt others. However, Alice concluded she needs Bill's experience, especially since she has no available replacement for Bill's job.

Bill is secure in his personal life. He owns a nice house and lives well. His wife works as a librarian, and their two children are grown and married. Alice has sensed that Bill thinks he is as high as he'll ever go in the company. This doesn't seem to bother him since he feels comfortable and likes his present job.

Questions

1. What would you do to try to motivate Bill if you were Alice Jeffries?
2. Suppose Alice could transfer Bill. Would you recommend that she do it?

References and Additional Readings

1. Cited in Paul Hersey and Kenneth H. Blanchard, *Management of Organizational Behavior: Utilizing Human Resources,* 4th ed. (Englewood Cliffs, NJ: Prentice Hall, 1982), p. 4.
2. Richard M. Steers and Lyman W. Porter, *Motivation and Human Behavior* (New York: McGraw-Hill, 1983), pp. 3–4.
3. J. Stacey Adams, "Toward an Understanding of Inequity," *Journal of Abnormal and Social Psychology,* November 1963, pp. 422–36. Also see Richard C. Huseman, John D. Hatfield, and Edward W. Miles, "A New Perspective on Equity Theory: The Equity Sensitivity Construct," *Academy of Management Review,* October 1987, pp. 322–34.
4. Abraham H. Maslow, *Motivation and Personality,* 2nd ed. (New York: Harper & Row, 1970).
5. Edwin A. Locke, "The Nature and Causes of Job Satisfaction," in *Handbook of Industrial and Organizational Psychology,* ed. Marvin D. Dunnette (New York: John Wiley & Sons, 1983).
6. David C. McClelland, *The Achievement Motive* (New York: Halsted Press, 1976).
7. Frederick Herzberg, Bernard Mausner, and Barbara Snyderman, *The Motivation to Work* (New York: John Wiley & Sons, 1959).
8. Victor H. Vroom, *Work and Motivation* (New York: John Wiley & Sons, 1967).
9. B. F. Skinner, *Science and Human Behavior* (New York: MacMillan, 1953); and B. F. Skinner, *Beyond Freedom and Dignity* (New York: Knopf, 1972).
10. Steers and Porter, *Motivation,* pp. 123–24.
11. Ibid., pp. 162–63.
12. P. M. Podsakoff, William D. Tudor, and Richard Skov, "Effects of Leader Contingent and Noncontingent Reward and Punishment Behaviors on Subordinate Performance and Satisfaction," *Academy of Management Journal,* December 1982, pp. 810–21.
13. Charles N. Greene, "The Satisfaction–Performance Controversy," *Business Horizons,* October 1972, p. 31. Also see D. R. Norris and R. E. Niebuhr, "Attributional Influences on the Job Performance–Job Satisfaction Relationship," *Academy of Management Journal,* June 1984, pp. 424–31.
14. Greene, "The Satisfaction–Performance Controversy," p. 40.
15. John M. Ivancevich, "The Performance to Satisfaction Relationship: A Causal Analysis of Stimulating and Nonstimulating Jobs," *Organizational Behavior and Human Performance* 22 (1978), pp. 350–64.
16. Donald P. Schwab and Larry L. Cummings, "Theories of Performance and Satisfactions: A Review," *Industrial Relations,* October 1970, pp. 408–29. Also see Locke, "Job Satisfaction," p. 1343, for a complete summary of the related research.

15

Developing Leadership Skills

Learning Objectives

After studying this chapter, you will be able to:

1. Define power.
2. Describe the sources of power in organizations.
3. Define leadership.
4. Describe the self-fulfilling prophecy in management.
5. Define the trait theory of leadership.
6. List and define the basic leadership styles.
7. Understand the Managerial Grid.
8. Define the contingency approach to leadership.
9. Explain the path–goal approach to leadership.
10. Define the situational leadership theory.
11. Define transactional and transformational leadership.
12. Define servant leadership.
13. Discuss some of the lessons that can be learned from leadership research.

Chapter Preview

The only American airline to post a profit since September 11, 2001, accredits its success to a servant-leadership culture. The approach involves changing focus from power and coercion to service to others and shared trust. After the terrorist attacks, Southwest Airlines gave hourly updates of events to its 35,000 employees. Its top three leaders chose to work without pay for the rest of the year, and staff voluntarily raised more than $1 million to keep the firm afloat. The firm promised no layoffs and no reduction in scheduled service. On September 14, 2001, the company put nearly $200 million into the employee profit sharing plan to show its commitment to staff. Last year, the airline was rated "Most admired airline" in *Fortune* magazine.

It was the worst of times for Toro. It was 1983, and this manufacturer of mowing, spraying, and irrigation equipment was on the brink of bankruptcy. The CEO and COO had left, and more than half of the company's employees had been given their walking papers.

New CEO Ken Melrose was called upon to motivate the remaining staff. "It was a very sobering time. We said we never wanted to have to do that again. So we set out to build a culture that would survive," Melrose said. "We saw an opportunity to really transform the company. It's easier to change a culture, mission statement, and behavior when you're about to go under. Everyone wants to be led in that environment."

After doing some research, Melrose embraced a concept called *service leadership* and weaved it tightly into Toro's corporation culture. Now, two decades later, the Bloomington, Minnesota–based company thrives, and Melrose still serves as CEO and chairman.

Sources: "People Policies Lift Southwest Airlines," *People Management,* May 29, 2003, p. 1; and Kenneth Hein, "Taking the Lead," *Incentive,* September 2003, p. 24.

Analyzing Management Skills

Can a person be taught how to be a leader? Why or why not? What leadership skills do you feel can be taught?

Applying Management Skills

Think of the leader that you most admire. What unique leadership skills does he or she possess?

Leadership is probably researched and discussed more than any other topic in the field of management. New suggestions, methods, and tips for improving leadership skills are offered each year. Everyone seems to acknowledge the importance of leadership to managerial and organizational success. This chapter reviews the research on leadership and offers perspectives on leadership processes and styles.

Power, Authority, and Leadership

power
A measure of a person's potential to get others to do what he or she wants them to do, as well as to avoid being forced by others to do what he or she does not want to do.

Before undertaking a study of leadership, a clear understanding must be developed of the relationships among power, authority, and leadership. **Power** is a measure of a person's potential to get others to do what he or she wants them to do, as well as to avoid being forced by others to do what he or she does not want to do.[1] Figure 15.1 summarizes several sources of power in organizations. The use of or desire for power is often viewed negatively in our society because power is often linked to the concepts of punishment, dominance, and control.

David C. McClelland has observed, "In American society in general, individuals are proud of having a high need to achieve, but dislike being told they have a high need for power."[2] McClelland's work, which was briefly described in Chapter 14, led him to study managers at AT&T where he found that managers high in need of power when they joined the company were more successful 16 years later if they were low in need for affiliation and high in self-control. McClelland con-

FIGURE 15.1
Sources of Power

Organizational Sources	Basis
Reward power	Capacity to provide rewards.
Coercive power	Capacity to punish.
Legitimate power	Person's position in the organizational hierarchy.

Personal Sources	Basis
Expert power	The skill, expertise, and knowledge an individual possesses.
Referent power	The personal characteristics of an individual that make other people want to associate with the person.

authority
The right to issue directives and expend resources, related to power but narrower in scope.

leadership
Ability to influence people to willingly follow one's guidance or adhere to one's decisions.

leader
One who obtains followers and influences them in setting and achieving objectives.

cluded power can have both a positive and negative form. Positive power results when the exchange is voluntary and both parties feel good about the exchange. Negative power results when the individual is forced to change. Power in organizations can be exercised upward, downward, or horizontally. It does not necessarily follow the organizational hierarchy from top to bottom.

Authority, which is the right to issue directives and expend resources, is related to power but is narrower in scope. Basically, the amount of authority a manager has depends on the amount of coercive, reward, and legitimate power the manager can exert. Authority is a function of position in the organizational hierarchy, flowing from the top to the bottom of the organization. An individual can have power—expert or referent—without having formal authority. Furthermore, a manager's authority can be diminished by reducing the coercive and reward power in the position.

Leadership is the ability to influence people to willingly follow one's guidance or adhere to one's decisions. Obtaining followers and influencing them in setting and achieving objectives makes a **leader.** Leaders use power in influencing group behavior. For instance, political leaders often use referent power. Informal leaders in organizations generally combine referent power and expert power. Some managers rely only on authority, while others use different combinations of power.

Leadership and Management

Leadership and management are not necessarily the same but are not incompatible. Effective leadership in organizations creates a vision of the future that considers the legitimate long-term interests of the parties involved in the organization, develops a strategy for moving toward that vision, enlists the support of employees to produce the movement, and motivates employees to implement the strategy. Management is a process of planning, organizing, staffing, motivating, and controlling through the use of formal authority.[3] In practice, effective leadership and effective management must ultimately be the same. Management Illustration 15.1 shows how one company feels about the importance of leadership in management.

Leader Attitudes

Douglas McGregor developed two attitude profiles, or assumptions, about the basic nature of people. These attitudes were termed *Theory X* and *Theory Y;* they are summarized in Figure 15.2. McGregor maintained that many leaders in essence subscribe to either Theory X or Theory Y and behave accordingly. A Theory X

Remarketing Services of America (RSA) has more than 600 employees. The company manages sales of repossessed and leased·vehicles for banks and automotive manufacturers. RSA attributes its surprisingly low turnover rate to its corporate values, which promote self-motivation, idea sharing, and personal growth. Every employee is encouraged to set career goals, and leadership development is the foundation of the company's program to advance its most promising staff members. "We are a highly entrepreneurial organization that was founded by strong leaders," said Rita Proulx, a manager in the company's center for learning and development. "We want to drive those leadership skills down to everyone."

To achieve this goal, every new manager is expected to complete a rigorous leadership-training curriculum. Regardless of whether they are promoted from within or newly hired, managers receive a complete evaluation to determine their leadership strengths and gaps. After six months on the job, they participate in a 360-degree assessment that rates them on 14 established leadership competencies such as building trust, coaching, communication, and delegating authority. Based on the results, a custom training program is established to meet their individual needs and potential. "The assessment process gives us an opportunity, early on, to guide their development as leaders," Proulx said.

But leadership development isn't limited to managers. It's also aimed at employees just below the first tier of management jobs who show management potential. "We want to build their leadership skills so that when a need arises for a new manager, we have a pool of talent to choose from," Proulx said.

Potential managers receive management and leadership training in skills they are most likely to need immediately on the job, such as relationship building and conflict resolution. Training in other skills, such as team building and peer assessment, which they may not need until they've been managers for a few months, is offered after the new position has been assigned.

To ensure that the training department is targeting the right people and effectively managing their training needs, RSA recently rolled out the Leadership Emerging and Development program. The 12-month program exposes motivated employees to leadership opportunities through formal mining, job rotations, and mentoring. Candidates nominate themselves and are chosen by the management team on the basis of their experience, skills, and past performance.

Source: Sarah Fister Gade, "Building Leaders at All Levels," *Workforce*, October 2002, pp. 82–92.

leader would likely use a much more authoritarian style of leadership than a leader who believes in Theory Y assumptions. The real value of McGregor's work was the idea that a leader's attitude toward human nature has a large influence on how that person behaves as a leader.[4]

self-fulfilling prophecy
The relationship between a leader's expectations and the resulting performance of subordinates.

The relationship between a leader's expectations and the resulting performance of subordinates has received much attention. Generally, it has been found that if a manager's expectations are high, productivity is likely to be high. On the other hand, if the manager's expectations are low, productivity is likely to be poor. McGregor called this phenomenon the **self-fulfilling prophecy.** It has also been called *Pygmalion in management.*

Framework for Classifying Leadership Studies

Many studies have been conducted on leadership. One useful framework for classifying these studies is shown in Figure 15.3.[5] *Focus* refers to whether leadership is to be studied as a set of traits or as a set of behaviors. *Traits* refer to what characteristics the leader possesses, whereas *behaviors* refer to what the leader does. The second dimension—*approach*—refers to whether leadership is studied from a universal or contingent approach. The universal approach assumes there is one best way to lead regardless of the circumstances. The contingent approach as-

FIGURE 15.2
Assumptions about People

Source: From Douglas McGregor, *The Human Side of Enterprise,* Copyright 1960 © The McGraw-Hill Companies. Reproduced with permission.

Theory X

1. The average human being has an inherent dislike of work and will avoid it if possible.
2. Because of their dislike of work, most people must be coerced, controlled, directed, or threatened with punishment to get them to put forth adequate effort toward the achievement of organizational objectives.
3. The average human being prefers to be directed, wishes to avoid responsibility, has relatively little ambition, and wants security above all.

Theory Y

1. The expenditure of physical and mental effort in work is as natural as play or rest.
2. External control and the threat of punishment are not the only means for bringing about effort toward organizational objectives. Workers will exercise self-direction and self-control in the service of objectives to which they are committed.
3. Commitment to objectives is a function of the rewards associated with their achievement.
4. The average human being learns, under proper conditions, not only to accept but to seek responsibility.
5. The capacity to exercise a relatively high degree of imagination, ingenuity, and creativity in the solution of organizational problems is widely, not narrowly, distributed in the population.
6. Under the conditions of modern industrial life, the intellectual potentialities of the average human being are only partially utilized.

sumes the best approach to leadership is contingent on the situation. Each of the studies shown in Figure 15.3 is discussed in the following sections.

Trait Theory

trait theory
Stressed what the leader was like rather than what the leader did.

Early research efforts devoted to leadership stressed what the leader was *like* rather than what the leader did—a **trait theory** of leadership. Many personality traits (such as originality, initiative, persistence, knowledge, enthusiasm), social traits (tact, patience, sympathy, etc.), and physical characteristics (height, weight, attractiveness) have been examined to differentiate leaders.[6]

At first glance, a few traits do seem to distinguish leaders from followers. These include being slightly superior in such physical traits as weight and height and in a tendency to score higher on tests of dominance, intelligence, extroversion, and adjustment. But the differences seem to be small, with much overlap.

Thus, the research in this area has generally been fruitless—largely because the traits related to leadership in one case usually did not prove to be predictive in other cases. In general, it can be said that traits may to some extent influence the capacity to lead. But these traits must be analyzed in terms of the leadership situation (described in detail later in this chapter).

FIGURE 15.3
Framework for Classifying Leadership Studies

Source: Arthur G. Yago, "Leadership Perspectives in Theory and Practice," *Management Science,* March 1982, p. 316.

Focus	Approach	
	Universal	**Contingent**
Traits	Trait theory	Fiedler's contingency theory
Behaviors	Leadership styles Ohio State studies Michigan studies Managerial Grid	Path–goal theory Situational theory

FIGURE 15.4
Relationship between Styles of Leadership and Group Members

Source: L. B. Bradford and R. Lippitt, "Building a Democratic Work Group," *Personnel* 22, no. 2, November 1945.

Autocratic Style

Leader

1. The individual is very conscious of his or her position.
2. He or she has little trust and faith in members of the group.
3. This leader believes pay is a just reward for working and the only reward that will motivate employees.
4. Orders are issued to be carried out, with no questions allowed and no explanations given.

Group members

1. No responsibility is assumed for performance, with people merely doing what they are told.
2. Production is good when the leader is present, but poor in the leader's absence.

Laissez-Faire Style

Leader

1. He or she has no confidence in his or her leadership ability.
2. This leader does not set goals for the group.

Group members

1. Decisions are made by whoever in the group is willing to do it.
2. Productivity generally is low, and work is sloppy.
3. Individuals have little interest in their work.
4. Morale and teamwork generally are low.

Democratic Style

Leader

1. Decision making is shared between the leader and the group.
2. When the leader is required or forced to make a decision, his or her reasoning is explained to the group.
3. Criticism and praise are given objectively.

Group members

1. New ideas and change are welcomed.
2. A feeling of responsibility is developed within the group.
3. Quality of work and productivity generally are high.
4. The group generally feels successful.

Basic Leadership Styles

Other studies dealt with the style of the leader. They found three basic leadership styles: autocratic, laissez-faire, and democratic. The main difference among these styles is where the decision-making function rests. Generally, the **autocratic leader** makes more decisions for the group; the **laissez-faire leader** allows people within the group to make all decisions; and the **democratic leader** guides and encourages the group to make decisions. More detail about each of the leadership styles is given in Figure 15.4. The figure implies that the democratic style is the most desirable and productive. However, current research on leadership, discussed later in this chapter, does not necessarily support this conclusion. The primary contribution of this research was identifying the three basic styles of leadership.

autocratic leader
Makes most decisions for the group.

laissez-faire leader
Allows people within the group to make all decisions.

democratic leader
Guides and encourages the group to make decisions.

Ohio State Studies

A series of studies on leadership was conducted at Ohio State University to find out the most important behaviors of successful leaders. The researchers wanted to find out what a successful leader does, regardless of the type of group being led: a mob, a religious group, a university, or a business organization. To do this, they developed a questionnaire called the **Leader Behavior Description Questionnaire (LBDQ).** Both the original form and variations of it are still used today.

In using the questionnaire, two leader behaviors emerged consistently as being the most important: consideration and initiating structure. The term **consideration** refers to the leader behavior of showing concern for individual group members and satisfying their needs. The term **initiating structure** refers to the leader behavior of structuring the work of group members and directing the group toward the attainment of the group's goals.

Since the Ohio State research, many other studies have been done on the relationship between the leader behaviors of consideration and initiating structure and their resulting effect on leader effectiveness. The major conclusions that can be drawn from these studies are[7]

1. Leaders scoring high on consideration tend to have more satisfied subordinates than do leaders scoring low on consideration.
2. The relationship between the score on consideration and leader effectiveness depends on the group being led. In other words, a high score on consideration was positively correlated with leader effectiveness for managers and office staff in a large industrial firm, whereas a high score on consideration was negatively correlated with leader effectiveness for production foremen.
3. There is also no consistent relationship between initiating structure and leader effectiveness; rather, the relationship varies depending on the group that is being led.

University of Michigan Studies

The Institute for Social Research of the University of Michigan conducted studies to discover principles contributing both to the productivity of a group and to the satisfaction derived by group members. The initial study was conducted at the home office of the Prudential Insurance Company in Newark, New Jersey.

Interviews were conducted with 24 managers and 419 nonmanagerial employees. Results of the interviews showed that managers of high-producing work groups were more likely

1. To receive general rather than close supervision from their superiors.
2. To like the amount of authority and responsibility they have in their job.
3. To spend more time in supervision.
4. To give general rather than close supervision to their employees.
5. To be employee oriented rather than production oriented.

Supervisors of low-producing work groups had basically opposite characteristics and techniques. They were production oriented and gave close supervision.

Rensis Likert, then director of the institute, published the results of his years of research in the book *New Patterns of Management,* which is a classic in its field.[8] Likert believes there are four patterns or styles of leadership or management employed by organizations. He has identified and labeled these styles as follows:

System 1: Exploitative authoritative. Authoritarian form of management that attempts to exploit subordinates.

System 2: Benevolent authoritative. Authoritarian form of management, but paternalistic in nature.

Leader Behavior Description Questionnaire (LBDQ)
Questionnaire to determine what a successful leader does, regardless of the type of group being led.

consideration
Leader behavior of showing concern for individual group members and satisfying their needs.

initiating structure
Leader behavior of structuring the work of group members and directing the group toward the attainment of group's goals.

System 3: Consultative. Manager requests and receives inputs from subordinates but maintains the right to make the final decision.

System 4: Participative. Manager gives some direction, but decisions are made by consensus and majority, based on total participation.

Likert used a questionnaire to determine the style of leadership and the management pattern employed in the organization as a whole. The results of his studies indicated that system 4 was the most effective style of management and that organizations should strive to develop a management pattern analogous to this system.

The Managerial Grid

Managerial Grid
A two-dimensional framework rating a leader on the basis of concern for people and concern for production.

Robert Blake and Jane Mouton have also developed a method of classifying the leadership style of an individual.[9] The **Managerial Grid**, depicted in Figure 15.5, is a two-dimensional framework rating a leader on the basis of concern for people and concern for production. (Notice that these activities closely relate to the leader activities from the Ohio State studies—consideration and initiating structure.) A questionnaire is used to locate a particular style of leadership or management on the grid.

Blake and Mouton identified five basic styles of management using the Managerial Grid. *Authority-obedience*—located in the lower right-hand corner (9,1 position)—assumes that efficiency in operations results from properly arranging the conditions at work with minimum interference from other people. The opposite view, *country club management*—located in the upper left-hand corner (1,9)—assumes that proper attention to human needs leads to a comfortable organizational

FIGURE 15.5
The Managerial Grid

Source: Robert R. Blake and Jane Srygley Mouton, *The New Managerial Grid* (Houston: Gulf Publishing, 1978), p. 11. Copyright © 1978 by Gulf Publishing Company. Reproduced by permission.

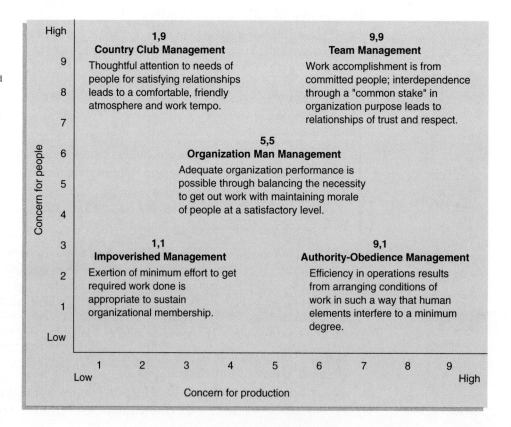

atmosphere and workplace. *Team management*—in the upper right-hand corner (9,9)—combines a high degree of concern for people with a high degree of concern for production. The other two styles on the grid are *impoverished management* (1,1) and *organization man management* (5,5). The Managerial Grid is intended to serve as a framework for managers to learn what their leadership style is and to develop a plan to move toward a 9,9 team management style of leadership.

Fiedler's Contingency Studies of Leadership

The leadership studies discussed so far are similar in that they did not specifically address the complex differences between groups (such as production workers versus accountants) and their influences on leader behavior. To imply that a manager should be employee-oriented rather than production-oriented (Michigan studies) or that the manager should exhibit concern for both production and people (Blake and Mouton) does not say much about what the manager should do in particular situations. Nor does it offer much guidance for daily leadership situations. As a result, research began to focus on the style of leadership that is most effective in particular situations.[10] This is called the **contingency approach to leadership.**

One of the first studies using the contingency approach was conducted by Fred Fiedler.[11] He studied the match between the leader's personality and the situation. Fiedler defined two basic leader personality traits—task and relationship motivation. Task-motivated leaders gain satisfaction from the performance of a task. Relationship-motivated leaders gain satisfaction from interpersonal relationships. Fiedler viewed task versus relationship as a leader trait that was relatively constant for any given person.

A scale, called the *least preferred co-worker scale* (LPC), was used to measure whether a person is a task- or relationship-oriented leader. Respondents were asked to think of all the people they had worked with and select the person with whom they could work least effectively. The respondents then described their least preferred co-worker on the LPC. Three sample items on the LPC are[12]

Pleasant	___	___	___	___	___	___	___	___	Unpleasant
	8	7	6	5	4	3	2	1	
Friendly	___	___	___	___	___	___	___	___	Unfriendly
	8	7	6	5	4	3	2	1	
Cooperative	___	___	___	___	___	___	___	___	Uncooperative
	8	7	6	5	4	3	2	1	

A person who described a least preferred co-worker in fairly favorable terms was presumed to be motivated to have close interpersonal relations with others; Fiedler classified these people as relationship-motivated leaders. On the other hand, people who rejected co-workers with whom they had difficulties were presumed to be motivated to accomplish or achieve the task; they were classified as task-oriented leaders.[13]

Fiedler next turned to the situation in which the leader was operating. He placed leadership situations along a favorable–unfavorable continuum based on three major dimensions: leader–member relations, task structure, and position power. **Leader–member relations** refer to the degree others trust and respect the leader and to the leader's friendliness. This compares somewhat to referent power. **Task structure** is the degree to which job tasks are structured. For example, assembly-line jobs are more structured than managerial jobs. **Position power** refers to the power and influence that go with a job. A manager has more position power who

---

contingency approach to leadership
Focuses on the style of leadership that is most effective in particular situations.

leader–member relations
Degree that others trust and respect the leader and the leader's friendliness.

task structure
Degree to which job tasks are structured.

position power
Power and influence that go with a job.

FIGURE 15.6 Fiedler's Classification of Situations

Situation	1	2	3	4	5	6	7	8
Leader–member relations	Good	Good	Good	Good	Poor	Poor	Poor	Poor
Task structure	Structured	Structured	Unstructured	Unstructured	Structured	Structured	Unstructured	Unstructured
Position power	Strong	Weak	Strong	Weak	Strong	Weak	Strong	Weak
	Favorable for leader						*Unfavorable for leader*	

FIGURE 15.7 Leadership Style and Leadership Situations

Situation	1	2	3	4	5	6	7	8
Leader–member relations	Good	Good	Good	Good	Poor	Poor	Poor	Poor
Task structure	Structured	Structured	Unstructured	Unstructured	Structured	Structured	Unstructured	Unstructured
Leader position power	Strong	Weak	Strong	Weak	Strong	Weak	Strong	Weak
	Favorable for leader						*Unfavorable for leader*	
Most productive leadership style	Task	Task	Task	Relationship	Relationship	No data	Task or relationship	Task

is able to hire, fire, and discipline. Position power compares to coercive, reward, and legitimate power. Using these three dimensions, an eight-celled classification scheme was developed. Figure 15.6 shows this scheme along the continuum.

Figure 15.7 shows the most productive style of leadership for each situation. In both highly favorable and highly unfavorable situations, a task-motivated leader was found to be more effective. In highly favorable situations, the group is ready to be directed and is willing to be told what to do. In highly favorable situations, the group welcomes having the leader make decisions and direct the group. In moderately favorable situations, a relationship-motivated leader was found to be more effective. In situation 7 (moderately poor leader–member relations, unstructured task, and strong position power), the task and relationship styles of leadership were equally productive.

Continuum of Leader Behaviors

Robert Tannenbaum and Warren Schmidt also contend that different combinations of situational elements require different styles of leadership. They suggest that there are three important factors, or forces, involved in finding the most effective leadership style: forces in the manager, the subordinate, and the situation.[14] Furthermore, all of these forces are interdependent.

Figure 15.8 describes in detail the forces that affect leadership situations. Since these forces differ in strength and interaction in differing situations, one style of leadership is not effective in all situations.

In fact, Tannenbaum and Schmidt argue that there is a continuum of behaviors that the leader may employ, depending on the situation (see Figure 15.9). These authors further conclude that successful leaders are keenly aware of the forces that are most relevant to their behavior at a given time. Successful leaders accurately understand not only themselves but also the other persons in the organizational and social environment, and they are able to behave correctly in light of these insights.

FIGURE 15.8   Forces Affecting the Leadership Situation

Forces in the Manager	Forces in the Subordinates	Forces in the Situation
Value system: How the manager personally feels about delegating, degree of confidence in subordinates.	Need for independence: Some people need and want direction, while others do not.	Type of organization: Centralized versus decentralized.
Personal leadership inclinations. Authoritarian versus participative.	Readiness to assume responsibility: Different people need different degrees of responsibility.	Work group effectiveness: How effectively the group works together.
Feelings of security in uncertain situations.	Tolerance for ambiguity: Specific versus general directions.	The problem itself: The work group's knowledge and experience relevant to the problem.
	Interest and perceived importance of the problem: People generally have more interest in, and work harder on, important problems.	Time pressure: It is difficult to delegate to subordinates in crisis situations.
	Degree of understanding and identification with organizational goals: A manager is more likely to delegate authority to an individual who seems to have a positive attitude about the organization.	Demands from upper levels of management.
	Degree of expectation in sharing in decision making: People who have worked under subordinate-centered leadership tend to resent boss-centered leadership.	Demands from government, unions, and society in general.

Path–Goal Theory of Leadership

path–goal theory of leadership
Attempts to define the relationships between a leader's behavior and the subordinates' performance and work activities.

The **path–goal theory of leadership** attempts to define the relationships between a leader's behavior and the subordinates' performance and work activities.[15] Leader behavior is acceptable to subordinates to the degree that they see it as a source of satisfaction now or as a step toward future satisfaction. Leader behavior influences the motivation of subordinates when it makes the satisfaction of their

FIGURE 15.9
Continuum of Leader Behavior

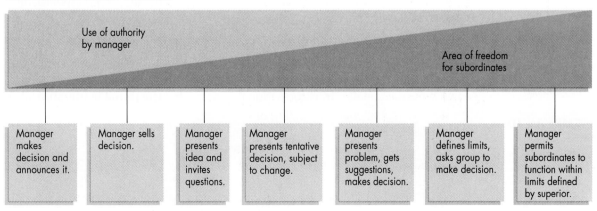

needs contingent on successful performance; and it provides the guidance, support, and rewards needed for effective performance (but that are not already present in the environment). The path–goal theory of leadership and the expectancy theory of motivation, which was described in the previous chapter, are closely related in that leader behaviors can either increase or decrease employee expectancies.

In path–goal theory, leader behavior falls into one of the four basic types: role classification, supportive, participative, and autocratic. *Role classification leadership* lets subordinates know what is expected of them, gives guidance as to what should be done and how, schedules and coordinates work among the subordinates, and maintains definite standards of performance. *Supportive leadership* has a friendly, approachable leader who attempts to make the work environment more pleasant for subordinates. *Participative leadership* involves consulting with subordinates and asking for their suggestions in the decision-making process. *Autocratic leadership* comes from a leader who gives orders that are not to be questioned by subordinates.

Under this theory, each of these leadership behaviors results in different levels of performance and subordinate satisfaction, depending on the structure of the work tasks. Role clarification leads to high satisfaction and performance for subordinates engaged in unstructured tasks. Supportive leadership brings the most satisfaction to those who work on highly structured tasks. Participative leader behavior enhances performance and satisfaction for subordinates engaged in ambiguous tasks. Autocratic leadership behavior has a negative effect on both satisfaction and performance in both structured and unstructured task situations.

Situational Leadership Theory

situational leadership theory
As the level of maturity of followers increases, structure should be reduced while socioemotional support should first be increased and then gradually decreased.

Paul Hersey and Kenneth Blanchard include maturity of the followers as an important factor in leader behavior.[16] According to the **situational leadership theory,** as the level of maturity of followers increases, structure (task) should be reduced while socioemotional support (relationship) should first be increased and then gradually decreased. The maturity level of the followers is determined by their relative independence, their ability to take responsibility, and their achievement–motivation level.

Figure 15.10 shows the cycle of the basic leadership styles that should be used by the leader, depending on the maturity of the followers. The situational leadership theory proposes that as the followers progress from immaturity to maturity, the leader's behavior should move from: (1) high task–low relationships to (2) high task–high relationships to (3) low task–high relationships to (4) low task–low relationships.

Transformational and Transactional Leaders

transactional leadership
Takes the approach that leaders engage in a bargaining relationship with their followers.

Another approach to the analysis of leadership has been based on how leaders and followers influence one another. Under this approach, leadership is viewed as either a transactional or transformational process. **Transactional leadership** takes

FIGURE 15.10
Situational
Leadership Theory

the approach that leaders engage in a bargaining relationship with their followers. Under this approach, the leader (manager)

1. Tells employees what they need to do to obtain rewards.
2. Takes corrective action only when employees fail to meet performance objectives.

transformational leadership
Involves cultivating employee acceptance of the group mission.

Transformational leadership involves cultivating employee acceptance of the group mission. The manager–employee relationship is one of mutual stimulation and is characterized by charisma on the part of the leader, inspiration by the leader, consideration by the leader of individual needs, and intellectual stimulation between the leader and followers.[17] Transformational leaders go beyond transacting with their followers and transform not only the situation but also the followers.

Servant Leadership

Servant leadership is based on the belief that the leader exists to meet the needs of the people who he or she nominally leads. The servant leader takes the fulfillment of followers' needs as his or her primary aim. The servant leader believes that the business exists as much to provide meaningful work to employees as it does to provide a quality product or service to the customer.

Lessons from Leadership Studies

How can all of these leadership theories be made relevant to the organization's need for effective managers? First, given the situational factors discussed in this chapter, it appears unlikely that a selection process will be developed to accurately predict successful leaders. The dynamic, changing nature of managerial roles further complicates the situation. Even if the initial process could select effective leaders, the dynamics of the managerial situation might make the selection invalid. Further, contrary to the conclusions of many studies, most leadership training today seems to assume there is one best way to lead. Management Illustration 15.2 describes how important the management of Unisys feels leadership is to the company's success.

However, leadership training designed to help leaders or potential leaders identify the nature of the leadership situation appears to have potential in developing more effective leaders. Such training is not so much a process of changing individual traits as it is one of ensuring that the person is operating in an appropriate situation or of teaching the individual how to act in a given situation. The following points on effective leadership can tentatively be made:

1. High consideration and initiating structure often provide a successful leadership style.
2. Under emergency or high-pressure situations, emphasis on initiating structure is desirable and often preferred by subordinates.
3. When the manager is the only information source for subordinates regarding their tasks, they often expect the manager to structure their behavior.
4. Subordinates have differing preferences regarding the degree of consideration and initiating structure exhibited by their managers.
5. Higher management often has set preferences regarding the leadership styles employed by lower-level managers.

It's a radical approach in a world where leadership development is usually saved for a few high-performing individuals. The management of Unisys Corporation, an information technology services and solutions company, feels that everyone could benefit from taking leadership training. In the three and a half years since the leadership school was launched at Unisys, 2,200 employees have gone through the program, which is open to anyone interested in expanding his or her leadership skills.

Unisys CEO Larry Weinbach started the program and opened it up to all levels of employees to foster a culture in which leadership skills are celebrated and encouraged. Weinbach is the leadership school's acting dean, a frequent class speaker, and a vocal champion of the program. He believes that developing leaders across the company will create an environment that can change and adapt to the economy, making Unisys a better company.

The leadership curriculum at Unisys features six courses within two tracks focusing on culture and leadership skills. The classroom-based courses are two to five days long and cover core topics such as developing management and team leadership skills, understanding culture-change issues, and understanding the impact that leaders have on performance.

The skills courses use traditional leadership-training formats, such as practicing communication skills with peers and working with assessment tools, whereas the culture courses are more informal, employing a conversational tone. In fact, the culture courses are referred to as "conversations," in which course leaders introduce specific topics, such as how to influence the Unisys culture through leadership or the roles that leaders play as learners and teachers. Participants discuss how those issues relate to their own job performance and brainstorm solutions to specific workplace problems.

Even though some courses last five days, the school has no trouble filling seats. Leadership training is seen as a priority at Unisys, even in lean times, because it's part of the culture. The entire executive team has gone through both training tracks, and they regularly return to day sessions, both as speakers and as peers, to share a problem or to monitor the leadership concerns of other employees.

The programs are not mandatory, nor are they limited to management. Almost anyone can sign up with the support of his or her superiors, and many of those junior employees who attend come at the urging of their bosses. At a recent junior session of the five-day cultural-leadership course, for example, 95 percent of attendees had been referred to the course after their managers completed it.

Source: Sarah Fister Gade, "Building Leaders at All Levels," *Workforce*, October 2002, pp. 82–92.

---

6. Some managers can adjust their behavior to fit the situation; while others, in attempting to make this adjustment, appear to be fake and manipulative.

Summary

1. *Define power.* Power is a measure of a person's potential to get others to do what he or she wants them to do, as well as to avoid being forced by others to do what he or she does not want to do.

2. *Describe the sources of power in organizations.* The sources of power in organizations are reward, coercive, legitimate, expert, and referent.

3. *Define leadership.* Leadership is the ability to influence people to willingly follow one's guidance or adhere to one's decisions.

4. *Describe the self-fulfilling prophecy in management.* The self-fulfilling prophecy basically postulates that what a manager expects of subordinates and the way he or she treats subordinates influence their performance and career progress.

5. *Define the trait theory of leadership.* The trait theory of leadership emphasizes what the leader is like rather than what the leader does. Personality traits and physical characteristics are examined to differentiate leaders. Few studies have been able to support this theory.

6. *List and define the basic leadership styles.* The autocratic leader makes most decisions for the group. The laissez-faire leader allows people within the group to make all decisions. The democratic leader guides and encourages the group to make decisions.

7. *Understand the Managerial Grid.* The Managerial Grid is a two-dimensional framework rating a leader on the basis of concern for people and concern for production.

8. *Define the contingency approach to leadership.* The contingency approach to leadership defines two basic styles of leadership: task-motivated and relationship-motivated. In both highly favorable and highly unfavorable situations, a task-motivated leader was found to be more effective. In moderately favorable situations, a relationship-motivated leader was found to be more effective.

9. *Explain the path–goal approach to leadership.* The path–goal theory of leadership attempts to define the relationships between a leader's behavior and the subordinates' performance and work activities. Leader behavior influences the motivation of subordinates when it makes the satisfaction of their needs contingent on successful performance; and it provides the guidance, support, and rewards needed for effective performance.

10. *Define the situational leadership theory.* According to the situational leadership theory, as the maturity of followers increases, structure (task) should be reduced while socioemotional support (relationship) should first be increased and then gradually decreased.

11. *Define transactional and transformational leadership.* Transactional leadership takes the approach that leaders engage in a bargaining relationship with their followers. Transformational leadership involves cultivating employee acceptance of the group mission.

12. *Define servant leadership.* Servant leadership is based on the belief that the leader exists to meet the needs of the people whom he or she nominally leads.

13. *Discuss some of the lessons that can be learned from leadership research.* The following lessons can be learned from leadership research:

    High consideration and initiating structure often provide a successful leadership style.

    Under emergency or high-pressure situations, emphasis on initiating structure is desirable and often preferred by subordinates.

    When the manager is the only information source for subordinates regarding their tasks, they often expect the manager to structure their behavior.

    Subordinates have differing preferences regarding the degree of consideration and initiating structure exhibited by their managers.

    Higher management often has set preferences regarding the leadership styles employed by lower-level managers.

    Some managers can adjust their behavior to fit the situation; while others, in attempting to make this adjustment, appear to be fake and manipulative.

Review Questions

1. Define power.
2. Describe sources of power in organizations.
3. Define leadership.
4. Describe in detail the following three leadership styles:
   a. Autocratic
   b. Laissez-faire
   c. Democratic
5. What was the purpose of the Ohio State leadership studies? What were the results of the Ohio State studies?
6. What was the purpose of the University of Michigan leadership studies? Explain the results of the Michigan studies.
7. Describe the Managerial Grid.
8. What is Fiedler's contingency approach to leadership?

9. Describe three important forces, or factors, that Tannenbaum and Schmidt think should be considered in determining which leadership style is most effective.

10. What is the path–goal theory of leader effectiveness?

11. What is the situational leadership theory?

12. Define transactional and transformational leadership.

13. Describe some of the implications of the studies on leadership for organizations and managers.

Skill-Building Questions

1. Discuss the following statement: Leaders are born and cannot be developed.

2. Do you agree or disagree with this statement: Leaders must have courage. Why?

3. Do you think the variance in leadership styles of such people as Adolf Hitler, Franklin D. Roosevelt, and Martin Luther King, Jr., can be explained by any of the theories discussed in this chapter? Elaborate on your answer.

4. Explain what people mean when they use this statement: Leaders lead by example. Do you believe it? Explain your answer.

Skill-Building Exercise 15.1

Insubordination?

The company installed a new performance management system this year. You distributed the information and forms several weeks ago, and they were due to be completed two weeks ago. One manager reporting to you has not yet returned his. This morning, you ran into him in the parking lot and asked him about it. He reacted angrily with: "I haven't had time to do it—I don't have enough time to get my job done as it is, much less to take the time necessary to have my people write a bunch of meaningless information."

You asked him to stop by your office later to discuss it. As you think about how to handle this situation in the meeting, you consider several alternatives.

1. In view of his attitude and behavior, it clearly is appropriate to exercise your authority. Tell him, in no uncertain terms, that this must be done if he expects to continue as a supervisor.

2. Tell him why this program is important and use your best persuasion technique to sell him on doing it willingly.

3. Remind him that no salary increases, including his own, will be processed until the forms are completed. Establish another deadline and let him know you expect it to be done then.

4. Explain to him that appraising employee performance is a part of every supervisor's job and that he himself is being evaluated on his performance in implementing this program.

5. Tell him you understand the difficulties of his job and the shortage of time available to do it, but remind him that this is a mandatory program that has top management's backing.

Other alternatives may be open to you, but assume these are the only ones you have considered. *Without discussion* with anyone, choose one of them and be prepared to defend your choice.

Skill-Building Exercise 15.2

Leadership Situations

Under the situational approach to leadership, different situations call for different leadership styles. Assuming this approach is correct, outline specific situations in which you would employ an autocratic style of leadership. In addition, outline situations in which you would employ a participative style of leadership. Be specific in describing the situation. Be prepared to present your list of situations for both leadership styles to the class.

Skill-Building Exercise 15.3

Test Your Leadership Style

Read both statements in each entry in the following list and circle either a or b to indicate whichever best describes you—or is the least incorrect about you. You must answer every question to arrive at a proper score.

1. *a.* You are the person people most often turn to for help.
    b. You are aggressive and look after your best interests first.

2. *a.* You are more competent and better able to motivate others than most people.
    b. You strive to reach a position where you can exercise authority over large numbers of people and sums of money.

3. *a.* You try hard to influence the outcome of events.
    b. You quickly eliminate all obstacles that stand in the way of your goals.

4. *a.* There are few people you have as much confidence in as yourself.
    b. You have no qualms about taking what you want in this world.

5. a. You have the ability to inspire others to follow your lead.
    b. You enjoy having people act on your commands and are not opposed to making threats if you must.

6. *a.* You do your best to influence the outcome of events.
    b. You make all the important decisions, expecting others to carry them out.

7. *a.* You have a special magnetism that attracts people to you.
    b. You enjoy dealing with situations requiring confrontation.

8. *a.* You would enjoy consulting on the complex issues and problems that face managers of companies.
    b. You would enjoy planning, directing, and controlling the staff of a department to ensure the highest profit margins.

9. *a.* You want to consult with business groups and companies to improve effectiveness.
    b. You want to make decisions about other people's lives and money.

10. *a.* You could deal with level upon level of bureaucratic red tape and pressure to improve performance.
    b. You could work where money and profits are more important than other people's emotional well-being.

11. *a.* You typically must start your day before sunrise and continue into the night six to seven days a week.
    b. You must fire unproductive employees regularly and expediently to achieve set targets.

12. *a.* You must be responsible for how well others do their work (and you will be judged on their achievements, not yours).
    b. You have a workaholic temperament that thrives on pressure to succeed.

13. *a.* You are a real self-starter and full of enthusiasm about everything you do.
    b. Whatever you do, you have to do it better than anyone else.

14. *a.* You are always striving to be the best, the tops, the first at whatever you do.
    b. You have a driving, aggressive personality and fight hard and tough to gain anything worth having.

15. *a.* You have always been involved in competitive activities, including sports, and have won several awards for outstanding performance.
    b. Winning and succeeding are more important to you than playing just for enjoyment.

16. *a.* You will stick to a problem when you are getting nowhere.
    b. You quickly become bored with most things you undertake.

17. *a.* You are naturally carried along by some inner drive or mission to accomplish something that has never been done.

    b. Self-demanding and a perfectionist, you are always pressing yourself to perform to the limit.

18. *a.* You maintain a sense of purpose or direction that is larger than yourself.

    b. Being successful at work is the most important thing to you.

19. *a.* You would enjoy a job requiring hard and fast decisions.

    b. You are loyal to the concepts of profit, growth, and expansion.

20. *a.* You prefer independence and freedom at work to a high salary or job security.

    b. You are comfortable in a position of control, authority, and strong influence.

21. *a.* You firmly believe that those who take the most risks with their own savings should receive the greatest financial rewards.

    b. There are few people's judgment you would have as much confidence in as your own.

22. *a.* You are seen as courageous, energetic, and optimistic.

    b. Being ambitious, you are quick to take advantage of new opportunities.

23. *a.* You are good at praising others and you give credit readily when it's due.

    b. You like people but have little confidence in their ability to do things the right way.

24. *a.* You usually give people the benefit of the doubt, rather than argue openly with them.

    b. Your style with people is direct, "tell it like it is" confrontation.

25. *a.* Although honest, you are capable of being ruthless if others are playing by devious rules.

    b. You grew up in an environment that stressed survival and required you to create your own rules.

Find Your Score

Count all the *a* responses you circled and multiply by 4 to get your percentage for leadership traits. Do the same with *b* answers to arrive at manager traits.

Leader (number of *a*'s) _____ × 4 = _____%

Manager (number of *b*'s) _____ × 4 = _____%

Interpret Your Score

Consider yourself a leader if you score more than 65 percent in the leader tally above; consider yourself a manager if you score more than 65 percent in the manager tally. If your scores cluster closer to a 50–50 split, you're a leader/manager.

The Leader

Your idea of fulfilling work is to motivate and guide co-workers to achieve their best and to reach common goals in their work by functioning in harmony. You are the sort of person who simply enjoys watching people grow and develop. You are commonly described as patient and encouraging in your dealings with people and a determined self-starter in your own motivation. Since you have a natural ability for inspiring top performances, there's usually little turnover among your employees, and staff relations are harmonious. At times, however, you may be too soft on people or overly patient when their performance lags. Where people are concerned, you may be too quick to let emotions get in the way of business judgments. Overall, you're the visionary type, not the day-to-day grinder.

The Manager

You are capable of getting good work out of people, but your style can be abrasive and provocative. You are especially competent at quickly taking charge, bulldozing through corporate red tape, or forcing others to meet tough work demands. Driven partly by a low threshold for boredom, you strive for more complexity in your work. But you love the "game" of power and the sense of having control over others. Also, your confidence in your own ideas is so strong that you may be frustrated by working as part of a team. Your tendency to see your progress as the battle of a great mind against mediocre ones is not the best premise for bringing out the best in others. Therefore, the further up the corporate ladder you go, the more heavily human-relations problems will weigh against you.

The Leader/Manager Mix

As a 50–50 type, you probably do not believe in the need to motivate others. Instead, you maintain that the staff should have a natural desire to work as hard as you do, without needing somebody to egg them on. You do your job well, and you expect the same from your subordinates. This means that while your own level of productivity is high, you are not always sure about how to motivate others to reach their full potential. Generally, however, you do have the ability to get others to do as you wish, without being abrasive or ruffling feathers. You may pride yourself on being surrounded by a very competent, professional staff that is self-motivated, requiring little of your own attention. But don't be too sure: almost everyone performs better under the right sort of encouraging leadership.

Source: Adapted from Michael Clugston, "Manager," *Canadian Business,* June 1988, pp. 268, 270.

Case Incident 15.1

Changes in the Plastics Division

Ed Sullivan was general manager of the Plastics Division of Warner Manufacturing Company. Eleven years ago, Ed hired Russell (Rusty) Means as a general manager of the Plastics Division's two factories. Ed trained Rusty as a manager and thinks Rusty is a good manager, an opinion based largely on the fact that products are produced on schedule and are of such quality that few customers complain. In fact, for the past eight years, Ed has pretty much let Rusty run the factories independently.

Rusty believes strongly that his job is to see that production runs smoothly. He feels that work is work. Sometimes it is agreeable, sometimes disagreeable. If an employee doesn't like the work, he or she can either adjust or quit. Rusty, say the factory personnel, "runs things. He's firm and doesn't stand for any nonsense. Things are done by the book, or they are not done at all." The turnover in the factories is low; nearly every employee likes Rusty and believes that he knows his trade and that he stands up for them.

Two months ago, Ed Sullivan retired and his replacement, Wallace Thomas, took over as general manager of the Plastics Division. One of the first things Thomas did was call his key management people together and announce some major changes he wanted to implement. These included (1) bring the operative employees into the decision-making process; (2) establish a planning committee made up of three management members and three operative employees; (3) start a suggestion system; and (4) as quickly as possible, install a performance appraisal program agreeable to both management and the operative employees. Wallace also stated he would be active in seeing that these projects would be implemented without delay.

After the meeting, Rusty was upset and decided to talk to Robert Mitchell, general manager of sales for the Plastics Division.

Rusty: Wallace is really going to change things, isn't he?

Robert: Yeah, maybe it's for the best. Things were a little lax under Ed.

Rusty: I liked them that way. Ed let you run your own shop. I'm afraid Wallace is going to be looking over my shoulder every minute.

Robert: Well, let's give him a chance. After all, some of the changes he's proposing sound good.

Rusty: Well, I can tell you our employees won't like them. Having them participate in making decisions and those other things are just fancy management stuff that won't work with our employees.

Questions

1. What different styles of leadership are shown in this case?
2. What style of leadership do you think Wallace will have to use with Rusty?
3. Do you agree with Rusty? Discuss.

Case Incident 15.2

Does the Congregation Care?

You are talking with a young pastor of an independent church with 300 adult members. The pastor came directly to the church after graduating from a nondenominational theological school and has been in the job for eight months.

Pastor: I don't know what to do. I feel as if I've been treading water ever since the day I got here; and frankly, I'm not sure that I will be here much longer. If they don't fire me, I may leave on my own. Maybe I'm just not cut out for the ministry.

You: What has happened since you came to this church?

Pastor: When I arrived, I was really full of energy and wanted to see how much this church could accomplish. The very first thing I did was to conduct a questionnaire survey of the entire adult membership to see what types of goals they wanted to pursue. Unfortunately, I found that the members had such mixed (and perhaps apathetic) feelings about the goals that it was hard to draw any conclusions. There were also a few who strongly favored more emphasis on internal things, such as remodeling the sanctuary, developing our music program, and setting up a day care center for the use of the members. Most of the members, however, didn't voice any strong preferences. A lot of people didn't return the questionnaire, and a few even seemed to resent my conducting the survey.

You: What have you done since you took the survey?

Pastor: To be honest about it, I've kept a pretty low profile, concentrating mainly on routine duties. I haven't tried to implement or even push any major new programs. One problem is that I've gotten the impression, through various insinuations, that my being hired was by no means an overwhelmingly popular decision. Evidently, a fairly substantial segment of the congregation was skeptical of my lack of experience and felt that the decision to hire me was railroaded through by a few members of the Pastoral Search Committee. I guess I am just reluctant to assume a strong leadership role until some consensus has developed concerning the goals of the church and I've had more time to gain the confidence of the congregation. I don't know how long that will take, though; and I'm not sure I can tolerate the situation much longer.

Questions

1. Analyze and explain the situation using any of the theories of leadership discussed in this chapter.
2. What would you recommend the young pastor do?

References and Additional Readings

1. John P. Kotter, *Power in Management* (New York: American Management Association, 1979), p. i.
2. David C. McClelland, *Power: The Inner Experience* (New York: John Wiley & Sons, 1975), p. 255.
3. John P. Kotter, *The Leadership Factor* (New York: Free Press, 1988), pp. 25–26.
4. For another view on Theory X and Theory Y, see T. C. Carbone, "Theory X and Theory Y Revisited," *Managerial Planning*, May–June 1981, pp. 24–27.

5. Arthur G. Jago, "Leadership: Perspectives in Theory and Research," *Management Science*, March 1982, pp. 315–36.

6. J. D. Barrow, "The Variables of Leadership: A Review and Conceptual Framework," *Academy of Management Review*, April 1977, p. 232.

7. Victor H. Vroom, "Leadership," in *Handbook of Industrial and Organizational Psychology*, ed. Marvin D. Dunnette (Skokie, IL: Rand McNally, 1976), p. 1531.

8. Rensis Likert, *New Patterns of Management* (New York: McGraw-Hill, 1961).

9. Robert R. Blake and Jane Srygley Mouton, *The New Managerial Grid* (Houston: Gulf Publishing, 1978); and Robert R. Blake and Jane S. Mouton, "How to Choose a Leadership Style," *Training and Development Journal*, February 1982, pp. 38–45.

10. C. L. Graeff, "The Situational Leadership Theory: A Critical Review," *Academy of Management Review*, April 1983, pp. 285–91.

11. Fred E. Fiedler, *A Theory of Leadership Effectiveness* (New York: McGraw-Hill, 1967).

12. Ibid., p. 269.

13. For more analysis on this subject, see Ramadhar Singh, "Leadership Style and Reward Allocation: Does Least Preferred Co-Worker Scale Measure Task and Relation Orientation?" *Organizational Behavior and Human Performance*, October 1983, pp. 178–97.

14. Robert Tannenbaum and Warren Schmidt, "HBR Highlights: Excerpts from How to Choose a Leadership Pattern," *Harvard Business Review*, July–August 1986, p. 131.

15. For an in-depth analysis of the path–goal theory, see J. F. Schriesheim and C. A. Schriesheim, "Test of the Path–Goal Theory of Leadership and Some Suggested Directions for Future Research," *Personnel Psychology*, Summer 1980, pp. 349–71; and Janet Falk and Eric R. Wendler, "Dimensionality of Leader–Subordinate Interactions: A Path–Goal Investigation," *Organizational Behavior and Human Performance*, October 1982, pp. 241–64.

16. Paul Hersey and Kenneth Blanchard, "Life-Cycle Theory of Leadership," *Training and Development Journal*, June 1979, pp. 94–100.

17. Ronald J. DeLuga, "Relationship of Transformational and Transactional Leadership with Employee Influencing Strategies," *Group and Organizational Studies*, December 1988, p. 457.

16

Managing Conflict and Stress

Learning Objectives

After studying this chapter, you will be able to:

1. Define conflict.
2. Discuss the useful effects of conflict.
3. Outline the stages of conflict development.
4. Name the five major types of conflict based on the entities involved.
5. Name five approaches for resolving interpersonal conflict.
6. Name and briefly discuss one method of positively managing conflicts created by diversity in the workforce.
7. Define stress.
8. Define burnout.
9. Outline the basic elements of a violence-prevention program.
10. Explain the three basic types of employee assistance programs.
11. Explain wellness programs.

Chapter Preview

In 1997, operations at United Parcel Service (UPS) were severely hampered when unionized drivers and truck loaders went on strike. Before the strike, UPS did not appear to be a likely candidate for a strike. The company had worked collaboratively with the Teamsters Union for 82 years—ever since UPS founder Jim Casey extended the invitation to the teamsters, saying that employees could be both good Teamsters and good "UPSers." After a stormy two-week strike, a settlement was reached and a new contract was signed. Recognizing the importance of individual contact between customers and drivers, the company was careful not to create negative images of its striking drivers during and after the strike. The company concentrated not only on rebuilding its customer base but also on rebuilding the relationship with its employees. First up was a video presentation to employees by chairman and CEO James Kelly. The theme of the video was to move forward and concentrate on what the company does best—deliver packages. At this same time, the management team held meetings in all of the 60 UPS districts around the country. They met with employees and held question-and-answer sessions.

Despite all the efforts by top management to diffuse hard feelings, relations between first-level supervisors and employees have continued to be strained in some areas. Many supervisors who crossed the picket lines to keep the company going were subjected to harsh language and even threats. Some of these supervisors have found it hard to forget.

The 1997 strike was still having repercussions five years later in the spring and summer of 2002. During this time, UPS's volume of business fell significantly because of a threatened strike by the Teamsters. Mindful of the 1997 strike and as a precautionary act, many customers took their business elsewhere. A strike was averted and many of the customers came back—but not all.

Sources: Robert J. Grossman, "Trying to Heal the Wounds," *HR Magazine,* September 1998, pp. 85–92; and Richard Thompson, "Some United Parcel Customers Fear Strike, Turn to Other Carriers," *Knight Ridder Tribune Business News,* July 24, 2002, p. 1.

Analyzing Management Skills

Why do you think conflict arises between parties that have had a good relationship for years? What might have happened if UPS had used press coverage and other means to portray its drivers negatively during and after the strike?

Applying Management Skills

Have you ever witnessed a dispute between friends or co-workers that turned out badly? Outline a set of guidelines that might be followed to help resolve such a dispute.

---

conflict
Overt behavior that results when an individual or a group of individuals thinks a perceived need of the individual or group has been blocked or is about to be blocked.

Conflict is an overt behavior that results when an individual or group of individuals thinks a perceived need of the individual or group has been blocked or is about to be blocked. Conflict occurs because individuals have different perceptions, beliefs, and goals. From an organizational perspective, conflict can be viewed as anything that disrupts the "normal" routine.[1]

Conflict in organizations is often assumed to be unnatural and undesirable, something to be avoided at all costs. Conflict can lead to rigidity in the system in which it operates, distort reality, and debilitate the participants in the conflict situation. Therefore, many organizations approach the management of conflict with the following assumptions:

1. Conflict is avoidable.
2. Conflict is the result of personality problems within the organization.
3. Conflict produces inappropriate reactions by the persons involved.
4. Conflict creates a polarization within the organization.

However, conflict is perfectly natural and should be expected to occur. Management must know when to eliminate conflict and when to build on it. Today's managers must accept the existence of conflict and realize that to attempt to stop all conflict is a mistake. The general consensus is that conflict itself is not undesirable; rather, it is a phenomenon that can have constructive or destructive effects.[2]

FIGURE 16.1
Myths and Truths about Conflict

Source: Jerry Wisinski, *Resolving Conflicts on the Job* (New York: American Management Association, 1993).

Myth	Truth
Conflict in the workplace is always dysfunctional.	Conflict is a normal part of life within an organization.
All conflicts can be resolved.	Most conflicts can be managed.
Conflict tends to go away if it is ignored.	Conflict can motivate change.
Conflicts always result in winners and losers.	Conflict can help build relationships between people.

For example, in a struggle between two people for a promotion, the winner will probably think the conflict was most worthwhile, while the loser will likely reach the opposite conclusion. However, the impact of the conflict on the organization must also be considered. If the conflict ends in the selection and promotion of the better-qualified person, the effect is good from the organization's viewpoint. If, by competing, the parties have produced more or made improvements within their areas of responsibility, the effect is also positive. At the same time, there may be destructive effects. The overall work of the organization may have suffered during the conflict. The loser may resign or withdraw as a result of the failure. The conflict may become chronic and inhibit the work of the organization. In extreme cases, the health of one or both participants may be impaired.

The destructive effects of conflict are often obvious, whereas the constructive effects may be more subtle. The manager must be able to see these constructive effects and weigh them against the costs. Some potentially useful effects of conflict include the following:

1. Conflict energizes people. Even if not all of the resulting activity is constructive, it at least wakes people up and gets them moving.
2. Conflict is a form of communication; the resolution of conflict may open new and lasting channels.
3. Conflict often provides an outlet for pent-up tensions, resulting in catharsis. With the air cleansed, the participants can again concentrate on their primary responsibilities.
4. Conflict may actually be an educational experience. The participants may become more aware and more understanding of their opponents' functions and the problems with which they must cope.

Figure 16.1 summarizes some general myths and truths about conflict. Management Illustration 16.1 describes the negative effects that some organizations have experienced as a result of trying to quell all types of conflict.

Progressive Stages of Conflict

A manager must be aware of conflict's dynamic nature. Conflict usually does not appear suddenly. It passes through a series of progressive stages as tensions build. These stages of development are as follows:

1. *Latent conflict:* At this stage, the basic conditions for conflict exist but have not yet been recognized. For example, racial differences may preclude basic communication channels between two employees.

"Leaders who are aggressive and unapproachable are uncomfortable having issues placed on the table," says Howard Guttman, a consultant who specializes in helping companies address conflict in the workplace. "They operate with the illusion that no news is good news."

Guttman emphasizes that companies that promote a conflict-free atmosphere are often sowing the seeds for disaster. Guttman gives three specific examples of well-known corporate disasters related to such an environment: (1) *The New York Times,* (2) Enron, and (3) NASA. At the *Times,* reporter Jayson Blair's fabrications of stories led to the resignation of two top editors. Indications are that these editors were oblivious to numerous warnings about Blair's work and that they were unapproachable. Enron's famous collapse is now being described as being partially caused by an environment in which top managers did not listen to the concerns of employees. Investigations into *Columbia*'s space disaster found that NASA became so fixed on making its scheduled flights that safety concerns raised by lower level employees were ignored. Guttman believes that each of these cases ultimately revealed a climate in which employees were encouraged not to create conflict situations by pressing legitimate concerns with top managers.

Source: Teresa M. McAlearry, "Ledgewood, N.J.–Based Consultant Helps Companies Bring Conflict out in Open," *Knight Ridder Tribune Business News,* October 26, 2003, p. 1.

2. *Perceived conflict:* One or both participants recognize the cause of the conflict. For example, an employee begins to complain that his or her manager doesn't like him or her.

3. *Felt conflict:* Tension is beginning to build between the participants, although no real struggle has begun. When employees become short-tempered with one another, this form of conflict begins to emerge.

4. *Manifest conflict:* The struggle is under way, and the behavior of the participants makes the existence of the conflict apparent to others not directly involved. Arguments or damaged feelings are no longer privately held. Disruptions begin to arise in public.

5. *Conflict aftermath:* The conflict has been ended through resolution or suppression. This establishes new conditions that will lead either to more effective cooperation or to a new conflict that may be more severe than the first. This form of conflict can result in firings, punishments, or future difficulties. In some instances, resolution can be positive and serve to end the issue.

Conflict does not always pass through all of these stages. Furthermore, the parties in conflict may not be at the same stage simultaneously. For example, one participant may be at the manifest stage of conflict while the other is at the perceived stage.

Analyzing Conflict

Conflict can be analyzed from many different perspectives. One approach is based on the entities involved: intrapersonal, interpersonal, intergroup, organizational, or political. Each of these types of conflict is discussed in the following sections.

Intrapersonal Conflict

intrapersonal conflict
Conflict internal to the individual.

Intrapersonal conflict is internal to the individual. It is probably the most difficult form of conflict to analyze. Intrapersonal conflict can result when barriers exist between the drive and the goal. When a drive or a motive is blocked before the goal is reached, frustration and anxiety can occur. Barriers can be either overt (rules and procedures) or covert (mental hang-ups). When a barrier exists, people tend to react with defense mechanisms, which are behaviors used to cope with frustration and anxiety. Figure 16.2 lists some typical defense mechanisms.

Responses to frustration and anxiety vary and can be expressed through withdrawal behavior (higher absenteeism and turnover rates), aggression (sabotage

FIGURE 16.2   Reactions to Frustration and Anxiety

Adjustive Reactions	Psychological Process	Illustration
Compensation	Individual devotes himself or herself to a pursuit with increased vigor to make up for some feeling of real or imagined inadequacy.	Zealous, hardworking president of the 25-Year Club who has never advanced very far in the company hierarchy.
Conversion	Emotional conflicts are expressed in muscular, sensory, or bodily symptoms of disability, malfunctioning, or pain.	A disabling headache keeping a staff member off the job the day after a cherished project has been rejected.
Displacement	Redirects pent-up emotions toward persons, ideas, or objects other than the primary source of the emotion.	Roughly rejecting a simple request from a subordinate after receiving a rebuff from the boss.
Fantasy	Daydreaming or other forms of imaginative activity provide an escape from reality and imagined satisfactions.	An employee's daydream of the day in the staff meeting when he corrects the boss's mistakes and is publicly acknowledged as the real leader of the group.
Negativism	Active or passive resistance, operating unconsciously.	The manager who, having been unsuccessful in getting out of a committee assignment, picks apart every suggestion anyone makes in the meetings.
Rationalization	Justifies inconsistent or undesirable behavior, beliefs, statements, and motivations by providing acceptable explanations for them.	Padding the expense account because "everybody does it."
Regression	Individual returns to an earlier and less mature level of adjustment in the face of frustration.	A manager, having been blocked in some administrative pursuit, busies himself with clerical duties or technical details more appropriate for his subordinates.
Repression	Completely excludes from consciousness impulses, experiences, and feelings that are psychologically disturbing because they arouse a sense of guilt or anxiety.	An employee "forgetting" to tell his boss the circumstances of an embarrassing situation.
Resignation, apathy, and boredom	Breaks psychological contact with the environment, withholding any sense of emotional or personal involvement.	Employee who, receiving no reward, praise, or encouragement, no longer cares whether or not he does a good job.
Flight or withdrawal	Leaves the field in which frustration, anxiety, or conflict is experienced, either physically or psychologically.	The salesman's big order falls through, and he takes the rest of the day off; constant rebuff or rejection by superiors and colleagues pushes an older employee toward being a loner and ignoring whatever friendly gestures are made.

Source: From *Psychology in Administration: A Research Orientation,* by T. W. Costello and S. S. Zalkind. Copyright © 1963 by Pearson Education, Inc. Reprinted by permission of Pearson Education, Inc., Upper Saddle River, NJ.

and other destructive work acts), excessive drinking, drug abuse, and more subtle responses such as ulcers or heart trouble.

Intrapersonal conflict can also result from goal conflict. Goal conflict occurs when an individual's goal has both positive and negative aspects or when goals exist. There are three basic forms of goal conflict:

1. *Conflicting positive goals.* This situation occurs when a person must choose between two or more positive goals. For example, say that a person is offered two equally attractive jobs. Suppose that a manager in Company A is approached by the human resources manager of Company B and offered a managerial job in Company B. If the manager likes the present job but also thinks that the new job would be very good, he or she is faced with conflicting positive goals. This situation produces intrapersonal conflict.

2. *Goals with both positive and negative aspects.* This situation occurs when a person is confronted by a goal that has both positive and negative aspects. For example, an employee may be offered a job promotion that requires the employee to relocate. The employee may really want the promotion but may also not want to move. Thus, a conflict internal to the employee emerges.

3. *Goals that have only negative aspects.* This situation occurs when a person is confronted with two or more negative goals. For example, a person may be working at a job he or she dislikes but may consider quitting and looking for another job just as undesirable.

dissonance
Feeling of conflict felt by individual trying to make a decision.

Since goal conflict forces the person to make a decision, decision making often creates a feeling of conflict within the individual. This **dissonance** or disharmony is a danger sign that managers must watch for, since it can lead to a loss of mental concentration and productivity in the workplace.

An extension of goal conflict is *cognitive conflict*, in which ideas or thoughts are perceived as incompatible in a given situation, and *affective conflict*, in which feelings or emotions are incompatible and the result is usually anger at the other person.

Managers can help deal with intrapersonal conflict only if they can identify when and why it is occurring. Therefore, managers must learn to identify intrapersonal conflict not only within employees but also within themselves.

Interpersonal Conflict

interpersonal conflict
Conflict between two or more individuals.

Interpersonal conflict, or conflict between two or more individuals, may result from many factors. Opposing personalities often result in interpersonal conflict. Some people simply rub each other the wrong way. The extrovert and the introvert, the boisterous individual and the reserved one, the optimist and the pessimist, the impulsive person and the deliberate person are but a few possible combinations that may spark conflict.

Prejudices based on personal background or ethnic origin can also cause interpersonal conflict. Obvious examples are racial and religious conflicts, but other, more subtle, prejudices exist. Examples include the college graduate versus the person with only a high school education, the married person versus the divorced person, and the longtime employee versus the new hire.

Another cause of interpersonal conflict arises when individuals become dissatisfied with their roles relative to the roles of others. For example, an employee may be perfectly satisfied with the relationship with both his or her managers and coworkers. However, if a peer is promoted to a management job, the employee may have difficulty accepting his or her role in relation to the former peer.

In a classic discussion of role conflict, Robert L. Kahn revealed that each individual organizational member has numerous roles to play. In many instances, role conflict occurs because of job overload (especially at the managerial level). In attempting to deal with role conflict, employees may cut themselves off from peers and support groups, suffer high anxiety, reduce their productivity, and eventually become demotivated.[3]

Intergroup (Structural) Conflict

intergroup (structural) conflict Conflict that results from the organizational structure; may be relatively independent of the individuals occupying the roles within the structure.

The organizational structure may be the cause of **intergroup** or **structural conflict.** Such conflict may be relatively independent of the individuals occupying the roles within the structure. For example, structural conflict between marketing and production departments is fairly common. The marketing department, being customer oriented, may believe some exceptions can and should be made in production for the sake of current and future sales. The production department may view such exceptions as unreasonable and not in the best interests of the organization. Hence, a structural conflict occurs. The conflict situation can be even more intense if the managers of each department are also experiencing interpersonal conflict. The following sections discuss various types of structural conflict.

Goal Segmentation and Rewards

Each functional unit of an organization has different functional goals. These can cause conflict that, when it emerges, may seem to be personality clashes. The classic problem of inventory levels illustrates this dilemma. The marketing department would like to keep finished-goods inventories high to supply all of the customers' needs on short notice. The finance department would like to keep inventories low because of the cost of maintaining these inventories. The end result is often a conflict between departments.

The reward system is a key source for reducing this type of conflict. A reward system that stresses the separate performances of the departments feeds the conflict. However, rewarding the combined efforts of the conflicting departments reduces the conflict.

Nevertheless, inadequate reward systems that lead to conflict are still very common. Four factors generally inhibit implementing effective reward systems:

- Insistence on an objective criterion (i.e., rewards are linked to one objective when in fact many objectives come into play).

- Overemphasis on highly visible behaviors (for example, difficult-to-observe concepts such as team building are rarely rewarded).

- Hypocrisy (having a reward system that actually encourages one type of behavior while claiming to encourage another).

- Emphasis on morality or equity rather than efficiency (many situations are not just either-or situations).[4]

Mutual Departmental Dependence

Sometimes two departments or units of an organization are dependent on each other to accomplish their respective goals, creating a potential for structural conflict. For instance, the marketing department's sales depend on the volume of production from the production department; at the same time, the production department's quotas are based on the sales of the marketing department. This type of mutual dependence exists in many organizations.

Unequal Departmental Dependence

Often departmental dependence is unequal and fosters conflict. In most organizations, for instance, staff groups are more dependent on line groups. The staff generally must understand the problems of the line, cooperate with the line, and sell ideas to the line. However, the line does not have to reciprocate. One tactic in this form of conflict is an attempt by the more dependent unit to interfere with the work performance of the independent group. In doing so, the more dependent group hopes the other group will cooperate once it realizes how the dependent group can hinder progress.

Functional Unit and the Environment

Functional units obviously perform different tasks and cope with different parts of the environment. Research has shown that the more the environments served by functional units differ, the greater the potential for conflict. Paul Lawrence and Jay Lorsch have developed four basic dimensions to describe these differences: (1) structure—the basic type of managerial style employed; (2) environment orientation—the orientation of the unit to the outside world; (3) time span orientation—the unit's planning-time perspectives; and (4) interpersonal orientation—the openness and permissiveness of interpersonal relationships.[5]

Role Dissatisfaction

Role dissatisfaction may also produce structural conflict. Professionals in an organizational unit who receive little recognition and have limited opportunities for advancement may initiate conflict with other units. Purchasing agents often demonstrate this form of conflict.

Role dissatisfaction and conflict often result when a group that has low perceived status sets standards for another group. For example, within academic institutions, administrators—whom the faculty may view as having less status—often set standards of performance and make administrative decisions that affect the faculty.

Role Ambiguity

Ambiguities in the description of a particular job can lead to structural conflict. When the credit or blame for the success or failure of a particular assignment cannot be determined between two departments, conflict is likely to result. For instance, improvements in production techniques require the efforts of the engineering and production departments. After the improvements are made, credit is difficult to assign; thus, conflict often results between these two departments.

Common Resource Dependence

When two organizational units are dependent on common but scarce resources, potential for conflict exists. This often occurs when two departments are competing for budget money. Each naturally believes its projects are more important and should be funded.

Communication Barriers

Semantic differences can cause conflict. For instance, purchasing agents and engineers generally use different language to describe similar materials, which leads to conflict. Communication-related conflict also occurs when a physical or organizational barrier to effective communication exists. Company headquarters and branch offices frequently suffer from this problem.

Figure 16.3 summarizes types of intergroup or structural conflict.[6]

FIGURE 16.3
Summary of Types of Intergroup (or Structural) Conflict

Type	Example
Goal segmentation and reward	Different inventory levels are desired by different functional departments.
Mutual departmental dependence	Marketing department's sales are dependent on the volume of production from the production department.
Unequal departmental dependence	Staff departments are generally more dependent on line departments.
Functional unit and environment	The environment faced by an applied research department and a sales department are different and can lead to conflict between these departments.
Role dissatisfaction	Professionals in an organizational unit who receive little attention.
Role ambiguities	When the credit or blame for the success or failure of a particular assignment cannot be determined between two departments.
Common resource dependence	Two departments competing for computer time.
Communication barriers	Purchasing agents and engineers may use different language to describe similar materials, and conflict can result from those semantic differences.

Organizational Conflict

organizational conflict
Conflict between employees and the organization itself.

Organizational conflict is conflict between employees and the organization itself. Organizational conflict pits employees or groups of employees against the organization. Changes in policies that negatively affect employees, such as a cutback in benefits offered, are one source of organizational conflict. Reorganizations, corporate downsizing, layoff of employees, and tightening of expenses are other examples of sources of organizational conflict.

Political Conflict

Intrapersonal, interpersonal, intergroup, and organizational conflict generally are not planned; they simply develop as a result of existing circumstances. But political (sometimes called *strategic*) conflict is started purposely and is often undertaken with an elaborate battle plan. Such conflict usually results from the promotion of self-interests on the part of an individual or a group. The instigator(s) has a clear goal, and those who stand in the way are the adversary. In organizations, the goal is usually to gain an advantage over the opponent within the reward system. The potential reward may be a bonus or commission, a choice assignment, a promotion, or an expansion of power. Whatever it is, usually one of the participants will receive it (or the greatest portion of it). As an example, the vice presidents of an organization may find themselves in a political conflict situation as the retirement of the president nears. An ambitious vice president, in an attempt to better his or her personal chances for the presidency, may create a political conflict with one or more of the other vice presidents.

Political conflict does not always imply that the participants are dishonest or unethical. Indeed, rewards are there to be pursued with vigor. But such conflicts can degenerate into unfair play because the participants cannot resist the temptation to win at all costs.

Managing Conflict

As described earlier, conflict is an inherent part of any organization. Even though some conflict may be beneficial to an organization, unresolved conflict or conflict that is resolved poorly usually results in negative consequences such as job withdrawal behaviors, unionization activity, low morale, and lower levels of goal attainment.[7] Successful resolution of conflict among employees often depends on the employees' immediate manager or managers. The objective of the manager is not to force a resolution to the conflict but act as a referee and counselor in helping the participant(s) reach an acceptable solution. Understanding the type of conflict—intrapersonal, interpersonal, intergroup, organizational, or political—and the stage of the conflict cycle will aid the manager.

Resolving Conflict Situations

Managers most frequently are faced with intrapersonal, interpersonal, and intergroup conflict. Therefore, these forms of conflict are discussed in more depth in this section.

As was stated earlier, intrapersonal conflict is often difficult to analyze. Managers should not go around looking for intrapersonal conflict in every situation. However, when an employee asks to discuss a personal problem, the manager should look for signs of *intrapersonal conflict*. When a manager detects what he or she believes to be an intrapersonal conflict situation with an employee, the employee should normally be referred to a person specifically trained in handling such matters.

Five general approaches can be used to deal with interpersonal conflict situations: (1) compromising, (2) smoothing over the conflicts, (3) withdrawal of one or more of the participants, (4) forcing the conflict to a conclusion, and (5) confrontation. Each of these methods is discussed below.

Compromising

Compromising occurs when both sides give some of what they want. Compromising is effective in dealing with interpersonal conflict when it benefits both parties. It can be used when the issue in question is not very important. It can also be used to expedite solutions under time pressures or to obtain temporary solutions to complex problems. Unfortunately, compromising often leaves the real cause of the conflict unsolved and provides the groundwork for future conflict.

Smoothing over the Conflict

Smoothing over the conflict happens when the manager acts like the conflict does not exist. Managers using this approach often pretend "we are all one big happy family." This approach rarely leads to long-term solutions and generally results in more conflict.

Withdrawal

Withdrawal of one or more of the participants involves actions such as firing, transferring, or having an employee quit. Another form of withdrawal is having one or more of the participants refuse to discuss the conflict. Withdrawal rarely addresses the underlying cause of the conflict and usually provides the basis for future conflict.

Forcing a Solution

Forcing a solution occurs when the manager or another third party steps in and forces a solution on the conflicting parties. For example, a manager, observing a

FIGURE 16.4
Tactics for
Managing
Interpersonal
Conflict with
Difficult People

Source: From *Coping with
Difficult People* by Robert M.
Bramson. Copyright © 1981
by Robert Bramson. Used by
permission of Doubleday, a
division of Random House,
Inc. and The Carol Mann
Agency.

Hostile-Aggressives

Stand up for yourself.
Give them time to run down.
Use self-assertive language.
Avoid a direct confrontation.

Complainers

Listen attentively.
Acknowledge their feelings.
Avoid complaining with them.
State the facts without apology.
Use a problem-solving mode.

Clams

Ask open-ended questions.
Be patient in waiting for a response.
Ask more open-ended questions.
If no response occurs, tell clams what
you plan to do, because no discussion
has taken place.

Superagreeables

In a nonthreatening manner, work hard
to find out why they will not take action.
Let them know you value them as
people.
Be ready to compromise and negotiate,
and do not allow them to make
unrealistic commitments.
Try to discern the hidden meaning in
their humor.

Negativists

Do not be dragged into their despair.
Do not try to cajole them out of their
negativism.
Discuss the problem thoroughly, without
offering solutions.
When alternatives are discussed, bring up
the negative side yourself.
Be ready to take action alone, without
their agreement.

Know-It-Alls

Bulldozers:

Prepare yourself.
Listen and paraphrase their main points.
Use the questioning form to raise
problems.

Balloons:

State facts or opinions as your own
perceptions of reality.
Find a way for balloons to save face.
Confront balloons alone, not in public.

Indecisive Stallers

Raise the issue of why they are hesitant.
If you are the problem, ask for help.
Keep the action steps in your own hands.
Possibly remove the staller from the
situation.

conflict between two employees, might step in and say, "this is the way it is going
to be, and that ends it." Like the previous methods, this one may only sow the
seeds for future conflict.

Confrontation

Confrontation occurs when both parties confront each other with what is really
bothering them. With this method, each party discusses their true feelings and
also listens to what the other parties have to say.

Although each of the above methods can work in certain situations, confrontation is generally considered to be the most effective method of resolving conflict;
third-party intervention has been found to be the least effective method.[8] One reason for this is that resolutions reached through confrontation tend to be more long
lasting.

In some instances, however, the profiles of the parties involved in conflict fall
into the category of "difficult people." Figure 16.4 suggests some rather interesting tactics for dealing with these personalities. The general rule for the manager
is to ensure that each situation involving interpersonal conflict is dealt with based
on the individual's and the situation's basic characteristics.[9]

Much intergroup conflict results from interdependencies among organizational
units that are inherent in the organizational structure. Some of this conflict potential may be removed by decoupling the conflicting units by reducing their common

resource dependencies; giving each control over its own resources; introducing buffer inventories; or invoking impersonal, straightforward rules for resource allocation. Decoupling may also occur by duplicating facilities for dependent departments. However, this approach may be too expensive for the organization. A more affordable approach to reducing interdependencies is the use of a "linking" position between dependent departments. The purpose is to ease communication and coordination among interdependent and potentially conflicting departments. Another approach is to design the work flow so that the system reflects more logical and complete work units in which responsibility and authority are more consistent. Finally, the matrix organization can offer a means for constructive confrontation, which, as stated earlier, is the most effective method of conflict resolution.[10]

The Conflict Interface

Besides acting as referees in enforcing these rules, managers can give valuable assistance to the participants without interfering with their responsibility to resolve the conflict. Managers can help the participants understand why the conflict exists and what underlying issues must be resolved. They can also help obtain information needed to reach a solution. To maximize the constructive aspects of the conflict and speed its resolution while minimizing the destructive consequences, the manager should make sure the participants are aware of the following ground rules for constructive confrontations:

1. Before the confrontation begins, review the past actions of the participants, and clarify the issues causing the conflict.
2. Encourage the participants to communicate freely. They should get their personal feelings out in the open and should not hold back grievances.
3. Don't try to place blame. This only polarizes the participants.
4. Don't surprise either party with confrontations for which either party is not prepared.
5. Don't attack sensitive areas of either party that have nothing to do with the specific conflict.
6. Keep to specific issues; do not argue aimlessly.
7. Identify areas of mutual agreement.
8. Emphasize mutual benefits to both parties.
9. Don't jump into specific solutions too quickly.
10. Encourage all of the participants to examine their own biases and feelings.
11. Maintain the intensity of the confrontation and ensure that all participants say all they want to say. If the basic issues have been resolved at this point, agree on what steps are to be taken toward resolving the conflict.

In interpersonal conflict, managers can regulate somewhat the frequency of contacts between the participants and perhaps establish a problem-solving climate when they meet. A manager's most important contribution, however, is to keep the individuals working toward a true resolution of the conflict. Confrontation of the conflict situation within the ground rules just described should encourage constructive conflict within the organization.[11]

Conflict and Diversity

Conflict can and does arise in the workplace when differences in thinking styles, speech patterns, lifestyles, national origins, ethnicity, religion, age, functional expertise, company experience, and a host of other variables are present.[12] The key

FIGURE 16.5 A Model of Organizational Diplomacy

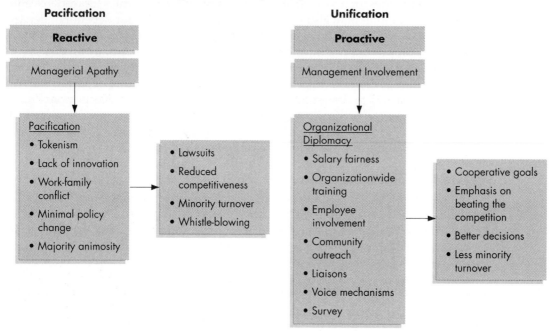

Source: Jacqueline A. Gilbert and John M. Ivancevich, "Organizational Diplomacy: The Bridge for Managing Diversity," *Human Resource Planning* 22, no. 3 (1999), p. 30.

organizational diplomacy
Strategies used to minimize conflict in a diverse workplace.

to using these differences to the organization's advantage is to properly manage the potential conflict. One method of positively managing the conflicts created by diversity is to use organizational diplomacy. **Organizational diplomacy** is broadly defined as strategies used to minimize conflict in a diverse workplace, in both domestic and international settings. Organizational diplomacy is based on a proactive, unifying approach to diversity, as opposed to a reactive and superficial approach. The model shown in Figure 16.5 outlines the causes and resulting solutions that accompany both a reactive and a proactive approach. Under the reactive or pacification approach, organizations do only the minimum required by law; diversity is viewed as a necessary evil to procure government contracts or to avoid litigation. The results produced by this approach are usually negative in the form of lawsuits, reduced competitiveness, turnover, and so on. With the proactive approach, employees work together toward mutually acceptable solutions, and differences among the organization's members are used to the organization's advantage. One of the primary tenets of the proactive approach using organizational diplomacy is to encourage employee suggestions for improving organizational climate and policies.

Workplace Stress

Just as conflict is an integral part of organizational life, so is stress. Stress is part of living and can contribute to personal growth, development, and mental health. However, excessive and prolonged stress generally becomes quite negative. For example, the American Institute of Stress reports that stress costs U.S. businesses between $200 billion and $300 billion a year in lost productivity, increased employee compensation claims, increased turnover, and increased health care costs.[13] Specifically, the Institute reports that stress is a factor in up to 80 percent of all work-related injuries, a major factor in 40 percent of all turnovers, and a major contributor in 75 to 90 percent of primary care physician visits.[14] Furthermore, the Bureau of Labor Statistics estimates that work-related stress claims cost employers about $10,000 per employee per year.[15]

stress
Mental or physical condition that results from a perceived threat of danger (physical or emotional) and the pressure to remove it.

Stress is the mental or physical condition that results from a perceived threat of danger (physical or emotional) and the pressure to remove it. The potential for stress exists when an environmental situation presents a demand that threatens to exceed the person's capabilities and resources for meeting it, under conditions in which the person expects a substantial difference in rewards and costs resulting from meeting the demand versus not meeting it. Northwestern National Life Company reports that 40 percent of employees say their jobs are "very or extremely stressful," and 25 percent view their job as the number one stressor in their lives.[16] While workplace violence culminating in bloodshed gets the most publicity, shouting matches and lost tempers occur much more frequently. A survey by the Marlin Group found that 42 percent of employees have jobs where yelling and verbal abuse occur frequently.[17]

In its earliest stages, stress manifests itself in exaggerated behavior such as cynical attitudes and increased use of alcohol, tobacco, and medications.[18] If allowed to continue, stress affects employees on the job in several ways, including increased absenteeism, job turnover, lower productivity, and mistakes on the job. In addition, prolonged excessive stress can result in both physical and emotional problems. Some common stress-related disorders include tension and migraine headaches; coronary heart disease; high blood pressure; and muscle tightness in the chest, neck, and lower back. From a psychological perspective, inordinate or prolonged stress can impair concentration, memory, sleep, appetite, motivation, mood, and the ability to relate to others. In addition, recent studies have shown that stress at work is carried to the home environment. Soon the employee becomes surrounded by stress and becomes dysfunctional.[19]

Stress strikes all levels of workers. While there is no single course of workplace stress, much of today's stress-related illnesses worldwide is the result of added demands placed on employees because of downsizing and the difficulties that women in particular force in juggling the demands of work and family.[20] In the face of reductions in workforces due to downsizing and reengineering, many employees have had to increase their job scopes and responsibilities. Those who experience "good job fit" do not seem to experience as much stress as those who are mismatched or overmatched in their expanded positions.[21] Figure 16.6 lists some of the more common sources and suggested causes of job-related stress.

The Workplace Stress Audit

The first step in managing workplace stress is to determine what the specific sources of stress are since they can and usually do vary from situation to situation. One method of doing this is to undertake a stress audit. A stress audit attempts to identify any work-related causes of stress. A stress audit can be undertaken by outside consultants or by internal personnel. Stress audits can be in the form of questionnaires filled out by employees or personal interviews conducted by qualified persons. Information can also be gathered on such factors as absenteeism, sick leave, and tardiness. When a company undertakes a stress audit, management is acknowledging that the workplace can be a source of stress and that it is not just the individual employees' personal problems.

FIGURE 16.6
Common Sources and Suggested Causes of Organizational Stress

Source: Charles R. Stoner and Fred L. Fry, "Developing a Corporate Policy for Managing Stress," *Personnel,* May–June 1983, p. 70.

Common Sources	Suggested Causes
Job mismatch	Job demands skills or abilities the employee does not possess (job incompetence).
	Job does not provide opportunity for the employee to fully utilize skills or abilities (underutilization).
Conflicting expectations	The formal organization's concept of expected behavior contradicts the employee's concept of expected behavior.
	The informal group's concept of expected behavior contradicts the employee's concept.
	The individual employee is affected by two (or more) strong influences.
Role ambiguity	Employee is uncertain or unclear about how to perform on the job.
	Employee is uncertain or unclear about what is expected in the job.
	Employee is unclear or uncertain about the relationship between job performance and expected consequences (rewards, penalties, and so forth).
Role overload	Employee is incompetent at job.
	Employee is asked to do more than time permits (time pressure).
Fear/responsibility	Employee is afraid of performing poorly or failing.
	Employee feels pressure for high achievement.
	Employee has responsibility for other people.
Working conditions	The job environment is unpleasant; there is inadequate lighting or improper regulation of temperature and noise, for example.
	The requirements of the job may unnecessarily produce pacing problems, social isolation, and so forth.
	The machine design and maintenance procedures create pressure.
	The job involves long or erratic work hours.
Working relationships	Individual employees have problems relating to, or working with, superiors, peers, or subordinates.
	Employees have problems working in groups.
Alienation	There is limited social interaction.
	Employees do not participate in decision making.

Organizational Guidelines for Managing Stress

Once the sources of stress have been identified, solutions for reducing the stress should be explored. There are many actions that organizations can take to reduce the amount of job-related stress experienced by their employees. Among these actions are

- Shortening hours of direct contact with customers.
- Granting special leaves (sabbatical programs).
- Introducing early retirement programs.
- Installing on-site exercise facilities.
- Actively involving employees in the decision-making processes.
- Fulfilling the realistic expectations of employees.

When the breakup of AT&T in the mid-1980s resulted in massive divestitures and reorganization of the so-called Baby Bells, Atlanta-based BellSouth Corporation realized that the changes were adversely affecting its employees. BellSouth decided to do something about it and implemented a companywide stress identification and management program.

BellSouth used an instrument called the Stress Navigator to help employees identify and quantify the effects of stress in their organization. Stress Navigator is a 264-question survey developed by Stress Directions Inc. of Lincoln, Massachusetts. Stress Navigator rates each participant on his or her degree of stress over the prior six months and predicts anticipated stress levels over the next six months. The instrument focuses on three areas: susceptibility to stress, sources of stress, and symptoms of stress.

BellSouth made Stress Navigator available to frequent users of health benefits. Participants received personal stress reports and the company received group data identifying companywide trends. BellSouth then used the findings to make changes to reduce employee stress loads. For example, the companywide profile showed that many night-shift employees were feeling stressed because they were not home to prepare their children for school. The company then created split shifts to help mothers go home and get their kids off to school. BellSouth estimates that it saved more than $13 million to health benefits and stress-related workers' compensation claims costs in the first year it implemented its stress reduction program.

Source: Joanne Wojcik, "Cutting Costs of Stress," *Business Insurance,* March 26, 2001, pp. 1, 22.

- Clearly defining employee jobs.
- Providing well-thought-out training programs.
- Introducing changes gradually.

Naturally, some of these actions are more appropriate in some situations than in others. For any of these actions to work, the organization must first have an awareness of its potential for dealing with stress-related problems. For example, in the case of North Sea oil rig workers, audits discovered that major sources of stress included long amounts of time away from the family, the foul weather and its effect on transporting and working conditions, living conditions, and a lack of opportunity for relaxing and exercising during free time.[22] Although all of these sources of stress seemed inherent to the job, remedies were discovered. The shift system could be rearranged, and exercise facilities, no-smoking areas, quiet rooms, and more private sleeping areas could be provided. Even the stress of having to fly back and forth to the rigs could be lessened by providing more information about the safety of helicopters. Management Illustration 16.2 discusses how BellSouth Corporation saved millions of dollars by implementing a stress reduction program.

Managing Personal Stress

In addition to reducing stress inherent in the industry and job, managers should learn to personally manage stress on a daily basis. The old strategy of waiting for an annual vacation to wind down is no longer a solution.[23] One or two weeks off rarely counterbalance 50 weeks of stress. Furthermore, many people don't take vacation time, even when it is available. According to one national stress survey, one out of four took no vacation. Of those who did take a vacation, people with lower levels of stress averaged 2.2 weeks of vacation, whereas those with higher levels of stress averaged only 1.4 weeks of vacation per year.

The first step in reducing personal stress is to determine if your life is reasonably balanced. The following behaviors are indications that your life may be out of balance:

- Hurrying everywhere; walking, talking, driving faster.
- Feeling depressed, apathetic, or bored most of the time.
- Changes in sleeping or eating patterns.
- Difficulty enjoying social activities.
- Emphasis on how much you get done, rather than how well you do it.
- Inability to accept praise or affection, even when you want it.
- More frequent accidents than usual.[24]

Recognizing the above signs in your life will let you know that you should search for ways of restoring balance. The following five-step approach can help you regain your balance:

1. Counter every yes with a no. If you add a new unscheduled activity to your day, cancel another. If you decide to make an unscheduled stop at the grocery store, reschedule your plan to stop at the post office.
2. Schedule only 80 percent of your time. Leave some breathing space for unpredictable events; remember most things take longer than you think.
3. Practice giving in. Constantly making decisions places demands on your time and energy. Occasionally giving in and letting someone else make the decisions can take the pressure off.
4. Be realistic. Set realistic deadlines and workloads. Usually, no one expects as much of you as yourself.
5. Focus on the five Fs. To find balance, focus on faith, family, finances, friends, and fitness. Examine each of these areas and balance your schedule each week by including activities in all five areas.[25]

Burnout

burnout
Condition that occurs when work is no longer meaningful to a person.

Burnout occurs when work is no longer meaningful to a person. Research has shown that chronic stress, rather than acute crises, and prolonged personal contact tend to bring about the highest degrees of burnout.[26] Figure 16.7 illustrates the sequence of events that often leads to professional burnout. As burnout has become more recognized, certain related myths have surfaced.[27]

> *Myth 1: Burnout is just a newfangled notion that gives lazy people an excuse not to work.* Although *burnout* is a relatively new term, the behavior has been around

FIGURE 16.7   **The Path to Professional Burnout**

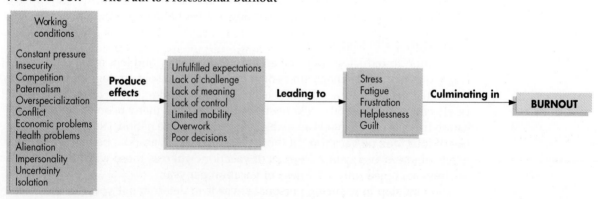

Source: Reprinted by permission from *State of Business Magazine*, "Helping Employees Cope with Burnout," by Donald P. Rogers, October–December 1984. Copyright © 1984 by the Robinson College of Business, Georgia State University, Atlanta.

FIGURE 16.8
Methods for Increasing Career Motivation

Sources: M. London and E. M. Moore, *Career Management and Survival in the Workplace* (San Francisco: Jossey-Bass, 1987), p. 5; and K. N. Wexley and J. Hinricks, eds., *Developing Human Resources* (Washington, DC: BNA Books, 1991), pp. 51–59.

1. Review your accomplishments and give yourself credit for them.
2. Take a moderate risk—one from which there will be some benefit.
3. Show others you can cooperate but that you also have your own ideas.
4. Inquire about how well you are doing.
5. Ask for information about career opportunities.
6. Set specific career goals for next year and general goals for the next five years.
7. Create your own job challenge by redesigning your job and generating new assignments.
8. If you want to be a leader, try it. Initiate and delegate work.
9. Take actions toward your goals.

for centuries. History abounds with examples of workers, such as writers, artists, and scientists, who gradually or suddenly stopped producing.

Myth 2: As long as people really enjoy their work, they can work as long and hard as they want and never experience burnout. Any work that inherently includes significant and continuing frustration, conflict, and pressure can lead to burnout.

Myth 3: Individuals know when they are burning out, and when they do, all they need to do is take off for a few days or weeks and then they will be as good as new. Unfortunately, most people do not realize that burnout is occurring until it reaches its later stages.

Myth 4: Individuals who are physically and psychologically strong are unlikely to experience burnout. Physically and psychologically strong individuals may indeed be able to work harder than less strong people. However, without proper stress skills, the inordinate amount of work can cause serious damage.

Myth 5: Job burnout is always job related. Burnout usually results from a combination of work, family, social, and personal factors.

Since chronic stress is one of the major causes of burnout, following the guidelines previously discussed for reducing workplace and personal stress should reduce burnout. A second step in reducing burnout is to identify those jobs with the highest potential for burnout. Certain jobs are more likely to lead to burnout than others. Once those jobs have been identified, several actions are possible. Some of the possibilities include redesigning the jobs, clarifying expectations, improving physical working conditions, and training the jobholders.

For top- and mid-level managers, a chief source of burnout is the "career plateau" (the point at which further promotion or advancement no longer seems possible). Studying career resilience, examining how one gains insight or learns about a career, and carefully matching individuals with their careers through career identity can dramatically reduce burnout. Figure 16.8 identifies several methods for increasing career motivation. Management Illustration 16.3 discusses one approach that some organizations are taking to help their employees avoid burnout.

Workaholism

workaholism
Working to the exclusion of everything else in one's life.

Workaholism is related to stress in that it can be a cause of stress. Workaholism is working to the exclusion of everything else in one's life.[28] It is an addiction that causes a person to become so obsessed with work that he or she is crippled emotionally and physically. Workaholics constantly think about work, work long hours, and often sacrifice sleep, food, exercise, family, and friends in favor of work.

More and more Americans are taking sabbaticals as a way of recharging themselves. Most sabbaticals allow the recipient to take time off with an appreciable pay cut while retaining benefits. The most common factor leading to the decision to take a sabbatical is burnout. Other factors include layoffs and the lingering effects of September 11, 2001.

According to New York–based Mercer Human Resource Consulting's 2000 Survey of Work/Life Initiatives, 15 percent of the 450 large employers surveyed offered paid sabbaticals, up from 11 percent in 1998. This same survey group reported that an additional 5 percent were considering adding sabbaticals to their benefits program. A similar 2000 survey by Hewitt Associates found that while only 6 percent of the 520 employers it polled offered sabbaticals, an additional 12 percent were considering offering such programs.

Source: Pamela Paul, "Time Out," *American Demographics,* June 2002, pp. 34–41.

One might think that having an organization full of workaholics would be desirable from the organization's viewpoint. However, a workaholic environment creates stress, burnout, and low morale. Also, workaholics are often not the most efficient employees because they frequently engage in doing unnecessary things.

Workplace Violence

Violence in the workplace has become a real concern. Consider the following facts: 2 million employees are victims of violence each year; one in six violent crimes in the United States occurs at work; and violence is the leading cause of death in the workplace.[29] Also, since the events of September 11, 2001, the threat of terrorism in the workplace has become a reality.

For many organizations, the danger from workplace violence comes not only from extreme violence, like shootings, but from nonfatal assaults, verbal threats, harassment and intimidation, sexual harassment, and other erratic behaviors suggesting emotional instability. Figure 16.9 shows the incidence of workplace violence found in a survey conducted by the Society for Human Resources Management (SHRM).

A poll of American employees found a significant lack of confidence in the ability of employers to successfully take precautions to prevent workplace violence.[30] The survey of 1,000 U.S. adults found that more than 25 percent believe their employers were ill-prepared to deal with workplace violence.

While there is no way to guarantee that an organization will not be victimized, the establishment of a workplace violence prevention program can greatly reduce the probability of a problem. A comprehensive workplace violence-prevention program should include the following elements:[31]

FIGURE 16.9
Violence Incidents in the Workplace

Source: "Safe, Not Sorry, Is the Best Approach," *HR Focus,* April 2000, pp. 51, 54.

Incidents	Percentage
Verbal threats	41
Pushing/shoving	19
Burglary/robbery	9
Fistfight	9
Stalking	9
Bomb threat	7
Shooting	1
Stabbing	1

- A written policy statement that communicates a clear commitment to promoting a workplace safe from violence, that prohibits threats and violence of every sort, and that requires employees to immediately report to management all circumstances that create a concern for safety from violence.

- A management response team that represents diverse segments of the organization, trained and charged with the responsibility of investigating and managing all reports of circumstances that raise a concern for an employee.

- A meaningful reporting and response mechanism that establishes clear lines of communication and responsibility for issues involving violence and ensures that the organization is both promptly notified of potential security risks and can take immediate steps to resolve underlying concerns.

- Clear standards of behavior that prohibit threats and violence of every sort and that require prompt, appropriate discipline of employees who breach safety rules.

- A wide array of other security, employment, legal, and administrative practices can help an organization prevent and manage on-site threats and violence. Such practices include a security inventory to assess the particular risks faced by the organization from violence; the development of security protocols to manage threats and violence; preemployment background checks; and the pursuit of legal remedies such as restraining orders (when needed) to guard against third-party threats.

- A system of periodic employee training addressing such issues as workplace policies; warning signs of violence; the requirement that employees report threats to management; methods for properly investigating complaints made under the workplace violence policy; defusing hostile situations; and strategies for addressing domestic violence.

Employee Assistance Programs (EAPs)

Many large organizations and a growing number of smaller ones are attempting to help employees with stress, burnout, and other personal problems that include not only alcohol and drug abuse but also depression, anxiety, domestic trauma, financial problems, and other psychiatric/medical problems. This help is not purely altruistic; it is based largely on cost savings. The help is generally offered in the form of an **employee assistance program (EAP).**

employee assistance program (EAP)
Program sponsored by the organization that attempts to help employees with stress, burnout, and other personal problems that include alcohol and drug abuse, depression, anxiety, domestic trauma, financial problems, and other psychiatric/medical problems.

A primary result of personal problems brought to the workplace is reduced productivity. A recent study published in the *Journal of the American Medical Association* reported that depression is a leading cause of lost productivity at work, costing employers $44 billion annually in lost time and medical treatment.[32] Absenteeism and tardiness also tend to increase with personal problems. Increased costs of insurance programs, including sickness and accident benefits, are a direct result of personal problems brought to the workplace. Lower morale, more friction among employees, more friction between supervisors and employees, and more grievances also result from troubled employees. Permanent loss of trained employees due to disability, retirement, and death is also associated with troubled employees. Frequently cited work-related stress problems that affect the employee's feeling of self-worth are lack of supervisor trust and respect, help disincentives (misdirected credit), conflict between job performance and reward, job communication, supervisor action or inaction, and job nonperformance (lack of control over job).[33] An intangible but very real cost associated with troubled employees is the loss of business and damaged public image.

Until recently, organizations attempted to avoid employees' problems that were not job related. Although aware of the existence of these problems, organizations did not believe they should interfere with employees' personal lives. In the past, organizations tended to get rid of troubled employees. In recent years, however, cost considerations, unions, and government legislation have altered this approach. The accepted viewpoint today is that employees' personal problems are private until they begin affecting their job performance. When and if that happens, personal problems become a matter of concern for the organization.

Studies have shown that absenteeism can be significantly reduced by employee assistance programs. EAPs have also been found to help reduce on-the-job accidents and grievances. Workers' compensation premiums, sickness and accident benefits, and trips to the infirmary also tend to decrease with an EAP.

Several types of employee assistance programs exist. In one type, which is rarely used, diagnosis and treatment of the problem are provided directly by the organization. In a second type of program, the organization hires a qualified person to diagnose the employee's problem; then the employee is referred to the proper agency or clinic for treatment. The third and most common type of program employs a coordinator who evaluates the employee's problem only sufficiently to make a referral to the proper agency or clinic for diagnosis. Sometimes the coordinator serves only as a consultant to the organization and is not a full-time employee. This type of program is especially popular with smaller employers and branch operations of large employers.

To be successful, an EAP must first be accepted by the employees; they must not be afraid to use it. Experience has shown that certain elements are critical to the success of an EAP. Figure 16.10 summarizes several of the most important characteristics of an EAP.

FIGURE 16.10
Ten Critical Elements of an EAP

Source: F. Dickman and W. G. Emener, "Employee Assistance Programs: Basic Concepts, Attributes, and an Evaluation," *Personnel Administrator,* August 1982, p. 56.

Element	Significance
Management backing	Without this at the highest level, key ingredients and overall effect are seriously limited.
Labor support	The EAP cannot be meaningful if it is not backed by the employees' labor unit.
Confidentiality	Anonymity and trust are crucial if employees are to use an EAP.
Easy access	For maximum use and benefit.
Supervisor training	Crucial to employees needing understanding and support during receipt of assistance.
Union steward training	A critical variable is employees' contact with the union—the steward.
Insurance involvement	Occasionally assistance alternatives are costly, and insurance support is a must.
Breadth of service components	Availability of assistance for a wide variety of problems (e.g., alcoholism, family, personal, financial, grief, medical).
Professional leadership	A skilled professional with expertise in helping who must have credibility in the eyes of the employee.
Follow-up and evaluation	To measure program effectiveness and overall improvement.

Toronto-based BMO Financial Group has its own in-house EAP. The program is a cornerstone of the company's holistic philosophy, which focuses on employee wellness and work-life balance. According to Rose Patten, executive vice president of human resources, many of BMO's supporting programs such as short paid leaves of absences, flextime, job sharing, and working from the home have grown out of the EAP.

Currently, more than a quarter of BMO's 34,000 employees have used the EAP, which provides counseling, information, and referral; child and eldercare advice and resources; trauma response and intervention; managers' support and training; and education, workshops, and programs on a variety of wellness, lifestyle, and work topics.

Of employees who have used the EAP, 62 percent reported that without the service, they would have had to take time off from work. According to Patten, "we correlate our EAP with higher productivity and reduced absenteeism as well as our ability to attract and retain workers."

Source: Maryann Hammers, "Banking on an In-House EAP," *Workforce*, April 2003, p. 18.

The Internet is increasingly becoming a fast and convenient way to link employees with an EAP. In addition to being convenient, some people feel more at ease confiding in their computer than talking directly to an EAP specialist. Management Illustration 16.4 discusses how one company is successfully utilizing an in-house EAP.

Wellness Programs

wellness program
Company-implemented program designed to prevent illness and enhance employee well-being.

In addition to the EAPs discussed in the previous section, many companies have installed programs designed to prevent illness and enhance employee well-being. These programs are referred to as **wellness programs** and include such things as periodic medical exams, stop-smoking clinics, education on improved dietary practices, hypertension detection and control, weight control, exercise and fitness, stress management, accident-risk reduction, immunizations, and cardiopulmonary resuscitation (CPR) training. Some of the documented results of wellness programs include fewer sick days, reduced coronary heart disease, and lower major medical costs. Many also believe that employee productivity increases for employees who participate in exercise and fitness programs. Numerous studies have reported a very attractive return on investment for most types of wellness programs.[34] Experts in the wellness field report that even small companies can offer wellness programs and that such programs do not have to be expensive.

One example of the many organizations now adopting wellness programs is Adolph Coors Company. Coors claims that its 25,000-square-foot wellness facility, designed for employees and their spouses, has helped the company save more than $2 million annually in medical claims and other health-related factors. The Coors program is designed around a six-step behavioral change model: awareness, education, incentives, programs, self-education, and follow-up and support. Chief among the elements that are critical for successful wellness programs are CEO support and direction, accessibility, inclusion of family, needs assessment, staffing with specialists, and establishment of a separate budget for wellness activities.[35]

Summary

1. *Define conflict.* Conflict is overt behavior that results when an individual or a group of individuals think a perceived need or needs of the individual or group has been blocked or is about to be blocked.

2. *Discuss the useful effects of conflict.* Some potentially useful effects of conflict are that it energizes people; is a form of communication; often provides an outlet for pent-up tensions, resulting in catharsis; and may actually be an educational experience.

3. *Outline the stages of conflict development.* The stages of conflict development are latent conflict, perceived conflict, felt conflict, manifest conflict, and conflict aftermath.

4. *Name the five major types of conflict based on the entities involved.* The five major types of conflict based on the entities involved are intrapersonal, interpersonal, intergroup, organizational, and political.

5. *Name five approaches for resolving interpersonal conflict.* There are five general approaches for resolving interpersonal conflict: (1) compromising for the sake of ending the conflict; (2) smoothing over the conflict and pretending it does not exist; (3) withdrawal of one or more of the participants; (4) forcing the conflict to a conclusion through third-party intervention; and (5) forcing a confrontation between the participants in an effort to solve the underlying source of conflict.

6. *Name and briefly discuss one method of positively managing conflicts created by diversity in the workplace.* One method for positively managing conflicts created by diversity in the workplace is organizational diplomacy. Organizational diplomacy is based on a proactive, unifying approach to diversity, as opposed to a reactive and superficial approach.

7. *Define stress.* Stress is the mental or physical condition that results from a perceived threat of danger (physical or emotional) and the pressure to remove it.

8. *Define burnout.* Burnout is a condition that occurs when work is no longer meaningful to a person.

9. *Outline the basic elements of a violence-prevention program.* The basic elements of a comprehensive violence-prevention program are a written policy statement communicating a clear commitment to promoting a workplace safe from violence; a management response team; a meaningful reporting and response mechanism; clear standards of behavior; a wide array of other security, employment, legal, and administrative practices; and a system of periodic employee training covering violence-prevention issues.

10. *Explain the three basic types of employee assistance programs.* In one type of EAP, diagnosis and treatment of the problem are provided directly by the organization. In a second type, the organization hires a qualified person to diagnose the employee's problem and then refers the employee to a proper agency or clinic for treatment. The third and most common type employs a coordinator who evaluates the employee's problem only sufficiently to make a referral to the proper agency or clinic for diagnosis.

11. *Explain wellness programs.* Wellness programs are company-implemented programs designed to prevent illness and enhance employee well-being.

Review Questions

1. What is conflict?
2. Describe some potentially useful effects of conflict.
3. Identify the five stages of conflict.
4. What causes intrapersonal conflict?
5. What are some typical defense mechanisms used when an individual is frustrated?
6. What are some causes of interpersonal conflict?
7. Name at least four types of intergroup conflict.
8. What is organizational conflict?
9. What is political conflict?
10. What are some methods that can be used to resolve interpersonal conflict?
11. Outline some key questions that need to be answered in conflict resolution.
12. What is organizational diplomacy?
13. Name several ways that stress can manifest itself in the workplace.

14. What is a workplace stress audit?
15. List several actions an organization can take to reduce job-related stress of its employees.
16. What is burnout?
17. What is workaholism?
18. What is a workplace violence-prevention program?
19. What are three basic types of employee assistance programs?
20. What is a wellness program?

Skill-Building Questions

1. Should managers attempt to avoid conflict at all times? Explain.
2. "Conflict is inevitable." Do you agree or disagree with this statement? Discuss.
3. How can managers reduce destructive stress in organizations?
4. How would you handle a situation in which you have two people working for you who "just rub each other the wrong way"?
5. Examine your personal situation and identify some ways that you might reduce stress in your day-to-day activities.

Skill-Building Exercise 16.1

Self-Evaluation: The Glazer Stress Control Lifestyle Questionnaire

As you can see, each scale below is composed of a pair of adjectives or phrases separated by a series of horizontal lines. Each pair has been chosen to represent two contrasting behaviors. Each of us belongs somewhere along the line between the two extremes. Since most of us are neither the most competitive nor the least competitive person we know, put a check mark where you think you belong between the two extremes.

	1	2	3	4	5	6	7	
1. Doesn't mind leaving things temporarily unfinished	—	—	—	—	—	—	—	Must get things finished once started
2. Calm and unhurried about appointments	—	—	—	—	—	—	—	Never late for appointments
3. Not competitive	—	—	—	—	—	—	—	Highly competitive
4. Listens well, lets others finish speaking	—	—	—	—	—	—	—	Anticipates others in conversation (nods, interrupts, finishes sentences for the other)
5. Never in a hurry, even when pressured	—	—	—	—	—	—	—	Always in a hurry
6. Able to wait calmly	—	—	—	—	—	—	—	Uneasy when waiting
7. Easygoing	—	—	—	—	—	—	—	Always going full speed ahead
8. Takes one thing at a time	—	—	—	—	—	—	—	Tries to do more than one thing at a time; thinks about what to do next
9. Slow and deliberate in speech	—	—	—	—	—	—	—	Vigorous and forceful in speech (uses a lot of gestures)
10. Concerned with satisfying himself or herself, not others	—	—	—	—	—	—	—	Wants recognition by others for a job well done
11. Slow doing things	—	—	—	—	—	—	—	Fast doing things (eating, walking, etc.)
12. Easygoing	—	—	—	—	—	—	—	Hard driving

	1	2	3	4	5	6	7	
13. Expresses feelings openly	___	___	___	___	___	___	___	Holds feelings in
14. Has a large number of interests	___	___	___	___	___	___	___	Few interests outside work
15. Satisfied with job	___	___	___	___	___	___	___	Ambitious; wants quick advancement on job
16. Never sets own deadlines	___	___	___	___	___	___	___	Often sets own deadlines
17. Feels limited responsibility	___	___	___	___	___	___	___	Always feels responsible
18. Never judges things in terms of numbers	___	___	___	___	___	___	___	Often judges performance in terms of numbers (how much, how many)
19. Casual about work	___	___	___	___	___	___	___	Takes work very seriously (works weekends, brings work home)
20. Not very precise	___	___	___	___	___	___	___	Very precise (careful about detail)

Source: Unknown to the authors.

Scoring

Assign a value from 1 to 7 for each score. Total them. The categories are as follows:

Total Score	Type	Explanation
110–140:	A_1	If you are in this category, and especially if you are over 40 and smoke, you are likely to have a high risk of developing cardiac illness.
80–109:	A_2	You are in the direction of being cardiac prone, but your risk is not as high as the A_1. You should, nevertheless, pay careful attention to the advice given to all type As.
60–79:	AB	You are an admixture of A and B patterns. This is a healthier pattern than either A_1 or A_2, but you have the potential for slipping into A behavior and you should recognize this.
30–59:	B_2	Your behavior is on the less-cardiac-prone end of the spectrum. You are generally relaxed and cope adequately with stress.
0–29:	B_1	You tend to the extreme of noncardiac traits. Your behavior expresses few of the reactions associated with cardiac disease.

Skill-Building Exercise 16.2

Social Readjustment Rating Scale

Everybody is confronted by both major and minor changes in the workplace and in their private lives. Some of these changes are predictable and some are not; some can be controlled and others cannot. The following list contains 43 life events. Please record the frequency with which you have confronted each of these within the past 12 months.

Life Events	Life Change Units		Number of Events in Past 12 Months		Total
Death of spouse	100	×	___	=	___
Divorce	73	×	___	=	___
Marital separation	65	×	___	=	___
Jail term	63	×	___	=	___
Death of close family member	63	×	___	=	___
Personal injury or illness	53	×	___	=	___
Marriage	50	×	___	=	___

Life Events	Life Change Units		Number of Events in Past 12 Months		Total
Fired at work	47	×	_____	=	_____
Marital reconciliation	45	×	_____	=	_____
Retirement	45	×	_____	=	_____
Change in health of family member	44	×	_____	=	_____
Pregnancy	40	×	_____	=	_____
Sex difficulties	39	×	_____	=	_____
Gain of new family member	39	×	_____	=	_____
Business readjustment	39	×	_____	=	_____
Change in financial state	38	×	_____	=	_____
Death of a close friend	37	×	_____	=	_____
Change to different line of work	36	×	_____	=	_____
Change in number of arguments with spouse	35	×	_____	=	_____
Mortgage over $100,000*	31	×	_____	=	_____
Foreclosure of mortgage or loan	30	×	_____	=	_____
Change in responsibility at work	29	×	_____	=	_____
Son or daughter leaving home	29	×	_____	=	_____
Trouble with in-laws	29	×	_____	=	_____
Outstanding personal achievement	28	×	_____	=	_____
Spouse begins or stops work	26	×	_____	=	_____
Begin or end school	26	×	_____	=	_____
Change in living conditions	25	×	_____	=	_____
Revision of personal habits	24	×	_____	=	_____
Trouble with boss	23	×	_____	=	_____
Change in work hours or conditions	20	×	_____	=	_____
Change in residence	20	×	_____	=	_____
Change in schools	20	×	_____	=	_____
Change in recreation	19	×	_____	=	_____
Change in church activities	19	×	_____	=	_____
Change in social activities	18	×	_____	=	_____
Mortgage or loan less than $100,000*	17	×	_____	=	_____
Change in sleeping habits	16	×	_____	=	_____
Change in number of family get-togethers	15	×	_____	=	_____
Change in eating habits	15	×	_____	=	_____
Vacation	13	×	_____	=	_____
Christmas or High Holy Days	12	×	_____	=	_____
Minor violations of the law	11	×	_____	=	_____
Life change units total				=	_____

*Figures adjusted by authors to reflect inflation.
Source: Reprinted from *Journal of Psychosomatic Research*, Vol. 11, by T. H. Holmes and R. H. Rahe, "The Social Readjustment Rating Scale." Copyright © 1967, with permission of Elsevier.

After you have gone through the list, compute your score by multiplying the assigned points times the number of times a specific event has occurred and summing the totals. Use the following information to interpret your score:

Score	More Susceptible to Illness Than Following Percentage of General Population
350–400	90%
300–349	80%
200–299	50%
150–199	37%
Up to 150	Low stress level

If your total score is under 150, your level of stress, based on life change, is low. If your score is between 150 and 300, your stress levels are borderline—you should minimize other changes in your life at this time. If your score is over 300, your life change level of stress is high—you should not only minimize any other changes in your life and work but should strive to practice some stress intervention techniques.

Case Incident 16.1

The Young College Graduate and the Old Superintendent

You are a consultant to the manager of a garment manufacturing plant in a small southern town. The manager has been having trouble with two employees: Ralph, the plant superintendent, and Kevin, the production scheduler. Ralph is 53 years old and has been with the company since he was released from military duty after World War II. He started in the warehouse with a sixth-grade education and worked his way up through the ranks. Until recently, Ralph handled—along with his many other duties—the production scheduling function. He was proud of the fact that he could handle it all "in my head." As the volume of production and the number of different products grew, however, the plant manager thought significant savings could be attained through a more sophisticated approach to scheduling. He believed he could save on raw materials by purchasing in larger quantities and on production setup time by making longer runs. He also wanted to cut down on the frequency of finished-goods stock-outs; when backlogs did occur, he wanted to be able to give customers more definite information as to when goods would be available. He wanted to have a planned schedule for at least two months into the future, with daily updates.

Kevin is 24 years old and grew up in the Chicago area. This is his first full-time job. He earned a master of science degree in industrial engineering from an eastern engineering school. He jumped right into the job and set up a computer-assisted scheduling system, using a time-sharing service with a teletype terminal in his office. The system is based on the latest production scheduling and inventory control technology. It is very flexible and has proven to be quite effective in all areas that were of interest to the plant manager.

Plant manager: Sometimes I just want to shoot both Ralph and Kevin. If those two could just get along with each other, this plant would run like a well-oiled machine.

Consultant: What do they fight about?

Manager: Anything and everything that has to do with the production schedule. Really trivial things in a lot of cases. It all seems so completely senseless!

Consultant: Have you tried to do anything about it?

Manager: At first, I tried to minimize the impact of their feuds on the rest of the plant by stepping in and making decisions that would eliminate the point of controversy. I also tried to smooth things over as if the arguments were just friendly disagreements. I thought that after they had a chance to get accustomed to each other, the problem would go away. But it didn't. It got to the point that I was spending a good 20 percent of my time stopping their fights. Furthermore, I began to notice that other employees were starting to take sides. The younger people seemed to support Kevin; everybody else sided with Ralph. It began to look as if we might have our own little war.

Consultant: What's the current situation?

Manager: I finally told them both that if I caught them fighting again, I would take very drastic action with both of them. I think that move was a mistake though, because now they won't even talk to each other. Kevin just drops the schedule printouts on Ralph's desk every afternoon and walks away. Ralph needs some help in working with those printouts, and Kevin needs some feedback on what's actually going on in the plant. Frankly, things aren't going as well production-wise now as when they were at each other's throats. And the tension in the plant as a whole is even worse. They are both good people and outstanding in their respective jobs. I would really hate to lose either of them, but if they can't work together, I may have to let one or both of them go.

Questions

1. Why is this conflict occurring?
2. What method did the manager use in dealing with this conflict situation? Was it effective?
3. Recommend an approach for resolving the conflict.

Case Incident 16.2

Problems at the Hospital

Smith County is a suburban area near a major midwestern city. The county has experienced such a tremendous rate of growth during the past decade that local governments have had difficulty providing adequate service to the citizens.

Smith County Hospital has a reputation for being a first-class facility, but it is inadequate to meet local needs. During certain periods of the year, the occupancy rates exceed the licensed capacity. There is no doubt in anyone's mind that the hospital must be expanded immediately.

At a recent meeting of the Hospital Authority, the hospital administrator, Kaye Austin, presented the group with a proposal to accept the architectural plans of the firm of Watkins and Gibson. This plan calls for a 100-bed addition adjacent to the existing structure. Kaye announced that after reviewing several alternative plans, she believed the Watkins and Gibson plan would provide the most benefit for the expenditure.

At this point, Randolph (Randy) Lewis, the board chairperson, began questioning the plan. Randy made it clear he would not go along with the Watkins and Gibson plan. He stated that the board should look for other firms to serve as the architects for the project.

The ensuing argument became somewhat heated, and a 10-minute recess was called to allow those attending to get coffee as well as allow tempers to calm down. Kaye was talking to John Rhodes, another member of the Hospital Authority board, in the hall and said, "Randy seems to fight me on every project."

Randy, who was talking to other members of the board, was saying, "I know that the Watkins and Gibson plan is good, but I just can't stand for Kaye to act like it's her plan. I wish she would leave so we could get a good administrator from the community whom we can identify with."

Questions

1. Is Randy's reaction uncommon? Explain.
2. What type of conflict exists between Kaye and Randy?
3. What methods would you use to reduce or resolve the conflict?
4. Could Kaye have done anything in advance of the meeting to maximize her chances of success? Explain.

References and Additional Readings

1. William Cottringer, "Conflict Management," *Executive Excellence*, August 1997, p. 6.
2. See Kenneth Thomas, "Conflict and Conflict Management," in *Handbook of Industrial and Organizational Psychology*, ed. Marvin D. Dunnette (New York: John Wiley & Sons, 1983).
3. Robert L. Kahn, "Role Conflict and Ambiguity in Organizations," *Personnel Administrator*, March–April 1964, pp. 8–13.
4. Steven Kerr, "On the Folly of Rewarding A, while Hoping for B," *Academy of Management Journal* 18 (1975), pp. 769–83.

5. P. R. Lawrence and J. W. Lorsch, *Organization and Environment* (Boston: Harvard Business School, Division of Research, 1967).

6. For more information, see Dean Tjosvold, Valerie Dann, and Choy Wong, "Managing Conflict between Departments to Serve Customers," *Human Relations*, October 1992, pp. 1035–54.

7. Julie Olson-Buchanan, Fritz Drasgow, Philip J. Moberg, Alan D. Mead, et al., "Interactive Video Assessment of Conflict Resolution Skills," *Personnel Psychology*, Spring 1998, pp. 1–24.

8. See also Philip B. DuBose and Charles D. Pringle, "Choosing a Conflict Management Technique," *Supervision*, June 1989, pp. 10–12.

9. R. M. Bramson, *Coping with Difficult People* (New York: Dell, 1981).

10. See also Evert Van de Vliert and Boris Kabanoff, "Toward Theory-Based Measures of Conflict Management," *Academy of Management Journal*, March 1990, pp. 199–209.

11. See also, Kenneth Thomas, "Conflict and Conflict Management: Reflections and Update," *Journal of Organizational Behavior*, May 1992, pp. 263–74.

12. Much of this section is drawn from Jacqueline A. Gilbert and John M. Ivancevich, "Organizational Diplomacy: The Bridge for Managing Diversity," *Human Resource Planning* 22, no. 3 (1999), pp. 29–39.

13. William Atkinson, "Helping Employees Deal with Stress," *Bulletin, Northwest Public Power Association*, April 2003, p. 19.

14. John Townsend, "Get Tough with Stress," *New Zealand Management*, August 2001, pp. 24–25.

15. Atkinson, "Helping Employees Deal with Stress."

16. "Is Job Stress Taking Its Toll in Your Facility?" *Safety Management*, February 2003, pp. 3–5.

17. Terry Schraeder, "Battling Workplace Stress," *PIM's Papermaker*, June 2001, p. 30.

18. "How to Reduce Workplace Stress," *Worklife Report* 10, no. 3 (1997), pp. 4–5.

19. Victoria J. Doby and Robert D. Caplan, "Organizational Stress as Threat to Reputation: Effects on Anxiety at Work and Home," *Academy of Management Journal* 38, no. 4 (1995), pp. 1105–23.

20. "Workplace Stress Equals Health Distress," *Worklife Report* 11, no. 1 (1997), p. 10.

21. Jia Lin Xie and Gary Johns, "Job Scope and Stress: Can Job Scope Be Too High?" *Academy of Management Journal* 38, no. 5 (1995), pp. 1288–1309.

22. "How to Reduce Workplace Stress."

23. Much of this section is drawn from Cecilia MacDonald, "Frayed to the Breaking Point," *Credit Union Management*, June 1996, pp. 30–31.

24. Ibid.

25. Ibid.

26. C. Maslach, *Burnout—The Cost of Caring* (Englewood Cliffs, NJ: Prentice Hall, 1982).

27. Michael E. Cavanagh, "What You Don't Know about Stress," *Personnel Journal*, July 1988, pp. 56–57.

28. Much of this section is drawn from Kathryn Tyler, "Spinning Wheels," *HR Magazine*, September 1999, pp. 34–40.

29. Mary Beth Matzek, "Safety, Prevention Important in Workplace Violence," *Knight Ridder Tribune Business News*, September 24, 2002, p. 1.

30. Virginia Foran, "Employees Concerned about Workplace Violence," *Occupational Hazards*, September 2001, p. 27.

31. Rebecca A. Speer, "Can Workplace Violence Be Prevented?" *Occupational Hazards*, August 1998, pp. 26–30.

32. Fonda Phillps, "Employee Assistance Programs: A New Way to Control Health Care Costs," *Employee Benefit Plan Review*, August 2003, pp. 22–24.

33. H. Richard Priesmeyer, *Organization and Chaos* (Westport, CT: Quorum Books, 1992), pp. 164–65.

34. For example, see Fred W. Schott and Sandra Wendel, "Wellness with a Track Record," *Personnel Journal*, April 1992, pp. 98–104.

35. Shari Caudron and Michael Rozek, "The Wellness Payoff," *Personnel Journal*, July 1990, pp. 54–62, as described in John M. Ivancevich, *Human Resource Management* (Burr Ridge, IL: Richard D. Irwin, 1995), pp. 636–37.

17

Managing Change and Culture

Learning Objectives

After studying this chapter, you will be able to:

1. Identify the three major categories of organizational change.
2. List the three steps in Lewin's model for change.
3. Discuss several reasons employees resist change.
4. Identify several prescriptions for reducing resistance to change.
5. Describe an approach that managers can use to lead change.
6. Summarize the four phases of an organizational development (OD) program.
7. Briefly describe the four essential principles that organizations must follow to manage innovation.
8. Explain what a learning organization is.
9. Define corporate culture.
10. Describe the generic types of organizational culture.
11. Identify two common sources of organizational subcultures.

Chapter Preview

Few industries have experienced more change in recent years than men's clothing. In the last decade, men have spent less and less on tailored wear, and as a result, many men's stores have faced financial difficulty and even bankruptcy. Men's Warehouse has fared well in these turbulent times largely due to its management approach. "We know that the only constant is change," said Eric Anderson, Men's Warehouse's director of training. The company believes that its key to managing change and its success is its relationship with its employees. "We have said for a long time that we are in the people business, not the men's clothing business. We happen to sell men's clothing, but by recognizing what is really important—the people—we have a different paradigm than many other businesses." Following this philosophy, the company invests extensively in its employees' abilities. According to Anderson, "We try to recognize and nurture the potential in people. Because we are in the people business, training permeates our company culture."

The company believes that its extensive training is one of the major factors that prepares its workforce for the constantly changing markets it faces.

Source: Victor D. Infante, "Men's Warehouse: Tailored for Any Change That Retail Brings," *Workforce,* March 2001, pp. 48–49.

Analyzing Management Skills

Do you believe that most organizations do a good job of preparing their employees for change? What are some specific things that managers can do to better prepare their employees for change?

Applying Management Skills

Pick a specific industry of interest to you. How was this industry affected by the tragic events of September 11, 2001? How has the industry responded to the changes brought about by these events?

In his book *Thriving on Chaos,* Tom Peters stresses the importance of change to the modern corporation: "To up the odds of survival, leaders at all levels must become obsessive about change." He adds, "Change must become the norm, not cause for alarm."[1] What does *change* mean from his perspective? Simply put, it means that unless managers have changed something, they have not earned their paychecks. This bold view is somewhat foreign to many organizations today.

Today, managing change and dealing with its impact on the corporate culture are essential skills that the manager must master if the organization is to compete globally. Furthermore, the manager must learn these skills rapidly, since change is occurring at an ever-increasing rate. The new bottom line for the twenty-first century will be to assess each and every action in light of its contribution to an increased corporate capacity for change.

An organization's affinity for change and its corporate culture are intrinsically intertwined; each affects the other. It is because of this interdependency that both of these topics are discussed in this chapter.

Managing Change

Organizations today are beset by change. Many managers find themselves unable to cope with an environment or an organization that has become substantially different from the one in which they received their training and gained their early experience. Other managers have trouble transferring their skills to a new assignment in a different industry. A growing organization, a new assignment, changing customer needs, changing employee expectations, and changing competition may all be encountered by today's managers. To be successful, managers must be able to adapt to these changes.

Change as a Global Issue

One of the driving pressures for change is the desire to compete globally. Since America's global trading partners (notably Japan, China, and Europe) have

FIGURE 17.1
Types of Changes
Affecting
Organizations

Technological	Environmental	Internal
Machines	Laws	Policies
Equipment	Taxes	Procedures
Processes	Social trends	New methods
Automation	Fashion trends	Rules
Computers	Political trends	Reorganization
New raw materials	Economic trends	Budget adjustment
Robots	Interest rates	Restructuring of jobs
	Consumer trends	Personnel
	Competition	Management
	Suppliers	Ownership
	Population trends	Products/services sold

adopted change as an essential ingredient of their long-term strategies, corporate America must follow suit. When asked about change in the international environment, Eric A. Cronson, vice president and managing director of Thomas Group Europe, commented, "Change has to be radical—if you stay in your comfort zone, you will not be internationally competitive."[2] Similarly, Joseph V. Marulli, president of information services at Eunetcom, commented at an international conference on change, "Transformation has to be in the leader's heart, in your heart, and in the hearts of all the senior people."[3] From comments such as these, the manager must understand that the challenge to compete is really the challenge to change.

Types of Change

technological changes
Changes in such things as new equipment and new processes.

environmental changes
All nontechnological changes that occur outside the organization.

internal changes
Budget adjustments, policy changes, personnel changes, and the like.

Change as it applies to organizations can be classified into three major categories: (1) technological, (2) environmental, and (3) internal to the organization. **Technological changes** include such things as new equipment and new processes. The technological advances since World War II have been dramatic, with computers and increased speed of communication being the most notable. **Environmental changes** are all the nontechnological changes that occur outside the organization. New government regulations, new social trends, and economic changes are all examples of environmental change. An organization's **internal changes** include such things as budget adjustments, policy changes, diversity adjustments, and personnel changes. Figure 17.1 lists several examples of each major type of change affecting today's organizations.

Any of the three types of changes can greatly affect a manager's job. Both technological and environmental changes occur outside an organization and can create the need for internal change. Internal change can also occur because of performance issues (such as conflict, quality, lack of productivity, and so forth) or as a result of regular self-assessment as part of the strategic management process.

Any of the three types of change can create the need for unplanned change or planned change. Since managers can control planned change, they should be periodically analyzing what changes are necessary. Thus, by being proactive rather than reactive, managers can have much more control over the change process.

The Change Process

As first discussed in the late 1940s by social psychologist Kurt Lewin, change is a function of the forces that support or promote the change and those forces that oppose or resist the change (Lewin referred to this approach as *force field analysis*).

One of Kurt Lewin's most significant examples of his theory at work occurred as a result of a commission from the U.S. government to develop a program to change the eating habits of American families during World War II. To help the war effort, the government was encouraging families, and especially housewives, to buy more of the visceral organs and less of the more normal muscle cuts of beef. The government attempted to explain the facts and logically tell the housewives why it was necessary to support this program—patriotism, economy, and nutrition. However, the government underestimated the restraining forces; people were simply not used to preparing or eating tongue, heart, and lungs. As a result, the housewives resisted the change until Lewin came in and developed a program to counteract the restraining forces. The cornerstone of the program was a grassroots campaign that organized discussion groups throughout the country where housewives could meet and discuss the issue. Once housewives actually got involved with the nature of the problem, they gradually broadened their thinking and came to understand how their change of diet could help the war effort. The result was that they did change their buying habits.

Source: Stephen Covey, "Work It Out Together," *Incentive*, April 1997, p. 26.

Change forces introduce something different about the organization over time. Resistance forces support the status quo, or keeping things as they are. The sum total of these forces determines the extent to which a change will be successfully implemented.

Lewin's Three-Step Model for Change

Lewin developed a three-step model for successfully implementing change:

1. Lewin's first step, *unfreezing*, deals with breaking down the forces supporting or maintaining the old behavior. These forces can include such variables as the formal reward system, reinforcement from the work group, and the individual's perception of what is proper role behavior.

2. The second step, *presenting a new alternative*, involves offering a clear and attractive option representing new patterns of behavior.

3. The third step, *refreezing*, requires that the change behavior be reinforced by the formal and informal reward systems and by the work group. It is in this step that the manager can play a pivotal role by positively reinforcing employee efforts to change.

Implicit in Lewin's three-step model is the recognition that the mere introduction of change does not ensure the elimination of the prechange conditions or that the change will be permanent. Unsuccessful attempts to implement lasting change can usually be traced to a failure in one of Lewin's three steps. Management Illustration 17.1 describes one of Lewin's early applications of his theory.

Resistance to Change

Most people profess to be modern and up to date. However, their first reaction is usually to resist change. This is most often true when the change affects their jobs. Resistance to change is a natural, normal reaction; it is not a reaction observed only in troublemakers. For example, most employees are apprehensive when there is a change in their immediate manager. It is usually not that the employees dislike the new manager but rather that they don't know what he or she will be like. All change requires adjustment; in fact, the adjustment may concern employees more than the actual change.

Resistance to change may be very open, or it may be very subtle. The employee who quits a job because of a change in company policy is showing resistance to change in an open and explicit manner. For example, two of the original founders left Manugistics, a software and services company based in Maryland, when the company decided to go global.[4] Other employees who stay but become sullen are resisting in a more passive manner.

Because organizations are composed of individuals, often there is organizational resistance to change. Organizational resistance to change occurs when the organization, as an entity, appears to resist change. For example, obsolete products or services and inappropriate organization structure are often the result of organizational resistance to change.

Reasons for Resisting Change

Employees resist change for many reasons. Some of the most frequent reasons are as follows.

1. *Fear of the unknown.* It is natural human behavior to fear the unknown. With many changes, the outcome is not foreseeable. When it is, the results are often not made known to all of the affected employees. For example, employees may worry about and resist a new computer if they are not sure what its impact will be on their jobs. Similarly, employees may resist a new manager simply because they don't know what to expect. A related fear is the uncertainty employees may feel about working in a changed environment. They may fully understand the change yet really doubt whether they will be able to handle it. For example, an employee may resist a change in procedure because of a fear of being unable to master it.

2. *Economics.* Employees fear any change they think threatens their jobs or incomes. The threat may be real or only imagined. In either case, the result is resistance. For example, a salesperson who believes a territory change will result in less income will resist the change. Similarly, production workers will oppose new standards they believe will be harder to achieve.

3. *Fear that skills and expertise will lose value.* Everyone likes to feel valued by others, and anything that has the potential to reduce that value will be resisted. For example, an operations manager may resist implementation of a new, more modern piece of equipment for fear the change will make him or her less needed by the organization.

4. *Threats to power.* Many employees, and especially managers, believe a change may diminish their power. For example, a manager may perceive a change to the organization's structure as weakening his or her power within the organization.

5. *Additional work and inconvenience.* Almost all changes involve work, and many result in personal inconveniences to the affected employees. If nothing else, they often have to learn new ways. This may mean more training, school, or practice. A common reaction by employees is that "it isn't worth the extra effort required."

6. *Threats to interpersonal relations.* The social and interpersonal relationships among employees can be quite strong. These relationships may appear unimportant to everyone but those involved. For example, eating lunch with a particular group may be very important to the involved employees. When a change, such as a transfer, threatens these relationships, the affected employees often resist. Employees naturally feel more at ease when working with people they know well. Also, the group may have devised methods for doing the work

based on the strengths and weaknesses of group members. Any changes in the group would naturally disrupt the routine.

Reducing Resistance to Change

As discussed previously, most employees' first reaction to change is resistance. However, how employees perceive the change's impact greatly affects their reaction to the change. While many variations are possible, four basic situations usually occur:

1. If employees cannot foresee how the change will affect them, they will resist the change or be neutral at best. Most people shy away from the unknown, believing that change may make things worse.
2. If employees perceive that the change does not fit their needs and hopes, they will resist the change. In this instance, employees are convinced the change will make things worse.
3. If employees see that the change is inevitable, they may first resist and then resign themselves to the change. The first reaction is to resist. Once the change appears imminent, employees often see no other choice but to go along with it.
4. If employees view the change as being in their best interests, they will be motivated to make the change work. The key here is for the employees to feel sure the change will make things better. Three out of four of these situations result in some form of resistance to change. Also, the way in which employees resist change can vary greatly. For example, an employee may not actively resist a change but may never actively support it. Similarly, an employee may mildly resist by acting uninterested in the change. At the other extreme, an employee may resist by trying to sabotage the change.

Figure 17.2 summarizes how employees might respond to change.

FIGURE 17.2
Employee Response Model

Source: Waldron Berry, "Overcoming Resistance to Change," *Supervisory Management*, February 1983.

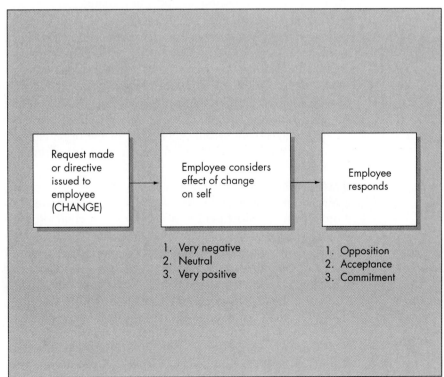

Before a manager can reduce resistance to a change, she or he must try to determine how the employees will react to the change. The following steps are recommended before issuing a change directive.

1. Determine the response needed from the employee to accomplish the task effectively.
2. Estimate the expected response if the directive is simply published or orally passed to the employee (as many are).
3. If a discrepancy exists between the needed response and the estimated response, determine how the two responses can be reconciled (opposition is never an acceptable response).[5]

The following paragraphs present several suggestions for reducing resistance to change and helping employees to accept and even commit themselves to change.

Build Trust   If employees trust and have confidence in management, they are much more likely to accept change. If an air of distrust prevails, change is likely to be strongly resisted. Management's day-to-day and long-term actions determine the degree of trust among employees. Managers can go a long way toward building trust if they discuss upcoming changes with employees and actively involve employees in the change process.

Discuss Upcoming Changes   Fear of the unknown is one of the major barriers to change. This fear can be greatly reduced by discussing any upcoming changes with the affected employees. During this discussion, the manager should be as open and honest as possible. The manager should explain not only what the change will be but also why the change is being made. The manager should also outline the impact of the change on each affected employee. Figure 17.3 presents a classical approach to change resistance that can help a manager who is attempting to explain and discuss an upcoming change.

Involve the Employees   Involving employees means more than merely discussing the upcoming changes with them. The key is to involve employees personally in the entire change process. It is natural for employees to want to go along with a change they have helped devise and implement. A good approach is to ask for employees' ideas and input as early as possible in the change process.

Make Sure the Changes Are Reasonable   The manager should always do everything possible to ensure that any proposed changes are reasonable. Often proposals for changes come from other parts of the organization. These proposals are sometimes not reasonable because the originator is unaware of all the pertinent circumstances.

Avoid Threats   The manager who attempts to force change through the use of threats is taking a negative approach. This is likely to decrease rather than increase employee trust. Most people resist threats or coercion. Such tactics also usually have a negative impact on employee morale.

Follow a Sensible Time Schedule   A manager can often influence the timing of changes. Some times are doubtless better than others for making certain changes. If nothing else, the manager should always use common sense when proposing a time schedule for implementing a change.

Most of the above suggestions for reducing resistance to change relate to the manner in which management communicates a change. It is often not the change itself that determines its acceptability but rather the manner in which the change is implemented. The importance of the manager's role in this process was rein-

FIGURE 17.3   Methods of Overcoming Resistance to Change

Approach	Commonly Used in Situations	Advantages	Drawbacks
Education + communication	Where there is a lack of information or inaccurate information and analysis.	Once persuaded, people will often help with the implementation of the change.	Can be time-consuming if lots of people are involved.
Participation + involvement	Where the initiators do not have all the information they need to design the change, and where others have considerable power to resist.	People who participate will be committed to implementing change, and any relevant information they have will be integrated into the change plan.	Can be time-consuming if participators design an inappropriate change.
Facilitation + support	Where people are resisting because of adjustment problems.	No other approach works as well with adjustment problems.	Can be time-consuming and expensive and still fail.
Negotiation + agreement	Where someone or some group will clearly lose out in a change, and where that group has considerable power to resist.	Sometimes it is a relatively easy way to avoid major resistance.	Can be too expensive in many cases if it alerts others to negotiate for compliance.
Manipulation + co-optation	Where other tactics will not work or are too expensive.	It can be a relatively quick and inexpensive solution to resistance problems.	Can lead to future problems if people feel manipulated.
Explicit + implicit coercion	Where speed is essential and the change initiators possess considerable power.	It is speedy and can overcome any kind of resistance.	Can be risky if it leaves people mad at the initiators.

Source: Reprinted by permission of *Harvard Business Review,* Exhibit from "Choosing Strategies for Change," by John P. Kotter and Leonard A. Schlesinger, March–April 1979. Copyright © 1979 by the Harvard Business School Publishing Corporation; all rights reserved.

forced by the finding of a recent study conducted by Watson Wyatt Worldwide. The study of more than 9,000 working Americans concluded that the three biggest barriers to managing change are (1) lack of management visibility and support, (2) inadequate management skills, and (3) employee resistance to change.[6] It is interesting to note that two relate directly to management and only one relates directly to employees.

Leading Change

Today's competitive world requires that managers at all levels be constantly looking for improvements via change. This fact, coupled with the realization that most people's natural reaction is to resist change, means that successful change implementation requires that managers make a conscious effort to lead change efforts. John Kotter has developed the eight-step method for leading change shown in Figure 17.4.[7] Each of these steps is discussed in the following paragraphs.

Establish a Sense of Urgency   Because so many large and small companies have a tendency to become complacent, managers must constantly be on the lookout for needed change. Success and the comfort of doing everything the same way are two frequently encountered reasons that organizations become complacent. Successful managers are constantly looking for the need to change, and once a need is identified, they establish an urgency for making it happen.

FIGURE 17.4
Model for Leading Change

1. Establish a sense of urgency

2. Create the guiding coalition

3. Develop a vision and strategy

4. Communicate the change vision

5. Empower broad-based action

6. Generate short-term wins

7. Consolidate gains and produce more change

8. Anchor new approaches in the culture

Create a Guiding Coalition Most successful change efforts require the participation and support of several managers and employees from many different levels in the organization. A group or coalition of managers and employees must be formed to lead the change. Most major changes are initiated by top management, but to be successful they must eventually involve middle managers, supervisors, and employees.

Develop a Vision and Strategy As discussed earlier in this chapter, most people are much more accepting of change when they can visualize its ultimate impact. Therefore, it is important that change leaders develop a clear image of what the results of the change will be and what the transition process will involve.

Communicate the Change Vision Change leaders should use every available means to communicate the change vision to organizational members and affected parties. All too often managers assume that employees have the same vision about a change that they do. The best approach is to use multiple channels and opportunities to communicate the change vision.

Empower Broad-Based Action The idea here is to actively involve managers and employees at all levels in the change process. Eliminate obstacles to the change process and empower employees to take the actions necessary to implement the change.

Generate Short-Term Wins Once the successes associated with a change are seen, even those who initially resisted will usually get on board. The key here is to not wait for the ultimate realization of the vision but rather to recognize and celebrate numerous small successes along the way. Take the opportunity to publicly recognize successes and the people responsible. Everyone likes to be a member of a winning team.

Consolidate Gains and Produce More Change   Don't rest on your laurels along the way. Maintain the ultimate vision, and don't get sidetracked or satisfied with the small successes. As you approach the original ultimate vision, look for new projects and changes.

Anchor New Approaches in the Culture   Take actions to ensure that the organization and its members don't slowly revert back to the old ways. Emphasize the positive results of the changes, and continually give credit to those who participated in the change process.

Organizational Development

The previous sections emphasized the change process from the viewpoint of individual managers. This section looks at the change process from the viewpoint of the entire organization.

organizational development (OD)
Organizationwide, planned effort, managed from the top, to increase organizational performance through planned interventions.

Organizational development (OD) is an organizationwide, planned effort managed from the top, with a goal of increasing organizational performance through planned interventions in the organization. In particular, OD looks at the human side of organizations. It seeks to change attitudes, values, and management practices in an effort to improve organizational performance. The ultimate goal of OD is to structure the organizational environment so that managers and employees can use their skills and abilities to the fullest.

An OD effort starts with a recognition by management that organizational performance can and should be improved. Following this, most OD efforts include the following phases:

1. Diagnosis
2. Change planning
3. Intervention/education
4. Evaluation

Diagnosis

The first decision to be made in the OD process is whether the organization has the talent and available time necessary to conduct the diagnosis. If not, an alternative is to hire an outside consultant. Once the decision has been made regarding who will do the diagnosis, the next step is to gather and analyze information. Some of the most frequently used methods for doing this are the following.

1. *Review available records.* The first step is to review any available records or documents that may be pertinent. Personnel records and financial reports are two types of generally available records that can be useful.
2. *Survey questionnaires.* The most popular method of gathering data is through questionnaires filled out by employees. Usually the questionnaires are intended to measure employee attitudes and perceptions about certain work-related factors.
3. *Personal interviews.* In this approach, employees are individually interviewed regarding their opinions and perceptions and certain work-related factors. This method takes more time than the survey questionnaire method but can result in better information.

4. *Direct observation.* In this method, the person conducting the diagnosis observes firsthand the behavior of organizational members at work. One advantage of this method is that it allows observation of what people actually do as opposed to what they say they do.

In the diagnosis stage, one should collect data for a reason. A plan for analyzing the data should be developed even before the data are collected. Too often data are collected simply because they are available and with no plan for analysis.

Change Planning

The data collected in the diagnosis stage must be carefully interpreted to determine the best plan for organizational improvement. If a similar diagnosis has been done in the past, it can be revealing to compare the data and look for any obvious differences. Because much of the collected data are based on personal opinions and perceptions, there will always be areas of disagreement. The key to interpreting the data is to look for trends and areas of general agreement. The end result of the change-planning process is to identify specific problem areas and outline steps for resolving the problems.

Intervention/Education

The purpose of the intervention/education phase is to share the information obtained in the diagnostic phase with the affected employees and help them realize the need for change. A thorough analysis in the change-planning phase often results in the identification of the most appropriate intervention/education method to use. Some of the most frequently used intervention/education methods are discussed next.

direct feedback
Process in which the change agent communicates the information gathered through diagnosis directly to the affected people.

Direct Feedback   With the **direct feedback** method, the change agent communicates the information gathered in the diagnostic and change-planning phases to the involved parties. The change agent describes what was found and what changes are recommended. Then workshops are often conducted to initiate the desired changes.

team building
Process by which a work group develops awareness of conditions that keep it from functioning effectively and takes action to eliminate these conditions.

Team Building   The objective of **team building** is to increase the group's cohesiveness and general group spirit. Team building stresses the importance of working together. Some of the specific activities used include (1) clarifying employee roles, (2) reducing conflict, (3) improving interpersonal relations, and (4) improving problem-solving skills.[8] Team building was discussed in depth in Chapter 11.

sensitivity training
Method used in OD to make one more aware of oneself and one's impact on others.

Sensitivity Training   **Sensitivity training** is designed to make one more aware of oneself and one's impact on others. Sensitivity training involves a group, usually called a *training group* or *T-group,* that meets and has no agenda or particular focus. Normally the group has between 10 and 15 people who may or may not know one another. With no planned structure or no prior common experiences, the behavior of individuals in trying to deal with the lack of structure becomes the agenda. While engaging in group dialogue, members are encouraged to learn about themselves and others in the nonstructured environment.

Sensitivity training has been both passionately criticized and vigorously defended as to its relative value for organizations. In general, the research shows that people who have undergone sensitivity training tend to show increased sensitivity, more open communication, and increased flexibility.[9] However, these same studies indicate that while the outcomes of sensitivity training are beneficial in general, it is difficult to predict the outcomes for any one person.

FIGURE 17.5   **Model for the Management of Organizational Development**

Source: James L. Gibson, John M. Ivancevich, and James H. Donnelly, Jr., *Organizations* (Burr Ridge, IL: Richard D. Irwin, 1994), p. 668.

Evaluation

Probably the most difficult phase in the OD process is the evaluation phase.[10] The basic question to be answered is: Did the OD process produce the desired results? Unfortunately, many OD efforts begin with admirable but overly vague objectives such as improving the overall health, culture, or climate of the organization. Before any OD effort can be evaluated, explicit objectives must be determined. Objectives of an OD effort should be outcome oriented and should lend themselves to the development of measurable criteria.

A second requirement for evaluating OD efforts is that the evaluation effort be methodologically sound. Ideally, an OD effort should be evaluated using hard, objective data. One approach is to compare data collected before the OD intervention against data collected after the OD intervention. An even better approach is to compare "before" and "after" data with similar data from a control group. When using this approach, two similar groups are identified, an experimental group and a control group. The OD effort is then implemented with the experimental group but not with the control group. After the OD intervention has been completed, the before and after data from the experimental group are compared with the before and after data from the control group. This approach helps to rule out changes that may have resulted from factors other than the OD intervention. Figure 17.5 summarizes the OD process.

Managing Innovation

The concept of innovation was briefly introduced in Chapter 4 as part of the discussion on creativity. As defined in Chapter 4, innovation refers to doing new things that inherently involve change. Many management experts today believe that innovation is an organization's best sustainable source of growth, competitive advantage, and new wealth.[11]

Because what worked in the past may not work today, many organizations are having to create new ways to foster innovation. Robert Tucker, author of the international best-seller *Managing the Future*, believes that organizations that successfully innovate in the future must embrace four essential principles. These four principles are discussed below.

1. An organization's approach to innovation must be comprehensive. Innovation cannot be confined to a few departments or to a small group of "innovations." Innovation must permeate the entire organization, and it must encompass all aspects of organization.

2. Innovation must include systematic, organized, and continual search for new opportunities. Traditionally, top management was the only organizational entity concerned with questions such as, What do these developments mean to our company? How could we take advantage of these developments? What threats are on the horizon that we must respond to now if we are going to capitalize on this development? The rapid pace of change today dictates much broader participation than just top management in these decisions.

3. Organizations must involve everyone in the innovation process. Up until very recent times, many employees were not asked or expected to innovate in their jobs. In some instances, employees were encouraged *not* to innovate. The dormant creativity of employees across the organization must be tapped.

4. An organization must work constantly on improving its climate for innovation. As used here, climate refers to the "feeling in the air" you get when you work for or visit an organization. Does the feeling in the air foster innovation and encourage employees to take risks? What happens when someone fails? Innovative climates expect a certain degree of failure, learn from failures, and share the learning throughout the organization. As the old saying goes, If you haven't failed, you haven't taken sufficient risks. Organization with favorable climates for innovation provide the context for people to collaborate in groups, teams, divisions, and departments without boundaries of fear.

As the rate of change increases for today's organizations, the ability to innovate becomes more and more critical. By subscribing to the above principles, managers at all levels can positively affect an organization's ability to innovate and remain competitive.

The Learning Organization

If organizations are to encourage change and innovation, they must establish environments that support these actions. Learning organizations establish such an environment. A learning organization has been defined as an organization skilled at creating, acquiring, and transferring knowledge, and in modifying behavior to reflect the new knowledge.[12] Peter Senge, whose book *The Fifth Discipline* popularized the learning organization, has identified five principles for creating a learning organization:[13]

1. *Systems thinking.* Managers must learn to see the big picture and not concentrate only on their part; they must learn to recognize the effects of one level of learning on another.

2. *Personal mastery.* Individual managers and employees must be empowered to experiment, innovate, and explore.

In the early 1990s, Royal Dutch Shell (RDS) had become the world's biggest oil firm with $107 billion in revenues, profits of $6.46 billion, and operations in over 100 countries. By 1998, RDS was being touted as a premier learning organization. However, less than a year later RDS reported the worst results in its century-long history—annual income was down 95 percent from the previous year!

How could this happen to one of the world's premier learning organizations? Unfortunately, by this time RDS had lost two of the key attributes of a successful learning organization: commitment and community. The company had alienated much of its workforce by its actions in the face of mounting adversity—such actions as eliminating its "job for life" program and massively restructuring the organization. It also became evident that RDS leadership had traditionally been suspicious, rather than supportive, of strong, visionary leaders. One result was that local units acted autonomously to the point that there was little control over capital spending.

Following the disastrous results of 1998, RDS took tighter control of capital spending, adopted a new style of management, reduced its number of business units, and used consultants to help rebuild organizationwide commitment. Now on the road to recovery, RDS learned the hard way that being recognized as a "premier learning organization" does not level itself to complacency—commitment and community must be preserved.

Source: "Learning at Royal Dutch Shell," *Strategic Direction,* June 2002, pp. 10–12.

3. *Mental models.* Managers and employees should be encouraged to develop mental models as ways of stretching their minds to find new and better ways of doing things.

4. *Shared vision.* Managers should develop and communicate a shared vision that can be used as a framework for addressing problems and opportunities.

5. *Team learning.* Team learning is the process of aligning a team so as to avoid wasted energy and to get the desired results.

Honda, Corning, and General Electric are examples of companies that have become good learning organizations.[14] In these organizations, learning, in whatever form, becomes an inescapable way of life for both managers and employees alike. These and other learning organizations are gaining the commitment of their employees at all levels by continually expanding their capacity to learn and change. Management Illustration 17.2 describes how one supposedly successful learning organization lost its edge by becoming complacent.

Managing Corporate Culture

culture
Set of important understandings (often unstated) that members of a community share.

The word *culture* is derived in a roundabout way from the Latin verb *colere*, which means "to cultivate."[15] In later times, *culture* came to indicate a process of refinement and breeding in domesticating a particular crop. The modern-day meaning draws on this agricultural derivation: It relates to society's control, refinement, and domestication of itself. A contemporary definition of **culture** is "the set of important understandings (often unstated) that members of a community share in common."[16]

Culture in an organization compares to personality in a person. Humans have fairly enduring and stable traits that help them protect their attitudes and behaviors. So do organizations. In addition, certain groups of traits or personality types are known to consist of common elements. Organizations can be described in similar terms. They can be warm, aggressive, friendly, open, innovative, conservative, and so forth. An organization's culture is transmitted in many ways, including long-standing and often unwritten rules; shared standards regarding what is important; prejudices; standards for social etiquette and demeanor; established customs for relating to peers, subordinates, and superiors; and other traditions that clarify to employees what is and is not appropriate behavior. Thus, corporate culture communicates how people in the organization should behave by establishing a value system conveyed through rites, rituals, myths, legends, and actions. Simply stated, **corporate culture** means "the way we do things around here."[17]

corporate culture
Communicates how people in an organization should behave by establishing a value system conveyed through rites, rituals, myths, legends, and actions.

Cultural Forms of Expression

Culture has two basic components: (1) substance, the meanings contained in its values, norms, and beliefs; and (2) forms, the practices whereby these meanings are expressed, affirmed, and communicated to members.[18]

How Does Culture Originate?

There is no question that different organizations develop different cultures. What causes an organization to develop a particular type of culture? Many organizations trace their culture to one person who provided a living example of the major values of the organization. Robert Wood Johnson of Johnson & Johnson, Harley Procter of Procter & Gamble, Walt Disney of Walt Disney Company, and Thomas J. Watson, Sr., of IBM all left their imprints on the organizations they headed. Research indicates, however, that fewer than half of a new company's values reflect the values of the founder or chief executive. The rest appear to develop in response both to the environment in which the business operates and to the needs of the employees.[19] Four distinct factors contribute to an organization's culture: its history, its environment, its selection process, and its socialization processes.[20]

History

Employees are aware of the organization's past, and this awareness builds culture. Much of the "way things are done" is a continuation of how things have always been done. The existing values that a strong leader may have established originally are constantly and subtly reinforced by experiences. The status quo is also protected by the human tendency to fervently embrace beliefs and values and to resist changes. Executives at Walt Disney Company reportedly pick up litter on the grounds without thinking because of the Disney vision of an immaculate Disneyland.

Environment

Because all organizations must interact with their environments, the environment plays a role in shaping their cultures. Deregulation of the telecommunications industry in the 1980s dramatically altered its environment. Before deregulation, the environment was relatively risk averse and noncompetitive. Increases in costs were automatically passed on to customers. As a result of deregulation, the environment changed overnight to become highly competitive and much more dynamic. No longer sheltered by a regulated environment, the cultures of the telecommunications companies were forced to change.

Staffing

Organizations tend to hire, retain, and promote people who are similar to current employees in important ways. A person's ability to fit in can be important in these processes. This "fit" criterion ensures that current values are accepted and that po-

FIGURE 17.6
Characteristics of a Strong Corporate Culture

Source: Terrence E. Deal and Allan A. Kennedy, *Corporate Cultures: The Rites and Rituals of Corporate Life* (Reading, MA: Addison-Wesley, 1982).

- Organizational members share clear values and beliefs about how to succeed in their business.
- Organizational members agree on which beliefs about how to succeed are most important.
- Different parts of the organization have similar beliefs about how to succeed.
- The rituals of day-to-day organizational life are well organized and consistent with company goals.

tential challengers of "how we do things" are screened out. Adjustment has to be carefully managed. For example, when Bill George took over Medronic, a leading producer of pacemakers, in 1991, he quickly found out that to survive in the rapidly growing high-tech health care business, he needed a change—but not at the expense of what had historically worked for the company. He opted for a merger with another company. The merger brought in "new blood" that was free-spirited and experimental in nature and teamed them with a highly disciplined, methodical existing culture. Though it was hard work, empowerment of people and a merger of cultures helped the company halve its development time and remain competitive in the industry.[21]

Entry Socialization

While an organization's values, norms, and beliefs may be widely and uniformly held, they are seldom written down. The new employee, who is least familiar with the culture, is most likely to challenge it. It is therefore important to help the newcomer adopt the organization's culture. Companies with strong cultures attach great importance to the process of introducing and indoctrinating new employees. This process is called **entry socialization.** Entry socialization not only reduces threats to the organization from newcomers but also lets new employees know what is expected of them. It may be handled in a formal or informal manner, as well as on an individual or group basis.

entry socialization
Adaptation process by which new employees are introduced and indoctrinated into the organization.

Strong and Weak Corporate Cultures

A strong corporate culture is clearly defined, reinforces a common understanding about what is important, and has the support of management and employees. Such a culture contributes greatly to an organization's success by creating an understanding about how employees should behave. Figure 17.6 identifies the characteristics of a strong corporate culture.

Weak cultures have the opposite characteristics. In a weak corporate culture, individuals often act in ways that are inconsistent with the company's way of doing things. Figure 17.7 summarizes some characteristics of a weak culture. Management Illustration 17.3 describes a strong culture developed by the SAS Institute.

Identifying Culture

Researchers have identified seven characteristics that, taken together, capture the essence of an organization's culture:[22]

1. *Individual autonomy.* The degree of responsibility, independence, and opportunities for exercising initiative that individuals in the organization have.
2. *Structure.* The number of rules and regulations and the amount of direct supervision that is used to oversee and control employee behavior.

The SAS Institute is the world's largest privately held software company with more than 8,000 employees. The company is renowned for its employee benefits, which are a major part of the corporate culture that the company has carefully crafted. The company views even the simplest perk as part of its highly developed business strategy to attract and retain high-quality employees. Before being adopted, every benefit is studied and reviewed to make sure it fits with the company's culture. Subsidized child care centers, on-site health care facility, fitness center, and free refreshments are examples of some of the perks available at the company's Cary, North Carolina, headquarters.

While many companies have cut back or even cut out nontraditional benefits, SAS has not cut benefits or personnel. This approach has reinforced its corporate culture. Jim Goodnight summarized the company's viewpoint, "Looking at . . . services that keep employees motivated, loyal, and doing their best work as merely an expense and not an investment is, I think, a little shortsighted."

Source: Jennifer Schu, "Even in Hard Times, SAS Keeps Its Culture Intact," *Workforce,* October 2001, p. 21.

3. *Support.* The degree of assistance and warmth provided by managers to their subordinates.

4. *Identification.* The degree to which members identify with the organization as a whole rather than with their particular work group or field of professional expertise.

5. *Performance–reward.* The degree to which reward allocations (i.e., salary increases, promotions) in the organization are based on performance criteria.

6. *Conflict tolerance.* The degree of conflict present in relationships between peers and work groups, as well as the willingness to be honest and open about differences.

7. *Risk tolerance.* The degree to which employees are encouraged to be aggressive, innovative, and risk seeking.

Each of these traits should be viewed as existing on a continuum ranging from low to high. A picture of the overall culture can be formed by evaluating the organization on each of these characteristics. The learning organization, discussed earlier in this chapter, is in essence a type of organization culture.

There are as many distinct cultures as there are organizations. Most can be grouped into one of four basic types, determined by two factors: (1) the degree of risk associated with the organization's activities and (2) the speed with which the

FIGURE 17.7
Characteristics of a Weak Corporate Culture

Source: Terrence E. Deal and Allan A. Kennedy, *Corporate Cultures: The Rites and Rituals of Corporate Life* (Reading, MA: Addison-Wesley, 1982).

- Organizational members have no clear values or beliefs about how to succeed in their business.
- Organizational members have many beliefs as to how to succeed but cannot agree on which are most important.
- Different parts of the organization have fundamentally different beliefs about how to succeed.
- Those who personify the culture are destructive or disruptive and don't build on any common understanding about what is important.
- The rituals of day-to-day organizational life are disorganized or working at cross-purposes.

FIGURE 17.8
Generic Types of
Organization
Culture

Speed of Feedback		Degree of Risk	
		High	**Low**
	Rapid	Tough-person, macho culture	Work-hard/play-hard culture
	Slow	Bet-your-company culture	Process culture

organization and its employees get feedback indicating the success of decisions. Figure 17.8 shows in matrix form the four generic types of culture.[23]

Tough-Person, Macho Culture

tough-person, macho culture
Characterized by individuals who take high risks and get quick feedback on whether their decisions are right or wrong.

The **tough-person, macho culture** is characterized by individualists who regularly take high risks and get quick feedback on whether their decisions are right or wrong. Teamwork is not important, and every colleague is a potential rival. In this culture, the value of cooperation is ignored; there is no chance to learn from mistakes. People who do best in this culture are those who need to gamble and who can tolerate all-or-nothing risks because they need instant feedback. Companies that develop large-scale advertising programs for major clients would be characterized by the tough-person, macho culture; these advertising programs are usually high-budget with rapid acceptance or failure.

Work-Hard/Play-Hard Culture

work-hard/play-hard culture
Encourages employees to take few risks and to expect rapid feedback.

The **work-hard/play-hard culture** encourages employees to take few risks and to expect rapid feedback. In this culture, activity is the key to success. Rewards accrue to persistence and the ability to find a need and fill it. Because of the need for volume, team players who are friendly and outgoing thrive. Companies that are sales based such as real estate companies often have a work-hard/play-hard culture.

Bet-Your-Company Culture

bet-your-company culture
Requires big-stakes decisions; considerable time passes before the results are known.

The **bet-your-company culture** requires big-stakes decisions, with considerable time passing before the results are known. Pressures to make the right decisions are always present in this environment. Companies involved in durable goods manufacturing are often characterized by a bet-your-company culture.

Process Culture

process culture
Involves low risk with little feedback; employees focus on how things are done rather than on the outcomes.

The **process culture** involves low risk coupled with little feedback; employees must focus on how things are done rather than on the outcomes. Employees in this atmosphere become cautious and protective. Those who thrive are orderly, punctual, and detail oriented. Companies in regulated or protected industries often operate in this type of culture.

Organizational Subcultures

In addition to its overall culture, organizations often have multiple subcultures. It is not uncommon for the values, beliefs, and practices to vary from one part of the organization to another. For example, newly acquired components of a company often have cultural differences that must be worked out over time. Global companies also tend to be faced with multiple cultures. Such factors as language, social norms, values, attitudes, customs, and religion naturally vary throughout the world.

The presence of different subcultures within an organization does not preclude the development of areas of commonality and compatibility.[24] For example, a company's emphasis on quality can be imbedded in the local culture at sites throughout the world. At the same time, however, successful companies have learned to look at the compatibility of cultures when considering acquisitions and mergers and new locations. Extreme cultural differences can make it very difficult for an acquisition or an expansion to be successful.

Changing Culture

Executives who have successfully changed organization cultures estimate that the process usually takes from 6 to 15 years.[25] Because organization culture is difficult and time consuming to change, any attempts should be well thought-out.

Allan Kennedy, an expert on organization culture, believes only five reasons justify a large-scale cultural change:[26]

1. The organization has strong values that do not fit into a changing environment.
2. The industry is very competitive and moves with lightning speed.
3. The organization is mediocre or worse.
4. The organization is about to join the ranks of the very large companies.
5. The organization is small but growing rapidly.

Some organizations attempt to change their cultures only when they are forced to do so by changes in their environments or economic situations; others anticipate a necessary change. While massive cultural reorientation may be reasonable in most situations, it is usually possible to strengthen or fine-tune the current situation. A statement of corporate mission consistently reinforced by systems, structures, and policies is a useful tool for strengthening the culture.

Because of the cost, time, and difficulty involved in changing culture, many people believe it is easier to change, or physically replace, the people. This view assumes most organizations promote people who fit the prevailing norms of the organization. Therefore, the easiest if not the only way to change an organization's culture is to change its people.

Summary

1. *Identify the three major categories of organizational change.* The three major categories of organizational change are technological changes, environmental changes, and changes internal to the organization.

2. *List the three steps in Lewin's model for change.* Lewin's model for change involves three steps: unfreezing, presenting a new alternative, and refreezing.

3. *Discuss several reasons employees resist change.* Employees resist change for many reasons. Six of the most frequently encountered reasons are (1) fear of the unknown, (2) economics, (3) fear that expertise and skills will lose value, (4) threats to power, (5) inconvenience, and (6) threats to interpersonal relations.

4. *Identify several prescriptions for reducing resistance to change.* Just as there are many reasons employees resist change, there are many approaches for reducing resistance to change. Several suggestions for reducing resistance to change include (1) building trust between management and employees; (2) discussing upcoming changes with affected employees; (3) involving employees in the change process as early as possible; (4) ensuring that the proposed changes are reasonable; (5) avoiding threats; and (6) following a sensible time schedule for implementing the change.

5. *Describe an approach that managers can use to lead change.* John Knotter has developed an eight-step method for leading change in organizations: (1) establish a sense of ur-

gency, (2) create a guiding coalition, (3) develop a vision and strategy, (4) communicate the change vision, (5) empower broad-based action, (6) generate short-term wins, (7) consolidate gains and produce more change, and (8) anchor new approaches in the culture.

6. *Summarize the four phases of an organizational development (OD) program.* Most OD efforts include a diagnosis phase, a change-planning phase, an intervention/education phase, and an evaluation phase. Diagnosis involves gathering and analyzing information to determine the areas of the organization in need of improvement. Change planning involves developing a plan for organization improvement. Intervention/education involves the sharing of diagnostic information with the people affected by it and helping them to realize the need for change. The evaluation phase attempts to determine the effects the OD effort has had on the organization.

7. *Briefly describe four essential principles that organizations must follow to manage innovation.* Essential principles for successfully innovating are (1) have a comprehensive approach; (2) include a systematic, organized, and continued search for new opportunities; (3) involve everyone in the innovation process, and (4) work constantly on improving the organization's climate for innovation.

8. *Explain what a learning organization is.* A learning organization is skilled at creating, acquiring, and transferring knowledge, and in modifying behavior to reflect the new knowledge. Learning organizations gain the commitment of their employees at all levels by continually expanding their capacity to learn and change.

9. *Define corporate culture.* Corporate culture communicates how people in the organization should behave by establishing a value system conveyed through rites, rituals, myths, legends, and actions. Simply stated, corporate culture means "the way we do things around here."

10. *Describe the generic types of organizational culture.* The tough-person, macho culture is characterized by individualists who regularly take high risks and get quick feedback on whether they are right or wrong. The work-hard/play-hard culture encourages employees to take few risks and to expect rapid feedback. The bet-your-company culture requires big-stakes decisions with considerable time lags before the results are known. The process culture involves low risk coupled with little feedback; employees must focus on how things are done rather than on the outcomes.

11. *Identify two common sources of organizational subcultures.* Two common sources of organizational subcultures are (1) acquisitions/mergers and (2) global or international operations.

Review Questions

1. Name the three major categories of change that apply to organizations.
2. Describe Lewin's model for change.
3. Name six common barriers (reasons for resistance) to change.
4. Describe the four basic reactions of employees to change.
5. Discuss six approaches to reducing resistance to change.
6. List Kotter's eight steps for leading change.
7. What is organizational development?
8. What principles can organizations follow to successfully innovate?
9. What is a learning organization?
10. What organizational characteristics determine corporate culture?
11. How is corporate culture originated and maintained?
12. Name and briefly define the four generic types of corporate culture.
13. What is an organizational subculture?

Skill-Building Questions

1. Take a position on the following statement and be prepared to defend it: Most people resist change, not because the change is harmful but because they are lazy.
2. Check recent literature (*Business Week, The Wall Street Journal,* and other library sources) and identify two or three industries that are currently experiencing major changes. How is each industry responding to the changes? Are these industries likely to be stronger or weaker as a result of these changes?
3. Pick an organization or industry you think will need to change its culture if it is to thrive in the future (as the telecommunication companies had to do in the 1980s and the airlines have had to do since September 11, 2001). Be prepared to explain why you think this change must occur.
4. Pick a company that you think has been particularly innovative. Why do you think they have been successful at promoting innovation?

Skill-Building Exercise 17.1

Change in the Airline Industry

Many organizations have had to change the way they do business since the tragic events of September 11, 2001. The airline industry has certainly been one of the most affected industries. Your instructor will divide the class into groups of four to six students per group. Once the groups have been formed, each group should respond to the following:

1. Identify what major changes have been implemented by or in the airline industry since September 11, 2001.
2. Does your group feel that these changes are positive or negative for the flying public? For airline employees?
3. Why does the group feel that these changes were not implemented before the tragic events took place?

After each group has answered the above questions, your instructor will ask each group to share their answers with the class.

Skill-Building Exercise 17.2

Resisting Change

One of the problems you face involves mistakes being made by employees who perform a particular operation. The same mistakes seem to occur in more than one department. You believe a training program for the people concerned will help reduce errors.

You are aware, however, that your supervisors may defend existing procedures simply because the introduction of training may imply criticism of the way they have been operating. You realize, too, that the supervisors may fear resistance by employees afraid of not doing well in the training program. All in all, you plan to approach the subject carefully.

1. Add to the agenda of your weekly staff meeting a recommendation that training be undertaken to help reduce errors.
2. Talk to all your supervisors individually and get their attitudes and ideas about what to do before bringing the subject up in the weekly staff meeting.
3. Ask the corporate training staff to come in, determine the training needs, and develop a program to meet those needs.
4. Since this training is in the best interests of the company, tell your supervisors they will be expected to implement and support it.
5. Appoint a team to study the matter thoroughly, develop recommendations, then bring it before the full staff meeting.

Other alternatives may be open to you, but assume these are the only ones you have considered. *Without discussion* with anyone, choose one of them and be prepared to defend your choice.

Case Incident 17.1

The Way We Do Things

Fitzgerald Company manufactures a variety of consumer products for sale through retail department stores. For over 30 years, the company has held a strong belief that customer relations and a strong selling orientation are the keys to business success. As a result, all top executives have sales backgrounds and spend much of their time outside the company with customers. Because of the strong focus on the customer, management at Fitzgerald emphasizes new-product development projects and growth in volume. The company rarely implements cost reduction or process improvement projects.

Between 1975 and 1985, Fitzgerald's 10 percent share of the market was the largest in the industry. Profitability was consistently better than the industry average. However, in the last 10 years, the markets for many of Fitzgerald's products have matured, and Fitzgerald has dropped from market share leader to the number three company in the industry. Profitability has steadily declined since 1991, although Fitzgerald offers a more extensive line of products than any of its competitors. Customers are complaining that Fitzgerald's prices are higher than those of other companies.

In June 1996, Jeff Steele, president of Fitzgerald Company, hired Valerie Stevens of Management Consultants, Inc., to help him improve the company's financial performance. After an extensive study of Fitzgerald Company and its industry group, Valerie met with Jeff and said, "Jeff, I believe the Fitzgerald Company may have to substantially change its culture."

Questions

1. Describe, in general terms, the corporate culture at Fitzgerald Company.
2. What does Valerie mean when she says Fitzgerald Company may have to change its culture? What are some of the necessary changes?
3. Discuss the problems the company may encounter in attempting to implement changes.

Case Incident 17.2

Upgrading Quality

Judy Franklin, the plant manager of Smart Manufacturing Company, was reviewing the Quality Control Department figures with despair. Once again, the department's figures indicated quality improvements were not being made. Judy was annoyed. "I don't understand it," she thought. "I've been stressing to my staff for over a year that I want to see some quality improvements, but it just doesn't seem to be happening. Quality may actually be worse now than it was a year ago!"

Judy called in David Berg, the quality control manager, and production manager Stuart Lewicki. "Look," Judy said, "I told both of you over a year ago I wanted to see some improvements in quality around here, and we've talked about it at every staff meeting since then. But nothing has happened. What's going on?"

David spoke up. "My department just inspects the products. The quality problems occur in production. All I can do is what I've been doing all along—tell Stuart about the problems we are seeing. I've already told him that 50 percent of the quality problems are caused by worker carelessness."

"I know," said Stuart. "I don't understand it. I've been stressing to my shift supervisors that we need to see quality improvements. They have all told me they are coming down really hard on quality problems and are telling their people they need to work harder on getting out a quality product. Just the other day, Frances Stanfield threatened to fire Joe Duncan if she got any more complaints from quality control about Joe's work."

Questions

1. Why have efforts to improve quality failed?
2. Design a quality improvement program that would have a better chance of being successful if used by Judy.

References and Additional Readings

1. Tom Peters, *Thriving on Chaos* (New York: Alfred A. Knopf, 1987), p. 464.

2. "The 1995 *Business Week* Europe Forum of Financial Directors," *Business Week,* January 15, 1996.

3. Ibid.

4. Gillian Flynn, "HR Translates Ideology into Action," *Workforce,* February 1997, p. 52.

5. Waldron Berry, "Overcoming Resistance to Change," *Supervisory Management,* February 1983, pp. 25–30.

6. Margaret Boles and Brenda Paik Sunoo, "Three Barriers to Managing Change," *Workforce,* January 1998, p. 25.

7. John Kotter, *Leading Change* (Boston: Harvard Business School Press, 1996).

8. Arthur G. Bedeian, *Management* (Hinsdale, IL: Dryden Press, 1986).

9. Michael Beer, "The Technology of Organizational Development," in *Handbook of Industrial and Organizational Psychology,* ed. Marvin D. Dunnette (New York: John Wiley & Sons, 1983), p. 941; and Michael Beer, *Organizational Change and Development: A Systems View* (Santa Monica, CA: Goodyear Publishing, 1980), pp. 194–95.

10. Much of this section is drawn from David E. Terpstra, "The Organization Development Evaluation Process: Some Problems and Proposals," *Human Resource Management,* Spring 1981, p. 24.

11. Much of this section is drawn from Robert B. Tucker, "Innovation Discipline," *Executive Excellence,* September 2001, pp. 3–4; and Robert B. Tucker, "Innovation: The New Core Competency," *Strategy and Leadership,* January–February 2001, pp. 11–14.

12. David Garvin, "Building a Learning Organization," *Harvard Business Review,* July 1993, p. 78.

13. Peter M. Senge, *The Fifth Discipline: The Art and Practice of the Learning Organization* (New York: Doubleday, 1990); and Peter M. Senge, "Learning Organizations," *Executive Excellence,* September 1991, pp. 7–8.

14. Garvin, "Building a Learning Organization."

15. Roy Wagner, *The Invention of Culture,* rev. ed. (Chicago: University of Chicago Press, 1981), p. 21.

16. Vijay Sathe, "Implications of Corporate Culture: A Manager's Guide to Action," *Organizational Dynamics,* Autumn 1983, p. 6.

17. Terrence E. Deal and Allan A. Kennedy, *Corporate Cultures: The Rites and Rituals of Corporate Life* (Reading, MA: Addison-Wesley, 1982), p. 4.

18. Harrison M. Trice and Janice M. Beyer, "Studying Organizational Cultures through Rites and Ceremonials," *Academy of Management Review* 9, no. 4 (1984), p. 645.

19. "The Corporate Culture Vultures," *Fortune,* October 17, 1983, p. 72.

20. Stephen P. Robbins, *Essentials of Organizational Behavior* (Englewood Cliffs, NJ: Prentice Hall, 1984), pp. 174–76.

21. Ron Stodghill, "One Company, Two Cultures," *Business Week,* January 22, 1996, p. 88.

22. Robbins, *Essentials of Organizational Behavior,* p. 171. © 1984; reprinted by permission of Prentice Hall, Inc.

23. This section is drawn from Deal and Kennedy, *Corporate Cultures,* pp. 107, 129–35.

24. Arthur A. Thompson, Jr., and A. J. Strickland III, *Strategic Management: Concepts and Cases,* 13th ed. (New York: McGraw-Hill/Irwin, 2003), p. 423.

25. "The Corporate Culture Vultures," p. 70.

26. Ibid.

Part 6

Controlling Skills

Gettyimages/Greg Kuchik

18

Controlling

Learning Objectives

After studying this chapter, you will be able to:

1. Explain why management controls are necessary.
2. Describe a feedback system.
3. Discuss the basic requirements of the control process.
4. Describe the control pyramid.
5. Identify the factors that affect how much control should be exercised in an organization.
6. Discuss the two categories of control methods.
7. Differentiate between preliminary, concurrent, and postaction controls.
8. List several methods or systems of control commonly used by managers.
9. List the four basic types of financial ratios.
10. Summarize the Sarbanes-Oxley Act of 2002.
11. Discuss the basic purpose of a break-even chart.

Chapter Preview

Well into 2001 Enron was flying high. The company was listed as number seven on the Fortune 500 list, had a total capitalization of $63 billion, was building a new $339 million office tower, and had obtained the naming rights of the Houston Astros' field, calling it "Enron Field." Founded in 1985, Enron had become the nation's largest and most innovative energy trader. Enron had brought high-tech and complex finance to energy trading and had been ultrasuccessful.

In a matter of weeks, if not days, Enron's stock fell from $90 a share to 61 cents a share, over 4,000 employees were laid off, and the company filed for bankruptcy. How could this possibly happen?

As it turned out, Enron businesses depended on the borrowing of lots of money. Institutions were anxious to lend Enron money as long as the company seemed healthy. However, when suspicions arose after some partnership problems were made public, the lenders began to become hesitant to lend money. What began as a trickle very soon became a flood. All of this was exacerbated by the failure of Enron's outside auditors, Arthur Andersen, to expose the problems.

Source: Allen Sloan, "Lights Out for Enron," *Newsweek,* December 10, 2001, pp. 50–51.

Analyzing Management Skills

How might Enron have prevented its problems? Why do you think a company as large as Enron might not have adequate controls?

Applying Management Skills

Suppose you have been elected treasurer of your sorority, fraternity, or some other social group of interest to you. What type of controls could you install to guard against any type of fraud by other officers or members of the organization? How do you think the other officers or members might react to your controls?

control
Process of ensuring that organizational activities are going according to plan; accomplished by comparing actual performance to predetermined standards or objectives, then taking action to correct any deviations.

The basic premise of organizations is that all activities will function smoothly; however, the possibility that this will not be the case gives rise to the need for control. **Control** simply means knowing what is actually happening in comparison to preset standards or objectives and then making any necessary corrections. The overriding purpose of all management controls is to alert the manager to an existing or a potential problem before it becomes critical. Control is accomplished by comparing actual performance to predetermined standards or objectives and then taking action to correct any deviations from the standard. However, control is a sensitive and complex part of the management process.

Controlling is similar to planning. It addresses these basic questions: Where are we now? Where do we want to be? How can we get there from here? But controlling takes place after the planning is completed and the organizational activities have begun. Whereas most planning occurs before action is taken, most controlling takes place after the initial action has been taken. This does not mean control is practiced only after problems occur. Control decisions can be preventive, and they can also affect future planning decisions.

Why Practice Management Control?

As we just noted, management controls alert the manager to potentially critical problems. At top management levels, a problem occurs when the organization's goals are not being met. At middle and lower levels, a problem occurs when the objectives for which the manager is responsible are not being met. These may be departmental objectives, production standards, or other performance indicators. All forms of management controls are designed to give the manager information regarding progress. The manager can use this information to do the following:

1. *Prevent crises.* If a manager does not know what is going on, it is easy for small, readily solvable problems to turn into crises.
2. *Standardize outputs.* Problems and services can be standardized in terms of quantity and quality through the use of good controls.
3. *Appraise employee performance.* Proper controls can provide the manager with objective information about employee performance.
4. *Update plans.* Even the best plans must be updated as environmental and internal changes occur. Controls allow the manager to compare what is happening with what was planned.

Allied Irish Banks PLC (AIB) has portrayed itself as the victim of a clever fraud that resulted in huge currency-trading losses at its Baltimore unit, Allfirst Financial Inc. However, there are signs that a lack of controls at Allfirst may have led to the problems. Initial evidence suggested that Allfirst's risk controls were not very sophisticated.

It has been alleged that Allfirst's currency trader, John Rusnak, fraudulently concealed losses of over $690 million over a five-year period. Larry Smith, Allfirst's back-office employee responsible for verifying the trades made by Rusnak, told investigators that his bosses instructed him not to bother confirming any trades involving banks in Asia. Furthermore, because Smith didn't always have access to a computer screen displaying currency rates, he sometimes had to ask Rusnak for verification. This situation obviously prevented independent verification. Another factor that helped disguise the extent of Rusnak's poor trading was that he used more than one prime broker to clear and settle his trades. This system may have helped conceal the extent of his trading from his colleagues. Looking at the entire situation, it appears that the controls used at Allfirst were extremely lax and not effective.

Source: Alessandra Galloni, Michael R. Sesit, and Benjamin Pedley, "Lax Controls May Explain Trading Loss at Allied Irish," *The Wall Street Journal*, March 8, 2002, p. 8.

5. *Protect the organization's assets.* Controls can protect assets from inefficiency, waste, and pilferage.

Management Illustration 18.1 illustrates what can happen to an organization when controls are inadequate.

Two Concerns of Control

When practicing control, the manager must balance two major concerns: stability and objective realization. To maintain stability, the manager must ensure that the organization is operating within its established boundaries of constraint. The boundaries of constraint are determined by policies, budgets, ethics, laws, and so on. The second concern, objective realization, requires constant monitoring to ensure that enough progress is being made toward established objectives.

A manager may become overly worried about one concern at the expense of another. Most common is a manager who becomes preoccupied with the stability of the operation and neglects the goal. This manager is overly concerned with day-to-day rules and policies and forgets about his or her goals. A manager who is obsessed with the manner or style in which a job is done is an example. On the other hand, a manager may lose sight of stability and have glamorous but short-lived success. A manager who sets production records by omitting safety checks is an example of this behavior.

The above concerns create a paradox. According to author Tom Peters, "control is an illusion . . . no one really controls anything . . . most success is due to luck."[1] This "illusion of control," according to Peters, leads to "the control paradox" wherein "you are out of control when you are 'in control' and you are in control when you are 'out of control.'"[2] He explains this rather interesting view by giving the example of the executive who "knows everything" (such executives are surrounded by layers of management and tons of paper documents telling them what is going on) but is inept because she or he is so removed from reality as to be really "out of control." In contrast is the manager who is "in control" despite the thousands of things going on (people taking initiatives, plans being made at various levels, and people exceeding their job descriptions as a part of tactical and operational decision making) because he or she sticks to the assigned task or plan and sees it to completion.[3] Using Peters's ideas, managers would do well to understand that control is as much an attitude as a physical reality.

The Management Control Process

Figure 18.1 is a simple model of the management control process. Outputs from the activity are monitored by some type of sensor and compared to preset standards (normally set during the planning process). The manager acts as the regulator; he or she takes corrective action when the outputs do not meet the standards. The manager's actions may be directed at the inputs to the activity or at the activity itself.

Such a system, in which outputs from the system affect future inputs into or future activities of the system, is called a **feedback system.** In other words, a feedback system is influenced by its own past behaviors. The heating system of a house is a common example of a mechanical feedback system. The thermostat sensor compares the temperature resulting from heat previously generated by the system to some predetermined standard (the desired temperature setting) and responds accordingly. Feedback is a vital part of the control process. Although preventive, before-the-fact steps can often aid the control process, total control cannot be practiced without feedback. Managers may receive and act on facts about the inputs or the activity itself. But in the end, they must know what is happening in the organization; feedback gives them this information.

feedback system
System in which outputs from the system affect future inputs or future activities of the system.

Three Requirements for Control

The process of control has three basic requirements: (1) establishing standards, (2) monitoring results and comparing them to standards, and (3) correcting deviations. The first step, setting standards, comes from the planning process, whereas the latter two, monitoring and correcting, are unique to the control process. All three are essential to effective control.

Setting Standards

standard
Value used as a point of reference for comparing other values.

A **standard** is a value used as a point of reference for comparing other values. As such, a standard outlines what is expected of the job or the individual. When used

FIGURE 18.1
The Control Process

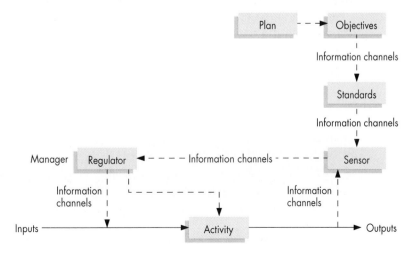

in management control, standards often come directly from objectives. In some instances, objectives may be used directly as standards. In other instances, performance indicators may be derived from the objectives. In certain situations, a standard may be determined by methods analysts, industrial engineers, or recognized experts. In any case, standards should be easy to measure and define. The more specific and measurable an objective is, the more likely it can be directly used as a standard. Standards may deal with output per hour, quality level, inventory level, or other indicators of individual or organizational performance.

Monitoring Performance

Obviously, the overall control system is no better than the information on which it operates, and much of this information is gathered from the monitoring process. Monitoring is often considered to be synonymous with control. In fact, it is only one part of the total control process. The main purpose of monitoring performance is to gather data and detect problem areas. The type of standards used often dictates the type of checks to be made.

The major problem in monitoring performance is deciding when, where, and how often to inspect or check. Checks must be made often enough to provide needed information. However, some managers become obsessed with the checking process. Monitoring can be expensive if overdone, and it can result in adverse reactions from employees. Timing is equally important. The manager must recognize a problem in time to correct it.

Correcting for Deviations

Too often, managers set standards and monitor results but do not follow up with actions. The first two steps are of little value if corrective action is not taken. The action needed may be simply to maintain the status quo. Action of this type would depend on standards being met in a satisfactory manner. If standards are not being met, the manager must find the cause of the deviation and correct it. It is not enough to treat only the symptoms. This action is comparable to replacing a car battery when the real problem is a faulty generator. In a short time, the battery will go dead again. It is also possible that a careful analysis of the deviation will require a change in the standard. The standard may have been improperly set, or changing conditions may dictate a change in standard. Figure 18.2 lists some potential causes of deviations between desired and actual performance.

Tools used to correct for deviations should have the following characteristics:

1. The tools should be used to eliminate the root causes of a problem (as in the battery example above).
2. Tools should be capable of correcting defects (which are bound to occur).
3. Tools should be relatively simple and straightforward so that all employees can use them (e.g., monitoring a gauge, turning a dial, reading a simple report).

FIGURE 18.2
Potential Causes of Performance Deviations

- Faulty planning.
- Lack of communication within the organization.
- Need for training.
- Lack of motivation.
- Unforeseen forces outside the organization, such as government regulation or competition.

4. Tools should be easy for employees to tie to goals or standards for improvement.

5. Tools should be applied totally, not piecemeal.[4]

Control Tolerances

control tolerances
Variation from the standard that is acceptable to the manager.

Actual performance rarely conforms exactly to standards or plans. A certain amount of variation will normally occur. Therefore, the manager must set limits on the acceptable degree of deviation from the standard. In other words, how much variation from standard is tolerable? For example, by how much can expenses be allowed to exceed expectations before the manager becomes alarmed? The manner in which the manager sets **control tolerances** depends on the standard and methods being used. If sampling is being used to monitor the activity, statistical control techniques can be used. The tolerance levels may be formalized, or they may merely exist in the mind of the manager. The important point is that the manager must develop some guidelines as to what deviation is acceptable (in control) and what is not acceptable (out of control).

The Control Pyramid

The control pyramid provides a method for implementing controls in the organization.[5] The idea is to implement simple controls first and then move to more complex controls at a later time. The first area to be considered using this method would be *foolproof controls,* wherein the control deals with repetitive acts and requires little thought (e.g., turning off lights). Surprisingly, many of these acts and controls already exist in an organization's normal course of business. The second area to consider is *automatic controls,* wherein a feedback loop can exist without much human interaction (e.g., regulation of plant temperature). These systems require monitoring, but the control can be machine or computer based. The third area is *operator controls,* which require a human response (e.g., a salesperson checking records). The key to this form of control is to make it meaningful for the controller. The fourth area is *supervisory control,* the layer that controls the person or persons implementing the controls (e.g., a department head checking an employee's reports). The organization must make sure that this form of control gets results and is not redundant. The final area is *informational controls* (e.g., report summaries). This is the ultimate feedback loop, wherein the manager must pull together all the information provided by the other controls.[6] Seeing the process as a whole helps the manager get a feel for how interrelated the control process is and how it must be synchronized. See Figure 18.3 for an explanatory diagram of this process.

How Much Control?

The effectiveness of any control system is a function of the number and types of controls that are used. When deciding just how much control should be exercised in an organization, three major factors must be appraised: (1) economic considerations, (2) behavioral considerations, and (3) flexibility and innovation considerations.

Economic Considerations

Installing and operating control systems cost money. A good quality control system, for instance, requires additional labor, if nothing else. The equipment costs of sophisticated electronic and mechanical control systems can be significant. Ideally, control systems should be installed as long as they save more than they cost.

FIGURE 18.3
The Control Pyramid

Source: J. M. Juran, *Managerial Breakthrough,* rev. ed. (New York: McGraw-Hill, 1995), p. 205.

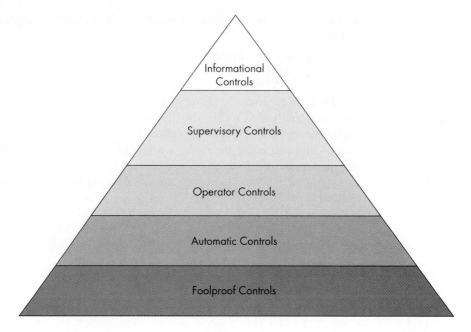

Figure 18.4 shows the general relationship between control costs and the benefits gained. The straight, upward-sloping line represents the costs associated with implementing and maintaining the controls (up-front installation expenses, labor costs, and so on). The S-shaped curve represents the performance or benefits received as a result of having the controls. Analyzing Figure 18.4, several points can be seen:

- There is some minimum amount of control necessary before the benefits of more control outweigh the costs (point A).
- There is some optimal amount of control (point B).
- There is some maximum amount of control that, if exceeded, can be very costly (point C).

FIGURE 18.4
General Relationship between Control Cost and Benefits

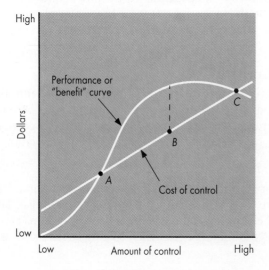

The costs of implementing a control system can usually be estimated or calculated much more accurately than the benefits. For example, it is difficult to quantify and measure the true benefits of a quality control system. A good quality control system supposedly increases goodwill; but how does one measure this attribute? The decision is obviously much easier when the costs of not maintaining control are either very high or very low. For example, because the cost of low quality control is so high, airlines go to great expense to ensure high control of quality. Despite the measurement problems, management should regularly attempt to evaluate the economic costs versus the benefits of controls.

Behavioral Considerations

Managers need to be aware of the potential impact of the control system on employees. Most people do not like to work where they think their every move is being watched or questioned. For example, most salespeople do not like to have to account for every penny spent on meals and entertainment. At the same time, however, very few people like to work where no control exists; an absence of control creates an environment in which people do not know what is expected of them.

Flexibility and Innovation Considerations

Too much control may restrict the flexibility and innovation required to be competitive. Overly restrictive controls often stifle the entrepreneurial spirit of employees and discourage them from trying new and creative options. The key is to maintain control without squelching innovation.

Many managers tend to increase controls whenever things are not going according to plan. Figure 18.5 shows a simplified version of a model developed by Alvin Gouldner that explains this behavior. Gouldner's model begins with top management's demand for control over operations. This is attempted through the use and enforcement of general and impersonal rules regarding work procedures. These rigid rules are meant to be guides for the behavior of the organization members; they also have the unintended effect of showing minimum acceptable

FIGURE 18.5
Simplified Gouldner Model of Organization Control

Source: From James G. March and Herbert A. Simon, *Organizations*, 2/e. Reprinted with permission of Blackwell Publishing Ltd.

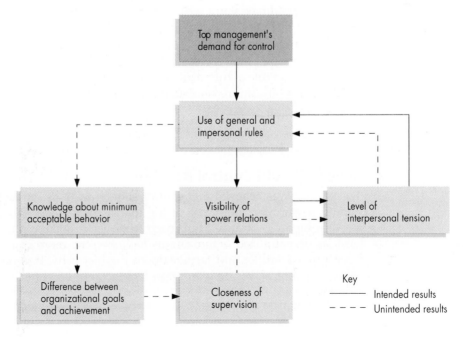

behavior. In organizations where there is little congruence between individual and organizational objectives or acceptance of organizational objectives is not high, the effect is a reduction of performance to the lowest acceptable level: People who are not highly committed to organizational objectives will perform at the lowest acceptable level. Managers view such behavior as resulting from inadequate control; they therefore respond with closer supervision. This increases the visibility of power, which in turn raises the level of interpersonal tension in the organization. Raising the tension level brings even stricter enforcement of the general and impersonal formal rules. Hence, the cycle repeats itself. The overall effect is increased control, increased interpersonal tension, and a lowering of performance.

One problem in deciding on the right degree of control is that different people react differently to similar controls. Research suggests that reactions differ according to personality and prior experiences.[7] Problems can occur from unforeseen reactions to control due to both compliance and resistance.[8] Problems from compliance arise when people adhere to the prescribed behavior even when it is inappropriate. The salesperson who will not vary from prescribed procedures to satisfy a customer complaint is an example of this. Problems resulting from resistance to controls arise when individuals attempt to preempt, work around, or sabotage the controls. Distorting a report and padding the budget are forms of control resistance.

Several things can be done to lessen negative reactions to controls. Most approaches are based on good common sense. However, they require a concerted effort by the manager. The tendency is to take these suggestions for granted. The guidelines are as follows:

1. Make sure the standards and associated controls are realistic. Standards set too high or too low turn people off. Make sure the standards are attainable yet challenging.

2. Involve employees in the control-setting process. Many of the behavioral problems associated with controls result from a lack of understanding of the nature and purpose of the controls. People naturally resist anything new, especially if they do not understand why it is being used. Solicit and listen to suggestions from employees.

3. Use controls only where needed. As the Gouldner model suggests, there is a strong tendency to overcontrol. Periodically evaluate the need for different controls. A good rule of thumb is to evaluate every control at least annually. Changing conditions can make certain controls obsolete. Remember, overcontrol can produce negative results.

Management Illustration 18.2 describes how Fiat is attempting to turn around its fortunes by tightening some of its internal controls.

Where Should Control Reside?

For years, it was believed that control in organizations is a fixed commodity that should rest only in the hands of top management. This viewpoint naturally favored a highly centralized approach to decision making and controlling. However, as decentralized organizations have become more common, controls have been pushed farther and farther down the hierarchy. It is now recognized that where the controls reside is an important factor in how much control is desirable.

James Champy, author of *Reengineering Management*, believes the modern approach to control should involve more "enabling" or learning to control at lower

In late February 2003, Guiseppe Morchio was hired as Fiat S.p.A's fourth chief executive in nine months. Morchio had been with tiremaker Pirelli for 21 years and is known as a change manager specialized in rescuing troubled companies. He is credited with successfully restructuring Pirelli's cable division. The announcement was made just as Fiat was to disclose a net loss of about 3 billion euros ($3.24 billion) for 2002.

Four months into his new job, Morchio had launched a $22 billion, four-year restructuring plan that involved more than 12,000 job cuts, the closure of 12 factories, and the raising of 1.8 billion euros ($2.1 billion) to recapitalize the ailing carmaker. Some of the more significant of Morchio's internal changes are aimed at tightening control over vari-

ous operations. For example, instead of getting regular 20-minute financial presentations from the heads of the main operating companies—autos, heavy trucks, farm and construction equipment—Morchio holds in-depth monthly meetings with each group. These meetings last up to five hours each and include discussions on everything from finances, productivity, quality, and personnel. The meetings also are used to review each division's business plans and include the top managers from each of the major sectors.

Sources: "Morchio Concentrates on Building Fiat's Credibility," *Automotive News*, July 14, 2003, p. 52; and "Can It Be Saved," *Economist*, June 26, 2003, p. 1.

levels.[9] Supporting this idea, Leon Royer, director of Learning Services at 3M, found that learning and enabling go hand in hand. Lower-level employees are valuable controllers if they are allowed to learn how to control.[10] The difficulty with enabling, however, is that it means senior management must be willing to relinquish control. One reason for pushing controls down in the organization is that the controllers then are close to the actual situations that require control.

Building on this material, evidence favors relatively tight controls as long as they are placed as far down in the organization as possible.[11] This approach has several advantages. First, it keeps higher-level managers from getting too involved in details. Second, it shows why the control is necessary. Third, it elicits commitment from lower-level managers. When controls are spread through many levels of an organization, caution must be taken to ensure that there are no disagreements about how the controls are distributed. In other words, managers at every level should clearly understand their authority and responsibility.

Types of Control

behavior (personal) control
Based on direct, personal surveillance.

output (impersonal) control
Based on the measurement of outputs.

There are two categories of control methods: behavior control and output control. **Behavior** or **personal control** is based on direct, personal surveillance. The first-line supervisor who maintains a close personal watch over employees is using behavior control. **Output** or **impersonal control** is based on the measurement of outputs. Tracking production records and monitoring sales figures are examples of output controls.

Research shows that these two categories of control are not substitutes for each other in the sense that a manager uses one or the other.[12] The evidence suggests that output control occurs in response to a manager's need to provide an accurate measure of performance. On the other hand, behavior control is exerted when performance requirements are well known and personal surveillance is needed to promote efficiency and motivation. In most situations, organizations need to use a mix of output and behavior controls because each serves different organizational needs.

preliminary (steering) control
Method of exercising control to prevent a problem from occurring.

concurrent (screening) control
Focuses on process as it occurs; designed to detect a problem when it occurs.

postaction control
Designed to detect an existing or a potential problem before it gets out of hand.

budget
Statement of expected results or requirements expressed in financial or numerical terms.

Preliminary, Concurrent, or Postaction Control?

In general, methods for exercising control can be described as either preliminary, concurrent, or postaction. **Preliminary control** methods, sometimes called **steering controls,** attempt to prevent a problem from occurring. Requiring prior approval for purchases of all items over a certain dollar value is an example. **Concurrent controls,** also called **screening controls,** focus on things that happen as inputs are being transformed into outputs. They are designed to detect a problem as it occurs. Personal observation of customers being serviced is an example of a concurrent control. **Postaction control** methods are designed to detect existing problems after they occur but before they reach crisis proportions. Written or periodic reports represent postaction control methods. Most controls are based on postaction methods.

Budgetary Control

Budgets are probably the most widely used control devices. A **budget** is a statement of expected results or requirements expressed in financial or numerical terms. Budgets express plans, objectives, and programs of the organization in numerical terms. Preparation of the budget is primarily a planning function; however, its administration is a controlling function.

Many different types of budgets are in use. Figure 18.6 outlines some of the most common types. Some may be expressed in terms other than dollars. For example, an equipment budget may be expressed in numbers of machines; material budgets may be expressed in pounds, pieces, gallons, and so on. Budgets not expressed in dollars can usually be translated into dollars for inclusion in an overall budget.

While budgets are useful for planning and control, they are not without their dangers. Perhaps the greatest danger is inflexibility. This is a special threat to organizations operating in an industry with rapid change and high competition. Rigidity in the budget can also lead to ignoring organizational goals for budgetary goals. The financial manager who won't go $5 over budget to make $500 is a classic example. Budgets can hide inefficiencies. The fact that a certain expenditure has been made in the past often becomes justification for continuing the practice even when the situation has greatly changed. Managers may also pad budgets because they anticipate that their budgets will be cut by superiors. Since the manager is never sure how severe the cut will be, the result is often an inaccurate, if not unrealistic, budget.

The answer to effective budget control may be to make the manager and any concerned employees accountable for their budgets. Performance incentives can

FIGURE 18.6
Types and Purposes of Budgets

Type of Budget	Purpose
Revenue and expense budget	Provides details for revenue and expense plans.
Cash budget	Forecasts cash receipts and disbursements.
Capital expenditure budget	Outlines specific expenditures for plant, equipment, machinery, inventories, and other capital items.
Production, material, or time budget	Expresses physical requirements of production, or material, or the time requirements for the budget period.
Balance sheet budgets	Forecasts the status of assets, liabilities, and net worth at the end of the budget period.

be tied to budget control, accuracy, and fulfillment. In other words, if it is worth budgeting, it is worth budgeting right! Others believe budgets should also be tied not only to financial data but also to customer satisfaction. Budget for what it takes to satisfy the customer would be the rule of thumb for this logic. Ron Rittenmeyer of Frito-Lay cautioned that organizations can get so hung up on measuring themselves by sticking to their own sets of rules, focusing internally, and watching their budgets that they forget their customers.[13] Yet the customer is what business is all about. Generally managers meet on a periodic basic (usually monthly or quarterly) with budget officials to discuss planned finances versus actual expenses. The budget officials are usually from the accounting department.

Zero-Base Budgeting

zero-base budgeting

Form of budgeting in which the manager must build and justify each area of a budget. Each activity is identified, evaluated, and ranked by importance.

Zero-base budgeting was designed to stop basing this year's budget on last year's budget. **Zero-base budgeting** requires each manager to justify an entire budget request in detail. The burden of proof is on each manager to justify why any money should be spent. Under zero-base budgeting, each activity under a manager's discretion is identified, evaluated, and ranked by importance. Then each year every activity in the budget is on trial for its life and is matched against all the other claimants for an organization's resources.

Financial Controls

In addition to budgets, many managers use other types of financial information for control purposes. These include balance sheets, income statements, and financial ratios. Regardless of the type of financial information used, it is meaningful only when compared with either the historical performance of the organization or the performances of similar organizations. For example, knowing that a company had net income of $100,000 last year doesn't reveal much by itself. However, when compared to last year's net income of $500,000 or to an industry average of $500,000, much more can be determined about the company's performance.

Financial Ratio Analysis

Financial ratios can be divided into four basic types: profitability, liquidity, debt, and activity ratios. *Profitability ratios* indicate the organization's operational efficiency, or how well the organization is being managed. Gross profit margin, net profit margin, and return on investment (ROI) are all examples of profitability ratios. *Liquidity ratios* are used to judge how well an organization will be able to meet its short-term financial obligations. The current ratio (current assets divided by current liabilities) and the quick ratio (current assets minus inventories divided by current liabilities) are examples of liquidity ratios. *Debt* (sometimes called *leverage*) *ratios* measure the magnitude of owners' and creditors' claims on the organization and indicate the organization's ability to meet long-term obligations. The debt to equity ratio and total debt to total assets ratio are two common debt ratios. *Activity ratios* evaluate how effectively an organization is managing some of its basic operations. Asset turnover, inventory turnover, average collection period, and accounts receivable turnover represent some commonly used activity ratios.

As mentioned earlier, financial ratios are meaningful only when compared to past ratios and to ratios of similar organizations. Also, financial ratios reflect only certain specific information, and therefore they should be used in conjunction with other management controls. Figure 18.7 presents a summary of several financial ratio calculations.

FIGURE 18.7   **Summary of Financial Ratio Calculations**

Ratio	Calculation	Purpose
Profitability Ratios		
Gross profit margin	$\dfrac{\text{Sales} - \text{Cost of goods sold}}{\text{Sales}} \times 100$	Indicates efficiency of operations and product pricing
	$\dfrac{\text{Net profit after tax}}{\text{Sales}} \times 100$	Indicates efficiency after all expenses are considered
Return on assets (ROA)	$\dfrac{\text{Net profit after tax}}{\text{Total assets}} \times 100$	Shows productivity of assets
Return on equity (ROE)	$\dfrac{\text{Net profit after tax}}{\text{Stockholders' equity}} \times 100$	Shows earnings power of equity
Liquidity Ratios		
Current ratio	$\dfrac{\text{Current assets}}{\text{Current liabilities}}$	Shows short-run debt-paying ability
Quick ratio	$\dfrac{\text{Current assets} - \text{Inventories}}{\text{Current liabilities}}$	Shows short-term liquidity
Debt Ratios		
Debt to equity	$\dfrac{\text{Total liabilities}}{\text{Stockholders' equity}}$	Indicates long-term liquidity
Total debt to total assets (debt ratio)	$\dfrac{\text{Total liabilities}}{\text{Total assets}}$	Shows percentage of assets financed through borrowing
Activity Ratios		
Asset turnover	$\dfrac{\text{Sales}}{\text{Total assets}}$	Shows efficiency of asset utilization
Inventory turnover	$\dfrac{\text{Cost of goods sold}}{\text{Average inventory}}$	Shows management's ability to control investment in inventory
Average collection period	$\dfrac{\text{Receivables} \times 365 \text{ days}}{\text{Annual credit sales}}$	Shows effectiveness of collection and credit policies
Accounts receivable turnover	$\dfrac{\text{Annual credit sales}}{\text{Receivables}}$	Shows effectiveness of collection and credit policies

Sarbanes-Oxley Act of 2002

On July 30, 2002, President Bush signed into law the Sarbanes-Oxley Act of 2002. The Sarbanes-Oxley Act, which has been called the most dramatic change to federal securities laws since the 1930s, radically redesigned federal regulation of public company corporate governance and reporting obligations. The law also significantly tightens accountability standards for corporate directors and officers, auditors, securities, analysts, and legal counsel. The purpose of the act is to prevent the kind of accounting and financial maneuvering that caused the meltdowns experienced at Enron (see the chapter preview) and WorldCom. Figure 18.8 summarizes the major points of the law.

One major concern related to the Sarbanes-Oxley Act is its hefty compliance costs. It has been estimated that the total compliance costs could top $7 billion the

FIGURE 18.8
Major Points of the Sarbanes-Oxley Act of 2002

Source: Reprinted by permission of CPE, Inc., 3700 Reed Road, Suite 227, Broomall, PA 19008, 800-514-1114, www.cpeonline.com.

The SEC will direct the NYSE and NASDAQ to prohibit listing any public company whose audit committee does not comply with a new list of requirements affecting auditor appointment, compensation, and oversight. The audit committee must consist solely of independent directors.

CEOs and CFOs must certify in each periodic report containing financial statements that the report fully complies with Sections 13(a) and 15(d) of the Securities Exchange Act of 1934 and that the information fairly presents the company's financial condition and results of operations.

Certifying officers will face penalties for false certification of $1,000,000 and/or up to 10 years' imprisonment for "knowing" violation and $5,000,000 and/or up to 20 years' imprisonment for "willing" violation.

No public company may make, extend, modify, or renew any personal loan to its executive officers or directors, with limited exceptions.

The act sets a deadline for insiders to report any trading in their companies' securities to within two business days after the execution date of the transaction.

Each company must disclose "on a rapid and current basis" additional information about the company's financial condition or operations as the SEC determines is necessary or useful to investors or in the public interest.

All annual reports filed with the SEC containing financial statements must include all material corrections identified by a public accounting firm.

The act creates several new crimes for securities violations, including
- Destroying, altering, or falsifying records with the intent to impede or influence any federal investigation or bankruptcy proceeding.
- Knowing and willful failure by an accountant to maintain all audit or workpapers for five years.
- Knowingly executing a scheme to defraud investors in connection with any security.

first year alone and that it will cost the average Fortune 500 company an additional $3 million to $8 million in annual compliance costs.[14] There is concern that the compliance costs will be especially hard on smaller companies.

Direct Observation

A store manager's daily tour of the facility, a company president's annual visit to all branches, and a methods study by a staff industrial engineer are all examples of control by direct observation. Although time-consuming, personal observation is sometimes the only way to get an accurate picture of what is really happening. One hazard is that employees may misinterpret a superior's visit and consider such action meddling or eavesdropping. A second hazard is that behaviors change when people are being watched or monitored. Another potential inaccuracy lies in the interpretation of the observation. The observer must be careful not to read into the picture events that did not actually occur. Visits and direct observation can have positive effects when viewed by employees as a display of the manager's interest.

Written Reports

Written reports can be prepared on a periodic or an as-necessary basis. There are two basic types of written reports: analytical and informational. Analytical reports interpret the facts they present; informational reports present only the facts. Preparing a report is a four- or five-step process, depending on whether it is informational or analytical. The steps are (1) planning what is to be done, (2) collecting the facts, (3) organizing the facts, (4) interpreting the facts (this step is omitted with informational reports), and (5) writing the report.[15] Most reports should be prepared for the benefit of the reader and not the writer. In most cases, the reader wants useful information not previously available.

Electronic Monitors

Today, a number of different types of electronic devices can be used to monitor what is going on. Examples include electronic cash registers that keep a record of what items are sold and when; video cameras that record employee and customer movements; phones that record how long each customer was engaged; Internet programs that track where and how long an employee or customer is at certain Internet sites; and other forms of automated reports.

Management Information Systems

As discussed in Chapter 4, management information systems (MISs) are computerized systems designed to produce information needed for successful management of a process, department, or business. Usually, the information provided by an MIS is in the form of periodic reports, special reports, and outputs of mathematical simulations.[16]

Audits

audit
Method of control normally involved with financial matters; also can include other areas of the organization.

management audit
Attempts to evaluate the overall management practices and policies of the organization.

break-even chart
Depicts graphically the relationship of volume of operations to profits.

Audits can be conducted by either internal or external personnel. External audits are normally done by outside accountants and are limited to financial matters. Most are conducted to certify that the organization's accounting methods are fair, are consistent, and conform to existing practices. Internal audits are performed by the organization's own personnel.

An audit that looks at areas other than finance and accounting is known as a management audit. **Management audits** attempt to evaluate the overall management practices and policies of the organization. They can be conducted by outside consultants or inside staff; however, a management audit conducted by inside staff can easily result in a biased report.

Break-Even Charts

Break-even charts depict graphically the relationship of volume of operations to profits. The break-even point (BEP) is the point at which sales revenues exactly equal expenses. Total sales below the BEP result in a loss; total sales above the BEP result in a profit.

Figure 18.9 shows a typical break-even chart. The horizontal axis represents output; the vertical axis represents expenses and revenues. Though not required, most break-even charts assume there are linear relationships and all costs are either fixed or variable. Fixed costs do not vary with output, at least in the short run. They include rent, insurance, and administrative salaries. Variable costs vary with output. Typical variable costs include direct labor and materials. The purpose of the chart is to show the break-even point and the effects of changes in output. A break-even chart is useful for showing whether revenue and costs are running as planned.

Time-Related Charts and Techniques

Gantt charts, the critical path method (CPM), and the program evaluation and control technique (PERT) (discussed in Chapter 7) are tools used to plan and schedule. These same tools can also be used for controlling once the plans have

FIGURE 18.9
Break-Even Chart

Expenses and revenues
(thousands of dollars)

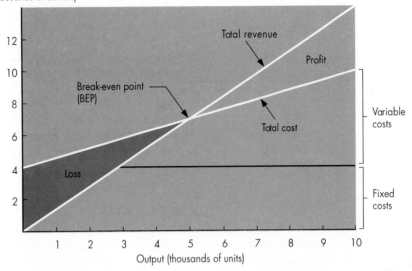

Output (thousands of units)

been put into action. By tracking actual progress compared to planned progress, activities that fall behind schedule can quickly be spotted.

Summary

1. *Explain why management controls are necessary.* The overriding purpose of all management controls is to alert the manager to an existing or a potential problem before it becomes critical. Specifically, management controls can be used to (1) prevent crises, (2) standardize outputs, (3) appraise employee performance, (4) update plans, and (5) protect an organization's assets.

2. *Describe a feedback system.* Any system in which the outputs from the system affect future inputs or future activities of the system is called a feedback system; in other words, a feedback system is influenced by its own past behavior.

3. *Discuss the basic requirements of the control process.* The control process has three basic requirements: (1) establishing standards, (2) monitoring results and comparing them to standards, and (3) correcting for any deviations between the standard and actual results.

4. *Describe the control pyramid.* The control pyramid is a method for implementing control in the organization. It consists of control through foolproofing, automatic controls, operator controls, control by personal supervision, and informational controls.

5. *Identify the factors that affect how much control should be exercised in an organization.* When deciding how much control should be exercised in an organization, three major factors must be appraised: (1) economic considerations, (2) behavioral considerations, and (3) flexibility and innovation considerations.

6. *Discuss the two categories of control methods.* Control methods can be either of two kinds: (1) behavior control or (2) output control. Behavior (or personal) control is based on direct, personal surveillance. Output (or impersonal) control is based on the measurement of outputs.

7. *Differentiate between preliminary, concurrent, and postaction controls.* Preliminary (steering) controls are designed to prevent a problem from occurring. Concurrent (screening) controls focus on things that happen as inputs are being transformed into outputs. They are designed to detect a problem as it occurs. Postaction controls are designed to detect existing or potential problems after they occur but before they reach crisis proportions.

8. *List several methods or systems of control commonly used by managers.* Many control methods or systems are in use today. Some of the most popular control methods/systems include all types of budgets, financial controls (balance sheets, income statements, and financial ratios), direct observations, written reports, management information systems, audits, break-even charts, and time-related charts and techniques.

9. *List the four basic types of financial ratios.* The four basic types of financial ratios are profitability, liquidity, debt, and activity ratios.

10. *Summarize the Sarbanes-Oxley Act of 2002.* The Sarbanes-Oxley Act of 2002 radically redesigned federal regulation of public company corporate governance and reporting obligations. The law also significantly tightens accountability standards for corporate directors and officers, auditors, securities analysts, and legal counsel.

11. *Discuss the basic purpose of a break-even chart.* A break-even chart graphically depicts the relationship of volume of operations to profits.

Review Questions

1. What is management control? What are the two major concerns in management control?
2. Describe a model of the management control process.
3. Outline the three basic requirements of control.
4. How much control should be exercised in an organization?
5. Describe the two categories of control methods.
6. Define preliminary, concurrent, and postaction controls.
7. Describe the following control methods and systems:
   a. Budgets
   b. Financial ratios
   c. Direct observation
   d. Written reports
   e. Management information systems
   f. Audits
   g. Break-even charts
8. Outline the major points of the Sarbanes-Oxley Act of 2002.

Skill-Building Questions

1. If you were implementing a new control system designed to track more closely the expenses of your salespeople, what actions might you take to minimize negative reactions?
2. Why are many managers reluctant to take the actions necessary to correct for deviations?
3. How should you deal with managers who are so "married" to their departmental budgets that they will not let you spend $1 to make $10?
4. Give an example of how you might enable a subordinate to control something at the line level. What might be the benefits of enabling?

Skill-Building Exercise 18.1

Breaking Even

As of January 1, 2004, UND Family Health Service Center had 15 employees with a total annual salary budget of $400,000. The annual maintenance cost was estimated at $80,000. Based on 2003 data, the monthly patient service in 2004 is forecast as 180 patients per month. For each patient serviced, the average variable cost incurred (e.g., paperwork, treatment materials, equipment depreciation, utility consumption) is estimated at $10, and average revenue per patient is projected to be $230.

1. Based on the above information, do you think the center manager can balance annual costs and annual revenues? Explain. What would you suggest to the manager?
2. If, by implementing more efficient operations management, the center's operating (variable) cost can be reduced to $8 per patient, do you think the center could balance its annual budget?
3. If dismissing employees becomes necessary to balance the budget, how many employees would you recommend be let go? Why?
4. At the end of June 2004, the manager showed you the following report:

	Jan.	Feb.	March	April	May	June
Number of patients	150	140	152	145	130	145

What comments would you make to the manager?

Source: This exercise was written by Jiaqin Yang, assistant professor, the University of North Dakota.

Skill-Building Exercise 18.2

Staying on Budget

As manager of the Ace Division of the Triple-A Company, you agreed to the following budget at the beginning of the current fiscal year: This budget was based on forecast sales of 30,000 units during the year.

Fixed costs	$80,000
Subcontracting costs (variable, per unit)	$4
Other variable costs (per unit)	$2
Sales price	$10

You are six months into the fiscal year and have collected the following sales data:

Month	Actual Sales (units)
1	2,000
2	2,200
3	1,700
4	1,800
5	2,300
6	2,200

By shopping around, you have held your subcontracting costs to an average of $3.60 per unit. The fixed and other variable costs are conforming to budgets.

1. What was the break-even point based on the original forecast in sales for the Ace Division?
2. What is the revised break-even point?
3. What trends in the above information, if any, concern you?
4. Based on the preceding information, prepare a brief report for your boss, summarizing the current status of the Ace Division.

Case Incident 18.1

"Bird Dogging" the Employee

Ace Electronics, Inc., is a small company located in Centerville. It is owned and operated by Al Abrams, a highly experienced electronics person who founded the company.

Ace's basic product is a walkie-talkie that is sold primarily to the U.S. military. The walkie-talkie units are relatively simple to produce; Ace merely purchases the parts—cables, wires, transistors, and so on—and assembles them with hand tools. Due to this moderate level of complexity, Ace employs semiskilled workers at low wage rates.

Although Ace has made a profit each year since it started production, Al Abrams was becoming increasingly concerned. Over the past six years, he had noticed a general decline in employee morale; furthermore, he had observed a decline in his employees' productivity and his company's profit margin.

As a result of his concern, Al asked his supervisors to keep a closer watch on the workers' hour-to-hour activities. In the first week, they discovered two workers in the restroom reading magazines. This "bird dogging" technique, as management called it, or "slave driving," as the workers called it, failed to increase either production or productivity.

Al recognized that the lack of performance on the part of some employees was affecting the production of everyone. This phenomenon was caused by the balanced assembly line under which the walkie-talkies were assembled. If an employee next to a normally productive employee did not work fast enough, walkie-talkies would back up on the line. Instead of having a backup, however, the assembly line was usually readjusted to the production rate of the slower employees.

In addition, another situation developed to lower productivity and increase unit costs. Ace was required by the government to meet monthly production and delivery schedules. If it failed, a very substantial financial penalty could result. In recent years, the production and delivery schedule had become more difficult to meet. For the last eight months, Al had scheduled overtime to meet the production and delivery schedule and thus avoid the financial penalty. This overtime increased unit production costs and caused another problem: Many employees began to realize that if they worked more slowly at the beginning of the month, they could receive more overtime at the end of the month. Even the senior employees were slowing down to increase their overtime wages.

Al was very reluctant to fire employees, especially senior employees. Even if he was inclined to do so, it was difficult to catch employees slowing down or provide any reasonable evidence for such a rash action. Al was frustrated and perplexed.

Questions

1. Describe in detail the control dilemma at Ace Electronics.
2. Are Al Abrams and the employees getting the same feedback? Why or why not?
3. What should Al do?

Case Incident 18.2

Mickey Mouse Controls

Jean: Hey, John, I could sure use some help. We regional supervisors are caught in the middle. What do you do about all this red tape we're having to put up with? The accounting department is all bothered about the way people are padding their expenses and about the cost of luncheons and long-distance calls. You know—their answer is nothing but more red tape.

John: Well, Jean, I don't know. I'm feeling the heat too. Upper management wants us to maintain our contacts with our brokers and try to get the money out in loans. So we push the district supervisors to see our best contacts or at least call them frequently. Yet lately, I've been having a heck of a time getting my people reimbursed for their expenses. Now the accounting department is kicking because we spend a few bucks taking someone to lunch or making a few long-distance calls.

Jean: I really don't know what to do, John. I'll admit that some of my people tend to charge the company for expenses that are for their personal entertainment. But how can I tell whether they're buttering up a broker or just living it up on the company? The accounting department must have some receipts and records to support expenses. Yet I think that getting a receipt from a parking lot attendant is carrying this control stuff too far. As a matter of fact, the other day, I caught a taxi at the airport and failed to get a receipt—I'll bet I have a hard time getting that money from the company even if I sign a notarized affidavit.

John: Well, the way I handle those things is to charge the company more for tips than I actually give—and you know they don't require receipts for tips. I just don't know how to decide whether those reimbursement receipts that I sign for my people are legitimate. If I call people up and ask about some items on a reimbursement request, they act as though I'm making a charge of grand larceny. So far, I've decided to sign whatever requests they turn in and leave the accounting department to scream if it wants to. The trouble is that I don't have any guidelines as to what is reasonable.

Jean: Yeah, but I don't want to ask questions about that because it would just result in more controls! It isn't up to me to be a policeman for the company. The accounting department sits back looking at all those figures—it should watch expenses. I ran into someone from the department the other day on what she called an internal audit trip, and she told me that they aren't in a position to say whether a $40 lunch at a restaurant is necessary to sell a loan. She said that the charge was made by one of my people and that I should check it out! Am I a regional production person or am I an accountant? I've got enough to do meeting my regional quota with my five district salespeople. I can't go snooping around to find out whether they're taking advantage of the company. They may get the idea that I don't trust them, and I've always heard that good business depends on trust. Besides, our department makes the company more money than any other one. Why shouldn't we be allowed to spend a little of it?

John: Well, I say that the brass is getting hot about a relatively small problem. A little fudging on an expense account isn't going to break the company. I learned the other day that the accounting department doesn't require any receipts from the securities department people. They just give them a per diem for travel and let them spend it however they want to, just so long as they don't go over the allotted amount for the days that they're on trips.

Jean: Now that sounds like a good idea. Why can't we do that? It sure would make my life easier. I don't want to get a guilt complex about signing reimbursement requests that may look a little out of line. Why should I call an employee on the carpet for some small expense that may be the reason we got the deal? Performance is our job, so why can't the company leave us alone? They should let us decide what it takes to make a deal. If we don't produce the loans, we should catch flak about something that's important—not about these trifling details.

John: Jean, I've got to run now. But honestly, if I were you, I wouldn't worry about these Mickey Mouse controls. I'm just going to do my job and fill in the form in order to stay out of trouble on the details. It's not worth getting upset about.

Questions

1. Has the company imposed overly restrictive controls? Explain why or why not.
2. Do you think the company has a good conception of control tolerances? Why or why not?
3. What should Jean do?

References and Additional Readings

1. Tom Peters, *Liberation Management* (New York: Alfred A. Knopf, 1992), pp. 486, 488.
2. Ibid., pp. 465–66.
3. Ibid.
4. Jeremy Main, *Quality Wars* (New York: Free Press, 1994), pp. 132–33.
5. J. M. Juran, *Managerial Breakthrough*, rev. ed. (New York: McGraw-Hill, 1995), pp. 203–205.
6. Ibid.

7. For a discussion of some relevant studies, see Arnold S. Tannenbaum, "Control in Organizations: Individual Adjustment in Organization Performance," *Administrative Science Quarterly,* September 1962, pp. 241–46; and Klaus Bartolke, Walter Eschweiler, Dieter Flechsenberger, and Arnold S. Tannenbaum, "Worker Participation and the Distribution of Control as Perceived by Members of Ten German Companies," *Administrative Science Quarterly* 27 (1982), pp. 380–97.

8. Gene W. Dalton and Paul R. Lawrence, *Motivation and Control in Organizations* (Homewood, IL: Richard D. Irwin, 1971), p. 8.

9. James Champy, *Reengineering Management* (New York: Harper Business, 1995), p. 130.

10. Ibid.

11. Timothy J. McMahon and G. W. Perritt, "Toward a Contingency Theory of Organizational Control," *Academy of Management Journal,* December 1973, pp. 624–35.

12. William G. Ouchi and Mary Ann Maguire, "Organizational Control: Two Functions," *Administrative Science Quarterly,* December 1975, pp. 559–71; and William G. Ouchi, "The Transmission of Control through Organizational Hierarchy," *Academy of Management Journal,* June 1978, pp. 174–76.

13. Champy, *Reengineering Management,* p. 140.

14. David Henry and Amy Borrus, "Honesty Is a Pricey Policy: Execs Are Grumbling about the Steep Costs of Complying with New Financial Controls," *Business Week,* October 27, 2003, p. 100; and Jeremy Kahn, "A Taste of Success," *Fortune,* September 1, 2003, p. 50.

15. C. W. Wilkinson, Dorothy Wilkinson, and Gretchen Vik, *Communicating through Letters and Reports,* 9th ed. (Homewood, IL: Richard D. Irwin, 1986).

16. James A. Seen, *Information Technology in Business,* 2nd ed. (Englewood Cliffs, NJ: Prentice Hall, 1998), p. 615; and Raymond McLeod, Jr., *Management Information Systems,* 4th ed. (New York: Macmillan, 1990), p. 30.

19

Appraising
and Rewarding
Performance

Learning Objectives

After studying this chapter, you will be able to:

1. Define performance appraisal.
2. Define performance.
3. Explain the determinants of performance.
4. List and describe the 10 major performance appraisal methods.
5. Define job analysis.
6. Explain the contents of a job description.
7. Discuss common errors made in performance appraisals.
8. Suggest ways to make performance appraisal systems more legally acceptable.
9. Define compensation.
10. Outline desirable preconditions for implementing a merit pay program.

Chapter Preview

Lincoln Electric Company celebrated its 100th anniversary in 1995. The Cleveland, Ohio–based manufacturer of arc welders has 2,000 blue-collar employees at its four U.S. plants. The employees do not belong to a union, have never gone out on strike, and deferred 614 weeks of vacation in 1994 to meet worldwide demand. Recent figures show that Lincoln's employees are two-and-a-half to three times more productive than employees of other, similar manufacturing companies.

The key to Lincoln's success is that the company bases pay on performance and sets virtually no limit on what employees can earn. Employees have not experienced a layoff since 1948 and have received an annual bonus every year since 1934. Once they have been with the company for three years, Lincoln employees are also guaranteed their jobs until retirement if they agree to pay cuts or reassignment within the company when necessary. In response to demand, employees may work overtime or work fewer hours. According to Jon Stropki, the president of Lincoln's North American branch, "Most of our people get paid by the number of parts they produce. [Years ago] the Lincolns had the foresight to know that if they didn't guarantee employment, people would say [to each other], 'Make less, so we'll have a job even when things are slow.' The way we can be successful is by having a high level of productivity all the time."

Sources: Eric Wahlgren, "Alternatives to the Ax," *Business Week Online,* February 9, 2001; and Jennifer Gill, "How 'No Layoffs' Can Work," *Business Week Online,* November 6, 2001.

Analyzing Management Skills

Do you feel that a person's pay should be based on his or her performance? Why or why not?

Applying Management Skills

Recall a time when you were rewarded for an activity based on how well you completed the task. Did the reward motivate you to do a better job?

Performance appraisal systems that are directly tied to an organization's reward system provide a powerful incentive for employees to work diligently and creatively toward achieving organizational objectives. When properly conducted, performance appraisals not only let employees know how well they are presently performing but also clarify what needs to be done to improve performance.[1]

performance appraisal
Process that involves determining and communicating to employees how they are performing their jobs and establishing a plan for improvement.

Performance appraisal is a process that involves determining and communicating to employees how they are performing their jobs and establishing a plan for improvement. Some of the more common uses of performance appraisals are to make decisions related to merit pay increases, promotions, layoffs, and firings. For example, the present job performance of an employee is often the most significant consideration for determining whether to promote the person. While successful performance in the present job does not necessarily mean an employee will be an effective performer in a higher-level job, performance appraisals do provide some predictive information.

Performance appraisal information can also provide needed input for determining both individual and organizational training and development needs. For example, it can be used to identify individual strengths and weaknesses. These data can then be used to help determine the organization's overall training and development needs. For an individual employee, a completed performance appraisal should include a plan outlining specific training and development needs.

Another important use of performance appraisals is to encourage performance improvement. In this regard, performance appraisals are used as a means of communicating to employees how they are doing and suggesting needed changes in behavior, attitude, skill, or knowledge. This type of feedback clarifies for employees the job expectations the manager holds. Often, this feedback must be followed by coaching and training by the manager to guide an employee's work efforts.

To work effectively, performance appraisals must be supported by documentation and a commitment by management to make them fair and effective. Typical standards for the performance appraisal process are that it be fair, accurate (facts,

Joseph Brundage, an African American male born in 1943, originally worked part-time for NBC, taking a full-time job as a remote computer operator at two of NBC's "remote" computer locations in New York City. His job was to make sure that the computer jobs run in Briarcliff, N.Y., were printed correctly and distributed to users at the two remote locations in New York City. Soon after becoming a full-time employee, a dispute arose between Brundage and NBC concerning his grade level and salary. He was under the impression that he was hired as a Grade H and that he would be eligible for a raise in six months. NBC claimed that he was hired as a Grade E. After filing a discrimination case with the EEOC, Brundage and NBC settled the issue with Brundage withdrawing his complaint to the EEOC, after being promoted to Grade G, as well as receiving a salary increase to Grade H salary.

During the period 1984–1986, Brundage had attendance and punctuality problems, and there were periods when he left the computer room unattended. This was in violation of an NBC memorandum indicating that when there are two operators on duty, both should not leave the computer center at the same time; and if there is only one operator on duty, a supervisor or manager at the other computer center should be notified before the operator leaves the center. Brundage's 1986 performance appraisal noted that he had a "habit" of leaving the computer center unattended. Following receipt of the 1986 performance

appraisal, Brundage expressed interest in being promoted to senior remote computer operator, as two positions had become vacant. He was informed that he was not qualified for promotion because of his poor performance evaluation, his lack of follow-up, and his failure to get along with management.

The following performance appraisal indicated that Brundage met only the basic requirements of the job, he spent an excessive amount of time on the phone and out of the computer room, his attitude toward superiors was counterproductive, and he reacted in a very negative manner when faced with constructive criticism. Brundage's performance was evaluated by two other raters on two more occasions with the same comments, as well as one that addressed his smoking in a nonsmoking area, the computer center. Brundage was subsequently discharged on June 6, 1989. Brundage again filed a charge with the EEOC from which he received a right-to-sue letter. However, NBC subsequently prevailed in the lawsuit, demonstrating that it had been more than fair with Brundage in all areas, merit pay, promotion, and discharge. The performance appraisal results buttressed all of NBC's actions.

Source: Kathryn M. Bartol, Robert H. Smith, and Patrick E. Kehoe, "The Legal Ramifications of Performance Appraisal: The Growing Significance," *Public Personnel Management*, Fall 2000, pp. 379–404.

not opinions, should be used), include as much direct observation as possible, be consistent, and contain as much objective documentation as possible.[2] The amount and types of documentation necessary to support decisions made by management vary, but the general rule of thumb is to provide enough varied documentation to allow anyone evaluating the performance of an employee to generally come to the same conclusion as the manager. Management Illustration 19.1 describes one use of performance approvals.

An additional concern in organizations is how often to conduct performance appraisals. No real consensus exists on this question, but the usual answer is as often as necessary to let employees know what kind of job they are doing and, if performance is not satisfactory, the measures they must take to improve. For many employees, this cannot be accomplished through one annual performance appraisal. Therefore, it is recommended that for most employees, informal performance appraisals should be conducted two or three times a year in addition to the annual performance appraisal.

performance
Degree of accomplishment of the tasks that make up an employee's job.

Understanding Performance

Performance refers to the degree of accomplishment of the tasks that make up an employee's job. It reflects how well an employee is fulfilling the requirements of the job. Often confused with effort, which refers to energy expended, performance is measured in terms of results. Because many American corporations have become very results oriented in the last decade, more and more emphasis is being placed on measuring performance.

Determinants of Performance

Job performance is the net effect of an employee's effort as modified by abilities, role perceptions, and results produced. This implies that performance in a given situation can be viewed as resulting from the interrelationships among effort, abilities, role perceptions, and results produced.

effort
Results from being motivated; refers to the amount of energy an employee uses in performing a job.

abilities
Personal characteristics used in performing a job.

role perception
Direction in which employees believe they should channel their efforts on their jobs.

Effort, which results from being motivated, refers to the amount of energy an employee uses in performing a job. **Abilities** are personal characteristics used in performing a job. Abilities usually do not fluctuate widely over short periods of time. **Role perception** refers to the direction in which employees believe they should channel their efforts on their jobs. The activities and behavior employees believe are necessary in the performance of their jobs define their role perceptions. The results produced are usually measured by standards created by the degree of attainment of management-directed objectives.

To attain an acceptable level of performance, a minimum level of proficiency must exist in each of the performance components. Similarly, the level of proficiency in any one of the performance components can place an upper boundary on performance. Studies indicate that the level of performance can be improved and boundaries raised if management empowers employees to become more active in determining and evaluating their performance measures and standards.[3] To accomplish this, however, management has to erase the natural fear of and resistance to empowerment and become advocates of employee involvement.[4]

Performance Appraisal Methods

An early method of performance appraisal used in the United States was described as follows:

> On the morning following each day's work, each workman was given a slip of paper informing him in detail just how much work he had done the day before, and the amount he had earned. This enabled him to measure his performance against his earnings while the details were fresh in his mind.[5]

This method of performance appraisal was effective in that it gave immediate feedback and tied pay to performance. Since then, the number and variety of performance appraisal methods have dramatically increased. The following sections describe the performance appraisal methods used in businesses today.

Goal Setting, or Management by Objectives (MBO)

In addition to being a useful method for directing the organization's objective-setting process, management by objectives (MBO) can also be used in the performance appraisal process. The value of linking the MBO program to the appraisal process is that employees tend to support goals if they agree the goals are acceptable and if they expect to be personally successful in their efforts.[6] Employee acceptance (by giving the employee a stake in the MBO process) is certainly a powerful motivator for considering the MBO process. The typical MBO process consists of

FIGURE 19.1
Sample Objectives

To answer all customer complaints in writing within three days of receipt of complaint.
To reduce order-processing time by two days within the next six months.
To implement the new computerized accounts receivable system by August 1.

1. Establishing clear and precisely defined statements of objectives for the work an employee is to do.
2. Developing an action plan indicating how these objectives are to be achieved.
3. Allowing the employee to implement this action plan.
4. Appraising performance based on objective achievement.
5. Taking corrective action when necessary.
6. Establishing new objectives for the future.

If an employee is to be evaluated on the objectives set in the MBO process, several requirements must be met. First, objectives should be quantifiable and measurable; objectives whose attainment cannot be measured or at least verified should be avoided where possible. Objectives should also be challenging, yet achievable, and they should be expressed in writing and in clear, concise, unambiguous language. Figure 19.1 lists some sample objectives that meet these requirements.

Production Standards

production standards approach
Performance appraisal method most frequently used for employees who are involved in physically producing a product; is basically a form of objective setting for these employees.

The **production standards approach** to performance appraisal is most frequently used for employees who are involved in physically producing a product and is basically a form of objective setting for these employees. It involves setting a standard or an expected level of output and then comparing each employee's performance to the standard. Generally, production standards should reflect the normal output of an average person. Production standards attempt to answer the question of what is a fair day's output. Several methods can be used to set production standards. Figure 19.2 summarizes some of the more common methods.

An advantage of the production standards approach is that the performance review is based on highly objective factors. Of course, to be effective, the standards must be viewed by the affected employees as being fair. The most serious criticism of production standards is a lack of comparability of standards for different job categories.

FIGURE 19.2
Frequently Used Methods for Setting Production Standards

Method	Areas of Applicability
Average production or work	When tasks performed by all employees are the same or approximately the same.
Performance of specially selected employees	When tasks performed by all employees are basically the same, and it would be cumbersome and time-consuming to use the group average.
Time study	Jobs involving repetitive tasks.
Work sampling	Noncyclical types of work in which many different tasks are performed and there is no set pattern or cycle.
Expert opinion	When none of the more direct methods (described above) applies.

Essay Appraisal

essay appraisal method
Requires the manager to describe an employee's performance in written narrative form.

The **essay appraisal method** requires the manager to describe an employee's performance in written narrative form. Instructions are often provided to the manager as to the topics to be covered. A typical essay appraisal question might be, "Describe, in your own words, this employee's performance, including quantity and quality of work, job knowledge, and ability to get along with other employees. What are the employee's strengths and weaknesses?"

The primary problem with essay appraisals is that their length and content can vary considerably (depending on the manager) and the method can be very subjective (whereas objective measures are more defensible). For instance, one manager may write a lengthy statement describing an employee's potential and saying little about past performance; another manager may concentrate on the employee's past performance. Thus, essay appraisals are difficult to compare. The writing skill of a manager can also affect the appraisal. An effective writer can make an average employee look better than the actual performance warrants.

Critical-Incident Appraisal

critical-incident appraisal
Requires the manager to keep a written record of incidents, as they occur, involving job behaviors that illustrate both satisfactory and unsatisfactory performance of the employee being rated.

The **critical-incident appraisal** method requires the manager to keep a written record of incidents, as they occur, involving job behaviors that illustrate both satisfactory and unsatisfactory performance of the employee being rated. As they are recorded over time, the incidents provide a basis for evaluating performance and providing feedback to the employee.

The main drawback to this approach is that the manager is required to jot down incidents regularly, which can be a burdensome and time-consuming task. Also, the definition of a critical incident is unclear and may be interpreted differently by different managers. Some believe this method can lead to friction between the manager and employees when the employees think the manager is keeping a "book" on them.

Graphic Rating Scale

graphic rating scale
Requires the manager to assess an employee on factors such as quantity of work, dependability, job knowledge, attendance, accuracy of work, and cooperativeness.

With the **graphic rating scale** method, the manager assesses an employee on factors such as quantity of work, dependability, job knowledge, attendance, accuracy of work, and cooperativeness. Graphic rating scales include both numerical ranges and written descriptions. Figure 19.3 gives an example of some of the items that might be included on a graphic rating scale that uses written descriptions.

The graphic rating scale method is subject to some serious weaknesses. One potential weakness is that managers are unlikely to interpret written descriptions in the same manner because of differences in background, experience, and personality. Another potential problem relates to the choice of rating categories. It is possible to choose categories that have little relationship to job performance or omit categories that have a significant influence on job performance.

Checklist

checklist
Requires the manager to answer yes or no to a series of questions concerning the employee's behavior.

With the **checklist** method, the manager answers yes or no to a series of questions concerning the employee's behavior. Figure 19.4 lists some typical questions. The checklist can also have varying weights assigned to each question.

Normally, the scoring key for the checklist method is kept by the human resource department; the manager is generally not aware of the weights associated with each question. But because the manager can see the positive or negative connotation of each question, bias can be introduced. Additional drawbacks to the checklist method are that it is time-consuming to assemble the questions for each job

FIGURE 19.3   **Sample Items on a Graphic Rating Scale Evaluation Form**

Quantity of work (the amount of work an employee does in a workday)

( )	( )	( )	( )	( )
Does not meet requirements.	Does just enough to get by.	Volume of work is satisfactory.	Very industrious, does more than is required.	Superior production record.

Dependability (the ability to do required jobs with a minimum of supervision)

( )	( )	( )	( )	( )
Requires close supervision; is unreliable.	Sometimes requires prompting.	Usually completes necessary tasks with reasonable promptness.	Requires little supervision; is reliable.	Requires absolute minimum of supervision.

Job knowledge (information that an employee should have on work duties for satisfactory job performance)

( )	( )	( )	( )	( )
Poorly informed about work duties.	Lacks knowledge of some phases of job.	Moderately informed; can answer most questions about the job.	Understands all phases of job.	Has complete mastery of all phases of job.

Attendance (faithfulness in coming to work daily and conforming to work hours)

( )	( )	( )	( )	( )
Often absent without good excuse, or frequently reports for work late, or both.	Lax in attendance or reporting for work on time, or both.	Usually present and on time.	Very prompt; regular in attendance.	Always regular and prompt; volunteers for overtime when needed.

Accuracy (the correctness of work duties performed)

( )	( )	( )	( )	( )
Makes frequent errors.	Careless; often makes errors.	Usually accurate; makes only average number of mistakes.	Requires little supervision; is exact and precise most of the time.	Requires absolute minimum of supervision; is almost always accurate.

category; a separate listing of questions must be developed for each job category; and the checklist questions can have different meanings for different managers.

Behaviorally Anchored Rating Scales (BARS)

behaviorally anchored rating scale (BARS)
Assesses behaviors required to successfully perform a job.

The **behaviorally anchored rating scale (BARS)** method of performance appraisal is designed to assess behaviors required to successfully perform a job. The focus of BARS (and, to some extent, the graphic rating scale and checklist methods) is not on performance outcomes but on behaviors demonstrated on the job. The assumption is that these behaviors result in effective performance on the job.

To understand the use and development of a BARS, several key terms must be understood. First, most behaviorally anchored rating scales use the term *job dimension* to mean those broad categories of duties and responsibilities that make up a job. Each job is likely to have several job dimensions, and separate scales must be developed for each one.

Figure 19.5 illustrates a BARS written for rating hotel managers' communication skills. Scale values appear on the left side of the table and define specific

FIGURE 19.4
Sample Checklist Questions

	Yes	No
1. Does the employee lose his or her temper in public?	_____	_____
2. Does the employee play favorites?	_____	_____
3. Does the employee praise people in public when they have done a good job?	_____	_____
4. Does the employee volunteer to do special jobs?	_____	_____

categories of performance. Anchors, which appear on the right side of the table, are specific written statements of actual behaviors that, when exhibited on the job, indicate the level of performance on the scale opposite that particular anchor. As the anchor statements appear beside each scale value, they are said to "anchor" the respective scale values along the scale.

Rating performance using a BARS requires the manager to read the list of anchors on each scale to find the group of anchors that best describes the employee's job behavior during the period being reviewed. The scale value opposite that group of anchors is then checked. This process is followed for all of the identified dimensions on the job. A total evaluation is obtained by combining the scale values checked for all of the job dimensions.

A BARS is normally developed through a series of meetings attended by both the manager and employees who are actually performing the job. Three steps are usually followed:

FIGURE 19.5   BARS for Rating Hotel Managers' Communication Skills

Relevant behavior: Attending departmental staff meetings and involving subordinates in discussions; visiting with executive committee regularly on personal basis; using memos to communicate special instructions and policies to departments; disseminating financial and other operating information to subordinates; conducting periodic meetings with employees.

Scale Values		Anchors
Communicates effectively with staff members and attends meetings frequently	7.00 | 6.00	This manager calls a "town hall" meeting to explain why the hotel will be cutting back staff. Employees are permitted to ask questions and discuss why certain positions in the hotel are being eliminated.
	| 5.00 |	During a busy expansion program, this manager increases the frequency of policy committee meetings to improve communications and coordination of the project.
Communicates satisfactorily with staff members and attends some meetings	4.00 | 3.00	Once a week, this manager invites several line employees into his or her office for an informal talk about hotel activities.
	| 2.00 |	This manager neglects to discuss with his or her front-office manager the problem of overstaffed bellmen during certain periods of the day, yet expresses concern to the resident manager.
Experiences difficulty in communicating with staff members and attends meetings infrequently	1.00	This manager misses departmental meetings and fails to visit with subordinates individually, but leaves memos around the hotel with instructions on what should be done.
		During weekly executive committee meetings, this manager dismisses most subordinate comments as stupid.

Source: Reprinted by permission of Elsevier Science from "Performance Appraisals: Making Them Fair and Making Them Work," by Terry W. Umbreit, Robert W. Eder, and Jon P. McConnell, *The Cornell Hotel and Restaurant Administration Quarterly,* February 1986, p. 65. Copyright © 1986 by Cornell University.

FIGURE 19.6
Sample Forced-Choice Set of Statements

Instructions: Rank the following statements according to how they describe the manner in which this employee carries out duties and responsibilities. Rank 1 should be given to the most descriptive and rank 4 to the least descriptive. No ties are allowed.

Rank	Description
_____	Easy to get acquainted with
_____	Places great emphasis on people
_____	Refuses to accept criticism
_____	Thinks generally in terms of money
_____	Makes decisions quickly

1. Manager and job incumbents identify the relevant job dimensions for the job.
2. Manager and job incumbents write behavioral anchors for each job dimension. As many anchors as possible should be written for each dimension.
3. Manager and job incumbents reach a consensus concerning the scale values to be used and the grouping of anchor statements for each scale value.

The use of a BARS can result in several advantages. First, such scales are developed through the active participation of both the manager and the job incumbents. This increases the likelihood that the method will be accepted. Second, the anchors are developed from the observations and experiences of employees who actually perform the job. Finally, a BARS can be used to provide specific feedback concerning an employee's job performance. One major drawback to the use of such scales is that they take considerable time and commitment to develop. Furthermore, separate rating scales must be developed for different jobs.

Forced-Choice Rating

forced-choice rating
Requires the manager to rank a set of statements describing how an employee carries out the duties and responsibilities of the job.

Many variations of the **forced-choice rating** method exist. The most common practice requires the manager to rank a set of statements describing how an employee carries out the duties and responsibilities of the job. Figure 19.6 illustrates a group of forced-choice statements. The statements are normally weighted, and the weights are generally not known to the manager. After the manager ranks all of the forced-choice statements, the human resource department applies the weights and computes a score. This method attempts to eliminate bias by forcing the manager to rank statements that are seemingly indistinguishable or unrelated. However, the forced-choice method can irritate managers who think they are not being trusted. Furthermore, the results of the forced-choice appraisal can be difficult to communicate to employees.

Ranking Methods

When it becomes necessary to compare the performance of two or more employees, ranking methods can be used. Three of the more commonly used ranking methods are alternation, paired comparison, and forced distribution.

Alternation Ranking

In this ranking method, the names of the employees to be evaluated are listed down the left side of a sheet of paper. The manager is then asked to choose the most valuable employee on the list, cross that name off the left-hand list, and put it at the top of the column on the right side of the paper. The manager is then asked to select and cross off the name of the "least valuable" employee from the left-hand column and move it to the bottom of the right-hand column. The manager then repeats this process for all of the names on the left-hand side of the paper. The resulting list of names in the right-hand column gives a ranking of the employees from most to least valuable.

Paired Comparison Ranking

This method is best illustrated with an example. Suppose a manager is to evaluate six employees. The names of these employees are listed on the left side of a sheet of paper. The manager then compares the first employee with the second employee on a chosen performance criterion, such as quantity of work. If the manager thinks the first employee has produced more work than the second employee, she or he places a check mark by the first employee's name. The first employee is then compared to the third, fourth, fifth, and sixth employees on the same performance criterion. A check mark is placed by the name of the employee who produced the most work in each of these paired comparisons. The process is repeated until each employee has been compared to every other employee on all of the chosen performance criteria. The employee with the most check marks is considered to be the best performer. Likewise, the employee with the fewest check marks is the lowest performer. One major problem with the paired comparison method is that it becomes unwieldy when comparing large numbers of employees.

Forced Distribution

This method requires the manager to compare the performances of employees and place a certain percentage of employees at various performance levels. It assumes the performance level in a group of employees is distributed according to a bell-shaped, or "normal," curve. Figure 19.7 illustrates how the forced distribution method works. The manager is required to rate 60 percent of the employees as meeting expectations, 20 percent as exceeding expectations, and 20 percent as not meeting expectations.

One problem with the forced distribution method is that for small groups of employees, a bell-shaped distribution of performance may not be applicable. Even where the distribution approximates a normal curve, it is probably not a perfect curve. This means some employees will probably not be rated accurately. Also, ranking methods differ dramatically from the other methods in that one employee's performance evaluation is a function of the performance of other employees in the job.

FIGURE 19.7
Forced Distribution Curve

A comprehensive way to evaluate employee feedback is through 360-degree feedback. It is used by some of the most successful companies in America, including UPS, AT&T, Amoco, General Mills, and Procter & Gamble. Traditionally, companies evaluate employee performance by relying almost exclusively on supervisor ratings that generally follow two types: measuring personality characteristics and technical abilities or appraisal by objectives. The first type of evaluation is usually in the form of a questionnaire with the evaluator ultimately making a subjective judgment. The second type of evaluation places emphasis on the achievement of recognized goals rather than personal characteristics.

With 360-degree feedback, a person's job performance is evaluated by his or her immediate supervisor as well as other individuals who have either direct or indirect contact with the person's work. The person also conducts a self-assessment of his or her performance. Co-workers also evaluate the person. Additionally, subordinates, customers, clients (internal as well as external), and anyone else who has contact with the person make an evaluation. Thus, a full circle (360 degrees) of evaluations is made by those people above, below, inside, outside, and anywhere in between. These evaluations are typically made by having all of the above mentioned individuals complete a lengthy, anonymous questionnaire.

Source: Marc Marchese, "Industry: The Poser of the 360-Degree Feedback," *Pennsylvania CPA Journal,* pp. 19–20, December 1995.

multirater assessment (or 360-degree feedback)
Method of performance appraisal that uses input from an employee's managers, peers, customers, suppliers, or colleagues.

Multirater Assessment (or 360-Degree Feedback)

The final method of performance appraisal is called **multirater assessment,** or **360-degree feedback.** With this method, managers, peers, customers, suppliers, or colleagues are asked to complete questionnaires on the employee being assessed. The person assessed also completes a questionnaire. The questionnaires are generally lengthy. Typical questions are: "Are you crisp, clear, and articulate? Abrasive? Spreading yourself too thin?" The human resources department provides the results to the employee, who in turn gets to see how his or her opinion differs from those of the group doing the assessment. Management Illustration 19.2 describes 360-degree feedback in more detail.

Selecting a Performance Appraisal Method

Whatever performance appraisal method an organization uses, it must be job related. Therefore, before selecting a performance appraisal method, job analyses must be conducted and job descriptions written.[7] Job analysis is a formal process of determining and reporting information relating to the nature of a specific job. It determines the tasks the job comprises and the skills, knowledge, abilities, and responsibilities required for successful performance of the job. Normally, job analyses are performed by trained specialists with the organization's human resource department or by outside consultants. Figure 19.8 summarizes the information a job analysis provides.

Job analysis involves not only determining job content but also reporting the results of the analysis. One product of a job analysis is a job description, a formal written document, usually one to three pages long, that should include the following:

- Date written.
- Job status (full-time or part-time).
- Job title.

FIGURE 19.8
Information
Provided by Job
Analysis

Area of Information	Contents
Job title and location within company	
Organizational relationship	A brief explanation of the number of persons supervised (if applicable) and the job title(s) of the position(s) supervised; a statement concerning supervision received.
Relation to other jobs	Describes and outlines the coordination required by the job.
Job summary	Condensed explanation of the content of the job.
Information concerning job requirements	Varies greatly from job to job and from organization to organization; typically includes information on such topics as machines, tools, and materials; mental complexity and attention required; physical demands; and working conditions.

leniency
Grouping of ratings at the positive end of the scale instead of spreading them throughout the scale.

central tendency
Tendency of raters to rate most employees as doing average or above-average work.

- Supervision received (to whom the jobholder reports).
- Supervision exercised (who reports to this employee).
- Job summary (a synopsis of the job responsibilities).
- Detailed list of job responsibilities.
- Principal contacts (in and outside the organization).
- Competency or position requirements.
- Required education or experience.
- Career mobility (position or positions employee may qualify for next).[8]

After a job description is written, the most appropriate performance appraisal method can be determined.

Potential Errors in Performance Appraisals

recency
Occurs when performance evaluations are based on work performed most recently, generally work performed one to two months before evaluation.

halo effect
Occurs when the interviewer allows a single prominent characteristic to dominate judgment of all other traits.

Several common errors have been identified in performance appraisals. **Leniency** is the grouping of ratings at the positive end of the performance scale instead of spreading them throughout the scale. **Central tendency** occurs when performance appraisal statistics indicate that most employees are evaluated similarly as doing average or above-average work. **Recency** occurs when performance evaluations are based on work performed most recently, generally work performed one to two months before evaluation. Leniency, central tendency, and recency errors make it difficult, if not impossible, to separate the good performers from the poor performers. In addition, these errors make it difficult to compare ratings from different managers. For example, it is possible for a good performer who is evaluated by a manager committing central tendency errors to receive a lower rating than a poor performer who is rated by a manager committing leniency errors.

Another common error in performance appraisals is the **halo effect**.[9] This occurs when managers allow a single prominent characteristic of an employee to influence their judgment on each separate item in the performance appraisal. This often results in the employee receiving approximately the same rating on every item.

Personal preferences, prejudices, and biases can also cause errors in performance appraisals. Managers with biases or prejudices tend to look for employee behaviors that conform to their biases. Appearance, social status, dress, race, and sex have influenced many performance appraisals. Managers have also allowed first impressions to influence later judgments of an employee. First impressions are only a sample of behavior; however, people tend to retain these impressions even when faced with contradictory evidence.

Because of all the potential problems just cited, some critics of the traditional process suggest that there may be a better way to evaluate employees. Tom Peters suggests that job descriptions and traditional evaluations are relevant only in stable, predictable, and very vertically oriented (functional) organizations.[10] Peters believes organizations that are better able to respond to dynamic competition are adopting "fluidity" concepts and are seriously reviewing the traditional forms of control (performance standards, MBO, and job descriptions).[11] Why? The reasoning is as follows. First, the focus should be on what is important (e.g., flexibility rather than rigidity). Second, the processes should be "living" ones that will encourage change on the part of both the organization and the employee. Third, a simple written contract will encourage creativity and reduce unnecessary and costly layers of bureaucracy.[12] Time will determine whether these ideas have merit.

Overcoming Errors in Performance Appraisals

A promising approach to overcoming errors in performance appraisals is to improve the skills of managers. Suggestions on the specific training managers should receive are often vague, but they usually emphasize that managers should be given training to observe behavior more accurately and judge it fairly.

More research is needed before a definitive set of topics for manager training can be established. However, at a minimum, managers should receive training in (1) the performance appraisal method(s) of the company, (2) the importance of the manager's role in the total appraisal process, (3) the use of performance appraisal information, and (4) the communication skills necessary to provide feedback to the employee.[13]

General dos and don'ts of the performance appraisal process can help managers to not only prevent but reduce the errors that always seem to plague the process. The dos include the following:

1. Base performance appraisal on job performance only and not other factors unrelated to the job.
2. Use only those rating scales that are relevant to the job itself and are indicators of objective performance and attainment.
3. Sincerely work at the appraisal interview process.
4. Be problem solving oriented.

The don'ts include the following:

1. Don't criticize. Be proactive.
2. Carefully avoid the halo effect and leniency errors.
3. Dominate conversations about performance. Encourage employees to speak and to address issues in the evaluation process themselves.
4. Avoid general prescriptions to fix performance. Always present concrete and realizable objectives. Performance goals are the foundation of productivity.[14]

Providing Feedback through the Appraisal Interview

After one of the previously discussed methods for developing an employee's performance appraisal has been used, the results must be communicated to the employee. Unless this interview is properly conducted, it can and frequently does result in an unpleasant experience for both manager and employee. Following are some of the more important factors influencing success or failure of appraisal interviews:

- The more employees participate in the appraisal process, the more satisfied they are with the appraisal interview and with the manager and the more likely they are to accept and strive to meet performance improvement objectives.
- The more a manager uses positive motivational techniques (e.g., recognizing and praising good performance), the more satisfied the employee is likely to be with the appraisal interview and with the manager.
- The mutual setting by the manager and the employee of specific performance improvement objectives results in more improvement in performance than does a general discussion or criticism.
- Discussing and solving problems that may be hampering the employee's current job performance improve the employee's performance.
- Areas of job performance needing improvement that are most heavily criticized are less likely to be improved than similar areas of job performance that are less heavily criticized.
- The more employees are allowed to voice their opinions during the interview, the more satisfied they will be with the interview.
- The amount of thought and preparation employees independently devote before the interview increases the benefits of the interview.
- The more the employee perceives that performance appraisal results are tied to organizational rewards, the more beneficial the interview will be.

The interviewer must also be aware that many employees are skeptical about the appraisal process because of its potential association with punishment. Research has shown that this most often happens because the employee does not trust the manager's motivation; the feedback is unclear; the employee does not respect the manager's judgment; the feedback is inconsistent with the opinions of others; and the employee has had negative past experiences with the evaluation, appraisal, or feedback process.[15] Most of these problems can be overcome by simply accentuating the positive as the basis for the interview, feedback, and correction processes.

Performance Appraisal and the Law

Title VII of the Civil Rights Act permits the use of a bona fide performance appraisal system. Performance appraisal systems generally are not considered to be bona fide when their application results in adverse effects on minorities, women, or older employees.[16]

Many suggestions have been offered to make performance appraisal systems more legally acceptable. Some of these include (1) deriving the content of the appraisal system from job analyses; (2) emphasizing work behaviors rather than personal traits; (3) ensuring that the results of the appraisals are communicated to employees; (4) ensuring that employees are allowed to give feedback during the appraisal interview; (5) training managers in conducting proper evaluations; (6) ensuring that appraisals are written, documented, and retained; and (7) ensuring that personnel decisions are consistent with the performance appraisals.[17]

Rewarding Performance

The previously described systems and methods of appraising employee performance are useful only if they are closely tied to the organization's reward system. Appraising performance without a system that ties the results of the appraisal to the organization's reward system creates an environment where employees are poorly motivated.

organizational rewards
All types of rewards, both intrinsic and extrinsic, received as a result of employment by the organization.

intrinsic rewards
Rewards internal to the individual and normally derived from involvement in work activities.

extrinsic rewards
Rewards that are directly controlled and distributed by the organization.

compensation
Composed of the extrinsic rewards offered by the organization and consists of the base wage or salary, any incentives or bonuses, and any benefits employees receive in exchange for their work.

Organizational Reward System

The organizational reward system consists of the types of rewards the organization offers. **Organizational rewards** include all types of rewards, both intrinsic and extrinsic, that are received as a result of employment by the organization. **Intrinsic rewards** are internal to the individual and are normally derived from involvement in work activities. Job satisfaction and feelings of accomplishment are examples of intrinsic rewards. Most **extrinsic rewards** are directly controlled and distributed by the organization and are more tangible than intrinsic rewards. Figure 19.9 provides examples of both intrinsic and extrinsic rewards.

Though intrinsic and extrinsic rewards are different, they are also closely related. Often an extrinsic reward provides the recipient with intrinsic rewards. For example, an employee who receives an extrinsic reward in the form of a pay raise may also experience feelings of accomplishment (an intrinsic reward) by interpreting the pay raise as a sign of a job well done.

Compensation consists of the extrinsic rewards offered by the organization and includes the base wage or salary, any incentives or bonuses, and any benefits employees receive in exchange for their work. The base wage or salary is the hourly, weekly, or monthly pay employees receive for their work. Incentives are rewards offered in addition to the base wage or salary and are usually directly related to performance. Benefits are rewards employees receive because of their employment with the organization. Paid vacations, health insurance, and retirement plans are examples of benefits.

Relating Rewards to Performance

The free enterprise system is based on the premise that rewards should depend on performance. This performance–reward relationship is desirable not only at the corporate level but also at the individual employee level. The underlying idea is

FIGURE 19.9
Intrinsic versus Extrinsic Rewards

Intrinsic Rewards	Extrinsic Rewards
Sense of achievement	Formal recognition
Feelings of accomplishment	Fringe benefits
Informal recognition	Incentive payments
Job satisfaction	Base wages
Personal growth	Promotion
Status	Social relationships

that employees will be motivated when they believe good performance will lead to rewards. Unfortunately, many extrinsic rewards provided by organizations do not lend themselves to being related to performance. For example, paid vacations, insurance plans, and paid holidays are usually determined by organizational membership and seniority rather than by performance.

Other rewards, such as promotion, can and should be related to performance. However, opportunities for promotion may occur only rarely. When available, the higher positions may be filled on the basis of seniority or by someone outside the organization.

A key organizational variable that can be used to reward individuals and reinforce performance is basing an employee's annual pay raise on his or her performance (often referred to as *merit pay*). Even though many U.S. companies have some type of merit pay program, most do a poor job of relating pay and performance.[18] Surveys repeatedly show that neither top management nor rank-and-file employees have much confidence that a positive relationship exists between performance and pay.[19]

If relating rewards to performance is desirable, why is it not more widespread? One answer is that it is not easy to do; it is much easier to give everybody the same thing, as evidenced by the ever-popular across-the-board pay increase. Relating rewards to performance requires that performance be accurately measured, and this is not easy. It also requires discipline to actually match rewards to performance. Another reason is that many union contracts require that certain rewards be based on totally objective variables, such as seniority. While no successful formula for implementing a merit pay program has been developed, a number of desirable preconditions have been identified and generally accepted:[20]

1. *Trust in management.* If employees are skeptical of management, it is difficult to make a merit pay program work.
2. *Absence of performance constraints.* Because pay-for-performance programs are usually based on individual ability and effort, the job must be structured so that an employee's performance is not hampered by factors beyond his or her control.
3. *Trained managers.* Managers must be trained in setting and measuring performance standards.
4. *Good measurement systems.* Performance should be based on criteria that are job specific and focus on results achieved.
5. *Ability to pay.* The merit portion of the salary-increase budget must be large enough to get employees' attention.
6. *Clear distinction between cost of living, seniority, and merit pay.* In the absence of strong evidence to the contrary, employees will naturally assume a pay increase is an economic or a longevity increase.
7. *Well-communicated total pay policy.* Employees must have a clear understanding of how merit pay fits into the total pay picture.
8. *Flexible reward schedule.* It is easier to establish a credible pay-for-performance plan if all employees do not receive pay adjustments on the same date.

Summary

1. *Define performance appraisal.* Performance appraisal involves determining and communicating to an employee how he or she is performing the job and establishing a plan for improvement.

2. *Define performance.* Performance refers to the degree of accomplishment of the tasks that make up an employee's job.

3. *Explain the determinants of performance.* Job performance is the net effect of an employee's effort in terms of abilities, role perceptions, and results produced. This implies that performance in a given situation can be viewed as resulting from the interrelationships among effort, abilities, role perceptions, and results produced. Effort refers to the amount of energy an employee expends in performing a job. Abilities are personal characteristics used in performing a job. Role perception refers to the direction in which employees believe they should channel their efforts on their jobs.

4. *List and describe the 10 major performance appraisal methods.*

    1. Evaluation by objectives involves using the objectives set in the management-by-objectives process as a basis for performance appraisal.

    2. The production standards approach involves setting a standard or expected level of output and then comparing each employee's performance to the standard.

    3. The essay appraisal method requires the manager to describe an employee's performance in written narrative form.

    4. The critical-incident appraisal method requires the manager to keep a written record of incidents, as they occur, involving job behaviors that illustrate both satisfactory and unsatisfactory performance by the employee being rated.

    5. The graphic rating scale method requires the manager to assess an individual on factors such as quantity of work, dependability, job knowledge, attendance, accuracy of work, and cooperativeness.

    6. The checklist method requires the manager to answer yes or no to a series of questions concerning the employee's behavior.

    7. The behaviorally anchored rating scale (BARS) method is designed to assess behaviors required to successfully perform a job.

    8. The forced-choice rating method requires the manager to rank a set of statements describing how an employee carries out the duties and responsibilities of the job.

    9. Ranking methods (alternation, paired comparison, and forced distribution) require the manager to compare the performance of an employee to the performance of other employees.

    10. Multirater assessment, or 360-degree feedback, involves managers, peers, customers, suppliers, or colleagues completing questionnaires on the employee being assessed.

5. *Define job analysis.* Job analysis is a formal process of determining and reporting information related to the nature of a specific job.

6. *Explain the contents of a job description.* A job description should include the following: date written, job status, job title, supervision received, supervision exercised, job summary, detailed list of job responsibilities, principal contacts, competency or position requirements, required education or experience, and career mobility.

7. *Discuss common errors made in performance appraisals.* Leniency is the grouping of ratings at the positive end of the performance scale instead of spreading them throughout the scale. Central tendency occurs when performance appraisal statistics indicate that most employees are evaluated similarly as doing average or above-average work. Recency occurs when performance evaluations are based on work performed most recently. The halo effect occurs when managers allow a single prominent characteristic of an employee to influence their judgment on each separate item in the performance appraisal.

8. *Suggest ways to make performance appraisal systems more legally acceptable.* Some suggestions include deriving the content of the appraisal system from job analyses; emphasizing work behaviors rather than personal traits; ensuring that the results of the appraisals are communicated to employees; ensuring that employees are allowed to give

feedback during the appraisal interview; training managers in conducting proper evaluations; ensuring that appraisals are written, documented, and retained; and ensuring that personnel decisions are consistent with performance appraisals.

9. *Define compensation.* Compensation consists of the extrinsic rewards offered by the organization and includes the base wage or salary, any incentives or bonuses, and any benefits employees receive in exchange for their work.

10. *Outline desirable preconditions for implementing a merit pay program.* Desirable preconditions are trust in management; absence of performance constraints; trained managers; good measurement systems; ability to pay; a clear distinction among cost of living, seniority, and merit pay; a well-communicated total pay policy; and a flexible reward schedule.

Review Questions

1. Define performance appraisal.
2. What is performance? What factors influence an employee's level of performance?
3. Identify at least three uses of performance appraisal information.
4. Describe the following methods used in performance appraisal:
   a. Evaluation by objectives
   b. Production standards
   c. Essay
   d. Critical incident
   e. Graphic rating scale
   f. Checklist
   g. Behaviorally anchored rating scale
   h. Forced-choice rating
   i. Ranking methods
   j. Multirater assessment, or 360-degree feedback
5. Define the following types of performance appraisal errors:
   a. Leniency
   b. Central tendency
   c. Recency
   d. Halo effect
6. Outline some factors that influence the success or failure of performance appraisal interviews.
7. Describe some suggestions for making performance appraisal systems more legally acceptable.
8. Identify three basic components of compensation and give examples of each.
9. Outline some preconditions for implementing a merit pay program.

Skill-Building Questions

1. What are your thoughts on discussing salary raises and promotions during the performance appraisal interview?
2. Which method of performance appraisal do you think is the fairest? Why? (You may have to cite an example to explain your reason.) Under which method would you like to work? Why?
3. It has been said that incentive plans work for only a relatively short time. Do you agree or disagree? Why?
4. Why do you think management frequently uses across-the-board pay increases?

Skill-Building Exercise 19.1

Developing a Performance Appraisal System

A large public utility has been having difficulty with its performance evaluation program. The organization has an evaluation program in which all operating employees and clerical employees are evaluated semiannually by their supervisors. The form they have been using is given in Exhibit 1. It has been in use for 10 years. The form is scored as follows: excellent = 5; above average = 4; average = 3; below average = 2; and poor = 1. The scores for each facet are entered in the right-hand column and are totaled for an overall evaluation score.

In the procedure used, each supervisor rates each employee on July 30 and January 30. The supervisor discusses the rating with the employee and then sends the rating to the personnel department. Each rating is placed in the employee's personnel file. If promotions come up, the cumulative ratings are considered at that time. The ratings are also supposed to be used as a check when raises are given.

The system was designed by Joanna Kyle, the personnel manager, who retired two years ago. Her replacement was Eugene Meyer. Meyer graduated 15 years ago with a degree in commerce from the University of Texas. Since then he's had a variety of experiences, mostly in utilities. For about five of these years, he did personnel work.

Eugene has been reviewing the evaluation system. Employees have a mixture of indifferent and negative feelings about it. An informal survey has shown that about 60 percent of the supervisors fill out the forms, give about three minutes to each form, and send them to personnel without discussing them with the employees. Another 30 percent do a little better. They spend more time completing the forms but communicate about them only briefly and superficially with their employees. Only about 10 percent of the supervisors seriously try to do what was intended.

Eugene also found that the forms were rarely used for promotion or pay-raise decisions. Because of this, most supervisors may have thought the evaluation program was a useless ritual. In his previous employment, Eugene had seen performance evaluation as a much more useful experience. It included giving positive feedback to employees, improving future employee performance, developing employee capabilities, and providing data for promotion and compensation.

EXHIBIT 1 Performance Evaluation Form

Performance Evaluation

Supervisors: When you are asked to do so by the personnel department, please complete this form on each of your employees. The supervisor who is responsible for 75 percent or more of an employee's work should complete this form on him or her. Please evaluate each facet of the employee separately. Circle the rating for each facet.

Facet	Rating				
Quality of work	Excellent	Above average	Average	Below average	Poor
Quantity of work	Poor	Below average	Average	Above average	Excellent
Dependability at work	Excellent	Above average	Average	Below average	Poor
Initiative at work	Poor	Below average	Average	Above average	Excellent
Cooperativeness	Excellent	Above average	Average	Below average	Poor
Getting along with co-workers	Poor	Below average	Average	Above average	Excellent

Supervisor's signature _____

Employee name _____

Employee number _____

Eugene has had little experience with design of performance evaluation systems. He believes he should seek advice on the topic.

Write a report summarizing your evaluation of the strengths and weaknesses of the present appraisal system. Recommend some specific improvements or data-gathering exercises to develop a better system for Eugene Meyer.

Skill-Building Exercise 19.2

Who Are "Normal" Employees?

Assume your company has just adopted the form shown in Skill-Building Exercise 19.1 for its performance evaluation system. Assume further that your company has also instituted a policy that every manager's performance appraisals must conform to the accompanying bell-shaped curve. Using this curve, a manager that has 10 employees would have one that would be ranked as excellent, one that would be ranked above average, six that would be ranked average, one that would be ranked as below average, and one that would be ranked unsatisfactory.

Prepare a 10-minute presentation summarizing the problems, advantages, and disadvantages of using such a system.

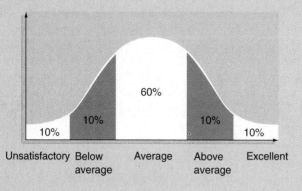

Case Incident 19.1

Determining Pay Raises

About four months ago, Judy Holcomb was promoted to supervisor of the claims department for a large, eastern insurance company. It is now time for all supervisors to make their annual salary increase recommendations. Judy doesn't feel comfortable in making these recommendations because she has been in her job only a short time. To further complicate the situation, the former supervisor has left the company and is unavailable for consultation.

There are no formal company restrictions on the kind of raises that can be given, but Judy's boss has said the total amount of money available to Judy for raises would be 8 percent of Judy's payroll for the past year. In other words, if the sum total of the salaries for all of Judy's employees was $200,000, then Judy would have $16,000 to allocate for raises. Judy is free to distribute the raises any way she wants, within reason.

Summarized below is the best information on her employees that Judy can find from the files of the former supervisor of the claims department. This information is supplemented by feelings Judy has developed during her short time as supervisor.

John Thompson: John has been with Judy's department for only five months. In fact, he was hired just before Judy was promoted into the supervisor's job. John is single and seems to be a carefree bachelor. His job performance, so far, has been above average, but Judy has received some negative comments about John from his co-workers. Present salary, $28,000.

Carole Wilson: Carole has been on the job for three years. Her previous performance appraisals have indicated superior performance. However, Judy does not believe the previous evaluations are accurate. She thinks Carole's performance is, at best, average. Carole appears to be well liked by all of her co-workers. Just last year, she became widowed and is presently the sole support for her five-year-old child. Present salary: $29,000.

Evelyn Roth: Evelyn has been on the job for four years. Her previous performance appraisals were all average. In addition, she had received below-average increases for the past two years. However, Evelyn recently approached Judy and told her she believes she was discriminated against in the past due to both her age and sex. Judy thinks Evelyn's work so far has been satisfactory but not superior. Most employees don't seem to sympathize with Evelyn's accusations of sex and age discrimination. Present salary: $27,000.

Jane Simmons: As far as Judy can tell, Jane is one of her best employees. Her previous performance appraisals also indicate she is a superior performer. Judy knows Jane badly needs a substantial salary increase because of some personal problems. She appears to be well respected by her co-workers. Present salary: $28,500.

Bob Tyson: Bob has been performing his present job for eight years. The job is very technical, and he would be difficult to replace. However, as far as Judy can discern, Bob is not a good worker. He is irritable and hard to work with. Despite this, Bob has received above-average pay increases for the past two years. Present salary: $23,000.

Questions

1. Indicate the size of the raise you would give each of these employees.
2. What criteria did you use in determining the size of the raise?
3. What do you think would be the feelings of the other people in the group if they should find out what raises you recommend?
4. Do you think the employees would eventually find out what raises others received? Would it matter?

Case Incident 19.2

Conducting a Performance Appraisal

Plant manager Paul Dorn wondered why his boss, Leonard Hech, had sent for him. Paul thought Leonard had been tough on him lately; he was slightly uneasy at being asked to come to Leonard's office at a time when such meetings were unusual. "Close the door and sit down, Paul," invited Leonard. "I've been wanting to talk to you." After preliminary conversation, Leonard said that because Paul's latest project had been finished, he would receive the raise he had been promised on its completion.

Leonard went on to say that since it was time for Paul's performance appraisal, they might as well do that now. Leonard explained that the performance appraisal was based on four criteria: (1) the amount of high-quality merchandise manufactured and shipped on time, (2) the quality of relationships with plant employees and peers, (3) progress in maintaining employee safety and health, and (4) reaction to demands of top management. The first criterion had a relative importance of 40 percent; the rest had a weight of 20 percent each.

On the first item, Paul received an excellent rating. Shipments were at an all-time high, quality was good, and few shipments had arrived late. On the second item, Paul also was rated excellent. Leonard said plant employees and peers related well to Paul, labor relations were excellent, and there had been no major grievances since Paul had become plant manager.

However, on attention to matters of employee safety and health, the evaluation was below average. His boss stated that no matter how much he bugged Paul about improving housekeeping in the plant, he never seemed to produce results. Leonard also rated Paul below average on meeting demands from top management. He explained that Paul always answered yes to any request and then disregarded it, going about his business as if nothing had happened.

Seemingly surprised at the comments, Paul agreed that perhaps Leonard was right and that he should do a better job on these matters. Smiling as he left, he thanked Leonard for the raise and the frank appraisal.

As weeks went by, Leonard noticed little change in Paul. He reviewed the situation with an associate:

It's frustrating. In this time of rapid growth, we must make constant changes in work methods. Paul agrees but can't seem to make people break their habits and adopt more efficient ones. I find myself riding him very hard these days, but he just calmly takes it. He's well liked by everyone. But somehow, he's got to care about safety and housekeeping in the plant. And when higher management makes demands he can't meet, he's got to say, "I can't do that and do all the other things you want, too." Now he has dozens of unfinished jobs because he refuses to say no.

As he talked, Leonard remembered something Paul had told him in confidence once. "I take Valium for a physical condition I have. When I don't take it, I get symptoms similar to a heart attack. But I only take half as much as the doctor prescribed." Now, Leonard thought, I'm really in a spot. If the Valium is what is making him so lackadaisical, I can't endanger his health by asking him to quit taking it. And I certainly can't fire him. Yet, as things stand, he really can't implement all the changes we need to fulfill our goals for the next two years.

Questions

1. Do you think a raise was justified in Paul's situation? Explain.
2. What could have been done differently in the performance appraisal session?
3. What can be done now to change the situation?

References and Additional Readings

1. For more discussion on effective performance appraisals, see Dean Elmuti, Yunus Kathawala, and Robert Waylend, "Traditional Performance Appraisal Systems: The Deming Challenge," *Management Decision* 30 (1992), pp. 42–48.
2. Michael Smith, "Documenting Employee Performance," *Supervisory Management*, September 1979, p. 30.
3. Dori Jones Young, "Letting Go Is Hard to Do," *Business Week/Enterprise*, 1993, pp. 218–19.
4. Ibid.
5. Frederick W. Taylor, *Scientific Management* (New York: Harper & Row, 1911), p. 52.
6. Bob Wooten, "Using Appraisals to Set Objectives," *Supervisory Management*, November 1981, pp. 30–35.
7. James A. Buford, Bettye B. Burkhulter, and Grover T. Jacobs, "Link Job Descriptions to Performance Appraisals," *Personnel Journal*, June 1988, pp. 132–40.
8. Judith A. DeLapa, "Job Descriptions That Work," *Personnel Journal*, June 1989, p. 156.
9. For a more in-depth discussion of the halo effect, see William K. Blazer and Lorne M. Sulsky, "Halo and Performance Appraisal Research: A Critical Examination," *Journal of Applied Psychology*, December 1992, pp. 976–85.
10. Tom Peters, *Thriving on Chaos* (New York: Alfred A. Knopf, 1987), p. 500.
11. Ibid., p. 501.
12. Ibid., p. 494.
13. For additional information on training for performance appraisals, see Robert N. Buckham, "Appraisal Training: Not Just for Managers," *Training and Development Journal*, June 1990, pp. 18, 21.
14. Edward L. Levine, "Let's Talk: Discussing Job Performance," *Supervisory Management*, October 1980, p. 25.
15. Michael Smith, "Feedback as a Performance Management Technique," *Management Solutions*, April 1987, pp. 20–29.
16. For an update on the legal status of performance appraisals, see David C. Martin and Kathryn M. Bartol, "The Legal Ramifications of Performance Appraisals: An Update," *Employee Relations Law Journal*, Autumn 1991, pp. 257–86.
17. Ginger C. Reed, "Employers' New Burden of Proof in Discrimination Cases," *Employment Relations Today*, Summer 1989, p. 112.
18. Frederick S. Hills, Robert M. Madigan, K. Dow Scott, and Steven E. Markham, "Tracking the Merit of Merit Pay," *Personnel Administrator*, March 1987, p. 50.
19. E. James Brennan, "The Myth and the Reality of Pay for Performance," *Personnel Journal*, March 1985, p. 73.
20. The following preconditions are drawn from Hills et al., "Tracking the Merit," pp. 56–57.

20

Operations Control

Learning Objectives

After studying this chapter, you will be able to:

1. Understand the basic requirements for controlling operating costs.
2. Define quality from the perspective of an operations manager.
3. List the eight common dimensions of design quality.
4. Explain the concept of quality assurance.
5. Explain the concept of total quality management (TQM).
6. Define the following terms: *continuous improvement, kaizen, six sigma, lean manufacturing,* and *quality at the source.*
7. Describe ISO 9000, ISO 14000, and the zero-defects approaches to quality.
8. Identify and define the two major types of quality control.
9. Recount the major reasons for carrying inventories.
10. Explain the concept of just-in-time (JIT) inventory.
11. Describe the ABC classification system for managing inventories.
12. Summarize the economic order quantity (EOQ) concept.
13. Describe the basic purposes of material requirements planning (MRP).

Chapter Preview

Performing Arts Center (PAC) Builders is a consortium of three construction firms hired by Miami–Dade County to build the new $260 million Performing Arts Center of Greater Miami. A recent audit by the county's Office of Inspector General questioned the quality of construction on the project. The audit, conducted when the project was more than halfway completed, described the quality control efforts of PAC Builders as half-hearted and plagued by poor record-keeping, under-staffing, and the use of apparently unqualified inspectors. The audit reported that in many cases the required inspections were not performed, and in some cases it was unclear if the inspections had taken place. In other cases where inspections had taken place, documentation had not been filed or was incomplete. According to the audit, these deficiencies were compounded by a cavalier attitude toward quality control by PAC Builders. Referring to the quality control program that is part of the contractual agreement, the county's inspector general summarized the situation: "Unfortunately, our audit disclosed that the builders of the Performing

Arts Center, though contractually required to, failed to provide this critical program. We hope, as a result of the OIG (Office of Inspector General) audit, they will do so without further hesitation or delay."

Jim Gray, a principal of PAC Builders, has defended the quality of the firm's work, its dedication to quality control, and the adequacy of its inspection program. Gray contends that the problems identified by the audit amount to little more than "inadequate documentation." Gray further stated that the problems will be remedied by a revamped quality control program that was recently presented to the county.

While the audit did not attempt to assess the quality of work at the site, it did express concern that it has no way of evaluating what it's getting in the way of quality. The county and PAC Builders have already been involved in a dispute over alleged cost overruns that could run into the millions of dollars and delays that have already pushed back completion of the Center by at least a year. County administrators have also raised concerns about what they call an "abnormal" number of work deficiencies.

Source: "Miami-Area Performing Arts Center Falls Short on Quality Control, Audit Says," *Knight Ridder Tribune Business News,* November 14, 2003, p. 1.

Analyzing Management Skills

Why do you think that cost, quality, or inventory problems are often allowed to get "relatively out of control" before they are detected? What can managers do to help prevent this from happening?

Applying Management Skills

Think of a retail store that you have visited in the last month that provided poor service to you. If you were manager of this store (or department), what would you do to improve the service to customers?

There are two aspects to an effective operating system: design and control. These aspects are related in that after a system has been designed and implemented, day-to-day operations must be controlled. With respect to efficient operation, the system processes must be monitored; quality must be assured; inventories must be managed; and all of these tasks must be accomplished within cost constraints. In addition to ensuring that things do not get out of control, good operations control can be a substitute for resources. For example, good quality control can reduce scrap and wasted materials, thus cutting costs. Similarly, effective inventory control can reduce the investment costs in inventories.

Effective operations control is attained by applying the basic control concepts to the operations function of the organization. Operations controls generally relate to one of three areas: costs, quality, or inventories.

Controlling Operations Costs

Ensuring that operating costs do not get out of hand is one of the primary jobs of the operations manager. The first requirement for controlling costs is to understand the organization's accounting and budgeting systems. Operations managers

FIGURE 20.1
Budget Costs: The Basis for Cost Control

Source: N. Gaither, *Production and Operations Management* (Fort Worth: Dryden Press, 1980).

Type of Cost	Components
Direct labor—variable	Wages and salaries of employees engaged in the direct generation of goods and services. This typically does not include wages and salaries of support personnel.
Materials—variable	Cost of materials that become a tangible part of finished goods and services.
Production overhead—variable	Training new employees, safety training, supervision and clerical, overtime premium, shift premium, payroll taxes, vacation and holiday, retirement funds, group insurance, supplies, travel, repairs and maintenance.
Production overhead—fixed	Travel, research and development, fuel (coal, gas, or oil), electricity, water, repairs and maintenance, rent, depreciation, real estate taxes, insurance.

variable overhead expenses
Expenses that change in proportion to the level of production or service.

fixed overhead expenses
Expenses that do not change appreciably with fluctuations in the level of production or service.

quality
For the operations manager, quality is determined in relation to the specifications or standards set in the design stages—the degree or grade of excellence specified.

are primarily concerned with costs relating to labor, materials, and overhead. Figure 20.1 describes the major components of each of these costs. **Variable overhead expenses** change with the level of production or service. **Fixed overhead expenses** do not change appreciably with the level of production or service.

Normally, operations managers prepare monthly budgets for each of the major cost areas. Once these budgets have been approved by higher levels of management, they are put into effect. By carefully monitoring the ensuing labor, material, and overhead costs, the operations manager can compare actual costs to budgeted costs. The methods used to monitor costs naturally vary, but typically they include direct observation, written reports, break-even charts, and so on.

Usually a cost control system indicates only when a particular cost is out of control; it does not address the question of *why* it is out of control. For example, suppose an operations manager determines from the monthly cost report that the labor costs on product X are exceeding budget by 20 percent. The manager must then attempt to determine what is causing the cost overrun. The causes could be many, including unmotivated employees, several new and untrained employees, low-quality raw materials, or equipment breakdown. The wise manager not only investigates the cause but also plans for prevention. The logical conclusion of a monitoring process is the implementation of prevention measures.[1]

Determining the cause may require only a simple inspection of the facts, or it may call for an in-depth analysis. Whatever the effort required, the operations manager must ultimately identify the source of the problem and then take the necessary corrective action. If the same cost problems continue to occur, chances are the manager has not correctly identified the true cause of the problem or the necessary corrective action has not been taken.

Quality Management

Quality is a relative term that means different things to different people. The consumer who demands quality may have a different concept than the operations manager who demands quality. The consumer is concerned with service, reliability, performance, appearance, and so forth. The operations manager's primary concern is that the product or service specifications be achieved, whatever they may be. For the operations manager, **quality** is determined in relation to the specifications or standards set in the design stages. Thus, the design quality refers to

FIGURE 20.2
The Dimensions of
Design Quality

Sources: John S. Oakland,
Total Quality Management
(London: Heinemann
Professional Publishing,
Ltd., 1989), pp. 291–92; and
Richard B. Chase, F. Robert
Jacobs, and Nicholas J.
Aquilano, *Operations
Management for Competitive
Advantage,* 10th ed. (Burr
Ridge, IL: McGraw-
Hill/Irwin, 2004), p. 276.

Dimension	Meaning
Performance	Primary product or service characteristics
Features	Added touches; bells and whistles; secondary characteristics
Reliability	Consistency of performance over time; probability of failing
Durability	Useful life
Serviceability	Ease of repair
Response	Characteristics of the human-to-human interface (speed, courtesy, competence)
Aesthetics	Sensory characteristics (sound, feel, look, and so on)
Reputation	Past performance and other intangibles (perceived quality)

the inherent value of the product or service in the marketplace.[2] Figure 20.2 lists the eight common dimensions of design quality.

The quality of an organization's goods and services can affect the organization in many ways. Some of the most important of these areas are (1) loss of business, (2) liability, (3) costs, and (4) productivity.[3] The reputation of an organization is often a direct reflection of the perceived quality of its goods or services. In today's legalistic environment, an organization's liability exposure can be significant and the associated costs can be high. Higher-quality goods and services generally have less liability exposure than lower-quality goods and services. In addition to liability costs, quality can affect other costs, including scrap, rework, warranty, repair, replacement, and other similar costs. Productivity and quality are often closely related.[4] Poor-quality equipment, tools, parts, or subassemblies can cause defects that hurt productivity. Similarly, high-quality equipment, tools, parts, and subassemblies can boost productivity.

Because of the many different ways quality can affect an organization, it is often difficult to determine precisely the costs associated with different quality levels. Also, it must be realized that consumers and customers are willing to pay for quality only up to a point. In response, many firms have instituted a total customer response program in which quality in the workplace is transferred to dealings with customers. To implement the program, firms must (1) develop a new attitude toward customers, (2) reduce management layers so that managers are in contact with customers, (3) link quality and information systems to customer needs and problems, (4) train employees in customer responsiveness, (5) integrate customer responsiveness throughout the entire distribution channel, and (6) use customer responsiveness as a marketing tool.[5]

Quality Assurance

For years, the responsibility for quality in almost all organizations rested with a quality control department.[6] The idea under this approach was to identify and remove defects or correct mistakes before they got to the customer. Some systems emphasized finding and correcting defects at the end of the line; others focused on detecting defects during the production process. Both approaches focused on only the production part of the process; they gave little or no consideration to the design of the products/services or to working with suppliers. Suppliers were usually treated as adversaries.

Today's quality management emphasizes the prevention of defects and mistakes rather than finding and correcting them. The idea of "building in" quality as op-

FIGURE 20.3
Deming's 14 Points

Source: From W. Edwards Deming, *Out of the Crisis,* 1986. Copyright © 1986 by The MIT Press. Reprinted with permission.

1. Create and publish to all employees a statement of the aims and purposes of the company or other organization. The management must demonstrate constantly their commitment to this statement.
2. Learn the new philosophy, top management and everybody.
3. Understand the purpose of inspection, for improvement of processes and reduction of cost.
4. End the practice of awarding business on the basis of price tag alone.
5. Improve constantly and forever the system of production and service.
6. Institute training.
7. Teach and institute leadership.
8. Drive out fear. Create trust. Create a climate for innovation.
9. Optimize toward the aims and purposes of the company the efforts of teams, groups, and staff.
10. Eliminate exhortations for the workforce.
11a. Eliminate numerical quotas for production. Instead learn and institute methods for improvement.
11b. Eliminate management by objective. Instead learn the capabilities of processes and how to improve them.
12. Remove barriers that rob people of pride of workmanship.
13. Encourage education and self-improvement for everyone.
14. Take action to accomplish the transformation.

posed to "inspecting it in" is also known as *quality assurance.* This approach views quality as the responsibility of all employees rather than the exclusive domain of a quality control department. Furthermore, suppliers are treated as partners.

While there have been many individuals who have championed the prevention approach to quality, W. Edwards Deming is perhaps most responsible. Deming was a statistics professor at New York University in the 1940s who went to Japan after World War II to assist in improving quality and productivity. While he became very much revered in Japan, Deming remained almost unknown to U.S. business leaders until the 1980s when Japan's quality and productivity attracted the attention of the world. Figure 20.3 presents a list compiled by Deming of 14 points he believed are needed to achieve quality in any organization. The underlying philosophy of Deming's work in this area is that the cause of poor quality and low productivity is the system and not the employees. He also stressed that it is management's responsibility to correct the system so that the desired results can be achieved.

Total Quality Management

Total quality management (TQM) is a management philosophy that emphasizes "managing the entire organization so that it excels in all dimensions of products and services that are important to the customer."[7] TQM, in essence, is an organizationwide emphasis on quality as defined by the customer. Under TQM, everyone from the CEO on down to the lowest-level employee must be involved. TQM can be summarized by the following actions:[8]

1. Find out what customers want. This might involve the use of surveys, focus groups, interviews, or some other technique that integrates the customer's voice in the decision-making process.
2. Design a product or service that will meet (or exceed) what customers want. Make it easy to use and easy to produce.

3. Design a production process that facilitates doing the job right the first time. Determine where mistakes are likely to occur, and try to prevent them. When mistakes do occur, find out why so that they are less likely to occur again. Strive to mistake-proof the process.

4. Keep track of results, and use those results to guide improvement in the system. Never stop trying to improve.

5. Extend these concepts to suppliers and to distribution.

As stated previously, TQM is an organizationwide emphasis on quality as defined by the customer. It is not a collection of techniques but a philosophy or way of thinking about how people view their jobs and quality throughout the organization.

Implementing TQM

Today's managers are bombarded with advice and literature telling them how to implement TQM. Three of the most popular approaches for implementing TQM are the Deming method, the Juran method, and the Crosby method, each named after the person who championed the respective approach. These three men, W. Edwards Deming, Joseph M. Juran, and Philip Crosby, are known as the "quality gurus." The Deming method emphasizes statistical quality control through employee empowerment. The Juran method emphasizes the reformulation of attitudes, comprehensive controls, and annual objective reviews. The Crosby method emphasizes conformance to requirements and zero defects. All of these approaches are sound; however, the best approach for implementing TQM is to custom-tailor the process for each application. In a study conducted by Frank Mahoney, the following initiatives were those most often cited by senior executives who had successfully implemented TQM.[9]

1. Demonstrate top-down commitment and involvement-push.
2. Set *tough* improvement goals, not just stretch goals.
3. Provide appropriate training, resources, and human resource backup.
4. Determine critical measurement factors; benchmark and track progress.
5. Spread success stories, especially those about favorable benchmarking; always share financial progress reports.
6. Identify the costs of quality and routes to improvement; prove the case that quality costs decline with quality progress.
7. Rely on teamwork, involvement, and all-level leadership.
8. Respect the "gurus," but tailor every initiative for a good local fit.
9. Allow time to see progress, analyze the system's operation, reward contributions, and make needed adjustments.
10. Finally, recognize that the key internal task is a culture change and the key external task is a new set of relationships with customers and suppliers.

Although it would seem to make good sense to transform an organization in the direction of total quality management, there is still resistance from the traditionalists. Figure 20.4 compares traditional organizations with those using TQM. The most often cited barriers to adopting TQM are (1) a lack of consistency of purpose on the part of management, (2) an emphasis on short-term profits, (3) an inability to modify personnel review systems, (4) mobility of management (job hopping), (5) lack of commitment to training and failure to instill leadership that is change oriented, and (6) excessive costs.[10] Management Illustration 20.1 describes one company's experience with TQM.

FIGURE 20.4
Comparison of Traditional Organizations with Those Using TQM

Source: From William J. Stevenson, *Production and Operations Management* 4th edition. Copyright © 1993 The McGraw-Hill Companies, Inc. Reprinted with permission.

Aspect	Traditional	TQM
Overall mission	Maximize return on investment	Meet or exceed customer satisfaction
Objectives	Emphasis on short term	Balance of long term and short term
Management	Not always open; sometimes inconsistent objectives	Open; encourages employees' input; consistent objectives
Role of manager	Issue orders; enforce	Coach, remove barriers, build trust
Customer requirements	Not highest priority; may be unclear	Highest priority; important to identify and understand
Problems	Assign blame; punish	Identify and resolve
Problem solving	Not systematic; by individuals	Systematic; by teams
Improvement	Erratic	Continual
Suppliers	Adversarial	Partners
Jobs	Narrow, specialized; much individual effort	Broad, more general; much team effort
Focus	Product oriented	Process oriented

Specific Approaches for Improving Quality

Continuous improvement, kaizen, quality at the source, six sigma, and *lean manufacturing* are all terms that have particular relevance to TQM. Each of these approaches is discussed in the following sections.

continuous improvement
Refers to an ongoing effort to make improvements in every part of the organization relative to all of its products and services.

Continuous improvement in general refers to an ongoing effort to make improvements in every part of the organization relative to all of its products and services.[11] With regard to TQM, it means focusing on continuous improvement in the quality of the processes by which work is accomplished. The idea here is that the quest for better quality and better service is never ending.

kaizen
"Good change"; a process of continuous and relentless improvement.

Kaizen is a philosophy for improvement that originated in Japan and that has recently enjoyed widespread adoption throughout the world. Many people consider *kaizen* and *continuous improvement* to be synonymous terms; others consider kaizen to be a subset of or a particular type of continuous improvement. The word *kaizen* comes from two Japanese words: *kai,* meaning "change," and *zen,* meaning "good."[12] Hence, *kaizen* literally means "good change," and in today's context it describes a process of continuous and relentless improvement. Kaizen is not based on large technical leaps but on the incremental refining of existing processes. Kaizen is basically a system of taking small steps to improve the workplace. It is based on the belief that the system should be customer driven and involve all employees through systematic and open communication. Under kaizen, employees are viewed as the organization's most valued asset. This philosophy is put into practice through teamwork and extensive employee participation. In summary, kaizen applies the principles of participatory management toward incremental improvement of the current methods and processes. Kaizen does not focus on obtaining new and faster machines but rather on improving the methods and procedures used in the existing situation.

quality at the source
The philosophy of making each employee responsible for the quality of his or her own work.

Quality at the source refers to the philosophy of making each employee responsible for the quality of his or her work.[13] In effect, this approach views every employee as a quality inspector for his or her own work. A major advantage of this approach is that it removes the adversarial relationship that often exists between quality control inspectors and production employees. It also encourages employees to take pride in their work.

six sigma
Both a precise set of statistical tools and a rallying cry for continuous improvement.

Six sigma is both a precise set of statistical tools and a rallying cry for continuous improvement.[14] Six sigma was pioneered by Motorola during the 1980s and literally means, in statistical terms, six standard deviations from the mean. The philosophy of six sigma is that in order to realize the very high level of quality demanded by six sigma (most processes traditionally have used three sigma), the entire production or service system must be examined and improved. Customer focus and data-driven rigor are at the heart of six sigma. Six sigma addresses the question of "what does the customer want in the way of quality." The answer to this question is then translated into statistical terms and rigorously analyzed.

lean manufacturing
A systematic approach to identifying and eliminating waste and non-value-added activities.

Lean manufacturing is a systematic approach to identifying and eliminating waste and non-value-added activities.[15] The essence of lean manufacturing is to look at the entire production or service process to eliminate waste or unnecessary activities wherever possible.

All of the above terms (*continuous improvement, kaizen, quality at the source, six sigma,* and *lean manufacturing*) are approaches for improving quality of the product or service offered. These approaches are not mutually exclusive but rather are complementary; the differences are that each offers a different emphasis. It should also be pointed out that each of these approaches can be applied in nonmanufacturing environments such as service, education, and government.

As stated earlier, TQM is an organizationwide emphasis on quality as defined by the customer. It is not a collection of techniques but a philosophy or way of thinking about how people view their jobs and quality through the organization.

Reengineering

reengineering
Searching for and implementing radical change in business processes to achieve breakthroughs in costs, speed, productivity, and service.

Some people confuse the concept of reengineering with TQM. **Reengineering,** also called *business process engineering,* is "the search for and implementation of radical change in business processes to achieve breakthrough results in costs, speed, productivity, and service."[16] Unlike TQM, reengineering is not a program for making marginal improvements in existing procedures. Reengineering is rather a onetime concerted effort, initiated from the top of the organization, to make major improvements in processes used to produce products or services. The essence of reengineering is to start with a clean slate and redesign the organization's processes to better serve its customers.

Other Quality Standards

While TQM is a highly effective, organizationwide philosophy about quality, there are other techniques and approaches that organizations may adopt to encourage quality. Most of these can be used alone or in conjunction with TQM. Quality circles were discussed in Chapter 11. Two additional approaches are discussed below.

ISO 9000

ISO 9000

A set of quality standards for international business.

ISO 9000 is a series of quality standards created in 1987 by the International Organization for Standardization (ISO), in Geneva, Switzerland. ISO currently is composed of the national standards bodies of more than 110 countries with the major objective of promoting the development of standardization and facilitating the international exchange of goods and services. The American National Standards Institute (ANSI) is the member body representing the United States in the ISO.

Originally, the ISO published five international standards designed to guide internal quality management programs and to facilitate external quality assurance endeavors. In essence, ISO 9000 outlines the quality system requirements necessary to meet quality requirements in varying situations. ISO 9000 focuses on the design and operation processes, not on the end product or service. ISO 9000 requires extensive documentation in order to demonstrate the consistency and reliability of the processes being used. In summary, ISO certification does not relate to the quality of the actual end product or service, but it guarantees that the company has fully documented its quality control procedures.

While ISO issues the standards, it does not regulate the program internationally; regulation is left to national accreditation organizations such as the U.S. Register Accreditation Board (RAB). RAB and other such boards then authorize registrars to issue ISO 9000 certificates. The number of worldwide organizations certified in ISO 9000 has increased dramatically, reaching over 510,000 in 161 countries by the end of 2001.[17]

New ISO 9000 standards were implemented beginning fall of 2000. The new standards, referred to as ISO 9000:2000, emphasize international organization and in-house performance, rather than engineering, as the best way to deliver a product or service. In essence, ISO 9000:2000 focuses more on continuous improvement and customer satisfaction. Management Illustration 20.2 illustrates how one company successfully implemented ISO 9000:2000.

ISO 14000

ISO 14000

Addition to the ISO 9000 to control the impact of an organization's activities and outputs on the environment.

Sparked by the success of ISO 9000, ISO has developed a similar series of international standards for environmental management. **ISO 14000** is a series of voluntary international standards covering environmental management tools and systems.[18] While many countries have developed environmental management system standards, these standards are often not compatible. The goal of ISO 14000 is to provide international environmental standards that are compatible. Similar to ISO 9000, which does not prescribe methods to integrate quality processes into an organization, ISO 14000 does not prescribe environmental policies. ISO 14000 does provide an international standard for environmental management systems so that organizations will have a systematic framework for their environmental activities. ISO 14000 focuses heavily on strategic issues such as setting goals and developing policies. Ultimately, ISO 14000 will include 20 separate standards covering everything from environmental auditing to labeling to assessing life cycles of products. ISO 14000 certification requires compliance in four organizational areas:[19] (1) implementation of an environmental management system, (2) assurance that procedures are in place to maintain compliance with laws and regulations, (3) commitment to continual improvement, and (4) commitment to waste minimization and prevention of pollution.

Many people believe that the impact of ISO 14000 will far exceed that of ISO 9000. As of the end of 2001, an ISO survey reported that over 36,000 certificates in 112 countries had been registered worldwide, compared with just over 5,000 at the end of 1997.[20]

Zero-Defects

The name *zero-defects* is somewhat misleading in that this approach doesn't literally try to cut defects or defective service to zero. Such an approach would obviously be very cost ineffective in many situations. A **zero-defects program** attempts to create a positive attitude toward the prevention of low quality. The objective of a zero-defects program is to heighten awareness of quality by making everyone aware of his or her potential impact on quality. Naturally, this should lead to more attention to detail and concern for accuracy.

zero-defects program
Increasing quality by increasing everyone's impact on quality.

Most successful zero-defects programs have the following characteristics:

1. Extensive communication regarding the importance of quality—signs, posters, contests, and so on.
2. Organizationwide recognition—publicly granting rewards, certificates, and plaques for high-quality work.
3. Problem identification by employees—employees point out areas where they think quality can be improved.
4. Employee goal setting—employees participate in setting quality goals.[21]

The Malcolm Baldrige National Quality Award

In 1987, the U.S. Congress passed the Malcolm Baldrige National Quality Improvement Act. The purpose of this legislation was to inspire increased efforts by

Management Illustration

BALDRIGE RECIPIENTS FOR 2002

www.motorola.com
www.branchsmith.com
www.stlbmbaa.org/Sponsor/8

20.3

On November 21, 2002, President George W. Bush and Commerce secretary Don Evans announced three winners of the 2002 Malcolm Baldrige National Quality Award. These winners included for the first time a winner in the health care category. The 2002 Baldrige Award recipients were: Motorola Inc., Commercial, Government and Industrial Solutions Sector, Schaumburg, Illinois (manufacturing category); Branch-Smith Printing Division, Fort Worth, Texas (small business category); and SSM Healthcare, St. Louis, Missouri (health care category).

Secretary Evans described the recipients, "The three 2002 Baldrige Award winners are role models of world-class excellence, and they have achieved extraordinary results. The men and women of these organizations represent the highest ethical standards in public responsibility and corporate stewardship."

Source: National Institute of Standards and Technology (NIST), news release, November 21, 2002.

Malcolm Baldrige Award
Recognition of U.S. companies' achievements in quality.

U.S. businesses to improve the quality of their products and services. The **Malcolm Baldrige Award** is named after the late Malcolm Baldrige, who was a successful businessman and a former U.S. secretary of commerce. The award is administered by the National Institute of Standards and Technology and can only be awarded to businesses located in the United States. The purpose of the award is to encourage efforts to improve quality and to recognize the quality achievements of U.S. companies. A maximum of three awards may be given annually in each of the following categories: manufacturing, service, small business, and beginning in 1999, education and health care. Management Illustration 20.3 describes the Baldrige award winners for 2002.

Types of Quality Control

product quality control
Relates to inputs or outputs of the system; used when quality is evaluated with respect to a batch of existing products or services.

Quality control relating to the inputs or outputs of the system is referred to as **product quality control** (sometimes called *acceptance control*). Product quality control is used when the quality is being evaluated with respect to a batch of products or services that already exists, such as incoming raw materials or finished goods. Product quality control lends itself to acceptance sampling procedures, in which some portion of a batch of outgoing items (or incoming materials) is inspected to ensure that the batch meets specifications with regard to the percentage of defective units that will be tolerated in the batch. With acceptance sampling procedures, the decision to accept or reject an entire batch is based on a sample or group of samples.

process control
Relates to equipment and processes used during the production process; used to monitor quality while the product or service is being produced.

Process control concerns monitoring quality while the product or service is being produced. Process control relates to the control of the equipment and processes used during the production process. Under process control, periodic samples are taken from a process and compared to a predetermined standard. If the sample results are acceptable, the process is allowed to continue. If the sample results are not acceptable, the process is halted and adjustments are made to bring the machines or processes back under control.

acceptance sampling
Statistical method of predicting the quality of a batch or a large group of products by inspecting a sample or group of samples.

Acceptance sampling is a method of predicting the quality of a batch or a large group of products from an inspection of a sample or group of samples taken from the batch. Acceptance sampling is used for one of three basic reasons:

1. The potential losses or costs of passing defective items are not great relative to the cost of inspection; for example, it would not be appropriate to inspect every match produced by a match factory.

415

2. Inspection of some items requires destruction of the product being tested, as is the case when testing flash bulbs.

3. Sampling usually produces results more rapidly than does a census.

Acceptance sampling draws a random sample of a given size from the batch or lot being examined. The sample is then tested and analyzed. If more than a certain number (determined statistically) are found to be defective, the entire batch is rejected, as it is deemed to have an unacceptably large percentage of defective items. Because of the possibility of making an incorrect inference concerning the batch, acceptance sampling always involves risks. The risk the producer is willing to take of rejecting a good batch is referred to as the *producer's risk*. The risk of accepting a bad batch is referred to as the *consumer's risk*. Obviously, one would desire to minimize both the producer's risk and the consumer's risk. However, the only method of simultaneously lowering both of these risks is to increase the sample size, which also increases the inspection costs. Therefore, the usual approach is to decide on the maximum acceptable risk for both the producer and the consumer and design the acceptance sampling plan around these risks.

process control chart
Time-based graphic display that shows whether a machine or a process is producing items that meet preestablished specifications.

A **process control chart** is a time-based graphic display that shows whether a machine or a process is producing output at the expected quality level. If a significant change in the variable being checked is detected, the machine is said to be out of control. Control charts do not attempt to show why a machine is out of control, only whether it is out of control.

The most frequently used process control charts are called *mean* and *range charts*. Mean charts (also called *X-charts*) monitor the mean or average value of some characteristic (dimension, weight, etc.) of the items produced by a machine or process. Range charts (also called *R-charts*) monitor the range of variability of some characteristic (dimension, weight, etc.) of the items produced by a machine or process.

The quality control inspector, using control charts, first calculates the desired level of the characteristic being measured. The next step is to calculate statistically the upper and lower control limits, which determine how much the characteristic can vary from the desired level before the machine or process is considered to be out of control. Once the control chart has been set up, the quality control inspector periodically takes a small sample from the machine or process outputs. Depending on the type of chart being used, the mean or range of the sample is plotted on the control chart. By plotting the results of each sample on the control chart, it is easy to identify quickly any abnormal trends in quality. Figure 20.5 shows a sample mean chart. A range chart looks like a mean chart; the only difference is that the range, as opposed to the mean, of the characteristic being monitored is plotted.

inventory
Quantity of raw materials, in-process goods, or finished goods on hand; serves as a buffer between different rates of flow associated with the operating system.

A mean or range chart used by itself can easily lead to false conclusions. For example, the upper and lower control limits for a machined part might be 0.1000 millimeter and 0.0800 millimeter, respectively. A sample of four parts of 0.1200, 0.1100, 0.0700, and 0.0600 would yield an acceptable mean of 0.0900; yet every element of the sample is out of tolerance. For this reason, when monitoring variables, it is usually desirable to use mean and range charts simultaneously to ensure that a machine or a process is under control.

Inventory Control

Inventories serve as a buffer between different rates of flow associated with the operating system. **Inventories** are generally classified into one of three categories, depending on their location within the operating system: (1) raw material, (2) in

FIGURE 20.5
Mean Chart

process, or (3) finished goods. Raw material inventories serve as a buffer between purchasing and production. In-process inventories are used to buffer differences in the rates of flow through the various production processes. Finished-goods inventories act as a buffer between the final stage of production and shipping.

Inventories add flexibility to the operating system and allow the organization to do the following:

1. Purchase, produce, and ship in economic lot sizes rather than in small jobs.
2. Produce on a smooth, continuous basis even if the demand for the finished product or raw material fluctuates.
3. Prevent major problems when forecasts of demand are in error or when unforeseen slowdowns or stoppages in supply or production occur.

If it were not so costly, every organization would attempt to maintain very large inventories to facilitate purchasing, production scheduling, and distribution. However, many costs are associated with carrying inventory. Potential inventory costs include such factors as insurance, property taxes, storage costs, obsolescence costs, spoilage, and the opportunity cost of the money invested in the inventory. The relative importance of these costs depends on the specific inventory being held. For example, with women's fashions, the obsolescence costs are potentially high. Similarly, the storage costs for dangerous chemicals may be high. Thus, management must continually balance the costs of holding the inventory against the costs of running short of raw materials, in-process goods, or finished goods. Management Illustration 20.4 illustrates an approach to inventory control that many restaurants and bars have found helpful.

Just-in-Time Inventory Control

just-in-time inventory control (JIT)
Inventory control system that schedules materials to arrive and leave as they are needed.

Just-in-time inventory control (JIT) was pioneered in Japan but has become popular in the United States. JIT systems are sometimes referred to as *zero inventory systems*, *stockless systems*, or *kanban systems*. JIT is actually a philosophy for production to ensure that the right items arrive and leave as they are needed. Traditionally, incoming raw materials are ordered in relatively few large shipments and stored in warehouses until needed for production or for providing a service.

Under JIT, organizations make smaller and more frequent orders of raw materials. JIT depends on the elimination of set-up time between the production of different batches of different products. JIT can be viewed as an operating philosophy whose basic objective is to eliminate waste. In this light, waste is "anything other than the minimum amount of equipment, materials, parts, space, and workers' time which are absolutely essential to add value to the product or service."[22]

The JIT philosophy applies not only to inventories of incoming raw materials but also to the production of subassemblies or final products. The idea is not to produce an item or a subassembly until it is needed for shipment. JIT is called a *demand pull system* because items are produced or ordered only when they are needed (or pulled) by the next stage in the production process. Figure 20.6 summarizes the benefits of JIT. One potential hazard is that the entire production line can be shut down if the needed parts or subassemblies are not available when needed. JIT has been successfully implemented by many American companies, including Hewlett-Packard, Motorola, Black & Decker, General Motors, Ford, Chrysler, General Electric, Goodyear, and IBM.[23]

Despite the popularity of JIT in American business, it is not a quick fix for all the quality and operations problems a company may face. In fact, JIT may take many years to really catch hold in a company. Beginning in the early 1960s, it took Toyota over 20 years to fully implement the concept.[24] Although JIT was a key to Toyota's lean production system, it also exposed many defects in the inventory system, because JIT enables easier detection of defective inventory. Fixing these

FIGURE 20.6
Benefits of JIT System

Source: N. Gaither, *Production and Operations Management* (Fort Worth: Dryden Press, 1992).

1. Inventory levels are drastically lowered.
2. The time it takes products to go through the production facility is greatly reduced. This enables the organization to be more flexible and more responsive to changing customer demands.
3. Product/service quality is improved and the cost of scrap is reduced because defective parts and services are discovered earlier.
4. With smaller product batches, less space is occupied by inventory and materials-handling equipment. This also allows employees to work closer together, which improves communication and teamwork.

forms of defects (finding where and how the defects occurred) is sometimes time-consuming and difficult to accomplish.

Tom Peters offers a new twist on JIT. He believes that instead of using JIT just to assist suppliers in improving their products (i.e., resulting in fewer defective parts), a company can push JIT forward in the distribution channel to proactively seek out opportunities to assist customers (using some variant of JIT as a marketing strategy) and link them to the company's processes. In other words, by examining and solving customers' problems by supplying them with exactly what they need, the company not only improves its quality control but also builds ties to its customer base.[25]

Tracking Inventory

Before computers, tracking inventory was a tedious and time-consuming task. It was difficult to keep accurate inventory records. Employees recorded every sale and purchase, and a bookkeeper would subtract all sales and add all purchases at the end of the week. This determined how much inventory remained in stock. However, employees often forgot to record transactions. Bookkeepers frequently made mistakes computing figures. Both kinds of errors made it difficult for businesses to know how much inventory they actually had in stock.

Bar-Code Technology

Technology has improved inventory tracking. Most items are marked with *bar codes*, patterns of bars and spaces that an electronic scanner recognizes. Barcoding has reduced errors in tracking inventory. When a company purchases or sells an item, an employee scans the item's bar code. A computer program recognizes the information contained in the bar code and automatically adds or subtracts the item from inventory.

Physical Inventory

Even if computers track inventory, managers need to take physical inventory. A **physical inventory** involves actually counting the number of units of inventory a company holds in stock. Most businesses perform a physical inventory once or twice a year.

Managers need to conduct physical inventories because actual inventory is often different from the level of inventory tracked. The discrepancy may reflect errors or unauthorized withdrawals, including theft. Managers who do not adjust their inventory occasionally may experience shortages.

physical inventory
Counting the number of units of inventory a company holds in stock.

Independent versus Dependent Demand Items

Independent demand items are finished goods or other end items. For the most part, independent demand items are sold or shipped out as opposed to being used in making another product. Examples of independent demand environments include most retail shops, book publishing, and hospital supplies.[26] **Dependent demand items** are typically subassemblies or component parts that will be used in making some finished product. In these cases, the demand for the items depends on the number of finished products being produced. An example is the demand for wheels for new cars. If the car company plans to make 1,000 cars next month, it knows it must have 5,000 wheels on hand (allowing for spares).[27] With independent demand items, forecasting plays an important role in inventory stocking decisions. With dependent demand items, inventory stocking requirements are determined directly from the production plan.

independent demand items
Finished goods ready to be shipped out or sold.

dependent demand items
Subassembly or component parts used to make a finished product; their demand is based on the number of finished products being produced.

FIGURE 20.7
ABC Inventory Classification
Shows the inventory value for each group versus the group's portion of the total list.

Source: From Richard B. Chase, et al., *Operation Management for Competitive Advantage with CD-ROM and PowerWeb.* Copyright © 2004 The McGraw-Hill Companies, Inc. Reprinted with permission.

ABC classification system
Method of managing inventories based on their total value.

safety stocks
Inventory maintained to accommodate unexpected changes in demand and supply and allow for variations in delivery time.

ABC Classification System

One of the simplest and most widely used systems for managing inventories is the ABC approach. The **ABC classification system** manages inventories based on the total value of their usage per unit of time. In many organizations, a small number of products or materials, group A, account for the greatest dollar value of the inventory; the next group of items, group B, accounts for a moderate amount of the inventory value; and group C accounts for a small amount of the inventory value. Figure 20.7 illustrates this concept. The dollar value reflects both the cost of the item and the item's usage rate. For example, an item might be put into group A through a combination of either low cost and high usage or high cost and low usage.

Grouping items in this way establishes appropriate control over each item. Generally, the items in group A are monitored very closely; the items in group B are monitored with some care; and the items in group C are checked only occasionally. Items in group C are usually not subject to the detailed paperwork of items in groups A and B. In an automobile service station, gasoline would be considered a group A item and monitored daily. Tires, batteries, and transmission fluid would be group B items and might be checked weekly or biweekly. Valve stems, windshield wiper blades, radiator caps, hoses, fan belts, oil and gas additives, car wax, and so forth would be group C items and might be checked and ordered only every two or three months.[28]

One potential shortcoming of the ABC method is that although the items in group C may have very little cost/usage value, they may be critical to the operation. It is possible, for instance, for an inexpensive bolt to be vital to the production of a costly piece of machinery. One way to handle items such as this is to designate them as group A or B items regardless of their cost/usage value. The major advantage of the ABC method is that it concentrates on controlling those items that are most important to the operation.

With computer technology and information systems becoming increasingly commonplace in small and medium-size firms, the ABC method can be computerized and categories can be monitored or changed with greater skill and accuracy. An additional value of computerizing the operation and control of the classification system is the power it brings to ordering cycles and stock control.

Safety Stocks

Most organizations maintain **safety stocks** to accommodate unexpected changes in demand and supply and allow for variations in delivery time. The optimal size of the safety stock is determined by the relative costs of a stock-out of the item versus the costs of carrying the additional inventory. The cost of a stock-out of the item is often difficult to estimate. For example, the customer may choose to go elsewhere rather than wait for the product. If the product is available at another branch location, the stock-out cost may be simply the cost of shipping the item from one location to another.

The Order Quantity

Most materials and finished products are consumed one by one or a few units at a time; however, because of the costs associated with ordering, shipping, and handling inventory, it is usually desirable to purchase materials and products in large lots or batches.

When determining the optimal number of units to order, the ordering costs must be balanced against the cost of carrying the inventory. *Ordering costs* include such things as the cost of preparing the order, shipping costs, and setup costs. The capacity to order online has reduced the ordering costs for many organizations. *Carrying costs* include storage costs, insurance, taxes, obsolescence, and the opportunity costs of the money invested in the inventory. The smaller the number of units ordered, the lower the carrying costs (because the average inventory held is smaller) but the higher the ordering costs (because more orders must be placed). The optimal number of units to order, referred to as the **economic order quantity (EOQ),** is determined by the point at which ordering costs equal carrying costs, or where total cost (ordering costs plus carrying costs) is at a minimum.

economic order quantity (EOQ)
Optimal number of units to order at one time.

The greatest weakness of the EOQ approach is the difficulty in accurately determining the actual carrying and ordering costs. However, research has shown that the total costs associated with order sizes that are reasonably close to the economic order quantity do not differ appreciably from the minimum total costs associated with the EOQ.[29] Thus, as long as the estimated carrying and ordering costs are in the ballpark, this approach can yield meaningful results. Variations of this basic model have been developed to take into account such things as purchase quantity and other special discounts.

Material Requirements Planning

material requirements planning (MRP)
Dependent inventory planning and control system that schedules the right amount of materials needed to produce the final product on schedule.

Material requirements planning (MRP) is a special type of inventory system in which the needed amount of each component of a product is figured on the basis of the amount of the final product to be produced. When each component is needed depends on when the final assembly is needed and the lead time required to incorporate the component into the assembly.

The purpose of MRP is to get the right materials to the right places at the right times. It does little good to have some of the parts needed to produce a product if the organization does not have all of them. Because carrying parts that are not being used is costly, the idea behind MRP is to provide either all or none of the necessary components. Figure 20.8 outlines some of the advantages of MRP.

Japanese organizations have used MRP to support their highly productive manufacturing and assembly process. Their planning systems include strategic industrial outsourcing. Under this concept, help with the MRP process is gained by relying on strategic partners to supply critical components. From their traditional vertically integrated system, entry and exit of resources and products are extremely efficient. Most suppliers' modernization attempts have been aided by the parent manufacturer so that the outsourcer and the manufacturer's systems match. Once the MRP systems are in alignment, significant gains can be made in cost savings and production efficiency.[30]

Almost all MRP systems, regardless of the competitive system in which they operate, utilize a computer because of its ability to store inventory records, production

FIGURE 20.8
Potential Advantages of Material Requirements Planning (MRP)

Source: From James B. Dilworth, *Production and Operations Management* 4th edition, McGraw-Hill, 1989. Reprinted with permission of the author.

1. Reduces the average amount of inventory for dependent demand items (raw material, parts, and work-in-progress inventory).
2. Improves work flow, resulting in reduced elapsed time between the start and finish of jobs.
3. Enables delivery promises to be more reliable.
4. Minimizes parts shortages.
5. Keeps priorities of work items up to date so that shop work is more effective and appropriate.
6. Helps plan the timing of design changes and aids in their implementation.
7. Can simulate and evaluate changes in the master schedule.
8. Tells management ahead of time if desired delivery dates appear achievable.
9. Changes (expedites or deexpedites) due dates for orders.
10. Facilitates capacity requirements planning.

sequences, and production lead times and then rapidly convert these data into period-by-period production schedules and inventory levels.

MRP utilizes three basic documents: (1) the master production schedule, (2) the bill of materials, and (3) the inventory status file. The *master production schedule* is derived from the aggregate production plan and forecasts the number of end products to be produced for a given period. The *bill of materials* is a listing of all parts and subassemblies that make up each end product. The *inventory status file* is a record of parts currently in inventory.

The MRP system uses these three files to create schedules that identify the specific parts and materials required to produce end items, the precise numbers

FIGURE 20.9
Overall View of the Inputs to a Standard Material Requirements Planning Program and the Reports Generated by the Program

Source: From Richard B. Chase, et al., *Operation Management for Competitive Advantage with CD-ROM and PowerWeb.* Copyright © 2004 The McGraw-Hill Companies, Inc. Reprinted with permission.

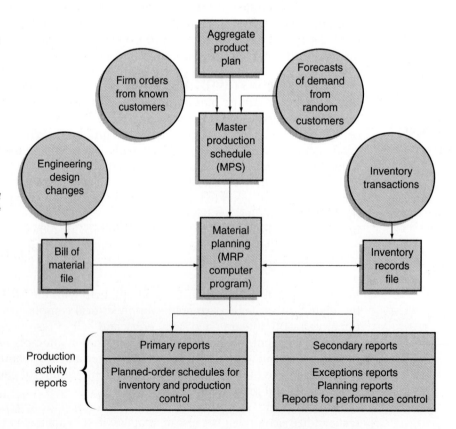

FIGURE 20.10
Differences between JIT and MRP

Source: From Nicholas J. Aquilano and Richard B. Chase, *Fundamentals of Operations Management.* Copyright © 1991 The McGraw-Hill Companies, Inc. Reprinted with permission.

Operating System Characteristics	JIT	MRP
Focus	Physical operations	Information system
Rates of output	Level schedule	Variable production plan
Work authorization	Kanban pull	Master schedule push
Data philosophy	Minimize data captured	Capture all data
Problem response	Resolve and fix	Regenerate
Clerical personnel	Decreased	Increased
Forms of control	Shop floor, visual, line workers	Middle management reports, staff
Capacity adjustment	Visual, immediate	Capacity requirements planning, deferred

needed, and the dates when orders for these materials should be placed and be received or completed. For example, if the master production schedule determines that a manufacturer needs to have 100 end items assembled and ready for shipment by June, the company may need to order some subcomponents in April and make additional subcomponent orders in May. Use of an MRP system allows a production planner to take the requirements for end items and "back schedule" the production and ordering of subcomponents. The MRP printout would indicate how much of each subcomponent and when to order so as to meet the end item production requirements. Figure 20.9 presents an overall view of the inputs to and the reports generated by a basic MRP system.

MRP differs from JIT in that MRP generally produces to forecasts (a push system) rather than to actual demands (a pull system). MRP allows for large batch production of parts, whereas JIT strives for small batches. Many companies combine elements of both MRP and JIT.[31] In these instances, companies use basic MRP for ordering purposes and materials management and then execute using JIT procedures. Figure 20.10 provides a general comparison between JIT and MRP.

Summary

1. *Understand the basic requirements for controlling operating costs.* The first requirement for controlling costs is to understand the organization's accounting and budgeting system. Once the budgets have been put into effect, they must be carefully monitored for any unexpected cost variances. Any cost variances detected must then be analyzed to determine the cause.

2. *Define quality from the perspective of an operations manager.* The operations manager's primary concern is that the product or service specifications be achieved. For the operations manager, quality is determined in relation to the specifications or standards set in the design stages.

3. *List the eight common dimensions of design quality.* The eight common dimensions of design quality are performance, features, reliability, durability, serviceability, response, aesthetics, and reputation.

4. *Explain the concept of quality assurance.* Quality assurance refers to the idea of "building in" quality as opposed to "inspecting it in."

5. *Explain the concept of total quality management (TQM).* Total quality management is a management philosophy that emphasizes managing the entire organization so that it excels in all dimensions of products and services that are important to the customer. In essence, TQM is an organizationwide emphasis on quality as defined by the customer.

6. *Define the following terms: continuous improvement, kaizen, six sigma, lean manufacturing, and* quality at the source. Continuous improvement refers to an ongoing effort to make improvements in every part of the organization relative to all of its products and services. Kaizen is a philosophy for improvement that originated in Japan and that literally means "good change." Kaizen is basically a system of taking small steps to improve the workplace. Six sigma is a precise set of statistical tools and a rallying cry for continuous improvement. The philosophy of six sigma is that in order to realize the very high level of quality demanded by six sigma (most processes traditionally have used three sigma), the entire production or service system must be examined and improved. Lean manufacturing is a systematic approach to identifying and eliminating waste and non-value-added activities. Quality at the source refers to the philosophy of making each employee responsible for the quality of his or her work.

7. *Describe ISO 9000, ISO 14000, and the zero-defects approach to quality.* ISO 9000 is a series of quality standards established in 1987 by the International Organization for Standardization (ISO). ISO 9000 focuses on the design and operations processes and not on the end product or service. ISO 9000 requires extensive documentation in order to demonstrate the consistency and reliability of the processes being used. The ISO 14000 series was developed to control the impact of an organization's activities and outputs on the environment. A zero-defects program attempts to create a positive attitude toward the prevention of low quality.

8. *Identify and define the two major types of quality control.* The two major types of quality control are product quality control and process control. Product quality control is used when the quality is being evaluated with respect to a batch of products or services that already exist, such as incoming raw materials or finished goods. Under process control, machines or processes are periodically checked to detect significant changes in the quality produced by the process.

9. *Recount the major reasons for carrying inventories.* Inventories add flexibility to the operating system and allow the organization to do the following:
   • Purchase, produce, and ship in economic lot sizes rather than in small jobs.
   • Produce on a smooth, continuous basis even if the demand for the finished product or raw material fluctuates.
   • Prevent major problems when forecasts of demand are in error or when unforeseen slowdowns or stoppages in supply or production occur.

10. *Explain the concept of just-in-time (JIT) inventory.* JIT is a philosophy for scheduling so that the right items arrive and leave at the right time. The basic idea under JIT is to have materials arrive just as they are needed.

11. *Describe the ABC classification system for managing inventories.* The ABC classification system is a method of managing inventories based on the total value of their usage per unit of time. In many organizations, a small number of products, group A, account for the greater dollar value of the inventory; the next group of items, group B, accounts for a moderate amount of the inventory value; and group C accounts for a small amount of the inventory value. The purpose of grouping items in this way is to establish appropriate control over each item. Generally, the items in group A are monitored closely; the items in group B are monitored with some care; and the items in group C are checked only occasionally.

12. *Summarize the economic order quantity (EOQ) concept.* When determining the optimal number of units to order, the ordering costs must be balanced against the cost of carrying the inventory. Ordering costs include such things as the cost of preparing the order, shipping costs, and setup costs. Carrying costs include storage costs, insurance, taxes, obsolescence, and the opportunity costs of the money invested in the inventory. The smaller the number of units ordered, the lower the carrying costs (because the average inventory held is smaller) but the higher the ordering costs (because more orders must be placed). The optimal number of units to order, referred to as the economic order quantity (EOQ), is determined by the point where ordering costs equal carrying costs, or where total cost (ordering costs plus carrying costs) is at a minimum.

13. *Describe the basic purposes of material requirements planning (MRP).* Material requirements planning is a special type of inventory system in which the needed amount of each component of a product is figured on the basis of the amount of the final product to be produced. When each component is needed depends on when the final assembly is needed and the lead time required to incorporate the component into the assembly. The purpose of MRP is to get the right materials to the right places at the right times.

Review Questions

1. Name the three major categories of costs that usually concern operations managers from a control standpoint. Give several examples of each category.
2. What is the difference between fixed and variable overhead expenses?
3. What are the eight common dimensions of design quality?
4. Define quality assurance.
5. Explain the concept of total quality management.
6. Define continuous improvement and kaizen. How are they related?
7. Define six sigma and lean manufacturing.
8. What is the meaning of "quality at the source"?
9. What is reengineering?
10. Explain the thrust of ISO 9000 and ISO 14000.
11. What is the objective of a zero-defects program?
12. What is the Malcolm Baldrige Award?
13. Differentiate between product quality control and process quality control.
14. What are the purposes of inventories?
15. What is just-in-time inventory control?
16. Explain the difference between independent and dependent demand items.
17. How does the ABC classification system work?

Skill-Building Questions

1. Given that quality is a relative concept, how does a manager ever know if the quality level is optimal?
2. Total quality management has gotten a lot of attention over the last several years. How do you account for this phenomenon? Do you think it is justified or just a lot of hype about nothing new?
3. What do you think are the most significant barriers to the implementation of TQM programs? What would you recommend to fix the problems?
4. Suppose you are manager of a drive-in restaurant and your business fluctuates dramatically from season to season as well as from day to day within a season. Discuss the production control problems such a situation presents.
5. It has been said that good inventory management can make the difference between success and failure in certain industries. Name several industries in which this statement is particularly applicable, and discuss the reasons for your answer.

Skill-Building Exercise 20.1

Out of Control?

Situation 1
The manager of a fast-food hamburger chain must ensure that the hamburger advertised as a quarter-pounder is actually 4 ounces, more or less. The company policy states that the quarter-pounder must come within 3/10 of an ounce of being 4 ounces in order to be used. The following chart reflects the expected weight of the patty (4 ounces), the upper control limit (4.3 ounces), and the lower control limit (3.7 ounces). A sample of patties has been taken each day for the last eight days, and the average weight recorded for each day is recorded on the chart.

1. Should the patty preparation process be investigated?
2. Why do you think so?

Situation 2

You are the owner of a car repair shop that specializes in tune-ups. On each work order, the mechanic records the time at which he began the tune-up and the time when finished. From these data, you can determine how long each mechanic spends on each job. You expect each job to take about 40 minutes; however, you know that if someone were in a hurry, the job could be done in as few as 20 minutes. Also, you believe that under no circumstances should a tune-up take over one hour. A recently hired mechanic has recorded the times shown on the following chart for his last 11 tune-up jobs:

1. Should you have a talk with this mechanic? Is there a problem?
2. Why do you think so?

Source: This exercise is adapted from Henry L. Tosi and Jerald W. Young, *Management Experiences and Demonstrations* (Homewood, IL: Richard D. Irwin, 1982), pp. 45–47.

Case Incident 20.1

Production Problems

Braddock Company of Sea Shore City fabricates stamped metal parts used in the production of wheelbarrows. Braddock fabricates two basic styles of wheelbarrow trays: One is for a deep, four-cubic-foot construction model, and the other is for a shallow, two-cubic-foot homeowner's model. Braddock's process is simple. Raw metal sheets are picked up from inventory (Braddock presently maintains about 7 days' worth of the large metal sheets for the construction model and about 10 days' worth of the smaller sheets for the homeowner model) and fed into a large machine that bends and shapes the metal into the desired tray. The trays are then inspected and packaged, 10 to a box, for shipping.

In the past few days, Braddock has been experiencing quality problems with both tray styles. Undesirable creases have been forming in the corners following the stamping operation. However, the problem with the construction model tray is more pronounced and appeared almost three full days before it did on the homeowner's model.

Several incidents have occurred at Braddock during the past week that Hal McCarthy, the operations manager, thinks may have a bearing on the problem. Shorty McCune, a machine operator and labor activist, was accused of drinking on the job and released a few days before the problem began. Since his release, Shorty has been seen in and around the plant talking to several other employees. About two weeks ago, Braddock also began receiving raw metal from a new supplier because of an attractive price break.

The only inspection the company performs is the postfabrication inspection.

Questions

1. What do you think is causing Braddock's problem?
2. Why is the problem more pronounced on the construction model than on the homeowner model?
3. How can Braddock eliminate its problem?

Case Incident 20.2

The Purchasing Department

The buyers for a large airline company were having a general discussion with the manager of purchasing in her office Friday afternoon. The inspection of received parts was a topic of considerable discussion. Apparently, several parts had recently been rejected six months or more after being received. Such a rejection delay was costing the company a considerable amount of money, since most of the items were beyond the standard 90-day warranty period. The current purchasing procedures state that the department using the parts is responsible for the inspection of all parts, including stock and nonstock items. The company employs an inspector who is supposedly responsible for inspecting all aircraft parts, in accordance with FAA regulations. However, the inspector has not been able to check those items purchased as nonaircraft parts because he is constantly overloaded. Furthermore, many of the aircraft parts are not being properly inspected because of insufficient facilities and equipment.

One recent example of the type of problem being encountered was the acceptance of a batch of plastic forks that broke easily when in use. The vendor had shipped over 100 cases of the forks of the wrong type. Unfortunately, all the purchase order specified was "forks." Another example was the acceptance of several cases of plastic cups with the wrong logo. The cups were put into use for in-flight service and had to be used because no other cups were available. A final example was the discovery that several expensive radar tubes in stock were found to be defective and with expired warranty. These tubes had to be reordered at almost $900 per unit.

It was apparent that the inspection function was inadequate and unable to cope with the volume of material being received. Purchasing would have to establish some guidelines as to what material should or should not be inspected after being processed by the material checker. Some of the buyers thought the material checker (who is not the inspector) should have more responsibility than simply checking quantity and comparing the packing sheet against purchase orders. Some believed the checker could and should have caught the obvious errors in the logo on the plastic cups. Furthermore, if the inspector had sampled the forks, they would have been rejected immediately. As for the radar tubes, they should have been forwarded by the inspector to the avionics shop for bench check after being received. Such a rejection delay was costing the company a considerable amount of money, since most of the items were beyond the standard 90-day warranty period. The current purchasing procedures state that the department using the parts is responsible for the inspection before the part is placed in stock. Some buyers thought the inspector should be responsible for inspection of all materials received, regardless of its function or usage. It was pointed out, however, that several landing gears had been received from the overhaul/repair vendor and tagged by the inspector as being acceptable. These gears later turned out to be defective and unstable and had to be returned for repair. This generated considerable discussion concerning the inspector's qualifications, testing capacity, work load, and responsibility for determining if the unit should be shop checked.

Much of the remaining discussion centered around what purchasing should recommend for the inspection of material. One proposal was that everything received be funneled through the Inspection Department. Another proposal was that all material be run through inspection except as otherwise noted on the purchase order. Other questions were also raised. If purchasing required all material to be inspected, would this demand additional inspection personnel? Who would be responsible for inspection specifications? Furthermore, who should determine what items should be shop checked?

The meeting was finally adjourned until the following Friday.

Questions

1. What do you think of the current system of inspection?
2. Do you think the inspector is at fault? Explain.
3. What would you suggest happen at the meeting next Friday?

References and Additional Readings

1. Y. S. Chang, George Labovitz, and Victor Rosansky, *Making Quality Work* (New York: Harper Business, 1993), p. 65.
2. Richard B. Chase, F. Robert Jacobs, and Nicholas J. Aquilano, *Operations Management for Competitive Advantage,* 10th ed. (New York: McGraw-Hill/Irwin, 2004), p. 276.
3. William J. Stevenson, *Production/Operations Management,* 4th ed. (Burr Ridge, IL: Richard D. Irwin, 1993), p. 99.
4. Ibid., p. 100.
5. Tom Peters, *Thriving on Chaos* (New York: Alfred A. Knopf, 1987), pp. 118–19.
6. Parts of this section were drawn from Stevenson, *Production/Operations Management,* p. 101.
7. Chase, Jacobs, and Aquilano, *Operations Management for Competitive Advantage,* p. 274.
8. Stevenson, *Production/Operations Management,* pp. 104–105.
9. Adapted from Francis X. Mahoney and Carl G. Thor, *The TQM Trilogy* (New York: AMACOM, 1994), pp. 132–37. Excerpted by permission of the publisher. All rights reserved.
10. Ibid., p. 134.
11. Richard B. Chase and Nicholas J. Aquilano, *Production and Operations Management: A Life Cycle Approach,* 6th ed. (Homewood, IL: Richard D. Irwin, 1992), p. 196; other parts of this section are drawn from this section.
12. Vivienne Walker, "Kaizen—The Art of Continual Improvement," *Personnel Management,* August 1993, pp. 36–38.
13. Stevenson, *Production/Operations Management,* p. 105; other parts of this section are drawn from Chase, Jacobs, and Aquilano, *Production and Operations Management,* p. 202.
14. Erik Einset and Julie Marzano, "Six Sigma Demystified," *Tooling and Production,* April 2002, p. 43.
15. Esther Durkalski, "Lean Times Call for Lean Concepts," *Official Board Markets,* October 26, 2002, p. 38.
16. Thomas B. Clark, "Business Process Reengineering," working paper, Georgia State University, November 1997, p. 1.
17. "ISO 9000, ISO 14000 Certificates Reach Record Levels in 2001," *Quality Progress,* October 2002, pp. 21–22.
18. Much of this section is drawn from Suzan L. Jackson, "ISO 14000: What You Need to Know," *Occupational Hazards,* October 1997, pp. 127–32; and Cecily A. Raiborn, Brenda E. Joyner, and James W. Logan, "ISO 14000 and the Bottom Line," *Quality Progress,* November 1999, pp. 89–93.
19. Katherine M. Pratt, "Environmental Standards Could Govern Trade," *Transportation and Distribution,* February 1997, p. 68.

20. Sharon Hogarth, "On the Horizon: ISO 14000," *Manufacturing Engineering*, March 1999, pp. 118–28; and "ISO 9000, ISO 14000 Certificates Reach Record Levels in 2001."

21. Chase and Aquilano, *Production and Operations Management*, pp. 654–55.

22. Nicholas J. Aquilano and Richard B. Chase, *Fundamentals of Operations Management* (Homewood, IL: Richard D. Irwin, 1991), p. 586.

23. Norman Gaither, *Production and Operations Management*, 5th ed. (Fort Worth: Dryden Press, 1992), p. 377.

24. Jeremy Main, *Quality Wars* (New York: Free Press, 1994), p. 115.

25. Peters, *Thriving on Chaos*, p. 117.

26. Chase and Aquilano, *Production and Operations Management*, p. 481.

27. Stevenson, *Production/Operations Management*, p. 585.

28. Chase and Aquilano, *Production and Operations Management*, p. 677.

29. John F. Magee, "Guides to Inventory Policy: I. Functions and Lot Size," *Harvard Business Review*, January–February 1956, pp. 49–60.

30. Adapted from a book review by Paul Shrivastava found in the *Academy of Management Review* 21, no. 1 (1996), p. 286, of Toshibiro Nishiguchi, *Strategic Industrial Sourcing: The Japanese Advantage* (New York: Oxford University Press, 1994).

31. Aquilano and Chase, *Fundamentals of Operations Management*, p. 581.

Glossary of Key Terms

A

ABC classification system   Method of managing inventories based on their total value.

abilities   Personal characteristics used in performing a job.

absolute advantage   The ability to produce more of a good than another producer.

acceptance sampling   Statistical method of predicting the quality of a batch or a large group of products by inspecting a sample or group of samples.

active listening   Absorbing what another person is saying and responding to the person's concerns.

activity scheduling   Develops the precise timetable to be followed in producing a product or service.

affirmative action plan   Written document outlining specific goals and timetables for remedying past discriminatory actions.

Age Discrimination in Employment Act of 1968
Passed in 1968, initially designed to protect individuals ages 40 to 65 from discrimination in hiring, retention, and other conditions of employment. Amended in 1978 to include individuals up to age 70. Specifically, forbids mandatory retirement at 65 except in certain circumstances.

aggregate operations planning   Concerned with overall operations and balancing major sections of the operating system; matches the organization's resources with demands for its goods and services.

Americans with Disabilities Act of 1990 (ADA)
Gives individuals with disabilities sharply increased access to services and jobs.

apprenticeship training   System in which an employee is given instruction and experience, both on and off the job, in all of the practical and theoretical aspects of the work required in a skilled occupation, craft, or trade.

aptitude tests   Measure a person's capacity or potential ability to learn.

assembly chart   Depicts the sequence and manner in which the various components of a product or service are assembled.

assessment center   Utilizes a formal procedure to simulate the problems a person might face in a real managerial situation to evaluate the person's potential as a manager and determine the person's development needs.

audit   Method of control normally involved with financial matters; also can include other areas of the organization.

authority   Legitimate exercise of power; the right to issue directives and expend resources; related to power but narrower in scope.

autocratic leader   Makes most decisions for the group.

avoidance   Giving a person the opportunity to avoid a negative consequence by exhibiting a desirable behavior. Also called *negative reinforcement.*

B

behavior (personal) control   Based on direct, personal surveillance.

behaviorally anchored rating scale (BARS)   Assesses behaviors required to successfully perform a job.

balance of trade   Difference between the value of the goods a country exports and the value of the goods it imports.

bet-your-company culture   Requires big-stakes decisions; considerable time passes before the results are known.

board of directors   Carefully selected committee that reviews major policy and strategy decisions proposed by top management.

bottom-up management   Philosophy popularized by William B. Given that encouraged widespread delegation of authority to solicit the participation of all employees from the bottom to the top of the organization.

brainstorming   Presenting a problem to a group and allowing group members to produce a large quantity of ideas for its solution; no criticisms are allowed initially.

brainwriting   Technique in which a group is presented with a problem situation and members anonymously write down ideas, then exchange papers with others, who build on ideas and pass them on until all members have participated.

break-even chart   Depicts graphically the relationship of volume of operations to profits.

budget   Statement of expected results or requirements expressed in financial or numerical terms.

burnout   Condition that occurs when work is no longer meaningful to a person.

business game   Generally provides a setting of a company and its environment and requires a team of players to make decisions involving company operations.

business strategies   Focus on how to compete in a given business.

C

case study   Training technique that presents real and hypothetical situations for the trainee to analyze.

central tendency   Tendency of raters to rate most employees as doing average or above-average work.

centralization   Little authority is delegated to lower levels of management.

checklist   Requires the manager to answer yes or no to a series of questions concerning the employee's behavior.

Civil Rights Act of 1991   Permits women, persons with disabilities, and persons who are religious minorities to have a jury trial and sue for punitive damages if they can prove intentional hiring and workplace discrimination. Also requires companies to provide evidence that the business practice that led to the discrimination was not discriminatory but was related to the performance of the job in question and consistent with business necessity.

coaching   Carried out by experienced managers, emphasizes the responsibility of all managers for developing employees.

code of ethics   A document that outlines the principles of conduct to be used in making decisions within an organization.

combination strategy   Used when an organization simultaneously employs different strategies for different parts of the company.

committee   Organization structure in which a group of people are formally appointed, organized, and superimposed on the line or line and staff structure to consider or decide certain matters.

communication   The act of exchanging information.

comparative advantage   Exists when a country can produce goods more efficiently or cheaply than other countries because of its specific circumstance.

compensation   Composed of the extrinsic rewards offered by the organization and consists of the base wage or salary, any incentives or bonuses, and any benefits employees receive in exchange for their work.

competitive advantage   Sometimes called *business-specific advantage;* refers to some proprietary characteristic of the business, such as a brand name, that competitors cannot imitate without substantial cost and risk.

computer-aided design (CAD)   Generates various views of different components and assemblies.

computer-aided engineering (CAE)   Uses a product's characteristics to analyze its performance under different parameters.

computer-aided manufacturing (CAM)   Uses stored data regarding various products to provide instructions for automated production equipment.

computer-based training   Training that allows the trainee to absorb knowledge from a preset computer program and advance his or her knowledge in a self-paced format.

computer-integrated manufacturing (CIM)   Uses computer technology to incorporate all of the organization's production-related functions into an integrated computer system to assist, augment, or automate most functions.

conceptual skills   Involve understanding the relationship of the parts of a business to one another and to the business as a whole. Decision making, planning, and organizing are specific managerial activities that require conceptual skills.

concurrent (screening) control   Focuses on process as it occurs; designed to detect a problem when it occurs.

conflict   Overt behavior that results when an individual or a group of individuals thinks a perceived need or needs of the individual or group have been blocked or are about to be blocked.

consideration   Leader behavior of showing concern for individual group members and satisfying their needs.

contingency approach to leadership   Focuses on the style of leadership that is most effective in particular situations.

contingency approach to management   Theorizes that different situations and conditions require different management approaches.

contingency (situational) approach to organization structure   States that the most appropriate structure depends on the technology used, the rate of environmental change, and other dynamic forces.

contingency plans   Address the what-ifs of the manager's job; get the manager in the habit of being prepared and knowing what to do if something does go wrong.

continuous flow system   Operating system used by companies that produce large amounts of similar products/services flowing through similar stages of the operating system.

continuous improvement   Refers to an ongoing effort to make improvements in every part of the organization relative to all of its products and services.

contract   An agreement between two parties to carry out a transaction.

control   Process of ensuring that organizational activities are going according to plan; accomplished by comparing actual performance to predetermined standards or objectives, then taking action to correct any deviations.

control tolerances   Variation from the standard that is acceptable to the manager.

controlling   Measuring performance against objectives, determining the causes of deviations, and taking corrective action where necessary.

copyright   The protection provided to a creative work.

corporate culture   Communicates how people in an organization should behave by establishing a value system conveyed through rites, rituals, myths, legends, and actions.

corporate strategies   See *grand strategies*.

corporation   A business formed under state or federal statutes that is authorized to act as a legal person.

creativity   Coming up with an idea that is new, original, useful, or satisfying to its creator or to someone else.

critical-incident appraisal   Requires the manager to keep a written record of incidents, as they occur, involving job behaviors that illustrate both satisfactory and unsatisfactory performance of the employee being rated.

critical path method (CPM)   Planning and control technique that graphically depicts the relationships among the various activities of a project; used when time durations of project activities are accurately known and have little variance.

culture   Set of important understandings (often unstated) that members of a community share.

customer departmentation   Defining organizational units in terms of customers served.

D

data processing   Capture, processing, and storage of data.

decentralization   A great deal of authority is delegated to lower levels of management.

decision making   In its narrowest sense, the process of choosing from among various alternatives.

decision process   Process that involves three stages: intelligence, design, and choice. Intelligence is searching the environment for conditions requiring a decision. Design is inventing, developing, and analyzing possible courses of action. Choice is the actual selection of a course of action.

defensive (retrenchment) strategy   Used when a company wants or needs to reduce its operations.

democratic leader   Guides and encourages the group to make decisions.

departmentation   Grouping jobs into related work units.

dependent demand items   Subassembly or component parts used to make a finished product; their demand is based on the number of finished products being produced.

direct feedback   Process in which the change agent communicates the information gathered through diagnosis directly to the affected people.

dissonance   Feeling of conflict felt by individual trying to make a decision.

diversity   Including people of different genders, races, religions, nationalities, ethnic groups, age groups, and physical abilities.

E

economic order quantity (EOQ)   Optimal number of units to order at one time.

effort   Results from being motivated; refers to the amount of energy an employee uses in performing a job.

embargo   Involves stopping the flow of exports to or imports from a foreign country.

employee assistance program (EAP)   Program sponsored by the organization that attempts to help employees with stress, burnout, and other personal problems that include alcohol and drug abuse, depression, anxiety, domestic trauma, financial problems, and other psychiatric/medical problems.

empowerment   Form of decentralization in which subordinates have authority to make decisions.

entrepreneur   An individual who conceives the idea of what product or service to produce, starts the organization, and builds it to the point where additional people are needed.

entry socialization   Adaptation process by which new employees are introduced and indoctrinated into the organization.

environmental changes   All nontechnological changes that occur outside the organization.

equal employment opportunity   The right of all people to work and to advance on the bases of merit, ability, and potential.

Equal Pay Act of 1963   Prohibits wage discrimination on the basis of sex.

equity theory   Motivation theory based on the idea that people want to be treated fairly in relationship to others.

ergonomics   Study of the interface between human and machines.

essay appraisal method   Requires the manager to describe an employee's performance in written narrative form.

ethics   A set of moral principles or values that govern behavior.

evaluation phase   Third phase in strategic management, in which the implemented strategic plan is monitored, evaluated, and updated.

exception principle   States that managers should concentrate on matters that deviate significantly from normal and let subordinates handle routine matters; also called *management by exception.*

expectancy   Employee's belief that his or her effort will lead to the desired level of performance.

expectancy approach   Based on the idea that employees' beliefs about the relationship among effort, performance, and outcomes as a result of performance and the value employees place on the outcomes determine their level of motivation.

exports   Goods and services that are sold abroad.

external environment   Consists of everything outside the organization.

extinction   Providing no positive consequences or removing previously provided positive consequences as a result of undesirable behavior.

extrinsic rewards   Rewards that are directly controlled and distributed by the organization.

F

facilities layout   Process of planning the optimal physical arrangement of facilities, including personnel, operating equipment, storage space, office space, materials-handling equipment, and room for customer or product movement.

Family and Medical Leave Act (FMLA)   Enables qualified employees to take prolonged unpaid leave for family- and health-related reasons without fear of losing their jobs.

feedback   The flow of information from the receiver to the sender.

feedback system   System in which outputs from the system affect future inputs or future activities of the system.

fixed overhead expenses   Expenses that do not change appreciably with fluctuations in the level of production or service.

fixed-position layout   A type of facilities layout where the product is too large to move and remains in one place.

flat structure   Organization with few levels and relatively large spans of management at each level.

flow process chart   Outlines what happens to a product or service as it progresses through the facility.

forced-choice rating   Requires the manager to rank a set of statements describing how an employee carries out the duties and responsibilities of the job.

formal plan   Written, documented plan developed through an identifiable process.

formal work group   Work group established and formally recognized by the organizing function of management.

formulation phase   First phase in strategic management, in which the initial strategic plan is developed.

free trade area   A region within which trade restrictions are reduced or eliminated.

functional departmentation   Defining organizational units in terms of the nature of the work.

functional plans   Originate from the functional areas of an organization such as production, marketing, finance, and personnel.

functional strategies   Concerned with the activities of the different functional areas of the business.

G

Gantt chart   Planning and controlling device that graphically depicts work planned and work accomplished in their relation to each other and to time.

geographic departmentation   Defining organizational units by territories.

glass ceiling   Refers to a level within the managerial hierarchy beyond which very few women and minorities advance.

global economy   Economy in which companies compete actively with businesses from around the world.

Gordon technique   Differs from brainstorming in that no one but the group leader knows the exact nature of the real problem under consideration. A key word is used to describe a problem area.

grand or corporate strategies   Address which businesses an organization will be in and how resources will be allocated among those businesses.

grapevine   Informal channels of communication within an organization.

graphic rating scale   Requires the manager to assess an employee on factors such as quantity of work, dependability, job knowledge, attendance, accuracy of work, and cooperativeness.

group cohesiveness   Degree of attraction each member has for the group, or the "stick-togetherness" of the group.

group conformity   Degree to which the members of the group accept and abide by the norms of the group.

group norms   Informal rules a group adopts to regulate and regularize group members' behavior.

groupthink   Dysfunctional syndrome that cohesive groups experience that causes the group to lose its critical evaluative capabilities.

growth strategy   Used when the organization tries to expand, as measured by sales, product line, number of employees, or similar measures.

H

halo effect   Occurs when the interviewer allows a single prominent characteristic to dominate judgment of all other traits.

Hawthorne effect   States that giving special attention to a group of employees (such as involving them in an experiment) changes their behavior.

Hawthorne studies   Series of experiments conducted in 1924 at the Hawthorne plant of Western Electric in Cicero, Illinois; production increased in relationship to psychological and social conditions rather than to the environment.

horizontal or lateral communication
Communication across the lines of the formal chain of command.

horizontal structure   Consists of two groups. One group is composed of senior management who are responsible for strategic decisions and policies. The second group is composed of empowered employees working together in different process teams.

human asset accounting   Determining and recording the value of an organization's human resources in its statement of financial condition.

human resource forecasting   Process that attempts to determine the future human resource needs of the organization in light of the organization's objectives.

human resource planning (HRP)   Process of "getting the right number of qualified people into the right job at the right time." Also called *personnel planning*.

hybrid departmentation   Occurs when an organization simultaneously uses more than one type of departmentation.

I

idiosyncrasy credit   Phenomenon that occurs when certain members who have made or are making significant contributions to the group's goals are allowed to take some liberties within the group.

implementation phase   Second phase in strategic management, in which the strategic plan is put into effect.

importing   The purchasing of goods from a foreign company.

imports   Goods and services purchased abroad.

In Search of Excellence   Book by Thomas J. Peters and Robert H. Waterman, Jr., that identifies 36 companies with an excellent 20-year performance record. The authors identified eight characteristics of excellence after interviewing managers in each company.

in-basket technique   Simulates a realistic situation by requiring each trainee to answer one manager's mail and telephone calls.

income tax   A tax levied against a business's profits.

independent demand items   Finished goods ready to be shipped out or sold.

inequity   Exists when a person perceives his or her job inputs and outcomes to be less than the job inputs and outcomes of another person.

informal organization   Aggregate of the personal contacts and interactions and the associated groupings of people working within the formal organization.

informal work group   Work group that results from personal contacts and interactions among people and is not formally recognized by the organization.

initiating structure   Leader behavior of structuring the work of group members and directing the group toward the attainment of the group's goals.

innovation   Process of applying a new and creative idea to a product, service, or method of operation.

inputs   What an employee perceives are his or her contributions to the organization (e.g., education, intelligence, experience, training, skills, and the effort exerted on the job).

instrumentality   Employee's belief that attaining the desired level of performance will lead to desired outcomes.

intellectual property   Ownership of ideas; gives creators of the intellectual property the exclusive right to market and sell their work.

interest tests   Determine how a person's interests compare with the interests of successful people in a specific job.

intergroup (structural) conflict   Conflict that results from the organizational structure; may be relatively independent of the individuals occupying the roles within the structure.

intermittent flow system   Operating system used when customized products and services are produced.

internal changes   Budget adjustments, policy changes, personnel changes, and the like.

international trade   The exchange of goods and services by different countries.

Internet   A global collection of independently operating, but interconnected, computers.

interpersonal communication   An interactive process between individuals that involves sending and receiving verbal and nonverbal messages.

interpersonal conflict   Conflict between two or more individuals.

intranet   A private, corporate, computer network that uses Internet products and technologies to provide multimedia applications within organizations.

intrapersonal conflict   Conflict internal to the individual.

intrinsic rewards   Rewards internal to the individual and normally derived from involvement in work activities.

intuitive approach   Approach used when managers make decisions based largely on hunches and intuition.

inventory   Quantity of raw materials, in-process goods, or finished goods on hand; serves as a buffer between different rates of flow associated with the operating system.

ISO 9000   A set of quality standards for international business.

ISO 14000   Addition to the ISO 9000 to control the impact of an organization's activities and outputs on the environment.

J

job analysis   Process of determining, through observation and study, the pertinent information relating to the nature of a specific job.

job content   Aggregate of all the work tasks the jobholder may be asked to perform.

job depth   Refers to the freedom of employees to plan and organize their own work, work at their own pace, and move around and communicate as desired.

job description   Written statement that identifies the tasks, duties, activities, and performance results required in a particular job.

job design   Designates the specific work activities of an individual or a group of individuals.

job enlargement   Giving an employee more of a similar type of operation to perform.

job enrichment   Upgrading the job by adding motivator factors.

job knowledge tests   Measure the job-related knowledge possessed by a job applicant.

job method   Manner in which the human body is used, the arrangement of the workplace, and the design of the tools and equipment used.

job rotation   Process in which the trainee goes from one job to another within the organization, generally remaining in each job from six months to a year.

job satisfaction   An individual's general attitude about his or her job.

job scope   Refers to the number of different types of operations performed on the job.

job specification   Written statement that identifies the abilities, skills, traits, or attributes necessary for successful performance in a particular job.

just-in-time inventory control (JIT)   Inventory control system that schedules materials to arrive and leave as they are needed.

K

kaizen   "Good change"; a process of continuous and relentless improvement.

L

laissez-faire leader   Allows people within the group to make all decisions.

law of comparative advantage   Producers should produce the goods they are most efficient at producing and purchase from others the goods they are less efficient at producing.

layoff   Occurs when there is not enough work for all employees; employees will be called back if and when the workload increases.

leader   One who obtains followers and influences them in setting and achieving objectives.

Leader Behavior Description Questionnaire (LBDQ)   Questionnaire designed to determine what a successful leader does, regardless of the type of group being led.

leader–member relations   Degree to which others trust and respect the leader and the leader's friendliness.

leadership   Ability to influence people to willingly follow one's guidance or adhere to one's decisions.

leading   Directing and channeling human behavior toward the accomplishment of objectives.

lean manufacturing   A systematic approach to identifying and eliminating waste and non-value-added activities.

leniency   Grouping of ratings at the positive end of the scale instead of spreading them throughout the scale.

level of aspiration   Level of performance that a person expects to attain; determined by the person's prior successes and failures.

line and staff structure   Organization structure that results when staff specialists are added to a line organization.

line functions   Functions and activities directly involved in producing and marketing the organization's goods or services.

line structure   Organization structure with direct vertical lines between the different levels of the organization.

linking-pin concept   Because managers are members of overlapping groups, they link formal work groups to the total organization.

long-range objectives   Go beyond the current fiscal year; must support and not conflict with the organizational mission.

long-range plans   Typically span at least three to five years; some extend as far as 20 years into the future.

M

Malcolm Baldrige Award   Recognition of U.S. companies' achievements in quality.

management   A form of work that involves coordinating an organization's resources—land, labor, and capital—toward accomplishing organizational objectives.

management audit   Attempts to evaluate the overall management practices and policies of the organization.

management development   Process of developing the attitudes and skills necessary to become or remain an effective manager.

management information system (MIS)   Integrated approach for providing interpreted and relevant data that can help managers make decisions.

management theory jungle   Term developed by Harold Koontz referring to the division of thought that resulted from the multiple approaches to studying the management process.

Managerial Grid   A two-dimensional framework rating a leader on the basis of concern for people and concern for production.

material requirements planning (MRP)   Dependent inventory planning and control system that schedules the right amount of materials needed to produce the final product on schedule.

matrix structure   Hybrid organization structure in which individuals from different functional areas are assigned to work on a specific project or task.

maximax approach   Selecting the alternative whose best possible outcome is the best of all possible outcomes for all alternatives; sometimes called the *optimistic* or *gambling approach* to decision making.

maximin approach   Comparing the worst possible outcomes for each alternative and selecting the one that is least undesirable; sometimes called the *pessimistic approach* to decision making.

McCormick multiple-management plan   Developed by Charles McCormick, a plan that uses participation as a training and motivational tool by selecting promising young employees from various company departments to form a junior board of directors.

mechanistic systems   Organizational systems characterized by a rigid delineation of functional duties, precise job descriptions, fixed authority and responsibility, and a well-developed organizational hierarchy through which information filters up and instructions flow down.

middle management   Responsible for implementing and achieving organizational objectives; also responsible for developing departmental objectives and actions.

mission   Defines the basic purpose(s) of an organization: why the organization exists.

motivation   Concerned with what activates human behavior, what directs this behavior toward a particular goal, and how this behavior is sustained.

motivation maintenance   An approach to work motivation that associates factors of high-low motivation with either the work environment or the work itself. Also called *motivation hygiene.*

multinational corporation (MNC)   Business that maintains a presence in two or more countries, has a considerable portion of its assets invested in and derives a substantial portion of its sales and profits from international activities, considers opportunities throughout the world, and has a worldwide perspective and orientation.

multirater assessment (or 360-degree feedback)   Method of performance appraisal that uses input from an employee's managers, peers, customers, suppliers, or colleagues.

N

need hierarchy   Based on the assumption that individuals are motivated to satisfy a number of needs and that money can directly or indirectly satisfy only some of these needs.

needs assessment   Systematic analysis of the specific training activities a business requires to achieve its objectives.

nominal group technique (NGT)   Highly structured technique for solving group tasks; minimizes personal interactions to encourage activity and reduce pressures toward conformity.

nonprogrammed decisions   Decisions that have little or no precedent; they are relatively unstructured and generally require a creative approach by the decision maker.

O

objectives   Statements outlining what the organization is trying to achieve; give an organization and its members direction.

Occupational Safety and Health Act (OSHA) of 1970   Federal legislation designed to reduce job injuries; established specific federal safety guidelines for almost all U.S. organizations.

on-the-job training (OJT)   Normally given by a senior employee or supervisor, training in which the trainee is shown how to perform the job and allowed to do it under the trainer's supervision.

operating systems   Consist of the processes and activities necessary to turn inputs into goods or services.

operations management   Application of the basic concepts and principles of management to those segments of the organization that produce its goods or services.

operations or tactical planning   Short-range planning; done primarily by middle- to lower-level managers, it concentrates on the formulation of functional plans.

operations planning   Designing the systems of the organization that produce goods or services; planning the day-to-day operations within those systems.

optimizing   Selecting the best possible alternative.

optimizing approach   Includes the following steps: recognize the need for a decision; establish, rank, and weigh criteria; gather available information and data; identify possible alternatives; evaluate each alternative with respect to all criteria; and select the best alternative.

organic systems   Organizational systems characterized by less formal job descriptions, greater emphasis on adaptability, more participation, and less fixed authority.

organization   Group of people working together in some concerted or coordinated effort to attain objectives.

organization structure   Framework that defines the boundaries of the formal organization and within which the organization operates.

organizational conflict   Conflict between employees and the organization itself.

organizational development (OD)   Organizationwide, planned effort, managed from the top, to increase organizational performance through planned interventions.

organizational diplomacy   Strategies used to minimize conflict in a diverse workplace.

organizational morale   An individual's feeling of being accepted by, and belonging to, a group of employees through common goals, confidence in the desirability of these goals, and progress toward these goals.

organizational rewards   All types of rewards, both intrinsic and extrinsic, received as a result of employment by the organization.

organizing   Grouping activities, assigning activities, and providing the authority necessary to carry out the activities.

orientation   Introduction of new employees to the organization, their work units, and their jobs.

orientation kit   Normally prepared by the human resource department, provides a wide variety of materials to supplement the general organizational orientation.

output (impersonal) control   Based on the measurement of outputs.

outsourcing   Practice of subcontracting information systems work to an independent outside source.

P

paralanguage   A form of nonverbal communication that includes the pitch, tempo, loudness, and hesitations in verbal communication.

parity principle   States that authority and responsibility must coincide.

partnership   An association of two or more persons who jointly own a for-profit business.

patent   The document the federal government issues to inventors and companies that gives them the exclusive right to their inventions for 17 years.

path–goal theory of leadership   Attempts to define the relationships between a leader's behavior and the subordinates' performance and work activities.

perception   The mental and sensory processes an individual uses in interpreting information received.

performance appraisal   Process that involves determining and communicating to employees how they are performing their jobs and establishing a plan for improvement.

period of solidification   A period in the 1920s and 1930s in which management became recognized as a discipline.

Peter Principle   Tendency of individuals in a hierarchy to rise to their levels of incompetence.

physical inventory   Counting the number of units of inventory a company holds in stock.

planning   Process of deciding what objectives to pursue during a future time period and what to do to achieve those objectives.

policies   Broad, general guides to action that constrain or direct the attainment of objectives.

polygraph   A device that records physical changes in the body as the test subject answers a series of questions.

polygraph tests   Record physical changes in the body as the test subject answers a series of questions; popularly known as *lie detector tests.*

position power   Power and influence that go with a job.

positive reinforcement   Providing a positive consequence as a result of desirable behavior.

postaction control   Designed to detect an existing or a potential problem before it gets out of hand.

power   Ability to influence, command, or apply force; a measure of a person's potential to get others to do what he or she wants them to do, as well as to avoid being forced by others to do what he or she does not want to do.

preliminary (steering) control   Method of exercising control to prevent a problem from occurring.

principle   A basic truth or law.

principle of bounded rationality   Assumes people have the time and cognitive ability to process only a limited amount of information on which to base decisions.

principle of individual rights   Involves making decisions based on protecting human dignity.

problem solving   Process of determining the appropriate responses or actions necessary to alleviate a problem.

procedure   Series of related steps or tasks expressed in chronological order for a specific purpose.

process approach to management   Focuses on the management functions of planning, controlling, organizing, staffing, and leading.

process control   Relates to equipment and processes used during the production process; used to monitor quality while the product or service is being produced.

process control chart   Time-based graphic display that shows whether a machine or a process is producing items that meet preestablished specifications.

process culture   Involves low risk with little feedback; employees focus on how things are done rather than on the outcomes.

process layout   Facilities layout that groups together equipment or services of a similar functional type.

process selection   Specifies in detail the processes and sequences required to transform inputs into products or services.

product departmentation   Grouping all activities necessary to produce and market a product or service under one manager.

product layout   Facilities layout that arranges equipment or services according to the progressive steps by which the product is made or the customer is served.

product quality control   Relates to inputs or outputs of the system; used when quality is evaluated with respect to a batch of existing products or services.

production planning   Concerned primarily with aggregate operations planning, resource allocation, and activity scheduling.

production standards approach   Performance appraisal method most frequently used for employees who are involved in physically producing a product; is basically a form of objective setting for these employees.

professional manager   Career manager who does not necessarily have a controlling interest in the organization and bears a responsibility to employees, stockholders, and the public.

proficiency tests   Measure how well the applicant can do a sample of the work that is to be performed.

program evaluation and review technique (PERT)   Planning and control technique that graphically depicts the relationships among the various activities of a project; used when the durations of the project activities are not accurately known.

property tax   Tax levied against the property, buildings, and land owned by a business.

psychological tests   Attempt to measure personality characteristics.

psychomotor tests   Measure a person's strength, dexterity, and coordination.

punishment   Providing a negative consequence as a result of undesirable behavior.

Q

quality   For the operations manager, quality is determined in relation to the specifications or standards set in the design stages—the degree or grade of excellence specified.

quality at the source   The philosophy of making each employee responsible for the quality of his or her own work.

quality circle   Composed of a group of employees (usually from 5 to 15 people) who are members of a single work unit, section, or department; the basic purpose of a quality circle is to discuss quality problems and generate ideas that might help improve quality.

quota   Establishes the maximum quantity of a product that can be imported or exported during a given period.

R

recency   Occurs when performance evaluations are based on work performed most recently, generally work performed one to two months before evaluation.

recruitment   Seeking and attracting a supply of people from which qualified candidates for job vacancies can be selected.

reengineering   Searching for and implementing radical change in business processes to achieve breakthroughs in costs, speed, productivity, and service.

regulations   Rules that government agencies issue to implement laws.

Rehabilitation Act of 1973   Prohibits discrimination in hiring of persons with disabilities by federal agencies and federal contractors.

reinforcement theory   States that the consequences of a person's present behavior influence future behavior.

resource allocation   Efficient allocation of people, materials, and equipment to meet the demand requirements of the operating system.

responsibility   Accountability for the attainment of objectives, the use of resources, and the adherence to organizational policy.

reverse discrimination   Providing preferential treatment for one group (e.g., minority or female) over another group (e.g., white male) rather than merely providing equal opportunity.

risk-averting approach   Choosing the alternative with the least variation among its possible outcomes.

role   Set of behaviors associated with a particular job.

role perception   Direction in which employees believe they should channel their efforts on their jobs.

routing   Finds the best path and sequence of operations for attaining a desired level of output with a given mix of equipment and personnel.

rules   Require specific and definite actions to be taken or not to be taken in a given situation.

S

safety stocks   Inventory maintained to accommodate unexpected changes in demand and supply and allow for variations in delivery time.

satisficing   Selecting the first alternative that meets the decision maker's minimum standard of satisfaction.

scalar principle   States that authority in the organization flows through the chain of managers one link at a time, ranging from the highest to the lowest ranks; also called *chain of command*.

Scanlon plan   Incentive plan developed in 1938 by Joseph Scanlon to give workers a bonus for tangible savings in labor costs.

scientific management   Philosophy of Frederick W. Taylor that sought to increase productivity and make the work easier by scientifically studying work methods and establishing standards.

self-directed work teams (SDWT)   Teams in which members are empowered to control the work they do without a formal supervisor.

self-fulfilling prophecy   The relationship between a leader's expectations and the resulting performance of subordinates.

semantics   The science or study of the meanings of words and symbols.

sensitivity training   Method used in OD to make one more aware of oneself and one's impact on others.

short-range objectives   Generally tied to a specific time period of a year or less and are derived from an in-depth evaluation of long-range objectives.

short-range plans   Generally cover up to one year.

situation of certainty   Situation that occurs when a decision maker knows exactly what will happen and can often calculate the precise outcome for each alternative.

situation of risk   Situation that occurs when a decision maker is aware of the relative probabilities of occurrence associated with each alternative.

situational leadership theory   As the level of maturity of followers increases, structure should be reduced while socioemotional support should first be increased and then gradually decreased.

situation of uncertainty   Situation that occurs when a decision maker has very little or no reliable information on which to evaluate the different possible outcomes.

six sigma   Both a precise set of statistical tools and a rallying cry for continuous improvement.

skills inventory   Consolidates information about the organization's current human resources.

small business   A company that is independently owned and operated and is not dominant in its field; generally has fewer than 100 employees.

social audit   A method used by management to evaluate the success or lack of success of programs designed to improve the social performance of the organization.

social responsibility   The obligation that individuals or businesses have to help solve social problems.

sociotechnical approach   Approach to job design that considers both the technical system and the accompanying social system.

soldiering   Describes the actions of employees who intentionally restrict output.

sole proprietorship   A business owned by a single individual, or proprietor.

span of management   Number of subordinates a manager can effectively manage; also called *span of control*.

stability strategy   Used when the organization is satisfied with its present course (status quo strategy).

staff functions   Functions that are advisory and supportive in nature; designed to contribute to the efficiency and maintenance of the organization.

staffing   Determining human resource needs and recruiting, selecting, training, and developing human resources.

stakeholders   The people—employees, customers, suppliers, and the community—who are affected by the actions of a business.

standard   Value used as a point of reference for comparing other values.

strategic business unit (SBU)   Distinct business that has its own set of competitors and can be managed reasonably independently of other businesses within the organization.

strategic management   Formulation, proper implementation, and continuous evaluation of strategic plans; determines the long-run directions and performance of an organization. The essence of strategic management is developing strategic plans and keeping them current.

strategic planning   Analogous to top-level long-range planning; covers a relatively long period; affects many parts of the organization.

strategy   Outlines the basic steps management plans to take to reach an objective or a set of objectives; outlines how management intends to achieve its objectives.

stress   Mental or physical condition that results from a perceived threat of danger (physical or emotional) and the pressure to remove it.

subsidies or subsidized protection   Widely used practice of government support of domestic industries to make their prices cheaper than the prices of imports.

supervisory management   Manages operative employees; generally considered the first or lowest level of management.

synectics   Creative problem-solving technique that uses metaphorical thinking to "make the familiar strange and the strange familiar."

systems approach to management   A way of thinking about the job of managing that provides a framework for visualizing internal and external environmental factors as an integrated whole.

T

tariffs   Government-imposed taxes charged on goods imported into a country.

task structure   Degree to which job tasks are structured.

team building   Process by which the formal work group develops an awareness of those conditions that keep it from functioning effectively and then requires the group to eliminate those conditions.

technical skills   Involve being able to perform the mechanics of a particular job.

technological changes   Changes in such things as new equipment and new processes.

test reliability   Consistency or reproducibility of the results of a test.

test validity   Extent to which a test predicts a specific criterion.

tests   Provide a sample of behavior used to draw inferences about the future behavior or performance of an individual.

Theory Z   A theory developed by William Ouchi that attempts to integrate American and Japanese management practices by combining the American emphasis on individual responsibility with the Japanese emphasis on collective decision making, slow evaluation and promotion, and holistic concern for employees.

Title VII of the Civil Rights Act of 1964   Designed to eliminate employment discrimination related to race, color, religion, sex, or national origin in organizations that conduct interstate commerce.

top or senior management   Establishes the objectives of the business, formulates the actions necessary to achieve them, and allocates the resources of the business to achieve the objectives.

tough-person, macho culture   Characterized by individuals who take high risks and get quick feedback on whether their decisions are right or wrong.

trademark   A word, name, symbol, or slogan a business uses to identify its own goods.

training   Acquiring skills or learning concepts to increase the performance of employees.

trait theory   Stressed what the leader was like rather than what the leader did.

transactional leadership   Takes the approach that leaders engage in a bargaining relationship with their followers.

transaction-processing system   Substitutes computer processing for manual recordkeeping procedures.

transformational leadership   Involves cultivating employee acceptance of the group mission.

U

unity of command principle   States that an employee should have one, and only one, immediate manager.

user-friendly computer   Computer that requires very little technical knowledge to use.

V

valence   Employee's belief about the value of the outcome.

value   A conception, explicit or implicit, that defines what an individual or a group regards as desirable. People are not born with values; rather, they acquire and develop them early in life.

value-added chain   Process by which a business combines the raw material, labor, and technology into a finished product, markets the product, and distributes the product.

variable overhead expenses   Expenses that change in proportion to the level of production or service.

vestibule training   System in which procedures and equipment similar to those used in the actual job are set up in a special working area called a vestibule.

virtual organization   Temporary network of independent companies—suppliers, customers, and even rivals—linked by information technology to share skills, costs, and access to one another's markets.

W

wellness program   Company-implemented program designed to prevent illness and enhance employee well-being.

workaholism   Working to the exclusion of everything else in one's life.

work-hard/play-hard culture   Encourages employees to take few risks and to expect rapid feedback.

Z

zero-base budgeting   Form of budgeting in which the manager must build and justify each area of a budget. Each activity is identified, evaluated, and ranked by importance.

zero-defects program   Increasing quality by increasing everyone's impact on quality.

Name Index

Subject Index